UNDERSTANDING ELECTRICITY AND ELECTRONICS TECHNOLOGY

UNDERSTANDING ELECTRICITY AND ELECTRONICS TECHNOLOGY

Fifth Edition

PETER BUBAN
MARSHALL L. SCHMITT
CHARLES G. CARTER, JR.

McGRAW-HILL BOOK COMPANY

New York   Atlanta   Dallas   St. Louis   San Francisco   Auckland
Bogotá   Guatemala   Hamburg   Johannesburg   Lisbon   London
Madrid   Mexico   Milan   Montreal   New Delhi   Panama   Paris
San Juan   São Paulo   Singapore   Sydney   Tokyo   Toronto

ABOUT THE AUTHORS

Peter Buban, late instructor of electricity and electronics at the Quincy (Ill.) Area Vocational Technical Center. He received his M.A. degree from Northeast Missouri State University. His many years of practical military and industrial experience in the electrical and electronics fields included such jobs as electronics technician, chief radioman, and electrician.

Marshall L. Schmitt is a Senior Program Specialist, Division of Educational Replication, U.S. Department of Education. He has responsibilities for industrial arts and technology programs in this division. He received his doctorate from Pennsylvania State University. He has taught courses in electricity and electronics for U.S. Navy personnel and at the high school level in New York State. He also taught in the Industrial Arts Department at North Carolina State University, Raleigh, N.C.

Charles G. Carter, Jr. teaches Electricity and Electronics at Wayne Valley High School, Wayne, New Jersey. He received his M.A. in Industrial Arts Education from Montclair State College, Montclair, New Jersey. In addition to his teaching duties, he is Supervisor of Student Computing Experiences for the Wayne district, and a consultant to New Jersey school districts in the field of educational computing technology. Mr. Carter also teaches microcomputer repair at the secondary and adult levels.

Sponsoring Editor: Gordon Rockmaker
Editing Supervisor: Nicola von Schreiber
Design and Art Supervisor: Patricia Lowy
Production Supervisor: Mirabel Flores

Text Designer: Karin Batten
Cover Designer: Phyllis Lerner
Cover Photographer: Geoffrey Gove

Library of Congress Cataloging-in-Publication Data

Buban, Peter.
  Understanding electricity and electronics
  technology.
  (McGraw-Hill publications in industrial education)
  Includes index.
  Summary: A textbook of the theory and practical
  applications of electricity and electronics.
  1. Electric engineering—Juvenile literature.
  2. Electronics—Juvenile literature. [1. Electric
  engineering. 2. Electronics] I. Schmitt, Marshall
  Langdon, 1919–   . II. Carter, Charles G. III. Buban,
  Peter. Understanding electricity and electronics.
  IV. Title. V. Series.
  TK148.B85 1987   621.3   86-12502
  ISBN 0-07-008646-X

Understanding Electricity and Electronics Technology, Fifth Edition

Copyright © 1987 by McGraw-Hill, Inc. All rights reserved. Copyright © 1982, 1975, 1969, 1962 as *Understanding Electricity and Electronics* by McGraw-Hill, Inc. All rights reserved. Printed in the United States of America. Except as permitted under the United States Copyright Act of 1976, no part of this publication may be reproduced or distributed in any form or by any means, or stored in a data base or retrieval system, without the prior written permission of the publisher.

 4 5 6 7 8 9 0   DOCDOC   8 9 3 2 1 0 9

ISBN 0-07-008646-X

EDITOR'S FOREWORD

The McGraw-Hill Publications in Industrial Education constitute a comprehensive series of textbooks covering important areas of industrial education. *Understanding Electricity and Electronics Technology*, a volume in this series, has proved to be one of the most widely used textbooks in its field. To remain effective in such a rapidly changing and expanding field, a textbook must be updated, improved, and expanded. This fifth edition incorporates all the vital aspects of theory and practice necessary to keep pace with the latest technology and pedagogy.

This book reflects the authors' many years of teaching experience at various educational levels and their broad knowledge of the practical side of the field. Their ingenuity and resourcefulness are constantly being tested and refined in the classroom and laboratory. The result is a textbook that is a superior source of information for the junior and senior high school student, as well as for the technical student taking electricity and electronics for the first time.

A two-color format has been used throughout this book to highlight outstanding concepts. A highly readable typeface and an open, pleasing overall design sustain the student's interest. Discussion topics, learning-by-doing exercises, individual-study activities, and construction projects are all designed to challenge the theoretical and practical minds of boys and girls having a wide range of backgrounds, interests, and abilities.

The authors, editor, and publisher hope that the fifth edition of *Understanding Electricity and Electronics Technology* will stimulate the interest of students in this most important area. Perhaps the inspiration fostered by study of this fascinating field of energy and communication will result in satisfying the need for future electrical and electronics specialists. Indeed, it might stimulate the imaginations of potential electrical engineers and technicians, those who will contribute to the society of tomorrow.

Chris H. Groneman

McGraw-Hill Publications in Industrial Education
Chris H. Groneman, Consulting Editor

Books in Series
GENERAL INDUSTRIAL EDUCATION AND TECHNOLOGY Groneman and Feirer
GENERAL METALS Feirer
GENERAL POWER MECHANICS Crouse, Worthington, Margules, and Anglin
GENERAL WOODWORKING Groneman
GETTING STARTED IN DRAWING AND PLANNING Groneman and Feirer
GETTING STARTED IN ELECTRICITY AND ELECTRONICS Groneman and Feirer
GETTING STARTED IN METALWORKING Groneman and Feirer
GETTING STARTED IN WOODWORKING Groneman and Feirer
TECHNICAL ELECTRICITY AND ELECTRONICS Buban and Schmitt
TECHNICAL WOODWORKING Groneman and Glazener
UNDERSTANDING ELECTRICITY AND ELECTRONICS TECHNOLOGY Buban, Schmitt, and Carter

CONTENTS

PREFACE ix

Section 1

INTRODUCTION

1. Atoms, Electrons, and Electric Charges 2
2. Electric Circuits 7
3. Circuit Diagrams and Symbols 10
4. Safety Rules, Practices, and Devices 19
5. Occupations in Electricity and Electronics 32

Section 2

ELECTRIC CIRCUITS AND DEVICES

6. Voltage, Current, and Power 42
7. Conductors and Insulators 47
8. Resistance and Resistors 52
9. Ohm's Law and Power Formulas 60
10. Series Circuits 69
11. Parallel Circuits 77
12. Series-Parallel Circuits 86
13. Measuring Electrical Quantities 94
14. Capacitance and Capacitors 103
15. Magnetism 113
16. Electromagnetism 120
17. Electromagnetic Induction and Inductance 126

Section 3

ENERGY SOURCES

18. Chemical Cells and Batteries 144
19. Generators 154
20. Other Sources of Electric Energy 161

Section 4

SEMICONDUCTORS AND INTEGRATED CIRCUITS

21. Semiconductors and Diodes 169
22. Transistors 176
23. Special Devices and Integrated Circuits 183
24. Printed Circuits 197

Section 5

ELECTRICAL WIRING: MATERIALS, TOOLS, AND PROCESSES

25. Wires and Cubles 206
26. Wiring Tools and Devices 218
27. Soldering 232
28. Making a Sheet-Metal Chassis 240

Section 6

ELECTRICITY AT WORK

29. Lamps and Lighting   249
30. Producing Chemical Reactions   260
31. Home Electrical Systems   265
32. Electric Motors   278
33. Producing Heat   292
34. Refrigeration and Air Conditioning   304
35. The Automobile Electrical Systems   309

Section 7

ELECTRONICS IN AN INFORMATION AGE

36. Basic Concepts in Communication   320
37. Common Information Systems   326
38. Audio Systems   344
39. Radio and Satellite Communications   364
40. Television and Facsimile Systems   386
41. Digital Electronic Circuits   415
42. Fundamentals of Computers   427
43. Interacting With the Microcomputer   447

Section 8

ELECTRICITY AND INDUSTRY

44. The Electric Power Industry   468
45. Research and Development in Electronics   476
46. Product Manufacturing   481

Section 9

TESTING AND TROUBLESHOOTING

47. Electronic Test Instruments   485
48. Troubleshooting and Repair   491

Section 10

PROJECT PLANNING AND SUGGESTED PROJECTS

49. Project Planning   498
50. Suggested Projects and Technical Problem Solving   505

Glossary   517
Index   525

vii

LEARNING BY DOING ACTIVITIES

1. Making a Neon Lamp Handitester 29
2. Installing a Loudspeaker "Fader" Control 57
3. Making a Relaxation Oscillator 111
4. Making an Electromagnetic Experimenter 139
5. Experiences With the Photoconductive Cell 194
6. Making Thermocouples 195
7. The Safe Current-Carrying Capacity of Wires 214
8. Experiences in Soldering 238
9. Making a Saltwater Rheostat 264
10. Wiring With Nonmetallic Sheathed Cable 276
11. A Simple Two-Pole Universal Motor 289
12. AM Radio Transmission 382
13. Making a Logic Probe 425
14. Surface Roughness Guage 463
15. Reaction Timer 464

PREFACE

Understanding Electricity and Electronics Technology is intended for a basic course in electricity and electronics. While the organization of the book has been especially designed to adapt easily to varying course lengths, more than sufficient material has been included for a full-year course.

Two publications are correlated with the text to provide a complete basic electricity and electronics learning program. They are an *Activities Manual* and a *Teacher's Resource Guide*.

The *Activities Manual* contains procedures for performing 62 experiments. Special attention has been given to the use of readily available and relatively low-cost components and materials. A unique feature of the laboratory program that this manual presents is instructions for the construction of the circuit board, the power supply, and the coils that are to be used in performing the experiments. Experiments in digital circuitry and in interfacing the computer with the real world are included. The *Activities Manual* also contains *Learning Guides*. The Learning Guides consist of objective questions that are directly related to the 50 textbook units. These guides provide a convenient way to check individual progress and to identify those topics that require further attention.

The *Teacher's Resource Guide* provides suggestions for using the student text and for conducting the correlated laboratory activities and experiments. The overall goals of the electricity-electronics program are presented as well as the performance objectives for each text unit and the student behavioral statements related to the performance objectives. The *Teacher's Resource Guide* contains a list of all components and other items needed to perform the experiments. Answer keys are provided for the *Activities Manual*, for the *Learning Guides*, and for the Self-Tests provided after each textbook unit.

Early in this text the student is introduced to the fundamental theories on which later discussions of practical applications are based. This logical development of the subject is particularly effective in relating the technological advances in electricity and electronics to basic concepts in physics, mechanics, and chemistry, to which the student is introduced. This approach is strengthened by a judicious use of basic mathematics, primarily in problem-solving situations that involve fundamental electrical relationships.

Classroom experience with the previous editions and many useful suggestions from users of the text have helped shape the general organization and content of this edition. The career and avocational opportunities in electricity and electronics open to both men and women are explored in detail. The discussions of materials, devices, and processes reflect the latest developments in their respective areas. In keeping with the objective of relating the subject to the real world, basic consumer information on electrical products and their use is included when pertinent. The unit on other sources of energy looks toward the future, touching on energy problems likely to affect the lives of everyone. This edition includes coverage of all major technological areas, including computers and peripherals, data communications, cellular radio, satellite broadcasting, digital audio, synthesized speech, and modern solid state devices.

The text consists of 10 main sections that present a total of 50 units of instruction and suggestions for the construction of several projects. End-of-unit materials include learning-by-doing exercises, self-tests, review and discussion topics, and individual-study activities. Each is designed to achieve a particular objective in motivating, evaluating, and reinforcing the student's comprehension of what has been studied. *Learning-by-doing* exercises provide practical "hands-on" experiences in the use of circuit diagrams, tools, and test equipment. They may be used as individual or group assignments or as demonstrations by the instructor. Each of the exercises has been designed to use inexpensive materials usually available in the school shop or laboratory. The *self-test* sections provide a way for students to assess their own progress through each unit in a challenging and independent fashion. The *review and discussion* topics may be used effectively by the teacher to stimulate classroom discussions of specific topics, to highlight particular points, and to develop topics more fully. In this manner the instructor can very easily expand the treatment of certain subject matter as the needs and interests of the class demand. The *individual-study* activities that are particularly suited as project assignments for those students showing special interests or aptitudes. Small groups of two, three, or four students can also be assigned these activities. The primary purpose is to encourage students to make use of school, community, and industry resources to prepare a report and then to use their oral or written skills to communicate the information to their class. The pursuit of these objectives can serve as an effective method of extending the scope of the student's learning experiences beyond the classroom.

Section 10 is devoted to suggestions for projects that will provide practical experiences in the design and construction of useful electrical and electronic devices. These projects are free of detailed step-by-step instructions since the authors feel such details are best left to instructors, who are familiar with the facilities available to them and the abilities of their students. Section 10 also includes selected technical problems to solve. The basic purpose is to provide situations where students will have to apply their knowledge, skills, and creativity to derive an appropriate solution.

As in the previous edition, metric units are included with the customary U.S. units. With the United States destined to join the rest of the industrial world in the adoption of the metric system of measurements, it is important that students obtain a working knowledge of these units early in their industrial education.

The authors wish to acknowledge the companies, organizations, and individuals who generously contributed material for use in this book. Specific reference to these sources is given, where appropriate, throughout the text. They gratefully acknowledge the special assistance, contributions, and information extended by the following companies and organizations: Admiral Home Appliances; American National Standards, Inc.; The American Radio Relay League; Ametek; Analog Devices; AT&T; Ball Corp.; Bell Atlantic Mobile Systems; Black Box Corp.; Burr-Brown Corp.; Electronic Industries Association; Exide Corp.; Exxon Corp.; Fayette Manufacturing Corp.; Federal Communications Commission; The Foxboro Co.; General Electric Co.; GTE Laboratories, Inc.; Hayes Microcomputer Products, Inc.; Hunter Associates; ICOM AMERICA, Inc.; ILC Data Device Corp.; Infolink Corp.; Institute of Electrical and Electronics Engineers; Lead Industries Association, Inc.; Magnetic Shield Division-Perfection Mica Co.; Mid-Atlantic Finishing, Inc.; Mostek Corp.; NEC America, Inc.; Pitney Bowes; RCA Corp.; Reference Technology, Inc.; Sencore; Siemens Opto; Sony Corporation of America; Sunbeam Appliance Co.; Tandy Corp./Radio Shack; Teletype Corp.; Toroid Corp. of Maryland; Varta Batteries, Inc.; Veeco Instruments, Inc.; Virginia Electric and Power Co.; U.S. Department of Energy; and Zenith Electronics Corp.

The authors wish to express their sincere appreciation to Doris L. Schmitt and Elizabeth G. Carter, who have provided encouragement and assistance in the preparation of this edition. A special acknowledgement is made to the late Peter Buban. He will be remembered for his dedication to his profession, his concern for students, and his many contributions to the previous editions of this text.

Comments and suggestions for the improvement of this edition are most welcome.

Marshall L. Schmitt
Charles G. Carter, Jr.

INTRODUCTION

Why study electricity and electronics? Try to imagine living today without using electricity and electronics. You would have no electric lights, no telephone, no television, and no doorbell to announce your friends. You could not buy a radio, a computer, or a flashlight. There would be no electricians, computer programmers, or electrical engineers. Electricity and electronics have made life not only easier and more interesting but also more complicated.

Because electricity has had such an impact on our lives, we need to know something about its uses, its dangers, and its potential for the future. This is true today more than ever before. For example, computers are already available to play chess, to retrieve information at lightning speed, to aid doctors in treating disease, and to control robots in manufacturing automobiles.

As you grow older, you will probably be called on as a citizen to help make many decisions. One of these decisions will, no doubt, deal with the fuels used to *generate,* or produce, electric energy. Unit 44 discusses the generating plants that change various forms of energy to electric energy. The advantages and disadvantages of the different generating methods are also presented. Studying this information will help you make informed judgments today and in the future about the fuels that produce electric energy.

In a more personal way, we live with an ever-increasing variety of electrical and electronic products. If we are to choose and use them wisely, we should know something about them. For example, we should know how they are designed, manufactured, and made more efficient. Also, we should know what their limits are and to what uses they can best be put. The study of electricity and electronics can open new avenues of interest for you. This study may suggest career or hobby opportunities you may like. Perhaps your future work station may be in your own home and your connection with fellow workers may be through a computer terminal.

Only by expanding your knowledge can you hope to deal with living in this fast-moving world of ours. Studying this text will help give you this base.

UNIT 1   Atoms, Electrons, and Electric Charges

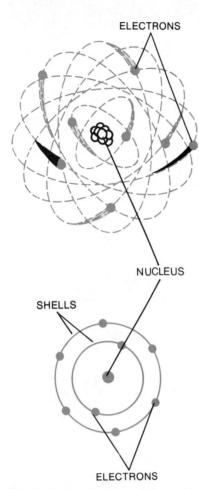

ELECTRONS

NUCLEUS

SHELLS

ELECTRONS

Fig. 1-1. Artist's view of the inside of an atom, containing eight electrons that move around the nucleus in two shells

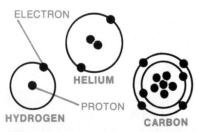

ELECTRON

HELIUM

PROTON

HYDROGEN

CARBON

Fig. 1-2. Atoms of hydrogen, helium, and carbon

Before we discuss the basics of electricity and electronics, we need to understand what matter is. *Matter* is anything that occupies space and has *mass,* or weight. Wire, rubber, and glass are examples of matter. Scientists study the properties of matter in order to know how it works. Scientists are also concerned with the study of energy. *Energy* is the capacity for doing work. Energy has different forms, such as heat energy and electric energy. Electric energy results from the motion of tiny bits of matter called *electrons.* Energy can make changes in materials, such as putting them together, taking them apart, or simply moving them from one place to another.

The basic unit of matter is the *atom.* In studying electricity and electronics, it is important for you to understand the atom because the electron is one of its parts. In this unit, the structure of the atom and its electrical properties are discussed.

STRUCTURE OF THE ATOM

An atom is made up of tiny particles. Two of these particles, the *electron* and the *proton,* are important to our studies.

Electrons move around the center, or *nucleus,* of an atom in paths. These paths are usually called *shells* (Fig. 1-1). An atom can have several shells around its nucleus. Each of these shells can have only up to a certain number of electrons. This number is called the *quota* of a shell. When every shell of the atom contains its quota of electrons, the atom is said to be in a stable condition. The nucleus of the atom is made up of particles called *protons* and *neutrons.* These are held together tightly by a binding energy.

All electrons are alike, and all protons are alike. Thus, atoms differ from one another only in the number of electrons and protons they contain (Fig. 1-2). The number of protons in the nucleus is the *atomic number* of that atom. Neutrons weigh about the same as protons. The term *atomic weight* refers to the total number of particles (both protons and neutrons) in the nucleus of an atom.

While scientists have provided much information about the atom, the search for more information continues. For example, new theories indicate that the nucleus of the atom contains other kinds of particles that are dynamic and complex. A discussion of these subatomic particles is beyond the scope of this text. These particles, however, are being studied intensively by scientists in the field called *high-energy physics.*

ELEMENTS, COMPOUNDS, AND MOLECULES

When all the atoms in a substance are alike, the substance is called an *element.* Copper, iron, and carbon are among the more than 100 different elements known to exist. Different elements can combine to form a

Fig. 1-3. Molecules of water and sulfuric acid. A molecule is made up of a number of atoms.

HYDROGEN ATOMS

HYDROGEN ATOMS

OXYGEN ATOM

WATER MOLECULE

OXYGEN ATOMS

SULFUR ATOM

OXYGEN ATOMS

SULFURIC ACID MOLECULE

substance called a *compound*. Water, sugar, and plastic materials are examples of compounds.

The smallest particle of a compound that has all the properties of that compound is called a *molecule*. A molecule contains atoms of each of the elements that form the compound (Fig. 1-3).

CHARGES

Electrons and protons have tiny amounts of energy known as *electric charges*. Electrons have negative (−) charges. Protons have positive (+) charges. Neutrons have no electric charge. Thus, they are neutral. The amount of the negative charge of each electron is equal to the amount of the positive charge of each proton. These opposite charges attract each other. This attraction helps hold the atom together.

Under normal conditions, the negative and the positive charges in an atom are equal in value. This is because the atom has an equal number of electrons and protons. An atom in this condition is said to be electrically neutral (Fig. 1-4).

ELECTRONS

PROTONS

Fig. 1-4. An electrically neutral atom

VALENCE ELECTRONS

Electrons in the outermost shell of an atom are called *valence electrons*. In the study of electricity and electronics, we are concerned mostly with the behavior of valence electrons. They can, under certain conditions, leave their "parent" atoms. The number of valence electrons in atoms also determines important electrical and chemical characteristics of the substance.

ENERGY LEVELS AND FREE ELECTRONS

The electrons in any shell of an atom are said to be located at certain energy levels. These are related to the distance of the electrons from the nucleus of the atom. When outside energy such as heat, light, or electricity is applied to certain materials, the electrons within the atoms of these materials gain energy. This may cause the electrons to move to a higher energy level. Thus, they move farther from the nuclei of their atoms (Fig. 1-5A).

FREE ELECTRONS

A   B

Fig. 1-5. Some electrons within an atom may move to higher energy levels within the atom or leave the atom as a result of the absorption of energy.

3

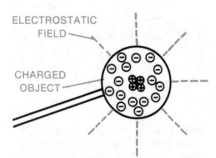

Fig. 1-6. Ions: (A) negatively charged ion; (B) positively charged ion

Fig. 1-7. Opposite electric charges attract each other and thus cause a rubber balloon to "stick" to a wall.

Fig. 1-8. An invisible electrostatic field is present around every charged body.

When an electron has moved to the highest possible energy level (or the outermost shell of its atom), it is least attracted by the positive charges of the protons within the nuclei of the atom. If enough energy is then applied to the atom, some of the outermost-shell, or valence, electrons will leave the atom. Such electrons are called *free electrons* (Fig. 1-5B).

IONS

An *ion* is a charged atom. If a neutral atom gains electrons, there are then more electrons than protons in the atom. Thus, the atom becomes a negatively charged ion (Fig. 1-6A). If a neutral atom loses electrons, protons outnumber the remaining electrons. Thus, the atom becomes a positively charged ion (Fig. 1-6B). Ions with unlike charges attract one another. Ions with like charges repel one another. The process by which atoms either gain or lose electrons is called *ionization*.

ELECTRIC CHARGES IN ACTION

A simple way of generating an electric charge is to create friction. For example, if you rub a rubber balloon briskly with a wool cloth, electrons will move from the cloth to the balloon, causing the balloon to become negatively charged. If you then put the balloon against a wall, the balloon's negative charge will repel electrons from the surface of the wall (Fig. 1-7). This will, in turn, cause the surface of the wall to become positively charged. The attraction between the opposite charges of the balloon and a small surface area of the wall is strong enough to hold the balloon in place. Other substances, such as glass, when rubbed briskly with a silk cloth, lose their electrons and therefore have a positive charge.

STATIC ELECTRICITY

The attraction between the charged balloon and wall represents work done by *electrostatic energy,* which is often called *static electricity.* An *electrostatic field* is the energy that surrounds every charged object (Fig. 1-8). In this kind of electricity, there is no movement of electrons between the balloon and the wall. Thus, the electricity is said to be *static,* or at rest.

Static electricity is sometimes thought of as a nuisance. However, devices such as capacitors and air cleaners and industrial processes such as the manufacture of abrasive paper make use of it.

USEFUL APPLICATIONS OF STATIC ELECTRICITY

Figure 1-9 shows how static charges are used in making abrasive paper. *Sandpaper* is a common term for abrasive paper. Such paper is used to smooth the surfaces of wood or metal. A conveyor belt carries the abrasive particles over a negatively charged plate. The abrasive particles are negatively charged by contact. At the same time, the paper, which is tacky from an adhesive coating, is moving under a positively

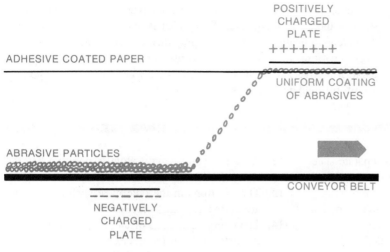

POSITIVELY CHARGED PLATE
++++++

ADHESIVE COATED PAPER

UNIFORM COATING OF ABRASIVES

ABRASIVE PARTICLES

CONVEYOR BELT

NEGATIVELY CHARGED PLATE

BELT AND PAPER MOVE TOGETHER

Fig. 1-9. Electrostatic charges used in making abrasive paper

DIRTY AIR

PRE-FILTER

POSITIVELY CHARGED PLATES

CLEAN AIR

FILTER NEGATIVELY CHARGED

Fig. 1-10. An electrostatic air cleaner

charged plate. This makes the paper positive. Since opposite charges attract, the abrasive particles are attracted to the paper. These particles form a very uniform and dense abrasive surface on the paper.

Static electricity can also be used in an air cleaner (Fig. 1-10). This device can be used in home heating systems to clean the air as it circulates through the furnace. A similar device can be used by industry to reduce air pollution. Electrostatic air filters are much more efficient than simple cloth or paper filters. Those remove only large particles from the air. An electronic filter can remove tiny particles. As shown in Fig. 1-10, the dirty air passes through a paper prefilter that removes large pieces of dirt and lint. The air then moves through a series of plates that give a positive charge to the dirt and dust particles. Finally the air moves through a negatively charged filter. The positive particles are attracted to the negative filter. They become trapped there. After the filters become very dirty, the system must be shut down and cleaned.

Another practical use of static electricity is shown in Fig. 1-11. Spray painting is a common way of producing beautifully finished surfaces.

NO SPRAY DUST

ELECTROSTATIC CHARGES

Fig. 1-11. Electrostatic spray painting

However, it is wasteful. Much of the paint never sticks to the surface. It stays in the air as *spray dust*. Spray dust is not only wasteful but also dangerous to health. Most of the spray dust can be eliminated by positively charging the object to be painted and negatively charging the paint. Moreover, since the charge decreases where the paint is applied, a uniform thickness of paint is produced.

SELF-TEST

Test your knowledge by writing, on a separate sheet of paper, the word or words that most correctly complete the following statements:

1. _____ is anything that occupies space and has mass.
2. The capacity for doing work is called _____ .
3. Electrons move around the nucleus of an atom in paths that are usually called _____ .
4. The nucleus of an atom is made up of particles called _____ and _____ .
5. Atoms differ from one another only in the number of _____ and _____ they contain.
6. The number of protons in the nucleus of an atom is known as the atomic _____ of that atom.
7. When all the atoms within a substance are alike, the substance is called an _____ .
8. Common examples of elements are _____ , _____ , and _____ .
9. Different elements can combine to form a substance called a _____ .
10. A _____ is the smallest particle of a compound that has all the properties of that compound.
11. Electrons are _____ charges. Protons are _____ charges.

12. An electrically neutral atom is one that has the same number of _____ and _____ .
13. The electrons in the outermost shell of an atom are called _____ electrons.
14. The energy _____ of an electron is related to its distance from the nucleus of an atom.
15. An ion is an atom that is either _____ charged or _____ charged.
16. If a neutral atom gains electrons, it becomes a _____ ion.
17. If a neutral atom loses electrons, it becomes a _____ ion.
18. Ions with unlike electric charges _____ each other. Ions with like electric charges _____ each other.
19. The process by which atoms either gain or lose electrons is called _____ .
20. A simple way of generating an electric charge is by _____ .
21. The attraction between two opposite electric charges is an example of _____ electricity.
22. A charged object is surrounded by an _____ field.

FOR REVIEW AND DISCUSSION

1. Define the term *energy*.
2. Identify two different forms of energy. Can you list more?
3. Describe the makeup of an atom.
4. How do atoms differ from one another?
5. What is an element? What is a compound? What is a molecule?
6. Define the atomic number of an atom.
7. Explain what is meant by an *electrically neutral atom*.
8. What are valence electrons?

9. Explain the relationship between electron energy levels and free electrons.
10. How does an atom become a negative ion? A positive ion?
11. State the laws of electrical attraction and repulsion.
12. Describe a simple way of generating an electric charge.
13. Explain static electricity. Give an example of its presence.
14. What is meant by an *electrostatic field*?

1. Prepare a written or an oral report on the electron theory as it relates to the study of electricity.
2. Prepare a written or an oral report on the field of high-energy physics. Include in your report the function of an accelerator as it pertains to this field of inquiry.

UNIT 2   Electric Circuits

An *electric circuit* is a combination of parts connected to form a complete path through which electrons can move. The purpose of a circuit is to make use of the energy of moving electrons. Therefore, a circuit is also a system of parts, or components, by which electric energy can be changed into other forms of energy, such as heat, light, or magnetism.

PARTS OF A CIRCUIT

A basic complete circuit has four parts: (1) the energy source, (2) the conductors, (3) the load, and (4) the control device (Fig. 2-1).

Energy Source. The *energy source* in a circuit produces the force that causes electrons to move. It is like a pump that forces water through a pipe. In electricity, this force is called *voltage,* or *electromotive force.* The basic unit of force is the *volt.* The flow of electrons is called *current.* The most common energy sources used in electric circuits are chemical cells and electromechanical generators. These devices do the work needed to move electrons through the parts of the circuit.

Fig. 2-1. A basic electric circuit

CONTROL DEVICE
(SWITCH)

CONDUCTORS (WIRES)

LOAD (BUZZER)

SOURCE OF ENERGY (BATTERY)

Conductors. The *conductors* in a circuit provide an easy path through which electrons can move through the circuit. Copper is the most commonly used conductor material. It is formed into wire, bars, or channels (Fig. 2-2). Copper wire may be bare or covered with some kind of insulating material. The insulation prevents electrons from moving outside the wire (Fig. 2-3).

Fig. 2-2. Wire is manufactured by pulling copper rods through dies (*Rome Cable Corporation*)

Fig. 2-3. Insulated wire. Some common insulating materials are neoprene, rubber, nylon, polyethylene, Teflon, vinyl, cotton, asbestos, paper, and enamel.

In some circuits, metal objects other than copper conductors form the conducting paths. In an automobile, for example, the entire car frame serves as a conductor. It completes a number of circuits that connect the voltage source (the car battery) to various electrical and electronic devices (the loads). The metal *chassis*, or frame, that supports the components of electrical devices is also used as a common conductor for the electric circuit. Figure 2-4 shows an experimental circuit that uses a novel method to achieve a common conducting path. Many of the component leads of this circuit are soldered directly to the copper-clad surface of the laminated circuit board. The copper-clad surface forms a common conducting path for these components.

Fig. 2-4. The copper-clad surface of a circuit board provides a common conductor for the experimental circuit. (*QST, Journal of American Radio Relay League*)

Load. The *load* is that part of a circuit that changes the energy of moving electrons into some other useful form of energy. A light bulb is a very common circuit load. As electrons move through the filament of the lamp, the energy of the electrons in motion is changed into heat energy and light energy (Fig. 2-5).

Control Device. A simple circuit-control device is the common mechanical wall switch. It lets us open or close a circuit (Fig. 2-6). When the switch is ''on,'' it acts as a conductor to keep electrons moving through the circuit. The circuit is said to be *closed*. In this condition, the circuit has a *closed loop*. When the switch is ''off,'' the circuit path is interrupted. Electrons can no longer move through the circuit. The circuit is said to be *open*, that is, it has an *open loop*.

In addition to the familiar on-off switches, other devices can provide a switching action and control the flow of electrons in a circuit. Examples are electromagnetic relays, diodes, transistors, and logic circuits, all discussed later in this book.

KINDS OF CIRCUITS

Loads can be connected into a circuit in *series,* in *parallel,* or in *series-parallel* combinations. A series circuit provides only one path, or one loop, through which electrons can move from one terminal of the energy source to the other (Fig. 2-7A). In a parallel circuit, there may be two or more different paths, or loops, through which electrons can flow (Fig. 2-7B). A series-parallel circuit is shown in Fig. 2-7C. Note that series and parallel circuits are combined to form one circuit with several paths, or loops.

Fig. 2-5. A typical electrical load. The light bulb converts electric energy into heat and light energy. (*General Electric Company*)

Fig. 2-7. Circuit connections: (A) series circuit; (B) parallel circuit; (C) series-parallel circuit. Arrows indicate a closed current loop.

Fig. 2-6. A typical on-off switch

SELF-TEST

Test your knowledge by writing, on a separate sheet of paper, the word or words that most correctly complete the following statements:

1. An electric circuit makes it possible to use the energy of moving _____.

2. In a circuit, electric energy is changed into other forms of energy, such as _____, _____, or _____.

3. The four basic parts of a complete circuit are the
_____, the _____, the _____, and the
_____.
4. Common sources of energy used in electric circuits are _____ and _____.
5. The most common conductor material is _____.

6. That part of a circuit that changes electric energy into another form of energy is the _____.
7. The series circuit provides only _____ path through which electrons can move.
8. In a _____ circuit, there may be two or more electron paths.

FOR REVIEW AND DISCUSSION

1. What is an electric circuit?
2. Name and define the four parts of a basic complete circuit.
3. Describe basic series and parallel circuits.
4. What is the main feature of a series-parallel circuit?

INDIVIDUAL-STUDY ACTIVITY

Prepare a written or an oral report describing familiar electric circuits you use in everyday activities. Identify each of the parts of the circuits and tell what each does in its circuit.

UNIT 3   Circuit Diagrams and Symbols

Once you have developed a circuit on paper to do a task, you should plan how to build it. In electrical and electronics work, the basic part of such a plan is usually a diagram. A *diagram* shows how the different parts are connected to form the complete circuit. Developing the diagram is an important step in designing circuits. The diagram will guide those who will maintain and repair the circuit. The diagram also serves as a record for those who may want to copy or study it or for those who wish to change the circuit.

This unit discusses several common kinds of diagrams. It also offers much useful information about reading and drawing diagrams.

PICTORIAL DIAGRAMS

If you build a project from a do-it-yourself kit, one of the items included in the construction manual will be a *pictorial diagram*. This is a drawn picture of the parts of the circuit. It shows how the parts are connected and where they are to be located within the assembly (Fig. 3-1). The pictorial diagram also shows the wiring devices, such as lugs and sockets, that are to be used. The pictorial diagram is usually drawn *to scale*. That means that the *relationships* of the sizes and locations of the parts are accurate whether they are shown full-size, smaller, or larger.

Pictorial diagrams are easy to follow. For this reason, they are used

Fig. 3-1. Pictorial diagram of a one-transistor radio

10

with do-it-yourself kits and in manufacturing to show what finished products will look like.

One disadvantage of a pictorial diagram is that it does not give clear electrical information about the circuit. It simply shows what the circuit will look like after it is put together. Such diagrams do not show the electron path or the way the parts relate to one another electrically. Pictorial diagrams usually take a lot of time to prepare and often take up much space.

SCHEMATIC DIAGRAMS

The *schematic diagram* is the standard way of communicating information in electricity and electronics. On this diagram, the components are shown by *graphic symbols*. These are letters, drawings, or figures that stand for something. In electricity and electronics, a graphic symbol shows the connecting points of a part in a circuit. Because the symbols are small, the diagrams can be drawn small. The symbols and related lines are used to show how the parts of a circuit are connected and how they relate to one another.

Examine the schematic diagram of the two-transistor radio circuit shown in Fig. 3-2. If you read this diagram from left to right, you see

Fig. 3-2. Schematic diagram of a two-transistor radio

Identification of components

BT1	Battery
C1	Variable capacitor (The arrow crossing the symbol indicates the value of the component can be varied.)
C2, C3, and C4	Fixed capacitors
CR1	Crystal diode
HT	Double headset
J1 and J2	Insulated tip jacks
L1	Antenna coil (variable ferrite-core inductor)
Q1 and Q2	p-n-p transistors
R1, R2, and R3	Carbon-composition resistors
S1	Single-pole—single-throw switch

Conductor symbols:

Conductors crossing but not connected.

Conductors electrically connected (the dot is often omitted when the connection is obvious).

NOTE: The letters B, C, and E near the transistor symbols indicate the Base, Collector, and Emitter leads of the transistors.

11

the components in the order in which they are used to convert radio waves into sound energy. The antenna (at the left) collects the radio waves (energy), and the headset (at the right) converts this energy into sound. By using the diagram, you can trace the operation of the circuit from beginning to end. Because of this, schematic diagrams are used widely by engineers and technicians. They are used in all kinds of circuit design, construction, and maintenance activities.

Identification of Components. As shown in Fig. 3-2, the components on a schematic diagram are also identified by *class designation letters*. These include R for resistors, C for capacitors, and Q for transistors. You will learn later what these are and what they do. For now, you should simply be able to recognize their assigned letters. Table 3-1

TABLE 3-1 SELECTED CLASS DESIGNATION LETTERS

Designation Letter(s)	Class of Items	Designation Letter(s)	Class of Items
AR	Amplifier (other than rotating) Repeater	Q	Semiconductor controlled rectifier Phototransistor (three terminals) Transistor
BT	Battery Solar cell	R	Potentiometer Resistor Rheostat
D or CR	Crystal diode Metallic rectifier Varactor	S	Contactor (manually, mechanically, or thermally operated) Disconnecting device (switch) Switch Telegraph key Thermostat
DS	Alphanumeric display device Light-emitting solid-state device Signal light		
HT	Earphones Electrical headset Telephone receiver	V	Electron tube Phototube Voltage regulator (electron tube)

shows the class designation letters for selected items. The letters are further combined with numbers, such as R1, R2, and R3, to distinguish different components of the same kind. The numerical values of components are often shown directly on the schematic diagram, together with the component identifications. When these are not given in this way, they are stated in the parts list in the notes that come with the diagram. Very often symbol letters are shown slanted (called *italic*) on diagrams.

Other Symbols. A number of other common symbols used with schematic diagrams are shown in Fig. 3-3. One of the organizations responsible for standardizing these and other symbols is the American National Standards Institute (ANSI). Complete listings of the symbols used in electricity and electronics are available from this organization. Standards used in other technical fields are also available from the ANSI.

The symbols for a *ground connection* and for a *chassis,* or *frame, connection* are commonly found on schematic diagrams. These symbols serve as common reference points in a circuit. The symbol for the ground connection stands for a common circuit return to a structure, such as the frame of an air, space, or land vehicle, that is not conductively connected to the earth. If the circuit, however, has a direct connection to the earth or a body of water, additional information should be placed adjacent to the symbol. The word (*earth*) adjacent to a ground symbol, for example, indicates an earth ground. An earth ground connection is often made by fastening the wire to a water pipe or to a metal rod that is driven into the earth. The symbol for a chassis, or frame, connection also stands for a common circuit return. This symbol represents a conduction connection to a chassis, or frame, or to a common wire or area on a printed circuit board. This connection, however, may be at a higher voltage level with respect to the earth or structure in which this chassis frame (or printed circuit board) is mounted. In complex circuits, such as those for television and radio, many connections have a common return. The use of these symbols makes it possible to show all common connecting points without cluttering up the diagram with extra lines.

READING THE SCHEMATIC DIAGRAM

The ability to read schematic diagrams is important. Most circuits you may want to study, build, or repair are probably illustrated by such a diagram. Reading a diagram is not so hard as it first may appear. With some practice, you will find that reading a schematic is convenient and saves time.

To begin to learn how to read schematic diagrams, look at the pictorial and the schematic diagrams of the same circuit shown in Fig. 3-4. Read from left to right. Find and identify the same components in both. Trace the wire connections. Some connections in the pictorial diagram may be covered by other components. Try to find these wires in the schematic diagram.

Unlike a pictorial diagram, a schematic diagram does not show where the parts or connecting wires are located on the chassis. The *chassis* is the frame or base on which the parts are mounted. Also note that the schematic diagram does not show any wiring devices such as lugs and sockets. Whether and where to use other wiring devices depends on the sizes and shapes of the components and the space available. Wiring also depends on the electrical characteristics of the parts of the circuit. They must be wired according to the schematic diagram.

Alternating-current source

Amplifier, general

Buzzer

Cell (chemical)

Chassis or frame connection

Circuit breaker, general

Connector (plug)
2-conductor, nonpolarized

Diode, rectifier, semiconductor

Electron tube, triode with
indirectly heated cathode

Fuse
or

Ground, general

Lamp, incandescent

Lamp, neon

Loudspeaker

Meter

*Insert appropriate
designation . . . .

A   -   ammeter
G   -   galvanometer
MA   -   milliammeter
OHM   -   ohmmeter
V   -   voltmeter

Microphone

Motor, general

Potentiometer, variable resistor

Terminal

Transformer, with Iron Core

or

Transistor, n-p-n

Wire, shielded, single conductor

Fig. 3-3. Common symbols used on schematic diagrams. Other symbols are shown throughout the book.

Fig. 3-4. (A) Pictorial (bottom view) and (B) schematic diagrams of a rectifier circuit

WIRING FROM A SCHEMATIC DIAGRAM

To wire a circuit from a schematic diagram, you must know how to read the diagram. You also need to know about kinds and sizes of wires, about how to make connections, and about wiring tools and devices. These are discussed in Section 5, ''Electrical Wiring: Materials, Tools, and Processes.''

DRAWING A SCHEMATIC DIAGRAM

Sometimes you will wire a circuit without using a schematic diagram. At other times, you may have to work on a wired circuit for which no diagram is available. In such cases, you may often need or want to make a schematic diagram directly from the wired circuit. The following suggestions will help you make a neat, readable diagram:

1. Use standard symbols for all the components. If there is no standard, adapt a symbol for your use. Note its meaning on the diagram and in a separate symbol list.
2. Locate the symbols so that the lines that will show the conductors connecting them will not be too close together. Use as few line crossings and bends as possible (Fig. 3-5A.)
3. Do not draw the symbols so close to one another that they crowd the diagram and make it hard to read.

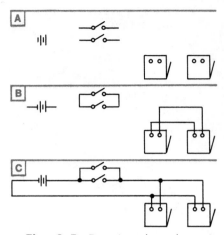

Fig. 3-5. Drawing the schematic diagram

4. Use unruled paper for schematic diagrams to keep from confusing drawn lines with the lines printed on the paper.
5. After drawing the symbols, connect them with straight vertical and horizontal lines (Fig. 3-5B and C).
6. Use the dot symbol when it is necessary to show that conductors are electrically connected.

WIRING, OR CONNECTION, DIAGRAMS

Wiring diagrams are used to show circuit-system connections in a simple way. They are commonly used with home appliances and automobile electrical systems.

The typical wiring diagram shows the components of a circuit in a pictorial manner. The components are usually identified by name (Fig. 3-6). Such a diagram also often shows the positions of the components in relation to each other. A color code may identify certain wires.

BLOCK DIAGRAMS

A block diagram provides a convenient means to quickly convey information about complex electrical systems (Fig. 3-7). Each block represents electrical circuits that perform specific functions in the system. The functions the circuits perform are written in each block. Where appropriate, block diagrams are often combined with graphic symbols. Block diagrams are usually read from left to right. Arrows connecting the blocks indicate the general direction of the current paths. Wires and individual components are not shown on block diagrams. The *power supply* block has arrows pointing toward the other blocks. This means that its function is to supply electrical power to all the circuits. The power supply block is sometimes omitted in block diagrams because it is assumed that all electrical circuits need power to operate properly.

ARCHITECTURAL FLOOR-PLAN DIAGRAMS

Architects, electrical designers, and contractors use floor-plan diagrams to show where the parts of a building's electrical system are to be located. These include receptacle outlets, switches, lighting fixtures, and conduit and other wiring devices. These are shown with symbols (Fig. 3-8). A basic floor-plan diagram sometimes omits the conduit system and associated wiring. These and their sizes are shown, however, on the contractor's working drawings. It is from these that the electrician does the wiring job.

Fig. 3-6. Wiring diagram of an automobile starting circuit

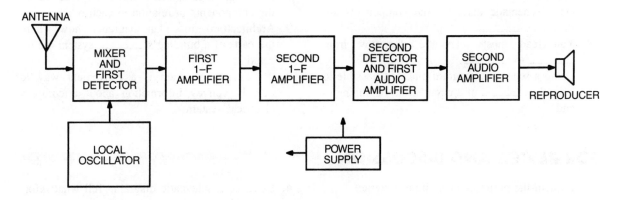

Fig. 3-7. Block diagram of a superheterodyne radio receiver

Other symbols used with architectural floor-plan diagrams

⊖G	Duplex receptacle outlet, grounding type	▫•	Push button
⊖WP	Duplex receptacle outlet, weatherproof	▫◦	Bell
⊖R	Range outlet	▨	Power panel
S₃	Three-way switch	◦ⓒ	Clock outlet, wall mounted
S₄	Four-way switch	BT	Bell ringing transformer

Fig. 3-8. A simple architectural floor-plan diagram and some standard symbols used on these diagrams

SELF-TEST

Test your knowledge by writing, on a separate sheet of paper, the word or words that most correctly complete the following statements:

1. A _____ shows how the different parts are connected to form the complete circuit.
2. The pictorial diagram is usually drawn to _____.
3. On a schematic diagram, the components are shown by _____.
4. You read most schematic diagrams from _____ to _____.
5. Using a schematic diagram makes it possible to trace the _____ of a circuit from beginning to end.
6. Examples of class designation letters used to identify components on a schematic diagram are _____ for resistors, _____ for capacitors, and _____ for transistors.
7. The dot symbol is used to show that wires are electrically _____ at that point.
8. A wiring diagram often shows the _____ of the components in relation to each other.
9. Architectural floor-plan diagrams show where the parts of a building's _____ system are located.
10. A _____ diagram is a convenient way to quickly convey information about a complex electrical system.

FOR REVIEW AND DISCUSSION

1. Explain the purposes of a circuit diagram.
2. Describe a pictorial diagram.
3. Name some disadvantages of the pictorial diagram.
4. Describe a schematic diagram. Tell what information is given by such a diagram.
5. How are the different components identified on a schematic diagram?

6. Draw and identify the symbols for 10 familiar electrical and/or electronic components.
7. List several practices to be followed when drawing a schematic diagram.
8. Describe a wiring diagram.
9. What are the advantages of a block diagram?
10. Explain how the ground symbol can be used to reduce the number of lines in Fig. 3-2.
11. What is the purpose of an architectural floor-plan diagram?

INDIVIDUAL-STUDY ACTIVITIES

1. Prepare a written or an oral report on the development of standard electrical symbols in this country.
2. Obtain large-size pictorial and schematic diagrams. Explain to the students in your class what they show. Tell about the advantages of each type of diagram.
3. Obtain an architectural floor-plan diagram from a local architect, contractor, or electrician. Explain it to your class.
4. Prepare an architectural floor-plan diagram of one room in your home.
5. Obtain an electronic assembly (wired chassis, printed circuit board, etc.). Make a schematic diagram of the assembly. Explain in written form or orally how the process was done.

UNIT 4   Safety Rules, Practices, and Devices

Safety is everybody's business. Developing safe work habits depends on the right attitude—a feeling that you *want* to work safely. With this attitude, you will try to understand the safety rules and practices for your activities. And you will find yourself following these rules and practices. You will want to do these things not only for your own safety but also for the safety of others.

Failing to follow electrical safety rules and practices can injure you or others and destroy property. Shock and burns may result when the body conducts electricity. Property may be damaged by electrical fires started by overheated wires or sparks. These must be prevented if we are to use electric energy safely and efficiently.

ELECTRIC SHOCK

An *electric shock* is a physical sensation caused by the reaction of the nerves to electric current. In minor cases, there is only a harmless "jerking" of the affected muscles. In more severe cases, the breathing and heart muscles become paralyzed. If the muscles are permanently damaged, the result is often death by *electrocution*. That means "to be killed by electricity." If the muscles are not permanently damaged, they can often be restored to normal operation by *artificial respiration*. Mouth-to-mouth artificial respiration is an effective way to restore normal breathing. In this method, you periodically blow air into the victim's mouth. At the same time, you pinch the victim's nostrils shut.

Fig. 4-1. Current paths through the chest region of the body

Call a medical doctor at once. If a doctor is not available, call the nearest rescue squad.

The amount of current that can cause serious damage to the muscles of a person's body depends on his or her physical condition. Records show that people have been electrocuted by very low values of current. Serious muscular damage is likely to result if an excessive current passes through the chest area. This happens when the conducting path goes from hand to hand or from one hand to the feet (Fig. 4-1). The danger of a severe shock is increased when the skin becomes wet.

Under normal conditions, the *epidermis,* or outer layer of skin, presents a high resistance to current. If the epidermis becomes wet from sweat or another liquid, its resistance is greatly lowered. Under this condition, a voltage lower than 120 volts (V) can cause a dangerous amount of current to pass through the body.

BURNS

In addition to shock, an excessive current passing through the body can cause severe burns. Such burns result from heat produced by friction between electrons and body tissues. Electrical burns often occur inside the body along the path followed by current. Burns of this kind can be very painful and difficult to heal.

GENERAL SAFETY RULES AND PRACTICES

Understanding the causes and effects of electric shocks and burns is important. Safety rules and practices are designed to prevent such accidents. No set of rules and practices can cover all cases. However, the list that follows will help you use and work with electricity safely.

1. Always treat electrical wires in a circuit as being potentially dangerous.
2. Always unplug the power cord of a piece of equipment before removing the case or cabinet in which the wiring is contained.
3. Do not touch a water or gas pipe, a sink, a bathtub, or any wet surface while handling the metal parts of electrical equipment that is plugged in.
4. Never place any plugged-in equipment where it can fall into a sink or a bathtub containing water.
5. Be sure to read and follow all instructions supplied with electrical or electronic equipment before attempting to use it.
6. Make it a habit to periodically inspect all the electrical appliances and tools you use. In this way, you will find any potentially dangerous conditions, such as loose wires, undesirable bare wires, and frayed cords (Fig. 4-2).
7. Always unplug or disconnect equipment that does not seem to be working normally.
8. Do not work on any equipment unless you know the right proce-

Fig. 4-2. Points at which electrical cord defects most often occur: (A) where cords enter appliances; (B) where cords enter attachment plugs

dures to follow. It is always a good practice to call in an expert when you are unsure about the safe and proper way to handle any equipment.

9. If you must work with the exposed parts of a circuit that is plugged in, handle the parts with one hand only. Keep the other hand behind your back or in a pocket. This will keep the current from passing through your chest. Do not wear rings or watches when touching live electric circuits.

10. It is always a safe practice to use only equipment that has the Underwriters' Laboratories label (Fig. 4-3). This shows that the item has been made according to strict safety standards.

11. Find and learn to work the main power switch in your home and in other places where you work with electricity. This will let you quickly turn off all the circuits in an emergency.

12. During an electric shock, the muscles will often cause the fingers to hold the point of contact tightly. Use all available means to separate from a point of electrical contact as quickly as possible. The possibility of serious muscular damage and burns increases the longer current passes through your body.

13. If an electric shock causes breathing to stop, a doctor should be called immediately. Artificial respiration must be started right after the electrical contact has been broken. Extreme care must be taken in removing a person from the point of contact. Otherwise, the path of current can pass through the rescuer, causing her or him to suffer severe shock also.

14. Although an electric shock may not be dangerous, it will almost always startle or frighten you. This may, in turn, cause you to fall or to bump against hard surfaces, resulting in serious injury.

Fig. 4-3. The Underwriters' Laboratories label

GROUNDING FOR PERSONAL SAFETY

The *ground*, or earth, usually is a good conducting point for electrons when a path exists between it and a *live,* or charged, wire. Because of this, putting any part of your body between the ground and such a wire presents the danger of severe shock. *Grounding wires* and *devices* are designed to reduce this hazard.

If a bare wire of an electrical appliance comes into contact with the bare metal of its cabinet, the cabinet becomes an extension of the wire. If the cabinet is *ungrounded,* or not connected to the ground, the line voltage will appear between the cabinet and ground. In most homes, the line voltage is about 115 V. Thus, there is a danger of severe shock if a person makes contact between the cabinet and any surface that is in close contact with the ground.

Grounding Wires, Plugs, and Outlets. Metal cabinets, cases, and frames of appliances, tools, and machines are usually grounded by a separate grounding wire. This grounding wire is part of their power

Fig. 4-4. Grounding plug and receptacle outlet

TO APPLIANCE TERMINALS

RECEPTACLE OUTLET

GROUNDING WIRE TO APPLIANCE CABINET OR FRAME

TO BUILDING GROUND

SYMBOLS

3-CONDUCTOR POLARIZED CONNECTOR FEMALE CONTACTS

3-CONDUCTOR POLARIZED CONNECTOR MALE CONTACTS

cords. The grounding wire is connected to the cabinet, case, or frame of the device and to the round prong of the cord's plug. It is not connected to any part of the device's electric circuit. When the plug is put into a grounded outlet, the grounding wire of the cord is automatically connected to the building ground. This connection is made through a grounding wire in the cord leading to the outlet (Fig. 4-4). Since the cabinet, case, or frame is then at the same voltage as the ground, a shock hazard cannot exist between it and any grounded surface.

The three-pronged grounded plug is called a *polarized plug*. Its prongs will fit into the outlet only when they are lined up properly. For example, the round prong connected to the equipment ground wire can fit only into the round hole in the outlet. When this happens, the other two prongs automatically line up with their slots in the outlet. One is connected to the "hot" wire. The other is connected to the "neutral" wire. For a description of the hot and neutral wires, see Unit 31.

Individual Grounding. Metal cabinets of appliances and frames of machines do not always use grounding plugs and outlets. These devices are grounded by connecting them directly to water pipes or to ground rods (Fig. 4-5). Because plastic plumbing is often used, the plumbing system must be inspected to make sure the water pipe is an adequate ground. Gas pipes should never be used for grounding.

Green Wire. Some appliances have cords that have a two-pronged plug but still contain three wires. One of these, a grounding wire, is green. It extends a short distance from the side of the plug. A *spade lug* is connected to this end of the green wire. This lug is used to connect the green wire to a grounding point. The other end of the green wire is attached to the metal case of the electrical appliance or tool. When

Fig. 4-5. Grounding metal cabinets of appliances: (A) grounding to a water pipe; (B) use of a ground rod

connected properly, the green wire provides adequate protection against electric shock.

Two-to-three-wire Adapter. A two-to-three-wire *adapter* is a handy device. It makes it possible to use a grounding plug in a two-socket outlet (Fig. 4-6). Such an adapter does not automatically ground the device. It must be connected, using the grounding wire, to the ground point.

Fig. 4-6. A typical two-to-three-wire adapter

NEON LAMP HANDITESTER

An inexpensive device called a *neon lamp handitester* can be used to see whether an exposed wire is touching the metal cabinet or case of an electrical appliance. This condition presents, of course, the danger of severe shock. To use a handitester, simply press one tip firmly against a bare metal surface of the cabinet or case under test and hold the other tip in your hand (Fig. 4-7). The neon lamp of the tester will glow if a dangerous voltage exists between the cabinet and ground. If it does, the appliance or the tool should be unplugged at once and fixed as soon as possible.

WIRED-TO-CHASSIS CIRCUITS

One wire of the line cord of some radios and television sets is connected directly to the chassis. This then serves as a circuit conductor. This presents a definite shock hazard. A dangerous voltage may exist between the chassis and ground. Check the chassis with a neon lamp

Fig. 4-7. Using a neon lamp handitester to check for the presence of voltage between an appliance cabinet and ground

23

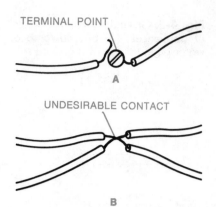

Fig. 4-8. Examples of (A) open circuit; (B) short circuit

Fig. 4-9. Medium-base plug fuse: (A) fuse in good condition; (B) blown or broken fuse link; (C) blown fuse link indicated by darkened "window"; (D) method of connecting a fuse to a circuit (*Bussmann Manufacturing Division, McGraw-Edison Company*)

handitester. If the test lamp glows, unplug the line cord. Then reverse the plug by turning it halfway around. Put the plug back in. In most cases, this will eliminate the dangerous condition. If not, unplug the device at once. Have it checked by a service technician.

DOUBLE, OR REINFORCED, INSULATION

Many appliances and portable motor-driven tools now offer protection against shock by means of *double*, or *reinforced, insulation*. In these devices, the wiring is kept from grounding by special kinds of insulation between the wiring and the equipment cabinet or case. To further protect against shock, certain gears and screws that hold the assembly together are often made of nylon or some other insulating material. Very often, the entire case is made of strong plastic material. This kind of construction makes it unnecessary to ground the cabinet or case.

OPEN AND SHORT CIRCUITS

When a wire becomes broken, burned out, or disconnected at some point, its circuit becomes open. When this occurs, the current will stop flowing (Fig. 4-8A). An open circuit can be dangerous. The voltage of the circuit will appear across the point at which the circuit is broken. Wires or equipment with a broken connection must be handled carefully if the equipment is still plugged in.

If two bare live wires come in contact with one another in such a way as to bypass the load, an excessive amount of current will flow in the circuit. This condition is known as a *short circuit* (Fig. 4-8B). Short circuits are very dangerous. They are dangerous because the excessive current is usually high enough to damage the insulation of the wire and perhaps start a fire. In most circuits, fuses and circuit breakers are used to automatically open the circuit if there is excessive current flow. These devices are discussed below.

FUSES

A *fuse* is a safety device that works as a switch to turn a circuit off when the current goes over a specified value. Too much current may be due to a short circuit within the load. It may result from a condition known as *overloading*. Overloading happens when a circuit delivers more current to the load than the conductors can carry safely. Then the circuit becomes overheated. Overloading generally happens because too many appliances are plugged into the outlets served by the circuit.

Plug Fuses. Plug fuses are commonly used in household circuits. Such a fuse has a strip of metal called a *fuse link*, or *element* (Fig. 4-9). The link is usually made of zinc. It is designed to melt or burn out when more than the rated value of current passes through it. The electrical size of a fuse is equal to this value of current. It is given in a unit called an *ampere* (A). The number of amperes is usually printed on the body of a fuse, for example, 15 A or Amp. This means that the fuse will open if the current goes over 15 A. Plug fuses are put into a circuit by screwing them into special sockets. Some plug fuses have a metal screw base like the base of an ordinary light bulb. This kind of plug fuse is known as an *Edison,* or *medium, base.* The use of medium-base plug fuses is generally being discontinued. Most electrical building codes now prohibit their use. However, they are still quite common in older buildings.

Tamperproof Fuse. The tamperproof fuse is designed to prevent a fuse from being replaced with one of a different electrical size. For this reason, it is also called a *noninterchangeable plug fuse.* A socket is used that will accept only certain sizes of fuses. For example, 25-A or 30-A fuses will not fit into sockets for 15-A and 20-A fuses. In order to use these fuses in a medium-base socket, an adapter must be installed (Fig. 4-10). The adapter is first screwed into the fuse socket. Then the fuse is screwed into the adapter. Once in place, the adapter cannot be easily removed.

Fig. 4-10. Tamperproof fuse: (A) plug fuse; (B) fuse adapter (*Bussmann Manufacturing Division, McGraw-Edison Company*)

Dual-Element Plug Fuse. A dual-element, or time-delay, plug fuse is used in many homes. It is designed to withstand a current larger than its rated value for a short time. If the excessive current continues after this time, the fuse blows out just like an ordinary plug fuse. It must then be replaced.

The construction of a dual-element plug fuse is shown in Fig. 4-11. When too much current passes through the thermal cutout of the fuse, the solder holding the fuse link to the thermal cutout becomes hot. If this current continues, the solder is softened. This allows the spring to pull the fuse link out of the thermal cutout and break its connection.

Dual-element plug fuses are most often used in motor circuits. A motor draws much more current on starting than it does after reaching full speed. A dual-element plug fuse will withstand this short period of high current. It then continues to protect the motor circuit after the current has decreased to its running value. An ordinary plug fuse would probably burn out during the starting period. The dual-element plug fuse is slow to act under normal conditions. However, a sudden, heavy flow of current will cause its fuse link to quickly melt and open the circuit just like the ordinary plug fuse.

Fig. 4-11. Cutaway view showing construction of a dual-element plug fuse (*Bussmann Manufacturing Division, McGraw-Edison Company*)

Cartridge Fuses. Like plug fuses, cartridge fuses are available in either ordinary or dual-element versions (Fig. 4-12A). Some of these fuses are the renewable-link kind (Fig. 4-12B). A burned-out link in such a fuse can be replaced. The cartridge case can be used over and over again.

Cartridge fuses are mounted in clip holders (Fig. 4-12C). Small-size glass cartridge fuses are sometimes enclosed in spring-loaded fuse holders (Fig. 4-12D).

Fig. 4-12. Cartridge fuses and holders: (A) typical fuse cases; (B) cutaway view of renewable-link fuse; (C) clip-style fuse holders; (D) spring-loaded fuse holder (*Bussmann Manufacturing Division, McGraw-Edison Company*)

FUSE SAFETY RULES

Fuses will protect circuits only if they are used in the right way. The following rules will help you use fuses correctly and handle them safely:

1. Never replace a fuse of the proper size with a larger one.
2. Do not try to repair any blown fuse unless it is the renewable-link kind.
3. Call an electrician or some other qualified person if you are in doubt about the right size fuse to use in a circuit.
4. Never put a coin or any other object in a fuse socket.
5. Whenever possible, disconnect the main switch at the load center or switch box before replacing a fuse that is blown.
6. When replacing a fuse in a load center or switch box while the main switch is on, stand on a dry surface (preferably wood or a rubber mat). Use one hand to make the replacement. Keep the other hand behind your back or in a pocket.
7. To prevent overheating and sparking, make sure that a fuse is firmly inserted into its socket or fuse holder.
8. Remember that even an ordinary fuse of the right size will often blow out if used in a circuit with a motor in it. Use a dual-element fuse instead.
9. If a fuse of the right size blows out repeatedly, then you know that the circuit is overloaded or that there is a short circuit somewhere in

OPERATING LEVER

SYMBOL

CURRENT PIGTAIL

LATCH

RETAINER

MAGNETIC ARMATURE

LATCH LEVER

CALIBRATION SCREW
(SEALED BY U.L. LABEL)

MAGNETIC POLE PIECE

CURRENT BI-METAL

CONTACT
FINGER

LINE TERMINAL

LINE CONTACT
CLIP

ARC CHUTE

MOUNTING CLIP

CONTACT
CLIP SPRING

CONTACTS

SLIDER

OVER-CENTER
TOGGLE SPRING

AMBIENT COMPENSATION
BI-METAL

Fig. 4-13. Construction of a typical circuit breaker (*Cutler-Hammer*)

the circuit. Such conditions must be corrected before the circuit is put back into use.

10. Never try to bypass a fuse by connecting a wire between the terminals of its socket or holder. Always keep a supply of spare fuses of the right sizes on hand in case of emergency.

CIRCUIT BREAKERS

A *circuit breaker* is a mechanical device that performs the same protective function as a fuse. Unlike a fuse, however, it can also serve as an ordinary on-off switch. Some circuit breakers have a switch mechanism that works by *thermal,* or heat, control. Others use a magnetic switch mechanism. Larger circuit breakers have switchlike mechanisms that are both thermally and magnetically controlled (Fig. 4-13). Thermal control involves the use of a bimetallic element, discussed in Unit 33. Magnetic control involves the use of a solenoid, discussed in Unit 16.

Like fuses, circuit breakers are rated according to the amount of current in amperes that can pass through them before they are *tripped,* or opened. However, unlike a fuse, a circuit breaker can be reset after being tripped. Some circuit breakers have adjustable trip sizes. Others have only a single trip value.

When a circuit breaker of the kind shown in Fig. 4-13 trips, its lever moves to or near the off position. To reset it, simply move the lever back to the on position.

Fig. 4-14. A portable ground-fault circuit interrupter (GFCI) (*Harvey Hubbel, Inc.*)

GROUND-FAULT CIRCUIT INTERRUPTER

The *ground-fault circuit interrupter* (GFCI) is a device that gives added personal protection against electric shock. Devices such as fuses, equipment grounds, and double insulation are used for personal and equipment protection, but they have shortcomings. An electric current of about 60 milliamperes (mA) can cause the heart action of adults to become irregular or to stop altogether. A 15-A fuse or circuit breaker disconnects the circuit only when the current exceeds 15 A. This amount is much greater than 60 mA.

Figure 4-14 shows a portable ground-fault circuit interrupter. Such interrupters are also available built into circuit breakers and duplex outlets. It is small enough to fit into a pocket. This GFCI can be plugged into a common duplex receptacle. However, it must be grounded properly to the receptacle. Before connecting an electrical cord of an appliance to a GFCI, you should test the GFCI to see if it is working properly. Do this by following the specific instructions for the GFCI being used. Ground-fault circuit interrupters work on the basic electrical principle that the current flowing in the hot wire to the device should equal the current flowing in the neutral wire from the same device. Any difference in the currents in these wires indicates that the current is taking another path to complete the circuit. The other path could be an unwanted ground in the electrical equipment. Ground-fault circuit interrupters sense the difference between the currents in the hot and neutral wires. If there is a difference of more than 5 mA, a safety switch trips in the GFCI and interrupts the circuit. This protects the person who is operating the electrical equipment from a serious electric shock. The GFCI does not completely eliminate the feeling of an electric shock. However, it does open the circuit quickly enough to prevent injury to a person of normal health. Thus, a GFCI provides protection against dangerous currents that do not overload 15- or 20-A fuses or circuit breakers. Nevertheless, do not use a GFCI in place of a separate grounding wire. Moreover, a GFCI does not protect a person who accidentally touches bare hot and neutral wires at the same time.

SAFETY GLASSES

The use of safety glasses is strongly recommended in electrical and electronics shops. Safety glasses should be worn when soldering, cutting wires, handling chemicals or television picture tubes, and using machines such as the drill press, portable electric drill, or grinder. All these activities could injure the eyes. It is always good practice to wear safety glasses while doing them.

POWER STRIPS

Electrical devices, such as microcomputers, printers, and monitors, function as a complete electrical system. Each device, however, requires an individual electrical outlet. The electrical wiring systems of most homes and business offices do not have a sufficient number of electrical outlets located in one place to meet this new need. The electrically grounded plug-in power strips help meet this new need (Fig. 4-15).

The power strip shown in Fig. 4-15A can accommodate six electrical devices. It has an on-off switch with a "power-on" indicator and a push-to-reset circuit breaker. Power strips used in homes are generally rated at 15 A, 125 V ac. A 6-ft electrical cord makes it possible to reach most electrical equipment.

Some power strips provide surge protection for the electrical equipment. *Power surges,* or excessive current or voltage, are often caused by switching on and off inductive loads, such as air conditioners and furnace fans. Lightning from thunderstorms causes most damage due to the sudden high-voltage discharge of atmospheric electricity. Entire computer systems, for example, can be damaged by lightning or other electrical surges unless protection is provided.

Fig. 4-15. Electrically grounded plug-in strips: (A) six-outlet; (B) four-outlet (*Radio Shack, A Division of Tandy Corp.*)

OSHA

As a future worker, you should become familiar with the *Occupational Safety and Health Act,* commonly called OSHA. The U.S. Congress passed this act in 1970. Its basic purpose is to ensure that every worker in the nation has safe and healthful working conditions.

The act does several things. It encourages employers and employees to reduce hazards in the workplace. It establishes responsibilities and rights for employers and employees. It develops required job safety and health standards and enforces them.

Both the worker and the employer have responsibilities under the act. The worker must read the OSHA posters at the job sites. The worker must obey all OSHA standards that apply. The worker must follow all the employer's safety and health rules and regulations. The employer must tell all employees about OSHA. The employer must provide a hazard-free workplace. The employer must make sure employees have and use safe tools and equipment. It is not possible to describe OSHA in detail in this textbook. However, much information about OSHA is available from the U.S. Department of Labor. That is the government agency that administers the act.

LEARNING BY DOING

1. *Making a Neon Lamp Handitester.* This device can be used to conveniently check for the presence of voltage at receptacle outlets and terminals and between ungrounded appliance and tool housings and ground. A voltage of at least about 60 V is needed to light the lamp. A direct-current (dc) voltage will cause only the electrode of the neon lamp connected to the negative terminal to glow. Thus, the handitester can be used to test dc-voltage polarity.

MATERIALS NEEDED

1 clear, hard plastic (Lucite or vinyl) tube, ½ in. (12.7 mm) OD, ¼ in. (6.35 mm) ID, 4 in. (101.6 mm) long
1 neon lamp, type NE-2
1 carbon-composition or film resistor; 220,000 Ω; ½ watt
12-in. (305-mm) test-prod wire, black, no. 18 AWG (1.00 mm)
12-in. (305-mm) test-prod wire, red, no. 18 AWG (1.00 mm)
1 test solderless prod, black, 4-in. (102-mm) handle
1 test solderless prod, red, 3-in. (76-mm) handle
plastic insulating tubing (spaghetti)
epoxy cement
clear liquid casting plastic (optional)

Procedure

1. Make the neon lamp, resistor, and test-prod-wire connections shown in Fig. 4-16. Make sure that all solder joints and bare wires of the assembly are completely insulated.
2. Carefully put the assembly into the plastic tube.
3. Seal the ends of the tube with epoxy cement or with some other suitable sealing compound. Put the cement or sealing compound on the lamp end of the tube a little at a time to keep it from covering a part of the lamp.

NOTE: A more attractive handitester can be made by sealing the test-prod-wire end of the tube with clear liquid casting plastic after the parts have been put into it. You then place the tube upright and fill it with the casting plastic from the lamp end.

Fig. 4-16. Neon lamp handitester assembly and circuit diagram

Test your knowledge by writing, on a separate sheet of paper, the word or words that most correctly complete the following statements:

1. An electric shock is a physical sensation caused by the reaction of the nerves to _____ .
2. The danger of severe shock is greatly increased if the skin becomes _____ .
3. In addition to shock, an excessive current through any part of the body can cause severe _____ .
4. Electrical wires, wherever they may be found in a circuit, should always be treated as being potentially _____ .
5. It is always safe practice to read and thoroughly understand all available operating _____ supplied with electrical and electronic products.
6. You should make it a habit to periodically _____ all electrical and electronic equipment you use.
7. A plug-in device should be immediately _____ if it does not seem to be working normally.
8. An _____ Laboratories label on a product shows that it has been made according to strict _____ standards.
9. Putting any part of your body between the _____ and a live wire presents the danger of severe shock.
10. A grounding wire is used to prevent a shock hazard from existing between a metal cabinet and _____ .
11. Grounding plugs and outlets automatically connect power cords to the building _____ .
12. The color of the grounding wire in the power cords of tools and appliances is _____ .
13. The use of _____ , or _____ , insulated products significantly lessens the danger of severe electric shock.
14. A fuse is a safety device that works as a _____ to turn a circuit _____ when there is too much current.
15. When a circuit is overloaded, it becomes _____ .
16. The electrical size of an ordinary plug fuse is given in _____ .
17. Dual-element fuses are usually needed in _____ circuits.
18. Never replace a fuse of the proper size with a _____ one.
19. A _____ is a mechanical device that, like a fuse, protects a circuit from excessive current.
20. Ground-fault circuit interrupters sense the difference between the currents in the _____ and _____ wires.
21. OSHA stands for _____ .

FOR REVIEW AND DISCUSSION

1. Describe an electric shock.
2. Why is it especially important not to allow the body to become a conductor of current from hand to hand or from hand to foot?
3. Explain why moisture on the skin greatly increases the danger of severe electric shock.
4. What causes electrical burns?
5. Discuss several general safety rules and practices.
6. Why is it important to ground metallic cabinets of appliances and metallic housings of portable electric tools?
7. Discuss grounding plugs and outlets.
8. For what purpose is a two-to-three-wire adapter used?
9. Explain the use of a neon lamp handitester as a safety aid.
10. Why does a wired-to-chassis circuit present a dangerous condition when operated at the standard house voltage of 115 V?
11. What is meant by *double*, or *reinforced, insulation construction?*
12. For what purpose is a fuse used? Explain the operation of this device.

13. Name and describe four common kinds of fuses.
14. In what kinds of circuits are dual-element plug fuses commonly used? Why?
15. Discuss several fuse safety rules.
16. What is a circuit breaker?
17. How is a typical circuit breaker reset after it has tripped?
18. What is the major advantage of using a ground-fault circuit interrupter?
19. Name several activities that require wearing safety glasses.
20. Identify three responsibilities OSHA requires of a worker and of an employer.
21. What is meant by the term *surge protection?*

INDIVIDUAL-STUDY ACTIVITIES

1. Prepare a written or an oral report about electric shock.
2. Prepare a list of the electrical safety practices that could be improved or that should be begun in your home.
3. Prepare a written or an oral report about the purposes and the policies of the Underwriters' Laboratories.
4. Give a demonstration showing various kinds of fuses and their general uses.
5. Obtain publications on artificial respiration from your local chapter of the American Red Cross or other area health agencies. Discuss the steps involved in mouth-to-mouth respiration.
6. Obtain examples of polarized plugs. Discuss the different kinds that are available.
7. Discuss how the Occupational Safety and Health Act (OSHA) affects your school.

UNIT 5 Occupations in Electricity and Electronics

The rapidly growing fields of electricity and electronics provide jobs for a large portion of the nation's workers (Table 5-1). According to those who study employment trends, many more workers will be needed in these fields in the future. This is due to the development and the use of new systems, products, and processes. Some of these new systems are now in operation in telecommunications, computer technology, automated manufacturing (robotics), and data processing.

Perhaps you, too, will be one of the ever-increasing number of young people entering these areas of employment. Your participation in an electricity and electronics course is a good start in this direction. Such a course can provide you with many interesting and useful educational experiences. It can serve to stimulate your interest in preparing for a job in the field. An introduction to these occupations at this time may suggest some career ideas. These will help make the rest of the course more meaningful. This information may also help you plan a school schedule. You should study those subjects that are recommended for an introduction to and/or preparation for entry into a particular occupation.

TABLE 5-1 APPROXIMATE NUMBER OF PERSONS EMPLOYED IN SELECTED ELECTRICAL AND ELECTRONICS OCCUPATIONS (1985)

Occupation	No. of Persons Employed in U.S.
Air-conditioning, refrigeration, and heating mechanics	210,000
Appliance repairers	145,000
Automobile mechanics	860,000
Broadcast technicians	40,000
Business-machine repairers	63,000
Central-office-equipment installers (telephone)	21,000
Computer operating personnel	660,000
Computer service technicians	63,000
Drafters	296,000
Electrical and electronic engineers	300,000
Electric sign repairers	15,000
Electricians (construction)	270,000
Electricians (maintenance)	300,000
Engineering and science technicians	600,000
Line installers and cable splicers	21,400
Programmers	247,000
Systems analysts	182,000
Telephone and PBX installers and repairers	59,000
Television and radio service technicians	131,000

EDUCATION AND TRAINING

A high school education can and does provide the necessary background for entry into many electrical and electronics jobs. For those who go into jobs immediately after graduation, continued education and training generally are needed. This training is often acquired in on-the-job apprenticeship programs. Attendance at special training sessions and evening classes is very helpful, too. Individualized programs such as approved correspondence courses can meet special training needs. In general, the more education you have, the better are your employment opportunities.

The basic education and training needed for entry into professional and skilled occupations are usually obtained through formal training programs. These include programs at both public and private 2- and 4-year colleges, technical institutes, and trade schools. In addition to these programs, participation in technical activities in the military services can often qualify you for entry into many different jobs. Military experience also may prepare you for jobs that require education and training beyond the high school level.

Whatever training program you may choose, you should begin at once to make the necessary plans for entering such a program. Much information about this can be obtained from your school instructor and guidance counselor. College and school representatives, labor unions, and those who are working at jobs can provide additional information.

ELECTRICAL OR ELECTRONIC ENGINEERING

Engineers are creators of ideas and problem solvers. They understand the principles of electrical theory, mathematics, physics, and chemistry. With this knowledge, they design and develop new systems and products (Fig. 5-1). They also improve the performance of systems and products already in use.

Most engineers are graduates of colleges or universities. Courses leading to a bachelor of science degree in electrical engineering (EE) are usually completed in 4 years. However, some engineers continue their education in specialized areas for which advanced study is needed. A master of science degree in computer science or electronics engineering is an example of advanced study. Specialized areas in such master's degree programs include communications, automatic controls, robotics, microelectronics, and signal processing.

In addition to the electrical engineering degree, another 4-year bachelor of science engineering degree is offered by some colleges. This is the electronics engineering technology (EET) degree. Graduates of this program are highly trained in the fields of science and mathematics. Their training also includes much work in the more practical areas of electricity and electronics. This training involves the improvement of systems and products already in use. In addition, the installation and maintenance of complicated electrical systems and equipment are studied.

ELECTRIC POWER AND LIGHTING DESIGNERS

Electrical designers are responsible for the design of electrical systems. Electrical systems are found in all kinds of indoor and outdoor facilities, such as buildings, highways, bridges, and stadiums. The systems electrical designers design provide power for air-conditioning equipment, business machines, pumps, elevators, and lighting. In fact, they design almost any equipment connected to a power supply. Electrical designers are usually employed by engineering companies in the construction field or by architectural firms. Many designers work for the contractors who install the systems designed. A designer normally works under the direction of an engineer. The engineer takes legal responsibility for the designer's work by officially signing the plans and specifications produced. A designer's formal education may include a full 4-year engineering course of study. Some designers have only a 2-year technical education or on-the-job training. These persons begin as electrical *drafters*. A drafter's work includes drawing detailed plans for the entire

Fig. 5-1. Electrical engineer designing control systems for manned flight operations (*National Aeronautics and Space Administration*)

electrical system. Electrical designers must be extremely knowledgeable about the various building codes. These codes govern the design and installation of electrical systems in the area in which the facilities will be built.

ENGINEERING TECHNICIANS

Engineering technicians are skilled workers whose jobs require a broad knowledge of scientific and mathematical principles. They apply this knowledge to activities involving the design, construction, operation, installation, and maintenance of electrical equipment. It is also important for engineering technicians to be skilled in writing and in public speaking. This is because their duties include selling, preparing reports, and speaking before various groups. This is particularly true of technicians who work directly with engineers in developing and producing new products (Fig. 5-2). Many engineering technicians advance to their jobs after a long period of on-the-job training. Another route to becoming an engineering technician is to complete an approved course of study at a community college or technical institute. Many of these schools offer an associate in science degree in electronic engineering technology. This degree usually requires successful completion of a 2-year program of study.

Fig. 5-2. Electronic technicians give final systems tests to professional videotape recorders (*Ampex Corporation*)

TELEVISION AND AUDIO SERVICE TECHNICIANS

Skilled television and audio service technicians are experts in the use of test instruments and hand tools. These technicians use troubleshooting techniques and adjustment procedures to repair, maintain, and install electronic appliances and devices (Fig. 5-3). Most of these technicians specialize in home television sets. However, they also work on a wide variety of other electronic equipment, such as video cassette recorders and cameras and personal computers.

Technical skills are not the only requirement for successful audio and television service technicians. These technicians work both in the shop and in customers' homes. Because of this, they must be courteous, neat, and businesslike in their conduct with other people. Many employers consider this an important quality when selecting new people for permanent jobs.

Fig. 5-3. Television and radio service technician testing the performance of a television receiver

The employment of consumer electronics service technicians is expected to increase sharply during the coming years. There will also be a marked increase in the complexity of the systems with which the technicians will work. Any plan for becoming a service technician should include attending a technical or vocational school. Many schools offer programs that emphasize this kind of training. These programs normally last from 9 to 18 months. Regardless of training and experience, service technicians must stay up to date. New television sets, for example, serve increasingly as personal computer monitors, bulletin boards, and teletext displays. Special courses and workshops about new products and techniques, such as microprocessors, digital amplifiers, new test equipment, and diagnosis of circuit troubles, are offered at technical schools. These courses often are taught by factory personnel. Attending these courses provides an effective way for consumer electronics technicians to improve their skills.

BROADCAST TECHNICIANS

Broadcast technicians set up, operate, and maintain the equipment used to record and transmit radio and television programs. This equipment includes transmission consoles, microphones, record and tape recording and playback equipment, television cameras, videotape recorders, motion-picture projectors, and lighting and sound-effects devices (Fig. 5-4).

Broadcast technicians receive their basic training on the job or by taking courses in the technical aspects of broadcasting. In addition to the technical skills needed, any person who operates broadcast transmitters is required by federal law to have a radiotelephone license issued by the Federal Communications Commission (FCC). Applicants for the license must pass a series of written examinations. These examinations test knowledge of transmitting and receiving equipment and electromagnetic wave theory. In addition, the examinations include questions about governmental and international regulations and practices concerning broadcasting. Preparation for the license examinations is available in special school programs and correspondence courses.

Fig. 5-4. Technical director monitoring programs at a television broadcasting station (*WRC-TV, Washington, D.C.*)

TELECOMMUNICATION WORKERS

A large number of skilled technicians and craft workers are needed in the telecommunication industry. Telephone workers install, maintain, and repair the vast amount of wiring and equipment used in this industry. Telephone companies frequently employ young, inexperienced men and women with the proper technical aptitude for this work. Then they are trained for some of these jobs.

Central-office-equipment Installers. These workers assemble, adjust, and wire the switching and dialing equipment in central offices of telephone companies (Fig. 5-5). Their jobs may involve installing a completely new central-office system. They may also add equipment to an existing system or replace outdated equipment. New employees receive their training both on the job and by classroom instruction. Because of the complexity of the work, this training continues as new techniques and equipment are developed and introduced.

Fig. 5-5. Telephone central-office-equipment installer at work on a distributing frame (*American Telephone and Telegraph Company*)

Telephone Installers. The principal responsibility of these workers is to install, rearrange, and remove telephones and related equipment in homes and offices. New telephone installers usually begin their training with classroom instruction. This is followed by work with an experienced installer for on-the-job training. In many telephone companies, especially the smaller ones, an installer may work on private branch exchange (PBX) equipment. Private-branch-exchange systems are often found in private companies. These systems generally have special requirements. For example, in some private companies, incoming night calls must be switched automatically to different telephones. These telephones are often on the desks of persons who are working overtime or late shifts.

Repair Personnel. Repair personnel and installers together make up the largest group of craft workers employed by the telephone industry. Repair personnel locate and correct troubles that occur in customer telephones and related equipment. Those who work with private-branch-exchange equipment test and maintain switchboards, batteries, relays, and power plants. Others maintain the equipment used for radio and television broadcasts, radiotelephones, and teletypewriters. They may also repair and maintain equipment such as electric-signal systems, public-address systems, and time clocks.

Line Workers and Cable Splicers. Line workers install wires, cables, and optical fiber systems and do other jobs associated with telephone transmission lines. Although new installations are a very important part of their work, line workers also inspect, repair, and maintain existing telephone lines.

Cable splicers make line connections between cables after they have been installed by line workers underground or on poles. Splicers work on aerial platforms, underground, and in basements of large buildings. The principal duty of cable splicers is to connect the individual wires that run in large cables. Cable splicers also rearrange wire connections at cable splices whenever telephone line circuits are changed, and they maintain and repair cables (Fig. 5-6).

Fig. 5-6. Cable splicers at work (*Chesapeake and Potomac Telephone Company*)

HIGH-TECH OCCUPATIONS

Opportunities for jobs in the high-tech industries are expected to continue and to expand in the future. These industries employ, for example, computer service technicians, electronic engineers, programmers, systems designers, and communications specialists (Fig. 5-7). Workers who have a strong background in electricity and electronic technology are in demand by these industries.

High-tech, or *high technology, industries* are engaged in a variety of activities. Some design and manufacture industrial equipment, such as robot-controlled welding machines, sophisticated undersea research vehicles, computers, telecommunications equipment, and space satellites. Other high-tech industries are engaged in developing software, systems engineering, and research and development. Although these

Fig. 5-7. Technicians at work in a service laboratory of a high-tech industry (*Black Box Corporation*)

latter high-tech industries can be classified as "nonmanufacturing industries," their workers provide the interconnecting link for the emerging information age.

Individuals interested in preparing for technical occupations in these high-tech industries need in-depth study in courses such as digital electronics, circuit analysis, integrated circuits, microprocessors, and communications systems. *Programmers,* or computer software specialists, in addition to a technical background, need to have good communications skills and to be able to think logically.

Depending on an individual's interest and drive, preparing to enter into the high-tech industries can take as much as 4 to 5 years of formal education for a degree in electrical engineering or computer science. Graduation from a 2-year electronic or computer technology program at a 2-year college is another way to prepare for work in these industries. These schools usually offer associate degree programs in various technical and occupational fields. Many industries provide on-the-job training for their employees. Salaries are generally high and promotion is rapid.

APPLIANCE SERVICE WORKERS

Appliance service workers install, repair, and rebuild large and small electrical appliances. They work on appliances such as ranges, refrigerators, washing machines, clothes dryers, irons, and toasters (Fig. 5-8). In small shops, they work on all kinds of appliances. In larger shops, they usually specialize in one general kind.

Appliance service workers are generally employed by the service departments of stores, wholesale houses, and appliance manufacturers. Others work in electrical-repair shops or operate their own shops. As the number of appliances grows, so will the need for qualified service workers.

Most workers who service appliances begin as helpers and learn their skills through practical experience. These workers often attend training sessions sponsored by appliance manufacturers. They also meet with factory representatives to learn about new products and the general procedures for servicing them.

Fig. 5-8. Appliance service worker repairing an electric coffee pot (*U.S. Department of Labor*)

The repair of simple appliances can be learned by on-the-job training in several months. However, to become competent in servicing a variety of complicated appliances takes several years of study and training. This training period can be shortened if the beginning service worker has some knowledge of electricity. Knowing about electrical theory and the use of basic test instruments provides a good foundation for training. In addition, an understanding of the characteristics and operation of electrical and electronic devices is helpful.

BUSINESS-MACHINE SERVICE WORKERS

Business-machine service workers maintain and repair the rapidly increasing numbers and kinds of office equipment. This includes electric typewriters, calculating machines, cash registers, word processors, computer systems, dictating and transcribing machines, duplicating and copying machines, and microfilm equipment. All these are combinations of mechanical and electrical or electronic systems. Business-machine service workers must have a strong background in electrical and electronic theory and applications. They must also have the ability to analyze a mechanical system. This is essential to understand the system's relationship to the circuits and devices that control it. Much of the work of business-machine service workers is done in offices during regular business hours. Therefore, it is important that they be neat and cooperative in addition to being technically able. Many business-machine service workers begin as inexperienced helpers. Then, after several years of on-the-job training, they become qualified to work on some machines. Because of the nature of this work, a person who plans to become a business-machine service worker needs a good background in mechanical, electrical, and electronic technology.

CONSTRUCTION ELECTRICIANS

The occupation of construction electrician is one of the most important in the skilled building trades. These workers lay out, assemble, install, connect, and test electric circuits, fixtures, devices, machinery, and control equipment. They work in houses, factories, hospitals, schools, and offices. Since most of their work is done indoors, year-round employment is more common for electricians than it is for other workers in the building trades. Most construction electricians are employed by electrical or building contractors. Others are self-employed (Fig. 5-9).

Fig. 5-9. A self-employed construction electrician at work

Construction electricians usually begin their careers as apprentices. During this time, they work under the close supervision of experienced workers. Apprenticeship training also involves classroom instruction in all phases of wiring and installation techniques. The beginner should have some previous training in basic mathematics, electrical theory, and the use of common hand and power tools. Technical and vocational schools often offer courses in electrical wiring, machinery, and control devices.

MAINTENANCE ELECTRICIANS

Maintenance electricians form the largest group of skilled electrical workers. They inspect, troubleshoot, repair, and maintain electrical wiring, machinery, motors, generators, and other electrical equipment. Most of this work is done in industrial plants. Machinery in factories must be constantly maintained and repaired to prevent costly interruptions in production. Maintenance electricians also work in hospitals, commercial and institutional buildings, and large apartment developments (Fig. 5-10).

AUTOMOTIVE SERVICE

The electrical system of the modern automobile must be periodically checked and tested. In small garages, this is usually done by an auto-

Fig. 5-10. A maintenance electrician repairing a motor of an air-conditioning unit (*U.S. Department of Labor*)

Fig. 5-11. Making electrical connections for a "jump start" on an automobile (*Ford Motor Company*)

Fig. 5-12. Utility line worker

Fig. 5-13. Scientist working in the space program shown with a model of the Orbiting Solar Observatory (*National Aeronautics and Space Administration*)

motive mechanic who has experience with the electrical system (Fig. 5-11). In larger garages, automotive electrical work is done by specialists. These people are trained to interpret the readings of a variety of electronic testing instruments and to make the needed repairs.

ELECTRICAL UTILITY LINE WORKERS

Line workers install and repair transmission and distribution cables and equipment of electrical utility companies. These companies supply power to residential, commercial, and industrial users. Line work is performed on both low- and high-voltage systems. Work is also performed overhead on tall towers or underground with duct and conduit systems (Fig. 5-12). High-voltage line workers are highly skilled. They are especially trained and experienced in the problems connected with voltages that may be as high as 750,000 V. Most line workers receive their training on the job. However, theoretical and practical training in general electricity may be obtained in high schools, special technical institutes, and community colleges.

PREPARING FOR THE FUTURE

What you have just read are brief introductions to some of the important electrical and electronic occupations. These occupations will be open to young women and men in the years ahead. There is much more to be said about each of them. In addition, there are many more occupations from which to choose (Fig. 5-13). If you plan to enter an electrical or electronic occupation, taking an electricity and electronics course is an important step in that direction. Do not forget that your prospective employer will be interested in both your technical skills and aptitude and your personal qualities. Will you be interested in your job and in becoming better at it? Will you be willing to cooperate with coworkers? Are you trustworthy and dependable? Developing these qualities can be your best preparation for the future.

SOURCES OF INFORMATION

Much useful information about many different kinds of occupations can be found in the *Occupational Outlook Handbook,* published by the U.S. Department of Labor, Bureau of Labor Statistics. This handbook is available at your school or local library. Valuable occupational information can also be obtained from your school counselors. In addition, discuss your job interests with local technicians and with representatives of colleges, technical schools, and community colleges.

Test your knowledge by writing, on a separate sheet of paper, the word or words that most correctly complete the following statements:

1. There are approximately _____ television and radio service technicians employed in the United States.
2. It usually takes _____ years to complete the formal education necessary to become an electrical engineer.
3. Persons who draw the plans for electrical systems are called _____.
4. _____ installers are likely to be found working on private-branch-exchange (PBX) systems.
5. Construction _____ are persons who install, connect, and test electrical circuits in buildings.
6. A U.S. Department of Labor publication entitled _____ provides much useful information on occupations.
7. Computer service technicians are likely to be found in the _____ industries.

FOR REVIEW AND DISCUSSION

1. Discuss why a high school education has become standard for American workers.
2. Name several high school courses that are helpful in preparing for technical occupations.
3. Name several kinds of post-high school education and training programs that are useful in preparing for technical occupations.
4. What personal characteristics do you consider to be important qualifications for entering a technical occupation?
5. List the types of occupations frequently found in the high-technology industries. Discuss the training needed to enter each of the occupations on your list.

INDIVIDUAL-STUDY ACTIVITIES

1. Prepare a written or an oral report telling about your possible choice of a future occupation and the steps to be taken to achieve this goal.
2. Visit a local electrical or electronics service shop or manufacturing plant and tell the class about your experiences.
3. Prepare a written or an oral report on the growth of the high-tech industries in your state.

ELECTRIC CIRCUITS AND DEVICES

UNIT 6   Voltage, Current, and Power

Fig. 6-1. (A) Two charged objects; (B) electrons are attracted to the positively charged object; (C) a source of energy provides a continuous supply of electrons.

Static electricity is electrical energy at rest. Although this form of electricity can be very useful, it cannot operate a load such as lamps, heaters, motors, and other devices. This takes dynamic, or active, electricity.

Dynamic electricity involves the transfer of energy from a source to a load. This is done by the movement of electrons through a circuit. The energy that forces the electrons through a circuit is the *electromotive force*. The electromotive force, abbreviated emf, is measured in units called *volts*. Because of this, it is often referred to as *voltage*. When you hear or read the term *voltage,* you will know that it is the force that moves electrons through a circuit.

As electrons flow through the load, their energy is changed into some other form of energy. In an electric heater, for example, the electrons passing through the heater wire, or element, give up their energy in the form of heat. This is how moving electrons can be used to transfer energy from a source to a load.

Because electrons are negatively charged, they are attracted by positive charges and repelled by negative charges. If two charged objects are connected by a conducting material such as a wire, a *current* of electrons will flow from the negative object to the positive object. To produce a continuous electric current in the wire, energy must be supplied continuously (Fig. 6-1). In a circuit, this energy is provided by a source such as a *dry cell*, a *battery*, or a *generator*.

Electrons are not used up as they move through a circuit. Therefore, the number of electrons that returns to the positive (+) terminal of a source of energy is the same as the number of electrons that leaves the negative (−) terminal of the source of energy (Fig. 6-2).

THE VOLT AND THE AMPERE

The basic unit of voltage is the volt. It is named after Alessandro Volta. He was an Italian professor who lived from 1745 to 1798. Most of the electrical and electronic equipment found in homes operates at about 120 V. A common flashlight dry cell produces 1.5 V. A modern automobile battery produces 12 V. The voltage used to operate a television picture tube may be as high as 30,000 V. The letter symbol for voltage is *E*.

The basic unit of current is the *ampere*. It is named after André Marie Ampère. He was a French physicist and mathematician who lived from 1775 to 1836. One ampere of current equals the movement of 6,280,000,000,000,000,000 electrons past any point in a circuit during one second of time. By using *scientific notation,* such a large number can be written as 6.28×10^{18}.

A 100-W light bulb requires about 0.8 A of current to operate. A ¼-horsepower electric motor needs about 4.6 A of current to operate. The cranking motor of an automobile may use over 200 A when the starter switch is turned on. The letter symbol for current is *I*.

Fig. 6-2. Electrons are not consumed as they move through a circuit.

VOLTAGE AND CURRENT REQUIREMENTS

If an electrical device is to work properly, the source of energy must be able to do two things. First, it must supply the voltage. Second, it must deliver the current for which the device was designed. For example, you can connect eight flashlight dry cells together in such a way as to form a battery that produces 12 V. However, if you tried to start an automobile engine with this battery, it would not work. This is because it does not have the ability to deliver the large amount of current needed to operate the automobile's electric cranking motor. To do that, a larger battery, also producing 12 V but having a much larger current-delivering capacity, must be used. It is important, therefore, to know both the voltage and current requirements of electrical appliances and tools. These requirements are often given on the nameplates attached to these products. They may also be found in the technical literature that accompanies the products.

UNIT PREFIXES

Very small and very large values of voltage and current are usually expressed in a shorthand way. This is done by using a system of *decimal prefixes*. The most common of these prefixes used in electricity and electronics and the numerical values they represent are given in Table 6-1. As shown in this table, the prefix *milli-* (m) means one-thousandth (0.001). A current of 0.001 ampere can then be expressed as a current of 1 milliampere, or more simply, 1 mA. Likewise, a voltage of 1000 volts can be expressed as 1 kilovolt, or 1 kV.

DIRECT CURRENT

Direct current (dc) is produced in a circuit by a steady voltage source. That is, the positive and negative *terminals,* or poles, of the voltage

43

Fig. 6-3. Direct current: (A) steady direct current; (B) varying direct current; (C) pulsating direct current

TABLE 6-1 COMMON NUMERICAL PREFIXES USED WITH METRIC AND OTHER UNITS

Prefix and Symbol	Numerical Equivalent	Powers of 10
Giga (G)	1 000 000 000	= 10^9 (thousand-millions*)
Mega (M)	1 000 000	= 10^6 (millions)
Kilo (k)	1 000	= 10^3 (thousands)
Milli (m)	0.001	= 10^{-3} (thousandths)
Micro (μ)	0.000 001	= 10^{-6} (millionths)
Nano (n)	0.000 000 001	= 10^{-9} (billionths or thousand-millionths)
Pico (p)	0.000 000 000 001	= 10^{-12} (trillionths or million-millionths)

*In the United States, we call this number a billion; in England a million-million (1,000,000,000,000) is called a billion.

source do not change their charges over time. These terminals are said to have *fixed polarity*. Therefore, the direction of the current does not change over time. Such a voltage is provided by electric cells, batteries, and dc generators. Direct current may be constant, or steady, in value (Fig. 6-3A). It may vary, or change, in value (Fig. 6-3B). The current also may be pulsating, or interrupted (Fig. 6-3C). The applied voltage and the nature of the load determine the kind of direct current supplied.

ALTERNATING CURRENT

Alternating current (ac) is produced by a voltage source whose polarity changes, or alternates, with time. This causes the current in the circuit to move in one direction and then in the other (Fig. 6-4). The most common source of alternating voltages is alternating-current generators, or alternators.

In addition to changing direction, most kinds of alternating current change in value with time. For example, the variation of current with time may follow the form of a sine wave. This is called *sinusoidal alternating current*. Most electric utilities in this country supply sinusoidal alternating current and voltage to their customers.

Sine Wave. A graph called a *sine wave* shows the direction and the value of the current that passes through a given point in a circuit during a certain period of time (Fig. 6-5). One complete wave is a *cycle* of alternating current. The time it takes to complete one cycle is the *period* of the wave.

In Fig. 6-5, points on the vertical line AB represent current values. Base line CD is the time line. The heavy curved line, the sine wave, shows how the current changes in value during one cycle. That part of

Fig. 6-4. The polarity of the voltage in an ac circuit alternates, or changes, at regular intervals.

the sine wave above the base line represents the movement of current in one direction. The part of the sine wave below the base line represents the movement of current in the other direction.

During one alternation, or one-half, of the sine-wave cycle, the current moving in one direction increases from zero to a maximum value, and then returns to zero. At that time, the current begins to increase again but in the opposite direction. It again increases to a maximum value and then decreases to zero. This completes one cycle.

Fig. 6-5. A sine wave describes the variation in the value of current with time in the usual ac circuit.

Frequency. The number of times that a cycle of alternating current is repeated during one second of time is called the *frequency* of the current. The basic unit of frequency is the *hertz* (Hz). It is named after Heinrich Rudolph Hertz. He was a German physicist who lived from 1857 to 1894. The hertz has replaced cycles per second (cps) as the unit of frequency. However, cps still appears in some older books and other literature.

In this country, the frequency supplied by power companies is generally 60 Hz, although 50 Hz is used in some areas. Frequencies in the thousands and millions of hertz are used in radio and television broadcasting and microwave communications. They are usually expressed in terms of kilohertz (kHz), megahertz (MHz), and gigahertz (GHz) units (see Table 6-1).

You will learn in Unit 39 how the frequency affects the *wave length* of an alternating current and voltage. The wave length, for example, is the distance between a point on a sine wave to a similar point on the next consecutive sine wave.

USING DIRECT OR ALTERNATING CURRENT

Electric energy is most often supplied in the form of alternating current. Therefore, most electrical and electronic products are designed to operate with it. However, many of these products will work with either alternating or direct current. This is true, for example, of common lamps and almost all equipment with heating elements, such as toasters and irons. The right voltage must, of course, be applied to these devices.

Direct current is needed to operate devices such as transistors and electron tubes. Radios that are not battery-operated must be provided with a source of direct current. A special circuit in the radio changes the power-line alternating current into the necessary direct current. This special circuit is called a *rectifier circuit*. Direct current must also be used for certain electrochemical processes such as charging batteries and electroplating.

Direct-current power supplies are designed to provide direct-voltage outputs that can usually be varied from zero to a certain maximum voltage. These power supplies are used wherever a controlled variable voltage is needed, such as in experimental work and testing of circuits.

45

Fig. 6-6. Nonsinusoidal ac waveforms: (A) square waveform; (B) sawtooth waveform; (C) peaked waveform

Alternating current must be used to operate the induction motors used in appliances such as washing machines and refrigerators. Other motors, called *universal motors,* can be operated with either alternating or direct current. Transformers must be operated with alternating current or with varying or pulsating direct current. Inverters are used to change direct current to alternating current.

NONSINUSOIDAL ALTERNATING CURRENTS

Alternating voltages and currents may have waveforms that are not like sine waves. These are *nonsinusoidal waveforms* (Fig. 6-6). Television sets, radios, and other devices may have circuits in which these voltage waveforms are present.

ELECTRIC POWER AND ENERGY

Power is the time rate of doing work. In an electric circuit, power may also be defined in two other ways. First, it is the rate at which electric energy is delivered to a circuit. Second, it is the rate at which an electric circuit does the work of converting the energy of moving electrons into some other form of energy. The basic unit of power is the *watt* (W). It is named after James Watt. He was a Scottish inventor who lived from 1736 to 1819. Much of the electrical equipment we use is rated in terms of the power or watts it consumes. Thus, a light bulb is rated as 60 W, 100 W, 200 W, and so on. Toasters, irons, clothes dryers, and other appliances also have a certain wattage rating. Since electric power is the rate at which energy is delivered to the circuit, it is easy to calculate. You simply multiply the power by some time unit. This will give you the total energy delivered to the circuit. The time unit usually used is the hour. The power unit is usually given in terms of kilowatts (1,000 watts). Therefore, the energy unit on which most electric companies base their bills is the kilowatthour (kWh).

SELF-TEST

Test your knowledge by writing, on a separate sheet of paper, the word or words that most correctly complete the following statements:

1. Electromotive force causes _____ to move through a circuit.
2. Electromotive force is measured in units called _____ .
3. The flow of electrons in a circuit is called an electric _____ .
4. Electrons flow through a circuit from the _____ terminal of the energy source to the _____ terminal of the energy source.
5. A source of energy must be able to supply the _____ and deliver the _____ for which the load was designed.
6. Direct current moves through a circuit in one _____ only.
7. The action of a sinusoidal current is best described by what is called a _____ wave.
8. In this country, the frequency of the alternating current in power lines is usually _____ Hz.
9. Examples of devices or products that can be operated with either direct or alternating current are _____ and _____ .

10. Direct current must be used for the operation of _____ and _____ tubes.
11. A _____ circuit is one that changes alternating current into direct current.
12. Electric companies base their bills on a unit called the _____ .

---

1. Define *voltage* and *current*.
2. Name the basic units of voltage and current.
3. What are the letter symbols for voltage and current?
4. Explain why it is impossible to start a 12-V automobile cranking motor with a typical 12-V dry-cell battery.
5. Write the numerical values of the prefixes *mega-, kilo-, milli-,* and *micro-*.
6. Describe steady direct current, varying direct current, and pulsating direct current.

FOR REVIEW AND DISCUSSION

7. Give two important characteristics of sinusoidal alternating current.
8. Draw a sine wave. Explain how it can be used to describe a cycle of sinusoidal alternating voltage or current.
9. Define frequency. Name the basic unit of frequency.
10. Name three kinds of loads that must be operated with direct current.
11. What is the basic unit of power?
12. What is the unit used for electric energy?

INDIVIDUAL-STUDY ACTIVITIES

---

1. Prepare a written or an oral report telling about the numerical prefixes used with metric and other units. Discuss prefixes not included in

Table 6-1.
2. Give a demonstration that will be helpful in explaining sinusoidal waveforms.

UNIT 7   Conductors and Insulators

Since moving electrons have energy, they can be made to do work for us. What electrons do and how they can be controlled in a circuit depends mostly on the kinds of materials through which they flow. There are also certain materials through which electrons cannot flow easily. Knowing about these materials will help you understand better the many ways in which electric energy is used.

CONDUCTORS

A *conductor* is a material through which electrons flow easily. In such materials, valence electrons of the outermost shell can be quite easily removed from their parent atoms by the force of voltage. To put it another way, a conductor is a material having many free electrons.

Three good electrical conductors are silver, copper, and aluminum. In fact, metals generally are good conductors. Certain gases also can be used as conductors under special conditions. For example, neon gas, argon gas, mercury vapor, and sodium vapor are used in lamps.

How Electrons Flow. The basic way electrons flow through a wire is shown in Fig. 7-1 The action begins as the positive terminal of the cell attracts a valence electron away from atom 3. Atom 3 is now positively charged, having lost part of its negative charge. Thus, it attracts an electron from atom 2. Atom 2, in turn, attracts an electron from atom 1. As atom 1 loses its electron, an electron leaves the negative terminal of the cell and is attracted to atom 1.

Fig. 7-1. In a conductor material, voltage causes some electrons to be removed from their atoms. These "free" electrons then move through the conductor.

In a circuit, this action continues among very large numbers of atoms within the conductor. It produces a steady flow of free electrons through the conductor. The direction of this electron flow is always from the negative to the positive terminal of the source of energy.

Electrical Impulse. Individual electrons flow through a conductor at a relatively slow speed, usually less than 1 inch (25.4 mm) per second. However, an *electrical impulse,* or force, travels through a conductor at the speed of light, 186,000 miles (300 000 km) per second. This means that after a voltage is applied to a circuit, it produces a flow of free electrons through all points in that circuit at the speed of light.

It might be hard for you to imagine that an electrical impulse travels at the speed of light. Maybe this example will help. Suppose you could build an electric circuit 186,000 miles (300 000 km) long. This is more than seven times the distance around the Earth at the equator. One second after you closed the switch on such a circuit, the electrical impulse would take place throughout it.

RESISTANCE

As electrons flow through a conductor, they collide with other electrons and with other atomic particles. These collisions tend to reduce the number of electrons that flow through the conductor. This is like the difficulty that water has in passing through a hose or pipe that is partly filled with dirt or sand.

The opposition to current that results from electronic collisions within a conductor is called *resistance*. The basic unit of resistance is the *ohm*. It is named after Georg Simon Ohm. He was a German physicist who lived from 1787 to 1854. The letter symbol for resistance is *R*.

One ohm of resistance is that amount of resistance that will limit the current in a circuit to 1 A when 1 V is applied to the circuit (Fig. 7-2). Larger values of resistance are often expressed by using the prefixes *kilo-* and *mega-*. For example, a resistance of 2,000 ohms can be written as 2 kilohms, and a resistance of 2,000,000 ohms can be written as 2 megohms. The Greek capital letter omega (Ω) is used as an abbreviation for ohms after a numerical value, for example, 25 Ω. A resistance of 2 kilohms can also be written as 2 kΩ. A resistance of 2 megohms can be written as 2 MΩ.

Fig. 7-2. One ohm is the amount of resistance that will allow one ampere of current to pass through a circuit to which a voltage of one volt is applied.

RESISTANCE OF METAL CONDUCTORS

The resistance of a metal conductor depends mainly on four things: (1) the kind of metal from which it is made, (2) its temperature, (3) its length, and (4) its cross-sectional area.

Different metals have different properties of electrical resistance. The resistances of several common metals compared with that of copper are given in Table 7-1.

In general, as a metal gets hotter, its resistance increases. A hot wire has more resistance than the same wire when it is cold. For example, the resistance of the tungsten wire filament in a 100-W light bulb is about 10 Ω when the bulb is off. When the bulb is lit, the resistance of the white-hot filament increases to about 100 Ω. As in any conductor, heat causes atoms within the wire to move about much more rapidly than usual. This increases the number of collisions between free electrons

TABLE 7-1 RELATIVE RESISTANCE

Metals	Relative Resistance Compared with Annealed Copper*
aluminum (pure)	1.70
brass	3.57
copper (hard-drawn)	1.12
copper (annealed)	1.00
iron (pure)	5.65
silver	0.94
tin	7.70
nickel	6.25–8.33

*For example, a silver wire has only 0.94 times as much resistance as the same-size copper wire, whereas an aluminum wire has 1.70 times, or 170%, the resistance of copper.

and other atomic particles within the wire. As a result, the resistance to the flow of electrons through the wire also increases.

Just as resistance increases with an increase in temperature, a decrease in temperature will produce a decrease in resistance. If the temperature is reduced to absolute zero ($-273.16°C$, or $-459.69°F$), the resistance of the conductor will be zero. This is so because all molecular activity in the material will stop at absolute zero. There will thus be nothing to resist the flow of electrons. This condition is called *superconductivity*. Temperatures very close to absolute zero have been produced in the laboratory. This has made it possible to operate circuits having almost no resistance.

The resistance of a wire increases as its length increases. If two wires of different lengths have the same cross-sectional area, the longer wire will have the greater resistance. There are two reasons for this. First, electrons must move a greater distance in the longer wire. Second, they collide with more particles in the longer wire.

If two wires are of the same length, the wire with the larger cross-sectional area will have less resistance. This is because the thicker wire has more free electrons. It also has more space through which these electrons can move.

INSULATORS

An electrical *insulator* is a material that does not easily conduct an electric current. Such materials contain valence electrons that are tightly bound to the nuclei of their atoms. As a result, it takes an unusually high voltage to produce significant numbers of free electrons in them. Such materials are also called *nonconductors* and *dielectrics*.

Common insulators are glass, porcelain, mica, rubber, plastics, paper, and wood. These materials are used to separate conductors electrically so that the currents they carry will flow in the right paths (Fig. 7-3).

Fig. 7-3. Common insulating materials and their uses

STRAIN-TYPE ANTENNA INSULATOR, GLASS OR PORCELAIN

PORCELAIN STAND-OFF INSULATOR

WIRE

PHENOLIC, NYLON, TEFLON, OR PORCELAIN FEED-THROUGH INSULATORS, GROMMETS, OR STRAIN-RELIEFS

ENAMEL (PAINT) INSULATION

WIRE INSULATION: PAPER, RUBBER, PLASTIC, ASBESTOS, AND COTTON, ALONE OR IN COMBINATION

There is no sharp line dividing conductors from insulators. All insulating materials will conduct electric current if a high enough voltage is applied across them. For example, air is usually thought of as being a fairly good insulator. However, during a thunderstorm, the huge voltages generated between clouds and the earth cause air to conduct current in the form of lightning.

The ability of a material to insulate is known as its *dielectric strength*. The dielectric strengths of several common insulators are given in Table 7-2.

TABLE 7-2 DIELECTRIC STRENGTHS OF COMMON INSULATING MATERIALS

Material	Dielectric Strength Breakdown Voltage in Volts per 0.001 in. (0.0254 mm)
Bakelite	300
Formica	450
glass (window)	200–250
mica	3,500–5,000
polystyrene	500–700
porcelain	50–100
Teflon	1,000–2,000
air	75
kraft paper (glazed)	150
wood	125–750

SELF-TEST

Test your knowledge by writing, on a separate sheet of paper, the word or words that most correctly complete the following statements:

1. A conductor is a material through which electrons can flow _____.
2. In a conductor, there are many _____ electrons.
3. In addition to metals, certain _____ are also used as conductors.
4. Electrons move through a circuit conductor in a _____ to _____ direction.
5. The _____ to current that results from electronic collisions within a conductor is known as *resistance*.
6. The basic unit of resistance is the _____.
7. The Greek capital letter _____ is used as an abbreviation for ohms after a numerical value. This letter is written as _____.
8. In almost all metal conductors, the resistance _____ as the temperature increases.
9. With two wires of the same length, the wire with the larger cross-sectional area has _____ resistance.
10. All insulating materials will conduct current if a high enough _____ is applied to them.

FOR REVIEW AND DISCUSSION

1. Define an electrical conductor. Name at least three good conductor materials.
2. Describe the movement of electrons through a conductor.
3. What is meant by an *electrical impulse?*
4. Define *electrical resistance*.
5. Name and define the basic unit of resistance.
6. What are the four things that determine the resistance of a metal conductor?
7. Explain why, with most metal conductors, the electrical resistance increases as the temperature of the conductor increases.
8. Define an *electrical insulator*. Name five common insulating materials.
9. Under what condition can a material that is normally an insulator become a conductor?
10. What is meant by the *dielectric strength* of a material?

INDIVIDUAL-STUDY ACTIVITY

Prepare a written or oral report on a common household appliance, electric tool, or other electrical device. Indicate those parts that serve as conductors in the electric circuit and those parts that are insulators or insulation. Investigate and identify the materials from which the conductors and insulation are made.

UNIT 8   Resistance and Resistors

Resistance may or may not be useful in practical circuits. When too much current passes through a conductor, the resistance of the conductor may cause it to become hot. This, in turn, can create a fire hazard or cause the conductor to burn out. In this case, resistance is not desirable.

In other cases, resistance is deliberately put into a circuit. When this is done, the resistance is the circuit load. In an electric range, for example, the heating elements are made of a special wire called *resistance wire*. As current passes through this wire, the energy of moving electrons is changed into useful heat energy. Resistance is also put into many different circuits by the use of resistors.

RESISTORS

A *resistor* is a device with a known value of resistance. Resistors are very common parts of many electric and electronic circuits (Fig. 8-1). They are used to control voltage and current.

FIXED RESISTORS

A *fixed resistor* has a single value of resistance. This value remains the same under normal conditions. The three common kinds of fixed resistors are carbon-composition resistors, film resistors, and wire-wound resistors.

VARIABLE
RESISTORS
(POTENTIOMETERS)

OFF/ON
SWITCH
MOUNTED
ON
REAR OF
CONTROLS

Fig. 8-1. Resistors are made in many sizes and shapes.

Carbon-Composition Resistors. The resistance element in a carbon-composition resistor is mainly graphite or some other form of solid carbon. The carbon material is measured carefully to provide the right resistance (Fig. 8-2). These resistors generally have resistance values from 0.1 Ω to 22 MΩ.

OUTER INSULATION
COVER

SYMBOL

COLOR CODING
STRIPES

SOLID
CARBON-COMPOSITION
RESISTANCE
ELEMENT

SOLIDLY
EMBEDDED
LEADS OF TINNED
(SOLDER-COATED)
WIRE

Fig. 8-2. The main elements of a fixed carbon-composition resistor (*Allen-Bradley Company*)

Fig. 8-3. Metal-glaze resistor

Fig. 8-4. Wire-wound resistor (*Ohmite Manufacturing Company*)

Film Resistors. Resistors of this kind have a ceramic core called the *substrate*. A film of resistance material is deposited on the substrate. This serves as the resistance element. The film may be a carbon or metallic compound. It may also be a mixture of metal and glass called *metal glaze* (Fig. 8-3).

Wire-Wound Resistors. The resistance element of a fixed wire-wound resistor is usually nickel-chromium wire. This wire is wound around a ceramic core. This whole assembly is usually coated with a ceramic material or a special enamel (Fig. 8-4). Wire-wound resistors generally have resistance values from 1 Ω to 100 kΩ.

Tolerance. The actual resistance of a resistor may be greater or less than its rated value. This variation is called the *tolerance*. Carbon-composition, film, and wire-wound resistors each have a given tolerance. For example, common tolerances of carbon-composition resistors are ±5 percent, ±10 percent, and ±20 percent. This means that a resistor with a stated resistance of 100 Ω and a tolerance of ±5 percent can actually have a resistance of any value between 95 and 105 Ω. General-purpose wire-wound resistors usually have a tolerance of ±5 percent.

Resistors having tolerances as high as ±20 percent are used in many electric and electronic circuits. The advantage in using high-tolerance resistors is that they are less expensive to make than low-tolerance resistors. However, they can be used only in circuits where the variation is not important.

Precision Resistors. Some wire-wound and film resistors have actual values that are nearly equal to their rated values. These are called *precision resistors*. They are used in special circuits such as in test instruments.

Power Rating. The power rating of a resistor indicates how much heat a resistor can throw off before burning out. Since it is current that produces the heat, the power rating also gives some indication of the maximum current a resistor can safely carry. The power rating of a resistor is given in watts.

Carbon-composition resistors have power ratings from $\frac{1}{16}$ W to 2 W. Wire-wound resistors have power ratings from 3 W to hundreds of watts.

The physical size of a resistor has nothing to do with its resistance. A very small resistor can have a very low or a very high resistance. The physical size of a resistor does, however, suggest its wattage rating. For a given value of resistance, the physical size of a resistor increases as the wattage rating increases (Fig. 8-5). With experience, you can soon learn to tell the wattage ratings of resistors from their physical sizes.

Fig. 8-5. Relationship between the physical size of carbon-composition resistors and their wattage ratings (*Allen-Bradley Company*)

1,000 Ω, ±5%

RESISTOR COLOR CODE

The resistance and wattage values of wire-wound resistors are usually printed directly on them. The resistance values of fixed carbon-composition resistors and some kinds of film resistors are shown by a *color code*. The colors of the code and the numbers they stand for are given in Table 8-1. Three stripes are used for resistance values. A fourth stripe is often used to show the tolerance. A fifth stripe, when used, tells the *failure rate*. That is the amount the resistance will change over a period of time, such as 1,000 hours. The color code is read as follows:

1. The first, or end, stripe indicates the *first number* of the resistance value.

56,000 Ω, ±10%

470,000 Ω, ±20%

TABLE 8-1 RESISTOR COLOR CODE

Resistance Values, First Three Stripes	Tolerance Values, Fourth Stripe	
black = 0	gold = ±5%	
brown = 1	silver = ±10%	
red = 2	none = ±20%	
orange = 3		
yellow = 4	**Failure Rate, Fifth Stripe**	
green = 5		
blue = 6		
violet = 7	brown = 1%	
gray = 8	red = 0.1%	
white = 9	orange = 0.01%	
gold = divide by 10	yellow = 0.001%	
silver = divide by 100		

3.3 Ω, ±10%

Note: The fifth stripe, if present, indicates the failure rate, or the amount by which the resistance will change during a given period of time, usually 1,000 hours.

FIFTH STRIPE
(refer to Table 8-1)

Fig. 8-6. Reading the resistor color code

Fig. 8-7. Variable resistors: (A) potentiometer; (B) wire-wound rheostat (*Ohmite Manufacturing Company*)

2. The second stripe indicates the *second number* of the resistance value.
3. The third stripe indicates the *number of zeros* that follow the first two numbers of the resistance value. If the third stripe is black, no zeros are added after the first two numbers since black represents zero.
4. If the third stripe is gold, the number given by the first two stripes is divided by ten.
5. If the third stripe is silver, the number given by the first two stripes is divided by 100.

Several examples of resistance values given by the color code are shown in Fig. 8-6.

VARIABLE RESISTORS

Variable resistors are used when it is necessary to change the amount of resistance in a circuit. The most common variable resistors are called *potentiometers* and *rheostats*. Potentiometers generally have carbon-composition resistance elements. The resistance element in a rheostat is generally made of resistance wire. In both devices, a sliding arm makes contact with the resistance element (Fig. 8-7). In most variable resistors, the arm is attached to a shaft that can be turned in almost a full circle. As the shaft is turned, the point of contact of the sliding arm on the resistance element changes. This changes the resistance between the sliding-arm terminal and the terminals of the element (Fig. 8-8).

Rheostats are commonly used to control rather high currents, such as those in motor and lamp circuits. An example of how a rheostat is connected into a lamp circuit is shown in Fig. 8-9. Although similar to a potentiometer, a rheostat is usually larger because its resistance element carries greater currents and throws off greater amounts of heat.

A potentiometer can be used to vary the value of voltage applied to a circuit, as shown in Fig. 8-10. In this circuit, the input voltage is applied across terminals A-C of the resistance element. When the position

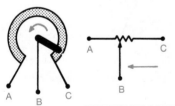

Fig. 8-8. When the sliding arm of a variable resistor is moved, the resistance between the center terminals and the end terminals changes.

of the sliding arm (terminal B) is changed, the voltage across terminals B-C will change. As the sliding arm moves closer to terminal A, the output voltage of the circuit increases. As the sliding arm moves closer to terminal C, the output voltage of the circuit decreases.

Potentiometers are commonly used as control devices in amplifiers, radios, television sets, and different kinds of meters. Typical uses include volume and tone controls; balance controls; linearity, brightness, and width controls; and zeroing adjustments.

The rating of a rheostat or of a potentiometer is the resistance of the entire resistance element. This resistance is measured from one end terminal to the other. The resistance and the wattage ratings of these devices are sometimes printed directly on them. They can also be found in manufacturers' specifications.

Fig. 8-9. Rheostat used to control current in a lamp circuit

Fig. 8-10. Basic potentiometer action

RESISTOR DEFECTS

Resistors are rugged devices. They seldom become defective unless too large a current passes through them. This may happen when there is a short circuit somewhere in the circuit.

A carbon-composition or a film resistor that becomes overheated will often be burned completely apart. In other cases, overheating will cause such a resistor to be scorched, to crack, or to bulge out. The value of the resistance may then increase to many times normal.

When a wire-wound resistor becomes overheated, the resistance wire will often burn out at one point. This makes the resistor open. A carbon-composition, film, or wire-wound resistor also can become open if one of its wires is disconnected from the resistance element inside its body.

FUSIBLE RESISTORS

The most common kinds of *fusible resistors* are wire-wound devices that look like wire-wound resistors (Fig. 8-11). They are used often as fuses in amplifiers and in television sets to protect particular circuits. These fusible resistors usually have resistance values of less than 14 Ω. The resistance element, like the fuse link in a cartridge fuse, is designed to burn out when too much current passes through it.

Fig. 8-11. Fusible resistors

LEARNING BY DOING

2. Installing a Loudspeaker "Fader" Control. The following circuit shows a very practical use of a potentiometer. It can be used to adjust the volume of two loudspeakers, such as the front and rear loudspeakers in an automobile.

MATERIALS NEEDED

potentiometer, 350 Ω, 2 W

loudspeaker, if necessary. If this loudspeaker is to be added to an existing system, it should have the same electrical characteristics as the loudspeaker already in use.

hook-up wire, no. 20 AWG (0.8 mm), as needed

SAFETY

Many devices using loudspeakers, such as radios, televisions, and phonographs, *should not be expanded into multiple-speaker systems.* Often these devices are directly connected to the power lines. This means that the metal chassis *and the speaker wires* can be at a dangerous potential, or voltage, with respect to ground. Manufacturers of such equipment almost always disapprove of modifications. Check with a qualified technician before making any connections to these circuits.

Some equipment can be damaged by connecting the wrong speaker load. Again, check with a qualified technician or service center before attaching extra speakers to such equipment.

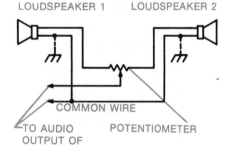

Fig. 8-12. Circuit used for Learning by Doing No. 2, "Installing a Loudspeaker 'Fader' Control"

Procedure

1. Wire the circuit shown in Fig. 8-12. If the chassis of an automobile is used as one conductor of the loudspeaker circuit, the common wire is not necessary. In this case, one terminal of each loudspeaker is connected to a nearby part of the chassis as shown by the dotted lines.

2. Test the circuit by turning the shaft of the potentiometer first in one direction and then the other. As this is done, one of the loudspeakers should approach full volume while the volume of the other loudspeaker decreases. At the center position, the loudspeakers' volume should be equal.

SELF-TEST

Test your knowledge by writing, on a separate sheet of paper, the word or words that most correctly complete the following statements:

1. Resistors are used to put _____ into a circuit or part of a circuit.

2. Resistors are used to control _____ and _____.

3. A fixed resistor has a _____ value of resistance.

4. The resistance element in a carbon-composition resistor is mainly _____ or _____.

5. In a film resistor, a film of _____ is deposited on a ceramic core.

6. The resistance element of a wire-wound resistor is made of _____ wire.

7. The amount by which the actual resistance of a resistor may vary from its indicated value is known as the _____ of the resistor.

8. A resistor that has a resistance that is very nearly equal to its indicated resistance is called a _____ resistor.
9. The _____ rating of a resistor indicates how much current the resistor can conduct before _____ .
10. The physical size of a resistor has nothing to do with its _____ .
11. A larger resistor of a given value has a greater _____ rating than a smaller resistor of the same value.
12. The first three stripes of the resistor color code indicate the _____ value of a resistor. The fourth stripe shows the _____ of the resistor.
13. The two most common kinds of variable resistors are called _____ and _____ .
14. A potentiometer is most often used to change the value of the _____ applied to a circuit or to part of a circuit.
15. The sliding arm of a potentiometer or a rheostat is connected to the _____ of the device.
16. The resistance of a potentiometer or of a rheostat is measured between its _____ terminals.
17. The most common resistor defect is an open or burned-out condition caused by too large a _____ passing through.
18. The overheating of a carbon-composition or film resistor often causes the resistance of the resistor to _____ .
19. A resistor that serves as a fuse is called a _____ resistor.

FOR REVIEW AND DISCUSSION

1. What is a resistor?
2. Name and describe three kinds of fixed resistors.
3. Define the tolerance of a resistor.
4. What is a precision resistor?
5. Explain the meaning of the wattage rating of a resistor.
6. Does the physical size of a resistor give some information about its resistance? Its wattage rating?
7. Describe the resistor color code and explain how it is used.
8. Describe the construction of a variable resistor. Name the two most common kinds of variable resistors.
9. For what purpose is a potentiometer most commonly used?
10. What condition most often causes a resistor to become defective?
11. For what purpose is a fusible resistor used?

INDIVIDUAL-STUDY ACTIVITIES

1. Prepare a written or an oral report on the uses of resistors in common household appliances and devices such as radio and television sets, dimming switches for lights, and so on. If possible, show examples of these resistors in the device discussed.
2. Explain to your class how the resistor color code is used.

UNIT 9   Ohm's Law and Power Formulas

In any circuit where the only opposition to the flow of electrons is resistance, there are definite relationships among the values of *voltage, current,* and *resistance*. These relationships were discovered by Georg Simon Ohm in 1827. They are known as *Ohm's law*.

According to Ohm's law:

1. The voltage needed to force a given amount of current through a circuit is equal to the product of the current and the resistance of the circuit.
2. The amount of current in a circuit is equal to the voltage applied to the circuit divided by the resistance of the circuit.
3. The resistance of a circuit is equal to the voltage applied to the circuit divided by the amount of current in the circuit.

THE OHM'S LAW FORMULAS

By using the letter symbols for voltage *(E)*, current *(I)*, and resistance *(R)*, the relationships given by Ohm's law can be expressed in the following formulas:

$$E = I \times R$$

By solving for *I*, this same formula can be written as

$$I = \frac{E}{R}$$

By solving for *R*, it can be written as

$$R = \frac{E}{I}$$

where E = voltage in volts
I = current in amperes
R = resistance in ohms

The arrangement of terms in a formula allows us to state certain general rules about the relationships of current, voltage, and resistance. For example, in the Ohm's law formula

$$I = \frac{E}{R}$$

the E in the numerator tells us that I (current) will change in step with E (voltage), providing the denominator R (resistance) does not change.

Thus, if the voltage in a circuit doubles, the resulting current will be double its original value. For example, if $E = 20$ V and $R = 2$ Ω, $I = ?$

$$I = \frac{E}{R} = \frac{20}{2} = 10 \text{ A}$$

If $E = 40$ V and $R = 2$ Ω, $I = ?$

$$I = \frac{E}{R} = \frac{40}{2} = 20 \text{ A}$$

If the voltage in a circuit is reduced to one-half its original value, the current will adjust itself to one-half of its original value. For example, if $E = 120$ V and $R = 20$ Ω, $I = ?$

$$I = \frac{E}{R} = \frac{120}{20} = 6 \text{ A}$$

If $E = 60$ V and $R = 20$ Ω, $I = ?$

$$I = \frac{E}{R} = \frac{60}{20} = 3 \text{ A}$$

Thus, Ohm's law shows us that the current is *directly* proportional to the voltage. Provided that the resistance does not change, the current increases if the voltage increases, and the current decreases if the voltage decreases.

Let us now look closely at the resistance R in the formula

$$I = \frac{E}{R}$$

The R in the denominator tells us that with E (voltage) remaining the same, I (current) is inversely proportional to R (resistance).

As resistance increases, current decreases in the same way. If the resistance in a circuit is increased to twice its original value, the current will decrease to one-half the original value. For example if $E = 16$ V and $R = 4$ Ω, $I = ?$

$$I = \frac{E}{R} = \frac{16}{4} = 4 \text{ A}$$

If $E = 16$ V and $R = 8$ Ω, $I = ?$

$$I = \frac{E}{R} = \frac{16}{8} = 2 \text{ A}$$

61

Thus, when the voltage remains the same, the current decreases as the resistance increases.

Similarly, a decrease in resistance results in an increase in current. If the resistance is decreased to one-third its original value, the current will increase to three times its original value. For example, if $E = 60$ V and $R = 30$ Ω, $I = ?$

$$I = \frac{E}{R} = \frac{60}{30} = 2 \text{ A}$$

If $E = 60$ V and $R = 10$ Ω, $I = ?$

$$I = \frac{E}{R} = \frac{60}{10} = 6 \text{ A}$$

The preceding example illustrates that the current is inversely proportional to the resistance. In this case, as the resistance decreases, the current increases, provided that the voltage remains the same.

USING OHM'S LAW

The Ohm's law formulas can be learned easily by using a circle, divided as shown in Fig. 9-1A. To use this circle, choose and cover one of the quantities ($E, I,$ or R). The relationship of the other two quantities in the circle will show how the chosen quantity can be figured (Fig. 9-1B).

Ohm's law is important in understanding the behavior of circuits. It is also important because it makes it possible to find the value of any one of the three basic circuit quantities (voltage, current, or resistance) if the values of the other two are known. Thus, circuits and their parts can be designed mathematically. This cuts down on measurements and experiments that would waste time and might damage equipment. The use of Ohm's law in solving practical circuit problems is shown in the following examples.

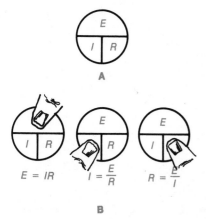

Fig. 9-1. The Ohm's law circle

Problem 1: An electric light bulb uses 0.5 A of current when operating in a 120-V circuit. What is the resistance of the bulb?

Fig. 9-2. Diagram for Problem 1

Solution: The first step in solving a circuit problem is to sketch a schematic diagram of the circuit itself. The second step is to label each of the parts and show the known values (Fig. 9-2).

In this problem, the values for *I* and *E* are known. To solve for *R*, we use the formula

$$R = \frac{E}{I}$$

or

$$R = \frac{120}{0.5}$$

$$= 240 \ \Omega$$

Problem 2: A bicycle horn has a current rating of 0.1 A printed on it. The resistance of the horn coil is known to be 15 Ω. Compute the voltage that must be applied to the horn circuit if it is to operate correctly (Fig. 9-3).

Fig. 9-3. Diagram for Problem 2

Solution: Since voltage is the unknown quantity, use the formula

$$E = I \times R$$
$$= 0.1 \times 15$$
$$= 1.5 \ \text{V}$$

Problem 3: To use the right size fuse in an automobile circuit, it is necessary to find the current needed by a certain device. The device is to be connected to the 12-V battery and has a resistance of 4.35 Ω (Fig. 9-4). Find the current.

Fig. 9-4. Diagram for Problem 3

Solution: Since current is the unknown quantity, use the formula

$$I = \frac{E}{R}$$

$$= \frac{12}{4.35}$$

$$= 2.76 \ \text{A}$$

POWER FORMULAS

The power formulas show the relationships between electric power and voltage, current, and resistance in a dc circuit. The basic power formula is

$$P = E \times I$$

where *P* = power in watts
   E = voltage in volts
   I = current in amperes

From this formula, it is possible to get two other commonly used power formulas. For example, Ohm's law states that $E = I \times R$.

63

By putting $I \times R$ in place of E in the basic power formula,

$$P = I \times R \times I$$
$$= I^2R$$

Also, from Ohm's law we know that $I = E/R$. By putting E/R in place of I in the basic power formula,

$$P = E \times \frac{E}{R}$$

$$= \frac{E^2}{R}$$

USING THE POWER FORMULAS

The power formulas can be used to find the wattage ratings of circuit parts. They can be used to find the value of current in a circuit. And they can be used to find the cost of operating electrical and electronic products. The use of these formulas in solving practical circuit problems is shown in the following examples.

Problem 1: The current through a 100-Ω resistor to be used in a circuit is 0.15 A. What should the wattage rating of the resistor be?

Solution: Since the two known quantities in this problem are current and resistance, use the formula $P = I^2R$:

$$P = I^2R$$
$$= 0.15^2 \times 100$$
$$= 2.25 \text{ W}$$

To keep a resistor from becoming overheated, its wattage rating should be about twice the wattage rating computed from a power formula. Thus, the resistor used in this circuit should have a wattage rating of about 5 W.

Problem 2: Find the current that flows through a 60-W incandescent lamp operating at 120 V. Also find the current through a 200-W lamp and a 300-W lamp operating at 120 V.

Solution: In this problem, the power and voltage are known, and we wish to find the current. The simplest formula to use, therefore, is $P = E \times I$, from which we solve for I:

$$I = \frac{P}{E}$$

For the 60-W, 120-V lamp:

$$I = \frac{60}{120}$$

$$= 0.5 \text{ A}$$

For the 200-W, 120-V lamp:

$$I = \frac{200}{120}$$

$$= 1.67 \text{ A}$$

For the 300-W, 120-V lamp:

$$I = \frac{300}{120}$$

$$= 2.5 \text{ A}$$

In this problem, the voltage applied to each of the lamps is the same (120 V). As the wattage of the lamps increases, the current in the circuit also increases. This means that there is a direct relationship between the power dissipated in the load and the current flowing through it.

Problem 3: The current in a house wiring system increases to twice the original value, from 2 to 4 A. What effect does this have on the temperature of the wires in the circuit? Assume a resistance of 25 Ω.

Solution: According to the formula $P = I^2R$, if the resistance does not change, power is directly proportional to the square of the current. Thus, if the current is doubled, the power increases four times.

$$P = I^2R = 2^2 \times 25$$
$$= 4 \times 25 = 100 \text{ W}$$

If the current is doubled from 2 to 4 A,

$$P = 4^2 \times 25$$
$$= 16 \times 25 = 400 \text{ W}$$

In this problem, doubling the current increases the power four times—from 100 to 400 W. Power can be thought of as the rate at which the energy of moving electrons is changed into heat in the wires. If the current is doubled, the wires will become heated to four times the original temperature. This relationship between power and current is important to know. It means that even a small increase in current will cause a large increase in wire temperature. Overheated wires are a major cause of fires in houses and in other buildings.

KILOWATTHOUR FORMULA

The kilowatthour (kWh) is the unit of electric energy on which electric companies base their bills. Kilowatts multiplied by hours is equal to kilowatthours. For example, if a toaster rated at 1,000 W is operated for 30 minutes (0.5 hour), the energy used is $1 \text{ kW} \times 0.5 \text{ hour} = 0.5 \text{ kWh}$.

The amount of energy in kilowatthours used by an appliance or some other product can be computed by the following formula:

$$kWh = \frac{\text{wattage rating} \times \text{no. of hours used}}{1{,}000}$$

$$kWh = \frac{P \times h}{1{,}000}$$

where P = power in watts
h = time in hours

The electric energy in kilowatthours supplied by electric power companies is measured by a watthour meter. Such a meter is usually mounted on the side of a building. It is "read" at certain times. This reading is used to calculate the electric bill for a period of time, usually 1 month.

The average price of electric energy in the United States in 1985 was about 7.5¢ per kWh. The average home in this country in 1985 used about 870 kWh of electric energy per month.

USING THE KILOWATTHOUR FORMULA

The kilowatthour formula can be used to find the cost of operating a product for any period of time if the cost per kilowatthour is known. This is shown in the problems below.

Problem 1: The average price of electric energy in a certain town is 6¢ per kWh. Find the cost of operating a 250-W television set for 1.5 hours.

Solution:

$$kWh = \frac{P \times h}{1{,}000}$$

$$= \frac{250 \times 1.5}{1{,}000}$$

$$= 0.375$$

Since the energy costs 6¢ per kWh, the cost of operating the television set for 1.5 hours is $0.375 \times 6 = 2.25¢$.

Problem 2: At a price of 10¢ per kWh, what is the cost of operating a 1,200-W clothes iron for 2 hours?

Solution:

$$kWh = \frac{P \times h}{1,000}$$

$$= \frac{1,200 \times 2}{1,000}$$

$$= 2.4$$

Total cost $= 2.4 \times 10$, or 24¢

Problem 3: At a price of 7¢ per kWh, what is the cost of operating a 100-W lamp for 6 hours?

Solution:

$$kWh = \frac{P \times h}{1,000}$$

$$= \frac{100 \times 6}{1,000}$$

$$= 0.6$$

Total cost $= 0.6 \times 7$, or 4.2¢

Problem 4: A residential home used 1,210 kWh of electricity in 1 month. What is the total cost for the month at 8¢ per kWh?

Total cost $= kWh \times$ cost per $kWh = 1,210 \times \$0.08 = \$96.80$

SELF-TEST

Test your knowledge by writing, on a separate sheet of paper, the word or words that most correctly complete the following statements:

1. Ohm's law states the relationships among _____, _____, and _____.
2. The voltage applied to a circuit is equal to the product of the _____ and the _____ of the circuit.
3. The current in a circuit is equal to the applied _____ divided by the _____.
4. The resistance of a circuit is equal to the applied _____ divided by the _____.
5. If the voltage applied to a circuit is doubled and

67

the resistance remains constant, the current in the circuit will increase to _____ the original value.
6. If the voltage applied to a circuit remains constant and the resistance is doubled, the current will decrease to _____ the original value.
7. The three most commonly used power formulas are _____, _____, and _____.
8. If the current through a conductor is doubled and the resistance remains unchanged, the power dissipated by the conductor will increase to _____ times the original amount.
9. The unit of electric energy on which electric companies base their bills is the _____.
10. The kilowatthours of energy used by an appliance can be calculated by multiplying the _____ of the appliance by the _____ it is used and dividing by 1,000.

FOR REVIEW AND DISCUSSION

1. State the relationships among voltage, current, and resistance as given by Ohm's law.
2. Using correct letter symbols, write the three forms of the Ohm's law formula.
3. A soldering iron uses 2 A of current when it is plugged into a 120-V outlet. How much power does it use?
4. An automobile spotlight has a resistance of 2 Ω while using 6 A of current. What is the voltage of the car battery?
5. The heating element of an electric range has a resistance of 10 Ω. How much current does the element use when connected to a voltage of 115 V?
6. The value of current through a 285-Ω resistor in a radio circuit is 0.3 A. What is the voltage across the resistor?
7. The voltage across an 8,000-Ω resistor in a television circuit is 256 V. How much current passes through the resistor?
8. What voltage is applied to a circuit with 2 A of current and a resistance of 57.5 Ω?
9. Using correct letter symbols, write the three basic power formulas.
10. Calculate the current used by a 100-W incandescent lamp that is operated at a voltage of 120 V.
11. Calculate the current used by a 1,000-W toaster operated at 117 V.
12. At a price of 7¢ per kWh, what is the cost of operating a 300-W television receiver for 6 hours?
13. At a price of 6¢ per kWh, what is the cost of operating a 60-W lamp for 24 hours?
14. Explain the general procedure for calculating an electric bill.
15. What happens to the amount of power used in a circuit when the voltage is decreased to one-half its original value?

INDIVIDUAL-STUDY ACTIVITIES

1. Prepare a written or an oral report telling about Georg Simon Ohm and his discovery of the relationships among voltage, current, and resistance.
2. Give a demonstration that will show your class at least one practical application of Ohm's law and one power formula.
3. Give a demonstration that will show your class the relationship between the physical sizes of resistors and their wattage ratings. Use similar resistors for your demonstration.
4. Make a list of appliances and other products in your home that show the wattage rating on a nameplate or elsewhere. After finding out what the average price of electric energy per kilowatthour is in your community, figure the cost of operating each of the products for 1 hour.

UNIT 10 Series Circuits

In previous units, you learned that a complete circuit contains four basic parts: (1) the energy source, (2) the control device, (3) the conductor, and (4) the load (Fig. 10-1A). You also learned that loads can be connected in series, in parallel, or in series-parallel combinations. This unit discusses the series circuit in detail. Topics such as open and closed loop, direction of current flow, polarity, nodes, and fundamental laws governing series circuits are explained. Parallel circuits are discussed in Unit 11. Series-parallel circuits are discussed in Unit 12.

THE SERIES CIRCUIT

The series circuit provides only one path through which electrons can flow. When the switch is closed, the energy source forces the electrons to flow through the closed switch, through the conductor, through the load, and back to the energy source. In a direct current circuit, the electron flow (current) is unidirectional.

The filaments of some types of Christmas tree lamps illustrate loads that are connected in series. In a radio or television system, many of the circuits are connected in series. Resistors or a combination of resistors and other devices make up these series circuits. Energy sources such as dry cells can be connected in series. These connections are also discussed in this unit.

OPEN AND CLOSED LOOP

Figure 10-1B represents a simplified drawing of Fig. 10-1A. It assumes that the switch is closed, a voltage is present, and the circuit is complete. The arrow labeled *current loop* indicates the direction of the current. Current can flow only if the loop is closed. The path, or circuit, must be complete. As you learned in Unit 6, the current flows from the negative (−) terminal of the energy source to the positive (+) terminal of the energy source. An *open circuit*, or an *open loop*, means that the circuit is not complete. A broken conductor or an open switch causes a

Fig. 10-1. The series circuit: (A) the basic parts of a series circuit; (B) simplified drawing of a series circuit break in the external circuit. If such a circuit is broken or open at any point, the whole circuit is turned off. This feature is used to control and protect electrical systems. Such devices as switches, fuses, and circuit breakers are connected in series with the load.

EXAMPLES OF SERIES CIRCUITS

Figure 10-2 shows several sketches of series circuits. When more than one resistance or load is shown, the loads are connected to the conductors one after the other. Thus, there is only one path through which current can pass as it moves from one terminal of the energy source to the other. Notice that different symbols or letters are used to represent the energy sources. Figure 10-2A provides details about the voltage and resistance. This sketch is more complete than the others. However, all sketches are meaningful and represent the ways technicians and engineers convey information about series circuits. Verbal and written instructions are needed whenever complete information is omitted from a sketch.

Fig. 10-2. Sketches illustrating series circuits

POLARITY

The polarity, or electrical charges at the energy source, are indicated on diagrams with a common electrical symbol or positive (+) and negative (−) signs. However, polarity charges exist in other parts of the circuit, too. Figure 10-2B shows the polarity (charges) at the resistances, or loads, in a circuit. The polarity is negative (−) at the end where the current enters the resistance. The polarity is positive (+) where the current leaves the resistance. It is necessary to know the polarity in direct-current circuits to properly connect instruments to the circuit.

NODES AND JUNCTIONS

A *node* is a terminal or connection point between two or more elements or parts in a circuit. Figure 10-2C illustrates where two nodes are located in the circuit. They are identified by large dots between the resistances $R1$, $R2$ and $R2$, $R3$. When three or more circuit elements such as resistances are connected at one point, a *junction* is formed. Junctions are discussed in Unit 11 on parallel circuits. Nodes and junctions form reference points for voltage and current measurements.

RESISTANCE IN A SERIES CIRCUIT

Figure 10-3 shows three resistances in series. Since the circuit has only one path for current to flow, the current must pass through all the resistances in the circuit. Therefore, the total resistance is the sum of all the resistances in the series circuit. The following formula is used to calculate the total resistance R_t in a series circuit:

$$R_t = R1 + R2 + R3 + \cdots + R(n)$$

NOTE: The small n in $R(n)$ stands for any number of resistances.

Fig. 10-3. Diagram for Problem 1

Problem 1: Find the total resistance of the three resistances connected in series (Fig. 10-3).

Solution:

$$R_t = R1 + R2 + R3$$
$$= 5\ \Omega + 35\ \Omega + 95\ \Omega$$
$$= 135\ \Omega$$

Problem 2: A series circuit contains six resistors: $R1 = 6\ \Omega$, $R2 = 14\ \Omega$, $R3 = 7\ \Omega$, $R4 = 10\ \Omega$, $R5 = 150\ \Omega$, $R6 = 2\ \Omega$. Calculate the total resistance.

71

Solution:

$$R_t = R1 + R2 + R3 + R4 + R5 + R6$$
$$= 6\ \Omega + 14\ \Omega + 7\ \Omega + 10\ \Omega + 150\ \Omega + 2\ \Omega$$
$$= 189\ \Omega$$

Problem 3: A series circuit contains five resistors. The total resistance of the circuit is 186 Ω. The values of the four resistors are: $R1 = 20\ \Omega$, $R2 = 14\ \Omega$, $R3 = 10\ \Omega$, and $R4 = 100\ \Omega$. What is the value of the resistance $R5$? Manipulate the formula for resistance in a series circuit and solve for $R5$.

Solution:

$$R_t = R1 + R2 + R3 + R4 + R5$$

Rewrite the formula to put $R5$ on the left side of the equal sign:

$$R1 + R2 + R3 + R4 + R5 = R_t$$

Subtract $R1$, $R2$, $R3$, and $R4$ from both sides of the formula:

or $\qquad R5 = R_t - R1 - R2 - R3 - R4$
$$R5 = R_t - (R1 + R2 + R3 + R4)$$
$$= 186\ \Omega - (20\ \Omega + 14\ \Omega + 10\ \Omega + 100\ \Omega)$$
$$= 186\ \Omega - 144\ \Omega$$
$$= 42\ \Omega$$

CURRENT IN A SERIES CIRCUIT

Since a series circuit has only one current path, as many electrons flow *from* any point of the circuit as flow *to* that point. This means that there is the same amount of current in all parts of a series circuit at any time.

Problem 4: A series circuit has three resistors: $R1 = 6\ \Omega$, $R2 = 12\ \Omega$, $R3 = 7\ \Omega$ (Fig. 10-4). Find the total current in the circuit.

Solution:

1. Determine the total resistance of the circuit.

$$R_t = R1 + R2 + R3$$
$$= 6\ \Omega + 12\ \Omega + 7\ \Omega$$
$$= 25\ \Omega$$

2. Since the total resistance and total voltage are known, use Ohm's law formula to calculate the total current.

$$I_t = \frac{E_t}{R_t} = \frac{100\ \text{V}}{25\ \Omega} = 4\ \text{A}$$

Fig. 10-4. Current in a series circuit is the same in all parts of the circuit.

The total current calculated in Problem 4 is 4 A. If the current is measured at the nodes (Fig. 10-4), you will find it to be the same at each node.

VOLTAGE

The total voltage applied to a series circuit is automatically spread across the loads or devices in the circuit. The voltage across any load will be that amount needed to force the circuit current through the resistance of the load. This is also called a *voltage drop*. According to Ohm's law, the voltage drop across any load in the circuit is equal to the product of the current through the load and the resistance of the load:

$$E \quad = \quad I \quad \times \quad R$$
(Voltage drop   (current   (resistance
across load)   through load)   of load)

In a series circuit, the sum of the voltage drops across the individual loads is equal to the total voltage applied to the circuit. This is known as Kirchhoff's voltage law.

Problem 5: Three resistances are connected in series (Fig. 10-5A). Calculate the total voltage drop across each resistance. This problem involves several steps.

Solution:

1. Find the total resistance.

$$R_t = R1 + R2 + R3 = 1\ \Omega + 2\ \Omega + 3\ \Omega = 6\ \Omega$$

2. Since the total voltage and total resistance are known, calculate the total current.

$$I_t = \frac{E_t}{R_t} = \frac{12}{6} = 2\ \text{A}$$

3. Now that the total current is known, you can figure the voltage drops across each resistance by using Ohm's law for that part of the circuit.

Voltage drop across $R1$: $E = IR = 2 \times 1 = 2$ V
Voltage drop across $R2$: $E = IR = 2 \times 2 = 4$ V
Voltage drop across $R3$: $E = IR = 2 \times 3 = \underline{6\ \text{V}}$

Total voltage drops $= 12$ V

Notice that the sum of the voltage drops across the resistances equals the applied voltage (Fig. 10-5A). If any one of the resistances is changed in

A

B

Fig. 10-5. Voltage drops: (A) diagram for Problem 5; (B) diagram for Problem 6

such a circuit, all the voltage drops will change. However, the individual voltage drops will still add up to the source voltage.

Problem 6: Figure 10-5B is the same as Fig. 10-5A except that $R1$ has a resistance of 5 Ω instead of 1 Ω. Compute the voltage drops across each resistor.

Solution:

1. Find the total resistance.

$$R_t = R1 + R2 + R3 = 5 \; \Omega + 2 \; \Omega + 3 \; \Omega = 10 \; \Omega$$

2. Calculate the total current.

$$I_t = \frac{E_t}{R_t} = \frac{12}{10} = 1.2 \; \text{A}$$

3. Determine the voltage drops across each resistance.

Voltage drop across $R1$: $E = IR = 1.2 \times 5 = 6.0 \; \text{V}$
Voltage drop across $R2$: $E = IR = 1.2 \times 2 = 2.4 \; \text{V}$
Voltage drop across $R3$: $E = IR = 1.2 \times 3 = \underline{3.6 \; \text{V}}$

Total voltage drops $= 12.0 \; \text{V}$

Notice that if any one of the resistances is changed in a circuit, the current changes and all the voltage drops change. But the sum of the individual voltage drops across each resistance will always be equal to the applied voltage.

VOLTAGE DIVIDER

A series voltage-divider circuit, or network, is often used when different values of voltage are needed from a single energy source. A simple voltage divider is shown in Fig. 10-6. In this circuit, a voltage of 12 V is applied to three resistors in series. The total resistance of these resis-

Fig. 10-6. A voltage-divider circuit

tors limits the current through them to 1 A. The individual voltages are found as follows:

Total current:

$$I = \frac{E}{R} = \frac{12}{2 + 4 + 6} = \frac{12}{12} = 1 \text{ A}$$

Voltage drop across CD: $E = I \times R = 1 \times 6 = 6 \text{ V}$
Voltage drop across DE: $E = I \times R = 1 \times 4 = 4 \text{ V}$
Voltage drop across EF: $E = I \times R = 1 \times 2 = 2 \text{ V}$

Total voltage drop CF: $= 12 \text{ V}$

Voltage drop across CE: $E = I \times R$
$$= 1 \times (6 + 4) = 1 \times 10 = 10 \text{ V}$$

CELLS IN SERIES (AIDING VOLTAGES)

Energy sources such as cells and batteries often are connected in series. These connections affect the total voltage and the total current. Cells that are connected in series get a higher voltage than can be obtained from one cell. The connections are made so that the positive terminal of one cell is connected to the negative terminal of the next cell. When the cells are connected this way, total voltage is equal to the sum of the individual voltages (Fig. 10-7). The current-delivering capacity of the combination is equal to that of the cell with the lowest capacity. Batteries are made up of a number of cells that are usually connected in series so that the individual cells are aiding each other.

Fig. 10-7. Cells connected in series (aiding voltages)

CELLS IN SERIES (OPPOSING VOLTAGES)

In some circuits, the energy sources are connected so that the polarity of the connected terminals oppose each other (Fig. 10-8). The resultant voltage to the load is the difference between the two voltages. In Fig. 10-8, the 70-V battery has the higher energy level but will be reduced by the opposing 30-V battery.

Problem: What is the total voltage applied to the load in Fig. 10-8?

Solution:

$$E_t = E2 - E1 = 70 \text{ V} - 30 \text{ V} = 40 \text{ V dc}$$

The polarity is negative (−) at point A and positive (+) at point B.

Fig. 10-8. Batteries connected in series (opposing voltages)

SELF-TEST

Test your knowledge by writing, on a separate sheet of paper, the word or words that most correctly complete the following statements:

1. A complete series circuit has four basic parts: (1) the energy source, (2) the control device, (3) the conductor, and (4) the _____ .

2. An open circuit, or open loop, means that the circuit is _____ .
3. A terminal that connects two or more elements of a circuit is called a _____ .
4. The total resistance of a series circuit is equal to the _____ of all the resistances in the circuit.
5. In a series circuit, the _____ voltage is equal to the _____ of the voltage drops across all the loads in the circuit.
6. There is the same amount of _____ in all parts of a series circuit.

7. A series network of resistors used to provide different voltages from a single source of energy is called a _____ .
8. When cells are connected in series with the voltages aiding, the total voltage of the combination is equal to the _____ of the individual voltages.
9. When cells are connected in series with the voltages opposing, the total voltage of the combination is equal to the _____ of the individual voltages.

FOR REVIEW AND DISCUSSION

1. Describe in your own words what is meant by an *open loop* and a *closed loop*.
2. Draw three series circuits. In the first circuit, include two loads; in the second circuit, include four loads; and in the third circuit, six loads. Identify the nodes with a small dot. Explain the use of a node.
3. State Kirchhoff's voltage law as it applies to series circuits.
4. An automobile spotlight has a resistance of 2 Ω and 6 A of current flowing through it. What is the voltage of the car battery?
5. The heating element of an electric range has a resistance of 10 Ω. How much current flows in the circuit when connected to a voltage of 115 V?
6. The value of current through a 285-Ω resistor in a radio circuit is 0.3 A. What is the voltage across the resistor?
7. The voltage across an 8,000-Ω resistor in a television circuit is 256 V. How much current passes through the resistor?
8. What voltage must be applied to a circuit to have 2 A of current flow through a resistance of 57.5 Ω?
9. What is true about the value of current in all parts of a series circuit?
10. State the relationship between the voltage drops and the total applied voltage in a series circuit. Express this with a formula.
11. State the relationship between the total resistance and the individual resistances in a series circuit. Express this with a formula.
12. A number of incandescent lamps in a circuit are connected in series. Suddenly, they all go out at the same time. Explain the probable reason for this (the wire connecting the lamps is in perfect condition).
13. Four resistors with the values of 7 Ω, 13 Ω, 27 Ω, and 96 Ω are connected in series. What is their total resistance?
14. Three resistors with the values of 5 Ω, 12 Ω, and 28 Ω are connected in series with a 90 V battery. What is the value of current in the circuit?
15. Loads A, B, and C are connected in series. Loads A and B each have a resistance of 20 Ω. When the circuit is plugged into a 115-V outlet, 2 A of current pass through it. What is the resistance of load C?
16. Six 1.5-V dry cells are connected in series (positive terminal of one cell connected to the negative terminal of another cell) to form a transistor radio battery. What is the voltage of the battery?
17. A 12-V automobile battery has six cells connected in series. What is the voltage of each cell?
18. Two 12-V batteries are connected in a series circuit so that they oppose each other. There are three resistances (4 Ω, 6 Ω, and 8 Ω) in series with the batteries. What are the total current and total resistance of the circuit?

1. Give a demonstration that will show your class at least one practical application of Ohm's law in a series circuit.
2. Obtain the electrical troubleshooting manual for a late-model automobile. Locate and trace the circuit for the fuel gage from the fuel tank to the instrument panel. Draw and explain the circuit diagram.
3. Write a report on the contributions of Gustav R. Kirchhoff (1824 to 1887) to the field of physics.
4. Identify common devices that use more than one direct-current energy source in their operation.

UNIT 11   Parallel Circuits

In the previous unit you learned that series circuits obey certain fundamental laws. Parallel circuits also obey certain laws. In this unit you will learn how Ohm's and Kirchhoff's laws are useful in determining how parallel circuits function.

This unit explains the relationship of voltage, current, and resistance in parallel circuits. Basic parallel-resistance formulas are presented. The behavior of currents as they enter and leave junction points is discussed. Circuit problems are solved in a step-by-step manner. This approach allows you to follow closely the mathematical process. You will also use the concept of the "equivalent resistance" in solving parallel circuits. And you will learn how to connect batteries in parallel in order to increase the current capacity of the energy source.

PARALLEL CIRCUIT

In a *parallel circuit*, the loads are connected "across the line." That is, they are connected between the two conductors that lead to the source of energy (Fig. 11-1). The loads and their connecting wires often are called the *branches* of the circuit. Parallel connections also are called *multiple connections* and *shunt connections*.

In a parallel circuit, the loads operate independently. Therefore, if one of the branches is disconnected, turned off, or burned out (as an electric light bulb), the remaining branches will continue to operate.

Fig. 11-1. A parallel circuit with three branches

EXAMPLES OF PARALLEL CIRCUITS

Sketches of various parallel circuits are shown in Fig. 11-2. Although the drawings look very different, all the loads are connected "across the line." That is, the energy source provides the same voltage to the loads. In Fig. 11-2F and H, the energy source is not shown. The terminals, however, provide the connecting point for the energy source. Notice that each load (resistance) can function independently since the voltage

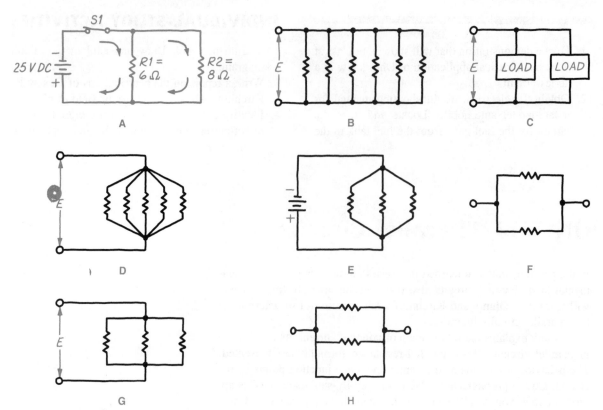

Fig. 11-2. Sketches illustrating various parallel circuits

source is common to all loads. Figure 11-2A shows many more details about the circuit, including the direction of current flow in the branches.

VOLTAGE AND CURRENT

Note that all the branches of a parallel circuit have the same voltage (Fig. 11-3). The total current, however, is distributed among the branches. The amount of current in any branch can be found by using the Ohm's law formula $I = E/R$. The lower the resistance in any branch, the greater the current. Thus, while all the loads in a parallel circuit have the same voltage, they may or may not have the same amount of current. In a house wiring system, for example, lights and small appliances that operate at the same voltage require different amounts of current. Therefore, they are connected in parallel (Fig. 11-4).

Fig. 11-3. The voltage is the same across all the branches in a parallel circuit.

The total current delivered to a parallel circuit is equal to the sum of the branch currents. This is why a fuse in a household circuit blows out when too many lights or appliances are plugged into its outlets. As each light or appliance is added to the circuit, the current required increases until the total current is greater than the ampere rating of the fuse or circuit breaker. The circuit is then said to be *overloaded*. It is at this point that the fuse blows or the circuit breaker trips.

Suppose, for example, that the circuit in Fig. 11-4 has a 20-A fuse. What will happen if another toaster is connected to the circuit? The 20-A fuse will burn out, or "blow." The fuse will blow because the circuit is overloaded. Remember, *the total current delivered to a parallel circuit is equal to the sum of the branch circuits.* In Fig. 11-4, the current in each branch is:

Toaster   =   9.00 A
Light   =   0.85 A
Coffee maker =   <u>4.50 A</u>
    Total   = 14.35 A

The total current in Fig. 11-4 is 14.35 A. This current is well within the range of the 20-A fuse. If another toaster is connected into the circuit, there will be four branches. The current in each branch is:

Toaster 1   =   9.00 A
Toaster 2   =   9.00 A
Light   =   0.85 A
Coffee maker =   <u>4.50 A</u>
    Total   = 23.35 A

With the second toaster connected in the circuit, the total current is 23.35 A. This circuit is now overloaded. The circuit is fused for 20 A and the load requires 23.35 A. The fuse, therefore, will blow.

OHM'S LAW IN PARALLEL CIRCUITS

Whenever the voltage is the same across each branch of the circuit, Ohm's law can be used to determine the current in that branch of the

Fig. 11-4. Parallel circuits are used for the operation of household appliances, lights, and other electrical devices.

79

Fig. 11-5. The total current in a parallel circuit is equal to the sum of the currents in each branch.

circuit (Fig. 11-5). For example, for branch A the current is:

$$I = \frac{E}{R} = \frac{6}{2} = 3 \text{ A}$$

For branch B, the current is:

$$I = \frac{E}{R} = \frac{6}{3} = 2 \text{ A}$$

The total current is:

$$
\begin{aligned}
I_t &= I_{\text{branch A}} + I_{\text{branch B}} \\
&= \quad 3 \quad + \quad 2 \\
&= 5 \text{ A}
\end{aligned}
$$

In parallel circuits, therefore, the current in that part of the circuit is equal to the voltage across that part of the circuit divided by the resistance of that part of the circuit.

RESISTANCE IN PARALLEL CIRCUITS

As branches are added to a parallel circuit, there are more paths through which current can flow. Therefore, the total resistance to the current decreases. The total resistance of a parallel circuit is always less than that of the branch with the lowest resistance (Fig. 11-6). The three resistances (25, 50, and 100 Ω) when connected in a parallel circuit have the *equivalent resistance* of 14.29 Ω (Fig. 11-6B). An equivalent resistance (R_{eq}) is electrically equal to the circuit parts that it replaces. An equivalent resistance represents the same load as the parallel circuit. It is convenient to use in analyzing parallel and more complex circuits. If these three resistances in Fig. 11-6 are connected in a series circuit, the total resistance is 175 Ω (25 + 50 + 100 = 175 Ω). The total resistance, therefore, is quite different when the same resistances are connected in a circuit in series or in parallel. Let us now solve some parallel circuit problems that illustrate this difference. The following parallel-resistance formulas are used in solving these circuits.

Fig. 11-6. The concept of the equivalent resistance (R_{eq})

80

PARALLEL-RESISTANCE FORMULAS

The total resistance of loads connected in parallel can be found by using one of the following parallel-resistance formulas.

1. If there are two resistances of unequal value,

$$R_t = \frac{R1 \times R2}{R1 + R2}$$

where R_t = total resistance
$R1$ and $R2$ = parallel resistances

2. If all the resistances are equal in value,

$$R_t = \frac{\text{value of one resistance}}{\text{number of resistances}}$$

3. If the resistances are not all of equal value,

$$R_t = \frac{1}{\dfrac{1}{R1} + \dfrac{1}{R2} + \dfrac{1}{R3} + \ldots + \dfrac{1}{R(n)}}$$

NOTE: This is a general formula that can be used with any kind of parallel circuit, including the ones in formulas 1 and 2 above.

Problem 1: Two resistors with resistances of 20 Ω and 30 Ω are connected in parallel (Fig. 11-7). Calculate the total resistance.

Fig. 11-7. Diagram for Problem 1

Solution: Formula 1 is the easiest one to use in this case.

$$R_t = \frac{R1 \times R2}{R1 + R2} = \frac{20 \times 30}{20 + 30} = \frac{600}{50} = 12 \ \Omega$$

Problem 2: Five resistors, each with a resistance of 10 Ω are connected in parallel (Fig. 11-8). Calculate the total resistance.

Fig. 11-8. Diagram for Problem 2

Solution: Since the resistances have the same value, use formula 2.

$$R_t = \frac{\text{value of one resistance}}{\text{number of resistances}} = \frac{10}{5} = 2 \ \Omega$$

Problem 3: Three resistors with resistances of 2 Ω, 2.5 Ω, and 10 Ω are connected in parallel (Fig. 11-9). Find the total resistance.

Fig. 11-9. Diagram for Problem 3

Solution: Since there are more than two resistances of unequal value, use formula 3.

$$R_t = \cfrac{1}{\cfrac{1}{R1} + \cfrac{1}{R2} + \cfrac{1}{R3}}$$

$$= \cfrac{1}{\cfrac{1}{2} + \cfrac{1}{2.5} + \cfrac{1}{10}}$$

$$= \cfrac{1}{0.5 + 0.4 + 0.1}$$

$$= \cfrac{1}{1} = 1\ \Omega$$

NOTE: This solution verifies the fundamental law: The total resistance of a parallel circuit is always less than the branch with the lowest resistance (see also Fig. 11-6).

Fig. 11-10. Diagram for Problem 4

Problem 4: An experimenter obtained a surplus circuit board that has a circuit shown in Fig. 11-10. What resistance must be connected in parallel with the circuit to obtain a total resistance of 1,482 Ω?

Solution: Use formula 3.

1. Manipulate formula 3 algebraically and solve for R3.

$$R_t = \cfrac{1}{\cfrac{1}{R1} + \cfrac{1}{R2} + \cfrac{1}{R3}}$$

$$\frac{1}{R_t} = \frac{1}{R1} + \frac{1}{R2} + \frac{1}{R3}$$

$$\frac{1}{R3} = \frac{1}{R_t} - \left(\frac{1}{R1} + \frac{1}{R2}\right)$$

$$\frac{1}{R3} = \frac{1}{1,482} - \left(\frac{1}{4,700} + \frac{1}{22,000}\right)$$

$$\frac{1}{R3} = 0.0006747 - (0.0002127 + 0.0000454)$$

$$\frac{1}{R3} = 0.0004166$$

$$R3 = \frac{1}{0.0004166}$$

$$R3 = 2400.38 = 2.4\ \text{k}\Omega$$

2. Verify the results by substituting the calculated resistance (2.4 kΩ) for $R3$.

$$R_t = \cfrac{1}{\cfrac{1}{R1} + \cfrac{1}{R2} + \cfrac{1}{R3}}$$

$$= \cfrac{1}{\cfrac{1}{4,700} + \cfrac{1}{22,000} + \cfrac{1}{2,400}}$$

$$= \cfrac{1}{0.0002127 + 0.0000454 + 0.0004166}$$

$$= \cfrac{1}{0.0006747} = 1482.4 = 1,482 \ \Omega$$

NOTE: This verifies the results. The calculated resistance of 2.4 kΩ connected in parallel with 4.7 kΩ and 22 kΩ equals 1,482 Ω.

Problem 5: Three resistances 50 Ω, 100 Ω, and 1,000 Ω are connected in parallel (Fig. 11-11). Calculate the total resistance, the total current, and the current in each of the branches.

Fig. 11-11. Diagram for Problem 5

Solution:

1. This problem involves several steps. First, determine the total resistance in the circuit. Then find the total current and individual branch currents. Use formula 3.

$$R_t = \cfrac{1}{\cfrac{1}{R1} + \cfrac{1}{R2} + \cfrac{1}{R3}}$$

$$= \cfrac{1}{\cfrac{1}{50} + \cfrac{1}{100} + \cfrac{1}{1,000}}$$

$$= \cfrac{1}{0.02 + 0.01 + 0.001}$$

$$= \cfrac{1}{0.031}$$

$$= 32.3 \ \Omega$$

2. Calculate the total current in the circuit. Since the total voltage and total resistance are known, use Ohm's law.

$$I_t = \frac{E_t}{R_t} = \frac{120}{32.3} = 3.72 \text{ A}$$

3. Calculate the individual currents in each branch circuit. Use Ohm's law for each part or branch in the circuit.

$$I_{\text{branch A}} = \frac{E}{R1} = \frac{120}{50} = 2.4 \text{ A}$$

$$I_{\text{branch B}} = \frac{E}{R2} = \frac{120}{100} = 1.2 \text{ A}$$

$$I_{\text{branch C}} = \frac{E}{R3} = \frac{120}{1{,}000} = 0.12 \text{ A}$$

Total = 3.72 A

4. Compare the total current of the individual branch circuits with step 2. Notice that the total current is the same. This verifies another fundamental law: that the sum of the individual branch currents equals the total current in a parallel circuit (Fig. 11-12).

Fig. 11-12. The direction of current in the branch circuits from Problem 5. Notice that the current flowing from a junction point equals the current flowing to that junction point.

CURRENT AT JUNCTION POINTS

In the study of series circuits, you learned that the sum of the voltage drops is equal to the applied voltage. This is known as Kirchhoff's voltage law. Kirchhoff's current law is equally important. It states that the total current flowing out of a junction point equals the current flowing into that junction point. This is illustrated in Fig. 11-12. Notice that the current flowing from junction point 2 equals the current flowing to junction point 2.

CELLS IN PARALLEL

Cells or batteries are connected in parallel to get more current than can be obtained from one unit. With a parallel connection, the total voltage of the combination is equal to the voltage of each unit (Fig. 11-13). The current-delivering capacity of the combination is equal to the sum of the capacities of all the cells or batteries.

Using a "booster" battery is an interesting and useful example of connecting batteries in parallel. The booster battery is temporarily connected to an automobile battery that cannot deliver enough current to start a car. The voltage applied to the automobile electrical system is

Fig. 11-13. The total voltage obtained when cells are connected in parallel is equal to the voltage of the individual cells.

still 12 V. However, the booster battery can supply enough extra current to turn the cranking motor and start the engine. The plus terminal of the booster battery is connected to the plus terminal of the automobile's battery, and the two negative terminals are also connected. Using booster batteries is called *jump starting*. Safety goggles or similar eye protection should be used when connecting a booster battery to the terminals.

SELF-TEST

Test your knowledge by writing, on a separate sheet of paper, the word or words that most correctly complete the following statements:

1. In a parallel circuit, the loads are connected across or between the two _____ that lead to the source of energy.
2. All branches of a parallel circuit have the same _____.
3. The total current in a parallel circuit is equal to the _____ of the _____ currents.
4. The total resistance of a parallel circuit is always _____ than that of the branch with the lowest resistance.
5. The formula for finding the total resistance of two parallel resistances having unequal values is _____.
6. The formula for finding the total resistance of two or more resistances that are equal in value and connected in parallel is _____.
7. The general formula for finding the total resistance of two or more resistances not all of equal value and connected in parallel is _____.
8. Cells and batteries are connected in parallel to get more _____ than can be obtained from one cell or battery.
9. When cells of equal voltage are connected in parallel, their combined voltage is equal to the voltage of _____ cell.

FOR REVIEW AND DISCUSSION

1. Describe the voltage and current conditions in a parallel circuit.
2. What is the relationship between the total resistance and the lowest resistance in a parallel circuit?
3. A number of incandescent lamps in a circuit are connected in parallel. When one of them burns out, the rest continue to operate normally. Explain the characteristics of a parallel circuit that make this possible.
4. Describe what is meant by the statement: "The circuit is overloaded."
5. The term *equivalent resistance* is used frequently in this unit. Explain what this term means.
6. Explain Kirchhoff's current law.
7. Two parallel resistors have values of 40 Ω and 60 Ω. What is the total resistance?
8. A parallel circuit has three branches. The loads in these branches each have a resistance of 150 Ω. Calculate the total resistance.
9. Three resistors connected in parallel have values of 4 Ω, 5 Ω, and 20 Ω. Find the total resistance.
10. Four resistors connected in parallel have values of 2.5 kΩ, 10 kΩ, 50 kΩ, and 150 kΩ. Find the total resistance.
11. A three-branch parallel circuit is connected to a 120-V dc source. The branch currents are 3 A, 2 A, and 4 A. What is the total voltage across the branches? Find the total current.
12. A two-branch parallel circuit draws a total current of 3 A from a 75-V dc source. One of the resistances $R1$ is 30 Ω. Resistor $R2$ is not specified. Calculate the total resistance, the individual branch currents, and the resistance of $R2$.

13. Describe how you would connect two batteries of equal voltage to get more current than could be obtained from one battery.
14. Obtain an owner's manual for a late-model automobile and explain to the class the procedure recommended in the manual for jump starting a vehicle with a "dead battery." Emphasize the safety cautions.

INDIVIDUAL-STUDY ACTIVITY

1. Make a list of all the parallel circuits in your home.
2. Identify the electrical devices that are used in the kitchen of your home. Determine if this circuit is overloaded if all the devices are operated simultaneously.
3. Obtain a circuit from some home electrical device such as a clothes dryer, toaster, or electric fry pan. Identify the loads that are connected in parallel.

UNIT 12   Series-Parallel Circuits

The two previous units discussed circuit loads that were connected in series or in parallel. This unit discusses ways in which series and parallel circuits are connected together. When connected together, they form circuits called *series-parallel circuits*, or *combination circuits*. Several interconnected series-parallel circuits are often called a *network*, or *electrical system*. Most electrical devices are made up of combination circuits. Automobiles, television sets, radios, and computers have many combination circuits that make up their electrical systems.

SERIES-PARALLEL CIRCUIT

Figure 12-1 is an example of a series-parallel circuit. Load 1 is in series with a parallel circuit made up of loads 2 and 3. Notice that the current must first pass through load 1. Then the current separates into two paths at junction point A where it enters the parallel circuit. The two paths join again at junction point B where the current leaves the parallel circuit on its return to the energy source. This illustration represents only one way in which a series-parallel circuit is connected.

Fig. 12-1. A series-parallel, or combination, circuit

EXAMPLES OF SERIES-PARALLEL CIRCUITS

Figure 12-2 shows several sketches of series-parallel circuits. Some are simple, others complex. The sketches show how the loads, represented by the symbol for a resistance, are connected together. In every sketch, one or more loads are in series with loads that are in parallel. You may wish to compare the similarity and differences of these sketches with

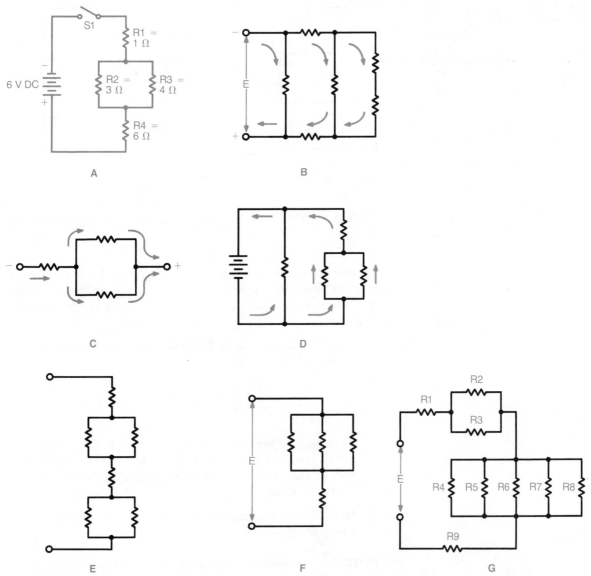

A

B

C

D

E

F

G

Fig. 12-2. Sketches illustrating various series-parallel circuits

those shown in the two previous units. When you want to convey more complete information about a series-parallel circuit, draw your sketch as shown in Fig. 12-2A. This sketch contains basic information about the circuit. All sketches, however, are meaningful and are the type used often by technicians and engineers to quickly convey information about series-parallel circuits.

RESISTANCE

Let us take a close look at the series-parallel circuit shown in Fig. 12-3. In this circuit, loads 1 and 4 are in series with the combination of loads 2 and 3. Loads 2 and 3 make up a parallel circuit.

87

Fig. 12-3. Diagram for Problem 1: (A) series-parallel circuit; (B) equivalent resistance (2.4 Ω) of parallel circuit in series with R1 and R4; (C) equivalent resistance of entire circuit

Problem 1: What is the total resistance of the circuit shown in Fig. 12-3A?

Solution: To find the total resistance of a series-parallel combination, it is helpful to consider the individual parts that make up the total circuit. In this series-parallel circuit, for example, the parallel circuit is considered first.

1. Find the total resistance of the parallel part of the circuit made up of R2 and R3 (Fig. 12-3A).

$$R_t = \frac{R2 \times R3}{R2 + R3} = \frac{4 \times 6}{4 + 6} = \frac{24}{10} = 2.4 \ \Omega$$

Since the parallel part of the circuit has an equivalent resistance of 2.4 Ω, you can now redraw the circuit showing the 2.4 Ω in series with R1 and R4 (Fig. 12-3B). This completes the first step in solving the problem.

2. Find the total resistance of the circuit. Use the redrawn circuit shown in Fig. 12-3B.

NOTE: In the following formula the mathematical symbol ‖ means "parallel to." In step 1, the equivalent resistance of $R2 \parallel R3$ is 2.4 Ω.

$$R_t = R1 + R2 \parallel R3 + R4$$
$$= 8 + 2.4 + 12$$
$$= 22.4 \ \Omega$$

Figure 12-3 shows the steps followed in calculating the total resistance of this series-parallel circuit. In summary, first, analyze carefully each series-parallel circuit to determine its individual parts. Second, consider each individual part as a unit. In this circuit, the parallel circuit was considered as a separate unit. Third, combine the individual parts to form a simple series "equivalent" circuit.

Problem 2: Four resistors are connected as a series-parallel circuit (Fig. 12-4). Resistance $R1$ is in series with a parallel circuit. The parallel circuit consists of two branches. One branch of the parallel circuit is made up of resistance $R2$, and the other branch is made up of resistances $R3$ and $R4$. Find the total resistance.

Fig. 12-4. Diagram for Problems 2 and 3

Solution:

1. Since $R3$ and $R4$ are in series with each other in one branch of the parallel circuit, determine the total resistance R_{t1} of the this series "string."

$$R_{t1} = R3 + R4 = 5\ \Omega + 5\ \Omega = 10\ \Omega$$

2. Determine the total resistance R_{t2} of the parallel part of the circuit.

$$R_{t2} = \frac{R2 \times R_{t1}}{R2 + R_{t1}} = \frac{5 \times 10}{5 + 10} = \frac{50}{15} = 3.3\ \Omega$$

3. Since the parallel part of the circuit has an equivalent resistance of $3.3\ \Omega$, calculate the total resistance R_{t3} of the series-parallel circuit.

$$R_{t3} = R1 + R2 \parallel R_{t1} = 10 + 3.3 = 13.3\ \Omega$$

CURRENT AND VOLTAGE

The previous problems illustrate the process of determining the resistance of a series-parallel circuit. The next problems explain how Kirchhoff's voltage and current laws are applied in series-parallel circuits. You already know that Kirchhoff's voltage law in series circuits states that the sum of the voltage drops around a circuit must equal the applied voltage. This is also true with series-parallel circuits. However, the voltage across any parallel branch must be considered as one of the voltage drops in the total circuit. The current in these combination circuits also follows Ohm's law if the proper voltage and resistance are considered for that part of the circuit. Let us now examine the behavior of current and voltage in series-parallel or combination circuits.

Problem 3: Refer to the series-parallel circuit in Fig. 12-4. Find the total current in the circuit, the current in each resistance, and the voltage drops across each resistance.

Solution:

1. Since the total voltage is given and the total equivalent resistance (as calculated in Problem 2) is known, use Ohm's law formula to determine the total current.

$$I_t = \frac{E_t}{R_t} = \frac{100}{13.3} = 7.5 \text{ A}$$

2. Calculate the voltage drop across $R1$. Since the total current is known and $R1$ is in series with the parallel circuit, you can use the Ohm's law formula for *this part of the circuit.*

$$E = IR = 7.5 \times 10 = 75 \text{ V}$$

3. Find the voltage drop across the parallel circuit. We know from Kirchhoff's voltage law that the sum of the voltage drops around the circuit is equal to the applied voltage. Since the voltage drop across $R1$ is 75 V, the voltage drop across the parallel circuit is 100 V − 75 V or 25 V. The following calculation verifies that the sum of the voltage drops equals the applied voltage.

$$
\begin{aligned}
E_t &= IR1 + I[R2 \parallel (R3 + R4)] \\
&= 7.5 \times 10 + 7.5 \times 3.3 \\
&= 75 + 24.75 \\
&= 99.75 \text{ V}
\end{aligned}
$$

The voltage drop calculated across the series and parallel circuit is 99.75 V. This is approximately equal to the applied voltage. The slight difference is due to rounding of numbers during the calculations.

4. Since the voltage (25 V) across the parallel circuit is known, find the current in resistances $R2$, $R3$, and $R4$. Use Ohm's law for calculating the current for this part of the circuit.

$$I = \frac{E}{R2} = \frac{25}{5} = 5.0 \text{ A}$$

$$I = \frac{E}{R3 + R4} = \frac{25}{10} = 2.5 \text{ A}$$

$$\text{Total} = 7.5 \text{ A}$$

The current in the parallel branch with resistance $R2$ is 5 A. The current in the parallel branch with resistances $R2$ and $R3$ is 2.5 A. Since $R2$ and $R3$ form a series "string," the current is the same in each resistance. Notice that the total current that passes through the parallel part is 7.5 A—the calculated total current for the entire circuit. The current in the various parts of this circuit is shown in Fig. 12-5. Notice that the current separates at junction point A and joins again at point B. The same amount of current flows out from point B as flows into point B. This verifies Kirchhoff's current law: The sum of the currents entering a point must equal the sum of the currents leaving that point.

5. Calculate the voltage drops across the series string $R3$ and $R4$ within the parallel circuit. We know that the total voltage across the parallel circuit is 25 V and the current in the resistance string is 2.5 A. Use Ohm's law to figure the voltage drops across this part of the circuit.

$$E = IR1 = 2.5 \times 5 = 12.5 \text{ V}$$
$$E = IR2 = 2.5 \times 5 = 12.5 \text{ V}$$

$$\text{Total} = 25.0 \text{ V}$$

ANALYZING COMPLEX CIRCUITS

In analyzing complex series-parallel circuits, it is often convenient to rearrange the network into an electrically equivalent circuit so that the series-parallel parts are recognized easily. This is illustrated in the next problem.

Problem 6: Find the total resistance and total current of the circuit in Fig. 12-6A.

Solution:

1. Analyze the circuit shown in Fig. 12-6A and redraw it to show more clearly the series and parallel parts of the total circuit (Fig. 12-6B).
2. Determine the equivalent resistance (R_{eq1}) of the parallel circuit consisting of $R3$ and $R4$.

91

A

B

C

D

E

Fig. 12-6. Diagrams for Problem 6

$$R_{eq1} = \frac{R3 \times R4}{R3 + R4} = \frac{6 \times 4}{6 + 4} = \frac{24}{10} = 2.4 \ \Omega$$

3. The circuit now can be illustrated as shown in Fig. 12-6C. Calculate the total equivalent resistance (R_{eq2}) of the upper branch.

$$R_{eq2} = R2 + R_{eq1} + R5 = 8 + 2.4 + 10 = 20.4 \ \Omega$$

4. The circuit can now be redrawn as a simple parallel circuit (Fig. 12-6D). Find the resistance of this parallel circuit.

$$R_t = \frac{R_{eq2} \times R1}{R_{eq2} + R1} = \frac{20.4 \times 24}{20.4 + 24} = \frac{489.6}{44.4} = 11.03 \ \Omega$$

The total resistance of the circuit can be represented by a single resistance equal to 11.03 Ω (Fig. 12-6E).

5. Find the total current in the circuit. Use Ohm's law.

$$I_t = \frac{E_t}{R_t} = \frac{12}{11.03} = 1.09 \ A$$

The process of determining the total resistance of a complex network can be summarized as follows:

1. Analyze the network so that you can identify the loads that make up

the parallel circuits of the network. Do the same for the loads that are in series with the parallel circuits.

2. If necessary, redraw the network so that the loads in parallel and the loads in series with the parallel circuits are shown clearly.

3. Identify the parallel circuit most distant from the energy source and figure its equivalent resistance. Sum any resistances that are in series with it.

4. If necessary, redraw the result of step 3. Look carefully at the redrawn diagram for the existence of another parallel circuit. If another parallel circuit exists, repeat step 3 until a single resistance can represent the entire load for the network.

SELF-TEST

Test your knowledge by writing, on a separate sheet of paper, the word or words that most correctly complete the following statements:

1. A circuit with several interconnected series-parallel circuits is called a _____ .

2. A series-parallel circuit is often referred to as a _____ circuit.

3. Combination circuits have some loads connected in series and some in _____ .

4. In solving series-parallel circuits, the resistances in the parallel circuits are first reduced to their _____ .

5. In a series-parallel circuit, if two of the resistors are in series with the energy source, the current is the _____ in each resistor.

6. The current in a series-parallel circuit divides when it enters a parallel circuit and _____ when it leaves the parallel circuit.

7. A series-parallel circuit has two resistances in series with a parallel circuit. The parallel circuit has three branches. There are a total of _____ voltage drops in the circuit.

8. To find the voltage drop across a parallel circuit, you must know the _____ and the _____ of the parallel circuit.

9. A series-parallel circuit is shown in Fig. 12-7. In solving the problem, the equivalent resistance of parallel circuit _____ should be determined first.

Fig. 12-7. Diagram for self-test question 9

10. The current flowing from a junction point _____ the current flowing to that junction point.

FOR REVIEW AND DISCUSSION

1. Write a description of the circuit sketch in Fig. 12-2G.

2. Describe in your own words the process to follow in solving complex series-parallel circuits for total resistance, current, and voltage.

3. A series-parallel circuit is shown in Fig. 12-8. Calculate the total resistance, the total current,

the currents through $R2$ and $R3$, and the voltage drop across each resistor in this circuit.

4. A series-parallel circuit is shown in Fig. 12-9. Find the voltage across $R6$.

5. A series circuit has two resistances in series with a parallel circuit that has five branches. Describe the flow of a 5-A current in the circuit.

Fig. 12-8. Diagram for review and discussion question 3

Fig. 12-9. Diagram for review and discussion question 4

INDIVIDUAL-STUDY ACTIVITY

Obtain a schematic circuit diagram of some electrical device such as a radio, a television set, a toaster, or an electric clothes dryer. Identify the parts in the diagram that are considered as loads. Indicate the combinations of loads that make up series, parallel, and series-parallel circuits.

UNIT 13 Measuring Electrical Quantities

Electricity cannot be seen. However, electrical quantities such as voltage, current, resistance, and power can be measured with instruments called *meters*. In this unit, you will learn about the most common kinds of meters. These are used in the design, the manufacturing, and the servicing or repairing of all kinds of electrical and electronic products.

THE MOVING COIL METER

A typical moving coil meter works like a small electric motor. This "motor action" causes the meter pointer to move. The amount of this movement depends on the amount of current that passes through the meter circuit. Although the pointer moves because of current, other electrical quantities, such as voltage and resistance, can be measured. The "face" of the meter can be marked to show the different electrical quantities. The arrangement of parts that causes the pointer to move is called the *meter movement*. Many meters use a *permanent-magnet moving coil movement* (Fig. 13-1). The coil is wound around a frame mounted between pivot points so that the coil is free to turn. The pointer is fastened to the coil assembly. A small spring holds the coil so that the pointer is at zero on the meter scale. The ends of the coil are connected to the stationary terminals of the meter.

Fig. 13-1. The permanent-magnet moving coil meter movement (*Triplett Corporation*)

When current passes through the coil, a small electromagnet is produced. The poles of the electromagnet are repelled by the poles of the permanent magnet. Since the movement of the coil and pointer depends on current, the pointer will move. From zero it moves a distance determined by the value of the current. The amount of current needed to move the pointer to the highest reading on the meter scale is called the *full-scale deflection current* of the meter. This type of meter is called an *analog meter*. It is called an analog meter because it operates with a continuous variable quantity. In this meter, the continuous variable quantity is the current flowing through the coil of the meter.

VOLTMETERS AND AMMETERS

Voltage is measured with a *voltmeter*. Current is measured with an *ammeter*. Microammeters measure current in millionths, and milliammeters, in thousandths, of an ampere. Very small amounts of current are measured with an instrument called a *galvanometer*.

Voltmeters and ammeters can be built as individual instruments. They can also be part of an instrument called a *multimeter*. Multimeters use a single meter movement but different internal circuits to measure voltage, current, and resistance. *Panel meters* are single-purpose instruments. They usually are made to be mounted on a test or an instrument panel (Fig. 13-2). Panel voltmeters measure either direct or alternating voltage. Panel ammeters measure either direct or alternating current.

OHMMETERS

Electrical resistance is measured with an *ohmmeter*. The meter movement of the ohmmeter is the same as that in voltmeters and ammeters. An ohmmeter can be an individual panel instrument, or it can be a part of a multimeter.

Fig. 13-2. Panel meters: (A) dc voltmeter; (B) ac ammeter (*Triplett Corporation*)

95

An ohmmeter circuit requires a source of energy such as a cell, a battery, or both. These are contained in the case of the meter. You should measure periodically the voltage on the cells or batteries of the ohmmeter. This measurement should be at or slightly above the rated voltages on the cells or batteries. The proper voltage is important to maintain because this source of energy in the ohmmeter is used to measure the resistance of components. If the ohmmeter's cells or batteries are below their rated voltage, improper measurement of resistances will result.

A *megohmmeter* is used to test materials with very high resistances. Equipment and wire insulation are examples. A high voltage in the megohmmeter is needed to measure these resistances. The source of energy in the megohmmeter is often a hand-cranked generator that provides this high voltage.

MULTIMETER

The most common kind of multimeter is the volt-ohm-milliammeter (VOM) (Fig. 13-3A). This instrument can be used as a voltmeter, an ammeter, or an ohmmeter. All you need to do is set its selector switch correctly. Some VOMs are also equipped with a decibel (dB) scale. This is used to measure the sound-output level of audio amplifiers for public-address systems.

The field-effect volt-ohm-milliammeter (FET VOM) has one or more devices called *field-effect transistors*. These cause the instrument to have a very high input impedance, or resistance, to current (Fig. 13-3B). As a result, the FET VOM is able to measure voltages without disturbing the circuit. This is very important when low voltages must be measured accurately.

The transistorized voltmeter (TRVM) and vacuum-tube voltmeter (VTVM) are combination voltmeters and ohmmeters (Fig. 13-3C). As with the FET VOM, the outstanding feature of these instruments is their high input impedance.

Fig. 13-3. Multimeters: (A) volt-ohm-milliammeter (*Triplett Corporation*); (B) field-effect VOM (*Sencore*); (C) vacuum-tube voltmeter (VTVM) (*Heath Company*)

SELECTOR SWITCH

RUBBER-INSULATED ALLIGATOR CLIP

TEST PROD

A

B

C

96

Fig. 13-4. Using the voltmeter

CARE AND SAFE USE OF METERS

All meters are delicate instruments. They must be used with care to keep from damaging them mechanically or electrically. You must choose a voltmeter or an ammeter with the right *range*. This means that the instrument must be able to handle safely the highest voltage or largest current being tested. You should always learn how to operate any meter before trying to use it. One of the best ways to do this is to read carefully the operation and application manual for the meter. This manual provides detailed instructions on how to use and read the meter safely.

Voltmeters and ammeters are connected to energized circuits or in circuits to which a voltage will be applied. It is very important, therefore, to follow the right safety rules while using them. Voltmeters and ammeters are often connected to a circuit with clips or screw terminals. It is always safer to turn off the power supply before making these connections. The circuit can then be turned on to make the measurement. Also be careful not to touch bare circuit wires when using test prods to connect a meter to a circuit.

USING THE VOLTMETER

A voltmeter is always connected to the two points of a device or a circuit across which the voltage is to be measured (Fig. 13-4A). A dc voltmeter is a *polarized* instrument. This means that it must be connected to a circuit in the correct polarity, or + to + and − to − (Fig. 13-4B). If this is not done, the pointer of the meter will move in the wrong direction. This can damage the pointer mechanism. An ac voltmeter can be connected across two points under test without regard to polarity.

USING THE AMMETER

The ammeter is normally connected in series with the conductors and load being tested (Fig. 13-5). It may be permanently damaged if it is

Fig. 13-5. Using the ammeter

Fig. 13-6. Using the ohmmeter

connected across an energy source or into a circuit with too much current. A dc ammeter must be connected into a circuit with the right polarity. If the pointer of a dc ammeter moves in the wrong direction during testing, reverse its connections to the test points. An ac ammeter can be connected into a circuit without regard to polarity.

USING THE OHMMETER

An ohmmeter is connected in parallel to the terminals of the device or circuit to be tested (Fig. 13-6). To get an accurate measurement, an ohmmeter must be "zeroed" before being used. To zero a volt-ohm-milliammeter, bring the test prods together. Next turn the zero adjustment knob until the pointer is at zero on the ohm scale. If you switch the meter to another ohm range, you will have to zero it again.

If an ohmmeter cannot be zeroed, it is usually because of a weak cell or battery in the meter circuit. To keep from ruining an ohmmeter battery, always make sure that the tips of the test prods do not touch, except when zeroing the meter. To prevent accidental short circuiting of the contacts, turn the meter off if possible. Unplug the test leads when the ohmmeter is not in use. When using an ohmmeter, always be sure that voltage is not being applied to the device or the circuit under test. The meter may be damaged if it is connected across two points between which even a low voltage is present.

Do not let the fingers of both hands touch the tips of the test prods while measuring resistance. If you do so, the ohmmeter will measure the combined resistance of your body and the circuit being tested. Be very careful of this in measuring high values of resistance, when you might not suspect the problem.

READING METER SCALES

Reading the value of an electrical quantity from the position of the pointer on a meter scale is not always easy. To read meter scales quickly and accurately, you must know how they are marked off. In many circuits, small changes in voltage and current will take place, causing the pointer to move only a little. Accurate meter reading means looking and judging carefully.

Panel-Meter Scales. Studying the panel-ammeter scales in Fig. 13-7 will help you learn how to read all meter scales. You will notice that the scale of Fig. 13-7A is marked off into 4 main divisions. The values of these are 0.5, 1.0, 1.5, and 2 A. Each main division is, in turn, divided into 10 subdivisions. The value of each is then equal to 0.5/10, or 0.05 A.

If the meter pointer is at a position of less than 0.5, the value of the current is equal to the sum of the values of the subdivisions through which the pointer has passed in moving to that position. If the pointer has moved past one of the first three main divisions, the value of the

Fig. 13-7. Reading the scales of a panel meter

current is equal to the value of that main division plus the sum of the values of the subdivisions to the right of the main division.

When the pointer stops between the two lines of a subdivision, you must estimate the last figure of the reading according to the pointer's position within the subdivision.

In Fig. 13-7B, the 0-to-5-A scale is marked off into 5 main divisions. Each of these is divided into 10 subdivisions. The value of each subdivision on this meter scale is then equal to 1/10, or 0.1 A.

Volt-Ohm-Milliammeter Scales. The face of a volt-ohm-milliammeter has a combination of scales. These scales are used to measure a wide range of values in dc voltage and current, ac voltage, resistance, and output levels (Fig. 13-3A). For this reason, the scale is more complicated than that of a panel meter.

Though several different kinds of volt-ohm-milliammeters are used, all have similar scales and work in similar ways.

Part of a volt-ohm-milliammeter ac scale and range-selector switch is shown in Fig. 13-8. The selector-switch values show the ranges of the meter.

If the range of the voltage being measured is not known, set the selector switch to the highest value, in this case 1,200 V. Once an approximate value for the unknown voltage has been obtained, the selector switch can be set to the position closest to this value but not less than it. For example, if the selector is set at 1,200 and the pointer moves a little to show that the measured voltage is about 10 V, the selector switch can be set at 12. By doing this, it is possible to get a more accurate reading of the actual voltage, say, 10.8 V. Note that, although the selector has positions for 3, 12, 60, 300, and 1,200 V, the face of the meter has only the 12-, 60-, and 300-V scales. If the 3-V position on the selector is used, the voltage values read directly on the 300 scale must be divided by 100. With the selector switch set at the 3-V position and the pointer indicating 153 on the 300-V scale, the actual voltage being measured is 153/100, or 1.53 V. Similarly, with the selector on the 1,200-V position, the voltage shown on the 12-V scale must be multiplied by 100 to get the actual voltage. Remember that you can always get a reading on a higher position of the selector switch for any voltage less than this value. The lower positions are used merely to get a more accurate reading. You must never set the selector switch to a value less than the actual voltage. If this were done, the pointer might be damaged in swinging past the full-scale deflection. The coil in the meter movement might also burn out.

Measuring Resistance with the Volt-Ohm-Milliammeter. The ohms or resistance scale of a typical VOM is read from right to left (Fig. 13-9). The main divisions of this scale are not marked off evenly. Such a meter scale is said to be *nonlinear*. While this may be a bit confusing at first, you will find that such a scale is not at all unusual or difficult to read.

Fig. 13-8. Reading an ac VOM scale. The selector switch shows the full-scale deflection.

Fig. 13-9. Reading the ohms scale on a VOM

99

14 × 1,000 = 14,000 Ω

10

20

Ω

x1
x10   Ω
x1,000
x100,000

COM

V-Ω-A

RANGE-SELECTOR
SWITCH

RESISTOR UNDER
TEST

Fig. 13-10. The selector switch on the VOM indicates the multiplier to be used in measuring resistance.

Fig. 13-11. Making a continuity test with an ohmmeter

Figure 13-10 shows how one type of VOM is used to measure resistance. The ohms-range selector switch of the instrument is set at the × 1,000 position. This means that the resistance-scale reading must be multiplied by 1,000. In Fig. 13-10, the reading of the meter is 14,000 Ω (14 × 1,000). If the range-selector switch were at any other position, the reading of the scale should be multiplied by the number at that position.

The extreme left-hand end of a VOM ohm scale may be marked with an infinity symbol (∞). This means that if the pointer is at this position when the range-selector switch is at the highest ohms range, the resistance being tested is so high that it cannot be measured with the instrument.

CONTINUITY TEST

In addition to measuring resistance, an ohmmeter is used to make continuity tests. These show whether or not there is a continuous electron path from one test point to another. Continuity tests are very useful for checking hidden conductors of coils and other devices in which the complete path cannot be seen. Continuity tests are commonly used for checking switches and transformer and relay coils.

When making a continuity test, the ohmmeter (or the VOM) is usually adjusted first to the $R \times 1 \Omega$ range. It is then connected to the terminals of the device or to the points of the circuit being tested. If the meter pointer does not move from the high resistance end of the ohms scale at any ohms range, a conductor of the device or the circuit being tested is broken or open (Fig. 13-11A).

If, on the other hand, the ohmmeter pointer moves to a position that indicates some resistance, there is continuity between the terminals (Fig. 13-11B). The amount of resistance will be determined by the characteristics of the device or the circuit being tested. When the resistance is very low, as shown when the meter pointer moves to or near zero on the resistance scale, there is said to be *direct continuity* between the points under test.

A continuity test is also very useful in checking for "shorts" or "grounds." In the test shown in Fig. 13-11C, direct continuity exists between one terminal of a coil wound with insulated wire and the core.

OHMS

OPEN

A

OHMS

B

OHMS

SHORT

IRON
CORE

C

In this case, the wire insulation has become defective at some point. There is a short circuit between the wire and the core. Since this condition might be dangerous or cause the circuit to work improperly, the coil should be replaced.

CLAMP-ON METER

Most meters must be connected directly into a circuit in order to get a reading. The clamp-on meter is designed to avoid this. Clamp-on meters are generally used to measure alternating current and voltage. They are used to measure current by opening the jaws and then closing them around the conductors of the circuit being tested (Fig. 13-12). This makes it easy to measure currents in wires that cannot be disconnected quickly from their terminals.

DIGITAL METERS

The digital meter, like the analog meter, operates with a continuous variable quantity. The main difference, however, is that the digital meter circuits change or convert the analog quantity, for example, voltage, into a digital form. The device that does this is called an *analog-to-digital converter,* or ADC. The electrical concepts involved in the conversion system used by the ADC are discussed in Unit 41, "Digital Electronic Circuits."

Digital meters are rapidly replacing many of the analog meters previously used to measure electrical quantities. There are three main reasons for this. First, the digital meter is easy to read. Second, the measurements are accurate. Third, the cost of purchasing a digital meter is becoming more competitive with the cost of an analog meter.

DIGITAL MULTIMETER

A portable digital multimeter is shown in Fig. 13-13A. This meter is designed to measure volts, ohms, and milliamperes. Some of its features include a power switch, function selector for desired measurement, negative-sign indicator when measuring dc volts or dc milliamperes, a digital readout provided by LED (light-emitting diode) numerals, automatic positioning decimals, and a range selector. The meter leads have a special "touch-on" probe. This probe has a finger-action push button that applies power to the unit when it is pressed. The meter requires four (size C) batteries. The batteries are the disposable alkaline types or the rechargeable nickel-cadmium type. The nickel-cadmium batteries can be recharged by using a *power adapter* (Fig. 13-13B). If the voltage of the rechargeable batteries is less than 4.8 V, the batteries should be recharged by the power adapter. It normally takes about 2 to 3 hours to bring the voltage of the battery back to normal. Before using any electrical meter, it is good practice to become familiar with its instruction manual. Other digital meters are discussed in Unit 47, "Electronic Test Instruments."

Fig. 13-12. Using a clamp-on meter to measure motor current (*Columbia Electric Manufacturing Company*)

A

B

Fig. 13-13. Digital meter: (A) portable digital multimeter; (B) ac power adapter (*Sencore, Inc.*)

Test your knowledge by writing, on a separate sheet of paper, the word or words that most correctly complete the following statements:

1. Voltage is measured with a _____. Current is measured with an _____.
2. A _____ measures very small amounts of current.
3. A _____ is a combination of voltmeter, ammeter, and ohmmeter.
4. A voltmeter is always connected to the two _____ of a circuit between which the voltage is to be measured.
5. Direct-current voltmeters and ammeters are _____ instruments that must be connected to a circuit in the correct _____.
6. The typical ammeter is connected in _____ with one of the conductors of the circuit being tested.
7. An ac voltmeter or ammeter can be connected to a circuit without regard to _____.
8. Electrical resistance is measured with an _____.
9. If an ohmmeter cannot be zeroed, this is often due to a weak _____ or _____ within the meter circuit.
10. An ohmmeter may be seriously damaged if it is connected to two points across which even a low _____ is present.
11. A _____ test is done to find if there is a continuous path for electrons between two points of a circuit or of a device.

FOR REVIEW AND DISCUSSION

1. Name the instruments with which voltage and current are measured.
2. What is a multimeter?
3. What is the advantage of using an FET VOM or a vacuum-tube voltmeter instead of an ordinary VOM?
4. Draw a diagram showing how a voltmeter is connected to circuit points being tested.
5. Draw a diagram showing how a typical ammeter is connected into a circuit.
6. Give a general explanation of how meter scales are read.
7. What condition often makes it impossible to zero an ohmmeter?
8. Briefly describe how an ohmmeter is used for measuring the resistance of a device or of a circuit.
9. What instrument is used to make a continuity test? Why is such a test made?
10. Describe a clamp-on meter.
11. Explain the difference between an analog and digital meter.

INDIVIDUAL-STUDY ACTIVITIES

1. Give a demonstration showing how an ohmmeter is used to measure resistance and to make continuity tests. Explain to your class how a continuity test can be used to determine the condition of devices such as switches, incandescent lamps, and coils.
2. Give a demonstration showing how fixed resistors and a potentiometer are tested with an ohmmeter.
3. Give a demonstration describing a typical volt-ohm-milliammeter. Show how it is used to measure voltage and current in a circuit.
4. Investigate the various methods of converting a continuous variable quantity into a digital form that can be used in a meter. Report your findings to the class.

UNIT 14 Capacitance and Capacitors

Capacitance is the ability of a circuit or a device to "store" electric energy. Although almost all alternating-current circuits have capacitance, it may or may not be desirable. In circuits where a specific value of capacitance is needed, a device known as a *capacitor* may be used (Fig. 14-1). The basic form of a capacitor is two conductors called *plates* separated by insulating material called the *dielectric*.

Capacitors are one of the most common components of electric circuits. They perform several different circuit functions. Since they do not provide a continuous conducting path for electrons, they are used to block a direct current. An alternating current, however, can still flow in the circuit. Capacitors are used with resistors and with coils to filter, or smooth out, a varying direct current. Capacitors, along with resistors, form timing circuits that control other circuits. In radio and television receivers, capacitors are used with coils to form tuning circuits. These let us choose the stations to which we want to listen. Capacitors are also very important components of oscillator circuits. These produce high-frequency alternating voltages.

Fig. 14-1. Capacitors are manufactured in many different sizes and shapes. (*Cornell-Dubilier Electric Corporation*)

CAPACITOR ACTION

The action of a simple capacitor is shown in Fig. 14-2. When the plates are connected to a battery, electrons from the plate connected to the positive terminal of the battery move to the battery. This causes the plate to become positively charged. At the same time, an equal number of electrons are repelled to the other plate by the negative terminal of the battery. That plate becomes negatively charged. This produces a voltage across the plates (Fig. 14-2A). Because of the dielectric separating the plates, electrons cannot move directly from one plate to the other. Electrons have simply been taken off one plate and put on the other through the circuit that connects them. This flow of electrons in the wires connecting the capacitor to the battery continues until the voltage

Fig. 14-2. Charging and discharging actions of a capacitor: (A) charging; (B) discharging

DIELECTRIC   PLATES

A   BATTERY

SPARK   B

across the plates is equal to the voltage of the battery. When this happens, the capacitor is fully *charged*. An *electrostatic field* exists between the plates of a charged capacitor. Energy is stored in this field.

When the battery is taken out of the circuit, the plates keep their charges. A voltage continues to exist across them. If the plates are now connected, electrons will flow through the circuit in the opposite direction. They will flow from the negatively charged plate to the positively charged plate (Fig. 14-2B). When the voltage across the plate decreases to zero, the flow of electrons stops. Now the capacitor is fully *discharged*.

Fig. 14-3. The voltage across a fully charged capacitor is equal in value and polarity to the applied voltage. Thus, no current will flow in the circuit.

Blocking Action. The voltage across the plates of a fully charged capacitor is equal to the voltage of the battery to which it is connected. The capacitor voltage is also of the opposite polarity from the battery voltage. Because of this, a fully charged capacitor blocks current in a circuit (Fig. 14-3). The blocking action of a capacitor is used in many electronic circuits.

Action in an Alternating-Current Circuit. When a capacitor is connected to a source of alternating voltage, the polarity of the applied voltage changes each half cycle. As a result, the capacitor is alternately charged, discharged, and recharged. It has the opposite polarity during each cycle (Fig. 14-4). However, there is no current flow through the dielectric that separates the plates.

Capacitive Reactance. A capacitor allows the alternating current in a circuit to flow, but it does oppose the current. The opposition of a capacitor to the flow of alternating current is called *capacitive reactance*. The symbol for capacitive reactance is X_c. Its unit of measure is the ohm. The formula for figuring capacitive reactance is

$$X_c = \frac{1}{2\pi fC}$$

where X_c = capacitive reactance in ohms
    f = frequency in hertz
    C = capacitance in farads
    π = 3.14 (pi), a constant

Capacitive reactance is inversely proportional to both frequency and capacitance. This means that when the capacitance of a circuit is increased, the capacitive reactance decreases. The capacitive reactance also decreases when the frequency of the current in a circuit increases. These relationships are very important in tuning circuits in which capacitors determine the frequency at which the circuits operate.

Impedance. The total opposition to current in a circuit containing a combination of resistance and capacitive reactance is called *impedance.* It is also measured in ohms. The letter symbol for impedance is Z. Another component of impedance, called *inductive reactance,* is discussed in Unit 17.

CAPACITANCE

The capacitance of a capacitor—its ability to store electric energy—depends mainly on three things: (1) the area of its plates—the greater the area, the greater the capacitance; (2) the spacing, or distance, between plates—the closer the spacing, the greater the capacitance; and (3) the dielectric material. Energy is stored by a capacitor in the form of an electrostatic field within its dielectric. Different materials have different abilities to maintain an electrostatic field and, thus, to store electric energy. The measure of this ability is known as the *dielectric constant.* Common dielectric materials are air, Mylar, mica, oxide films, and certain ceramic materials. Other capacitor dielectric materials are paper, glass, and polystyrene.

UNIT OF CAPACITANCE

The basic unit of capacitance is the *farad,* abbreviated F. It is named in honor of Michael Faraday. He was an English scientist who lived from 1791 to 1867. A capacitor has a capacitance of one farad when an applied voltage that changes at the rate of one volt per second produces a current of one ampere in the capacitor circuit.

The capacitance of capacitors is most often given in microfarads (μF) or in picofarads (pF). One microfarad is equal to one-millionth of a farad. One picofarad is equal to one-millionth of a microfarad, or one-trillionth of a farad. The prefix *pico-* means 1/1,000,000,000,000 (one-trillionth).

Fig. 14-4. Action of a capacitor in an ac circuit

KINDS OF CAPACITORS

Capacitors are made in different ways. They are divided into two general classes: *fixed capacitors* and *variable capacitors.* Fixed capacitors have a specific single value of capacitance. Fixed capacitors are either *nonelectrolytic* or *electrolytic* (Fig. 14-5). This refers to the structure of the dielectric.

Capacitors with a capacitance of not more than one microfarad are generally nonelectrolytic capacitors. The capacitances of electrolytic capacitors usually range from one microfarad to hundreds of thousands of microfarads. Capacitance values and working voltages are usually printed on the body of the capacitor or are shown by means of a color code.

SYMBOL

MYLAR   SILVERED MICA   CERAMIC DISK

A

SYMBOL

ALUMINUM   TANTALUM

B

Working Voltage. In addition to capacitance, fixed capacitors are also rated in terms of their working voltage (WVDC). This is given in volts. It is the largest value of direct voltage that can safely be applied to a capacitor. If a higher voltage is applied, the dielectric breaks down and begins to conduct current. When this happens in a nonelectrolytic capacitor, the capacitor is said to be *leaking*. It must be replaced.

Mylar Capacitors. A Mylar capacitor is made of thin metal-foil plates and a Mylar dielectric. These are cut into long, narrow strips and rolled together into a compact unit (Fig. 14-6). Capacitance values range from 0.001 to 1 microfarad. Working-voltage ratings are as high as 1,600 V.

Ceramic Capacitors. Ceramic capacitors have disk-shaped or tubular dielectrics. These are made of ceramic materials such as titanium dioxide and barium titanate. The plates are thin coatings of a silver compound deposited on each side of the dielectric. Capacitances range from 5 pF to 0.05 μF. Working-voltage ratings exceed 10,000 V.

Silvered-Mica Capacitors. A silvered-mica capacitor is made of a thin sheet of mica (the dielectric) with coatings of a silver compound on each side (the plates). Silvered-mica capacitors have capacitance values that range from 1 to 10,000 pF. The working voltage is about 500 V.

ELECTROLYTIC CAPACITORS

The dielectric of electrolytic capacitors is a thin film of oxide. It is formed by electrochemical action directly on a plate of metal foil. The other plate is a a paste electrolyte, either borax or a carbon salt. The very thin dielectric provides a large capacitance within a much smaller volume than would be possible with other materials.

Many electrolytic capacitors have more than one section. Some have two or more individual capacitor units within a single case. Multi-

WIRE LEAD CONNECTED TO PLATE 1

FOIL PLATE 1

MYLAR DIELECTRIC

WIRE LEAD CONNECTED TO PLATE 2

FOIL PLATE 2

Fig. 14-6. Basic construction of a Mylar capacitor

section capacitors have a positive lead for each of the capacitor units. They have a single negative lead common to all the capacitor units (Fig. 14-7).

The typical electrolytic capacitor used in electronic circuits is polarized. It must be connected into a circuit according to the plus and minus markings on the case (Fig. 14-8). Otherwise, the capacitor will overheat. This happens because of excessive leakage of current through the dielectric. Enough gas may be produced to cause the capacitor to explode. Nonelectrolytic capacitors are not polarized. They can be connected into a circuit without regard to polarity.

Electrolytic capacitors are used in rectifier circuits to smooth out varying direct currents. They are also often used as blocking capacitors. These block a direct current from a circuit while letting an alternating current pass.

Although electrolytic capacitors made from an aluminum foil are very popular, the tantalum electrolytic has very low leakage. It can be made much smaller than the aluminum electrolytic capacitor for the same capacity and working voltage. However, for extremely large values of capacitance for filtering power supplies, the aluminum electrolytic is generally preferred.

SYMBOL

Fig. 14-7. Examples of dual, or two-section, electrolytic capacitors (*Sprague Electric Company*)

VARIABLE CAPACITORS

Variable capacitors are used primarily to tune circuits. This involves giving the circuits the least opposition to currents with a certain frequency (Fig. 14-9). One kind of variable capacitor, called a *trimmer*, is made of two metal plates separated by a sheet of mica dielectric. The space between the plates can be adjusted with a screw. As the distance between the plates is increased, the value of capacitance decreases.

Another kind of variable capacitor is made of two sets of metal plates separated either by air or by sheets of mica insulation. One set of plates, the *stator assembly*, does not move. It is insulated from the frame of the capacitor, on which it is mounted. The other set of plates, the *rotor assembly*, is connected to the shaft. It can be turned. The rotor plates can move freely in or out between the stator plates. Thus, the capacitance of the capacitor can be adjusted easily from the lowest (plates apart) to the highest (plates together) value.

CAPACITORS IN PARALLEL

Capacitors are often connected in parallel. This is done to get a capacitance value that cannot easily be obtained from one capacitor (Fig. 14-10). The total capacitance of such a combination is equal to the sum of the individual capacitances. The working voltage of the combination is equal to the lowest individual working-voltage rating.

+12 V

Fig. 14-8. The polarized electrolytic capacitor must be connected into a circuit according to its polarity markings.

SINGLE-GANG
CAPACITOR

SYMBOL

TRIMMER CAPACITOR

TWO-GANG CAPACITOR

SHAFT

STATOR
PLATES

FRAME

ROTOR
PLATES

Fig. 14-9. Variable capacitors

0.03 μF   0.02 μF   0.05 μF

Fig. 14-10. When capacitors are connected in parallel, the total capacitance is equal to the sum of the individual capacitances.

CHARGING RATE OF A CAPACITOR

Unlike a dry cell, a capacitor does not generate a voltage by its own action. However, the voltage developed across the plates of a charged capacitor can be used as a voltage source. One of the important characteristics of a capacitor is that it can be charged. The charge can be stored for a time and then discharged through a load when needed.

The process of charging and discharging a capacitor can be illustrated in Fig. 14-11. At the instant the switch is closed from position 1 to position 2, electrons are transferred from one plate of the capacitor to the other (Fig. 14-11A). This causes a current I to flow in the circuit. At this same instant, the voltage E across the capacitor C is at a minimum since the voltage drop IR across R is at a maximum (Fig. 14-11B). As the current flow continues, the capacitor gradually becomes charged and a voltage begins to develop across the capacitor. This voltage opposes the battery voltage that is applied to the circuit. The opposing capacitor voltage is called a *counter electromotive force* (cemf). As a result, the current in the capacitor also decreases. Figure 14-11B illustrates the rise in voltage E and the corresponding decrease in current I during the process of charging a capacitor.

If the switch is closed from position 1 to position 3, the capacitor immediately begins to discharge through the resistor (Fig. 14-11C). Since the voltage E across the capacitor is at maximum, the initial discharge current I is also at maximum (Fig. 14-11D). As the capacitor continues to discharge, the current gradually decreases until both the current in the circuit and the voltage become zero.

The rate at which a capacitor charges and discharges can be controlled by varying the resistance in the capacitor circuit. The time needed for the voltage across a charging capacitor to reach 63.2 percent of the applied voltage is known as the *time constant* of the circuit. After five time-constant periods, the voltage across the capacitor will be very near 100 percent of the applied voltage. The time-constant formula is

$$T = R \times C$$

where T = the time constant in seconds
R = the resistance in ohms
C = the capacitance in farads

Capacitor charge and discharge rates can be used to control many circuits, including electronic timers and flashers. The circuit in Fig. 14-12 is a good example. In this circuit, the variable resistor R1 is used to change the time constant. During the first time constant, the capacitor will charge to 63.2 percent of 100 V, or 63.2 V. This may be enough voltage across the neon lamp to ionize the neon gas, causing it to conduct current. At low voltages, the neon acts as an insulator, so no current passes through it.

If the 63.2 V ionizes the lamp, the capacitor will quickly discharge through the lamp. There will be a flash of light. Now the capacitor will again begin to charge. The cycle is repeated. The time between flashes depends on the time constant of the circuit. A smaller value of resistance will let the capacitor charge more quickly. Flashes will occur more often. A larger resistance or capacitance will lengthen the time constant. Flashes will occur less often. This kind of circuit is often called a *relaxation oscillator*.

CAPACITOR COLOR CODES

Capacitance values are often printed directly on the body of capacitors. The values may also be shown by a color code. The numbers represented by colors in this code are the same as those used in the resistor color code. Unless otherwise stated, capacitance values given by the color code are in picofarad units.

How the color code is used with three kinds of nonelectrolytic capacitors is shown in Fig. 14-13. As with the resistor color code, the multiplier color gives the number of zeros that are to be added to the first two numbers of the capacitance value. The temperature-coefficient color in each of the codes shows the degree to which the capacitance will change with an increase of temperature.

CAPACITOR SAFETY

Many capacitors, such as the electrolytic capacitors used in high-voltage rectifier circuits of television receivers, keep their charges for some time after the charging voltages have been removed. There could be dangerous voltages across these capacitors for many hours after their circuits have been turned off. These could give a person a bad electric shock or badly damage test instruments.

To prevent this, all electrolytic capacitors in high-voltage circuits should be discharged before the circuits are handled in any way. This can be done safely by briefly shorting the terminals of the capacitors with an insulated wire. A 10,000-Ω resistor can be connected in series with the wire to reduce sparking at the terminals.

CAPACITOR DEFECTS

Fixed capacitors often become shorted because of a direct contact between their plates. This happens when the dielectric becomes worn or burned through because of age or the application of a voltage higher than the working voltage. A shorted capacitor must be replaced. The capacitor not only may not work properly but also may let too much current pass through other components in its circuit. A capacitor can, but seldom does, become open. This happens when one of its leads becomes disconnected from its plate. Electrolytic capacitors can become defective if the chemical materials inside dry out. Such a capacitor has much less capacitance and should be replaced.

A variable capacitor becomes defective because of shorted plates. This often happens because the plates are bent while the capacitor is being installed or while its circuit is being repaired. A shorted variable

Fig. 14-11. The effect of capacitance on voltage and current in a dc circuit

Fig. 14-12. Lamp-flasher circuit

NORMALLY STAMPED FOR VALUE

MOLDED TUBULAR PAPER OR MYLAR

CERAMIC DISK

AXIAL LEAD CERAMIC

Fig. 14-13. How the capacitor color code is used

Fig. 14-14. Isolating a capacitor for test purposes

capacitor can often be repaired by simply bending the touching plates back into place.

When replacing capacitors, it is best to replace them with a capacitor having not only the same capacity or tolerance but the same type of dielectric and temperature characteristics as well.

TESTING CAPACITORS

Capacitors can also be tested for short circuits with an ohmmeter. The ohmmeter (or volt-ohm-milliammeter) is connected across the terminals of the capacitor being tested. If the capacitor is shorted, the ohmmeter will show continuity or a very low resistance. Leaky or shorted capacitors should be replaced. When testing a capacitor that is wired into a circuit, you should always take it out of, or isolate it from, the circuit (Fig. 14-14). This will keep the ohmmeter from also measuring the resistance of the circuit in parallel with the capacitor.

Good nonelectrolytic capacitors have a very high resistance or no continuity between their terminals. Electrolytic capacitors have a lower resistance between their terminals. This is true even if they are in good condition. The amount of resistance will depend on the capacitance and working-voltage rating. With practice, you can soon learn how to tell if a capacitor is defective by testing it with an ohmmeter. If such a test is indefinite, the capacitor should be tested with a capacitor tester.

An ohmmeter applies a voltage to the component or part of a circuit to which it is connected. To keep from damaging an electrolytic capacitor while testing it with an ohmmeter, make sure that the ohmmeter voltage is not greater than the working-voltage rating of the capacitor. When testing an electrolytic capacitor with an ohmmeter, it is also important to connect the ohmmeter to it in the right polarity, or + to + and − to −.

To test a variable capacitor for short circuits, connect an ohmmeter to its terminals. Then slowly turn the shaft as far as it will go in both directions. If the capacitor is shorted at a point, the ohmmeter will show direct continuity at that point.

Accurate measurements of capacitors can be made with a capacitor analyzer (Fig. 14-15). This type of meter performs two functions. It measures both capacitance and inductance. It is called a *Z meter* because it measures the total impedance Z of the component (capacitor or inductor) being tested. This unit discusses how the meter measures capacitance. You will learn in Unit 17 how the meter is used to measure inductance.

The capacitor analyzer, such as the type shown in Fig. 14-15, can provide measurements (within 1 percent) of the rated capacitance of the capacitor. The following steps represent the general procedure to determine the capacitance of a capacitor.

1. Remove the power from the circuit if the capacitor to be checked has one end removed from the circuit but the other end still con-

nected to the circuit. Whenever possible, completely remove the capacitor from the circuit.

2. Connect the cord of the meter to a properly grounded 117-V ac outlet.
3. Turn on the meter power switch.
4. Connect the test leads to the capacitor to be tested. Polarity of the test leads is important only if you are checking a polarized capacitor, such as an electrolytic capacitor. The red lead should be connected to the positive terminal of a polarized capacitor.
5. Depress the VALUE button under the capacitor section of the push button switch.
6. Read the value of the capacitor on the front panel digital readout. The value of the capacity will be in microfarads (μF) if the LED in front of the μF indicator is lighted. The capacity is in picofarads (pF) if the LED in front of the pF indicator is lighted. (The indicators are in the upper right-hand portion of the meter panel.)

Fig. 14-15. Capacitor analyzer: "Z meter" capacitor-inductor analyzer (*Sencore, Inc.*)

The foregoing procedures illustrate the ease with which this meter can be used to measure the capacitance of a capacitor. Many other tests and measurements on capacitors can be performed by this meter. It can, for example, detect leakage, dielectric absorption (the inability of a capacitor to discharge to zero), and intermittent capacitors.

LEARNING BY DOING

3. Making a Relaxation Oscillator. In this interesting circuit, the charge-discharge action of a capacitor causes a neon lamp to flash on and off. When the resistance or the capacitance of the circuit is varied, the time constant is changed. This causes the lamp to flash at a different rate.

MATERIALS NEEDED

circuit board, prepunched, 6 × 8 in. (152 × 203 mm)
1 potentiometer, 1 megohm, ½ W
1 carbon-composition or film resistor, 1 megohm, ½ W
2 capacitors, 0.5 μF, 200 WVDC
1 neon lamp, type NE-2
90-V battery or a dc power supply

Procedure

1. Wire the circuit shown in Fig. 14-16.
2. Connect the battery or the power supply to the circuit. If a power supply is used, adjust it to produce an output voltage of 90 V.
3. Adjust the potentiometer so that the lamp flashes about once per second. The time between flashes can be calculated using the formula $T = RC$. T is time in seconds, R is resistance in ohms, and C is capacitance in farads. This is because 63.2 percent of 90 V is the approximate ionization voltage of an NE-2 lamp.

Fig. 14-16. Schematic diagram used for Learning by Doing No. 3, "Making a Relaxation Oscillator"

4. By using the formula $T = RC$, figure the total resistance of R1 and R2 when the lamp is flashing at the rate of one flash per second.
5. Adjust the potentiometer so that the lamp flashes at a faster speed. Has the total resistance of R1 and R2 been increased or decreased? Explain your answer.
6. Adjust the potentiometer to again get one flash per second. After disconnecting the battery or the power supply from the circuit, connect the other capacitor in parallel with C1. Does this cause the lamp to flash more or fewer times per second? Explain the reason for this.

SELF-TEST

Test your knowledge by writing, on a separate sheet of paper, the word or words that most correctly complete the following statements:

1. Capacitance is the ability of a circuit or a device to store _____ energy.
2. The basic form of a capacitor is two _____ separated by the _____.
3. A capacitor is charged by removing _____ from one of its plates and adding _____ to the other plate.
4. The voltage across the plates of a fully _____ capacitor is equal to the voltage of the source of energy.
5. The energy stored in a charged capacitor is in the form of an _____ field between its plates.
6. The discharge current of a capacitor is in a direction _____ to the direction of the charging current.
7. A capacitor prevents direct current from flowing in a circuit by what is referred to as a _____ action.
8. The opposition of a capacitor to the flow of alternating current in a circuit is called _____. This opposition is measured in _____. Its letter symbol is _____.
9. The total opposition to current by resistance and capacitive reactance in a circuit is known as _____. This total opposition is measured in _____. Its letter symbol is _____.
10. The measure of the ability of a dielectric material to maintain an electrostatic field between the plates of a capacitor is known as its _____.

11. A capacitor has a capacitance of one farad when an applied voltage that changes at the rate of one volt per _____ produces a current of one _____ in the capacitor circuit.
12. The most common units of capacitance are the _____ and the _____.
13. One _____ is equal to one-millionth of a microfarad.
14. The two general classes of capacitors are _____ capacitors and _____ capacitors.
15. The _____ voltage of a capacitor is the highest dc _____ that can be applied to it without causing the dielectric to break down and conduct current.
16. Three common kinds of fixed nonelectrolytic capacitors are _____ capacitors, _____ capacitors, and _____ capacitors.
17. The typical _____ capacitor is polarized. It must be connected into a circuit with the right _____.
18. An _____ capacitor is used to smooth out the varying dc output of a rectifier circuit.
19. The primary use of variable capacitors is to _____ circuits.
20. When capacitors are connected in parallel, the total capacitance of the combination is equal to the _____ of the individual capacitances.
21. The time needed for the voltage across a charging capacitor to reach 63.2 percent of the applied voltage is known as the _____ of the circuit.
22. For safety, charged high-voltage electrolytic capacitors should be _____ before they are handled in any way.

1. Define capacitance.
2. Describe the basic form of a capacitor.
3. Describe the charging and the discharging action of a capacitor.
4. What is meant by the blocking action of a capacitor?
5. Define capacitive reactance and impedance.
6. What are the three main things that determine the capacitance of a capacitor?
7. What is meant by the dielectric constant of a material?
8. What is meant by the working-voltage rating of a capacitor?
9. Describe the construction of a Mylar capacitor and of a ceramic capacitor.
10. The typical electrolytic capacitor is polarized. What does this mean?
11. Describe the construction of a variable capacitor.
12. What is the effect of connecting capacitors in parallel?
13. Explain the time-constant feature of a resistor-capacitor combination in a circuit.
14. Why is it important to discharge electrolytic capacitors in high-voltage circuits before the circuits are handled in any way?
15. Describe the most common capacitor defects.

INDIVIDUAL-STUDY ACTIVITIES

1. Give a demonstration showing your class the basic charging action of a capacitor. Use diagrams to explain each step of the charging process.
2. Give a demonstration showing your class how capacitors can be tested with an ohmmeter and with a capacitor tester.
3. Assemble the circuit as shown in Fig. 14-16 with a 90-V battery or three 30-V batteries connected

in series aiding. Adjust the potentiometer so that the lamp flashes about once every 2 seconds. Put the assembled and operating circuit in a closet. Check to see that it is still operating once a month. How long do you think the circuit will continue to operate? Do you think it takes a large or small amount of current to operate this circuit? Explain your findings to your class.

UNIT 15   Magnetism

Certain metals and metallic oxides are able to attract other metals (Fig. 15-1). This attraction is called *magnetism*. Materials that have magnetism are called *magnets*. Some magnets are found naturally in metallic ores. Others are manufactured. Magnets that keep their magnetism for a long time are called *permanent magnets*.

Magnetism is produced as a result of electrons spinning on their own axes while rotating about the nuclei of atoms (Fig. 15-2).

In magnetic materials, the atoms within certain of their areas, called *domains,* are aligned. When this happens, most of their electrons spin in the same direction (Fig. 15-3A). Magnetization usually results in two *magnetic poles* being formed at the ends of the magnet. These are called the *north pole* and the *south pole*. In the absence of magnetization, the domains within a material are not aligned (Fig. 15-3B). The electrons spin in all directions.

Fig. 15-1. Metal tools held in place by a magnetic tool holder (*Master Magnetics, Inc.*)

Fig. 15-2. An electron spinning on its own axis while revolving about the nucleus of an atom produces a magnetic field

ATTRACTION AND REPULSION

The law of magnetic attraction and repulsion states that *unlike* magnetic poles attract each other and *like* magnetic poles repel each other (Fig. 15-4). The force of the attraction or repulsion depends on the strength of the magnets and the distance between them.

As the strengths of magnets increase, the force of attraction or repulsion between them also increases. The force of attraction or repulsion decreases as the distance between the poles of the two magnets increases. If the distance between the unlike poles of two magnets is doubled, the force of attraction between the magnets decreases to one-fourth the original value. If the distance between the poles is reduced by one-half, the force of attraction between the magnets is increased four times. There is another way of stating these relationships. It can be said that the force of attraction or repulsion between the poles of two magnets is inversely proportional to the square of the distance between them.

MAGNETIC FIELD

The energy of a permanent magnet is in the form of a *magnetic field*. This field surrounds the magnet. The magnetic field is made of invisible *lines of force,* or *flux.* Outside the magnet, the lines of force run from the north pole to the south pole (Fig. 15-5). Magnetic lines of force form an unbroken loop. They do not cross one another. The strength of the magnetic field is directly related to the number of domains that have been aligned within the magnet during magnetization. When all the domains have been aligned, the magnetic field is as strong as possible. The magnet is then said to be *saturated.*

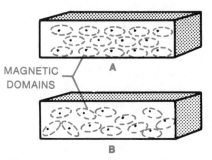

Fig. 15-3. Magnetic domains: (A) aligned; (B) not aligned

MAGNETIC AND NONMAGNETIC MATERIALS

A *magnetic material* is one that is attracted to a magnet and can be made into a magnet. Among these materials are steel and the metallic elements iron, nickel, and cobalt. These are commonly called *ferromagnetic elements. Ferro* refers to iron and to other materials and alloys that have certain properties similar to those of iron. Permanent magnets were originally natural magnets made of an iron ore called *magnetite,* or

Fig. 15-4. The law of magnetic attraction and repulsion

lodestone (Fig. 15-6). During the twelfth century, it was learned that a lodestone needle, when suspended so that it was free to turn, would point to the Earth's magnetic poles. Thus, it could serve as a magnetic compass. Lodestone is no longer used commercially as a magnetic material.

The magnetic materials most often used for making modern permanent magnets are metallic alloys and compounds. These are usually combinations of iron oxide and certain other elements. These materials have a high *retentivity*, the ability to keep a magnetic domain alignment for a long time. They also have high *permeability*, the ability to conduct magnetic lines of force. The magnetic permeability of a material is measured by comparing its ability to conduct magnetic lines of force to the ability of air to do so. Air, a vacuum, or other nonmagnetic substances are assumed to have a permeability of one.

Metals that are not attracted by a magnet and that cannot be made into a magnet are *nonmagnetic materials*. Copper, aluminum, gold, silver, and lead are nonmagnetic. Most nonmetallic materials such as cloth, paper, porcelain, plastic, and rubber are also nonmagnetic.

Alloys. One of the most common magnetic alloys is alnico. This alloy is made of aluminum, nickel, cobalt, and iron. Permanent alnico magnets come in different shapes and grades. They are used in such products as motors, generators, loudspeakers, microphones, and meters (Fig. 15-7). Other good magnetic alloys are Permalloy (nickel and iron, or cobalt, nickel, and iron), Supermalloy (nickel, iron, molybdenum, and manganese), and platinum-cobalt.

Ceramic Materials. Some hard ceramic magnetic materials are called *ferrites*. They are made by first grinding a combination of iron oxide and an element such as barium into a fine powder. The powder mixture is then pressed into the desired shape and baked at a high temperature. This produces a magnetic material that is very efficient and, unlike alloy materials, has a high electrical resistance.

Ceramic magnets are formed into many shapes (Fig. 15-8). Permanent magnets of this kind are used as latches on refrigerator doors. Such a magnet is in the form of a plastic strip filled with barium ferrite and bent to fit the shape of the door.

HOW MAGNETS ARE MADE

In order to make a magnet, energy in the form of a magnetic field must be applied to some magnetic material. This is called *magnetic induction*.

An example of magnetic induction is shown in Fig. 15-9. A nail made of steel is placed parallel to and near a permanent magnet. Since steel is more permeable than air, the force lines from the permanent magnet pass easily through the nail. This causes some of the domains in

Fig. 15-5. The magnetic field surrounding a bar-shaped magnet

Fig. 15-6. Magnetite, commonly known as lodestone, is a natural magnetic material.

Fig. 15-7. Alnico permanent magnets. The soft-iron keeper placed across the poles of the horseshoe magnet helps the magnet keep its full strength for a longer period of time.

Fig. 15-8. Ceramic permanent magnets can be made in many shapes and sizes. (*Allen-Bradley Company*)

the steel to become aligned. Thus, the magnetic induction process produces magnetic poles at the ends of the nail. Note that the magnetic polarity of the nail is opposite to the polarity of the permanent magnet. The nail thus becomes a magnet and is able to attract objects made of magnetic materials.

Commercially, permanent magnets are made with a *magnetizer*. One kind of magnetizer uses electric coils as the source of the magnetization energy (Fig. 15-10). To use the magnetizer, the object to be magnetized is placed over the pole pieces formed by two ends of the metal cores over which the coils are wound. When the switch is turned on, a direct current passes through the coils. This current produces a strong magnetic field that magnetizes the object quickly. The magnetism produced by the current is called *electromagnetism*. (See Unit 16, "Electromagnetism.")

MAGNET SHIELDING

The property of permeability is widely used to protect or shield certain components and instruments from the effects of magnetic fields. In many instruments and other circuits, the effects of "stray" magnetic fields can cause significant errors in measurement or other forms of interference.

A basic form of magnetic shield is shown in Fig. 15-11. In this type of shielding, a cover or "can" made of a high-permeability ferromagnetic material is placed over a circuit component. As a result, any external magnetic field that may be present in the vicinity of the component is "bypassed" (Fig. 15-12).

Fig. 15-9. Magnetic induction

ELIMINATING MAGNETISM

Although magnetism is useful in many ways, sometimes objects must be *demagnetized,* or have their magnetism removed. Wristwatches made of magnetic materials, for example, will not keep correct time after becoming magnetized. If metal-cutting tools such as drills and reamers become magnetized, they will attract metal chips and filings. This causes the tools to become dull quickly.

Magnetism can be removed from an object by using a *demagnetizer*. In its simplest form, this is a coil of insulated wire through which alternating current passes. The object to be demagnetized is put within the coil. Then the object is slowly removed from the coil. The effect of the varying magnetic field that results is to disturb the alignment of the domains and thus eliminate the magnetism from the object (Fig. 15-13).

A permanent magnet can also be demagnetized or greatly weakened by heating. It can also be demagnetized by striking it sharply with a metal object such as a hammer. In both cases, the domain alignment within the magnet is severely disturbed. Demagnetization is sometimes called *degaussing*.

Fig. 15-10. An electromagnetic magnetizer

MAGNETIC COMPASS

A *magnetic compass* is a device that is used to find directions. In the compass, a small permanent magnet, the needle, is mounted on a pivot point so that it is free to turn. The poles of the magnet are attracted by the magnetic poles of the Earth. Because of this, the needle of the compass points in a general north-south direction (Fig. 15-14).

The magnetic poles of the Earth are actually about 1,500 miles (2414 km) from the geographic poles. Therefore, a compass needle does not point to the true geographic north and south. The difference between a compass reading and the true direction is known as the *angle of declination*. This angle must, of course, be considered in finding true geographic directions with a magnetic compass.

The angle of declination can be observed directly with a car compass similar to the one shown in Fig. 15-15. After the compass is mounted on the automobile's dashboard (Fig. 15-15A), it must be adjusted to compensate not only for the angle of declination in your geographic area but also for the metal parts on the automobile. Two small plastic screws at the bottom of this compass are used to make the adjustment (Fig. 15-15B). The plastic screws actually turn small compensating magnets within the body of the compass. The magnetic fields of the compensating magnets slightly influence the main permanent magnet of the compass in order to change its direction so that the compass points to the true geographic north. One plastic screw adjusts for the north-south direction. The other adjusts for the east-west direction. Do not use a steel (ferrous) screwdriver to turn the plastic screws since this will affect the compass (Fig. 15-15C). Adjustments should be made on roads that run in a true north-south and east-west direction.

MAGNETIC-PARTICLE INSPECTION

Magnetic-particle inspection is a process that uses magnetism to find defects on the surfaces of metal parts. In this process, the object is magnetized and then coated with an oil or other liquid that contains fine particles of iron. The edges of cracks and scratches become magnetic poles to which the particles are attracted. This causes the particles to form a pattern that can easily be seen (Fig. 15-16). Tests of this kind are called *nondestructive testing*.

FUTURE USES OF MAGNETISM

Scientists and engineers are constantly thinking of new and different ways in which to use magnetism. The possibility of using the magnetic energy high above the surface of the Earth is now being studied. Many scientists believe that magnetism may someday be used to counteract the force of gravity. These ideas and the study of other applications of magnetism in the field of electronics are creating a new scientific frontier.

Fig. 15-11. Cutaway view of a magnetic shield used to protect an inductor from the influence of external magnetic fields (*Bud Radio, Inc.*)

Fig. 15-12. Principle of magnetic shielding

Fig. 15-13. Using a demagnetizer to remove the magnetism from a metal tool-holding device (*R. B. Annis Company*)

117

Fig. 15-14. The needle of a magnetic compass is attracted by the magnetic poles of the Earth. The north pole of a magnet is so named because it points to the Earth's north magnetic pole.

A

B

C

Fig. 15-15. Car compass: (A) compass mounted on an automobile's dashboard; (B) east-west and north-south compensating adjustment screws; (C) using a nonmagnetic screwdriver to adjust the compass

Fig. 15-16. Cracks in the turbine blade of a jet aircraft engine discovered by magnetic particle inspection (*Magnaflux Corporation*)

Test your knowledge by writing, on a separate sheet of paper, the word or words that most correctly complete the following statements:

1. Magnetism is produced as electrons _____ on their own axes while rotating about the nuclei of atoms.
2. In a permanent magnet, atoms in certain areas called _____ are aligned.
3. Unlike magnetic poles _____ each other, while like magnetic poles _____ each other.
4. The force of attraction or repulsion between the poles of two magnets is inversely proportional to the _____ of the distance between them.
5. A magnetic field is made of invisible lines of _____, the direction of which is from the _____ pole to the _____ pole of a magnet.
6. A magnet is said to be _____ when all its domains have been aligned.
7. A magnetic material is one that is _____ to a magnet and can be _____ into a magnet.
8. The first permanent magnets were natural magnets made of an iron ore called _____, or _____.

9. Three metallic elements that are highly magnetic are _____, _____, and _____.
10. A material has a high _____ when it is able to keep its magnetic-domain alignment for a long time.
11. The _____ of a material is its ability to conduct magnetic lines of force, as compared to air's ability.
12. Permanent magnets are used in products such as _____, _____, _____, and _____.
13. Ceramic magnetic materials are also called _____.
14. Magnetizing an object by putting it in the magnetic field of a permanent magnet is called _____.
15. Permanent magnets are made commercially with a _____.
16. Demagnetization is sometimes called _____.
17. A nondestructive test using magnetic-particle inspection can be used to find _____ on the surfaces of metals.
18. Stray magnetic fields can be bypassed using a magnetic _____ made of high-permeability ferromagnetic material.

1. Explain magnetization in a permanent magnet.
2. State the law of magnetic attraction and repulsion.
3. Describe the magnetic field around a permanent magnet.
4. What is a magnetic material?
5. Define *magnetic retentivity* and *permeability*.
6. Name three magnetic and three nonmagnetic materials.
7. Give five uses of permanent magnets made of an alloy such as alnico.
8. Describe the makeup of a ceramic magnetic material.

FOR REVIEW AND DISCUSSION

9. Explain magnetic induction.
10. Describe the making of permanent magnets with a magnetizer.
11. Why must a magnetizer be operated with direct current to get the best results?
12. Give two examples of the undesirable effects of magnetism.
13. State three ways in which magnetism can be removed or greatly weakened.
14. Tell how a magnetic compass works.
15. For what purpose is magnetic-particle inspection used? Describe this process.
16. Explain the purpose of a magnetic shield.

INDIVIDUAL-STUDY ACTIVITIES

ficient magnetic materials.

1. Prepare a written or an oral report telling about the discovery of magnetism, the uses of permanent magnets, and the development of highly ef-
2. Prepare a written or an oral report about the Earth's magnetism.

UNIT 16   Electromagnetism

As you have learned, the magnetism in a permanent magnet is produced by the spinning of electrons on their own axes as they rotate about the nuclei of atoms. Magnetism is also produced as free electrons move through a conductor in the form of a current. This important relationship between electricity and magnetism is known as *electromagnetism,* or the magnetic effect of current. It is used in the operation of many different kinds of circuits, products, and devices. Some of these are discussed in this unit. Others are discussed in later units of this textbook.

ELECTROMAGNETIC FIELD

An *electromagnetic field* is the magnetic field produced by current. It is in the form of circles around the conductor. Its strength depends on the amount of current passing through the conductor. The larger the amount of current, the stronger the field. The direction of the magnetic field depends on the direction of the current (Fig. 16-1). If the current is a steady direct current, the magnetic field is constant in polarity and in strength. An alternating current produces a magnetic field that reverses in polarity and changes in strength. This is called a *moving magnetic field.*

Fig. 16-1. The magnetic field produced by current in a conductor

SOLENOID

To concentrate the magnetic field produced by current flowing in a wire, the wire is wound into a coil. When this is done, the magnetic fields around the turns of the coil are added together. This increases the magnetic strength of the coil. A coil wound in this manner is called a *solenoid* (Fig. 16-2). A solenoid has magnetic poles and a magnetic field that have the same properties as those of a permanent magnet.

If the solenoid is energized with direct current, the polarity of its magnetic poles remains fixed. If the solenoid is energized with alternating current, its magnetic polarity reverses with each reversal of the direction of the current.

Fig. 16-2. By winding wire in the form of a coil, or solenoid, the magnetic field can be concentrated in a small area.

Solenoid Control. A solenoid coil is usually made by winding many turns of wire around a hollow paper, cardboard, or plastic form. The strong magnetic field created by the coil can be made to produce useful motion.

An example of a solenoid is shown in Fig. 16-3A. In this assembly, a plunger, or *armature* (movable piece), made of iron or steel is placed partly inside the coil. When the coil is energized, the armature is drawn further into it. With the right coupling, the movement of the armature can be used to control things such as valves, switches, and clutch mechanisms. A typical example of this kind of control is found in automatic washing machines, where water valves are operated by solenoid assemblies (Fig. 16-3B).

Door-Chime Solenoid. The door chime is another common use of the solenoid. In this device, an iron or steel armature with a rubber or plastic tip is put inside the coil (Fig. 16-4A). When the coil is energized, the armature is attracted upward into it. This causes the tip to strike the chime bar and produce sound (Fig. 16-4B).

IRON-CORE ELECTROMAGNET

An electromagnet can be made more powerful by winding magnet wire around an iron core. This is because iron is more *permeable* than air. That means that iron can conduct magnetic lines of force more easily. As a result, many more lines of force can pass between the poles of the electromagnet, producing a stronger magnetic field (Fig. 16-5). If soft iron is used as the core, very little *residual*, or leftover, *magnetism* stays after the electromagnet has been deenergized, or turned off. This is because soft iron has a low *retentivity*, or little ability to stay magnetized.

The strength of an electromagnet is given by a unit called *ampere-turns*. This is the product of the coil current times the number of turns of

Fig. 16-3. Solenoid-control mechanism: (A) basic construction and operation; (B) typical solenoid assembly (*Cutler-Hammer*)

A

B

Fig. 16-4. Operation of a door chime

MAGNETIC FIELD

IRON CORE

INSULATED WIRE

Fig. 16-5. The use of a soft-iron core increases the strength of an electromagnet.

wire with which the coil is wound. The ampere-turns unit is useful for comparing the strengths of electromagnets that operate at the same voltage.

Electromagnets of different sizes and strengths are used in a large number of devices. These include doorbells, buzzers, horns, relays, circuit breakers, and electric clutches. As you will learn in later units of this book, electromagnetism or a combination of electromagnets and permanent magnets is used in many electronic products. Electromagnets are, for example, used in transformers, generators, loudspeakers, microphones, phonograph cartridges, and audio equipment for recording and playback.

BELLS AND BUZZERS

Electric doorbells, buzzers, and some kinds of horns are an interesting group of *vibrating devices*. In these devices, electromagnetism is used to produce a rapid back-and-forth motion of an armature. The basic construction and operation of a typical doorbell are shown in Fig. 16-6.

Before the doorbell button is pressed, the contact strip is held against the contact point by the tension of the spring (Fig. 16-6A). When the button is pressed, the circuit is completed and current flows through the coil. The electromagnet then attracts the armature to the position shown in Fig. 16-6B. This causes the armature to move away from the contact point. The circuit is now turned off, and the electromagnet is deenergized. The spring is then able to pull the armature back to the contact point. This action is repeated very rapidly as long as the button is pressed. The *clapper* attached to the armature strikes the gong each time the armature is pulled toward the electromagnet. This produces a continuous ringing sound. In a buzzer, the sounds are produced as the armature strikes against one end of the electromagnet core.

Fig. 16-6. Basic construction and operation of a doorbell

CLAPPER

CONTACT POINT

CONTACT STRIP

ARMATURE

SPRING ARM

GONG

ELECTROMAGNET

TERMINAL SCREWS

DOORBELL BUTTON

A

B

THE RELAY

A *relay* is a magnetically operated switch that makes or breaks one or more of the contacts between its terminals (Fig. 16-7). As with mechanical switches, the action of relays is described by the number of lines (poles) that are controlled and the number of contacts (throws) each pole can make. The relay in Fig. 16-7 controls one line (single-pole) and can touch either of two contacts (double-throw).

The basic operation of a single-pole–single-throw relay is shown in Fig. 16-8A. When the switch in the relay circuit is closed, the electromagnet is energized. It thus attracts the armature to the fixed contact point. There is now continuity between terminals 1 and 2, and the lamp is turned on. When the relay circuit switch is opened, the relay coil is deenergized. This lets the spring pull the armature from the fixed contact point. The circuit connected to terminals 1 and 2 is thus turned off. Some typical relay switching arrangements are shown in Fig. 16-8B.

Fig. 16-7. Single-pole–double-throw relay

A

SINGLE-POLE–
DOUBLE-THROW
(SPDT)

DOUBLE-POLE–
SINGLE-THROW
(DPST)

DOUBLE-POLE–
DOUBLE-THROW
(DPDT)

B

Fig. 16-8. Relay operation: (A) single-pole–single-throw relay; (B) switching action of other common relays

A relay can control a large load current at a high voltage by means of a small relay-energizing current at a low voltage. An example of this is shown by the circuit of Fig. 16-9. Here the relay is controlled by the intensity of the light striking the photoconductive cell. The current in the control circuit, which consists of the cell, the relay coil, and the battery, is quite small. However, since the motor circuit that is controlled by the relay has a different source of energy, the current in this circuit can be and is quite large.

Rating. The general-purpose power relay is rated in terms of (1) the operating-voltage rating of the relay coil and whether it is to be operated with an ac or a dc voltage, (2) the resistance of its coil, and (3) the current rating of its contacts. This indicates the largest safe load current the relay can control.

Fig. 16-9. A sensitive relay used in a light-activated control circuit

PHOTOCELL

VOLTAGE AMPLIFIER

RELAY

MOTOR

TO 115 V AC POWER LINE

Contacts. The contacts of a relay are often described as being normally open (N.O.) or normally closed (N.C.). Normally open contacts are those that are separated when the relay is not energized. Normally closed contacts are those that are closed, or in contact, when the relay is not energized.

GLASS TUBE

REEDS

Fig. 16-10. Magnetic-reed relay

The Magnetic-Reed Relay. The switching assembly of a typical magnetic-reed relay, or reed switch, is made of ferromagnetic reeds enclosed in a sealed glass tube (Fig. 16-10). In a complete relay assembly, the tube is placed in a coil. When the coil is energized, the reeds come together as a result of magnetic attraction. This kind of relay is very sensitive, which means that it can be operated with a very small amount of current.

In another kind of magnetic-reed relay, the make and break action of the reeds is controlled with a permanent magnet that is brought near to or removed from the reed enclosure. When used in this way, the reed relay is sometimes called a magnetic *proximity switch*.

MAGNETIC CIRCUIT BREAKER

The magnetic *circuit breaker* is a device that protects a circuit from too much current. In one kind of circuit breaker, the coil of an electromagnet and two contact points are connected in series with one wire of a circuit (Fig. 16-11).

When the current is more than the ampere rating, or the trip size, of the circuit breaker, the electromagnet becomes strong enough to attract the armature. This moves and latches the contact point in the open position, and the circuit is broken. After being reset mechanically, the circuit breaker is once again ready to protect the circuit.

CONTACT IN CLOSED POSITION

CONTACT IN OPEN POSITION

LATCH

ELECTROMAGNET

CONTACT POINTS

ARMATURE

TO LOAD

SPRING

TO POWER LINE

Fig. 16-11. Basic construction and operation of a magnetic circuit breaker

Test your knowledge by writing, on a separate sheet of paper, the word or words that most correctly complete the following statements:

1. The electromagnetic field produced by current is in the form of _____ around the conductor.
2. A direct current produces a magnetic field that is _____ in polarity and strength.
3. An alternating current produces a magnetic field that reverses in _____ and changes in _____ .
4. When current passes through a coil of wire, the magnetic fields around the turns of the coil are _____ together to produce the total electromagnetic field.
5. If a solenoid is energized with alternating current, its magnetic polarity reverses with each reversal of the _____ of the current.
6. A movable iron piece put in a control solenoid is called an _____ .
7. An electromagnet that is more powerful than a solenoid can be made by winding insulated wire around an _____ .
8. The magnetism remaining in the core of an electromagnet after its coil has been deenergized is called _____ magnetism.
9. Electromagnets are used in devices such as _____ , _____ , _____ , _____ , and _____ .
10. A relay is a _____ operated _____ .
11. The general-purpose power relay is rated in terms of _____ , _____ , and _____ .
12. Normally open relay contacts are those that are separated when the relay is not _____ .

1. Define *electromagnetism*.
2. What are the differences between the magnetic fields that are produced by direct current and by alternating current?
3. What is a solenoid?
4. Why does the magnetic polarity of a solenoid periodically reverse when it is operated with alternating current?
5. Describe a practical solenoid. Tell how it can be used as a control device.
6. Explain the operation of a door-chime solenoid.
7. What is the effect of adding an iron core to an electromagnetic coil? Explain the reason for this.
8. Define residual magnetism.
9. Tell how the strength of a given iron-core electromagnet can be increased without adding turns of wire to its coil.
10. Explain why adding turns of wire to an electromagnet coil beyond a certain point will cause the strength of the electromagnet to decrease.
11. Describe the construction of a typical doorbell. Explain its operation.
12. What is a relay? How is the switching action of a relay described?
13. Explain the operation of a simple relay.
14. What can a relay be used to control?

1. Prepare a written or an oral report on the uses of electromagnetism and electromagnetic devices.
2. Give a demonstration showing electromagnetic devices such as solenoids, buzzers, or relays. Describe these to your class and explain the operation of each.

UNIT 17　Electromagnetic Induction and Inductance

If a magnet is moved near a wire, its magnetic field cuts across the wire and produces a voltage across the ends of the wire. If the ends of the wire are connected to form a closed circuit, the voltage causes current to flow through the circuit (Fig. 17-1A). A voltage that is produced in this way is called an *induced voltage*. A current produced by an induced voltage is called an *induced current*. This important relationship between electricity and magnetism is called *electromagnetic induction*. When the magnet is moved in the opposite direction, the polarity of the induced voltage changes and the direction of the current in the circuit also changes (Fig. 17-1B).

Motion is needed to produce a voltage by electromagnetic induction. The magnetic field must move past the wire, or the wire must move past the magnetic field. If both the magnetic field and the wire are stationary, no voltage can be induced across the ends of the wire.

LENZ'S LAW

A Russian physicist, Heinrich F. E. Lenz (1804 to 1865) discovered that when a current is induced by moving a conductor across lines of magnetic force, the induced current in the conductor sets up a magnetic field that opposes the lines of magnetic force that produced it. He also found that the induced current and its surrounding magnetic field change direction depending upon which way the conductor is moved in the magnetic field. These important discoveries are known as *Lenz's law*.

Figure 17-2 illustrates these relationships in a single conductor. In Fig. 17-2A, the conductor is shown moving down through the lines of magnetic force of a permanent magnet. The arrows on the conductor indicate the direction of the induced current. The arrows around the

Fig. 17-1. Electromagnetic induction

Fig. 17-2. The effects of Lenz's law: (A) direction of the induced current and its magnetic field; (B) enlarged view of the opposing magnetic fields of the conductor and the permanent magnet

conductor indicate the direction of the magnetic field caused by the induced currents. Notice that the conductor's magnetic field opposes the permanent magnet's magnetic field. Work, therefore, must be done to overcome the magnetic effects of the induced currents. Figure 17-2B shows an enlarged view of these opposing magnetic fields. If the conductor is moved up through the magnetic field, the direction of the induced current reverses as does the magnetic field that surrounds the conductor. Again, work must be done to overcome the magnetic effects of the induced currents. You will learn in Unit 19 how mechanical energy is used to do the work needed to generate electricity.

One of the most important uses of electromagnetic induction is in *alternators* and other kinds of *generators*. These machines supply the electric energy that is distributed to our homes by electric power companies. Electromagnetic induction is also used to operate many other kinds of machines and devices. These include motors, transformers, microphones, phonograph cartridges, and tape-player recording and playback heads.

MOVING MAGNETIC FIELD

As you have learned, electromagnetic induction takes place only when there is relative motion between a magnetic field and a conductor. In a generator, this motion is produced by turning its *rotor* assembly or its *field-coil* assembly with an engine of some kind. In a device such as a transformer that does not have any moving parts, a moving magnetic field is produced as the result of changes in the value of the current.

Alternating Current. The magnetic field produced by an alternating current is shown in Fig. 17-3A. When the current is increasing, the magnetic field moves outward from the conductor. As the current decreases, the magnetic field moves toward the conductor. A moving magnetic field such as this can produce electromagnetic induction.

Direct Current. A steady direct current does not produce a moving magnetic field. For this reason, such a current cannot produce electromagnetic induction. When a steady direct current must be used with a device such as a transformer, the current must be broken up into *pulses*. A pulsating direct current does produce a moving magnetic field, which can cause electromagnetic induction (Fig. 17-3B). You will learn in Unit 35 how a pulsating direct current is used in automobile ignition systems.

Magnetic Air Gap. The magnetic field of a stationary permanent magnet can be made to vary in strength. This is done by changing the permeability of its *air gap,* or the space between its poles. The air gap is changed by moving a soft-iron armature within it.

As the armature moves farther into the air gap, the permeability of the gap increases. This allows a stronger magnetic field to exist between the poles of the magnet (Fig. 17-4A). When the armature moves away from the air gap, the permeability of the gap decreases. When this occurs, the

Fig. 17-3. Moving magnetic fields: (A) field produced by an alternating current; (B) field produced by a pulsating direct current

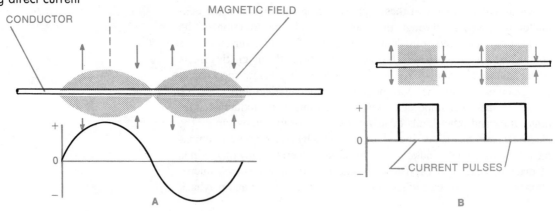

CONDUCTOR

MAGNETIC FIELD

CURRENT PULSES

A

B

strength of the magnetic field also decreases (Fig. 17-4B). This method of changing the strength of a magnetic field is used in a *magnetic phonograph cartridge*.

TRANSFORMER

The word *transform* means "to change." A *transformer* is used to change the value of voltage or current in an electrical system (Fig. 17-5). If it reduces a voltage, it is called a *step-down transformer*. If it increases a voltage, it is called a *step-up transformer*. Some transformers do not change the value of voltage. These are called *isolation transformers*. Isolation transformers are used when the electrical equipment must not be grounded through the power line.

Transformers are used to change the value of voltage in many kinds of circuits. For example, they are used to change the power line voltage of 120 V to a voltage needed to operate rectifier circuits. These circuits are used to change alternating current into direct current in products such as radios, television receivers, computers, and music systems. The ignition coil in an automobile ignition system is a step-up transformer that supplies a high voltage to the spark plugs. Both step-up and step-down transformers are used in systems that distribute electric energy from power plants to buildings.

The operation of a simple transformer is shown in Fig. 17-6. Here one winding, or coil, of the transformer is connected to the source of energy. This is called the *primary winding*. The other is electrically insulated from the primary winding and is connected to the load. This is called the *secondary winding*. Notice that there is *no direct electrical connection* between the primary and secondary windings.

The alternating current in the primary winding produces a moving magnetic field. This induces a voltage in the secondary winding. As a result, energy is transferred from the primary winding to the secondary winding. This is an example of what is known as *mutual induction*.

Fig. 17-4. Moving magnetic field produced by changing the position of a soft-iron armature within a magnetic air gap

Fig. 17-5. Small transformers: (A) audio transformer; (B) television high-voltage flyback transformer (*Triad-Utrad Distributor Division of Litton Precision Products Inc.*)

129

Fig. 17-6. Operation of a simple transformer

Polarity of Induced Voltage. The polarity of the voltage produced by electromagnetic induction depends on the direction in which magnetic lines of force cut across a conductor. Since a transformer is operated with alternating current or with a pulsating direct current, the magnetic field around the primary winding expands and collapses as it cuts across the secondary winding. This means that the magnetic field cuts across the secondary winding first in one direction, then in the other. Therefore, the voltage induced across the secondary winding of any transformer is an alternating voltage.

Transformer Cores. The transformer in Fig. 17-6 is an *air-core transformer.* The coils of transformers operated either with alternating currents of less than about 20,000 hertz or with pulsating direct currents are wound around *iron cores.* Despite their names, these cores are usually made of thin sheets of steel to which a small amount of silicon is added. These sheets are called *laminations.* Two kinds of cores and windings commonly used with iron-core transformers are shown in Fig. 17-7. Because the laminations are stacked together to form the core of these transformers, they are called *stacked-core transformers.*

The iron core allows a stronger magnetic field to exist in a transformer. This, in turn, permits a greater amount of energy to be transferred from the primary to the secondary winding.

Fig. 17-7. Transformer cores and windings: (A) types of cores used with iron-core transformers; (B) insulating the windings of transformer coils (*Kurz and Root Company*)

A laminated, as opposed to solid, core is used to lessen the amount of energy wasted in the form of heat. Some of this heat is produced by *eddy currents*. These are currents induced in the core of a transformer. Energy lost in the transformer core is known as a *hysteresis loss*. This is the heat produced within a core as its magnetic domains try to align themselves with the changes in the polarity of a magnetic field produced by an alternating current. Another energy loss is due to *copper losses*. This is the heat energy lost when current flows in the primary and secondary windings of the transformer.

Value of Induced Voltage. The value of the voltage induced across the secondary winding of a transformer depends on the number of turns of wire it has as compared with the number of primary-winding turns. This is called the *turns ratio* of the transformer. If the secondary winding has half as many turns as the primary winding, the voltage will be stepped down to one-half the primary-winding voltage (Fig. 17-8A). If the secondary winding contains twice as many turns as the primary winding, the voltage will be stepped up to twice the primary-winding voltage (Fig. 17-8B). This relationship can be expressed by the formula:

$$\frac{\text{Secondary voltage}}{\text{Primary voltage}} = \frac{\text{secondary turns}}{\text{primary turns}}$$

Problem: An experimenter has a 115 V ac transformer that has 725 turns of wire on the primary coil. Neglecting transformer losses, how many turns of wire are needed on the secondary winding to produce 10 V ac?

Solution: Use the preceding formula, and let χ = secondary turns.

$$\frac{\text{Secondary voltage}}{\text{Primary voltage}} = \frac{\text{secondary turns}}{\text{primary turns}}$$

$$\frac{10}{115} = \frac{\chi}{725} = 115\chi = 10 \times 725 = 115\chi = 7250 = \chi = 63 \text{ turns}$$

Fig. 17-8. The voltage induced across the secondary winding of a transformer depends on the winding turns ratio of the transformer. (A) Step-down transformer; (B) step-up transformer

115 V

$57\frac{1}{2}$ V

115 V

230 V

PRIMARY WINDING

SECONDARY WINDING

A

B

Fig. 17-9. Power transformer (*Triad-Utrad Distributor Division of Litton Precision Products Inc.*)

Fig. 17-10. Schematic of a power transformer showing the color code used to identify the various windings

POWER TRANSFORMERS

A transformer that supplies the voltages needed in electronic equipment is often called a *power transformer* (Fig. 17-9). A power transformer used in a rectifier circuit is often called a *rectifier transformer*.

Some power transformers have more than one secondary winding. Each of these windings is electrically insulated from the other. This makes it possible to obtain different values of output voltages (Fig. 17-10). A color code is often used to identify the different windings. Transformers of this kind are commonly found in older radios, amplifiers, and television sets that have electron tubes instead of transistors.

RELATIONSHIP BETWEEN VOLTAGE AND CURRENT

Although a power transformer can step up or step down voltage, it cannot deliver a greater amount of energy to a load from its secondary winding than is supplied to the primary winding. In fact, the energy delivered by the secondary winding is always less than that supplied to the primary winding. This is because of power losses within the core and the windings.

As an example, suppose that the primary winding of a transformer operating at 115 V has a current of 2 A. If the secondary winding has 10 times as many turns of wire as the primary, the voltage across the secondary winding will be stepped up to 115×10, or 1,150 V (Fig. 17-11).

Since $P = EI$, the wattage of the primary winding is equal to 115×2, or 230 W. Disregarding power losses within the transformer, the wattage of the secondary winding will also be 230 W. The largest current that the secondary winding can deliver to a load is then equal to

$$I = \frac{P}{E}$$

$$= \frac{230}{1,150} = 0.2 \text{ A}$$

Therefore, as the voltage is increased 10 times, the current in the secondary winding is decreased 10 times, or from 2 A to 0.2 A.

Fig. 17-11. Relationship between voltage and current in a transformer

Likewise, if a transformer steps down voltage, the largest current that can be delivered to a load by the secondary winding will be greater than the current in the primary winding. This condition must exist if the wattage ($P = EI$) of the secondary winding is to equal the wattage of the primary winding.

POWER TRANSMISSION LINE

The relationships between input and output voltages and currents in transformers are exemplified by a *transmission line*. Such a line is used to deliver electric energy from a power generating plant to homes and other buildings (Fig. 17-12). Here, the alternating voltage produced by the generator is stepped up by a transformer at the power plant. Because of this very high voltage, it is possible to deliver the required amount of energy from the plant to the users along the long-distance transmission line with a low current. This low current, in turn, lessens the power losses within the transmission line. It also permits the use of smaller conductors.

The substation transformers used with this power transmission system step down the high voltage of the transmission line to much lower voltages. These voltages are then further stepped down by distribution transformers. Because of this stepping down of voltages, the total current available to the users is many times greater than the current present in the transmission line. However, the total power is never greater than that produced originally by the generator. Actually, because of line losses, the available power is much less than that generated.

SELF-INDUCTANCE

When a current that is changing in value passes through a single coil, a moving magnetic field is produced around it. This action induces a voltage across the coil itself by means of electromagnetic induction.

Fig. 17-12. Simplified representation of a power transmission and distribution system

This is called *self-inductance,* or simply *inductance.* The voltage generated by self-inductance is always of a polarity that opposes any change in the value of the current through the coil.

Consider the circuits shown in Fig. 17-13. When the alternating voltage applied to these circuits is increasing in value during the first quarter of its cycle, the current through the coil also increases. This produces an expanding magnetic field around the coil (Fig. 17-13A). A voltage is now induced across the coil of a polarity that tends to oppose the change (increase) of the current through the coil.

When the applied voltage begins to decrease during the second quarter of its cycle, the magnetic field around the coil starts to collapse (Fig. 17-13B). As a result, the polarity of the voltage induced across the coil reverses. This voltage is now of a polarity that once again tends to oppose the change (decrease) of the current through the coil.

As the current moves through the second half of its cycle, the polarities of the applied voltage and the induced voltages reverse. However, the induced voltage continues to be of a polarity that tends to oppose any change in the value of the current. Because of this, the induced voltage also opposes the applied voltage that causes the current changes. For this reason, the voltage induced by self-inductance is called a *counter voltage* or a *counter electromotive force* (cemf).

The unit of inductance is the *henry.* It is named after Joseph Henry. He was an American teacher and physicist who lived from 1797 to 1878. A coil has an inductance of one henry when a current that changes at the rate of one ampere per second causes a voltage of one volt to be induced across it. The letter symbol for inductance is L.

INDUCTIVE REACTANCE

Inductive reactance is the opposition to a changing current in a coil that is caused by the inductance of the coil. The unit of inductive reactance is the ohm. Its letter symbol is X_L. The value of inductive reactance depends on the inductance of the coil and the frequency of the current that passes through it. The formula for inductive reactance is

$$X_L \text{ (in ohms)} = 2\,\pi\,fL$$

where f = the frequency of the current in hertz
L = the inductance of a coil in henrys
π = 3.14 (pi), a constant

Fig. 17-13. Self-inductance

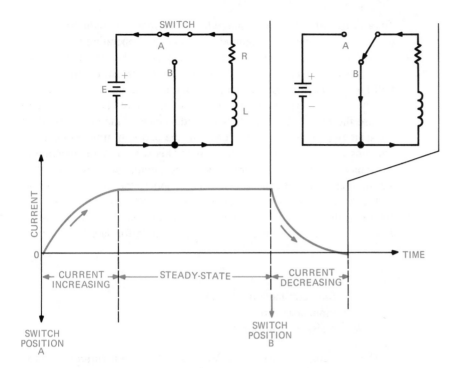

Fig. 17-14. Current responses in a typical *RL* circuit

This formula shows that inductive reactance is directly proportional to both frequency and inductance. As the frequency increases, the inductive reactance will increase. The inductive reactance will also increase if the inductance of a circuit is increased.

When inductive reactance and resistance are both present in a circuit, their total opposition to current is called *impedance*. The unit of impedance is the ohm. Its letter symbol is *Z*.

EFFECT OF INDUCTANCE IN A DC CIRCUIT

Since the counter electromotive force (cemf) induced across an inductive component always opposes the applied voltage, the current in an inductive circuit lags behind the applied voltage whenever there is a change in the magnitude of the current. Thus, the current in a direct-current inductive circuit is not in phase with the applied voltage during the period of time when the current is changing. The manner in which the current in such a circuit responds to a change in the magnitude of the applied voltage is referred to as the *transient response* of the circuit.

The current responses in a typical series *RL* circuit are illustrated in Fig. 17-14. Responses that occur when voltage is applied or removed are not instantaneous. The straight portion of the curve between the current-increasing and current-decreasing responses indicates the steady state of the circuit. During this time, no cemf is induced across the coil. Therefore, the current and the voltage are in phase because the current is limited only by the resistance of the circuit.

Time Constant. The time required for the current in an inductive circuit to rise to its maximum magnitude I_{max} after the operating voltage has been applied depends upon both the inductance and the resistance of the circuit. With a fixed amount of resistance in the circuit, the time period will be increased if the inductance is increased because the greater the inductance, the greater the magnitude of the cemf that is present to oppose the change in current. If the inductance of the circuit remains constant and the resistance is increased, the period of time required for attaining maximum current is decreased. This is because the increase in resistance reduces the current flow in the circuit, and, as a result, a smaller magnitude of cemf is generated to oppose the change in current.

The time required for the current in a series *RL* circuit to increase to 63.2 percent of its maximum (steady-state) magnitude is known as the *L/R* time constant of the circuit. Expressed as a formula,

$$t = \frac{L}{R}$$

where t = time constant, in seconds
L = inductance, in henrys
R = resistance, in ohms

The time constant also governs the rate at which a current decrease occurs after the source of the applied voltage is removed from a circuit (if a "discharge" path is provided by the remaining components of the circuit). Thus, if the current in a given circuit increases to 63.2 percent of its maximum in 0.25 second, it will also decrease by 63.2 percent of its maximum in 0.25 second.

Voltage Characteristics. During the time that the current in a series *RL* circuit is increasing, there are three different voltages present in the circuit: the applied voltage, the voltage drop across the resistance, and the cemf generated across the inductive component.

High Induced Voltages. When the current in an inductive circuit is increasing, the magnitude of the cemf induced across any coil in the circuit cannot become greater than the applied voltage. However, when the switch in such a circuit is opened, the resistance of the circuit suddenly approaches infinity. As a result, the time constant *L/R* becomes extremely small, and the current decreases toward zero very rapidly. This in turn causes a voltage many times greater than the applied voltage to be induced across the coil. A spark can often be observed between a switch and other contacts when an inductive circuit is suddenly opened.

INDUCTORS

Inductors are coils that are wound so as to have a certain amount of inductance. The inductance of an inductor depends mainly on four things: (1) the number of turns of wire with which it is wound, (2) the cross-sectional area of the coil, (3) the permeability of its core materials, and (4) the length of the coil.

Iron-core inductors are sometimes called *choke coils* or *reactors*. They often are used to *filter,* or smooth, the output current from a rectifier circuit (Fig. 17-15). Inductors are also used with capacitors in radio and television tuning circuits and in oscillator circuits.

TOROIDAL TRANSFORMERS

Toroidal transformers are being used more frequently in electronic circuits than ever before (Fig. 17-16A). Some of the major advantages of this type of transformer in contrast to the stacked-core types are: (1) low hum, (2) low stray magnetic fields, (3) low weight, and (4) small dimensions.

The term *toroid* is used to define the geometry of the doughnut-shaped magnetic core. The core is made of powdered iron or silicon steel. Since the toroidal transformer has no air gap, stray magnetic fields are minimized. They are also easy to mount on a circuit board (Fig. 17-16B). The wires that form the primary winding are insulated from the core and wound around it. A convenient method to wind a coil around the core is shown in Fig. 17-16C. The primary winding is wound first. The secondary winding, insulated from the primary, is wound and distributed evenly on top of the primary winding. The toroidal transformer, like the stacked-core type, can have several secondary windings.

Toroidal transformers and inductors are used in industrial control equipment, computers, audio amplifiers, and power supplies.

TESTING TRANSFORMERS AND INDUCTORS

The most common defects of transformers are these: (1) burned-out windings caused by too much current, (2) windings grounded or shorted to the core, (3) shorts between adjacent turns of wire, and (4) shorts between the primary and secondary windings. The first three of these defects also occur in inductors.

SYMBOL

Fig. 17-15. Choke coils (*Essex International, Inc.*)

Fig. 17-16. Toroidal transformer: (A) toroidal power transformer; (B) single bolt and mounting plates removed from transformer; (C) winding a toroidal coil with a bobbin

A

MOUNTING BOLT

MOUNTING PLATES

B

BOBBIN MADE FROM THIN PIECE OF WOOD

WIRE

TOROIDAL—SHAPED CORE

C

Continuity Tests. The different windings of a transformer can be identified easily by making *continuity tests*. A continuity test also can be made to see if there are any open windings or to see if there are any shorts between windings or between a winding and the core.

A short between the turns of a transformer or an inductor winding usually cannot be located with a continuity test. Such a short most often will cause a winding to become overheated even when it is operating with a normal amount of current.

Continuity tests of a transformer or an inductor should be made only after the device has been disconnected from its circuit. If this is not done, other components in the circuit may interfere with the tests.

Voltage Tests. After testing for continuity, the secondary winding should be given a voltage test. To do this, it is necessary to apply voltage to the primary winding. This should be done only after checking to see that bare ends of secondary-winding leads are not in contact with each other. Where very high secondary voltages are expected, a reduced primary voltage may be used and the voltage ratio determined. For example, a transformer with a 120-V primary and a 600-V secondary winding has a voltage ratio of 120:600, or 1:5. If 10 V is applied to the primary, the secondary should read about 50 V.

 CAUTION

> Power transformers often have one very high voltage winding. This winding is a severe shock hazard. Extreme care must be taken when applying the rated primary voltage. Never hold both winding leads at the same time when making tests.

After you have found the voltage of each secondary winding, label the leads for future reference.

Measuring Inductance. The digital meter discussed previously in Unit 14 (see Fig. 14-15) performs two functions. It measures both capacitance and inductance. It is called a *Z meter* because it measures the total impedance of the components (capacitor or inductor) being tested. This unit discusses how the meter measures inductance.

The following steps represent the general procedures to determine the inductance of an inductor (coil).

1. Turn the power off by disconnecting the ac line cord to the equipment under test.
2. Connect the cord of the meter to a properly grounded 117-V ac outlet.
3. Turn the meter power switch on.
4. Connect the test leads to the coil or transformer to be tested.
5. Depress the VALUE button under the inductor section of the push button switch (Fig. 14-15).

6. Read the value of inductance of the coil or transformer on the digital display. The LED will light in front of the μH if the value is in microhenrys or in front of the mH if the value is in millihenrys.

The foregoing procedures illustrate the ease with which the meter can be used to measure the inductance of a coil. Many other tests and measurements can be performed on inductors with this meter.

4. Making an Electromagnetism Experimenter. This assembly can be used as an electromagnet, a magnetizer, a demagnetizer, and for doing several very interesting experiments with electromagnetism. It can be operated at 115 V ac or with dc voltages of up to 6 V.

MATERIALS NEEDED

1 piece of wood, ¾ × 7½ × 10½ in. (19 × 191 × 267 mm)

2 round, plastic or Masonite disks, ⅛ × 4 in. (3.18 × 102 mm) in diameter

enough sheet metal (transformer iron) to form a laminated core 1½ × 1½ × 4 in. (38 × 38 × 102 mm) (The laminations from a large discarded transformer are excellent for this purpose.)

1 piece of band iron, ⅛ × 1½ × 7 in. (3.18 × 38 × 178 mm)

1 round, soft-iron rod, 1 × 4 in. (25.4 × 102 mm)

1 round, soft-iron rod, 1 × 10 in. (25.4 × 254 mm)

1 aluminum ring or washer, 1½ or 2 in. (38 or 50 mm) in diameter

1 round, sheet-copper or sheet-aluminum disk, 2½ in. (63.5 mm) in diameter

350 ft (107 m) PE magnet wire, no. 14 (1.60 mm)

18 ft (5.5 m) PE magnet wire, no. 18 (1.00 mm)

10 in. (254 mm) bare wire or PE magnet wire, no. 14 (1.60 mm)

5 ft (1.5 m) two-conductor service cord, no. 16 (1.25 mm)

2 ft (0.6 m) parallel lamp cord, no. 18 (1.00 mm)

1 pilot lamp, no. 40 or no. 46

1 miniature lamp socket, screw base

1 heavy-duty attachment plug

1 15-A surface toggle switch, spst, with mounting screws

2 wire nuts, medium size

5 insulated staples

3 flat-head machine screws, no. ¼ − 20 × 1 in. (M6 × 1)

3 round-head wood screws, no. 8 × ¾ in.

cambric cloth, medium thick

insulating varnish

plastic electrical tape

low-voltage, battery-eliminator dc power supply

LAMINATIONS
CAMBRIC CLOTH
TAPE
3"
BEND
PLASTIC OR
MASONITE DISKS
8-IN. BEGINNING
COIL LEAD
B

A

ELECTROMAGNET COIL
COIL-CORE POLE PIECE
BAND IRON
SERVICE CORD
INSULATED STAPLE
SWITCH
WIRE NUT

OBJECT TO BE MAGNETIZED
4-IN. IRON ROD
D

TAPE
#40 OR #46 LAMP
15 TURNS #18 MAGNET WIRE, $2\frac{1}{4}$" IN. DIA.
LAMP SOCKET
E

$\frac{5}{32}$" DIA. 3 HOLES
$\frac{9}{32}$" DIA. 3 HOLES
$1\frac{1}{8}$"
$2\frac{1}{2}$"
$\frac{1}{2}$"
$\frac{7}{8}$"
$1\frac{1}{2}$"
C

$3\frac{1}{2}$" APPROX.
$\frac{1}{4}$"-20 TAP
3 HOLES IN CORE
3
BASE AND COIL ASSEMBLY

$3\frac{1}{2}$"
DISK
3
I

DISK
J

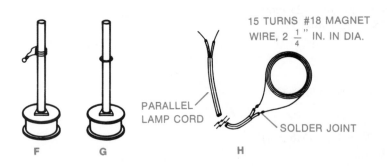

15 TURNS #18 MAGNET WIRE, $2\frac{1}{4}$" IN. IN DIA.
PARALLEL LAMP CORD
SOLDER JOINT
F
G
H

Fig. 17-17. Assemblies used for Learning by Doing No. 4, "Making an Electromagnetism Experimenter"

Procedure A (Basic Construction)

1. Assemble the electromagnet coil core and the coil form as shown in Fig. 17-17A.
2. Tightly wind the coil in layers with the no. 14 (1.6-mm) PE magnet wire (Fig. 17-17B). Insulate every third layer of the wire with a single layer of cambric cloth. After the coil is wound, apply a heavy coating of insulating varnish to its outside surfaces. Let it dry thoroughly.
3. Assemble materials and connect the circuit shown in Fig. 17-17C.

Procedure B (The Electromagnet)

Plug the experimenter into a 115 V ac receptacle outlet and turn the switch on. By holding an object made of a magnetic material near the coil-core pole piece, you will find that a strong electromagnetic field exists in the area near this pole piece.

 SAFETY

> The coil will overheat if operated continuously for an extended time. When this occurs, the circuit should be turned off and the coil allowed to cool.

Procedure C (Magnetizing and Demagnetizing)

1. To use the experimenter as a magnetizer, connect it to the power supply adjusted to a dc voltage of 6 V. Put the object to be magnetized across its pole pieces. One of the pole pieces is formed by placing the 4-in. (102-mm) iron rod over the band iron in an upright position (Fig. 17-17D). The rod can be moved as needed for the right spacing. Turn the switch on and, after a few seconds, turn it off. The object should now be magnetized. Explain this process of magnetization.
2. To use the experimenter as a demagnetizer, plug it into a 115 V ac receptacle outlet and turn the switch on. Hold the object to be demagnetized a little above the coil-core pole piece. Then slowly move it away from the pole piece for a distance of about 18 in. (457 mm). Repeat if necessary. Explain this process of demagnetization.

Procedure D (Transformer Action)

1. Assemble the coil and lamp shown in Fig. 17-17E.
2. Place the 10-in. (254-mm) iron rod on the coil-core pole piece in an upright position. Plug the experimenter into a 115-V ac receptacle outlet. Turn the switch on.
3. Slowly move the coil down over the iron rod. Do not let it touch the rod (Fig. 17-17F). As you do this, the lamp will begin to burn more and more brightly. Explain how energy is transferred from the electromagnet coil to the lamp circuit.

4. You will notice that the iron rod becomes quite warm after the experimenter is operated in this way for a short time. This is an example of induction heating. Induction heating is described in Unit 33, ''Producing Heat.''

Procedure E (The Jumping Ring and Coil)

1. Place the 10-in. (254-mm) iron rod on the coil-core pole piece in an upright position. Plug the experimenter into a 115-V ac receptacle outlet and turn the switch on.
2. Put the aluminum ring down over the end of the rod (Fig. 17-17G). Explain why the ring remains suspended above the coil-core pole piece. Turn the switch off.
3. Drop the ring over the iron rod and onto the coil-core pole piece. Put one hand over the end of the rod and turn the switch on. What happens? What causes this?
4. Form the coil shown in Fig. 17-17H.
5. Put the coil over the iron rod. With the switch on, slowly make and break contact between the ends of the lamp cord connected to it. Why does the coil jump upward when the ends of the lamp cord are in contact? Why does the coil remain stationary when the ends are not touching?

Procedure F (Motor Action)

1. Drill a $\frac{1}{16}$-in. (1.6-mm) hole through the center of the copper or aluminum disk. Pass the piece of no. 14 (1.6-mm) wire through the hole. Bend the wire as shown in Fig. 17-17I.
2. Put the legs of the disk-support wire into small holes drilled into the wood base of the experimenter. The disk should be midway between the coil and the 4-in. (102-mm) iron rod (Fig. 17-17J).
3. Plug the experimenter into a 115-V ac receptacle outlet. Turn the switch on.
4. Spin the disk with your fingers. It will continue to rotate. This is a simple induction motor. Induction motors are described in Unit 32, ''Electric Motors.''

SELF-TEST

Test your knowledge by writing, on a separate sheet of paper, the word or words that most correctly complete the following statements:

1. If a magnet is moved near a wire, a _____ is produced across the ends of the wire.
2. _____ is needed to produce a voltage by electromagnetic induction.
3. The magnetic field produced by an alternating current can be thought of as a _____ magnetic field.
4. If a transformer is operated with direct current, the current must be broken up into _____ .
5. The transformer is used to _____ the value of a voltage or current.
6. If a transformer reduces voltage, it is called a _____ transformer. If it increases voltage, it is called a _____ transformer.
7. The winding of a transformer that is connected to a source of energy is called the _____ winding.

8. A transformer is an example of _____ induction.
9. The voltage induced across the secondary winding of any transformer is an _____ voltage.
10. The thin sheets of steel from which transformer cores are made are called _____.
11. A laminated transformer core reduces the amount of energy that is wasted in the form of _____.
12. The voltage induced across a coil by its own moving magnetic field is an example of _____-inductance.

13. The total opposition to current presented by inductive reactance is called _____.
14. Coils that are wound so as to have a certain amount of inductance are called _____.
15. Iron-core inductors used to filter the output current from rectifier circuits are called _____ coils.
16. A _____ transformer is designed in such a way that it has no air gaps.

---

1. Define induced voltage and electromagnetic induction.
2. What condition must exist between a conductor and a magnetic field in order to produce electromagnetic induction?
3. How can the polarity of the voltage generated by electromagnetic induction be reversed?
4. Describe the moving magnetic field produced by an alternating current.
5. How can a moving magnetic field be produced by direct current?
6. Tell how a magnetic air gap can be used to pro-

FOR REVIEW AND DISCUSSION

duce a moving magnetic field.
7. Explain the construction and the operation of a simple transformer.
8. What is meant by a step-up transformer? A step-down transformer?
9. Name and define the unit of inductance.
10. Define inductive reactance. Write the symbol used to denote inductive reactance.
11. For what purpose are choke-coil inductors used?
12. How are transformers tested?
13. What transformer or inductor defects cannot be detected by making continuity tests?

---

1. Give a demonstration showing how adding an iron core increases the strength of an electromagnet. Explain why.
2. Obtain a variety of transformers. Explain the operation of each and give the purpose for which it is used.
3. Talk or write to a representative of the electrical company that serves your area and ask him or her for information about how transformers are used

INDIVIDUAL-STUDY ACTIVITIES

in their distribution system. Report orally to your class or prepare a written report about what you have learned.
4. Give a demonstration of a continuity test for a transformer.
5. Give a demonstration of a voltage test for a transformer.
6. Write a report on the importance of Heinrich F. E. Lenz's discovery regarding induced currents.

ENERGY SOURCES

UNIT 18 Chemical Cells and Batteries

SYMBOL

POSITIVE
TERMINAL

Fig. 18-1. A battery consists of two or more cells connected together. (*Union Carbide Corporation*)

A *voltaic chemical cell* is a combination of materials used to change chemical energy into electric energy in the form of voltage. The words *cell* and *battery* are often used to mean the same thing. However, this is not technically correct. A *cell* is a single unit. A *battery* is formed when two or more cells are connected together in series or in parallel (Fig. 18-1).

BASIC ACTION OF A CELL

A chemical cell is made up of two *electrodes,* or *plates,* in contact with a substance in which there are many ions. As you learned in Unit 1, an ion is a charged atom. A substance that has many ions is called an *electrolyte.* Water solutions made with acids, bases, or salts are electrolytes. Salt water, for example, is an electrolyte. It is also a good conductor of electricity.

The chemical actions that cause a combination of substances to produce a voltage are complicated. Studying how a very simple cell works, however, will help you understand the basics of how chemical cells work.

In the cell, the electrolyte ionizes to form positive and negative ions (Fig. 18-2A). At the same time, chemical action also causes the atoms within one of the electrodes to ionize. Because of this, electrons are deposited on the electrode. Positive ions from the electrode pass into the electrolyte. This creates a negative charge on this electrode. It leaves the area near it positively charged (Fig. 18-2B).

Some of the positive ions produced because of the ionization of the electrolyte are then repelled to the other electrode. At this electrode, these ions combine with electrons. Since this removes electrons from the electrode, it becomes positively charged. Because the chemical action has caused the electrodes to have opposite charges, there is now a voltage between them.

If a wire is connected between the electrodes of the cell, excess electrons from the negative electrode will pass through the wire and into the positive electrode (Fig. 18-2C). This current will continue until the materials in the cell become chemically inactive.

The electrolyte of a cell may be a liquid or a paste. If it is a liquid, the cell is often called a *wet cell*. Cells in which the electrolyte is a paste are called *dry cells*.

PRIMARY AND SECONDARY CELLS

Primary cells are those that cannot be *recharged*. This means they cannot be returned to good condition after their output voltage drops too low.

Secondary cells can be recharged. During recharging, the chemicals that provide electric energy are restored to their original condition. This is done by passing direct current through a cell in a direction opposite to the direction of the current that the cell delivers to a circuit.

A cell (or battery) is recharged by connecting it to a battery charger in ''like-to-like'' polarity as shown in Fig. 18-3. The charger is a rectifier circuit that can produce a variable output voltage. Many battery chargers have a voltmeter and an ammeter that show the charging voltage and current.

VOLTAGE AND CURRENT OF A CELL

The *voltage rating* of a cell is the voltage that the cell produces when it is not connected to a circuit. This is called the *open-circuit voltage*. The value of the open-circuit voltage depends on the materials from which the cell is made.

The *capacity* of a cell is its ability to deliver a given amount of current to a circuit. This depends on two things: the amount and condition of the electrolyte and the size of the electrodes. A large cell can usually deliver more current for a longer period of time than a smaller cell with the same kinds of electrodes and electrolyte.

In order to get a higher voltage, cells are connected in series. To get greater current, cells are connected in parallel. To review these connections, see Unit 10, ''Series Circuits,'' and Unit 11, ''Parallel Circuits.''

Fig. 18-2. Basic action of a chemical voltaic cell

Fig. 18-3. Battery charger and the charging circuit (*Schauer Manufacturing Corporation*)

145

SHELF LIFE

All dry cells, even when not in use, will lose energy to some extent. The *shelf life* of a cell is that period of time during which the cell can be stored without losing more than about 10 percent of its original capacity. A cell loses capacity because its electrolyte dries out and chemical actions change the materials within it. Since heat speeds both of these processes, the shelf life can be made longer by keeping a cell in a cool place.

CARBON-ZINC CELLS AND BATTERIES

The *carbon-zinc cell* is one of the oldest and most widely used primary dry cells. Its electrolyte is a paste of ammonium chloride and zinc chloride dissolved in water. These and other chemicals are contained in the *bobbin* of the cell (Fig. 18-4). The negative electrode is a zinc can.

Fig. 18-4. Principal parts of a typical carbon-zinc dry cell

The positive electrode is a mixture of a black mineral called *manganese dioxide* and powdered carbon. The carbon is used to decrease the resistance of the electrode. A solid carbon rod passes through the center of the mixture. The rod provides a good electrical contact between the positive electrode and the positive terminal of the cell.

Polarization. During the operation of a carbon-zinc cell, the carbon rod becomes coated with hydrogen gas by a process known as *polarization*. This gas is removed from the cell by the manganese dioxide, which in this case serves as a *depolarizing agent*. As a result, the cell is able to give much better service.

Sizes and Voltage. Carbon-zinc cells, which are available in several sizes, have an open-circuit voltage of from 1.5 to 1.6 V (Fig. 18-5). There are a number of different kinds of carbon-zinc batteries. The most

Fig. 18-5. Common sizes of carbon-zinc cells

Fig. 18-6. Construction of dry-cell batteries: (A) cylindrical-cell battery containing fifteen 1½-V cells connected in series to produce a total battery voltage of 22½ V; (B) flat-cell battery containing forty-five 1½-V cells connected in series to produce a total battery voltage of 67½ V

common have voltages of 3, 4.5, 6, 9, 13.5, 22.5 and 45 V. In some batteries, the cells are cylindrical (Fig. 18-6A). In others, they are flat (Fig. 18-6B).

Operating Efficiency. Ordinary carbon-zinc cells and batteries provide the most efficient service when they are used for short periods of time at relatively low currents. This lets the cells and batteries stay polarized.

ALKALINE CELLS

The *secondary,* or rechargeable, *alkaline cell* was a major advance in portable energy sources. In this dry cell, the electrolyte is potassium hydroxide. The negative electrode is zinc. The positive electrode is manganese dioxide (Fig. 18-7).

Secondary alkaline cells have an open-circuit voltage of 1.5 V. They commonly come in AA, C, and D sizes. They can be used as direct replacements for carbon-zinc cells of the same sizes. The most common secondary alkaline batteries have voltages of 4.5, 7.5, 13.5, and 15 V. Both the cells and batteries come in a fully charged condition. They should be allowed to discharge before being recharged. For best efficiency, recharging should be done as the manufacturer recommends.

Primary alkaline cells are similar in makeup to the rechargeable kinds and have the same open-circuit voltage. These dry cells last longer than carbon-zinc cells of the same size when used in the same way. Both the primary and secondary alkaline cells (and batteries) give good service when used with high-current loads. For this reason, they are widely used as sources of energy in radios, television sets, tape recorders, cameras, and cordless appliances.

MERCURY CELLS

In the typical *mercury cell,* the electrolyte is a paste of potassium hydroxide and zinc oxide. The negative electrode is a compound of zinc

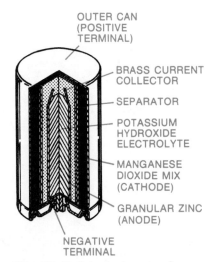

OUTER CAN
(POSITIVE
TERMINAL)

BRASS CURRENT
COLLECTOR

SEPARATOR

POTASSIUM
HYDROXIDE
ELECTROLYTE

MANGANESE
DIOXIDE MIX
(CATHODE)

GRANULAR ZINC
(ANODE)

NEGATIVE
TERMINAL

Fig. 18-7. Principal parts of a rechargeable alkaline cell (*Radio Corporation of America*)

and mercury. The positive electrode is mercuric oxide. Mercury cells are primary cells. They have an open-circuit voltage of 1.35 or 1.4 V, depending on the electrolyte mixture. Mercury batteries have a variety of voltage ratings.

Mercury cells and batteries have a very good shelf life and are extremely rugged. They have the ability to provide a rather constant output voltage under different load conditions. Thus, they are used in all kinds of products, including electric watches, hearing aids, test instruments, and alarm systems. They come in a wide range of shapes and sizes (Fig. 18-8).

Fig. 18-8. Mercury cells (*Gould Inc., Burgess Battery Division*)

NICKEL-CADMIUM CELL

The *nickel-cadmium cell* was originally developed in Europe as a secondary wet cell for use in automobiles. In the secondary nickel-cadmium dry cell, the electrolyte is potassium hydroxide. The negative electrode is nickel hydroxide. The positive electrode is cadmium oxide.

The open-circuit voltage of nickel-cadmium dry cells is 1.25 V. These cells come in several sizes, including the common AA, C, and D cells and the flat button shapes (Fig. 18-9). The most common nickel-cadmium batteries have voltages of 6, 9.6, or 12 V.

Fig. 18-9. Nickel-cadmium cells (*Gould Inc., Burgess Battery Division*)

Nickel-cadmium cells are rugged. They give good service under extreme conditions of shock, vibration, and temperature. They are used in many different kinds of products.

LITHIUM BATTERIES

Lithium batteries have excellent mechanical and electrical properties. They have high-energy density, low shelf discharge, long storage life, and operational reliability. Because of these advantages, they are ideally suited as power sources for the long-term supply of microelectronic circuitry, such as watches, calculators, and photo devices.

Lithium batteries are manufactured in button or cylindrical shapes (Fig. 18-10). Lithium, chemical symbol Li, is a very light metal. It has a silvery luster but quickly tarnishes when exposed to moist air. It is an active metal and gives up its electrons easily to form lithium ion, Li^+. One type of lithium battery contains lithium and manganese dioxide (Li/MnO_2). The voltage of this type of lithium battery is 3.0 V, dc. Button cells have an available capacity range of 30 to 200 mAh; cylindrical cells, 160 to 1400 mAh. The Li/MnO_2 cell uses lithium for the anode, an electrolyte containing lithium perchlorate in an organic solvent. The active cathode material is a specially prepared, heat-treated form of MnO_2. Figure 18-11A shows the construction of a button cell; and Fig. 18-11B, a cylindrical cell.

Fig. 18-10. Lithium batteries are manufactured in a variety of shapes to meet needs of industry (*Varta Batteries, Inc.*)

A

B

Fig. 18-11. Lithium batteries: (A) construction of an Li/MnO_2 button cell; (B) construction of an Li/MnO_2 cylindrical cell (*Varta Batteries, Inc.*)

TESTING DRY CELLS AND BATTERIES

The condition of a dry cell or battery can be checked by measuring its voltage when connected to a load. If the value of the voltage is less than 80 percent of the open-circuit voltage, the cell or battery should be replaced. The voltage test must be made with the load connected and the current flowing. This is because the load current will produce a voltage drop across the internal resistance of the cell or battery. If a dry cell or battery is not in good condition, its internal resistance is high. This is due to the drying out of the electrolyte. Moreover, a relatively large internal voltage drop occurs. Therefore, the voltage of the terminals is greatly reduced. If the cell or battery is tested under an open-circuit condition, there is only a very small internal voltage drop. As a result, the voltage across the terminals of the cell or the battery may be close to the rated voltage. This would be true even if the battery were not in good condition.

LEAD-ACID CELL AND BATTERY

The lead-acid secondary storage battery is mainly used in the automobile. In a fully charged *lead-acid cell,* the electrolyte is a solution of water and sulfuric acid. About 27 percent of the total volume is acid. The active material on the positive (brown-colored) plates is *lead perox-*

MICROPOROUS RUBBER SEPARATOR
PROTECTED CELL CONNECTOR
VENT PLUG
CELL COVER
VISUAL LEVEL FILL
TERMINAL POST
CELL COVER

PLATE BRIDGE
HARD RUBBER CASE
PLATE STRAP
SEDIMENT CHAMBER

Fig. 18-12. Principal parts of an automobile lead-acid battery (*Delco-Remy Division of General Motors Corporation*)

ide. The active material on the negative (gray-colored) plates is pure *lead* in a spongelike form.

The lead-acid cell has an open-circuit voltage of a little more than 2 V. In the typical automobile battery, six cells are connected in series to produce a total voltage of 12 V (Fig. 18-12).

Chemical Action. As a lead-acid cell discharges, some of the acid within the electrolyte leaves the electrolyte. The acid combines with the active material on the plates (Fig. 18-13). This chemical action changes the material on both plates to *lead sulfate*. When the cell is being charged, the reverse action takes place. Now the acid that was absorbed by the plates is returned to the electrolyte. As a result, the active materials on the plates are changed back into the original lead peroxide and lead.

The Hydrometer. The *hydrometer* (Fig. 18-14) is a device used to measure the specific gravity of the electrolyte in a lead-acid cell. The *specific gravity* of a liquid is its weight as compared to that of an equal volume of pure water. Since sulfuric acid is heavier than water, the specific gravity of the electrolyte in a lead-acid cell decreases as the cell discharges. Therefore, by measuring the specific gravity of the electrolyte, the charge condition of lead-acid cells can be determined.

Fig. 18-13. Chemical actions of a lead-acid cell: (A) discharging; (B) charging

CAUTION

The sulfuric acid used in a battery is a highly corrosive chemical. It can cause severe burns. When using a hydrometer, do not allow any of the electrolyte to touch your skin or clothing. In case of contact, immediately wash the affected area with large quantities of soap and water.

Fig. 18-14. Hydrometer used to test battery acid (*ESB Brands, Inc.*)

A sample of the electrolyte is obtained by squeezing the rubber bulb of the hydrometer while the end of the hydrometer is in the electrolyte. When the bulb is released slowly, the electrolyte will be drawn into the glass tube. The float in the hydrometer will then rise within the electrolyte to a level that depends on the specific gravity of the electrolyte. After the float has settled to its level, the specific gravity is read from the markings on the float (Fig. 18-15). Each cell of the battery must be tested. Since the cells are connected in series, any cell that is defective will cause the entire battery to be defective.

The specific gravity of the electrolyte within a fully charged automobile battery is about 1.280. As the cell discharges, the specific gravity gradually decreases to about 1.130. At that point, the cell is considered to be fully discharged.

Rating. The capacity rating of a lead-acid battery is usually given in ampere-hours (Ah) for a specific discharge period. The most commonly used rating system is based on the Society of Automotive Engineers (SAE) 20-hour rate. This means that a new battery rated at 100 Ah should deliver 5 A of current continuously for 20 hours and maintain at least 1.75 V per cell.

Dry Charge. Most lead-acid batteries are shipped from the manufacturer as dry-charge batteries. The plates of a dry-charge battery are in the condition of a fully charged battery. This means that one plate is lead and the other is lead peroxide. To prepare the battery for use, sulfuric acid of the proper specific gravity is added to each cell. The battery is then ready to be used.

BATTERY MAINTENANCE

Although the modern automobile battery is rugged, it must be used and maintained in the right way. The following suggestions will be helpful.

Battery cells must be kept properly filled at all times (Fig. 18-16). Terminals should be clean and free of corrosion. Battery-cable clamps should be connected solidly. The specific gravity of the electrolyte should be checked often.

A battery may show a low charge because of (1) faulty wiring in the electrical system of the automobile, which is causing the battery to be discharged, (2) a defect in the generator or regulator, or (3) a loose or

Fig. 18-15. Reading of a hydrometer scale when a battery is fully charged and when it is discharged

greasy alternator (fan) belt. Do not overcharge a lead-acid battery. This will weaken the electrolyte and may cause serious damage to the cell plates through overheating.

SAFETY

Hydrogen, an explosive gas, is released from a battery while it is being charged. For this reason, a battery should be charged in a well-ventilated area, away from open flames or sparks.

If a battery is to be stored, it should first be fully charged. The plates of a stored battery that is partly or fully discharged soon become coated with a sulfate compound. This compound hardens and causes the plate material to become chemically inactive. A partly or fully discharged battery will also freeze at a temperature of about 20°F (6.7°C).

Because of the problem of continuous maintenance needed on automobile batteries, some manufacturers have developed a low-maintenance battery. A *low-maintenance battery* usually means that the battery has a low water loss. This reduces routine maintenance such as adding water during the service life of the battery.

Most types of low-water-loss batteries produce very little gas at normal charging voltages. This reduces the rate of water loss. Some batteries have venting systems that consist of small vent holes, but water cannot be added. New developments in the design and manufacture of the battery plate grids that hold the active materials have helped make these types of lead-acid batteries possible. In conventional automobile batteries, antimony is used as an alloy in the plate grids to improve their strength. The presence of antimony, however, increases the rate of water loss and self-discharge. Other metals in low-maintenance batteries, such as cadmium and strontium, are substituted to provide the necessary strength but reduce gassing and self-discharge.

Although the newer batteries require little or no maintenance, you should always follow carefully the manufacturer's instructions in using and recharging these batteries.

Fig. 18-16. Adding water to a lead-acid battery (*Ford Motor Company*)

SELF-TEST

Test your knowledge by writing, on a separate sheet of paper, the word or words that most correctly complete the following statements:

1. A cell that changes chemical energy into electric energy is called a _____ cell.
2. A _____ is formed when two or more cells are connected.
3. A chemical cell is made up of two _____ in contact with an_____ .
4. A cell in which the electrolyte is a liquid is often called a _____ cell. A cell in which the electrolyte is a paste is called a _____ cell.
5. Cells that cannot be recharged are called _____ cells. Cells that can be recharged are called _____ cells.
6. A cell or a battery is recharged by passing current through it in a direction _____ to the direction of its discharge current.

7. When charging a battery, the positive terminal of the battery is connected to the _____ terminal of the battery charger. The negative terminal of the battery is connected to the _____ terminal of the charger.

8. The open-circuit voltage of a cell depends on the _____ from which it is made.

9. The amount of current that a cell can deliver to a load depends on the amount and condition of its _____ and the size of its _____.

10. The _____ of a cell is the period of time during which it can be stored without a significant loss of capacity.

11. The open-circuit voltage of carbon-zinc cells ranges from _____ to _____ V.

12. The open-circuit voltage of alkaline cells is _____ V.

13. Both primary and secondary alkaline cells give good service when used with _____ current loads.

14. Mercury cells have an open-circuit voltage of _____ or _____ volts.

15. Nickel-cadmium dry cells have an open-circuit voltage of _____ V.

16. Lithium batteries have a nominal voltage of _____ V dc.

FOR REVIEW AND DISCUSSION

1. What is the difference between a cell and a battery?

2. Describe the construction of a simple chemical cell.

3. Explain the basic action by means of which a chemical cell produces voltage.

4. Define primary and secondary cells.

5. State the correct way of connecting a battery charger to a battery.

6. On what does the open-circuit voltage of a cell depend?

7. What two factors determine the current-delivering capacity of a cell?

8. Define the shelf life of a cell or a battery.

9. Give several common sizes of carbon-zinc cells and identify their voltages.

10. Under what operating conditions will carbon-zinc cells provide the most efficient service?

11. Name the two kinds of alkaline cells. What advantages do these cells provide as compared to carbon-zinc cells?

12. State two desirable characteristics of mercury cells.

13. What is the outstanding feature of nickel-cadmium dry cells?

14. How are dry cells and batteries tested with a voltmeter?

15. Describe the basic construction of an automobile-battery lead-acid cell. What is the open-circuit voltage of such a cell?

16. How is a battery-test hydrometer used?

17. What is a dry-charge automobile battery?

18. What are the advantages of a low-maintenance battery?

INDIVIDUAL-STUDY ACTIVITIES

1. Show your class a number of different kinds and sizes of dry cells. Desribe these and tell the characteristics of each.

2. Give a demonstration showing your class how the condition of a dry cell or battery is tested with a voltmeter.

3. Prepare a written or an oral report telling about the proper care and use of a common lead-acid automobile battery.

4. Write a report on the procedure to test the efficiency of a low-maintenance battery. Discuss the report with your class.

UNIT 19   Generators

The term *to generate* means to produce. An *electric generator* is a machine that produces a voltage by means of electromagnetic induction. This is done by rotating coils of wire through a magnetic field or by rotating a magnetic field past coils of wire. The modern generator is the result of work done with electromagnetic induction by Michael Faraday and Joseph Henry in the early 1800s. Now more than 95 percent of the world's electric energy is supplied by generators.

BASIC GENERATOR

A continuous alternating voltage can be produced by rotating a coil of wire between the poles of a permanent magnet (Fig. 19-1). This is a simple generator. The coil is called the *armature*. The ends of the armature coil are connected to *slip rings*. These are insulated from each other and from the armature shaft on which they are mounted. The stationary brushes press against the slip rings. They make it possible to connect the rotating armature to an external circuit. The armature must be driven by mechanical force, Thus, a generator can be defined as a machine that changes mechanical energy into electric energy.

TO GENERATOR
OUTPUT TERMINALS

BRUSHES

SHAFT

TO SOURCE OF MECHANICAL
ENERGY USED TO DRIVE
THE GENERATOR

MAGNETIC FIELD

SLIP RINGS

ARMATURE

Fig. 19-1. A simple one-coil ac generator

GENERATOR ACTION

The value of the voltage induced by generator action at any instant of time depends on three things. These are (1) the flux density of the magnetic field through which a conductor is moving (the greater the flux density, the greater the induced voltage); (2) the velocity of the conductor motion (induced voltage increases as the velocity of the conductor increases); and (3) the angle at which a conductor cuts across flux lines (the greatest voltage is induced when the conductor cuts across flux lines at a 90° angle).

The action of a single coil in producing a complete cycle of alternating voltage is shown in Fig. 19-2. If a load is connected across the terminals, an alternating current will flow through the circuit.

Fig. 19-2. Generating one cycle of voltage with a single-coil ac generator

In Fig. 19-2, with the coil in position 1, no voltage is being induced because the armature is not cutting across any flux lines. No current flows through the load circuit.

As the armature moves from position 1 to position 2, it cuts across more and more flux lines. Thus, the voltage increases from zero to its highest value in one direction. This increase in voltage results in a similar increase in current. This is shown by the first quarter of the sine wave. At position 2, the coil is cutting flux lines at a 90° angle. This produces the highest voltage.

In moving from position 2 to position 3, the armature cuts across fewer flux lines at sharper angles but in the same direction. As a result, the voltage decreases from its highest value to zero. During this time, the current also decreases to zero. This is shown by the second quarter of the sine wave.

As the armature continues to rotate to position 4, each of its sides cuts across the magnetic field in the opposite direction. This changes the polarity of the voltage and the direction of the current. Once again, the voltage and current increase from zero to their highest values during the third quarter of the sine wave.

From position 4 to position 5, the armature rotates back to its starting point. During this time, the voltage and current decrease from their highest values to zero. This completes the cycle.

DIRECT-CURRENT GENERATOR

In a direct-current generator, the ends of the armature coil or coils are connected to a *commutator*. This device is needed to produce a direct current. In its basic form, a commutator is a ringlike device made up of metal pieces called *segments*. The segments are insulated from each other and from the shaft on which they are mounted.

The operation of a simple dc generator is shown in Fig. 19-3. In Fig. 19-3A, the armature coil is cutting across the magnetic field. This motion produces a voltage that causes current to move through the load circuit in the direction shown by the arrows. In this position of the coil, commutator segment 1 is in contact with brush 1. Commutator segment 2 is in contact with brush 2.

Fig. 19-3. Basic operation of a dc generator

Fig. 19-4. Main parts of a commercial dc generator (*Westinghouse Electric Corporation*)

Commutating Action. As the armature rotates a half turn in a clockwise direction, the contacts between the commutator segments and the brushes are reversed (Fig. 19-3B). Now segment 1 is in contact with brush 2. Segment 2 is in contact with brush 1. Because of this *commutating action,* the side of the armature coil in contact with either of the brushes is always cutting across the magnetic field in the same direction. Therefore, brushes 1 and 2 have a constant polarity. A direct voltage is applied to the external load circuit.

The Practical Generator. The main parts of a commercial dc generator are shown in Fig. 19-4. In this generator, the armature is made up of coils of magnet wire. These are placed in the slots of the laminated armature core. The ends of the coils are connected to the commutator segments. The field windings are electromagnets. They produce the magnetic field needed for the operation of the generator.

The direct current used to energize the field windings of a generator is called the *excitation current.* In a dc generator, this current is obtained from the output of the generator (Fig. 19-5).

Most small dc generators are driven by alternating-current motors or by gasoline engines. They are used in trains, in welders, for charging batteries, and for the operation of field telephone equipment.

Fig. 19-5. Schematic diagrams of common dc generators: (A) series generator with field windings connected in series with the armature; (B) shunt generator with field windings connected in parallel with the armature; (C) compound generator containing both series and shunt field windings

Fig. 19-6. A gasoline-engine-driven ac generator (*Fairbanks Morse and Company*)

Fig. 19-7. Slip rings mounted on the armature assembly of a rotating-armature ac generator (*Generac Corporation*)

Fig. 19-8. Principal parts of a rotating-field generator: (A) armature (stator); (B) field (rotor)

ALTERNATING-CURRENT GENERATORS

The rotating part of large ac generators is called the *rotor*. It is turned by steam turbines, hydro- (water-driven) turbines, or diesel engines. These generators produce the electric energy used in our homes and in industry. Small ac generators are usually driven by gasoline engines (Fig. 19-6). Such generators are commonly used to provide emergency power. Alternating-current generators are also called *alternators*.

Excitation. In the small ac generator, the excitation current needed to energize the field windings is often obtained from a battery or from the output of the generator itself. The excitation current must be direct, but the output current is alternating. Thus, the output current must first pass through a rectifier and be changed to direct current. In some alternators, the rectifier circuit is located within the generator housing itself. In a large ac generator, the excitation current is obtained from a dc *exciter generator*. This is either mounted on the shaft of the main generator or is located nearby.

Rotating-Armature Generator. In small ac generators, it is usually the armature that is the rotating part, or *rotor*. The rotor turns within the magnetic field produced by stationary field windings, called the *stator*. The rotor has a collector or slip rings that are in contact with carbon brushes (Fig. 19-7).

Rotating-Field Generator. In a rotating-field ac generator, the armature is stationary. It is made up of windings placed in the slots of the frame assembly (Fig. 19-8A). The field windings are wound around pole pieces on the rotor assembly. They are connected to slip rings (Fig. 19-8B). The excitation current is passed to the field windings by means of carbon brushes in contact with the slip rings. Generators of this kind are used in most large power generating plants.

Frequency. The frequency of the alternating current produced by a generator depends on the speed of the rotor (either the armature or the field windings) and on the number of magnetic poles formed by the field windings. The power-company generators in most parts of the United States produce a frequency of 60 Hz. Special-purpose generators may have a higher or lower frequency.

Voltage. The output voltage of a generator depends mostly on the speed of the rotor, the number of armature coils, and the strength of the magnetic field produced by the field windings. Power-station generators usually have an output voltage of 10,000 V or more.

Fig. 19-9. Rotor assembly of a typical magneto showing the bar-shaped permanent magnets embedded in the rotor (*Fairbanks Morse Engine Accessories Operation, Colt Industries*)

MAGNETO

A *magneto* is an ac generator in which the magnetic field is produced by one or more permanent magnets rather than by electromagnets. In some magnetos, the permanent magnets are in the rotor assembly (Fig. 19-9).

A flywheel magneto is commonly used with small gasoline engines. One or more permanent magnets of this generator are mounted on the flywheel assembly. As the flywheel turns, a magnetic field cuts across a stationary coil. This is the ignition coil, and it is a step-up transformer (Fig. 19-10). The voltage induced across the secondary winding of the ignition coil is applied to the spark plug.

THREE-PHASE GENERATOR

A generator with a single set of windings and one pair of slip rings will produce a single wave of voltage. This is known as a *single-phase system*.

A *three-phase generator* has three separate sets of windings. One end of each winding is connected to a slip ring (Fig. 19-11A). In such a

Fig. 19-10. Ignition circuit of a typical single-cylinder gasoline engine using a magneto

Fig. 19-11. Three-phase generator: (A) basic construction of a simple three-phase generator; (B) sine waveforms of a three-phase voltage

generator, each complete turn of the rotor produces three separate voltages (Fig. 19-11B). These are applied to a load by means of a three-conductor power line. A three-phase power system is usually protected with circuit breakers. A circuit breaker is connected in series with each of the conductors. A typical automobile alternator is an example of a three-phase generator.

A three-phase power system delivers a steadier supply of electric energy to a load. Because of this, three-phase systems are used for heavy-duty equipment that operates at a voltage of 208 V or more. Such equipment includes large motors, welders, and heating units.

Almost all power companies in this country use three-phase generators and three-phase power-distribution lines. Single-phase loads that operate at a voltage of about 120 V are connected to one of the three conductors of the power line and to a fourth conductor, called a *neutral wire*. Ordinary loads in homes and other buildings are so connected.

SELF-TEST

Test your knowledge by writing, on a separate sheet of paper, the word or words that most correctly complete the following statements:

1. An electric generator produces a voltage by means of _____.
2. A generator can be operated by rotating coils of wire through a _____ or by rotating a _____ past coils of wire.
3. A generator can be defined as a machine that converts _____ energy into _____ energy.
4. In its basic form, a commutator is a ringlike device made up of metal pieces called _____.
5. A commutator is used in a _____ generator.
6. Electromagnets that produce the magnetic field needed for the operation of a generator are called _____.
7. The direct current used to energize the field

windings of a generator is called the _____ current.
8. Most dc generators are driven by _____ or by _____.
9. Large ac generators are driven by sources of mechanical energy such as _____, _____, and _____.
10. Alternating-current generators are also called _____.
11. A rotating armature in an ac generator is equipped with _____ or _____ rings that are in contact with _____.
12. The frequency of the alternating current produced by the generator depends on the speed of the _____ and on the number of magnetic _____ formed by the field windings.
13. A three-phase generator has three separate sets of _____.

1. Define an electric generator.
2. Describe the construction of and explain the operation of a simple alternating-current generator.
3. What three things determine the value of the voltage induced by generator action?
4. What is the purpose of a commutator in a dc generator?
5. Explain commutating action.
6. Name the main parts of a practical dc generator.
7. What is meant by the excitation current of a generator?
8. How is the excitation current in a dc generator obtained?
9. Name three means by which the rotors of large ac generators are turned.
10. Are large ac generators usually the rotating-field kind?
11. What two things determine the frequency of an ac generator?
12. What is a magneto?
13. Explain the operation of the flywheel magneto commonly used on small gasoline engines.
14. Describe three-phase voltage.
15. What is the advantage of three-phase power as compared to single-phase power?

1. Prepare a written or an oral report on the development of large commercial generators.
2. Demonstrate the operation of a magneto. Describe its construction and explain how it is able to produce voltage.
3. Prepare a written or an oral report telling about three-phase power systems and the purposes for which they are used.

UNIT 20   Other Sources of Electric Energy

Energy sources are an important part of technology. Technology involves using scientific ideas in making machines that can do work for us. Countries such as the United States can maintain their social and technical standards only by using large amounts of energy. However, this use of energy creates several problems. These include: (1) the *depletion* (using up) of our fuel supplies, (2) the pollution of our environment, (3) a dependence on foreign countries for our fuel supplies, and (4) economic difficulties caused by the need to spend large amounts of money on fuels imported from other countries.

Electric energy is one of the cleanest forms of energy. It is easy to transport. If ways can be found to produce large quantities of electric energy at a reasonable cost, our society will be able to maintain its high living standards. At the same time, damage to the environment must be reduced. Consider an electric automobile powered by rechargeable batteries. Such a vehicle would be clean and quiet and would probably have few maintenance problems. More information about the electric automobile is given in Unit 35, "The Automobile Electrical System."

Today the production of most electric energy begins with heat energy. Fossil fuels, such as coal, oil, and natural gas, are burned to produce heat. This heat is used to heat water and change the water into steam. The steam is then used to power turbines that drive large generators.

Heat is also produced by atomic fission in nuclear power plants. The operation of these and other common kinds of power plants is discussed in Unit 44, "The Electric Power Industry."

The world's supplies of coal, oil, natural gas, and fissionable materials are limited. Thus, other sources of energy must be used. Some of these are sunlight, wind, ocean heat, wave motion, and *organic* (animal or plant) materials. These sources are particularly useful for producing electricity.

SUNLIGHT

The use of sunlight as a source of energy to generate electric power has many advantages. Sunlight is *inexhaustible* (cannot be used up) and is available everywhere. The use of sunlight should do little damage to the environment and produce few wastes. *Photovoltaic*, or *solar*, cells generate electricity directly from sunlight using no fuel. Changing sunlight into electricity may help solve the long-term energy problems of the United States.

Solar Cells. These cells usually are made up of a layer of *silicon*, a common nonmetallic element, that coats a metal base known as the substrate. The silicon is treated chemically to make what are called *p-type* and *n-type* forms. The area where these two forms touch each other is called a *p-n junction*.

A cross-section of a silicon solar cell is shown in Fig. 20-1. The top layer of p-type silicon is very thin. Light energy will pass through it and

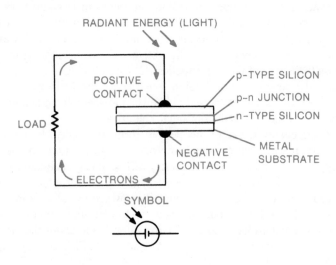

Fig. 20-1. Cross-sectional view of a silicon solar cell

reach the p-n junction. The light energy gives energy to the electrons in the p-type layer. This causes these electrons to move across the p-n junction and into the n-type layer. The n-type layer then becomes negatively charged. A voltage is produced across the layers on each side of the p-n junction.

The amount of voltage produced by a single solar cell is quite small. For this reason, many solar cells are often connected to form a *solar panel*. One very important use of solar panels is to provide energy for charging batteries and operating circuits in space vehicles.

Figure 20-2 shows a solar-powered water purifier. This experimental system uses several different solar cell designs mounted on panels. The solar cells produce 11 kW when the sun is at its highest point, generally around noon each day. Energy is also stored in 20 automotive lead-acid batteries. These are used during cloudy days and when more power is needed to start motors.

Fig. 20-2. Experimental water purifier powered by solar energy (*U.S. Department of Defense*)

WIND

Energy from the wind has been used in the United States for many years. The *windmill* is a machine that converts wind energy into useful work. In the rural United States, windmills were often used to pump water. Only recently have windmills been seriously considered as another means of generating electricity.

Figure 20-3 illustrates several wind-driven generators located on farmland near the Altamont Pass in California. Surveys indicate that the wind energy in this area averages 700 to 1,200 W per square meter for the 8-month wind season. A wind farm uses many wind generators in areas where there are strong and persistent winds. The wind farm industry is new but is growing in importance because the energy from the wind is nonpolluting and abundant. Single wind-driven generators, however, may be installed for residential or business use. Looking toward the future, one state has a goal to produce 10 percent of the state's electricity from wind energy by the year 2000. If this capacity were currently available, it would result in a direct saving of 40 million barrels of oil a year.

More details about wind-driven generators are shown in Fig. 20-4. This illustration shows workers installing a three-blade airplane-shaped propeller on one type of wind-driven generator. The blades of this wind-driven generator are 16.6 ft (5.1 m) in length. The blades, generator, and associated equipment are mounted on a tower up to 60 ft (18.3 m) high. It takes a ''cut-on'' wind speed of 10 miles per hour (16.1 km/h) to begin generating electricity. At a wind speed of 60 miles per hour (96.6 km/h), the wind generator will shut itself off. This wind speed is known as the ''cut-off'' wind speed. These wind-driven generators are designed, however, to withstand a wind speed of 125 miles per hour (201.2 km/h). They are rated at 95 kW at a wind speed of 40 miles per hour (64.4 km/h). The output of these wind generators is fed into the local utility system.

Fig. 20-3. In the future, wind farms may be a common sight over land areas where there is a strong and persistent wind. (*Fayette Manufacturing Corporation*)

NACELLE (ENCLOSED HOUSING) FOR ELECTRIC GENERATOR AND ASSOCIATED EQUIPMENT

LIFTING CRANE

TOWER

AIRPLANE PROPELLER-LIKE BLADES DRIVEN BY WIND

Fig. 20-4. Workers installing airplane propeller-like blades on a wind-driven generator (*Fayette Manufacturing Corporation*)

Fig. 20-5. Artist's concept of a floating structure for an ocean thermal energy conversion system (*Lockheed Missiles and Space Co., Inc.*)

OCEAN HEAT

Another possible way to generate electricity is to use the *thermal* (heat) energy of the ocean. This involves using the ocean water to collect and store energy from the sun. A system for doing this may take the form of a large floating structure anchored to the ocean floor (Fig. 20-5). This system makes use of the difference in temperature between the heated upper layers of water and the colder layers below. The warmer water can change a liquid such as ammonia into a gas. Gas pressure can be used to drive a turbine. An electric generator can be connected to the turbine. The gas, after passing through the turbine, can be changed back into a liquid by the colder water. This can go on and on. This system works somewhat like the steam electric plant described in Unit 44. However, an ocean thermal energy conversion system would operate at much lower temperatures and pressures. Very large amounts of ocean water would be used. Power would be transmitted to land by underwater cables where they would connect with regular power lines. Large numbers of such systems may be built. They would probably be located close to major population centers.

GEOTHERMAL

Scientists are working to find other natural sources of heat energy. One possible source, now little used, is *geothermal energy,* the natural heat of the Earth. This vast source could be tapped by drilling holes deep into the Earth. These holes release steam, which could be piped to turbines that drive large electric generators.

WAVE MOTION

Another source of energy being considered is the use of the motion of ocean waves. One way of doing this uses an anchored *buoy* (float). You may have seen buoys marking the entrances to channels and harbors. A buoy for using wave motion to produce electricity has two parts. The lower section is the part that floats. The upper part is shaped like a ball with its bottom open. Waves cause water to move up and down in this upper part. This forces air in and out through a tube containing a rotor with windmill-like blades. The air moves the blades of the rotor, which are designed to always turn in the same direction. Connected to the shaft of the rotor is an electric generator. Such a system could be an inexpensive way of generating electricity for countries with a seacoast.

ORGANIC MATERIALS

Organic materials that can be changed into usable fuels are another possible source of energy. Such materials include agricultural wastes from both crops and animals and sewage. These can be changed into methane gas, alcohol, and oil. Some crops can be grown specifically to be made into fuels. These fuels can replace some of the oil or gasoline used by the engines that turn electric generators.

HIGH-ALTITUDE TRANSMISSION OF POWER

Figure 20-6 shows an artist's idea of one kind of satellite power station, a Space-Based Power Conversion System. This system is being studied by the National Aeronautics and Space Administration (NASA). Such a system can be placed in a fixed *orbit* (path) around the Earth. There, it can collect pollution-free energy from the sun. This energy can be transmitted to the Earth in the form of *microwaves*. These are ultra-high-frequency radio waves. The receiving station on Earth can then change the microwaves to electricity. Located high above the Earth, this system would not be affected by clouds or night. Thus, it could operate continuously.

Fig. 20-6. Artist's concept of a space-based power conversion system (*National Aeronautics and Space Administration*)

FUEL CELLS

In a *fuel cell,* chemical reactions between oxygen and a fuel cause chemical energy to be changed directly into electric energy. The fuels most commonly used in such cells are hydrogen and methane.

The basic construction of a hydrogen-oxygen fuel cell is shown in Fig. 20-7. In this cell, hydrogen in either liquid or gas form is supplied

Fig. 20-7. Basic operation of a fuel cell

165

to the cathode, or negative electrode. The hydrogen then spreads through the electrolyte. This causes electrons to be released from the electrolyte. These electrons are deposited on the cathode, causing it to become negatively charged. The electrons then move through the load to the anode, or positive electrode.

At present, fuel cells are most commonly used in space vehicles (Fig. 20-8). In the future, larger fuel cells may be used to supply large amounts of electric energy for ordinary use.

Fig. 20-8. A space-vehicle fuel cell (*General Electric*)

FUEL CELL STACK

FUEL TANK

PRESSURE SENSOR & OXYGEN PURGE VALVE

COOLANT

PRODUCT WATER VALVE
HARNESS & BRACKET
HYDROGEN CONTROL VALVE

APPROXIMATE SIZE:
LENGTH—24 INCHES
DIAMETER—14 INCHES

COOLANT

MAGNETOHYDRODYNAMIC (MHD) CONVERSION

Another device that could generate large amounts of electricity is the *magnetohydrodynamic* (MHD) *converter*.

MHD converters are based on two principles. The first is that gases can be ionized by high temperatures and thus made into good conductors of electricity. The second is the principle of electromagnetic induction.

Figure 20-9 shows the basic elements of the MHD converter. Gas is heated to a temperature of about 5,000°F (2760°C). This ionizes the

FIELD COIL

CATHODE

HOT IONIZED GAS

ANODE

LOAD

FIELD SUPPLY

Fig. 20-9. Basic elements of a magnetohydrodynamic (MHD) converter

166

gas, which is then forced through a strong magnetic field. The electrical force that results makes contact with electrodes at the top and bottom of the gas stream. Current flows in the external circuit. The gas moves to a condenser unit and then back to the heat source to complete the cycle. The ionized gas thus takes the place of metal conductors.

MHD converters have few mechanical moving parts. New materials will allow them to withstand the tremendous heat and pressures needed. Someday it may be possible to design and build MHD converters with outputs of more than 1 million watts. These will be smaller, lighter, more efficient, and more reliable than equivalent turbine-generator combinations. Figure 20-10 is a flow diagram that shows the operation of an MHD converter.

Fig. 20-10. Flow diagram of a magnetohydrodynamic (MHD) electric power converter (*Avco Everett Research Laboratory*)

THERMIONIC ENERGY CONVERSION

Another system for changing heat directly into electricity is the *thermionic energy converter*. It consists of two electrodes in a vacuum (Fig. 20-11). The *emitter* electrode is heated to produce free electrons. The

Fig. 20-11. Coaxial thermionic energy converter

collector electrode, at a much lower temperature, receives the electrons released by the emitter.

The *coaxial thermionic energy converter* shown in Fig. 20-11 has a heat source in the center of the converter. This will heat the emitter. The heated emitter will give off electrons. The electrons will then move to the collector and on to the external load.

An alternating current can be produced directly in the thermionic converter. This is done by applying a small *modulating* (varying) *signal* to a *grid electrode* located between the emitter and the collector. Large thermionic converters could someday replace ordinary turbine-driven generators. (A general discussion of modulating signals can be found in Unit 39; the effect of grid electrodes is discussed in Unit 29.)

SELF-TEST

Test your knowledge by writing, on a separate sheet of paper, the word or words that most correctly complete the following statements:

1. _____ is an inexhaustible source of energy.
2. Devices that change sunlight directly into electricity are called _____.
3. The wind can be converted to electric energy by a _____.
4. Natural heat from the Earth is called _____ energy.
5. A satellite power station placed in a fixed orbit around Earth would transmit energy to Earth in the form of _____.
6. A device that converts chemical fuel energy directly into electric energy is the _____.
7. A device that changes heat energy into electric energy by using a hot ionized gas is the _____ converter.
8. A system for changing heat directly into electricity is called a _____.

FOR REVIEW AND DISCUSSION

1. List some of the problems created by a high rate of energy use.
2. List some of the advantages of an electric automobile.
3. Identify some sources of energy that may provide alternatives to today's fuels.
4. Discuss the advantages of sunlight as a source of energy.
5. Explain how a satellite power station might change sunlight into useful energy.

INDIVIDUAL-STUDY ACTIVITIES

1. Write a report on the world's present supplies of coal, oil, and gas. Discuss the immediate and long-term problems with these fuels.
2. Calculate the roof area of your school. Estimate how many silicon solar cells, each having an area of 1 square inch (645 square millimeters), could be placed on the roof. Assume that each silicon solar cell develops 0.2 V at 10 mA in bright sunlight. Calculate the power output for the entire sun battery.
3. Write a report on the development and production of large-scale wind-driven generators in the United States. Identify other countries having active wind-driven generator programs.

SEMICONDUCTORS AND INTEGRATED CIRCUITS

UNIT 21   Semiconductors and Diodes

A *semiconductor material* is one that, in its pure state and at normal room temperature, is neither a good conductor nor a good insulator. However, pure semiconductor materials are seldom used in electronics. Instead, small amounts of other substances are added by a process called *doping*. Thereby the resistance of semiconductor materials can be made much lower than that of the pure materials.

The most widely used semiconductor materials are the elements germanium and silicon. They are used in solid-state diodes and transistors. A *solid-state diode* is one that, unlike the electron tube, is made as a solid unit. It does not have a glass envelope or a filament (Fig. 21-1). Electron tubes are discussed in Unit 29, "Lamps and Lighting."

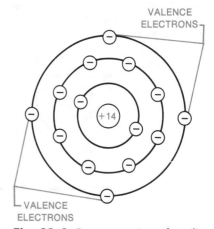

Fig. 21-1. Semiconductor solid-state devices (*Texas Instruments Incorporated*)

SEMICONDUCTOR STRUCTURE

The atoms of germanium and silicon have four *valence electrons,* those in the outermost shell (Fig. 21-2). In these materials, the atoms are arranged in what is called a *crystal-lattice structure*. Each atom shares each of its valence electrons with nearby atoms. This forms what are called *electron-pair,* or *covalent, bonds* between the atoms (Fig. 21-3).

Semiconductor Materials: n-type. One impurity with which a pure semiconductor material, such as silicon, is often doped is arsenic. Arsenic has five valence electrons. Four of the five valence electrons of each arsenic atom form electron-pair bonds with the valence electrons of four silicon atoms. One valence electron of each arsenic atom is then left unattached. It becomes a free electron (Fig. 21-4). Since the silicon then contains free electrons, or *negatively* charged particles, it is called an *n-type semiconductor material*. The arsenic donated free electrons to the silicon. Because of this, arsenic is called a *donor impurity*.

Fig. 21-2. Representation of a silicon atom

169

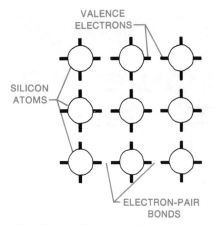

Fig. 21-3. Electron-pair, or covalent, bonds in the crystal-lattice structure of pure silicon

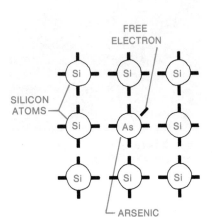

Fig. 21-4. Free, or excess, electron resulting from the addition of arsenic to silicon

Semiconductor Materials: p-type. Pure silicon is often doped with an impurity, such as the element indium, that has three valence electrons. In this case, the valence electrons of each indium atom form electron-pair bonds with the valence electrons of three silicon atoms. This leaves one valence electron of a nearby silicon atom without an electron-pair bond. As a result, there is a lack of one electron in the crystal-lattice structure of the silicon. This lack is called a *hole* (Fig. 21-5A).

If a voltage is applied to the silicon, an electron from an electron-pair bond can gain enough energy to break the bond and move into the hole. This creates a new hole. This hole is then ready to accept another electron that has broken its electron-pair bond. As this continues, the hole is said to *move* through the silicon, as shown in Fig. 21-5B.

Since a hole represents the lack of an electron, it can be considered a *positively* charged current carrier. Therefore, a semiconductor material containing many holes is called a *p-type material*. Indium is called an *acceptor impurity*. This is because each atom of indium added to silicon or germanium can accept an electron from an electron-pair bond.

THE P-N-JUNCTION DIODE

The basic solid-state diode is a combination of p-type and n-type semiconductor materials. It is made as a single unit through a chemical process. The section where the two types of materials meet is known as a *p-n junction* (Fig. 21-6).

The Depletion Region. When the p-n junction is formed, free electrons within the n section diffuse (spread out) across the junction to combine with (fill) holes that are near the junction in the p section. At the same time, holes from the p section diffuse across the junction to combine with free electrons that are within the n section near the junction. As a result of these combinations, the atoms near the junction of each section become ionized. Since this action reduces the number of n-section electrons and p-section holes, the area where the process of ionization occurs is called a *depletion region*.

Fig. 21-5. The semiconductor hole: (A) hole created when indium is added to silicon; (B) movement, or drift, of holes and electrons through a p-type material

Fig. 21-6. Electron and hole activity at a p-n junction: (A) diffusion of electrons and holes through the junction; (B) creation of potential barrier

Potential Barrier. Because of the electron-hole combinations within the depletion region, atoms within the p section gain electrons and become negatively charged (negative ions), while atoms within the n section lose electrons and become positively charged (positive ions). This condition creates a small voltage across the junction that is referred to as a *potential barrier* (Fig. 21-6). Because of the polarity of the potential barrier, there is no further significant diffusion of the electrons from the n section into the p section or of holes from the p section into the n section.

Diodes are enclosed in protective cases of various shapes with lugs or leads for making the needed circuit connections (Fig. 21-7A). The p-type material in a diode is called the *anode*. The n-type material is called the *cathode*. The anode and cathode terminals of a diode are identified in several different ways, as shown in Fig. 21-7B.

RECTIFICATION

Most power-company generating stations that supply electric energy to homes, businesses, and factories produce alternating current. One of the main reasons for this is that alternating-current energy can be sent over long distances very efficiently. Many processes and devices, however, can be operated only with direct current. For example, transistors, electron tubes, and certain control devices need direct current. If circuits containing these devices are to be operated from ordinary outlets, they must use rectifier circuits. *Rectifier circuits* change alternating current to direct current. Diodes are used as rectifiers in battery chargers and in other power-supply units that provide direct current. They also are used in rectifier circuits in radios, television receivers, computers, and other electronic and electrical products.

Fig. 21-7. Silicon rectifier diodes: (A) typical diodes (*International Rectifier*); (B) methods used to identify the cathode lead or terminal of small-size diodes (*International Rectifier*)

171

Fig. 21-8. Diode circuit with forward bias

HOW A DIODE WORKS

The common solid-state diode rectifier is made of silicon. It works by acting as a gate. A *gate* lets current pass through it in one direction but not in the other. The polarity of the voltage applied to a diode determines whether or not the diode will conduct current. The two polarities of an applied voltage are known as *forward bias* and *reverse bias*.

Forward Bias. A diode is forward-biased when the positive terminal of a voltage source, such as a battery, is connected to its anode and the negative terminal is connected to its cathode (Fig. 21-8A). Under this condition, the positive terminal of the battery repels holes within the p-type material toward the p-n junction. At the same time, free electrons within the n-type material are repelled toward the junction by the negative terminal of the battery. When holes and electrons reach the junction, some of them break through it (Fig. 21-8B). Then holes combine with electrons within the n-type material. Electrons combine with holes within the p-type material.

Each time that a hole combines with an electron or an electron combines with a hole near the junction, an electron from an electron-pair bond within the p-type material (anode) breaks its bond. This electron then enters the positive terminal of the battery. At the same time, an electron from the negative terminal of the battery moves into the n-type material (cathode) of the diode (Fig. 21-8C). This produces a negative-to-positive flow of electrons in the external circuit to which the diode is connected.

Reverse Bias. A diode is reverse-biased when its anode is connected to the negative terminal of the battery and its cathode is connected to the positive terminal of the battery (Fig. 21-9A). In this condition, holes within the p-type material are attracted toward the negative terminal of the battery and away from the p-n junction. At the same time, free electrons within the n-type material are attracted toward the positive terminal of the battery and away from the junction (Fig. 21-9B). This action causes the diode to present a high resistance to current. Under this condition, no current will flow in the external circuit.

Fig. 21-9. Diode circuit with reverse bias

Fig. 21-10. Half-wave-rectifier circuit

DIODE   CATHODE

AC INPUT VOLTAGE

DIODE FORWARD-BIASED

LOAD

FORWARD-BIAS

REVERSE-BIAS

WAVEFORM OF INPUT VOLTAGE

AC INPUT VOLTAGE

DIODE REVERSE-BIASED

LOAD

WAVEFORM OF PULSATING DIRECT CURRENT THROUGH LOAD

HALF-WAVE-RECTIFIER CIRCUIT

When a diode is connected to a source of alternating voltage, it is alternately forward-biased and then reverse-biased during each cycle. Therefore, when a single diode is used in a rectifier circuit, current passes through the circuit load during only one-half of each cycle of the input voltage (Fig. 21-10). For this reason, the circuit is called a *half-wave rectifier*.

Output. The output of a half-wave-rectifier circuit is a pulsating direct current. Such a current can be used in some circuits. However, it produces a loud hum in radios, television sets, and amplifiers. To eliminate or reduce this hum, the pulsating direct current is *filtered,* or smoothed out.

Filtering. The basic filtering component of rectifier circuits is an *electrolytic capacitor* (Fig. 21-11). The action of such a capacitor, when used in a half-wave-rectifier circuit, is shown in Fig. 21-12.

ELECTROLYTIC CAPACITOR

Fig. 21-11. Electrolytic capacitor used in the rectifier circuit of a timing assembly (*Gibbs Manufacturing and Research Corporation*)

CAPACITOR CHARGING   CAPACITOR DISCHARGING

CR1

R1

Fig. 21-12. Filtering action of an electrolytic capacitor in a half-wave-rectifier circuit

173

Fig. 21-13. Basic two-diode, full-wave-rectifier circuit: (A) diode CR1 conducting, diode CR2 not conducting; (B) diode CR2 conducting, diode CR1 not conducting

Fig. 21-14. Two-diode rectifier units

During the time that the diode is forward-biased, voltage builds up across the output circuit. The capacitor becomes charged. As the voltage decreases, the capacitor begins to discharge through the resistor R1. When the diode is reverse-biased, it ceases to conduct. Meanwhile the capacitor keeps discharging through R1. When the diode is forward-biased again, the capacitor, which was not fully discharged, is brought back to full charge. It then begins the discharge cycle again. Thus the output voltage and current are smoothed.

FULL-WAVE-RECTIFIER CIRCUIT

A *full-wave-rectifier* circuit is one that rectifies the entire cycle of an applied voltage. The basic full-wave-rectifier circuit uses two diodes. The action of these diodes during each half cycle of the applied voltage is shown in Fig. 21-13. The diodes may be individual units, or they may both be in a single package (Fig. 21-14).

The rectifier transformer used in this kind of circuit must have a center-tapped secondary winding. The dc output voltage of the rectifier circuit will depend mainly on the voltage across the secondary winding of the transformer.

Full-wave rectifiers have a smoother output voltage than half-wave rectifiers. The reason for this is that the full-wave rectifier produces a pulse of voltage in the output circuit during each half cycle of the applied voltage. After filtering, the load can be quite smooth.

Another kind of full-wave-rectifier circuit is called a *bridge circuit*. In this circuit, four diodes are used. The action of these diodes during each half cycle of the applied alternating input voltage is shown in Fig. 21-15. Note that the rectifier transformer used in a bridge circuit does not have a center-tapped secondary winding. The diodes may be individual units or be packaged into a single unit (Fig. 21-16).

DIODE RATINGS

Rectifier diodes are usually rated in terms of the largest current that they can safely conduct and their *peak inverse voltage* (PIV). The PIV rating of a diode is the highest reverse-bias voltage that can be applied to the diode. If more than this voltage is applied, the diode may be badly damaged or completely ruined.

TESTING DIODES

When a semiconductor diode becomes defective, it is usually open or shorted. Each of these conditions generally occurs because of overheating produced by too much current passing through the diode. This causes the atomic and molecular structures in the semiconductor material to become seriously disarranged.

Diodes are best tested with a diode tester. Rectifier diodes can also be checked with an ohmmeter.

174

Fig. 21-15. Bridge rectifier circuit: (A) diodes CR2 and CR4 conducting, diodes CR1 and CR3 not conducting; (B) diodes CR1 and CR3 conducting, diodes CR2 and CR4 not conducting

Ohmmeter testing of a diode is based on forward and reverse bias. When the negative terminal of the ohmmeter power supply is connected to the diode's cathode, the diode is forward-biased. Its resistance will be relatively low (Fig. 21-17A). If the positive terminal of the ohmmeter is connected to the diode's cathode, the diode is reverse-biased. Its resistance will be relatively high (Fig. 21-17B).

To test a diode with an ohmmeter, connect the meter to the diode. Then note the resistance of the diode. Next reverse the connections of the ohmmeter to the diode. If the resistance of the diode is much greater in one direction than in the other, you can assume that the diode is in good condition. If the test shows direct continuity or the same amount of resistance for both connections, the diode is defective and must be replaced.

Fig. 21-16. Four-diode bridge rectifier units (*Varo Semiconductor, Inc.*)

Fig. 21-17. Testing a diode with an ohmmeter

SELF-TEST

Test your knowledge by writing, on a separate sheet of paper, the word or words that most correctly complete the following statements:

1. The most widely used semiconductor materials are _____ and _____.
2. Impurities are added to pure semiconductor materials by a process called _____.
3. Atoms of semiconductors have _____ valence electrons.
4. The bonds between atoms in a crystal-lattice structure are called _____, or _____, bonds.
5. An n-type semiconductor contains many _____ electrons.
6. The lack of an electron in a crystal-lattice structure is called a _____.
7. A p-type semiconductor material contains many _____.

8. A hole can be considered as a _____ charged current carrier.

9. The two electrodes of a typical semiconductor diode are called the _____ and the _____ .

10. A diode will conduct when it is _____-biased.

11. The highest reverse-bias voltage that can be applied to a diode is its _____ rating.

FOR REVIEW AND DISCUSSION

1. Define a semiconductor. Name two semiconductor materials.
2. What is meant by a solid-state device?
3. Describe a crystal-lattice structure.
4. Define n-type and p-type semiconductor materials.
5. Explain how n-type and p-type semiconductor materials are formed by the process of doping.
6. What is a p-n junction?

7. Explain the conditions of forward and reverse bias in a semiconductor diode.
8. Describe a basic half-wave-rectifier circuit.
9. Describe a basic full-wave-rectifier circuit.
10. What is the purpose of a filter capacitor in a rectifier circuit?
11. What is meant by the peak inverse voltage of a diode?
12. How are diodes tested?

INDIVIDUAL-STUDY ACTIVITIES

1. Demonstrate the basic rectifying action of a diode.
2. Demonstrate the difference between a half-wave- and a full-wave-rectifier circuit.
3. Demonstrate how the condition of diodes can be

tested with the use of an ohmmeter alone and with a diode tester.

4. Write a report on how the depletion region and potential barrier are formed in a p-n junction. Discuss your findings with the class.

UNIT 22   Transistors

Transistors are semiconductor devices that can be used to control current or amplify an input voltage or current. In a transistor radio, for example, transistors are used to amplify the very small signal existing across the antenna coil. Thus a much larger signal, strong enough to operate the radio's loudspeaker, is created.

TRANSISTORS AND ELECTRON TUBES

In most electrical and electronic devices, transistors have almost completely replaced electron tubes. Transistors perform the same functions as electron tubes. However, they also have several important advantages. They are smaller, thus making more-compact products possible (Fig. 22-1). The transistor is also more rugged than the electron tube. It usually provides better performance over a longer period of time. Most important, the transistor usually needs much less current and voltage to work. This saves energy. For example, a 12-V automobile radio using tubes draws about 2.5 A. A similar transistor automobile radio draws

Fig. 22-1. Transistors used in an amplifier circuit (*David C. Richards*)

only a fraction of an ampere. The lower power needs of transistor circuits have made possible small, lightweight, portable products that work for long periods of time on small, low-voltage batteries.

KINDS OF TRANSISTORS

The two most common kinds of transistors are the *n-p-n transistor* and the *p-n-p transistor*. They are often called *bipolar transistors* because their operation depends on the movement of both holes and electrons. These transistors are made by combining n-type and p-type materials. The materials are arranged as two diodes connected in a "back-to-back" fashion. This arrangement forms three regions called the *emitter*, the *base*, and the *collector*. These regions are identified by the symbols *E, B,* and *C* (Fig. 22-2). The regions of a transistor are joined to wire leads or to pins, which connect the transistor to the circuit (Fig. 22-3).

Fig. 22-2. Transistor construction: (A) basic arrangement of materials; (B) typical construction of low-power, silicon-diffused n-p-n planar transistor; (C) typical construction of germanium alloy p-n-p power transistor

177

POWER TRANSISTORS

TO-3   TO-36   TO-5

C (CASE)   INDEX PIN

E   B   E   B   B   E

C (CASE)

TO-92   TO-98

B   C   C

E   C   E   B   E   B

Fig. 22-3. Common n-p-n and p-n-p transistor cases and a baseview identification of leads

Transistors enclosed in metal cases often have a fourth lead known as the *shield lead*. This lead is internally attached to the case and connected to a common point in a circuit. The metal case shields the transistor from nearby electrostatic and magnetic fields.

Symbol Interpretation. There is a convenient way to remember whether the symbol for a junction transistor represents the n-p-n or the p-n-p type. Note in what direction the arrow that stands for the emitter is pointing. If the arrow points away from the base, it can be thought of as "not pointing n." The symbol thus represents an n-p-n transistor. If the arrow points toward the base, it can be thought of as "pointing n." This symbol thus represents a p-n-p transistor (see Fig. 22-2A).

Identification. Most transistors are identified by a number-letter code, such as 2N, followed by a series of numbers as, for example, 2N104, 2N337, and 2N2556. Other transistors are identified by a series of numbers or by a combination of numbers and a letter, such as 40050, 40404, and 4D20.

Transistor Manuals. Transistor identification codes do not indicate whether the device is of the n-p-n or the p-n-p type. Such technical data are found in *transistor manuals* or *specification sheets*. These manuals also give information about the use of transistors in different kinds of circuits. Transistor outline drawings provide detailed information on their size, shape, and connections. The transistor connections (leads) usually are identified by a bottom view of the base of the transistor (Fig. 22-3).

Substitution. N-p-n and p-n-p transistors can never be directly substituted for each other. However, transistors can usually be replaced with other transistors that have different identifications but are designed to perform the same function. A listing of transistors that can substitute for other transistors is given in *transistor substitution guides* or *manuals*.

OPERATION OF THE TRANSISTOR

An *amplifier* is a device or circuit that can increase the value of a voltage or current. A transistor can act as an amplifier device. This is because a small signal in its input circuit can control a much larger signal in its output circuit. This action is called *power gain*. Voltages, called *bias voltages,* are applied to those parts of the transistor that form the input and the output circuits. When the bias voltage of the input circuit is varied, the transistor behaves as a variable resistor, the resistance of which increases or decreases.

The n-p-n Transistor. The most common transistor amplifier circuit is called a *common-emitter circuit* (Fig. 22-4A). It is so named because the emitter is common to, or is a part of, both the input and output circuits.

In this circuit, the base-emitter p-n junction of the input circuit is forward-biased by battery B1. Battery B2, which has a higher voltage than battery B1, is connected across the transistor from the collector to the emitter in the output circuit. This makes the collector more positive with respect to the emitter than the base is positive with respect to the emitter. The base is then negative with respect to the collector. The base-collector p-n junction is reverse-biased.

With the base-emitter p-n junction forward-biased, free electrons in the emitter move toward the junction. At the same time, holes within the base move toward the junction (Fig. 22-4B). Some of the holes and electrons combine in the area near the junction. This produces a current in the external base-emitter circuit. The base region is very thin. Thus, most of the electrons that move toward the base-emitter junction pass through it and into the collector. There these electrons are attracted to the positive terminal of battery B2.

At the same time, electrons from the negative terminal of battery B2 move into the emitter. The current in the external collector-emitter output circuit is much greater than the current in the input circuit. The circuit therefore acts as an amplifier.

Control of Output Current. There is another very important feature of the transistor amplifier circuit. The output current can be controlled by varying the current in the input circuit. How this can be done is shown in Fig. 22-5. Here a potentiometer R1 is connected across cell B1 in the input circuit. As the sliding arm moves toward point a, the base-emitter p-n junction becomes less and less forward-biased. As a result, the current in the input circuit decreases. This causes a greater decrease of current in the output circuit.

The p-n-p Transistor. When a p-n-p transistor is used in an amplifier circuit, the polarities of the bias voltages applied to the base-emitter and the base-collector p-n junctions are opposite to those in the n-p-n transistor circuit (Fig. 22-6A). As in the n-p-n transistor circuit, this causes the base-emitter junction to be forward-biased and the base-collector junction to be reverse-biased.

In this circuit, holes within the emitter move toward the base-emitter p-n junction. Electrons within the base also move toward the junction. Some of the holes and electrons combine in the area near the junction. However, most of the holes pass through the base and into the collector (Fig. 22-6B). Here the holes are attracted to the end of the collector connected to the negative terminal of battery B2. As this continues, electrons from the negative terminal of the battery enter the collector to combine with the holes. At the same time, an equal number of electrons within the emitter break their electron-pair bonds and enter the positive terminal of the battery. This again produces a much greater current in the external output circuit than is in the input circuit.

Fig. 22-4. A common-emitter n-p-n transistor amplifier circuit: (A) circuit diagram; (B) electron flow

Fig. 22-5. Basic method of controlling the output current in a transistor circuit

Fig. 22-6. A common-emitter p-n-p transistor amplifier circuit: (A) circuit diagram; (B) electron flow

PRACTICAL AMPLIFIER CIRCUITS

A simple, yet practical, one-transistor amplifier circuit is shown in Fig. 22-7. Note that, in this circuit, the bias voltages applied to the p-n-p transistor are supplied by a single source of energy, battery B1. Resistor R1 acts as a current limiter to provide the proper base-bias current. As in any transistor amplifier circuit, the base-collector p-n junction is reverse-biased.

The input signal from an audio-frequency source, such as a microphone, is applied to the input circuit. It is coupled to the base of the transistor through capacitor C1. As the input-signal voltage varies in value and reverses in polarity, it aids and opposes the forward bias applied to the base-emitter junction of the transistor by the battery. This causes the current in the input circuit to vary in direct proportion to the audio signal. It causes the larger output current to vary in the same way.

As the current in the output circuit changes in value, the voltage drop across R2 in the output circuit also changes in value. The transistor, the resistor R2, and the battery form a series circuit. Therefore, as the output current increases, the voltage drop across resistor R1 increases. The output voltage across the transistor, from collector to emitter, decreases. When the current in the output circuit decreases, the voltage drop across R1 decreases. The output voltage increases. The changes in the output-signal voltage are greater than those in the input-signal voltage. Thus, the input signal has been amplified. The amplified output voltage is then applied to the headset. There it is changed into sound waves. In more powerful amplifier circuits, two or more transistors are used. They are connected so that the output signal of each transistor is applied to the input circuit of the next transistor. Each transistor acts as an amplifier. Thus, this provides a much greater voltage amplification of the original input signal.

WORKING WITH TRANSISTORS

Although transistors are rugged devices, they can be damaged. Too much heat can permanently damage the crystal-lattice structure of the material.

Heat Sink. Transistors that must conduct large amounts of current are often mounted on *heat sinks* to keep them from overheating (Fig. 22-8). A heat sink absorbs heat from a transistor and dissipates it, or throws it

Fig. 22-7. Schematic diagram of a one-transistor common-emitter amplifier circuit. The transistor is identified by the letter Q.

off, more quickly than the transistor itself could. This lets the transistor work at a lower temperature.

Connections. Transistors are connected to a circuit in one of two ways. Either their leads are soldered to circuit terminals, or they are plugged into transistor sockets (Fig. 22-9). Sockets make it easier to put in or take out transistors. They also eliminate the danger of overheating the transistors. Overheating can happen when the leads are soldered to the circuit.

When soldering a transistor lead, it is best to use a soldering iron that does not produce more heat than is needed to do the job. A soldering iron rated at 30 to 50 W is usually hot enough. A heat sink should always be attached to a transistor lead that is being soldered. This can be the jaws of a longnose pliers or some other kind of heat sink (Fig. 22-10). A transistor should always be taken out of a socket when a socket terminal is being soldered or unsoldered.

Bias Voltages. Never put a transistor into a circuit until you are sure the right values of bias voltages will be applied to its terminals. As the base-emitter bias voltage in either the n-p-n or p-n-p transistors moves toward the collector voltage supply, the transistor is turned on. As the base voltage moves away from the collector voltage, the transistor is turned off. A base-emitter voltage, for example, is established usually midway between the cut-off and maximum region of operation. For amplifier operation, the base-emitter dc bias is approximately 0.3 V for germanium transistors and 0.6 V for silicon transistors. Excessive voltage applied to a p-n junction of a transistor will cause the transistor to conduct more current than it can handle safely. A transistor should never be taken out of or put into a live circuit. Otherwise, damaging surges of current can pass through the transistor.

Correct Polarity. A transistor can be damaged if bias voltages of the wrong polarity are applied to it. The danger of such damage is much less with common-emitter circuits. Nevertheless, it is always a good idea to check carefully to see that the transistor is properly connected before applying voltage to the circuit. This is particularly true with circuits that have been built in the shop and are being used for the first time.

TESTING TRANSISTORS

Transistors often become defective because of overheating. Overheating is caused by too much current flowing through the base-to-emitter diode section, the base-to-collector diode section, both these sections, or from emitter to collector. As with diodes, overheating seriously disrupts the crystal-lattice structure. This may result in either an open or a short circuited transistor.

Transistor Tester. One kind of transistor tester is shown in Fig. 22-11. Such a tester indicates transistor leakage and gain. Too much leakage occurs when a transistor conducts more than a normal amount of re-

Fig. 22-8. Power transistors mounted on a heat sink (*International Electronic Research Corporation*)

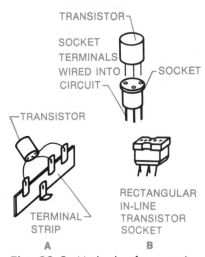

Fig. 22-9. Methods of connecting transistors: (A) leads soldered to circuit; (B) transistor plugged into socket

Fig. 22-10. Using a simple heat sink made of a small piece of sheet metal and an alligator clip

Fig. 22-11. Portable transistor tester (*Sencore, Inc.*)

verse-bias current between any two of its electrodes. The *current gain* of a transistor, referred to as *beta* (β), is the ratio of the collector current to the base current in a common-emitter circuit. Most transistor testers can be used to make either in-circuit or out-of-circuit tests.

Testing with an Ohmmeter. A transistor can be tested with an ohmmeter. If the transistor being tested is wired into a circuit, it should be isolated from the circuit by disconnecting its base lead. The ohmmeter, adjusted to a low or medium ohms range, is connected between the base and the emitter. The resistance reading is noted. The ohmmeter leads to the base and to the emitter are then reversed. If the resistance between the base and the emitter is significantly higher in one direction than in the other, the base-emitter diode section of the transistor can be assumed to be in good condition (Fig. 22-12). To test the base-collector diode section, the same procedure is followed, with the ohmmeter connected to the base and to the collector. As a final test, the ohmmeter is connected between the emitter and the collector.

If any of these tests show direct continuity, the transistor probably has a short circuit. If any of the tests show infinite resistance, the transistor is open. If there is some doubt about the accuracy of the ohmmeter test, recheck the transistor with a transistor tester.

CAUTION

Some ohmmeters on the R × 1 range, can supply enough voltage to damage some transistors. Also, some ohmmeters supply enough voltage on the highest range to break down transistor junctions.

Fig. 22-12. Testing n-p-n and p-n-p transistors with an ohmmeter

Test your knowledge by writing, on a separate sheet of paper, the word or words that most correctly complete the following statements:

1. N-p-n and p-n-p transistors are often called _____ transistors.
2. The three electrodes of an n-p-n or a p-n-p transistor are the _____, the _____, and the _____.
3. The arrow on the emitter of a p-n-p transistor symbol points _____ the base.
4. A transistor amplifier circuit in which the emitter is a part of both the input and output circuits is called a _____ circuit.
5. The n-p-n and p-n-p transistors are operated with their base-collector p-n junction _____-biased.
6. The input signal to a transistor amplifier stage is applied between the _____ and the _____ of the transistor.

1. What is a transistor?
2. What is the purpose of the shield in a transistor?
3. What is the purpose of an amplifier device or circuit?
4. Explain the basic operation of an n-p-n transistor.
5. Explain the basic operation of a p-n-p transistor.

FOR REVIEW AND DISCUSSION

6. What is the purpose of a heat sink?
7. Describe two ways of connecting transistors into circuits.
8. What precautions must be observed when soldering transistor leads?
9. What is meant by the beta of a transistor?

INDIVIDUAL-STUDY ACTIVITY

Give a demonstration showing your class how the condition of transistors can be tested with the use of an ohmmeter alone and with a commercial transistor tester.

UNIT 23 Special Devices and Integrated Circuits

In addition to the popular semiconductor silicon diodes and junction transistors, there are other solid-state rectification, current-control, light-sensitive, and amplifying devices. These include special forms of rectifiers, the field-effect transistor, and photocells. Another important solid-state product is the *integrated circuit*. An integrated circuit contains a large number of components built into tiny chips, or wafers, of certain materials.

DETECTOR DIODE

The *detector diode* is a semiconductor device used in radio and television circuits to produce a rectifying action known as *audio detection*, or *demodulation* (Fig. 23-1). This results in the separation of an audio signal (voice or music) from a high-frequency carrier signal. Carrier

SYMBOL

A

GERMANIUM CRYSTAL

CATWHISKER

B

Fig. 23-1. Germanium "crystal" detector diode: (A) typical diode; (B) interior construction (*Ohmite Manufacturing Company*)

signals are used in radio, television, and other communications systems. In order for a carrier signal to carry information, it is *modulated*, or made to vary, according to varying voice or music signals. These signals are mixed with or placed on the carrier signal at a broadcasting station.

A basic amplitude-modulated (AM) detector circuit is shown in Fig. 23-2. In this circuit, the modulated carrier signal is applied to detector diode CR1. This diode acts as a rectifier. As a result, a pulsating direct current passes through resistor R1. The value of this current varies according to the variations of the modulated carrier signal. This causes a voltage that represents the audio-modulating signal to be present across the resistor and the output of the detector circuit.

Fig. 23-2. Diode AM detector circuit

MODULATED INPUT SIGNAL

DETECTED SIGNAL PULSES

AUDIO SIGNAL OUTPUT

SILICON CONTROLLED RECTIFIER

The *silicon controlled rectifier* (SCR) is a four-layer semiconductor device equipped with three external connections. These are the *anode,* the *cathode,* and a control electrode called the *gate* (Fig. 23-3). Like the silicon diode, the silicon controlled rectifier conducts current in only one direction, from cathode to anode. However, the exact time at which it will begin to conduct, when an alternating voltage is applied between the anode and the cathode, can be controlled by applying a positive trigger voltage to the gate.

An example of a silicon controlled rectifier circuit is shown in Fig. 23-4. In this circuit, the amount of control voltage applied to the gate can be varied by adjusting variable resistor R1. As the control voltage is varied, the silicon controlled rectifier can be made to conduct early or late during the positive alternation. Early conduction produces the largest load current. Late conduction gives less load current. Because of this current-control feature, silicon controlled rectifiers are used in lamp-dimmer circuits and in speed controls for motors.

The silicon controlled rectifier is one of a group of devices commonly called *thyristors*. These are generally used in switching or current-control circuits in which a trigger voltage is applied to their control electrode.

CATHODE

GATE

ANODE

A

SYMBOL

ANODE

GATE

CATHODE

B

CATHODE

ANODE

GATE

Fig. 23-3. Silicon controlled rectifiers: (A) stud-mounted; (B) plastic-case (*International Rectifier*)

184

FIELD-EFFECT TRANSISTOR

In one common kind of *field-effect transistor* (FET), the control electrode is the *gate*. This is a region of p-type semiconductor material that forms an island within a block of n-type semiconductor material. The two other electrodes, the *source* and the *drain,* are the ends of the n-type material (Fig. 23-5).

When a direct voltage that makes the gate negative with respect to the source is applied to the transistor, an electrostatic field is created about the gate. This field acts on free electrons within the n-type material and limits current flow through the transistor from source to drain. As the voltage between the gate and the source is decreased, making the gate less negative with respect to the source, the transistor conducts more current from source to drain.

An amplifier circuit with one field-effect transistor is shown in Fig. 23-6. In this circuit, the input signal causes variations of the voltage applied between the gate and the source. As a result, greater variations of voltage appear across the output circuit. Therefore, the transistor acts as a voltage amplifier. Field-effect transistors are used in several kinds of circuits, including those found in audio amplifiers, electronic timers, and test instruments.

LOAD CURRENT WAVEFORM

EARLY SCR CONDUCTION
GIVES MAXIMUM LOAD CURRENT

LOAD CURRENT WAVEFORM

LATE SCR CONDUCTION
GIVES LESS LOAD CURRENT

Fig. 23-4. Simple silicon controlled rectifier current-control circuit

Fig. 23-5. An n-channel field-effect transistor: (A) basic construction; (B) transistor in TO-92 case

THERMISTORS

Thermistors, or thermal (heat) resistors, are devices that are usually designed so that their resistance decreases with an increase in temperature. They are made of compounds called *oxides*. Oxides are combinations of oxygen and metals, such as manganese, nickel, and cobalt. Thermistors come in various shapes, some of which are shown in Fig. 23-7.

Since the resistance of a thermistor varies with temperature, it operates as a heat-controlled resistor. Because of this, a thermistor can be used as a *heat sensor*. This is a device that converts a change in temperature into a corresponding change in the value of current in a circuit.

An example of such a circuit used for temperature measurement is shown in Fig. 23-8. The thermistor is connected in series with an ordinary dry cell and an ammeter. As the temperature around the thermistor changes, the value of the current also changes. The meter scale can be calibrated, or marked off, in degrees so that a direct temperature reading can be made.

Fig. 23-6. Field-effect-transistor amplifier circuit

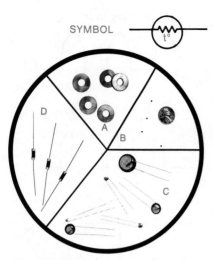

SYMBOL

Fig. 23-7. Thermistors: (A) washer; (B) bead; (C) disk; (D) rod (*Keystone Carbon Company*)

THERMOCOUPLE

A *thermocouple* is a solid-state device used to change heat energy into voltage. It consists of two different kinds of metals joined at a junction (Fig. 23-9A). When the junction is heated, the electrons in one of the metals gain enough energy to become free. These electrons then move across the junction and into the other metal. This movement produces a voltage across the terminals of the thermocouple. Several combinations of metals are used to make thermocouples. These include iron and constantan, copper and constantan, and antimony and bismuth.

Thermocouples are used as heat sensors in thermometer-like instruments called *pyrometers* (Fig. 23-9B). In a pyrometer, the voltage produced by a thermocouple causes current to pass through an electric meter. The meter is calibrated to indicate temperature. A thermocouple can be put in a furnace. As the temperature of the furnace increases, the voltage produced by the thermocouple also increases. As a result, more current passes through the meter. The meter then indicates the increase of current as a higher temperature. Temperatures ranging from 2,700 to above 10,800°F (1500 to 6000°C) can be measured very accurately with pyrometers.

PELTIER EFFECT

A change of temperature occurs at the junction of two different conducting materials when current passes through the junction. The change of temperature (increase or decrease) depends on the direction of the current. This is known as the *Peltier effect*. It is used with various kinds of semiconductor junctions to operate some heating and cooling systems.

INTEGRATED CIRCUITS

The *integrated circuit* (IC) represents a new way of building circuits. In such a circuit, components such as diodes, transistors, resistors, and capacitors either are formed into a common block of a base material, called the *substrate*, or are formed on the surface of the substrate. This process forms a *monolithic*, or single, block of material.

In the monolithic integrated circuit, diodes and transistors are formed into the substrate by a diffusion process. This process causes impurities to spread into given areas of the substrate. This creates p-type and n-type regions within the substrate. These regions then make up the sections of the diodes and transistors (Fig. 23-10).

In the thick- or thin-film integrated circuit, components such as resistors and capacitors are formed by placing or depositing certain materials on the substrate (Fig. 23-11). Hybrid integrated circuits are made up of components of both the monolithic type and the film type.

An integrated-circuit chip is shown in Fig. 23-12. Circuit assemblies of this size or smaller may have dozens of components. For this reason,

THERMISTOR   AMMETER

Fig. 23-8. A simple circuit using a thermistor as a heat-sensing or temperature measurement device integrated circuits have the very important advantages of being very small and light. This is often referred to as *microminiaturization.*

In its complete form, an integrated-circuit assembly is packaged in some kind of enclosure (Fig. 23-13). Each of these packages may contain the components of a specific circuit, such as an amplifier, or of a combination of circuits.

TYPES OF INTEGRATED CIRCUITS

There are several types, or families, of integrated circuits available today. Some of these types were developed to meet the need for high-speed switching circuits, called *logic gates,* in computers. Logic gates and digital circuits are discussed in Unit 41, "Digital Electronic Circuits." Types, or families, of integrated circuits include: *resistor-transistor logic* (RTL); *diode-transistor logic* (DTL); and *transistor-transistor logic* (TTL). Of these three types, the TTL has been one of the most successful. The TTL type IC is known as the "74 series." Examples of the 74 series integrated circuit are the 7400N and the 74LSO4N. These ICs are used in computers. The functions performed and the descriptions of these and other integrated circuits are available in various manufacturers' specification sheets and catalogs from electronic supply companies. Because of the method of manufacturing the TTL type ICs, the supply voltage is critical to its operation. The TTL supply voltage should be maintained between 4.5 and 5.5 Vdc.

Two other common types, or families, of integrated circuits are the *metallic-oxide semiconductor* (MOS) and the *complementary-metal-*

Fig. 23-9. The thermocouple: (A) basic construction and operation; (B) typical pyrometer thermocouple (*Minneapolis-Honeywell Regulator Company*)

Fig. 23-11. Thick-film integrated circuits (*Raytheon Company*)

Fig. 23-10. Basic fabrication of a monolithic n-p-n transistor

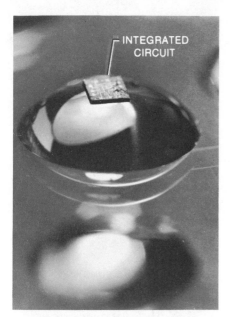

Fig. 23-12. Integrated circuit on a drop of water (*RCA Corporation*)

Fig. 23-13. Integrated-circuit packages: (A) TO-5 case; (B) dual inline case; (C) flatpack (*RCA Corporation*)

oxide semiconductor (CMOS). These integrated circuits are *unipolar* as contrasted to the *bipolar* TTL types. Bipolar TTL transistors have two charge carriers (holes and electrons). The MOS transistor is manufactured either as a p-type with positively charged carriers (holes) or as an n-type with negatively charged carriers (electrons). Since only one type of charge carrier is used, these are called *unipolar*.

Figure 23-14 illustrates the connections and graphic symbols of one type of MOS transistor. In the manufacture of the MOS transistor, a very thin piece of n-type silicon has two p-type regions diffused into it forming two p-type junctions in the n-type substrate. One p-type region is called the *source*; the other, the *drain*. The source and drain are manufactured with a very small gap between them. Over the gap an insulating layer of silicon oxide is formed. On top of the insulating layer, an aluminum layer is formed. This layer is called the *gate*. Notice in Fig. 23-14 that there is no direct connection between the gate and the junctions formed by the drain and source. The conductivity between the source and drain of the MOS transistor is controlled by the voltage on the gate.

When both the p-type channel and n-type channel MOS transistors are manufactured on the same integrated circuit chip, the CMOS family emerges. Some of the advantages of the MOS/CMOS integrated circuit include: low power consumption, small size in comparison to bipolar transistors, and capacity to operate at voltages of 3 to 15 Vdc.

Although the MOS/CMOS integrated circuits have several advantages, they must be handled carefully to prevent damage to the internal electrodes by electrostatic charges. Conducting plastic foam is used to provide an external conducting path for the pins until the IC is soldered in the circuit. Once soldered into a circuit, any damaging electrostatic charges are discharged through the resistances in the circuit.

One of the main advantages of both the MOS and CMOS integrated circuits is that large-scale integration (LSI) can be achieved. This has made possible the manufacture of complex electronic circuits within a single IC package, such as a *microprocessor* (Fig. 23-15). A microprocessor is a LSIC that can perform many functions. Microprocessors are used on some automobiles to monitor selected functions: the time of day, current rate of gas consumption, inside and outside temperature, and battery condition. The microprocessor is also used in automobiles to control the air-fuel mixture and engine timing. The microprocessor is discussed more fully in Unit 43, "Interaction with the Microcomputer."

There are other types of families of integrated circuits, and in the future, newer types no doubt will be developed. A more in-depth discussion, however, of integrated circuits is beyond the scope of this text.

OPTOELECTRONICS

Optoelectronics combines optics (properties of light) and electricity. An *optoelectronic device* is a device that has both optic and electric parts.

The field of optoelectronics is increasing in importance. Optoelectronic components, for example, are being used in the photographic industry, in infrared remote-control systems, in displays on instrument panels, and in signal transmission. Optoelectronic devices are also used in systems that control production, regulate equipment, and position machine tools for processing materials. The following optoelectronic components are discussed: photoconductive cell, light-emitting diodes, photodiodes, phototransistors, and optocouplers.

Photoconductive Cell. A typical cadmium sulfide photoconductive cell is shown in Fig. 23-16. Cadmium sulfide is a semiconductor compound consisting of cadmium and sulfur.

As light strikes the active material of the cell, some of the valence electrons in atoms of the material gain enough energy to escape from their parent atoms. They become free electrons. As the intensity of the light increases, more and more free electrons are made available. The resistance between the terminals of the cell decreases.

The use of a photoconductive cell as a light-sensing device is shown in Fig. 23-17. As light strikes the photocell, its resistance decreases. This allows more current to flow in the circuit. The reading of the ammeter is, at any instant of time, directly related to the intensity of the light.

Photoconductive cells are often used in a system that includes a light source and a relay. In such a system, when the path between the light source and the photocell is interrupted, the current in the relay circuit decreases. The relay, which acts as an on-off switch, is used to control counters, alarm systems, inspection or supervision equipment, and other devices.

Light-Emitting Diodes. The light-emitting diode (LED) is commonly found on many electronic devices as an indicating lamp (Fig. 23-18). It is used, for example, to indicate if a switch is closed or open or if a voltage is high or low. An LED is a p-n junction that emits or gives out light when the junction is forward-biased. The color of the light depends upon the materials used. Some LEDs emit a light that is red, green, yellow, or blue color. Others emit a light that is invisible to the eye, such as an *infrared light*. LEDs that emit invisible light are called *infrared emitters* (Fig. 23-19). Since the light is invisible to the eye, these emitters are used in combination with photodetectors in security systems.

In an LED, the material used that emits a red light is gallium arsenide phosphide (GaAsP). For a green light, gallium phosphide (GaP) is used. The LED is encapsulated, or embedded, in a plastic package. The package is shaped in the form of a lens where the light is emitted. Single lamps or arrays may be used individually or stacked together to form lines of any length. Arrays are used often on meters to indicate which meter scale is being used. Some LEDs have a colorless lens with two-

Fig. 23-14. Metallic-oxide semiconductors: (A) n-type channel and graphic symbol; (B) p-type channel with symbol

Fig. 23-15. Microprocessors (pencil provides comparison for size of integrated-circuit packages)

Fig. 23-16. Broad-area cadmium sulfide photoconductive cell (*RCA Corporation*)

Fig. 23-17. This circuit is an example of how a photoconductive cell can be used as a light-sensing device.

Fig. 23-18. LED lamps (*Siemens Opto*)

color operation, for example, red and green. These LEDs have two diodes and three leads, one of which is a common cathode.

The typical LED uses little electrical power. Selected ratings for one red miniature LED are: power dissipation (85 mW), forward voltage (2.4 Vdc), forward current (35 mA), viewing angle (100°), and a dominant red wavelength of 645 nanometers (nm). This wavelength is within the visible range. The wavelength normally visible to the human eye is approximately 400 to 700 nm. Specification sheets for each type of LED should be examined carefully so that maximum ratings are not exceeded.

Photodiodes. Photodiodes are semiconductor devices that can detect the presence of light (Fig. 23-20). The p-n junction is designed so that light can easily fall upon the light-sensitive, or radiant, area. When light strikes a reversed-biased p-n junction, charge carrier pairs (holes and electrons) are generated. The resulting current is called a *photocurrent*. It is proportional to the intensity of the light striking the radiant sensitive surface. A silicon photodiode can operate as a detector of light when it is reversed-biased. It can also operate as a photovoltaic cell. As a photovoltaic cell, it has a high open-circuit voltage. Because of this characteristic, it is used often in camera exposure meters.

The junction is often encapsulated in a plastic package with a round of flat glass lens exposing the radiant sensitive area. The types shown in Fig. 23-20 are easily mounted on printed circuit boards, and they are compatible with devices using integrated circuits. They can be designed to receive visible as well as invisible light. Photodiodes are used in light controlled regulating equipment, such as twilight switches, fire detectors, perforated tapes, and signal transmission.

Some of the characteristics of one type of silicon photodiode are as follows: maximum power dissipation (250 mW), reverse voltage (7 Vdc), photosensitivity to wavelength of 550 nm (within the visible range), and an open-circuit voltage of 390 mV.

Phototransistor. A phototransistor is similar in operation to the photodiode except that it has a built-in amplifier. It has over 100 times higher photosensitivity than a comparable photodiode. Phototransistors not only respond well to light of incandescent lamps but are also effective when combined with an infrared-emitting diode. Figure 23-21 illustrates this arrangement. Through carefully controlled manufacturing techniques, the emitter's light is focused in a narrow beam as in a flashlight. This beam can be pointed at the radiant sensitive area within a phototransistor. The resulting photocurrent is a function of the base diode current and the current amplification factor of the transistor. The combination of an infrared emitter and phototransistor is used as a beam interrupter in security and counting systems.

Optocouplers. The integrated circuit devices shown in Figure 23-22 are called *optocouplers,* or *isolators.* An optocoupler has two components in a single IC package. One component is a light source such as a light-emitting diode; the other is a photodetector. Together they form an optically coupled pair separated by a transparent insulator. The insulator provides very high isolation breakdown voltage, for example, 2,800 to 6,000 V. Because of this, they are especially suited for interfacing, or connecting, circuits that need to be isolated from each other. Connecting a circuit that operates at a high voltage to a circuit that operates at a low voltage is a common use of these devices. The optocoupler is used also to replace relays and transformers.

The material for the light source (transmitter) is often gallium arsenide (GaAs). The detector (receiver) is generally a phototransistor, but other semiconductors can be used. Figure 23-23 illustrates the application symbol and circuit diagram of one type of optocoupler.

Package and Pin Configuration. Figure 23-24 illustrates the specifications of a dual-channel phototransistor optoisolator. It has an optically coupled pair using gallium arsenide infrared LEDs and silicon n-p-n phototransistors. The drawings illustrate the standard method of providing detailed information on integrated dual-in-line packages (DIPs). These particular devices provide 100 percent minimum current transfer ratio, are compatible with the 7400 series IC, have an isolation breakdown voltage of 7,500 V, and have a coupling capacitance of 0.5 pF. They can be operated in a single channel or dual-circuit arrangement without *cross-talk,* or interference from another channel. The *dot,* or

Fig. 23-19. Infrared emitters (*Siemens Opto*)

Fig. 23-20. Photodiodes (*Siemens Opto*)

Fig. 23-21. Using an infrared emitter and phototransistor: (A) a narrow infrared beam focused on a phototransistor; (B) circuit diagram; (C) graphic symbols

small circle, on the top view identifies pin 1 for both the 8-pin dual and the 16-pin quad package. Other methods, such as a notch, are used to identify the location of pin 1 on a DIP.

OPERATIONAL AMPLIFER

The operational amplifier (op amp) is a very versatile integrated-circuit device. It can perform mathematical operations, such as addition, subtraction, and integration. The operational amplifier can also function as

Fig. 23-22. Optocouplers (*Siemens Opto*)

Fig. 23-23. Optocoupler or photon-coupled isolator: (A) symbol; (B) circuit diagram (top view) pin configuration. The dot identifies where pin 1 is located.

BASE   COLLECTOR   EMITTER

ANODE   CATHODE   NC

B

a comparator, oscillator, and linear amplifier. The op amp is a high-gain amplifier. Open-loop gains of 100,000 to 250,000 are not uncommon. It also has very high input impedance, for example, $10^{12}\ \Omega$. Op amps are designed primarily to be used with external circuit elements.

Figure 23-25 illustrates an internal view of a single op amp. The standard TO-99 package is shown with dimensions and pin identification (Fig. 23-25B). The pin configuration and functional diagram are shown in Fig. 23-25C. Notice that the input pins to the amplifier have an inverting input (pin 2) and a noninverting input (pin 3). The output of the single op amp is connected to pin 6. The power supply is connected to pins 7 and 4. Most op amp applications require a dual power supply, for example, ±12 V. The total supply current for an op amp is low, around 2.5 mA. The high open-loop gain ensures high linearity.

Inverting Input. The inverting input is identified with a negative $(-)$ polarity sign. And the noninverting input is identified with a positive $(+)$ polarity sign. These polarities should not be confused with the power-supply voltages. If the input signal is connected to the inverting input and the noninverting input is connected to the ground, there is a phase inversion at the output. With this type of circuit arrangement, the operational amplifier functions as an inverting amplifier (Fig. 23-26). Resistor R3 provides some feedback voltage from the output to the inverting input. This is known as *negative feedback voltage* because the

Maximum Ratings

Gallium Arsenide LED (each channel) Power Dissipation @ 25°C	150 mW
Derate Linearly from 25°C	1.33 mW/°C
Continuous Forward Current	100 mA
Detector Silicon Phototransistor (each channel) Power dissipation @ 25°C	150 mW
Derate Linearly from 25°C	2.0 mW/°C
Collector-Emitter Breakdown Voltage	30 V
Emitter-Collector Breakdown Voltage	7 V
Collector-Base Breakdown Voltage (IL-1)	70 V

Fig. 23-24. Specifications for the ILD-2 dual-channel phototransistor optoisolator (*Siemens Opto*)

PACKAGE DIMENSIONS IN INCHES AND (mm)

TOP VIEW

PIN NO.	FUNCTION
1	ANODE
2	CATHODE
3	CATHODE
4	ANODE
5	EMITTER
6	COLLECTOR
7	COLLECTOR
8	EMITTER

Fig. 23-25. Operational amplifier: (A) single operational amplifier; (B) outline dimensions; (C) pin configuration and functional diagram (*Analog Devices*)

op amp inverts the phase of the input signal. Although negative feedback reduces the gain somewhat, it improves the stability of the op amp and other operating characteristics.

Noninverting Input. If the input signal is connected to the noninverting input, the output signal changes in phase (in step) with the input signal. When the op amp is connected in this circuit arrangement, the output voltage follows the input voltage.

Fig. 23-26. Operational amplifier (op amp) connected as an inverting amplifier

5. *Experiences with the Photoconductive Cell.* By following the procedure outlined below, you will be able to see the effect an increase in light intensity has on the resistance of a typical photoconductive cell. You can then use the cell to see how it controls a circuit. The relay used in this circuit is a magnetically controlled switch. For more information about relays, see Unit 16, "Electromagnetism."

MATERIALS NEEDED

circuit board, prepunched, 4×6 in. (102×152 mm)
1 photoconductive cell, Clairex no. CL704M or equivalent
1 resistor, carbon-composition or film, 10,000 Ω, $\frac{1}{2}$ W
1 potentiometer, 100,000 Ω, $\frac{1}{2}$ or 1 W
2 transistors, p-n-p, SK-3004, GE-2, or equivalent
1 miniature sensitive relay, coil resistance 500 Ω, sensitivity about 40 mw, spdt, Radio Shack no. 275 B 004 or equivalent
1 pilot lamp, no. 40
1 miniature lamp socket, screw-base
a small desk lamp with a 60-W incandescent light bulb
9-V transistor radio battery or a dc power supply
6-V battery or a dc power supply with a current rating of at least 200 mA
volt-ohm-milliammeter

Procedure

TABLE 23-1 TABLE FOR LEARNING BY DOING NO. 5, "EXPERIENCES WITH THE PHOTOCONDUCTIVE CELL"

Dark Resistance	Normal Resistance	High-Intensity Resistance

1. On a sheet of paper, prepare a table like Table 23-1.
2. Connect the photoconductive cell across the VOM. Using the instrument as an ohmmeter, cover the cell with your hand. Measure its resistance. Record this resistance in the dark-resistance column of the table.
3. Remove your hand from the cell. Measure its resistance. Record this resistance in the normal-resistance column of the table.
4. Turn the desk lamp on. Move it toward the cell. As you do this, you will note that the resistance of the cell gradually decreases to a minimum value. Record this resistance in the high-intensity column of the table.
5. Connect the circuit shown in Fig. 23-27.
6. Put the 60-W lamp about 1 ft (300 mm) from the cell. Adjust the potentiometer until the relay contacts in the pilot lamp circuit are closed. When the relay contacts close, the pilot lamp will light.
7. Turn off the 60-W lamp and all other nearby lamps. This will cause the relay contacts to open. The pilot lamp will go out.
8. By moving the lighted 60-W lamp closer to and farther away from the cell, you will note that the pilot lamp can be made to go on and off. Explain the reason for this.

Fig. 23-27. Diagram for Learning by Doing No. 5, "Experiences With the Photoconductive Cell"

10 k

100 k

V1

R

DS1

RELAY

6 V

9 V

V1   PHOTOCONDUCTIVE CELL

(R)   RELAY

DS1   NO. 40 PILOT LAMP

6. Making Thermocouples. This activity shows how a voltage can be generated by heating the junction of two different kinds of metals.

MATERIALS NEEDED

1 piece each of sheet copper, tinplate, galvanized steel, brass,
  and zinc, 20 to 26 gage, 1 × 4 in. (25 × 102 mm)
1 wax candle or electric heating element
galvanometer with center-zero scale

Procedures

1. Lightly tin both surfaces to be joined. Then solder the copper and tinplate together as shown in Fig. 23-28.
2. Connect the unsoldered ends of the thermocouple to the galvanometer.
3. Heat the junction of the metals with the candle or electric heating element. Observe the reading of the galvanometer. Do not apply heat any longer than is needed for the pointer of the galvanometer to reach a steady, maximum position. Otherwise, the solder may melt.
4. Prepare on a piece of paper a table like the one in Fig. 23-28.
5. Record the maximum reading of the galvanometer on the table. Also indicate on the table the voltage polarity of the thermocouple, as, for example, copper (+) and tinplate (−).

(38.1 mm)

1 1/4"

COPPER   TINPLATE

METALS SOLDERED
TOGETHER

Fig. 23-28. Thermocouple assembly and table for Learning by Doing No. 6, "Making Thermocouples"

195

6. Repeat procedures 1 to 5 with the other combinations of the metals given in the table.
7. Refer to the data given in the table. Which of the metal combinations produced the most current, as indicated by the reading of the galvanometer?

Metals	Maximum Reading of Galvanometer	Polarity	
Copper-tinplate		copper ( )	tinplate ( )
Copper-galv. steel		copper ( )	galv. steel ( )
Copper-brass		copper ( )	brass ( )
Copper-zinc		copper ( )	zinc ( )
Tinplate-galv. steel		tinplate ( )	galv. steel ( )
Tinplate-brass		tinplate ( )	brass ( )
Tinplate-zinc		tinplate ( )	zinc ( )
Galv. steel-brass		galv. steel ( )	brass ( )
Galv. steel-zinc		galv. steel ( )	zinc ( )
Brass-zinc		brass ( )	zinc ( )

SELF-TEST

Test your knowledge by writing, on a separate sheet of paper, the word or words that most correctly complete the following statements:

1. Separating an audio signal from a radio-frequency carrier signal is called _____.
2. A detector diode acts as a _____.
3. The electrodes of a silicon controlled rectifier are the _____, the _____, and the _____.
4. Silicon controlled rectifiers are also commonly called _____.
5. The electrodes of a field-effect transistor are the _____, the _____, and the _____.
6. In a field-effect-transistor amplifier stage, the input signal is applied between the _____ and the _____.
7. Photocells belong to a group of devices often called _____.
8. The energy used to activate a photocell is _____.

9. The word *thermal* means _____.
10. Compounds of oxygen and metals are called _____.
11. A thermistor can be used in a circuit to operate as a _____ controlled resistor.
12. A thermocouple is a solid-state device used to change _____ energy into _____.
13. In a monolithic integrated circuit, transistors and diodes are formed into a substrate by a _____ process.
14. Several types, or _____, of integrated circuits are available today.
15. The TTL-type IC has a supply voltage between _____ and _____ Vdc.
16. A _____ is a LSIC that can perform many functions.
17. A field of study that combines optics and electricity is called _____.
18. A _____ is a p-n junction that emits or gives out light when the junction is forward-biased.

19. The wavelength normally visible to the human eye is approximately _____ to 700 nm.
20. _____ are semiconductor devices that can detect the presence of light.

21. A phototransistor is over _____ times more sensitive to light than a comparable photodiode.

1. Explain how a detector diode performs the function of detection.
2. Describe a silicon controlled rectifier. State the purpose for which this device is commonly used.
3. Draw the schematic diagram of a basic silicon controlled rectifier circuit. Explain how this circuit works.
4. Describe a field-effect transistor.
5. Draw the schematic diagram of a basic field-effect-transistor amplifier circuit. Explain how this circuit works.
6. What characteristic of a photoconductive cell enables it to act as a light sensor?
7. Describe the operation of a light-sensing device containing a photoconductive cell.
8. Explain the operation of a thermistor.
9. Describe the construction of a thermocouple. Explain how this device works.
10. For what purpose are thermocouples commonly used?
11. What is an integrated circuit?
12. Explain the differences between a light-emitting diode and a photodiode.
13. What are the advantages of optocouplers?

1. Give a demonstration showing the basic working action of a silicon controlled rectifier, a photoelectric cell, a thermistor, or a thermocouple.
2. Visit a bakery, a bottling plant, or a packaging company. Learn what electronic control devices are used for counting, inspecting, heat control, and so on. Report to your class on these devices and how they are used in the place you visited.
3. Write a report on the development of integrated circuits. Give an oral report to the class on your findings.
4. Give a demonstration to your class on how an optocoupler works.
5. Analyze the specifications of an operational amplifier. Identify the main characteristics and report your findings to the class.

UNIT 24   Printed Circuits

A *printed circuit* has conductors that are thin strips of metal, usually copper, bonded to a baseboard (Fig. 24-1A). The base is made of laminations, or layers, of special paper or glass mat joined by phenolic or epoxy resins. The electronic components are mounted on the other side of the base. They are connected to the conductors by soldering (Fig. 24-1B). Such a circuit assembly is more compact than one that is hand-wired. It can also be mass-produced efficiently. Because of these advantages, printed circuits are being used in all kinds of electrical and electronic products.

CONDUCTORS

BASE BOARD

A

B

Fig. 24-1. Printed-circuit assembly of a small transistor radio: (A) conductor or wiring side; (B) component side (Photos by *Maxwell*)

In this unit, you will learn about the basic processes used in the industrial manufacture of printed circuits. You will also learn how to make your own printed circuits.

MANUFACTURE OF PRINTED CIRCUITS

In its original form, at least one entire surface of a printed-circuit board is covered with copper foil that is bonded to it. This forms a copper-clad laminate (Fig. 24-2). For some printed circuits, both sides of the base-board are copper clad.

Layout Diagram. Before a printed-circuit board is made, a layout diagram must be prepared. This diagram is a pattern of the conductors that are to be on the board (Fig. 24-3). It shows which surfaces of the copper are to be protected from an etching solution. The solution is used to remove the unwanted copper foil from the board.

The layout diagram shown in Fig. 24-3 was made with adhesive printed-circuit tape. This tape comes in several different sizes and shapes. The tape is applied to a surface in a pattern representing the layout diagram. A layout diagram can also be drawn with ink.

Transfer of the Pattern. The simplest way to transfer a layout to the copper-clad laminate is to lay out the diagram directly on the surface of the laminate with tape. In industrial work, the pattern is usually transferred to the surface of the laminate by screen printing or by a photographic process.

Screen printing is a process by which a *resist* is put on the copper surface through a stencil of the layout diagram. The unwanted copper, the part not protected by the resist, is removed from the laminate with an etching solution.

A layout diagram can also be transferred to a printed-circuit board by using copper-clad material coated with a photosensitive resist compound. First, a picture of the layout diagram is taken. Second, the negative is carefully inspected to make sure that all dark areas are opaque (Fig. 24-4). Third, the negative is placed on the copper-clad laminate and exposed to strong light (Fig. 24-5). Light passes through the light-colored areas of the negative representing the diagram. The light strikes the copper surface in a pattern identical to the layout diagram. These surfaces then resist the effects of the etching solution.

Etching, Cleaning, and Drilling. After the layout diagram has been transferred to the copper surface, the copper-clad laminate is put in an acid or alkaline etching solution. This solution eats through the unpro-

198

tected copper, leaving only the copper under the layout (Fig. 24-6). Next, the tape or resist is simply removed from the base. The remaining conductors are then cleaned. As needed, holes are drilled or punched through the conductors and the base laminate for component wires. The baseboard is now ready for the components to be mounted.

Soldering. When all components have been mounted on the printed-circuit board, the assembly is ready for soldering. This is commonly done in a one-step process known as *wave soldering.* Waves of melted solder are washed into each of the joints that connect component leads to the conductors (Fig. 24-7). This kind of soldering takes only a short time. It is, therefore, well suited for use in mass production. After soldering, the assembly is ready for final inspection and testing.

MODULES

A single unit or board of a printed circuit is often called a *module,* or *circuit pack.* A module may contain the components of a specific circuit, such as a rectifier or an amplifier, or of a combination of circuits. In many electronic devices, modules are designed to be plugged into a

Fig. 24-2. Small sheets of copper-clad laminate with copper on one side (*Graymark Enterprises, Inc.*)

COPPER FOIL

BASE MATERIAL

Fig. 24-3. Printed-circuit layout diagram made with tape

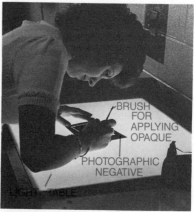

BRUSH FOR APPLYING OPAQUE

PHOTOGRAPHIC NEGATIVE

LIGHT TABLE

Fig. 24-4. Student using a light table and opaque (black coloring fluid) to "touch up" a negative for a printed-circuit board

circuit. Modules of this kind often have plated terminals that are inserted into clip sockets (Fig. 24-8).

Modules can be removed conveniently for inspection and testing. If a module proves to be defective, it can then be repaired or replaced without disturbing any other parts of the circuit system.

ORIGINAL ART

LIGHT SOURCE

PHOTOGRAPHIC NEGATIVE

COPPER-CLAD LAMINATE

Fig. 24-5. Basic photoengraving method of transferring a printed-circuit layout diagram to photosensitive, copper-clad laminate

MAKING YOUR OWN PRINTED CIRCUIT

If the printed-circuit board you are making is simple, you can draw the conductor layout directly on the copper foil with a soft lead pencil. However, if the conductor pattern is complicated, it is best to prepare a layout diagram first. You can then transfer it to the copper-clad laminate. Preparing the diagram is often the most difficult part of making a printed-circuit board. In any case, the final form of the printed-circuit conductor pattern will be determined by the size and number of components, by the overall circuit layout, and by design decisions.

Preparing the Layout Diagram. Though there are no rigid rules for making a layout diagram, the following guidelines should prove helpful:

1. Conductors must not cross each other.
2. The conductors should be about $\frac{1}{16}$ to $\frac{1}{8}$ in. (1.5 to 3.0 mm) wide.
3. There should be a space of at least $\frac{1}{8}$ in. (3.0 mm) between conductors.
4. The conductors, which may be straight or curved, should not be made longer than needed.
5. Conductor terminal points, through which holes will be drilled, should be at least $\frac{3}{16}$ in. (4.5 mm) wide.
6. The circuit layout should allow enough working space on the board without wasting laminate.

A good first step in preparing a layout diagram is to arrange the components of the circuit on a sheet of graph paper according to the schematic diagram. If this arrangement seems suitable for the printed-circuit board, the layout is then roughed in on paper with a pencil or pen. If this proves acceptable, the diagram is put into finished form.

A schematic diagram of a circuit and the layout diagram for the printed-circuit board of this project are shown in Fig. 24-9. Studying and comparing these diagrams will help you design your own layout diagrams.

Fig. 24-6. The effect of the etching process

RESIST OR TAPE (PROTECTIVE COATING)

COPPER FOIL

BASE MATERIAL

TERMINAL POINTS

COPPER FOIL

RESIST

MATERIAL BASE

BEFORE ETCHING

RESIST REMOVED EXPOSING PRINTED COPPER WIRE

COPPER FOIL ETCHED AWAY

AFTER ETCHING

Fig. 24-7. The process of wave soldering being used with a printed-circuit board (*ITT Industrial and Automation Systems*)

Cutting to Size. When the layout diagram has been prepared, the graph paper is cut to the final size. A border of at least ¼ in. (6.5 mm) should be left between any edge of the paper and conductor.

If a sheet of copper-clad laminate of the same size as the diagram paper is not available, it can be cut from a larger sheet. This is best done by using sheet-metal squaring shears or a fine-tooth hacksaw. Copper-clad laminate can be cut with tin snips. However, this will often cause the base laminate material to chip away at the edges. After you have cut the laminate to size, you should clean the copper surface thoroughly by rubbing it lightly with fine-grade steel wool.

Fig. 24-8. Both sides of a plug-in, printed-circuit module used in a computer (*AT&T*)

Transfer of the Pattern. You can transfer the layout diagram to the copper-clad laminate simply by redrawing the pattern on the copper surface, using a resist material. If done carefully, this will be accurate enough for most printed-circuit projects.

If tape resist is used, the correct lengths and shapes of tape are applied to the copper surface. Follow the layout diagram as closely as possible. The best way to apply an asphalt-base (tar) resist is to use a ball-point resist pen (Fig. 24-10). Asphalt-base resist is also available in liquid form. This resist can best be applied to the copper surface with a small artist's brush. The resist should be applied to the copper surface rather heavily. Let it dry for several hours before etching.

Fig. 24-9. Schematic diagram of a code-practice oscillator circuit and a sample of the printed-circuit layout diagram prepared for its construction

Etching. Etching compounds are available either as ready-to-use solutions or as powders that must be dissolved in water. For safe and good etching, never use an etching solution until you know the procedure. Safety glasses should be worn while working with an etching solution.

201

Fig. 24-10. Resist ink pen (*Injectorall Electronics Corporation*)

COMPONENT SIDE

CONDUCTOR — WIRING SIDE

Fig. 24-11. Mounting components on a printed-circuit board

PIN TERMINALS

Fig. 24-12. The transformer used on printed-circuit boards has pin terminals.

For most etching, a glass pan about $1\frac{1}{2} \times 6 \times 10$ in. ($38 \times 152 \times 254$ mm) will serve as a good container for the etching solution. Put the copper-clad laminate into the pan with the copper side up. Then slowly pour the etching solution into the pan to a depth of about 1 in. (25 mm). For best results, the solution should be heated to a temperature of about 100°F (38°C).

After the extra copper has been completely removed from the base laminate, take the printed-circuit board out of the solution. Wash it with water. Let it dry thoroughly. Next, remove the tape, or if asphalt-base resist has been used, remove this resist from the conductors with a suitable solvent. The surfaces of the conductors should then be cleaned by light rubbing with fine steel wool.

Before being etched, a copper-clad laminate is often a little warped. This is usually corrected by the etching process.

Tinning and Drilling. After the conductors of the printed-circuit board have been cleaned, the terminal points of the conductors are lightly tinned. The centers of the terminal points through which holes will be drilled should be center-punched to keep the drill from slipping over the copper surface. When doing this, use light pressure on the punch so that you will not damage the laminate. The holes are then drilled with a high-speed drill no larger than $\frac{1}{16}$ in. (1.59 mm) in diameter.

Mounting of Components. When mounting small components such as fixed resistors and capacitors on the printed-circuit board, first insert their full-length leads through the proper mounting holes. Be sure that the components are mounted so that any information written on them can be easily read. This will help you determine the specifications of any component if you should have to replace it.

The leads are then cut so that the ends extend about $\frac{1}{8}$ in. (3 mm) beyond the wiring side of the board. The lead ends are then bent at right angles. This is so that a larger surface of each end will be in contact with the terminal-point surface to which it is to be soldered (Fig. 24-11).

When mounting semiconductor devices such as diodes and transistors, leave their leads long enough to extend at least $\frac{3}{8}$ in. (10 mm) above the component side of the board. This will let you put a heat sink on each lead while soldering it.

Components such as transformers, potentiometers, variable capacitors, and multisection electrolytic capacitors that are designed for use with printed circuits have pin terminals (Fig. 24-12). These terminals are simply put into holes drilled in the board for them and soldered.

Soldering. Be careful not to use too much heat or solder when soldering component leads to printed-circuit conductors. Enough heat should be applied to the joint to let the solder flow onto all surfaces being joined. Too much heat may cause the conductor to separate from the baseboard (Fig. 24-13A). For most printed-circuit soldering, a light-duty soldering iron (25 or 40 W) will provide enough heat.

Using too much solder may cause it to flow to another conductor or terminal (Fig. 24-13B). Printed-circuit solders are in wire form. Fine work usually requires small-diameter solder wire. A 60/40 solder (60 percent tin, 40 percent lead) is normally acceptable for printed-circuit work.

REPAIR OF PRINTED CIRCUITS

It often takes a trained technician to troubleshoot and repair printed circuits. However, as a part of your electricity and electronics course, you may have an opportunity to do some printed-circuit repair work. This can give you interesting and valuable experience.

Repair jobs commonly done on printed circuits are replacing defective components, resoldering loose solder joints, and repairing broken conductors. Loose joints and conductor breaks are usually caused by dropping or bending a printed-circuit board.

The most important rule for doing any printed-circuit repair is not to use too much heat while soldering or desoldering. Too much heat will very often seriously damage conductors. Again, a light-duty soldering iron of 25 or 40 W is best.

Fig. 24-13. Printed-circuit defects caused by excessive heat or solder: (A) *delamination,* or separation, of the conductor from the surface of a board; (B) short circuits in adjacent conductors caused by excess solder

Replacing Components. Usually, the hardest part of replacing components is removing the defective components from the printed-circuit board. This must be done very carefully to keep from damaging conductors.

One way to remove a component such as a fixed resistor or capacitor is simply to cut its leads as near to the ''body'' of the component as possible. The leads of the replacement component are then soldered to the wire stubs (Fig. 24-14). This method is particularly good when the wiring side of the board cannot be conveniently reached.

When the wiring side of a printed-circuit board can be reached, a component can be replaced by desoldering its leads and slowly pulling them from the mounting holes. The leads of the replacement component are then put into the mounting holes and soldered into place (see Fig. 24-11). It may be necessary to melt the solder around the mounting hole before putting in the leads. This method makes for a neater job.

Fig. 24-14. Replacing a defective printed-circuit component: (A) cut the leads of the defective component; (B) solder the leads of the replacement component to the wire stubs.

Removing components such as potentiometers and multisection electrolytic capacitors that have fixed terminals is a more difficult job. In this case, the molten solder must be completely removed from all the terminal joints before the component itself can be taken out. Otherwise, a desoldered terminal joint will become resoldered while another joint is being heated. This problem can be solved by using a *desoldering tool*. It consists of a soldering iron and a suction device. First, the solder on a joint is melted with the hollow-tip soldering iron. The molten solder is then removed by suction into the rubber syringe bulb (Fig. 24-15). After all the terminals of a component have been desoldered in this way, the component can be easily taken out of the printed-circuit board.

Fig. 24-15. Using a desoldering-resoldering tool (*Enterprise Development Corporation*)

Fig. 24-16. Repairing broken conductors on a printed-circuit board

Loose Solder Joints. Loose solder joints on a printed-circuit board can often be repaired by reheating the joint without using more solder. If more solder must be put on a joint, this should be done carefully to keep any from flowing to a nearby terminal or conductor.

Broken Conductors. If the break in a conductor is a thin crack, it can usually be filled in with solder (Fig. 24-16A). On some printed-circuit boards, the conductors are coated with a kind of varnish that must be taken off before the crack can be soldered. This can be done by light rubbing with fine sandpaper or by light scraping with a knife blade.

A broken printed-circuit conductor can also be repaired by "bridging" over the break with hookup wire connected to the conductor terminal points (Fig. 24-16B). This method is best when a piece of a conductor has been destroyed or badly damaged.

Test your knowledge by writing, on a separate sheet of paper, the word or words that most correctly complete the following statements:

1. The conductors of a printed circuit are usually thin _____ of copper that are _____ to a baseboard.
2. Printed-circuit assemblies can be _____ efficiently.
3. The original form of the base on which a printed circuit is to be built is called _____.
4. The layout diagram is a pattern of the _____ that are to be used on a printed-circuit board.
5. In industrial work, the layout diagram is transferred to the surface of copper-clad laminate by _____ or by a _____ process.
6. The process for removing extra copper from a printed-circuit board is called _____.
7. A one-step manufacturing process for soldering components to a printed-circuit board is called _____ soldering.
8. A single printed-circuit unit is often called a _____.
9. A _____ is often used to coat conductor surfaces prior to etching.
10. Too much heat can cause a conductor on a printed-circuit board to _____ from the base.

FOR REVIEW AND DISCUSSION

1. Describe a printed-circuit assembly.
2. State two advantages of printed-circuit assemblies, as compared to those constructed by conventional hand wiring.
3. How is a printed-circuit layout diagram used?
4. State three ways in which a layout diagram can be transferred to a copper-clad laminate to make a printed circuit board.
5. What is a resist? How is it used in making a printed-circuit board?

INDIVIDUAL-STUDY ACTIVITY

You may wish to experiment with a technique of making an inexpensive printed circuit for your project using self-adhesive paper and nail polish as the resist. You will find that the self-adhesive paper sticks nicely to a copper-clad surface. Use carbon paper to transfer your circuit layout to the self-adhesive paper. With a sharp knife, cut along the printed circuit lines on your layout. Peel off the adhesive paper that represents the printed-circuit areas. This exposes the copper-clad surface that will form the printed circuit. Cover this exposed area with nail polish. When the nail polish dries, remove the remaining self-adhesive paper. Carefully inspect the copper surface to make sure it is free of all the adhesive paper. Etch the board. After the printed-circuit board is etched, clean off the nail polish with nail polish remover and fine-grade steel wool to expose the printed circuit. Discuss your results with the class.

ELECTRICAL WIRING: MATERIALS, TOOLS, AND PROCESSES

UNIT 25 Wires and Cables

SOLID WIRE

STRANDED WIRE

A

COLOR-CODED INSULATION

B

Fig. 25-1. Wires and cable

This unit is about wires and cables that are used as conductors in electrical and electronics circuits. It will help you choose the kind of wire or cable best suited for your job.

Wires used in electrical and electronics work are usually made of soft, annealed copper and are round. They may be solid or stranded, and bare or insulated (Fig. 25-1A). *Stranded wire* is made up of many smaller wires twisted together. It is more flexible than solid wire. Therefore, it is less likely to break if frequently bent or twisted. Several insulated wires contained within a single covering form a *cable* (Fig. 25-1B). Some kinds of flexible cables, especially those used with appliances and lamps, are called *cords*.

WIRE SIZE

An American wire gage (AWG) number tells the size of bare, round wire. This is based on its diameter. The larger the AWG number, the smaller the wire (Fig. 25-2). The American wire gage is also known as the Brown and Sharpe (B & S) wire gage.

Wire Gage. The AWG number and the diameter of wires can be conveniently found with a wire gage (Fig. 25-3). To use this gage, put the

Fig. 25-2. Actual American wire gage sizes

18 16 14 12 10   8   6   4   2   0   00

wire to be measured into the slot that gives the snuggest fit without binding (Fig. 25-4). You then read the AWG number of the wire at the bottom of the slot on one side of the gage. The diameter of the wire is given on the other side.

Circular-mil Area. The cross-sectional area of round wires is often stated in terms of circular mils. One *mil* is one-thousandth (0.001) of an inch (0.0254 mm). One *circular mil* is equal to the area of a circle with a diameter of 0.001 in (0.0254 mm). To find the circular-mil area of a wire, square its diameter, given in mils. Thus, a no. 20 AWG wire (closest standard size—0.80 mm), which has a diameter of 0.03196 in (0.81 mm), has a circular-mil area of 31.96^2, or about 1,022 circular mils.

Fig. 25-3. American standard wire gage (*The L. S. Starrett Company*)

SAFE CURRENT-CARRYING CAPACITY

The safe current-carrying capacity of a wire is that amount of current in amperes that the wire will conduct without overheating or damaging its insulation. The larger the cross-sectional area of a wire, the greater its current-carrying capacity. The safe current-carrying capacity of a wire also depends on its insulating material. For example, a wire insulated with heat-resistant plastic has a greater current-carrying capacity than a wire of the same size insulated with ordinary rubber. The safe current-carrying capacity of a wire is sometimes called the *ampacity* of the wire.

WIRE TABLE

Information about some of the physical and electrical characteristics of wires can be found in a wire table (Table 25-1). Other wire tables give the safe current-carrying capacities of wires insulated with different materials.

Fig. 25-4. Using the wire gage

Although the largest wire size in Table 25-1 is shown as 0000 (also written as 4/0 and pronounced "four-ought"), larger size wires are also in common use. Wires larger than 4/0 are generally used in transmission and distribution systems and in building electrical installations. These larger wires are measured in thousands of circular mils rather than in the AWG number systems.

COMMON WIRES

Many different kinds of wires are used for electrical and electronics wiring jobs. Each of these is best suited for a particular purpose because of its size, insulation, or composition. Some wires are *tinned*, or covered with a thin coat of solder. This prevents corrosion and makes it easier for one wire to be soldered to another.

Hookup Wire. Hookup wire is used mostly for wiring the components in a circuit. It is either solid or stranded copper wire with a plastic

TABLE 25-1 WIRE TABLE FOR STANDARD ANNEALED COPPER

AWG (B & S) Gage	Standard Metric Size (mm)	Diameter in mils	Cross-sectional Area		Ohms per 1,000 ft at 20°C (68°F)	Lbs per 1,000 ft	Ft per lb
			circular mils	square inches			
0000	11.8	460.0	211,600	0.1662	0.04901	640.5	1.561
000	10.0	409.6	167,800	0.1318	0.06180	507.9	1.968
00	9.0	364.8	133,100	0.1045	0.07793	402.8	2.482
0	8.0	324.9	105,500	0.08289	0.09827	319.5	3.130
1	7.1	289.3	83,690	0.06573	0.1239	253.3	3.947
2	6.3	257.6	66,370	0.05213	0.1563	200.9	4.977
3	5.6	229.4	52,640	0.04134	0.1970	159.3	6.276
4	5.0	204.3	41,740	0.03278	0.2485	126.4	7.914
5	4.5	181.9	33,100	0.02600	0.3133	100.2	9.980
6	4.0	162.0	26,250	0.02062	0.3951	79.46	12.58
7	3.55	144.3	20,820	0.01635	0.4982	63.02	15.87
8	3.15	128.5	16,510	0.01297	0.6282	49.98	20.01
9	2.80	114.4	13,090	0.01028	0.7921	39.63	25.23
10	2.50	101.9	10,380	0.008155	0.9989	31.43	31.82
11	2.24	90.74	8,234	0.006467	1.260	24.92	40.12
12	2.00	80.81	6,530	0.005129	1.588	19.77	50.59
13	1.80	71.96	5,178	0.004067	2.003	15.68	63.80
14	1.60	64.08	4,107	0.003225	2.525	12.43	80.44
15	1.40	57.07	3,257	0.002558	3.184	9.858	101.4
16	1.25	50.82	2,583	0.002028	4.016	7.818	127.9
17	1.12	45.26	2,048	0.001609	5.064	6.200	161.3
18	1.00	40.30	1,624	0.001276	6.385	4.917	203.4
19	0.90	35.89	1,288	0.001012	8.051	3.899	256.5
20	0.80	31.96	1,022	0.0008023	10.15	3.092	323.4
21	0.71	28.46	810.1	0.0006363	12.80	2.452	407.8
22	0.63	25.35	642.4	0.0005046	16.14	1.945	514.2
23	0.56	22.57	509.5	0.0004002	20.36	1.542	648.4
24	0.50	20.10	404.0	0.0003173	25.67	1.223	817.7
25	0.45	17.90	320.4	0.0002517	32.37	0.9699	1,031.0
26	0.40	15.94	254.1	0.0001996	40.81	0.7692	1,300
27	0.355	14.20	201.5	0.0001583	51.47	0.6100	1,639
28	0.315	12.64	159.8	0.0001255	64.90	0.4837	2,067
29	0.280	11.26	126.7	0.00009953	81.83	0.3836	2,607
30	0.250	10.03	100.5	0.00007894	103.2	0.3042	3,287
31	0.224	8.928	79.70	0.00006260	130.1	0.2413	4,145
32	0.200	7.950	63.21	0.00004964	164.1	0.1913	5,227
33	0.180	7.080	50.13	0.00003937	206.9	0.1517	6,591
34	0.160	6.305	39.75	0.00003122	260.9	0.1203	8,310
35	0.140	5.615	31.52	0.00002476	329.0	0.09542	10,480
36	0.125	5.000	25.00	0.00001964	414.8	0.07568	13,210
37	0.112	4.453	19.83	0.00001557	523.1	0.06001	16,660
38	0.100	3.965	15.72	0.00001235	659.6	0.04759	21,010
39	0.090	3.531	12.47	0.000009793	831.8	0.03774	26,500
40	0.080	3.145	9.888	0.000007766	1049.0	0.02993	33,410

insulation. The most common sizes range from no. 18 to no. 24 AWG (1.00 to 0.50 mm). Some large wiring jobs are hooked up or connected together with a wire harness. The wire in the harness is preshaped, tied, and wrapped to meet the needs of various applications (Fig. 25-5).

Magnet Wire. Magnet wire is solid wire. It is usually round and is insulated with a thin, tough coating of a varnishlike, plastic compound. This kind of wire is often referred to as *plain enamel* (PE) *magnet wire.* The most common sizes range from no. 14 to no. 40 AWG (1.60 to 0.08 mm). It is called magnet wire because it is used for winding the coils in electromagnets, solenoids, transformers, motors, and generators (Fig. 25-6).

Bus-Bar Wire. Bus-bar wire is solid, tinned, and uninsulated copper wire. Usual sizes range from no. 12 to no. 30 AWG (2.00 to 0.25 mm). It is used as a common terminal for several wires (Fig. 25-7).

Test-Prod Wire. Test-prod wire is a very flexible, stranded wire. It is insulated with rubber or with a combination of rubber and other materials. The most common sizes are no. 18 and no. 20 AWG (1.00 and 0.80 mm). It is used for making the test leads of instruments such as the volt-ohm-milliammeter.

Antenna Wire. Radio-antenna wire is a stranded wire that may be either bare or insulated. Each strand is usually made of Copperweld, which consists of a steel core coated with copper. This gives the wire a high tensile strength, which keeps it from sagging when a length of it is suspended between supports.

Television Lead-in Wire. This is a twin-lead, or two-conductor, wire used for connecting a television receiver to its antenna. The wires are most often made of Copperweld insulated with polyethylene plastic. They are usually contained within an outer jacket, also made of polyethylene (Fig. 25-8A). This allows for precise spacing between the wires. Because of that, they can conduct the maximum amount of signal energy from the antenna to the receiver. Twin-lead wire is also used to connect a frequency-modulation (FM) radio receiver with its antenna. The twin-lead, or two-conductor, wire is also known as a *300-Ω transmission line.*

Another common transmission line used is the 75-Ω coaxial cable. Coaxial cables are used to connect video cassette recorders and other electronic equipment to television receivers. These cables minimize interference from other lines due to the shield that surrounds the center wire.

Modern television receivers usually have two input connectors.

Fig. 25-5. Making a wire harness (*Kurz and Root Company*)

Fig. 25-6. Magnet wire used in a fan motor (*Delco Products Division of General Motors Corporation*)

Fig. 25-7. Bus-bar wire used as a common connecting point in a circuit

Fig. 25-8. (A) Television twin-lead lead-in wire (*Alpha Wire Division of Loral Corporation*); (B) indoor-outdoor matching transformer, reversible

300 OHMS

A

300 OHMS

MATCHING TRANSFORMER

75 OHMS

B

These connectors allow both the 300-Ω and 75-Ω transmission lines to be used when needed. It is important to have a good impedance match between the receiver and the transmission line so that the maximum amount of signal energy received from the antenna can be transferred. It is often necessary to connect a 75-Ω transmission line to a 300-Ω input on a television receiver or vice versa. You can match the different impedances with a *matching transformer*. A matching transformer has two connections: a cable connector for the 75-Ω coaxial cable and two metal screws for connecting the 300-Ω twin-lead line (Fig. 25-8B).

Grounding Wire. Grounding wire is usually a solid, bare wire made of copper or aluminum. It is used for connecting metal cabinets and certain parts of circuits, such as those in a house wiring system, to water pipes or to ground rods.

Building Wire and Cable. Building wire and cable are used to connect the devices and equipment in building wiring systems. These cables and wires are discussed in Unit 31, "Home Electrical Systems."

ELECTRICAL CORDS

Cords are used to connect electrical and electronic equipment and appliances to outlets. Cords are flexible. Thus, they are able to withstand the bending and twisting that occur as portable products are used.

Lamp Cord. The common lamp cord is made up of two parallel, stranded wires. Each wire is covered with rubber or plastic insulation that is joined into a single unit (Fig. 25-9A). The wires in a lamp cord are usually no. 16 or no. 18 AWG (1.25 or 1.00 mm). Lamp cord is used with products such as portable lamp fixtures, light-duty appliances, radios, and television sets.

Fig. 25-9. Electrical cords: (A) rubber-insulated lamp cord; (B) service cord (*General Electric Company*)

A

TYPE SJ CORD

B

Service Cords. Service cords have two or three stranded, bare-copper wires. These wires are insulated with rubber or plastic and put in a round outer jacket, also made of rubber or plastic (Fig. 25-9B). The wires usually range in size from no. 10 to no. 18 AWG (2.50 to 1.00 mm). The most common service cords are listed by the Underwriters' Laboratories as types S, SV, and SJ. These cords are most often used with portable power tools and with medium- and heavy-duty appliances. Service cords often have a separate grounding conductor.

Heater Cord. The wires in a heater cord are insulated with a material that can withstand high temperatures. Such cords are used with heat-producing appliances and with soldering irons and guns. Heater-cord wires are stranded and are usually no. 16 or no. 18 AWG (1.25 or 1.00 mm).

One common kind of heater cord looks much like ordinary rubber-insulated lamp cord. However, its insulation is made of a thermosetting plastic compound that can withstand high temperatures.

COMMUNICATION CABLES

Cables are most often used for connecting components or products that are some distance apart. Cables may be unshielded or shielded. A shielded cable is made up of one or more insulated wires. These are often contained within a sheath of copper wires woven together to form a braid (Fig. 25-10A). This protects the inner wire or wires from undesirable external electric or magnetic fields. It is placed directly beneath the outer covering jacket of a shielded cable. It may or may not serve as one conductor of the cable.

Fig. 25-10. Communication cables: (A) shielded cable; (B) audio cable; (C) coaxial shielded cable (*Alpha Wire Division of Loral Corporation*)

Audio Cable. Audio cable is commonly used in telephone circuits, in intercommunications circuits, and in circuits connecting the loudspeakers of public-address systems to amplifiers. This cable is made up of two or more solid or stranded wires. These are color-coded and placed in an outer jacket of plastic insulation (Fig. 25-10B). Wire sizes range from no. 20 to no. 24 AWG (0.80 to 0.50 mm).

Coaxial Cable. Most kinds of coaxial cable are made up of one stranded copper wire insulated with polyethylene and placed in the center of a copper-braid shield. The outer jacket of the cable is vinyl-plastic insulation (Fig. 25-10C). The braid is one conductor of the cable. Coaxial cable is used, for example, to connect a microphone to an audio amplifier. It is so named because the conductors in the cable have a common axis, or center.

Computer Cables and Connectors. The use of proper cables and connectors is essential to interface a computer with its peripherals. The point of connection between a device and the attached cables is called an *interface* (Fig. 25-11). Printers, disk drives, and modems are called *peripherals* since they are often external to the computer. These external devices are connected by cables to make up the total computer system.

CARD EDGE CONNECTOR (REUSABLE)

HOOD TO FIT 9–PIN PLUG OR SOCKET

9–PIN MALE PLUG

9–PIN FEMALE SOCKET

44–POSITION CARD EDGE SOCKET

25–CONDUCTOR RIBBON CABLE

25–PIN D–TYPE SUBMINIATURE MALE CONNECTOR (REUSABLE)

25–PIN D–TYPE SUBMINIATURE FEMALE CONNECTOR (REUSABLE)

Fig. 25-11. Common connectors for computers and peripherals (*Radio Shack, a Division of Tandy Corporation*)

Because computers generate high frequency in their operation, they must be manufactured to reduce the effects of electromagnetic interference (EMI) and radio frequency interference (RFI). The rules of the Federal Communications Commission set limits on how much "noise" or interference a computer system can legally emit. Since the rules cover the entire system, metallic shields and metallic hood covers are used on the cables and connectors that interface the peripherals with the computer.

212

Figure 25-12 illustrates the details of one type of six-wire twisted pair cable. This type of cable minimizes interference (EMI/RFI) due to its double layer of metallic shielding. Some types of twisted-pair/metallic-shield cables also use special insulation on the wires and the cable jacket. This makes them suitable for applications that extend beyond the standard 50-ft limit between terminal and peripherals. Before building a cable for installing a computer, terminal, or peripheral equipment at distances greater than 50 ft, make sure it offers both EMI/RFI shielding and low capacitance.

Fig. 25-12. Metallic shields reduce electromagnetic and radio interference. (*Black Box Corporation*)

*PVC = POLYVINYL CHLORIDE

CABLE FABRICATION TECHNIQUES

One of the most common types of cable connections used with computers and associated peripherals is the 25-pin D connector shown in Fig. 25-13. In assembling a cable, you should strive to obtain good electrical contact between the pins and the conductors and to minimize interference (EMI/RFI). Two general methods are used to connect a cable to a D-type connector. One method uses *pin insertion*; the other, soldering.

Fig. 25-13. A 25-pin D connector with cable: (A) male connector with hood; (B) female connector with hood (*Black Box Corporation*)

The pin insertion method allows you to service or change the pin locations in the connector. Male and female pins are used. The first task is to determine the number of conductors needed. Although the connector (solder or pin insertion type) has a fixed number of pins, not all pins are needed for a specific installation. To reduce cost, purchase a cable with the number of conductors required.

Figure 25-14 illustrates how individual male pins are connected to the conductors of a cable. A wire cutter/stripper is used to cut back the outer sheath 1 to 1.5 in. (25.4 to 38.1 mm). Each conductor in the cable is stripped to ⅛ to 3/16 in. (3.2 to 4.8 mm) from its end. The stripped conductors will have either a male or female pin/socket crimped to it. Each pin has two crimp locations, called *flags*. The first crimp makes

Fig. 25-14. Crimping a male pin to a conductor in a cable (*Black Box Corporation*)

Fig. 25-15. Assembling a D connector (*Black Box Corporation*)

Fig. 25-16. Attaching a hood to a cable connector (*Black Box Corporation*)

Fig. 25-17. Example of documenting an assembled cable (*Black Box Corporation*)

the electrical connection only with the conductor. The second flag crimps the insulation for strain relief. Special crimping tools are used to crimp the flags so that the connections are secure. Once the necessary crimps are made, a pin insertion/extraction tool is used to insert the pins in the correct shell holes. Male pins should be inserted only into male shells and female pins into female shells (Fig. 25-15).

The last step in fabricating a cable is to attach the hood (Fig. 25-16). The hood has a plastic or metal cover with two or three cover screws (with or without nuts). Some hoods have a strain relief screw. The completed cable shell assembly should be positioned between the two hood pieces and the cover screws inserted and partially screwed into place. Before the cover screws are tightened down, the device attachment washers and screws and the relief screw should be attached. After this is done, the cover screws can be tightened.

The soldering method uses a connector that has the pins embedded firmly within the shell (body) of the connector. The opposite end of each pin has a cup-shaped slot. A wire cutter/stripper is used to cut back the outer sheath of the cable 1 to 1.5 in. (25.4 to 38.1 mm). Strip away about 3/16 in. (4.8 mm) of the insulation from the ends of each conductor. Solder the ends of each conductor into the cup-shaped slot of the proper pin. Care must be used not to short circuit the connections by using too much solder. The hood is assembled as mentioned previously.

One of the most overlooked steps in cable assembly is the proper labeling and documentation of the assembled cable. The cable should have a stick-on label indicating where the pin documentation is located so that anyone can identify the electrical signals associated with each pin. An illustration of a typical master drawing is shown in Fig. 25-17. A male connector is indicated by the arrows pointing out; a female, by the arrows pointing in. The drawing should also identify the cable length, wire size, number of conductors, crossovers, type of connector (male, female, or both), jumpers, and any special information about the cable connection.

*RS-232 SIGNAL	WIRE COLOR	PIN NO		PIN NO	WIRE COLOR	RS-232 SIGNAL
GND	GRN	1		1	GRN	GND
TX	BLK	2		2	RED	TX
RX	RED	3		3	BLK	RX
RTS		4		4		RTS
CTS		5	CROSSOVER	5		CTS
DSR		6		6		DSR
SIG GND	WHT	7		7	WHT	SIG GND
DCD		8		8		DCD
DTR		20		20		DTR

FEMALE SIDE OF CABLE CONNECTOR   JUMPERS   MALE SIDE OF CABLE CONNECTOR

*SEE APPENDIX IN LABORATORY ACTIVITIES MANUAL FOR EXPLANATION OF ABBREVIATIONS FOR SIGNALS

7. The Safe Current-Carrying Capacity of Wires. The amount of current that any wire can conduct safely depends mainly on the wire's cross-sectional area. If too much current flows for that size of wire, the wire becomes overheated. This can damage the insulation and perhaps cause a fire. A simple experiment can show the fire hazard created when undersized wires are used to carry the load current of a circuit.

MATERIALS NEEDED

3½ in. (89 mm) PE magnet wire, no. 18 (1.00 mm)
4 in. (102 mm) PE magnet wire, no. 21 (0.71 mm)
4 in. (102 mm) PE magnet wire, no 25 (0.45 mm)
4 in. (102 mm) PE magnet wire, no. 30 (0.25 mm)
2 in. (51 mm) PE magnet wire, no. 36 (0.125 mm)
1 no. 6 dry cell, 1½ V

Procedure

1. Remove ½ in. (12.7 mm) of insulation from each end of the wires. Join them as shown in Fig. 25-18A.
2. Connect the joined wires to the dry cell as shown in Fig. 25-18B. This connection short-circuits the cell. Therefore, do not leave the wires connected any longer than needed to finish this procedure. Otherwise, the cell will be quickly ruined.

Fig. 25-18. Wiring diagram for Learning by Doing No. 7, "The Safe Current-Carrying Capacity of Wires"

Touch the no. 36 (0.125-mm) wire quickly and carefully. It will be hot enough to cause painful burns.

 CAUTION

215

3. After a few seconds, touch the no. 18 (1.00-mm), the no. 21 (0.71-mm), the no. 25 (0.45-mm), the no. 30 (0.25-mm), and the no. 36 (0.125-mm) wires. Which of these wires is the hottest? Why?
4. Using the power formula $P = I^2R$, explain why each of the wires is heated to a different temperature although the current is the same.

SELF-TEST

Test your knowledge by writing, on a separate sheet of paper, the word or words that most correctly complete the following statements:

1. Stranded wire is more _____ than solid wire.
2. A combination of insulated wires enclosed in a single covering is called a _____ .
3. Some kinds of flexible cables are called _____ .
4. The abbreviation for the _____ is AWG.
5. As the AWG size numbers of round wires increase, the diameters of the wires _____ .
6. The AWG numbers and the diameters of round wires are conveniently found by using a _____ .
7. The circular-mil area of a round wire is found by _____ the diameter of the wire expressed in _____ .
8. The safe current-carrying capacity of a wire is that amount of _____ that the wire will conduct without becoming _____ or _____ .
9. Wires are often tinned to prevent _____ .
10. Copperweld wire consists of a _____ core that is coated with _____ .
11. A television two-conductor antenna lead-in wire is also known as a _____ line.
12. Grounding wires are solid wires made of _____ or of _____ .
13. Heater cords are often insulated with a material that can withstand _____ .
14. Some cables have shields to protect the enclosed conductors from undesirable external _____ or _____ fields.
15. In a coaxial cable, all the conductors have a common _____ .
16. Wires that are preshaped and tied for a specific wiring job are called _____ .
17. Cables and connectors are used to _____ computers with peripherals.
18. Metallic shielding and hoods are used to reduce _____ interference.
19. Two common methods of connecting the wires of a cable to a connector are _____ and _____ .

FOR REVIEW AND DISCUSSION

1. State the difference between a solid wire and a stranded wire.
2. What is meant by a cable?
3. Define and describe the American wire gage.
4. How is a wire gage used?
5. How are circular-mil areas calculated?
6. What is meant by the safe current-carrying capacity of a wire?
7. Why are some wires tinned?
8. How is hookup wire used?
9. Why is it important for electrical cords to be flexible?
10. Name three kinds of electrical cords, and state the purpose for which each is commonly used.
11. Describe a coaxial cable.
12. Why is it important to have a good impedance match between a television transmission line and the television receiver?

INDIVIDUAL-STUDY ACTIVITY

Collect examples of as many different kinds of wires and cables as you can. Mount these on a panel and identify each. Exhibit this to your class. Describe the uses of each wire and cable. Small samples of wires and cables can often be obtained from local dealers or from manufacturers.

UNIT 26 Wiring Tools and Devices

Hand wiring involves using wires to connect the terminals of sockets and other devices from point to point. Integrated circuits and printed circuits have greatly lessened the need for wiring by hand. However, hand wiring is still used in manufacturing and in the repair and servicing of many products. To do hand wiring correctly, you must know about wires. You must also be familiar with the tools and the wiring devices used with circuits. Such knowledge will help you do new wiring or a repair job in a neat, efficient way.

PLIERS

Pliers are an essential wiring tool. There are many different kinds of pliers. The three kinds discussed below are generally used when working with wires.

Diagonal-Cutting Pliers. Diagonal-cutting pliers are only for cutting wires (Fig. 26-1A). They should never be used as a gripping tool or to notch sheet metal. This can damage the cutting jaws. The jaws can also be damaged if they are used to cut hardened iron or steel wires. As with other kinds of pliers, diagonal-cutting pliers are sized according to their length. The common sizes are 4, 5, and 6 in. (102, 127, and 152 mm).

Longnose Pliers. Longnose pliers are used most for gripping and bending small wires. They sometimes have wire-cutting jaws (Fig. 26-1B). The relatively weak jaws of these pliers may be bent out of shape if too much pressure is used to grip objects. Common sizes are 5 and 6 in. (127 and 152 mm).

Because of the shape of the *nose,* or gripping jaw, longnose pliers are very useful for bending wires into a loop. This is often done in fastening the end of a wire to a screw terminal. Pliers having longer and thinner gripping jaws than longnose pliers are often called *needlenose pliers.*

All-Purpose Pliers. These pliers are very handy to have around. Because of the shape of the jaws, they can be used as a nut wrench, stripper, cutter, or crimper (Fig. 26-1C). Common sizes are 5 and 6 in. (127 and 152 mm).

Fig. 26-1. Pliers: (A) diagonal-cutting, spring-return, insulated grips; (B) longnose, spring-return, insulated grips; (C) all-purpose (*Radio Shack, a Division of Tandy Corporation*)

WIRE STRIPPERS

Wire strippers are tools used to remove insulation from wires that are to be joined or connected.

Basic Wire Stripper. A simple wire stripper is shown in Fig. 26-2A. To use this tool, press the blades together until they cut through the insulation of the wire. You then pull the tool away from the wire, thereby removing the insulation. When using this kind of wire stripper, be careful not to press the blades together more than is needed to cut through the insulation. Otherwise, the blades may cut into the wire and weaken it.

Another common kind of wire stripper is shown in Fig. 26-2B. In removing insulation with this tool, it is important to use the right size stripping notch to keep from damaging the wires.

Automatic Wire Stripper. To use an automatic wire stripper, put the wire into the right size notch on the cutting jaws. Then squeeze the handles. This will cause the jaws to separate. The cutting jaws will cut through the insulation. At the same time, the clamping jaws will pull the insulation from the wire (Fig. 26-2C). Automatic wire strippers are very useful for removing tough plastic or fabric insulation from wires. Since they do not require any pulling, they are also good to use with wires that have one end connected to a terminal.

Other Stripping Methods. Thermal wire stripping involves using heat to remove insulation. Thermal wire strippers have adjustable, electrically heated "jaws." These melt through the insulation. The insulation of some wires, including some magnet wires, can be removed by the heat of a soldering iron without further stripping or cleaning of any kind. Wires with enamel or varnish insulation are often stripped chemically with a paint solvent.

USING PLIERS AS WIRE STRIPPERS

With practice, you can learn to use the wire-cutting jaws of pliers as a wire stripper, particularly on wires with a thin plastic insulation. To do this, first put a wire between the jaws. Then apply enough pressure to the handles to allow the jaws to cut through the insulation. Then pull the pliers away from the wire to remove the insulation (Fig. 26-3A). Be sure to use just the right amount of pressure so that the wire itself will not be nicked or cut.

When pliers are used to strip a wire covered with a heavy plastic or fabric insulation, it is often necessary to first crush the insulation. With most pliers, this can be done by inserting the wire between the handles just behind the pivot point and by applying enough pressure (Fig. 26-3B). The crushed insulation can then be either picked off the wire or removed with the cutting jaws.

PLUGS AND JACKS

Electrical plugs provide a convenient way to connect devices to a circuit. This is done by inserting a plug into a jack or a receptacle wired to the circuit.

Fig. 26-2. Wire strippers: (A) basic wire stripper; (B) notch-type wire stripper; (C) using the automatic wire stripper (*Ideal Industries, Inc.*)

Fig. 26-3. Using pliers as wire strippers

PAPER
COVER

UNDERWRITERS' KNOT

B

Attachment Plugs. Attachment plugs are used with lamp and service cords for making connections to outlets. On many products, molded attachment plugs are used (Fig. 26-4A). On others, attachment plugs are fastened to a cord by pressure contacts or screw terminals. Attachment plugs with screw terminals are wired as shown in Fig. 26-4B. To do this, first remove about ½ in. (12.7 mm) of the insulation from each wire of the cord. Then twist each bare end of the stranded wire tightly so that the strands form a compact bundle. Apply solder to the tips to keep them from separating. Otherwise, a loose strand might cause a short circuit. Wrap each wire around a terminal screw in a clockwise direction. This tends to keep the wire under the screwhead as the screw is tightened.

When space permits and when an attachment plug does not have a cord clamp, tie the two wires in an *Underwriters' knot*. This will keep the wires from pulling loose from the screw terminals if the cord is pulled (Fig. 26-5).

Fig. 26-5. Tying an underwriters' knot

FIRST STEP   SECOND STEP   THIRD STEP   FOURTH STEP

Banana Plugs and Jacks. Banana plugs and jacks are commonly used for connecting test leads to instruments and for other connections (Fig. 26-6). Wire leads are held in the plugs by set screws, pressure, or soldering.

Tip Plugs and Jacks. Tip plugs and jacks are used with test instruments (Fig. 26-7A). Because they are small, these devices are often used in spaces where other kinds of connecting devices could not fit.

PLUG

JACK

Fig. 26-6. Banana plug and jack

Phono Plugs and Jacks. Phono plugs and jacks are often used for connecting the phonograph cartridge output to the input of the amplifier and for making other audio-line connections (Fig. 26-7B). These devices are usually connected to shielded cables by soldering.

Phone Plugs and Jacks. Standard phone plugs and jacks are used for connecting headsets to radio receivers and audio amplifiers (Fig. 26-7C). The standard plug prong and the jack socket of these devices are ¼ in. (6.35 mm) in diameter.

Miniature phone plugs and jacks are used for the same purposes. They are also similar in construction. However, the prong and socket are ⅛ in. (3.18 mm) in diameter.

Open-Circuit and Closed-Circuit Phone Jacks. Phone jacks may be either open-circuit or closed-circuit (Fig. 26-8A). The closed-circuit jack allows a circuit to be completed through the jack contacts when a plug is not inserted into it. If, for example, a headset is plugged into a closed-circuit jack of a radio receiver, the circuit is completed through the headset. If, on the other hand, the headset is not plugged into the jack, the radio circuit is completed to the loudspeaker (Fig. 26-8B).

Fig. 26-7. Plugs and jacks: (A) tip; (B) phono; (C) phone

Fig. 26-8. Phone jacks: (A) symbols for open- and closed-circuit phone jacks; (B) operation of a closed-circuit phone jack

MICROPHONE CONNECTORS

Microphone connectors are used for connecting the coaxial cables of microphone cords to amplifiers (Fig. 26-9). They are also commonly used for connecting leads to various kinds of test instruments.

Fig. 26-9. Microphone connectors

WIRE NUTS

Wire nuts are devices used for making solderless connections in house wiring systems, motors, and various appliances (Fig. 26-10A).

Fig. 26-10. Wire nuts

221

To use a wire nut, strip about ⅜ in. (10 mm) of insulation from the ends of the wires to be connected. Put the wires into the wire nut. Then firmly screw the nut over the wires (Fig. 26-10B). Wire nuts come in different sizes. The size needed depends on the number and sizes of wire to be connected. Figure 26-10C shows two wires being inserted into a wire nut.

CLIPS

Various kinds of clips are used for making temporary wire connections to circuits. *Alligator clips* have spring-loaded jaws. These allow a firm wire connection to be made to a terminal point (Fig. 26-11A). They are used with instrument test leads and other temporary wiring systems.

Fahnestock clips have a spring lever. This is pushed down while a wire is inserted into the clip hasp (Fig. 26-11B). For a good connection, a wire must be thoroughly cleaned before it is inserted into such a clip. Fahnestock clips are often used for making temporary connections to experimental models.

Fig. 26-11. Clips: (A) alligator; (B) Fahnestock

TERMINAL STRIPS AND LUGS

Lug *terminal strips* consist of solder lugs and a mounting lug or lugs, usually fastened to a thin phenolic strip (Fig. 26-12A). They provide convenient solder terminals for wires and component leads (Fig. 26-12B). Whenever possible, soldered connections should be made on terminal strips.

Terminal, or *wire, lugs* are used for connecting wires to screw terminals. These lugs come in solder and solderless versions (Fig. 26-13A and B). Solderless lugs are fastened to the ends of wires with a terminal, or crimping, tool, as shown in Fig. 26-13C.

CLAMPING AND STRAPPING DEVICES

Clamping and strapping devices are used to hold wires and cables in place. They make the job look neater and lessen the physical strain on individual wires.

Cable clamps are made of either metal or plastic (Fig. 26-14A). They are used to secure wires and cables to the surfaces of metal, wood, or plastic.

Insulated staples are a form of wire or cable clamp with an insulating saddle. They are used to secure wires and cables to wood surfaces (Fig. 26-14B).

Plastic tie straps are used to secure a bundle of wires and cables (Fig. 26-14C). Wires and cables are also commonly tied or laced together with heavy lacing string, as shown in Fig. 26-14D.

Fig. 26-12. Terminal strips

COAXIAL CABLE CONNECTORS AND ADAPTERS

Figure 26-15 illustrates a variety of types of coaxial cables, connectors, and adapters available for use today. These devices make it possible to

A SOLDER TYPE

RING LUG

SPADE LUG

B SOLDERLESS TYPE

Fig. 26-13. Terminal or wire lugs: (A) solder lugs; (B) solderless lugs; (C) fastening a solderless lug to the end of a wire with a terminal or crimping, tool

TERMINAL TOOL

C

INSULATION

A

B

Fig. 26-14. Clamping and strapping devices: (A) cable clamps; (B) insulated staple; (C) plastic tie straps; (D) laced cables

MOUNTING HOLE

KEY SLOT

RIBS

LOCKING CLIP

C

D

Fig. 26-15. (A) through (L): Selected coaxial cable connectors and adapters; (M) heavy-duty "HEX" crimp tool (*Radio Shack, a Division of Tandy Corp.*)

interconnect with the proper cables, various video cassette recorders, television receivers, and FM equipment. For example, an rf plug and chassis mount are used with coaxial cables for citizen band communications. High-grade coaxial cables are used extensively for amateur radio, CB, TV, and FM equipment. Coaxial cables are available to meet various electrical specifications. They are made from low-loss polyethylene dielectric with a tough outer jacket. All conductors are made of copper. It is essential that the type of connector and cable match properly.

The following represent a brief description of the items illustrated in Fig. 26-15A through M.

A. *Cable reducer.* Reducing adapters make it possible to use different diameter cable with a larger standard-size plug.

B. *Chassis mount connector.* This type of connector is commonly found on amateur and citizen band radio equipment.

C. *Right-angle adapter.* This adapter is used on coaxial cables for television sets and FM radios. The adapter is especially useful when space is limited directly to the rear of a chassis.

D. *Antenna chassis connector.* This type of connector is used on television sets and FM radios to connect antennas to the equipment.

E. *Coaxial connector.* This connector is crimped onto a coaxial cable with a hex crimping tool. It is used extensively to connect coaxial cables to television sets. It is relatively easy to install and does not need soldering.

F. *RCA phono jack to male BNC connector.* This type of connector makes it possible to join two different types of connections. BNC connectors are very secure because of the coupling mechanism. The coupling mechanism has spiral ramps that engage in projections that lock the mating halves together. A phono plug can be pressed firmly into the jack at the other end to form a connection.

G. *Female F connector to RCA phono plug.* This type of coaxial connector has two different style ends. One end has threads to connect with a male F connector secured on a coaxial cable. The other end is pressed firmly into a mating socket.

H. *Male F connector to RCA phono plug.* This type of connector is used to connect a coaxial cable to a phono plug.

I. *Male BNC solderless connector.* This type of connector has a locking connector on one end and a solderless connector on the other end.

J. *Female BNC connector.* This type of connector is used on a chassis to provide a connector for a male BNC plug. It provides a very secure type of connection that can withstand considerable vibration.

K. *Right-angle adapter, BNC male to BNC female.* This type of adapter provides a convenient method to make a secure connection where space is limited between cables terminated with BNC connectors.

L. *Right-angle adapter.* This adapter is especially useful where space is limited to connect an antenna transmission line to a transmitter.

M. *Heavy-duty hex crimp tool*. This tool is used to crimp connectors to a coaxial cable. No soldering is necessary.

BREADBOARDS

In the early days of radio, a flat wooden board was used as a base for mounting components. Fahnestock clips, held fast to the board with wood screws, provided a convenient way to make temporary connections. This made it easy to experiment with different circuits. The flat wooden board was called a *breadboard* because of its appearance. Modern "breadboards" have many forms.

Solderless Connections. Figure 26-16 shows a solderless spring terminal. Mounted on a breadboard, this kind of terminal makes it possible to connect several leads from different components to a single terminal. Several terminals usually are mounted on a single breadboard.

The breadboard shown in Fig. 26-17 uses ordinary solid hookup wires. The wire size can vary between no. 22 and no. 30 AWG. Wire jumpers are measured from point to point. Short leads should be used. About ⅜ in. (10 mm) of insulation must be stripped from the wires. The bare wire lead is put into a hole in the board that contains a flat spring clip. The flat spring clip grips the wire tightly, making a solderless connection. Five of these spring clips are placed in a row of five holes. Then any lead pushed into a hole is connected automatically with all other holes in the row. Therefore, five connections, called a *tie point,* can be made in any row of five holes. Note that both discrete and integrated circuits are connected to the solderless breadboard. *Discrete circuits* are made up of separate components connected by leads. *Integrated circuits* contain many interconnected components in a single block of material.

Fig. 26-16. Solderless spring terminal (*Vector Electronic Company, Inc.*)

HOLES CONTAIN FLAT SPRING CLIPS THAT GRIP WIRES

INTEGRATED CIRCUITS

DISPLAY

WIRE JUMPERS

DISCRETE COMPONENTS

Fig. 26-17. Decade counter circuit with display arranged on a solderless breadboard (*Global Specialties Corporation*)

CIRCUIT BOARD

SOLDER TERMINALS

Fig. 26-19. Using push-in terminals that need to be soldered (*Vector Electronic Company, Inc.*)

Soldered Connections. Figure 26-18 shows a prepunched circuit board. This board is made of a phenolic material and comes in several sizes. Prepunched circuit boards make a convenient base for mounting and wiring circuit components. These circuit boards are often used as a breadboard. Sometimes a special pin is pushed into a hole, as in Fig. 26-19. These pins form convenient contact points for soldering the leads of components.

Manufacturers' surplus printed-circuit boards make another very useful and inexpensive breadboard. These can be found in many radio and electronic supply stores. Many of these boards do not have the components soldered in place. If they do, the components can be desoldered and removed. Remove the components carefully so they can be used again.

Although the circuit on the board is not the one you want for your experimental circuit, you can modify it. Figure 26-20 shows a breadboard made from a surplus printed-circuit board. This breadboard circuit is an experimental radio-frequency (rf) oscillator. The components are soldered to any convenient printed circuit. Even the predrilled mounting holes can be used to mount the circuit. Note that a tube socket is used in place of a regular crystal socket. Note also that jumper wires are used to modify the previously printed circuit to meet specific needs. Using surplus printed-circuit boards and old components saves time and money. Also, it avoids any mess in etching the circuits.

Advantages of Breadboard Circuits. Breadboards allow technicians and electronic engineers to design, build, and test circuits quickly. Breadboard circuits are used to make industrial *prototypes*, or first models, of circuits to see if they will work as planned. After being checked out completely, a prototype is rearranged as needed before the finished product is made.

Breadboards can help you build circuits more quickly, more easily, and less expensively. They also can help you test and improve your circuit.

INSULATING TAPES, DEVICES, AND MATERIALS

Insulation is used to prevent undesirable electrical contacts. *Electrical tapes* are made of plastic, rubber, or cloth, usually ¾ in. (19 mm) wide

TUBE SOCKET USED FOR CRYSTAL SOCKET

BATTERY CONNECTOR (SNAP)

JUMPER WIRES

MOUNTING HOLES

Fig. 26-20. Breadboard circuit of an rf oscillator mounted on a surplus printed-circuit board

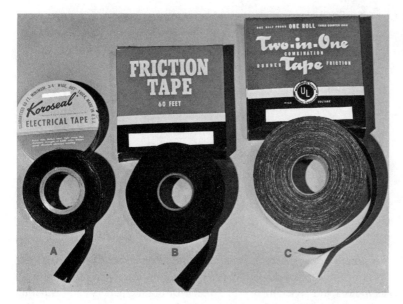

(Fig. 26-21). Plastic tape is thinner than rubber or cloth tape. It is also more adhesive and has a higher dielectric strength. Electrical tape made of black, coated cloth is generally called *friction tape.*

Tubing. Plastic insulating tubing, or *spaghetti,* provides a very convenient way to insulate wires (Fig. 26-22). The size of this tubing is usually specified by its inside diameter and the largest wire size that can fit into it. Heat-shrinkable tubing is also used to insulate a wire connection. This tubing fits around the connection and shrinks to half its original diameter when heated. A 40-W soldering iron, for example, held about ½ in. (12.7 mm) away from the tubing provides sufficient heat to shrink it. A hair blow-dryer can also be used to shrink the tubing. Heat-shrinkable tubing is available in sizes ⅟₁₆ to ½ in. diameter (1.6 to 12.7 mm).

Grommets. Grommets made of rubber or plastic are used to protect wires and cords that must pass through holes in metal (Fig. 26-23). The size of a grommet is the diameter of the mounting hole into which it will fit snugly.

Fiber Washers. Fiber shoulder washers are used to insulate devices such as jacks and mounting screws from metal surfaces (Fig. 26-24A). The shoulder of the washer insulates the device from the inside surface of the mounting hole. The use of a shoulder washer and a flat fiber washer to insulate a banana plug from a metal chassis is shown in Fig. 26-24B. The size of a shoulder washer is usually given by the inside and the outside diameters of its shoulder.

Fig. 26-22. (A) Using insulating tubing to cover exposed wiring at a terminal point; (B) tubing used to cover a splice

Fig. 26-23. A grommet being used to protect wires passing through a hole in a chassis

Fig. 26-24. Types of fiber washers: (A) shoulder and flat washers; (B) use of a shoulder and flat washer

Fig. 26-25. Insulating paper used to line the winding slots in the laminated stator of an electric motor (*Brook Motor Company*)

Fig. 26-26. Marking wire: (A) applying a clip-sleeve wire marker (*W. H. Brady Company*); (B) other practical methods of marking wires

Insulating Papers, Cloths, and Varnishes. Rag and kraft papers of various thicknesses and shapes are often used as insulation in machines such as motors and generators (Fig. 26-25). Insulating papers and insulating cloths made of glass fiber or varnished cotton, silk, or linen are also used to insulate the windings of transformer coils from the metal cores around which they are wound. Varnished linen is known as *varnished cambric*.

In addition to being applied to papers and cloths, insulating varnishes are used to strengthen the insulation of magnet wires and to repair defective insulation on these and other wires. These varnishes are applied by dipping, spraying, or brushing. Insulating varnishes are air-dried or are dried by being baked at a temperature of 220 to 270°F (104 to 132°C) for several hours.

WIRE MARKERS

Wire markers are used to identify wires, cables, and terminals in various wiring systems. They make it possible to quickly find and trace wires in a circuit. The marking of wires and terminals is also very useful in testing certain circuits and in replacing wires in them.

Many wires, individual or in cables, are color-coded. For more marking, wire markers with a letter or number are used (Fig. 26-26A). Other ways of marking wires are shown in Fig. 26-26B.

WIRE WRAPPING AND UNWRAPPING

Making an electrical connection by tightly coiling a wire around a metal terminal is called *wire wrapping*. This process is used because soldering is slow and has some disadvantages. For example, soldering uses heat. This can be dangerous to a worker and to the components being soldered. A soldered connection takes up a lot of space. Modern electronic circuits are very compact, with little space available. Also, unsoldering a connection is difficult. Wire wrapping and unwrapping meet the needs of many modern electronic circuits.

Terminal Post. To make a wire-wrapping connection, you will need a terminal post that has at least two sharp edges. Most terminal posts have four sharp edges. Terminal posts used in wire wrapping are generally square with each side 0.025×0.025 in. (0.64×0.64 mm). Insulated solid copper wire from no. 26 to no. 32 AWG (0.40 to 0.20 mm) is commonly used for wire wrapping.

Wire-Wrapping and Unwrapping Tools. Figure 26-27A shows a package containing a wire-wrapping tool, an unwrapping tool, and four spools of wire. Fig. 26-27B illustrates four wire-wrapped connections made to four terminal posts. Each wire wrap is made separately. Then the tool is moved to the next terminal post without cutting or stripping the wire.

The wire-wrapping tool shown in Fig. 26-27 uses a solid copper wire with a special insulation that can be pierced by the sharp corners of terminal posts. Thus, the bare copper wire from no. 26 to no. 32 AWG (0.40 to 0.20 mm) is commonly used for wire wrapping.

Fig. 26-27. (A) Wire-wrapping and unwrapping tools; (B) using the wire-wrapping tool (*OK Machine and Tool Corporation*)

WIRE-WRAPPING TOOL

WIRE SPOOLS

UNWRAPPING TOOL

A

B

- WIRE SPOOL
- WIRE
- WIRE-WRAPPING TOOL
- SLIDE
- WRAP
- CUT
- EYE
- HOLE FOR TERMINAL POST
- WIRE
- WRAPPING BIT

¼ IN. OR 6 mm

Fig. 26-28. Wire inserted in the wire-wrapping tool

Using the Wire-Wrapping Tool. When using a hand wire-wrapping tool, be sure the tool is designed to wrap around the terminal posts being used. In using the wire-wrapping tool, you must move the slide to the "wrap" position. Then feed the wire through the center hole in the body of the tool, through the eye, and through the wrapping bit. Allow about ¼ in. (6 mm) of wire to stick out of the wrapping bit (Fig. 26-28).

Put the tool over the terminal post. Rotate the tool clockwise about 8 to 10 turns. Keep a firm, but gentle, pressure on the tool while turning it. During the turning, the wire will be pulled down from the spool and wrapped tightly around the terminal. To make a point-to-point connection, lift the tool off the first terminal and put it over the next terminal. Repeat the clockwise turning, thereby making another connection. To cut the wire, move the slide to the "cut" position. Keep turning the tool in a clockwise direction. This cuts the wire close to the terminal.

Unwrapping. To unwrap a connection, put the *unwrapping tool* over the wire-wrapped terminal post so that it engages the post. Turn the unwrapping tool in a counterclockwise direction. This causes the wire to free itself from the terminal post. Thus, the connection is easily removed. Because wire is nicked by wrapping, it should be thrown away and only new wire used for wrapping.

Wire wrapping and unwrapping make it easy to change connections in a circuit. Therefore, these methods are often used in developing prototype circuits on breadboards.

Fig. 26-29. Wire wrapping using a fast-action tool (*OK Machine and Tool Corporation*)

EXAMPLE OF A DAISY CHAIN

P184 SLIT-N-WRAPS HEAVY TEFZEL INSULATED WIRE.

TERMINAL POSTS

cutaway view of post wrapped with Tefzel insulated wire

SLIT AND WRAP TOOL

WIRE SPOOL

P184

Fig. 26-30. Wire wrapping with a tool that slits the insulation before wrapping (*Vector Electronic Company, Inc.*)

Types of Wire-Wrapping Tools. A variety of wire-wrapping tools and unwrapping tools are available. Figure 26-29 shows a fast-action tool. Figure 26-30 shows another kind of wire-wrapping tool that slits the insulation on the wire just before wrapping it. With some wire-wrapping tools, you must strip the ends of the wire before wrapping. Usually, about 1 in. (25 mm) of insulation is stripped away.

Advantages of Wire Wrapping. These are some of the advantages of wire wrapping: (1) a wire-wrapped connection can be removed as easily as it is made; (2) the tools are simple to use and require little training; (3) wire wrapping can be done in tight spaces; (4) wire-wrapped connections are dependable; (5) wire-wrapped connections are as durable as most connections; (6) wire wrapping is economical.

IC TEST CLIP

An integrated circuit (IC) can be conveniently checked with an *IC test clip*. Figure 26-31 shows a test clip with a prewired cable. The test clip is clipped like a wide clothespin to the terminals of the integrated circuit. This test clip will make contact with 24 terminals—12 on each side of an integrated circuit. The ribbonlike cable brings the leads away from the work area. This makes it convenient for testing the integrated circuit or connecting it to another device.

Fig. 26-31. Integrated-circuit (IC) test clip with prewired cable (*Global Specialties Corporation*)

SELF-TEST

Test your knowledge by writing, on a separate sheet of paper, the word or words that most correctly complete the following statements:

1. Diagonal-cutting pliers should be used only for _____ wires.
2. An _____ plier can be used as a nut wrench, stripper, cutter, or crimper.
3. The size of pliers is given by their _____.
4. The _____ is a tool used to remove insulation from wires.
5. Attachment plugs are fastened to a cord by _____ or _____.
6. The _____ knot is used to keep wires from being pulled loose in an attachment plug.
7. The _____ phone jack allows a circuit to be completed through the jack contacts when a plug is not inserted into it.
8. A _____ nut is a device used for making solderless connections.
9. A terminal, or crimping, tool is used to fasten _____ to the ends of wires.
10. Plastic tie strips are used to secure a _____ of wires and cables.
11. _____ circuits are made up of separate components connected by leads.
12. A _____ is used by technicians and electronic engineers to design, build, and test circuits quickly.
13. Electrical tape made of black, coated cloth is called _____.
14. Plastic insulating tubing is also known as _____.
15. Wires and cords that pass through holes in metal are protected by _____.
16. Insulating varnishes are _____ or are dried by being _____.
17. Integrated circuits can be checked conveniently with an _____.

FOR REVIEW AND DISCUSSION

1. Name three common kinds of pliers. Describe their uses.
2. How is the size of pliers given?
3. What do you have to be careful of when using a wire stripper?
4. Describe how to remove insulation from wires with the wire-cutting jaws of ordinary pliers.
5. How are attachment plugs used? Describe how to attach wires to the screw terminals of a plug.
6. Why is an Underwriters' knot used in attachment plugs?
7. Name three common kinds of plugs and jacks. Tell how they are used.
8. Explain the difference between an open-circuit and a closed-circuit phone jack.
9. What is the purpose of a microphone connector?
10. What is a wire nut? How is it used?
11. How are terminal strips and lugs used?
12. Name three common clamping and strapping devices.
13. List the advantages of developing prototype circuits on breadboards.
14. How are wires and cables laced?
15. What are prepunched circuit boards and how are they used?
16. Describe where and how insulating tubing (spaghetti) is used.
17. What is a grommet? Why is it used?
18. Describe the different kinds of wire-wrapping tools and unwrapping tools available today.

INDIVIDUAL-STUDY ACTIVITIES

1. Give a demonstration showing your class the various kinds of wiring tools and devices. Tell how each is used.
2. Write a report on how wire wrapping and unwrapping is used in the electronic industries today.
3. Obtain an assortment of video rf connectors and adapters, TV and FM antenna connectors, and coaxial cables. Demonstrate to the class how the connectors, adapters, and cables can be used to interconnect different types of electronic equipment.

UNIT 27   Soldering

Soldering is the process of joining metals with another metal that has a low melting point. This metal is called *solder*. In electricity and electronics, the metals being joined are usually copper wires, lugs, terminal points, and the like. Electrical soldering is called *soft soldering*. Its main purpose is to make a good electrical contact between the soldered surfaces.

Fig. 27-1. Core solder: (A) single core; (B) multicore

SOLDER AND SOLDER FLUX

The solder used for electrical and electronic soldering is usually in the form of a wire. This wire-shaped solder has one or more cores of rosin *flux* (Fig. 27-1). When the solder is melted, the flux flows over the surfaces to be soldered. It acts as a cleaner to remove any oxides coating the surface. These oxides are produced when oxygen in the air combines chemically with the metal. They must be removed because solder will not stick to surfaces covered with oxides.

An acid flux should never be used when soldering copper wires. Acid causes copper to corrode. This produces a weak solder joint and a high resistance between the connected wires.

Composition and Melting Point of Solder. Soft solder is an alloy of tin and lead. It is usually 40 percent tin and 60 percent lead, 50 percent tin and 50 percent lead, or 60 percent tin and 40 percent lead. Of these three, the 60 percent-tin-40 percent-lead solder has the lowest melting point. It ranges from about 360 to 370°F (182 to 188°C). A solder with a low melting point makes it possible to solder with less heat. This lessens the danger of damaging components or insulation. This is very important in connecting semiconductor components.

Eutectic Solder. Eutectic solder is 63 percent tin and 37 percent lead. It has the lowest melting point of any tin-lead combination, 360°F (182°C).

Size. In addition to composition, solders are specified by diameter or by an AWG number. The most popular solders have diameters of 1/16 in. or 3/32 in. (1.59 or 2.38 mm).

SOLDERING IRONS

A *soldering iron* is a tool used to melt solder. In an electric soldering iron, heat is produced as current passes through a heating element. The heating element is usually a coil wound with high-resistance wire (Fig. 27-2). The amount of heat produced is proportional to the wattage rating of the heating element. For electrical and electronic work, soldering-iron sizes range from 25 to 100 W. Heavy-duty soldering irons used for soldering very large wires or for soldering wires to large objects may have a wattage rating of 250 W or more. A general rule is to choose a soldering iron that does not produce more heat than is needed for the job.

Fig. 27-2. Soldering irons: (A) switchable dual heat soldering iron, 15 or 30 watts, replaceable tip (*Radio Shack, a Division of Tandy Corporation*); (B) construction features of a typical electric soldering iron (*American Electric Heater Company*)

A

CHROME NICKEL HEATING ELEMENT SURROUNDS COPPER TIP

SPECIAL HEAT-TREATED NONOXIDE CORE

BAFFLE PLATE DEVICE (COOLER HANDLE)

CONNECTOR ASSEMBLY

CONNECTOR STRAIN BLOCK

WOOD HANDLE

SET SCREW

ASSEMBLY NUT

NONOXIDE COPPER TIP

ONE-PIECE STEEL SHELL AND SHANK

ELEMENT LEADS INSULATOR

STEEL NUT INSERT

CONDUCTOR CORD

B

Fig. 27-3. Soldering-iron holders (*Hexacon Electric Company*)

Soldering-Iron Holders. You should always keep a heated soldering iron in a holder or support while not using it (Fig. 27-3). This will keep work surfaces from being charred or burned by a carelessly placed iron. Holders enclosed with a perforated metal guard give the best protection against burning flesh or clothing. A heated soldering iron can cause a fire if not handled properly. Thus, you should be very careful when using any soldering iron.

Tips. Soldering-iron tips come in several different shapes (Fig. 27-4). They are usually made of copper. However, some are nickel plated or iron clad to reduce corrosion. Most soldering irons have replaceable tips. These are either screwed into the barrel socket or held in place by a set screw.

DIAMOND　　CHISEL　　SCREWDRIVER　　CONE

Fig. 27-4. Soldering-iron tips (*American Electrical Heater Company*)

TURNED DOWN

After a period of time, a soldering-iron tip will become coated with a thick layer of oxide. This reduces the amount of heat that is transferred from the iron to the tip. The oxide will also cause the tip to stick in the iron. To keep these things from happening, a tip should be removed from a soldering iron after it has been used for some time. It should be cleaned with sandpaper before being put back into the iron. When putting a tip into a soldering iron, make sure that it is fully inserted into the socket of the iron.

Tinning and Cleaning. Before being used, a soldering-iron tip should be *tinned*. This involves melting a thin coat of solder over its surfaces (Fig. 27-5A). This allows the most heat to be conducted from the tip to the surfaces being soldered. After tinning a tip, you should remove any extra solder from it by carefully rubbing it over a slightly damp sponge (Fig. 27-5B).

234

Fig. 27-5. Preparing the soldering-iron tip for use: (A) tinning; (B) removing excess solder

ROSIN-CORE SOLDER

DAMP SPONGE

A

B

After being used for some time, the faces, or flat surfaces, of the tip of a soldering iron become coated with the burned residue of solder flux. This coating lessens the amount of heat delivered to the surfaces being soldered. When using a soldering iron, always keep the tip clean and shiny by rubbing it over a damp sponge. This is necessary if a good soldering job is to be done. A plated tip should never be cleaned with a file or with a wire brush. This can damage its protective coating.

SOLDERING GUNS

A *soldering gun* is a solder-melting tool that has a step-down transformer. This applies a low voltage across the tip. The current passing through the tip produces enough heat to melt solder (Fig. 27-6). The gun is controlled by an on-off trigger switch. The switch often has two trigger positions. This allows the soldering gun to be operated at two heat levels. The wattage ratings for the two heats could be, for example, 100 and 140. After the switch is depressed to the first trigger position, the tip becomes heated to soldering temperature in a few seconds. To solder, touch the tip to the metal. Feed a little solder to the tip to release the flux. Then apply solder to the work until the solder flows freely. Withdraw the gun immediately and release the trigger. The second trigger position produces more heat for heavier jobs. Most soldering guns have one or more lamps that light up when the trigger is depressed. The lamps illuminate the surfaces being soldered and show that the iron is on.

Soldering guns have replaceable tips that have a variety of shapes. These are tinned and cleaned in the same way as those used with soldering irons.

A soldering gun with an open tip as shown in Fig. 27-6 should never be used for soldering semiconductor devices such as transistors and integrated circuits. This is because a strong magnetic field surrounds the tip. This field can seriously disturb the atomic arrangement within the devices, damaging or ruining them.

PREPARING WIRES FOR SOLDERING

For most soldering jobs, about ½ in. (13 mm) of insulation should be removed from the wire. Wires from which insulation has just been

A

LAMINATED CORE

SECONDARY WINDING

PRIMARY WINDING

TIP SOCKETS

SECONDARY WINDING

PRIMARY WINDING

TIP

TRIGGER SWITCH

B

Fig. 27-6. (A) A typical soldering gun; (B) construction details and schematic diagram of a common soldering gun (*Weller Electric Corporation*)

Fig. 27-7. Cleaning wire with sandpaper

SOLDER ─
WIRE BEING TINNED

Fig. 27-8. Using a soldering-iron holder when tinning a wire

1. REMOVE OUTER JACKET FOR A DISTANCE OF APPROXIMATELY $1\frac{1}{2}$ IN. (38.1 mm).

2. UNBRAID THE SHIELD WITH A SCRIBER OR OTHER SHARP POINTED TOOL.

─ TO SHIELD CONNECTION

3. TWIST UNBRAIDED PORTION OF SHIELD TOGETHER AND REMOVE A SHORT LENGTH OF THE INSULATION WHICH COVERS THE CONDUCTOR.

Fig. 27-9. Preparing shielded coaxial cable for soldering

removed are usually clean enough for soldering. However, bare wires such as capacitor and resistor leads may be coated with oil, dirt, or an oxide coating. These wires should be cleaned with an ink eraser, with fine sandpaper, or with the blade of a knife (Fig. 27-7). When cleaning any wire, you should be careful not to nick the wire or to remove too much copper.

After the insulation has been removed from a stranded wire, the strands should be twisted together to form a firm bundle. This will keep the loose strands from making contact with other wires and causing a short circuit.

Some magnet wires are coated with an insulation that will burn off as the wires are soldered. The insulation on all other magnet wires can be removed with fine sandpaper, a knife blade, or a chemical solvent.

Tinning. Bare copper wires should always be tinned before soldering. This will allow quicker and more effective soldering with less heat. Pretinned wires can often be soldered more quickly if they are retinned just before soldering.

A wire can be tinned quickly by using a soldering-iron holder, as shown in Fig. 27-8. To do this, first melt a drop of solder on the soldering-iron tip. Put the wire in the solder. Melt a small amount of additional solder on the tip, turning the wire until all its surfaces are thinly coated with solder.

Most terminals and lugs to which wires are soldered are pretinned. They do not need more tinning. Any bare surface to which a solder connection is to be made should be tinned beforehand.

Coaxial Cable. Figure 27-9 shows how to prepare shielded coaxial cable for soldering when the braid shield must be connected into a circuit. When working with coaxial cable, be careful not to damage the insulation between the shield and the inner conductor. This is particularly important when soldering a wire lead to the shield. If too much heat is applied to such a joint, the insulation may be melted enough to cause a short circuit between it and the inner conductor.

SOLDERING WIRES TO LUGS

A wire that is to be soldered to a lug should first be mechanically fastened to the lug to hold it in place (Fig. 27-10A). If the wire is the lead of a semiconductor device such as a diode or transistor, attach a heat sink to it (Fig. 27-10B).

Next melt a drop of solder on the tip of the soldering iron or gun. Press the tip to one side of the joint (Fig. 27-10C). The melted solder will allow more heat to be conducted from the tip to the joint. Briefly heat the joint. Then press one end of a length of solder wire to the other side of the lug until a small amount of the solder has melted (Fig. 27-10D). Let this solder flow thoroughly into the joint. Hold the tip in place a while longer. Then remove it from the joint. After the joint has cooled, remove the heat sink.

PLIERS USED TO TIGHTEN WIRE TO LUG

LEAD FROM COMPONENT

LUG

USE HEAT SINK IF NECESSARY

SOLDER

A   B   C   D

Use only enough solder to cover all surfaces of the joint without hiding the shape of the joint (Fig. 27-11). This will enable you to inspect the joint. It will also keep extra solder from causing a short circuit with nearby wires or terminals.

Do not move or otherwise handle a newly soldered wire until the solder has cooled enough. If a warm connection is moved, the solder will suddenly become less shiny. A dull-colored solder joint indicates that not enough heat was used. Such a joint, commonly called a *cold solder joint,* does not provide a good electrical contact.

Always handle a soldering iron or gun with care to keep from burning the insulation or damaging the components. Burned or charred insulation does not look good. In addition, it may cause a short circuit or ground.

SOLDERING WIRES TO HOLLOW TERMINALS

Soldering a wire to a hollow terminal, such as a phono plug, is shown in Fig. 27-12. To solder, first melt a small amount of solder on the tip of

Fig. 27-10. Soldering a wire to a lug

Fig. 27-11. Solder joints showing the correct amount of solder to be used

HOLD VERTICALLY

SOLDER

APPLY SOLDER TO TIP OF HEATED PIN. SOLDER WILL FLOW UP INTO PIN BY CAPILLARY ACTION.

SOLDER SHIELD TO BODY OF PLUG

REMOVE EXCESS WIRE AND SOLDER.

Fig. 27-12. Soldering a wire to a hollow-terminal device such as a phone plug

the soldering iron or gun. Hold the tip of the plug in place until the solder has been drawn up into it. Then add more solder if needed. Any extra solder or wire extending beyond the tip of the plug should be cut or filed away. This will keep the plug from binding when inserted into a jack.

SOLDERING WIRES TOGETHER

Wires are usually soldered at terminal points, such as lugs. However, it is sometimes necessary or desirable to solder two wires together without a lug. The wires are first twisted or hooked together tightly (Fig. 27-13A). They are then soldered.

Fig. 27-13. Soldering two wires together: (A) wires are twisted or hooked together tightly to provide mechanical strength before soldering; (B) solder joint covered with insulating tubing

The solder joint should be as short as possible. It should be covered with insulating tubing or other insulation (Fig. 27-13B). The tubing insulates the joint and makes the job look neater.

When soldering integrated-circuit components to a circuit board, concentration is needed. Paying close attention to each soldered joint prevents short circuits (Fig. 27-14).

Fig. 27-14. Soldering components to a prototyping board

LEARNING BY DOING

8. Experiences in Soldering. Soldering is done to ensure good electrical connections. The following soldering jobs will give you experience in this important wiring activity.

MATERIALS NEEDED

1 three- or four-lug terminal strip
1 phono plug
6 in. (150 mm) untinned insulated wire, any size, no. 18 through no. 22 AWG (1.00 through 0.63 mm)
18 in. (460 mm) tinned or untinned insulated wire, any size, no. 18 through no. 22 AWG (1.00 through 0.63 mm)
6 in. (150 mm) microphone cable
soldering iron, 40 or 60 W
solder wire, rosin core

Procedure

Do one or more of the following soldering jobs:

1. tinning a wire (Fig. 27-8)
2. soldering two wires together (Fig. 27-13)
3. soldering wires to the lugs of a terminal strip (Fig. 27-10)
4. soldering a microphone cable to a phone plug (Fig. 27-12)

After you have finished these, show them to your instructor for approval. The terminal strip can be conveniently mounted on a baseboard.

SELF-TEST

Test your knowledge by writing, on a separate sheet of paper, the word or words that most correctly complete the following statements:

1. Solder flux is used as a cleaner to remove any _____ coating from the surfaces to be soldered.
2. Never use _____ flux when soldering copper wires.
3. Soft solder is generally an alloy of _____ and _____.
4. The melting point of 60/40 solder ranges from about _____ to _____ °F.
5. The most popular solder wires have diameters of _____ or _____ in.
6. The electrical size of a soldering iron or gun is given by its _____ rating.
7. In doing a soldering job, it is always best to use a soldering iron or gun that does not produce more _____ than is needed.
8. A soldering-iron or -gun tip is tinned by coating its surfaces with _____.
9. Bare copper wires should always be _____ before soldering.
10. A wire that is to be soldered to a lug is first _____ fastened to the lug to hold it in place.
11. A solder joint to which enough heat has not been applied is called a _____ solder joint.
12. Always handle a soldering iron or gun with care to keep from burning the _____ or _____ the components.

FOR REVIEW AND DISCUSSION

1. Define *soldering*.
2. Describe the solder wire used for common electrical and electronics soldering jobs.
3. What is the purpose of soldering flux?
4. Why is an acid flux never used when soldering copper wires?
5. How is the electrical size of a soldering iron given?
6. What is the purpose of a soldering-iron holder?
7. Why is it important to keep the tip of a soldering iron well tinned?
8. How is a soldering-iron tip cleaned?
9. Why is a wire tinned before soldering?
10. Describe step by step the process of soldering a wire to a lug.
11. What is meant by a cold solder joint?

INDIVIDUAL-STUDY ACTIVITIES

1. Prepare a written or an oral report on the different kinds of soldering materials and processes used in writing.
2. Give a demonstration showing your class the correct way to solder a number of different common kinds of jobs.

UNIT 28 Making a Sheet-Metal Chassis

Sheet metal is used to build a chassis for mounting and enclosing components (Fig. 28-1). This unit will be very helpful if you choose to build a project that requires mounting components on a sheet-metal chassis. Designing and building such a chassis is an interesting and valuable experience. You will also learn how to use several tools and devices.

Fig. 28-1. Types of chassis: (A) open-end; (B) box; (C) sloping-panel

The most common sheet metals used for building chassis are aluminum and galvanized steel. Galvanized sheet metal is mild steel with a coating of zinc.

The thickness of ferrous sheet metals such as iron and steel is given by a United States Standard (USS) gage number. A *ferrous metal* is one made of iron or one that contains iron. The thickness of nonferrous sheet metals such as copper and aluminum is most often given by an American wire gage (AWG) number. In both cases, as the gage number increases, the thickness of the metal decreases. For example, a no. 10 (0.135-in. or 3.43-mm) sheet metal is thicker than no. 12 (0.105-in. or 2.69-mm) sheet metal. Chassis are usually made from no. 14 to no. 20 gage (0.080 to 0.035 in. or 2.03 to 0.89 mm) sheet metal.

CHASSIS LAYOUT DIAGRAM

A chassis layout diagram shows the size of the sheet metal to be used, the location and shape of the holes to be drilled or punched, and the places where the metal is to be bent (Fig. 28-2). The diagram is usually drawn to scale. That way its main features can be seen in proper relation to each other.

The diagram should be prepared carefully. You should consider all the circuit components to be used with the chassis. A good first step in making the layout diagram is to arrange the components in a suitable pattern on a sheet of unruled paper. This sheet stands for the chassis (Fig. 28-3). Designing a chassis will give you good experience in solving design problems that can have more than one solution.

LOCATION OF COMPONENTS

There are no standard rules for placing the components of a circuit on a chassis. However, you should consider the following when determining the locations.

in.	mm.
$\frac{1}{4}$	6
$\frac{5}{16}$	8
$\frac{3}{8}$	10
$\frac{1}{2}$	13
$\frac{3}{4}$	19
$\frac{7}{8}$	22
$1\frac{1}{8}$	28
$1\frac{1}{2}$	38
$1\frac{3}{4}$	44
$2\frac{3}{4}$	70

Fig. 28-2. Chassis layout diagram. Table shows metric equivalents.

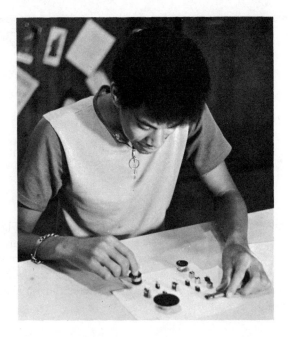

1. Transformers, transistors, and can-shaped electrolytic capacitors are usually mounted on the top surface of the chassis, with the capacitors upright.
2. Switches, input and output jacks, and receptacles are often mounted on the front or back of the chassis.
3. The shafts of potentiometers and variable capacitors are brought out at the front of a chassis.
4. Related components should be put in the same general area. (For example, a rectifier transformer should be mounted near the on-off switch and the electrolytic filter capacitor of the rectifier circuit.)
5. All components should be placed so that they can be connected with the shortest lengths and as little crossover of wires as possible.
6. The chassis should provide enough space for the mounting of wiring devices such as terminal strips and grommets.
7. There should be enough space to drill holes for wires connecting components on top of and underneath the chassis.
8. The chassis should be deep enough that components mounted beneath it will not extend below the sides.

CUTTING OUT THE CHASSIS BLANK

After preparing the chassis layout diagram, you have to choose the sheet metal for the chassis. The metal should be heavy enough to support the components without bending or buckling. You will probably cut the blank for the chassis from a larger sheet of metal after you have drawn the layout diagram on it. A soft lead pencil or a scriber and a square can be used for making the layout (Fig. 28-4).

Fig. 28-4. Combination square with scriber

SCRIBER

Sheet metal is cut with tin snips or with squaring shears (Fig. 28-5). With tin snips, a small piece of sheet metal can be cut from a larger sheet without disturbing other surfaces of the sheet. Squaring shears make a square, cleaner cut. However, when you use them, you have to cut completely across a larger sheet. This may result in too much waste of sheet metal.

LAYING OUT THE CHASSIS BLANK

When you have cut out the chassis blank, transfer information from the layout diagram to it. This information generally includes the location of bend lines and notch-cutting lines, the outline of square or rectangular holes, and the centers of round holes. The transfer can be done with a soft lead pencil or with a scriber. The centers of holes can then be marked with a prick-punch. The prick-punch marks should then be enlarged with a center punch. When using a center punch, hit the punch just hard enough to make a sharp indentation on the surface of the metal without causing it to bulge out on the other side.

SCRIBED CUT LINE

Fig. 28-5. Using tin snips to cut sheet metal

DRILLING HOLES

Round holes up to ½ in. (12.7 mm) in diameter are best cut through sheet metal with twist drills. These are used with a portable electric drill or with a drill press. The machines should be operated at medium speeds and with just enough pressure to cause the twist drill to cut into the metal. The diameter of a twist drill is given by a fraction, whole number, or letter stamped on its shank.

SAFETY

Always wear safety glasses while drilling holes in sheet metal. Never try to drill a hole unless the metal is securely clamped.

A safe way to drill a hole with a portable electric drill is shown in Fig. 28-6. The wood backing helps hold the metal in place. It also keeps the metal from bending as drill pressure is applied to it. Put a piece of wood or thick paper between the metal and the front vise jaw to keep the metal from being marked.

CHASSIS PUNCH

A *chassis punch* is a tool that cuts clean, accurate holes in sheet metal (Fig. 28-7). Round chassis punches come in sizes from ½ to 3⅛ in. (12.7 to 79.4 mm) in diameter. They are also available in square and other shapes.

To use a chassis punch, first drill a hole, a little larger in diameter than the drive screw of the punch, through the metal. Then assemble the tool with the sheet metal sandwiched between the die and punch. The drive screw passes through the die and is threaded into the punch. Turn the drive-screw nut with a wrench. This forces the cutting edges of the punch through the sheet metal and into the die. A hole of the same size and shape as the punch is cut.

FILES AND REAMERS

Rough edges of sheet metal can be smoothed with a flat file. A 10- or 12-in. (254- or 305-mm) second-cut file is best.

Round metal files, often called *rattail files*, are very useful for removing burrs from the edges of drilled holes and for enlarging holes in sheet metal.

Burrs can also be removed with a *countersink bit*, used with a bit brace. Another kind of reamer, the *taper reamer*, is very useful for enlarging holes in sheet metal. When using a taper reamer, use just enough pressure to let its cutting edges remove thin shavings of metal from the edges of the hole.

MAKING LARGE OPENINGS

A large opening in a sheet-metal blank can be made by first drilling small holes close to each other along the outline of the opening. The piece being removed is then completely cut out with a cold chisel. When doing this, use just enough hammer pressure on the chisel to cut through the metal without causing it to bulge on the other side. Use a hardwood or soft-metal plate under the sheet metal during the cutting. Then smooth the edges of the hole with a file.

Fig. 28-7. A chassis punch for making a 1-in (25-mm) diameter hole

FORMING THE CHASSIS

After all cutting and drilling have been done on the chassis blank, the flat sheet metal is ready to be formed or bent into shape. Two machines are used for this, the *box-and-pan brake* and the *bar folder* (Figs. 28-8 and 28-9). With practice, you can use these machines to make almost any shape you desire.

Fig. 28-8. Main parts of the box-and-pan brake

CLAMPING BAR FINGERS (REMOVABLE)

CLAMPING BAR

ADJUSTMENT KNOB

CLAMPING BAR LEVER

BENDING LEAF

BENDING LEAF HANDLE

Fig. 28-9. Main parts of the bar folder (*The Peck, Stow, and Wilcox Company*)

WING-ADJUSTING LEVER ON BACK OF WING

WING

45° AND 90° STOPS

HANDLE

DEPTH GAGE

GAGE-ADJUSTING SCREW

FRAME

LOCK SCREW

Fig. 28-10. Using the hand seamer to bend a flange

Hand Seamer. The *hand seamer* is a convenient tool for making simple bends or flanges in sheet metal (Fig. 28-10). It can be adjusted to bend flanges of up to 1 in. (25 mm).

Other Ways of Bending Sheet Metal. Right-angle (90°) bends in sheet metal can be made by clamping the chassis blank over the edge of a workbench and hammering the part to be bent with a mallet (Fig. 28-11A). A bend of up to 90° can also be made by clamping the sheet metal

244

Fig. 28-11. Bending small pieces of sheet metal

between pieces of wood and then shaping it to the desired angle with a mallet (Fig. 28-11B).

FINISHING THE CHASSIS

An attractive and inexpensive finish can be given to a sheet-metal chassis. This can be done by simply scratching the outside surface with coarse steel wool, medium-grit sandpaper, or a wire brush. If a painted surface is desired, many kinds of paints can be applied by either brushing or spraying. Among these is one that, when dry, produces a crinkled surface that is very attractive. Always consider chassis grounds (electrical connections to the chassis) before applying any finish. Most finishing materials act as insulators.

READY-MADE ENCLOSURES

Project cases, metal cabinets, and experimenter boxes are generally available in radio and electronic stores or mail order parts dealers. These enclosures make excellent chassis for electronic projects (Fig. 28-12). Some enclosures come with steel tops, an aluminum chassis, and rubber feet. Others are made of plastic with internal slots to hold PC boards (Fig. 28-12B). Ready-made enclosures are available in various heights, widths, and depths, for example, 3¼ × 2⅛ × 4 in. (82.6 × 54 × 101.6 mm) and 5¼ × 3 × 5⅞ in. (127 × 76.2 × 149.2 mm).

MACHINE SCREWS

Machine screws are used with nuts and lock washers for mounting components on the sheet-metal chassis (Fig. 28-13). A special kind of machine-screw nut, called a *locknut*, has a plastic insert. Under normal conditions, this prevents the nut from becoming loose and eliminates the need for a separate lock washer. Machine screws are usually made of metal. However, nylon screws are often used for electric and electronic circuit assemblies to insulate exposed hardware. The metal screws may be plain steel or brass. Screws may be plated with nickel or cadmium to prevent corrosion.

Fig. 28-12. Ready-made enclosures (chassis): (A) two tone enclosures, eggshell white bottoms, black tops; (B) blue plastic project case with cover (*Radio Shack, a Division of Tandy Corporation*)

245

Fig. 28-13. Machine screws and metal washers: (A) complete assembly; (B) flat washer; (C) types of lock washers

FLAT WASHER MACHINE SCREW SPLIT (SPRING) INTERNAL TOOTH

LOCK WASHER HEX NUT EXTERNAL TOOTH

A B C

BODY HOLE (OUTSIDE DIAMETER OF SELF-TAPPING SCREW)

ROOT DIAMETER

SELF-TAPPING SCREW

ROOT DIAMETER HOLE

A

PRE–DRILLED HOLES

B

Fig. 28-14. Fastening the sides of an enclosure: (A) using a self-tapping screw; (B) ready-made enclosure (chassis) with holes pre-drilled for self-tapping screws (*Radio Shack, a Division of Tandy Corporation*)

The U.S. customary size of a machine screw is given by the diameter of its threaded part, the number of threads per inch, and the length of the threaded portion. For sizes less than ¼ in., the diameter is given by a gage number, such as 4, 6, 8, 10, or 12. The larger the number, the greater the diameter. An example of a complete specification for a machine screw is no. 6-32 RH-1 in. Here, the 6 indicates the diameter, the 32 indicates threads per inch, RH means roundhead, and 1 in. gives the length of the threaded part. Other common sizes are 4-40, 8-32, and 10-32. The metric sizes of a machine screw are given by its nominal size (basic major diameter) and pitch. Both sizes are given in millimeters. Include the letter M in front of the nominal size to show it is metric. Use × between the nominal size and the pitch. An example would be M6 × 1. This size is close to a customary ¼-20. For a more complete explanation of metric threads, see a metric handbook.

SELF-TAPPING SCREWS

Self-tapping screws are a kind of sheet-metal screw. They are used for mounting components on a chassis and for fastening the panels and other parts of a chassis. These screws cut the threads in the hole into which they are screwed (Fig. 28-14). The size of self-tapping screws is given by a number that indicates the diameter and by the length of the threaded part.

SCREWDRIVERS

Standard screwdrivers are used with slotted-head screws (Fig. 28-15A). The size is usually given by the diameter and the length of the blade.

Phillips-head screwdrivers are with cross-slot screw heads. They have a stronger driving action than standard screwdrivers (Fig. 28-15B). The size is most often given by a number, such as 1, 2, 3, or 4. The larger the number, the larger the point of the screwdriver.

Fig. 28-15. (A) Standard screwdriver; (B) Phillips-head screwdriver (*Xcelite, Incorporated*)

A B

DISTANCE ACROSS "FLATS"

Allen screwdrivers fit the hexagonal holes found on some set screws (Fig. 28-16A). The size is given by the length of the blade and the distance across the *flats,* or parallel sides, of the blade.

Clutch-head screwdrivers are used with clutch-head screws to get a stronger driving action (Fig. 28-16B). They are sized according to the tip and the diameter of the blade.

NUTDRIVERS

Nutdrivers have a shaft and handle like a screwdriver and a hexagonal socket tip for use with hexagonal-head screws and nuts (Fig. 28-17A). The size of a nutdriver is given by the distance across the *flats,* or any two parallel sides, of its socket. Some tool manufacturers color-code the handles for easy size identification (Fig. 28-17B).

Fig. 28-17. Hollow-shaft nutdrivers: (A) typical set of nutdrivers; (B) color code used with nutdrivers (*Xcelite, Incorporated*)

Handle Color	Size	
	inches	millimeters
black	$3/16$	4.76
brown	$7/32$	5.55
red	$1/4$	6.35
orange	$9/32$	7.14
amber	$5/16$	7.94
green	$11/32$	8.73
blue	$3/8$	9.53

SELF-TEST

Test your knowledge by writing, on a separate sheet of paper, the word or words that most correctly complete the following statements:

1. Galvanized sheet metal consists of a base of mild _____ coated with _____ .
2. The thickness of sheet metal is given by a _____ gage number or by an _____ gage number. As the gage number increases, the thickness of the metal _____ .
3. A chassis layout diagram shows the _____ of the sheet metal to be used, the _____ and _____ of the holes to be drilled or punched, and the places where the metal is to be _____ .
4. Sheet metal is most often cut with _____ or with _____ .
5. The centers of holes to be drilled through sheet metal should be marked with a _____ .
6. The diameter of a twist drill is given by a _____ , by a whole _____ , or by a _____ .
7. _____ should always be worn while drilling holes.
8. Never try to drill a hole in sheet metal unless the metal is securely _____ .
9. Round holes from ½ to 3⅛ in. (13 to 79 mm) in diameter are often cut through sheet metal with a _____ punch.
10. Two-common tools used for reaming in sheet-metal work are the _____ and the _____ reamer.
11. All cutting and drilling operations should be done on a chassis blank before it is _____ or _____ into its final shape.
12. Two machines used for forming and bending sheet metal are the _____ and the _____ .
13. The hand seamer is used for making simple _____ or _____ in sheet metal.
14. The customary size of a machine screw is given by the _____ of its threaded part, the _____ of threads per inch, and the _____ of the threaded portion.
15. Self-tapping screws are a kind of _____ screw.
16. The size of a nutdriver is given by the distance across the _____ of its socket.

FOR REVIEW AND DISCUSSION

1. How is the thickness of sheet metal given?
2. Describe a chassis layout diagram.
3. Describe the first step in making a chassis layout diagram.
4. State five guidelines that are useful in determining the location of components on a chassis.
5. With what should you enlarge prick-punch marks?
6. How is the size of a twist drill given?
7. Describe the safe method of drilling a hole through sheet metal with a portable electric drill.
8. How is a chassis punch used?
9. Name two kinds of reaming tools. Tell the purpose for which each is used.
10. Describe the process of cutting a large opening through sheet metal.
11. Name two machines that are used for forming and bending sheet metal.
12. For what purpose is a hand seamer used?
13. How is the customary size of a machine screw given?
14. What are self-tapping screws?

INDIVIDUAL-STUDY ACTIVITIES

1. Demonstrate to your class how tools are used in working with sheet metal and/or plastics. Include in the demonstration hand, bench, and power tools. Show how common kinds of screws and screwdrivers are used.
2. Visit a local radio or electronics store and examine the various types and sizes of metal and plastic enclosures that could be used as a chassis for an electronics project. Discuss what you have learned with your class.

SECTION 6

ELECTRICITY AT WORK

UNIT 29   Lamps and Lighting

Electric energy can be changed into light energy in a number of different ways. The first practical device for producing light by electricity was the carbon-filament lamp invented by Thomas Edison in 1879. Since then, many kinds of lamps and other lighting devices have been developed.

INCANDESCENT LAMP

The word *incandescent* means "glowing from intense heat." In an *incandescent lamp,* current passes through a filament of the metal tungsten, causing the filament to become incandescent, or white hot (Fig. 29-1).

When an incandescent lamp is made, most of the air is removed from the glass bulb before it is sealed. This is done to keep oxygen from coming into contact with the filament. Oxygen would cause it to burn out quickly. A mixture of the gases nitrogen and argon is placed in the bulb to lessen the evaporation of the filament caused by its high temperature. This lengthens the life of the lamp.

The life of general-service incandescent lamps for home use ranges from 750 to 1,500 hours. The average life of a lamp is printed on the carton.

Watts and Lumens. Incandescent lamps come in a variety of sizes and shapes (Fig. 29-2). The electrical size of a general-service incandescent lamp is given in watts and in lumens (lm). The wattage rating indicates the amount of energy the lamp uses. The *lumen* rating indicates the amount of light it produces. A 100-W light bulb gives off about 1,000 lm.

Lamp Bases. Screw-base incandescent lamps are made in several sizes (Fig. 29-3A). Small lamps, such as those used in flashlights and as pilot lights, usually have miniature bases. The candelabra base is found on decorative lamps and large pilot lights. The medium base is used with

Fig. 29-1. Construction of a typical general-purpose incandescent lamp

249

Fig. 29-2. Sizes and shapes of common incandescent lamps. The numbers and letters beneath the lamps refer to manufacturers' standard types.

Fig. 29-3. Incandescent-lamp bases: (A) screw; (B) bayonet

Fig. 29-4. The three-lite lamp

general-purpose lamps rated at 300 W or less. The mogul base is used with lamps having a wattage of more than 300 W. Lamps rated at more than 1,500 W have special bases.

Miniature- and candelabra-base lamps often have a bayonet base (Fig. 29-3B). To put such a lamp in a socket, line up the pins on the base with the grooves or slots in the socket. Then press the lamp in and turn it clockwise until it locks into place.

THREE-LITE LAMP

A *three-lite lamp* can produce three different amounts of light. This kind of lamp is used in floor and table fixtures. It has two separate filaments. In the 50-100-150-W lamp, for example, one of these is a 50-W filament. The other is a 100-W filament (Fig. 29-4). The common wire of the filament is connected to the threaded part of the base. The second filament lead is connected to a ring on the bottom of the base. The third filament lead is connected to the center contact of the base. A special selector switch in the socket connects either or both of the filaments to the circuit. Thus, the lamp can be operated at 50, 100, or 150 (50 + 100) W.

ELECTRON TUBES

Electron tubes, like the incandescent lamp, have a filament contained within a glass or metal envelope (shell). Most of the air within the envelope has been removed. Early electron tubes had a high vacuum. For this reason, present-day tubes are called *vacuum tubes*. The light seen when the glass electron tube is on is caused by the glow of the heated filament. The heating process uses most of the energy supplied to an electron tube. The primary function of the electron tube is to control the movement of electrons within the tube and in radio and other communication circuits. Electron tubes have been largely replaced by solid-state devices. However, electron tubes are still found in some electronic products (Fig. 29-5). Special kinds of electron tubes used in oscilloscopes and television cameras and receivers are discussed in later units of this book.

BASIC OPERATION OF ELECTRON TUBES

The electrodes of a tube are connected internally to pins that extend from the base. An electron tube is put into a circuit by being plugged into a tube socket (Fig. 29-6). The tube and the rest of the circuit are connected by wires attached to the lugs of the socket. Some special miniature tubes have wire leads that are soldered directly into the circuit.

One of the electrodes in an electron tube is called a *cathode*. When this electrode is heated, it emits, or gives off, electrons. The cathode may be heated directly or indirectly. The process of electrons being emitted from a heated surface is known as *thermionic emission*.

Cathodes. A directly heated cathode is usually made of a nickel-alloy metal. It is in the form of a filament coated with a material that emits electrons. The filament is connected to a source of voltage. It is heated by the current that passes through it.

An indirectly heated cathode is in the form of a thin metal sleeve. It is also coated with a material that emits electrons when heated. This kind of cathode is heated by a heater wire inside the sleeve but not in contact with the sleeve.

Electrostatic Attraction. The cathode has a negative charge. The electrons emitted from the cathode are attracted to a positively charged tube electrode called the *plate* (Fig. 29-7). This is known as *electrostatic attraction*. When the plate is not positively charged, the electrons will not flow. (Actually, a small number of electrons will reach the plate even if it is not charged. This is called the *Edison effect* in honor of Thomas Edison, who discovered it.)

DIODE TUBE

A *diode* (*di* for two and *ode* for part) is the simplest kind of electron tube. It has two electrodes: a cathode and a plate.

If an alternating voltage is applied across the plate and cathode, the plate will be positive with respect to the cathode during one-half of each voltage cycle. Electrons will thus flow in the tube from the cathode to the plate only during this half of the cycle. As a result, the tube will emit

Fig. 29-5. Common types of electron tubes: (A) octal base—the center (insulated) post properly orients the metal pins in the tube socket; (B) 7-pin miniature; (C) 9-pin miniature; (D) 12-pin (duo-decar) base

Fig. 29-6. Electron tube sockets: (A) molded socket; (B) wafer socket

251

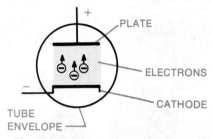

Fig. 29-7. Electrostatic attraction of electrons to the plate, or anode, of an electron tube

a pulsating direct current. Thus, a diode tube can act as a *half-wave rectifier*. A *rectifier* is a device or a circuit that changes alternating current into direct current.

The *full-wave-rectifier* electron tube has a cathode and two separate plates. The tube is connected to the ac voltage in such a way that one of the plates is always positive with respect to the cathode. Because of this, both halves of the cycle produce a current but always in the same direction. Rectification performed by the diode tube is like that of a solid-state p-n-junction diode discussed in Unit 21.

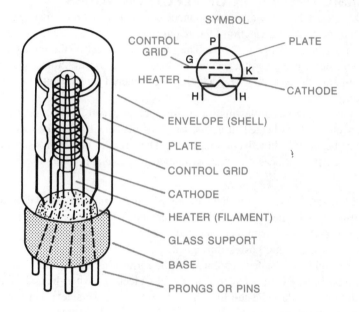

Fig. 29-8. The triode tube

Fig. 29-9. Action of the control grid in a triode

TRIODE TUBE

In a *triode* electron tube, a third electrode, called the *control grid,* is put between the cathode and the plate. The grid is usually a spiral of fine wire placed around the cathode and insulated from it (Fig. 29-8). The control grid controls the number of electrons that pass from the cathode to the plate. When the grid is positive with respect to the cathode, the grid lets electrons from the cathode reach the plate (Fig. 29-9A). When the grid is negative with respect to the cathode, the grid repels electrons, preventing many of them from reaching the plate (Fig. 29-9B).

A small change in the value of the voltage applied between the control grid and the cathode of a triode tube can control a large amount of current in the plate circuit of the tube. This action allows the tube to act as an amplifier. An *amplifier* is a device or circuit that increases the value of a voltage or a current. The grid, plate, and cathode of a triode electron tube perform an amplification function similar to that of the base, collector, and emitter of a bipolar transistor.

OTHER TUBES

Diodes and triodes are only two of the several kinds of electron tubes. Others have more electrodes, which are designed to improve electron flow. One such tube is the *pentode*. In addition to a control grid, it has a *screen grid* and a *suppressor grid*. Some tubes, commonly known as *multifunction* or *multisection tubes*, consist of two or three tubes in one envelope. Such tubes have the electrodes of a double diode and a triode, a triple diode, a double triode, or a triode and a pentode.

BASING DIAGRAMS

A tube basing diagram shows, by means of symbols, the kinds of electrodes in the tube. It also shows the particular base pin to which each electrode is connected (Fig. 29-10A). To identify the pins, look at a tube from its base. Then count each pin in a clockwise direction, beginning with the key (Fig. 29-10B).

Fig. 29-10. Identifying electron-tube base pins

G$_1$ = CONTROL GRID
G$_2$ = SCREEN GRID
G$_3$ = SUPPRESSOR GRID
H = HEATER
K = CATHODE
P = PLATE
NC = NOT CONNECTED

A

OCTAL BASE

7-PIN MINIATURE BASE

9-PIN MINIATURE BASE

B

TUBE DESIGNATION AND SUBSTITUTION

Electron tubes are identified by a combination of numbers and letters, such as 5U4GB, 12BA6, and 50C5. These are called *type designations*. The first number, for example, 12, is the voltage at which the heater filament is operated. Tubes with the same type designations have the same electrical characteristics even though they may have different brand names. In some circuits, it is possible to substitute one tube for another tube that has a different type-designation number. Tubes that can be used as replacements for another tube are listed in *tube-substitution manuals*.

TESTING ELECTRON TUBES

Electron tubes can be checked with a tube tester (Fig. 29-11). You can test a particular kind of tube with this instrument by adjusting its controls according to the operating-chart control settings for that tube. When using a tube tester, always be sure that the filament-voltage control is set to the right value for the tube being tested. Too much voltage applied to a filament or heater wire will cause it to burn out.

Fig. 29-11. Tube tester (*Courtesy Sencore, Inc.*)

Fig. 29-12. A common large photo-flash lamp (*General Electric Company*)

Labels on figure: OXYGEN, LACQUER, PRIMER, SHEARED ALUMINUM FOIL, GLASS, FILAMENT, BASE, LEAD-IN WIRES, SOLDER, EXHAUST TUBE

A continuity test done with an ohmmeter can be used to test for open filaments. You adjust the ohmmeter to a low or medium resistance range and then connect it to the heater pins. A tube manual will help you find the right pin numbers.

PHOTOFLASH LAMP

The *photoflash lamp,* used with flash cameras, is a special kind of incandescent lamp. It produces a large amount of light for a very short time. The lamp bulb contains pure oxygen and thin strips of aluminum or magnesium foil (Fig. 29-12).

The tungsten filament of the lamp is made to burn out with a spark when current passes through it. The spark ignites the aluminum or the magnesium, which burns very rapidly in the oxygen. This produces a very bright light that lasts for only a fraction of a second.

FLUORESCENT LAMP

The *fluorescent lamp* belongs to a group of light sources known as *electric-discharge lamps*. Such lamps produce light by passing current through a gas. The typical fluorescent lamp is a glass tube with a tungsten filament sealed into each of its ends. The inner surface of the tube is coated with a chemical called a *phosphor* (Fig. 29-13). When the lamp is made, most of the air is removed from the tube. A small amount of argon gas and mercury is sealed inside it.

SYMBOL

FILAMENT   GLASS TUBE

Fig. 29-13. View of one end of a typical preheat fluorescent lamp (*Westinghouse Electric Corporation*)

PHOSPHOR COATING
(INSIDE WALL OF TUBE)

Lamp Circuit. To operate what is called a *preheat* fluorescent lamp, a ballast and a starter must be used (Fig. 29-14A). The *ballast* is a coil of insulated magnet wire wound around an iron core. The *starter* acts as a switch that is automatically turned off when its moving element, a bimetal strip, reaches a certain temperature. Bimetal-strip switches (thermostats) are discussed in Unit 33.

In the lamp circuit, the filaments, the ballast, and the starter are connected in series (Fig. 29-14B). When the main lamp switch is turned on, current passes through the circuit and heats the filaments. As a result, the temperature in the lamp increases. This causes the mercury to turn to gas. The current is also heating the bimetal strip in the starter. After a brief preheat period, the starter opens the circuit.

The sudden stoppage of current produces several thousand volts across the terminals of the ballast by self-inductance. This high voltage also appears across the ends of the fluorescent tube. The high voltage ionizes the gas within the tube. This causes the gas to become a good conductor. Because of its high inductance, the ballast also limits the current through the lamp circuit to a safe value.

In an *instant-start* fluorescent lamp, a step-up transformer produces the high voltage needed to ionize the gas in the lamp. Most instant-start lamps have single-pin bases.

Fig. 29-14. The preheat fluorescent-lamp circuit: (A) auxiliary components; (B) complete lamp circuit

How Light Is Produced. Current flowing through the ionized gas mixture in the lamp excites the mercury atoms (Fig. 29-15). Their energy is released in the form of *ultraviolet light,* which people cannot see. When this light strikes the inside surface of the lamp tube, the phosphor *fluoresces,* or glows. This glow is the visible light produced by the fluorescent lamp.

Fig. 29-15. How light is produced by a fluorescent lamp (*Westinghouse Electric Corporation*)

Efficiency. Fluorescent lamps have been available since 1938. They have become a very common source of light in homes, stores, offices, factories, and schools. One of the main reasons for their popularity is their efficiency. A fluorescent lamp wastes much less energy in the form of heat than does an incandescent lamp. The modern fluorescent lamp system (which includes a ballast or transformer) is able to produce approximately three times more light than an incandescent lamp with the same wattage rating. Fluorescent lamps are available in the shape of common incandescent lamps with screw bases. These lamps can be used in ordinary lamp sockets. Lamps of this type have self-contained ballasts built into the lamp structure itself.

MERCURY LAMP

The *mercury,* or *mercury vapor, lamp* is widely used for producing large amounts of light (Fig. 29-16). Mercury lamps are used for street

OUTER BULB

ARC TUBE

STARTING ELECTRODE

RESISTOR

MAIN ELECTRODES

MOGUL SCREW BASE

Fig. 29-16. The mercury vapor lamp (*Westinghouse Electric Corporation*)

and bridge lighting, parking-area lighting, and lighting for other places where the lamp must be mounted high above the ground. The *arc tube,* or inner bulb, of this lamp is made of quartz, or rock crystal. The arc tube contains argon gas and a small amount of mercury. The outer bulb regulates and maintains the temperature of the inner bulb while the lamp is working.

To start the lamp, a high voltage from a transformer, called a ballast, is applied to the lower main electrode and to the starting electrode next to it. This produces a glow discharge between these electrodes that heats the mercury, causing it to turn to gas. The gas mercury presents a low-resistance path for current through the arc tube from one main electrode to the other. The current, which is seen as a brilliant arc, is the source of light.

GLOW LAMPS

In a *glow lamp,* two electrodes are placed very close to one another in a sealed glass bulb containing argon or neon gas (Fig. 29-17A). When the right dc voltage is applied to the electrodes, some valence electrons within atoms of the gas gain enough energy to escape from their parent atoms. As a result of this ionization, positive gas ions are produced. As these ions move toward the negative electrode, some of them collide with and regain electrons. This causes energy in the form of visible light to be released near the negative electrode. When a glow lamp is operated with alternating voltage, the electrodes become alternately negative and positive. This happens so quickly that both electrodes seem to be glowing at the same time (Fig. 29-17B).

The voltage needed to start a glow lamp is called the *starting,* the *striking,* or the *ionization* voltage. The typical glow lamp has a starting voltage of about 60 V.

Neon glow lamps of from $\frac{1}{25}$ to 3 W in size are used as test and pilot lights. One advantage of these lamps is that they start instantly when the

Fig. 29-17. (A) Neon and argon glow lamps. (B) Both electrodes seem to glow when the lamp is operated on alternating voltage. The numbers and letters beneath the lamps refer to manufacturers' standard types. (*General Electric Company*)

right voltage is applied to them. For this reason, glow lamps are very often used as high-speed indicators. When operated at 120 V, small glow lamps such as the neon NE-2 require a current-limiting resistor. This resistor has a resistance of about 100,000 Ω. It is connected in series with one of the lamp leads or terminals. The resistor may be connected externally. It may also be contained in an indicator-light assembly. Larger glow lamps often have high-resistance, current-limiting coils in their bases.

NEON SIGNS

In a *neon sign,* an electrode is sealed into each end of a glass tube filled with neon gas. The longer the tube, the higher the voltage that must be applied to the electrodes to sufficiently ionize the gas. In common neon signs, a voltage of 10,000 V or more may be needed. This high voltage is supplied by a step-up transformer (Fig. 29-18).

By using argon, helium, or a mixture of these and other gases, light of different colors can be obtained. Different colors are also obtained by using tinted glass tubes or coatings on the inside surface of the tubes.

Fig. 29-18. A step-up transformer is used with a neon sign.

LASER

The word *laser* comes from the phrase *l*ight *a*mplification by *s*timulated *e*mission of *r*adiation. Thus, a laser system is a means of producing and amplifying light.

Light is a form of electromagnetic energy radiated from a source of energy. Except that it has a much higher range of frequencies, its properties are like those of the electromagnetic waves radiated from the antenna of a radio or television transmitter.

The color of light depends on the frequency or frequencies of the radiation that reaches our eyes. The frequency range of visible light extends from about 400 million MHz (red) to about 700 million MHz (violet) (Fig. 29-19).

Incoherent Light. The light produced by a common incandescent lamp consists of electromagnetic radiations with a wide range of frequencies. The visible light from the lamp is then actually made up of a combination of colors. Our eyes see this as white light. Such light is called

Fig. 29-19. The frequency range of visible-light radiations. This is sometimes called the electromagnetic spectrum of light.

Fig. 29-20. Patterns of light radiation: (A) incoherent light; (B) coherent-light radiation of a laser beam

ORDINARY
LIGHT
SOURCE

A

LASER BEAM

B

incoherent, or *polychromatic,* light. An important characteristic of this light is that it spreads out very quickly after leaving the source (Fig. 29-20A). As a result, this light loses much of its energy when it travels over a long distance.

Coherent Light. The light produced by a laser consists of radiations that are very nearly of the same frequency. They are also in *phase,* or in step, with each other (Fig. 29-20B). This is called *coherent light.* A very important characteristic of coherent light is that it does not spread out very much even when it is far from its source. Because of this, the light stays highly concentrated. Thus, it has much energy as it strikes a target area.

Laser Beam. The light output from a laser is in the form of a narrow beam of light (Fig. 29-21). The color of the beam depends on the kind of laser used. A laser beam can be modulated by many different electri-

HELIUM-NEON
GAS LASER

LIGHT
BEAM

Fig. 29-21. Laser beam used for an optical communications experiment (*Bell Telephone Laboratories*) cal signals over long distances. Thus, it can be used in communications systems. (Modulation is explained in Unit 39.) The laser beam is also used for locating objects and measuring their distances from fixed points. More powerful laser beams are used for welding, metal cutting, and surgical cutting.

Operation. The working principle of a laser is that electrons in atoms can be raised from one energy level to another by applying external energy. Electrons that are raised from one energy level to the next higher energy level are said to be *excited*. Excited electrons tend to become deexcited and return to their original energy levels when external energy is no longer applied to their atoms. When this occurs in certain materials, energy in the form of light is released.

Laser materials that react in this way include ruby rods, combinations of gases, and special kinds of semiconductor p-n junctions. In several laser systems, the material is assembled into an *optical cavity,* which has mirrorlike ends.

The energy used to excite electrons in the laser is called *pumping energy.* In the ruby laser, the pumping energy is visible light supplied by a lamp. In the gas laser, it is a high-frequency electrostatic field. In the semiconductor laser, it is usually a high dc voltage.

SELF-TEST

Test your knowledge by writing, on a separate sheet of paper, the word or words that most correctly complete the following statements:

1. The word *incandescent* means "_____ from intense heat."
2. The filament of a common incandescent lamp is made of _____ .
3. Nitrogen gas and argon gas are put inside the bulb of an incandescent lamp to lessen the _____ of the _____ .
4. The life of general-service incandescent lamps usually ranges from _____ to _____ hours.
5. The lumen rating indicates the _____ of light a lamp produces.
6. The four main kinds of lamp bases are _____ , _____ , _____ , and _____ .
7. Electrons move from cathode to plate in a tube when the plate is _____ charged with respect to the cathode.
8. The full-wave-rectifier tube contains a cathode and two separate _____ .
9. The three electrodes of a triode tube are the _____ , the _____ , and the _____ .
10. The current-control action of a triode tube allows it to act as an _____ .
11. A tube _____ diagram shows the kinds of electrodes in a tube and the base _____ to which they are connected.
12. The fluorescent lamp belongs to a group of light sources known as _____ .
13. An instant-start fluorescent lamp is started by a _____ .
14. The word *laser* comes from the phrase _____ .
15. The laser beam is an example of _____ light.

FOR REVIEW AND DISCUSSION

1. Define the word *incandescent*. Explain how an incandescent lamp works.

2. Name the two units used to denote the size of general-service incandescent lamps.

3. Describe the basic construction of a typical electron tube.
4. What is the purpose of a cathode?
5. What is meant by thermionic emission?
6. What is electrostatic attraction in an electron tube?
7. Describe the construction of a diode tube.
8. Explain how a diode tube works as a rectifier.
9. Explain the function of the control grid in a triode tube.
10. How are electron tubes tested?
11. Describe the construction of a common fluorescent lamp tube.
12. Name the parts of a preheat-fluorescent-lamp circuit and explain how they work.
13. For what purposes are mercury lamps used?
14. What is meant by the starting voltage of a glow lamp?
15. Why must a step-up transformer be used with a neon sign?
16. Explain the origin of the term *laser*.
17. What factor determines the color of visible light?
18. Explain the difference between coherent and incoherent light.
19. What is meant by the pumping energy of a laser system?

INDIVIDUAL-STUDY ACTIVITIES

1. Prepare a written or an oral report about the nature of visible light.
2. Give a demonstration showing your class several different kinds of electron tubes. Give the name of each tube and explain what its type designation means.
3. Prepare a written or an oral report on the development and applications of lasers.

UNIT 30   Producing Chemical Reactions

A chemical reaction usually results in changes to the materials taking part in the reaction. For example, when oxygen reacts with iron, a new substance called *iron oxide* (rust) is formed. When paper is burned, it changes into ashes and smoke. In each case, the composition of the molecules in the substance is changed. New substances having different properties are produced.

The chemical reactions that take place when electric energy is applied to a substance result from the movement of charges through the substance. A liquid that ionizes to form positive and negative ions and that can conduct these charges is called an *electrolyte*.

In this unit, you will learn how electrolytes cause chemical changes by a process known as *electrolysis*. This process is widely used in industry for producing certain gases and chemicals, for electroplating, for refining copper, and for extracting metals such as aluminum and magnesium from their ores.

ELECTROLYSIS OF WATER

Pure water is a very poor conductor of electricity because it does not ionize easily. However, when certain chemical compounds are added to pure water, the solution becomes a good conductor. Applying a voltage to such a solution produces a process called *electrolysis*. Electrolysis is the breaking down of water into its two chemical elements, the gases hydrogen and oxygen.

In one industrial process for making hydrogen and oxygen gases, sulfuric acid is added to pure water. Each molecule of the acid ionizes into two positive hydrogen ions (H^+) and one negative sulfate ion having two negative charges (SO_4^{--}). The positive hydrogen ions are attracted to the cathode (negative electrode). At the same time, the negative sulfate ions are attracted to the anode (positive electrode) (Fig. 30-1). At the cathode, each hydrogen ion obtains an electron. It thereby becomes a neutral atom of hydrogen. Hydrogen, being a gas, rises from the solution. It collects at the cathode. At the anode, the negative sulfate ions deposit their excess electrons and become neutral. However, the sulfate reacts at once with the hydrogen of the water, forming sulfuric acid again. The oxygen in the water, which remains after the hydrogen has been removed, rises through the solution. It collects at the anode. This process continues as the sulfuric acid is recycled through the ionization and sulfate stages.

Fig. 30-1. Producing hydrogen and oxygen gases by electrolysis.

Fig. 30-2. Electroplating unit in an industrial plant. (*Atlantic Finishing, Inc.*)

ELECTROPLATING

Electroplating is a form of electrolysis used to coat a base material (usually a metal) with a thin layer of another metal. The base metals can be iron, steel, brass, or similar metals. They can be electroplated with one or more metals, which include cadmium, chromium, copper, gold, silver, and tin.

Cadmium plating will protect the base metal from corrosion (Fig. 30-2). Chromium is used to improve the appearance of base metals and to provide a much harder surface. Copper plating is generally used to provide an undercoating over which other metals are plated. Gold plating is used for decorative purposes and for improving the conductivity of contact points in some electrical equipment. Tin plating is used on surfaces likely to come in contact with food and to allow easy soldering of surfaces.

The Plating Solution. Electroplating requires the use of a plating solution, or electrolyte, that contains a compound of the plating metal. In copper plating, for example, the electrolyte consists mainly of a solution of water and copper sulfate ($CuSO_4$).

Basic Operation. The construction and operation of a basic copper-plating assembly is shown in Fig. 30-3. Here the object to be plated (the cathode) and a piece of pure copper (the anode) are suspended in the electrolyte and connected to a battery.

As the copper sulfate in the solution dissolves, it ionizes into positive copper ions (Cu^{++}) and negative sulfate ions (SO_4^{--}). The copper ions are attracted to the cathode. There they obtain the needed electrons and become metallic copper. This is deposited on the object being plated.

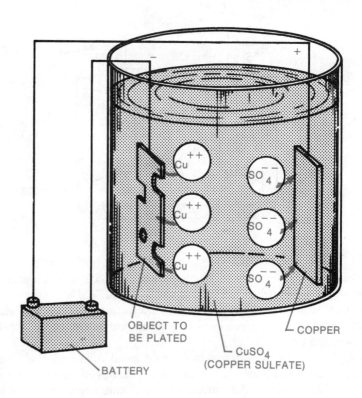

Fig. 30-3. The copper-plating circuit

The sulfate ions are attracted to the anode. There they combine with copper atoms to form copper sulfate. This goes into solution and ionizes. Thus, the copper sulfate replaces the copper removed from, or plated out of, the electrolyte. During this time, the current in the external circuit consists of electrons that move into the cathode from the negative terminal of the battery and electrons that move into the positive terminal of the battery from the anode.

As the electroplating process continues, the pure copper that forms the anode is gradually used up and must be replaced. At the same time, the coating of copper deposited on the object being plated gets thicker.

The time needed to electroplate a base metal to a given thickness depends on the kind of plating metal used and the density of the ions in the electrolyte. Ion density is indicated by the value of the current in the external circuit. For this reason, a practical electroplating assembly has meters that show the current in the external circuit and the voltage at which the circuit is operating. The circuit also has controls for increasing and decreasing the plating current as needed for electroplating different metals and adjusting the plating rate.

Partial Plating. Plated terminals on printed-circuit boards can be repaired by using a compact electroplating system and plating pen (Fig. 30-4). This system uses disposable cartridge pens and a power supply capable of supplying 12 Vdc at 5.0 A. Each plating pen contains its own nontoxic solution. Several types of pens are available for plating; for example, copper, gold, and silver.

To use the system, the surface to be plated is polished and then wiped clean. The part to be plated is connected to the negative (−) terminal of the power supply. An absorbent pen, connected to the positive (+) terminal, is used first. The absorbent pen operates on 12 Vdc and chemically cleans (degreases) the surface to be plated. This is done by rubbing the absorbent pen point back and forth on the surface to be plated. After degreasing, the surface is rinsed clean with water. The absorbent pen is disconnected and the plating pen is connected to the positive (+) terminal of the power supply. The operating voltage, for example, for a silver plating pen is adjusted between 5.0 and 6.0 Vdc. The plating process is accomplished by moving the pen lightly back and forth on the surface to be plated. In about 2 or 3 minutes, a silver plate is deposited upon the surface. After the plating process is complete, the part is rinsed with water and wiped with a soft clean cloth.

POSITIVE TERMINAL

POWER SUPPLY

ABSORBENT PEN USED TO CLEAN SURFACE TO BE PLATED

NEGATIVE TERMINAL

PLATING PEN

Fig. 30-4. Repairing the surface of terminals by plating with disposable plating pens (*Hunter Associates*)

Before rinsing surfaces, always turn off the power supply and disconnect the object to be plated.

 CAUTION

CARBON RODS
(ANODE)

CRUST OF
HARDENED
ELECTROLYTE

CARBON LINING
(CATHODE)

MOLTEN
ELECTROLYTE
(ALUMINA AND
CRYOLITE)

MOLTEN
ALUMINUM

Fig. 30-5. Basic construction of an electrolytic furnace used for producing aluminum

EXTRACTING METALS FROM ORES

The production of aluminum is the most common process in which electrolysis is used to extract metals from their ores. The first step in producing aluminum is changing the ore (bauxite) into a white powder called *alumina* (aluminum oxide). Then, in a method known as the *Hall process,* alumina is dissolved in molten cryolite (sodium aluminum fluoride) to form the electrolyte. The heat needed to keep the electrolyte liquid is produced by the current needed for electrolysis. Carbon rods and a carbon lining make up the cathode and the anode of what is referred to as an *electrolytic furnace* (Fig. 30-5).

Because of ionization, negative oxygen ions and positive aluminum ions are present in the electrolyte. The aluminum ions are attracted to the cathode. There they obtain electrons and are discharged to form aluminum atoms. The molten aluminum then collects at the bottom of the furnace and is withdrawn.

Several other metals are extracted from their ores by electrolysis. These include magnesium, sodium, potassium, and cesium.

LEARNING BY DOING

METER

LAMP

12 V DC

Fig. 30-6. Tumbler assembly and circuit for Learning by Doing No. 9, "Making a Saltwater Rheostat"

9. Making a Saltwater Rheostat. This kind of rheostat is not used in practical circuits. It does, however, clearly show the effect of ionization in a liquid solution.

MATERIALS NEEDED

medium-size glass or plastic tumbler filled with water, preferably distilled
2 pieces of sheet copper or aluminum, ½ × 2¼ in. (13 × 57 mm)
1 pilot lamp, no. 46
1 miniature lamp socket, screw-base
common table salt in shaker
glass or plastic stirring rod
2, 6-V batteries, or a low-voltage power supply with a current rating of at least 0.4 A
volt-ohm-milliammeter

Procedure

1. Bend the pieces of sheet metal. Put them in the tumbler containing the distilled water, as shown in Fig. 30-6.
2. With the volt-ohm-milliammeter adjusted to a range of about 0 to 250 mA, connect the circuit shown in Fig. 30-6. Explain why there is now no current in the circuit.
3. Slowly sprinkle salt into the water and stir. The current should gradually increase to a value that causes the lamp to light dimly.

4. Keep adding salt to the solution until the current has increased to 250 mA. The lamp should now be working normally.
5. Explain the ionization process that changed the nonconducting solution into an electrolyte able to conduct ionic charges.

SELF-TEST

Test your knowledge by writing, on a separate sheet of paper, the word or words that most correctly complete the following statements:
1. A solution that will produce positive and negative ions is called an _____.
2. Pure water is a very poor conductor because it does not _____ easily.
3. As a result of electrolysis, water is broken down into the gases _____ and _____.
4. Cadmium plating is done to protect a base metal from _____.
5. Metals extracted from their ores by electrolysis include _____, _____, _____, _____, and _____.

FOR REVIEW AND DISCUSSION

1. What is an electrolyte?
2. Why is pure water a very poor conductor?
3. What is meant by the electrolysis of water?
4. Describe an industrial process that uses electrolysis to produce the gases hydrogen and oxygen.
5. Define electroplating.
6. Name two metals used as base metals in electroplating.
7. Give the main reasons for plating base metals with cadmium, with chromium, and with gold.
8. Explain the basic copper-plating process.
9. Name three metals commonly extracted from their ores by electrolysis.

INDIVIDUAL-STUDY ACTIVITY

With the help of your instructor, make arrangements to visit an electroplating plant. Report your observations to the class. Provide details about one specific electroplating process.

UNIT 31 Home Electrical Systems

The electrical system in your home consists of conductors, devices, and various electrical equipment. The purpose of the system is to distribute electric energy throughout the building. Although this unit discusses mostly residential (house) wiring, many of the same materials are found in the electrical systems of other buildings. The main parts of a typical home electrical system are shown in Fig. 31-1.

Fig. 31-1. A typical home electrical system

NATIONAL ELECTRICAL CODE

The *National Electrical Code®* is a publication sponsored by the National Fire Protection Association in cooperation with the American National Standards Institute (ANSI). It includes recommendations and guidelines on wiring materials and methods. Following these guidelines will result in the safe use of electric energy for lighting, heating, communications, and other purposes. The code is reviewed continuously. A revised edition is issued every 3 years.

The *National Electrical Code* contains the basic minimum requirements needed to protect both persons and property from electrical hazards. Because of this, The *Code* is very useful for developing safety standards throughout the country. These standards, as well as those of local electrical codes, are used by electricians, contractors, and inspectors. Using these standards means that all building wiring will be done in an approved way. When the code is adopted by local governmental bodies, its provisions become legally enforceable.

SERVICE DROP

The *service drop* of a house wiring system is the part of the system that extends from a terminal point outside the house to the nearest electrical company distribution line. This line is fed from a distribution transformer. That device steps down the high voltage of a main power line to about the 115 and 230 V used in the house.

The service drop can be installed overhead or underground. An underground service drop is sometimes called a *service lateral*. The distribution transformer is mounted overhead on a utility pole, at ground level on a concrete pad, or underground in a vault (Fig. 31-2). The distribution transformer may supply electric energy to several houses.

Three-Wire Service. In order to supply two different voltages (115 and 230 V), the service drop is made up of three conductors (Fig. 31-3). One of these, called the *neutral,* is often bare. The other two conductors are insulated.

230-V Operation. The 230-V lines brought into a house are used to operate major appliances, such as ranges, hot-water heaters, and air-conditioning units. Comparable voltages used by different electric power companies include 208, 220, and 240 V. The reason higher voltages are used for these purposes can best be explained by referring to power formulas.

Suppose, for example, that a 1,725-W appliance is operated at 115 V. The amount of current used by the appliance under this condition is $I = P/E$, or $1,725/115 = 15$ A. Now, suppose that the same appliance is operated at 230 V. The current is then $1,725/230$, or 7.5 A.

The lower value of current (at 230 V) has two important advantages. First, the wires leading to the appliance can be smaller. This reduces the cost of installing them. Second, the lower current results in a smaller power loss in the wires. According to the formula $P = I^2R$, the loss is directly proportional to the square of the current.

SERVICE ENTRANCE

The *service-entrance conductors* extend from the point at which the service-drop conductors are attached at the house to the load center. The complete service entrance is generally thought to include the conductors, the watthour meter, and the load center. Usually the electric power company takes care of the wiring from the power line up to and including the meter.

Service-Entrance Cable. The service-entrance cable has three conductors (Fig. 31-4). One of these, the neutral conductor, is bare. It is usually in the form of individual strands of wire. When the cable is to be connected to a terminal point, the strands of the neutral conductor are twisted together to form a single-stranded conductor.

Fig. 31-2. Distribution transformer mounted overhead on a utility pole

Fig. 31-3. Voltages of a typical three-wire system used in homes

Fig. 31-4. Service-entrance cable (*General Electric Company*)

HEAT-AND MOISTURE-RESISTANT INSULATION

UNINSULATED COATED CONCENTRIC CONDUCTOR

FLAME-RETARDANT, MOISTURE-RESISTANT GLASS-COTTON BRAID

MOISTURE SEAL TAPES

75C 3 COND.

CONDUCTOR (COPPER OR ALUMINUM)

COLOR-CODED TREATED COTTON BRAID

CELLOPHANE WRAP

The Watthour Meter. The watthour meter measures and records the amount of electric energy (in kilowatthour units) supplied to a building. The meter is installed by the power company and belongs to it.

The Load Center. The load center, also called a *fuse* or *circuit-breaker panel,* is the unit from which electricity is distributed to different locations in a house (Fig. 31-5). It contains the main-line fuses and the switch. The latter can be used to disconnect all electrical service from a house. The load center also contains the fuses or circuit breakers that protect the branch circuits of the wiring system.

The size of the load center is designated by the number of fuses or circuit breakers that can be placed into it and by its load, or ampere, rating. The fuse panel shown in Fig. 31-5A is rated at 60 A. Larger load centers, equipped with more fuse holders, have ampere ratings of 100, 150, 200, or more amperes.

Fig. 31-5. Load centers: (A) fuse panel; (B) circuit-breaker panel (*Square D Company*)

GROUND TERMINALS (FASTENED TO BOX)

INPUT TERMINALS

BUS BAR

RANGE-CIRCUIT TERMINALS

KNOCKOUT

PULL-OUT-TYPE RANGE SWITCH

230-VOLT TAPS

A

FUSE SOCKETS

PULL-OUT-TYPE MAIN SWITCH

BRANCH-CIRCUIT TERMINALS

GROUND TERMINALS (FASTENED TO BOX)

B

The Service Ground. To reduce the danger of shock and to protect against lightning, the neutral conductor of the service-entrance cable is grounded. This is done by connecting it to the neutral bus bar in the load center. The bus bar is, in turn, grounded by being connected to a ground rod or in older homes, to a water pipe.

BRANCH CIRCUITS

The *branch circuits* of a house wiring system distribute electricity from the load center to the parts of the house. The three common kinds of branch circuits are discussed below.

General-Purpose Circuits. General-purpose branch circuits are used for lighting and outlets. The outlets are intended to serve radios, television sets, clocks, and small appliances other than those used for food preparation (such as toasters, broilers, and the like). Lighting circuits are usually wired with no. 12 (2.00-mm) or no. 14 (1.60-mm) wire and are protected with 20- or 15-A fuses or circuit breakers.

As shown in Fig. 31-6, one wire of each general-purpose circuit is connected to the neutral bus bar of the load center. The grounded neutral wire is color-coded white. The wire connected directly to the fuse or circuit breaker is generally black or red. This circuit wire is often called the *hot* wire.

Fig. 31-6. Wiring diagram of a four-pole fuse panel

The grounded white wire of a two-wire, general-purpose circuit is never used as a safety-grounding wire. When the cabinet or case of a product operated from such a circuit is to be grounded, a third grounding wire is used.

Small-Appliance Circuits. Small-appliance circuits are used for such appliances as refrigerators, toasters, broilers, coffee makers, and irons. They are wired with no. 12 (2.00-mm) wire and are protected with 20-A fuses or circuit breakers.

Individual Circuits. An individual branch circuit is generally used with only one piece of equipment. Examples of individual circuits are those used with electric ranges, dryers, water heaters, heating systems, and air conditioners.

A range circuit is usually a three-wire, 115–230-V circuit. It has two hot wires and a neutral wire. There is a fuse or circuit breaker in each of the hot wires. A 230-V individual circuit is a two-wire circuit. Both wires are hot and are protected with a fuse or circuit breaker.

The cabinet of an electric range is grounded by being connected to the neutral wire of the three-wire circuit (Fig. 31-7). However, a separate grounding wire is also connected from a terminal on the frame of the range to a grounding point of the wiring system. The cabinet or frame of an appliance or other equipment operated with a two-wire, 230-V circuit is grounded with an additional grounding wire. This wire is usually located in the connecting cable. Many electrical appliances and tools operated at 115 V, such as washing machines, dishwashers, and electric drills, present potential shock hazards. Therefore, they use a separate grounding wire. Refer also to grounding for personal safety discussed in Unit 4, "Safety Rules, Practices, and Devices."

Fig. 31-7. The cabinet of an electric range is grounded using a three-wire range plug and outlet.

230-V Taps. The 230-V taps in a panel are for wiring additional individual branch circuits. When they are used for such a circuit, extra fuses or circuit breakers must be installed outside the panel. These are necessary because the circuit is not protected with branch-circuit fuses or circuit breakers in the panel.

BRANCH-CIRCUIT WIRING

Branch circuits are wired with several kinds of approved wiring meant to protect the wire from mechanical damage. The most common of these in house wiring systems are discussed below.

Nonmetallic Sheathed Cable. Nonmetallic sheathed cable usually has two or three insulated wires. It may or may not contain a grounding wire (Fig. 31-8). NM cable is used for all kinds of indoor wiring work. It is never buried in cement or plaster. NM cable has a moisture-resistant overall covering. This allows it to be used for both exposed and con-

Fig. 31-8. Construction of two-conductor NM nonmetallic sheathed cable with a grounding wire

cealed work in dry, moist, and damp locations and in outside or inside walls of masonry, block, or tile.

Nonmetallic sheathed cable is made in several sizes, designated as 14/2, 12/2, 12/3, and the like. The number to the left of the slash is the AWG size of the individual conductors. The other number is the number of conductors in the cable other than the bare grounding wire. Therefore, a 12/2 cable has two no. 12 AWG (2.00-mm) insulated wires.

Armored Cable. In armored cable, the insulated wires are in a flexible armor sheath. The sheath is made of a single spiral of galvanized steel tape that is interlocked to form a tubelike enclosure. The cable also contains a bare-copper or aluminum bonding strip in contact with the armor along its entire length (Fig. 31-9). The purpose of the bonding strip is to provide continuity of the circuit's ground in case the armor is broken at any point. This is necessary because the armor is usually part of the grounding system.

AC cable is approved for use in dry locations where branch-circuit wiring must be protected against wear or be embedded in plaster. ACL cable is used in damp locations and where oil or other substances may corrode the wire insulation. In this cable, the insulated wires are covered with a lead sheath. The armor is put over this.

Fig. 31-9. Armored cable (*General Electric Company*)

Electrical Metallic Tubing. Electrical metallic tubing (EMT) is installed between wiring devices that are to be connected. Individual lengths of *building wire* are then inserted or pulled through the tubing and connected to the devices. For long lengths of tubing, the wires are pulled through with a *fish tape* made of springy steel.

ALUMINUM CONDUCTORS

Some building electrical systems are now being wired with aluminum conductors. Aluminum has a higher resistance than copper. Because of this, conductors made of aluminum must be larger than those made of copper when both could be used for the same purpose. For example, a circuit that could be wired with no. 14 AWG (1.60-mm) copper conductors would be wired with no. 12 AWG (2.00-mm) aluminum conductors.

Aluminum wiring requires special connectors. Wiring devices such as switches and outlets must also be approved for use with aluminum conductors. Aluminum building wires and cables are identified by the word *aluminum* or by its abbreviation, *Al.*

WIRING DEVICES

To complete a home electrical system, a number of wiring devices are used (Fig. 31-10). These are designed and installed to provide the safe, convenient, and reliable use and control of electricity.

Fig. 31-10. Common house wiring devices

SWITCH BOX   JUNCTION BOX

THREE-WAY SWITCH

FLUSH-TYPE SWITCH (SPST)

SURFACE-TYPE SWITCH (SPST)

DUPLEX CONVENIENCE OUTLET (RECEPTACLE)

CLEAT LAMP HOLDER

CEILING LAMP HOLDER

Switch Boxes. Most electrical codes require flush switches to be placed in metal enclosures. These enclosures, called *switch boxes,* are also used for mounting outlets. The boxes protect the devices mechanically. They also prevent switch sparking from becoming a fire hazard.

Junction Boxes. Junction boxes contain the connections in the branch-circuit wiring. The connections are often made with wire nuts or other solderless, pressure connectors (Fig. 31-11). Junction boxes are also used for mounting various kinds of lighting fixtures.

Fig. 31-11. Connecting wires with solderless, pressure connectors (*Ideal Industries, Inc.*)

Box Connectors. All cables entering a switch or a junction box must be securely fastened to the box. Some boxes have built-in cable clamps for this purpose. Otherwise, separate box connectors are used (Fig. 31-12).

1. STRIP WIRES AND TWIST TOGETHER

2. PLACE METAL SLEEVE CONNECTOR OVER WIRES AND CRIMP

3. CUT WIRES TO LENGTH

4. PLACE INSULATION OVER SLEEVE

ELECTRICIAN'S PLIERS EQUIPPED WITH CRIMPING DIE

Surface-Wiring Devices. Surface-wiring devices are particularly useful for changing an existing house wiring system (Fig. 31-13). They can be installed without breaking through plaster or wallboard.

Fig. 31-12. Box connectors (*Midwest Electric Manufacturing Company*)

LOCK NUT JUNCTION BOX

EMT CONNECTOR

BOX KNOCKOUTS

ARMORED CABLE CONNECTOR

NONMETALLIC SHEATHED CABLE CONNECTOR

SWITCH

DUPLEX CONVENIENCE OUTLET
(RECEPTACLE)

LAMP HOLDER

Fig. 31-13. Surface-wiring devices (*Bryant Division of Westinghouse*)

Multi-Outlet Strips. A *multi-outlet strip* is a rectangular metal enclosure with wires and outlets preinstalled (Fig. 31-14A). Such strips provide a very convenient way of adding to existing wiring. They are very useful for placing outlets in places that could not be reached easily by ordinary cable or conduit wiring. They also can provide several outlets in electrical repair stations (Fig. 31-14B).

Fig. 31-14. (A) Multi-outlet strip equipped with grounding outlets; (B) electrical repair stations equipped with multi-outlet strips (*The Wiremold Company*)

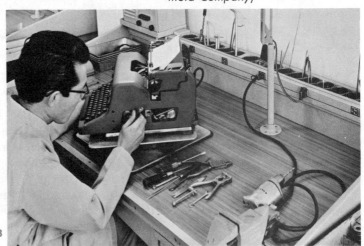

A

B

It is essential that the wiring devices installed on metal switch boxes and junction boxes be grounded properly. The aluminum bonding strip, or wire, in an armored cable or the bare copper wire in the nonmetallic sheathed cable provide the means to do this. The grounding wires are connected usually to the metal boxes by metal screws. When secured properly, these wires provide the grounding continuity for the entire electrical system. Some devices, such as duplex receptacles (grounding type) used in new residential houses, have an additional green-colored hexagonal ground terminal. This terminal is used to connect a jumper grounding wire to the metal box. When metal boxes or enclosures are not used, a separate continuous ground wire must be installed to provide adequate grounding.

THREE-WAY AND FOUR-WAY SWITCHES

Three-way switches are used to control a load from two points. Such switches are commonly used in lighting circuits in hallways, stairways, and doorways. The schematic diagram of a two-point control circuit using two three-way switches is shown in Fig. 31-15A.

A combination of three- and four-way switches can be used to control a load from any number of places. The diagram of a three-point control circuit using two three-way switches and one four-way switch is shown in Fig. 31-15B.

Fig. 31-15. Multipoint control circuits: (A) two-point; (B) three-point

REMOTE-CONTROL, LOW-VOLTAGE WIRING

Remote-control wiring makes it possible to control lights and appliances in various rooms and areas from a central place. In such systems, local control of lights is still possible. Remote-control wiring uses a low-voltage control circuit to operate line voltage circuits.

A basic remote-control circuit is illustrated in Fig. 31-16A. Additional components may be added to the basic circuit as needed to accomplish desired functions such as multipoint control or automatic control.

The low voltage for the basic circuit is provided by the transformer. It steps down the line voltage to 24 Vac. The rectifier in the circuit provides a pulsating direct current. The relay is controlled by a momentary contact switch. The relay permits the switching of line voltage loads with low-voltage control circuits.

The internal wiring of one type of relay is shown in Fig. 31-16B. This relay is mechanically *latched*. That is, the relay maintains its contacts in the last position without the need of maintaining current in the coil. The use of the split-coil design permits the use of pulses from selected equipment, such as computers, to operate only on or only off. The relays are usually mounted in relay-center boxes or cabinets, or they may be mounted in outlet boxes.

Some of the advantages of remote-control wiring are: (1) Flexibility is provided so that many switches (multipoint switching) can be used to control one relay inexpensively; (2) relays can be paralleled so that they can be controlled from one or more switches; (3) master switches (manual or motorized) can control many relays from one or more locations; (4) selected circuits can be deenergized when they are not needed by combining the remote-control system with automatic control devices, such as timers and photocells (thus saving energy); (5) the danger of shock and fire that is possible with line voltages is reduced (this is especially true in damp-location wiring); (6) when complex switching is required, remote-control wiring can substitute, for example, smaller low-voltage conductors that control relays for large power-handling devices; (7) the smaller, lower-voltage wire is less expensive to buy; and (8) most local electrical codes permit low-voltage wiring without conduits (this reduces initial installation cost, and future changes in wiring are simplified when conduits are eliminated).

SYMPTOMS OF INADEQUATE WIRING

In recent years, the number of electrical and electronic products used in the home has increased greatly. This has created the problem of overloaded branch circuits. In your own home, too many appliances may be connected to one or more branch circuits. This condition wastes electricity, creates a fire hazard, and often causes appliances to work improperly.

There are several signs of inadequate wiring. The most common of these are listed below:

1. Fuses blow and circuit breakers often open because of branch-circuit overloading.
2. Heating appliances do not warm up as quickly as they should or do not heat to the right temperature.
3. Lights dim when appliances are in use or when motors in appliances such as refrigerators start up.
4. The television picture shrinks when appliances are in use or when appliance motors start up.

Fig. 31-16. Remote-control, low-voltage wiring: (A) basic circuit; (B) internal wiring diagram of a split-coil, mechanically latched relay (*Wiring Device Department, General Electric Company*)

5. Appliance motors start with difficulty or fail to start at all.
6. Motors operate at a lower-than-normal speed, causing them to overheat.

If any of these signs are present, the wiring system should be thoroughly checked by a qualified electrician. In some cases, an inadequate wiring system can be corrected by simply adding branch circuits or by using wire of a larger size in a branch circuit. In some cases, the entire wiring system may have to be replaced.

LEARNING BY DOING

10. Wiring With Nonmetallic Sheathed Cable. These wiring jobs will help you learn how several common wiring devices are used in the home. They will also give you experience in connecting a load to three- and four-way switches.

MATERIALS NEEDED

baseboard, ¾ × 18 × 30 in. (19 × 457 × 762 mm)
1 junction box, octagonal, 4 × 1½ in. trade size
3 switch boxes, utility type, 4 × 2⅛ × 1½ in. trade size
1 junction-box cover
3 switch-box covers
1 switch, spst, flush mount
2 three-way switches, flush mount
1 four-way switch, flush mount
2 duplex receptacles
1 lampholder, keyless, medium-base, to fit 4-in. junction box
8 ft (2.4 m) nonmetallic sheathed cable, no. 14/3
5 ft (1.5 m) nonmetallic sheathed cable, no. 12/2
4 ft (1.2 m) parallel lamp cord, no. 18 (1.00-mm)
5 box connectors for nonmetallic sheathed cable
6 wire nuts for joining two no. 14 (1.60-mm) wires
1 rubber-handle attachment plug
1 incandescent lamp, medium-base, 40-, 60-, or 100-W
straps for nonmetallic sheathed cable

Procedures

1. Mount the three switch boxes (a, b, c) and the junction box (d) on the baseboard as shown in Fig. 31-17A.
2. Connect the lamp cord to the junction box as shown in Fig. 31-17B. The junction box is also used for mounting the lampholder.
3. *Job 1.* Wire and install the duplex receptacles in switch boxes a and b. Check the wiring by tracing the circuit.
4. *Job 2.* Wire a circuit to control the lamp using the spst flush switch mounted in switch box b.

Fig. 31-17. Assemblies for Learning by Doing No. 10, "Wiring With Nonmetallic Sheathed Cable"

A

PARALLEL LAMP CORD

WIRE NUT

NONMETALLIC SHEATHED CABLE

6 INCHES

6 INCHES

$\frac{5}{8}$ INCH BARE WIRE

B

#14/3 CABLE

THREE-WAY SWITCH

THREE-WAY SWITCH

C

THREE-WAY SWITCH

FOUR-WAY SWITCH

THREE-WAY SWITCH

D

5. *Job 3*. Wire a two-point control circuit (Fig. 31-17C).
6. *Job 4*. Wire a three-point control circuit (Fig. 31-17D).

SELF-TEST

Test your knowledge by writing, on a separate sheet of paper, the word or words that most correctly complete the following statements:

1. Information about wiring materials and methods that will result in the safe use of electric energy is given in the _____.
2. The bare wire of a service drop is called the _____ wire or conductor.
3. A three-wire service drop is used to supply two different _____.

4. An appliance operated at 230 V needs less _____ for its operation than that same appliance would need when operated at 115 V.
5. Electricity is distributed to different locations in a house from the _____. This unit is also commonly called a _____.
6. The load center contains the _____ or _____ that protect the branch circuits of a wiring system.
7. The neutral conductor of the service-entrance

cable is grounded to reduce the danger of _____ and to protect against _____.

8. Three common kinds of branch circuits are _____ circuits, _____ circuits, and _____ circuits.

9. One wire of each general-purpose 115 V branch circuit is connected to the neutral _____ of the load center. The insulation of the grounded neutral wire is colored _____.

10. The grounded wire of a two-wire, general-purpose circuit is never used as a _____ wire.

11. An electric-range circuit is an example of an _____ branch circuit.

12. Nonmetallic sheathed cable is never used outdoors or placed within _____ or _____.

13. A no. 14/3 nonmetallic sheathed cable contains _____ no. 14 AWG insulated wires.

14. Box _____ are used to securely fasten cables to switch and junction boxes.

FOR REVIEW AND DISCUSSION

1. What is the purpose of the *National Electrical Code?*
2. Why is a three-wire service drop used to supply a home electrical system?
3. Give at least two advantages of operating heavy-duty electrical equipment at 230 V as compared to 115 V.
4. Define the complete service entrance of a house wiring system.
5. What is the purpose of a load center? Describe two kinds of load centers.
6. How is the house wiring system grounded at the load center?
7. Name and define three kinds of branch circuits in the home.
8. Describe nonmetallic sheathed cable and armored cable.
9. What is the purpose of the bonding strip in armored cable?
10. Describe wiring with electrical metallic tubing.
11. Why are switches and outlets installed in switch boxes?
12. What is the purpose of junction boxes and of box connectors?
13. Describe a multi-outlet strip.
14. Draw diagrams of two-point and three-point control circuits. Explain how these circuits work.
15. What is meant by remote-control wiring?
16. Name five signs of inadequate wiring in a house wiring system.

INDIVIDUAL-STUDY ACTIVITIES

1. Show your class a copy of the latest *National Electrical Code®*. Describe its contents.
2. Visit a local electrical inspector, building contractor, or electrician and ask for information on the building wiring codes used in your community. Tell your class about what you have learned.
3. Collect and show to your class wiring devices, wires, and cables used in house wiring. Describe the purpose of each.

UNIT 32 Electric Motors

People are always looking for ways to do work faster, more efficiently, and more easily. Thus, many machines have been invented to replace manual labor. One of these is the electric motor. This machine changes electric energy into mechanical energy.

MOTOR ACTION

A basic example of how electric energy can be changed into mechanical motion is shown in Fig. 32-1. As current passes through the large wire from left to right, a magnetic field is produced around the wire. The polarity of this field causes it to be repelled by the magnetic field of the permanent magnet. The wire thus moves away from the magnet (Fig. 32-1A).

If the direction of the current through the wire is reversed, the polarity of the magnetic field around it also reverses. As a result, the wire moves toward the permanent magnet because of magnetic attraction (Fig. 32-1B.)

Fig. 32-1. Basic motor action

An example of how circular motion can be produced by simple motor action is shown in Fig. 32-2. A permanent magnet is mounted on a pivot so that it is free to turn between the poles of two electromagnet coils. These coils are connected in series with a battery and a reversing, or double-pole-double-throw (dpdt), switch (Fig. 32-2A). The reversing switch is used to change the polarity of the voltage applied to the coils.

When the reversing switch is closed in one direction, the current through the electromagnet coils produces magnetic poles of the polarity shown in Fig. 32-2B. These magnetic poles attract the poles of the permanent magnet. It begins to turn in a clockwise direction. As the magnet nears the poles, the switch is opened and the electromagnet is demagnetized. Because the permanent magnet is turning, it will continue to rotate beyond the coils.

The reversing switch is then closed in the opposite direction. The direction of current through the coils is thereby reversed. This, of course, changes the polarity of the electromagnets. Now the permanent magnet is repelled. It continues to turn in the clockwise direction (Fig. 32-2C).

COMMUTATOR ACTION

Using a dpdt switch would not be a practical way of changing the magnetic polarity in a motor. In a practical motor, a device called a *commutator* is used. The action of a commutator in a simple motor is shown in Fig. 32-3.

In this motor, an electromagnet coil, called the *armature,* is mounted on a shaft. It is placed between the poles of a permanent magnet. Since the armature rotates, it is also called a *rotor.* Each end of the rotor coil is connected to a segment of the commutator. The commutator is mounted on the motor shaft. The commutator has segments that are insulated from the shaft and from one another. As the rotor turns, the segments rub against stationary contacts called *brushes* at regular intervals.

In Fig. 32-3A, commutator segment 1 is connected to the negative terminal of the battery through brush 1. Segment 2 is connected to the positive terminal of the battery through brush 2. Under this condition, the rotor electromagnet is repelled by the poles of the permanent mag-

Fig. 32-2. Producing circular motion by simple motor action

Fig. 32-3. Motor commutator action

net, and the rotor begins to turn in a clockwise direction. The magnetic polarity of the rotor does not change as it continues to turn to the position shown in Fig. 32-3B. Now its poles are attracted by the poles of the permanent magnet.

When the rotor reaches the position shown in Fig. 32-3C, the commutator reverses its connections to the battery. Segment 1 is connected to the positive terminal of the battery. Segment 2 is connected to the negative terminal. This changes the direction of the current through the rotor coil and reverses its magnetic polarity. Like magnetic poles are once again near each other. Magnetic repulsion causes the rotor to continue to turn in a clockwise direction.

When the rotor reaches the position shown in Fig. 32-3D, the magnetic polarity of its poles does not change. They are attracted by the poles of the permanent magnet. This causes the rotor to continue to turn in a clockwise direction.

MOTOR SIZE

The size of an electric motor is given in terms of a mechanical unit of power called *horsepower* (hp). One horsepower is equal to 746 W of electric power. One horsepower is defined as the amount of work needed to raise a weight of 550 lb (250 kg) a distance of 1 ft (305 mm) in 1 second of time. In the metric system, motor sizes are given in watts.

Most of the motors discussed in the following paragraphs are known as *fractional-horsepower motors*. This means that their size is less than 1 hp. Other motors used for heavy-duty work may have power ratings of from 1 to 1,000 hp (0.746 to 746 kW) or more.

DIRECT-CURRENT MOTORS

Direct-current motors and direct-current generators are very similar. The magnetic fields of dc motors are produced by stationary windings called the *field* and by rotating windings in the rotor, or armature (Fig. 32-4A). The circuit through the rotor windings in the typical dc motor is completed through stationary carbon brushes. The brushes are in contact with commutator segments that are connected to the rotor windings. Several different kinds of motor brushes are shown in Fig. 32-4B.

The Series Motor. In a series dc motor, the field and the rotor windings are connected in series (Fig. 32-5A). The series motor has a high starting *torque,* or twisting force. This makes it good at starting while connected to heavy loads. The ordinary automobile cranking motor, or starter, is a series motor. Such motors are also used in cranes, hoists, cargo winches, and train engines.

LAMINATED FIELD
POLE PIECE
FIELD
WINDING
STATOR FRAME
END
BRACKET
BEARING
BRUSH
OIL
RESERVOIR
COMMUTATOR
ROTOR
A

B

Fig. 32-4. (A) Main parts of a dc motor (*Motor Division, Controls Company of America*); (B) carbon brushes used in dc motors and generators (*Helwig Carbon Products, Inc.*)

A series dc motor should never be operated without being connected directly to a load or coupled to a load through a gear assembly. Otherwise, the motor will continue to increase its speed to a point where it may be seriously damaged or even destroyed.

The Shunt Motor. In a shunt motor, the field and the rotor windings are connected in parallel (Fig. 32-5B). Shunt motors operate at a relatively constant speed when connected to varying loads. They are often used in heavy-duty drill presses, lathes, conveyors, and printing presses.

The Compound Motor. The compound motor is a combination of the series and the shunt types (Fig. 32-5C and D). This gives it the high-torque advantage of a series motor and the constant-speed advantage of a shunt motor. Compound motors may be long-shunt or short-shunt, depending on the way the shunt field is connected.

UNIVERSAL MOTORS

Universal motors work on either direct or alternating current. They are similar to the small, series dc motor (Fig. 32-5A). They come in sizes ranging from 1/100 to 2 hp (7.46 to 1492 W) with speeds up to 10,000 revolutions per minute (rpm).

Universal motors that work on 120 V are small but provide a relatively large horsepower output. The direction of rotation of universal motors can be reversed. Their speed can be controlled easily. Because of these features, the motors are used in a wide variety of small appliances and portable tools. These include sewing machines, vacuum cleaners, food mixers, drills, saws, and shears (Fig. 32-6).

Fig. 32-5. Schematic diagrams of dc motors: (A) series motor; (B) shunt motor; (C) long-shunt compound motor; (D) short-shunt compound motor

Fig. 32-6. Universal motor in a portable electric drill (*Black and Decker Manufacturing Company*)

FIELD WINDING

CHUCK

MOTOR ROTOR

BRUSH HOLDERS

BRUSH

COMMUTATOR

GEAR ASSEMBLY

BALL BEARINGS

VENTILATING FAN

HOUSING

SWITCH

FIELD WINDING

ROTOR

POWER LINE

BRUSH

REVERSING SWITCH

Fig. 32-7. A method of reversing a series motor

REVERSING A MOTOR

The direction of rotation of a dc motor or a universal motor can be reversed by interchanging the connections to the rotor windings or to the field windings. This is sometimes done by using a reversing switch connected to the brushes. An example of such a circuit arrangement using a dpdt switch with a series motor is shown in Fig. 32-7.

SPEED CONTROL

The speed of a dc motor can be varied by connecting a rheostat in series with its field or in parallel with its rotor (Fig. 32-8A).

The speed of a universal motor connected to an alternating current can be controlled by using a silicon-controlled rectifier (Fig. 32-8B). The main speed-controlling components of the circuit are potentiometer R1 and capacitor C1. The potentiometer is used to control the charging and the discharging rate of the capacitor. This, in turn, controls the voltage developed across the capacitor and the voltage applied to the gate of the silicon-controlled rectifier. By adjusting R1, the amount of current conducted by the silicon-controlled rectifier can be varied. As a result, the speed of the motor also changes.

ALTERNATING-CURRENT MOTORS

There are several different kinds of ac motors. The two most common are induction motors and synchronous motors. There are four general kinds of small, single-phase induction motors: (1) split-phase motors, (2) capacitor-start motors, (3) shaded-pole motors, and (4) repulsion-

Fig. 32-8. (A) Speed control of dc motors with a rheostat; (B) speed-control circuit using a silicon-controlled rectifier

start motors. Alternating-current motors that do not have windings in their rotor are known as *squirrel-cage motors.*

SPLIT-PHASE MOTOR

A typical split-phase motor, a widely used single-phase motor, is shown in Fig. 32-9. Split-phase motors come in sizes ranging from 1/20 to 1 hp (37.3 to 746 W). Because of their relatively low torque, these motors are used with loads that are easy to start. These include fans, blowers, small pumps, washing machines, clothes dryers, drill presses, grinders, and table saws.

Fig. 32-9. (A) Main parts of a single-phase, split-phase induction motor; (B) schematic diagram of the split-phase field circuit (*Delco Appliance Division, General Motors Corporation*)

LAMINATED STATOR CORE

MAIN (RUNNING) WINDING POLE

SLOT WEDGE

AUXILIARY (STARTING) WINDING POLE

Fig. 32-10. Stator assembly (field) of a split-phase motor (*Wagner Electric Corporation*)

END RINGS

COPPER OR ALUMINUM BARS

Fig. 32-11. The bars and end rings within the rotor of a split-phase motor. For clarity, the laminated rotor core through which the bars pass is not shown.

Running Winding. In the split-phase motor, electromagnetic fields are produced by current in the *running,* or *main, winding.* This winding consists of coils placed in insulated slots located around the inside of the stator, or stationary, core. These coils are connected in series. They form what are called *pole groups* or, simply, *poles* (Fig. 32-10).

Rotor. The rotor of a split-phase motor does not have windings. It is not connected to the power line in any way. The rotor is made up of a laminated iron core that has copper bars connected together by end rings (Fig. 32-11). As the rotor moves through the magnetic fields of the running winding, current is induced in the bars by electromagnetic induction. The induced current produces a secondary (rotor) magnetic field. This is always repelled by the poles of the running winding. This action causes the rotor to turn at a constant speed.

Starting Winding. In order to start a split-phase motor, additional magnetic energy is needed to make the rotor begin turning. This energy is supplied by a second set of stationary coils. These form what is called the *starting winding.* The coils are wound into the insulated slots that also contain the running winding (Fig. 32-10). The starting winding is connected to the motor circuit only during the time needed for the rotor to accelerate to about 80 percent of its full speed. After this, the winding is disconnected from the circuit.

Centrifugal Switch. The starting winding of a split-phase motor is automatically connected into and disconnected from the motor circuit by a centrifugally operated switch. This switch is turned on and off by a governor assembly mounted on the motor shaft (Fig. 32-12). When the motor is turned off or is running at a slow speed, the switch is turned on. The starting winding is now connected into the motor circuit. As the rotor speeds up, centrifugal force causes the governor assembly to move toward the rotor. This turns the switch off, causing the starting winding

GOVERNOR ASSEMBLY MOUNTED ON ROTOR

SWITCH ASSEMBLY MOUNTED ON END BRACKET

POWER CORD TERMINALS

Fig. 32-12. Centrifugal switch used in a split-phase motor (*Robbins and Myers, Inc.*)

to be disconnected from the motor circuit. The clicklike sound heard very soon after a split-phase motor is turned on or off is made by the movement of the governor assembly.

Reversing. A split-phase motor is usually reversed by interchanging the connections to the starting winding. A number of different kinds of reversing switches can be used for this purpose. The motor can also be reversed by interchanging the connections to the running winding. If both winding connections are interchanged, the motor will continue to run in its original direction.

Speed Control. The speed of a split-phase motor, unlike that of a universal motor, cannot be varied gradually by reducing the voltage across the field without losing too much torque. For this reason, the speed may be step-controlled by changing the number of running-winding poles. In a three-speed motor, for example, the running winding is arranged so that it can be switched to form two, four, or six poles. The approximate speed that each of these connections produces can be found by using the formula

$$rpm = \frac{120f}{N}$$

where rpm = revolutions per minute of the shaft
f = frequency of the operating current (expressed in hertz)
N = number of running-winding poles

This formula gives what is called the *synchronous speed* of a motor. In a nonsynchronous motor, the actual speed is always less than the synchronous speed. This is due to what is known as *slip,* which results from losses of electrical and mechanical energy in the motor.

CAPACITOR-START MOTOR

A typical capacitor-start induction motor is similar to a split-phase motor. However, this motor contains a nonpolarized electrolytic capacitor connected in series with the starting winding (Fig. 32-13). The electrical action of the capacitor gives the motor a much greater torque than the starting winding alone can produce. Because of this high torque, capacitor-start motors are used with hard-to-start loads. These include stokers, refrigerators, air conditioners, air compressors, and heavy-duty pumps.

SHADED-POLE MOTOR

The shaded-pole motor does not have a starting winding or a capacitor. Instead, the motor has heavy copper *shading coils*. These are wound

Fig. 32-13. Schematic diagram of a typical capacitor-start motor

Fig. 32-14. A two-pole, shaded-pole induction motor used in a record player (*The General Industries Company*)

around each pole piece or part of it (Fig. 32-14). The induced current in these coils produces a magnetic field. This acts with the field-winding magnetic field to provide the rotor with a rotating magnetic field.

Shaded-pole motors are usually less than ¼ hp (187 W) in size. Because of their low torque, they are used with light loads. These include small fans, small blowers, record players, tape recorders, and motion-picture projectors.

REPULSION-START MOTOR

The repulsion-start motor has a field winding and a wire-wound rotor similar to the rotor of a dc or a universal motor (Fig. 32-15). The rotor winding, however, is not connected to the power line. The motor also has a commutator and brushes. The brushes are shorted to one another.

Fig. 32-15. Cutaway view of a ½-hp (373-watt) repulsion-start induction motor (*Wagner Electric Corporation*)

When the motor is turned on, the magnetic fields of the field winding induce a voltage in the rotor winding. The secondary magnetic fields produced by the rotor current are then repelled by the electromagnetism of the field winding. This action provides the motor with its starting torque. After the motor reaches about 75 percent of its full speed, a centrifugally operated mechanism short-circuits the rotor commutator segments. The motor then continues to work as an ordinary induction motor.

The most common repulsion-start motors range from ½ to 8 hp (373 to 5,970 W) in size. They are operated at 220 V. Because of their extremely high torque, these motors are used with heavy-duty loads, such as large air-conditioning units, compressors, and pumps.

SYNCHRONOUS MOTOR

A synchronous motor keeps in step with the frequency of the ac power source. For this reason, the motor runs at a more constant speed than other motors. One kind of small synchronous motor is called a *hysteresis motor*.

A common use of synchronous motors is in electric clocks. Such motors are also used to operate time switches, business machines, and several kinds of control mechanisms. A shading coil makes these motors self-starting (Fig. 32-16).

Fig. 32-16. A small synchronous timing motor (*General Electric Company*)

THREE-PHASE INDUCTION MOTOR

In the three-phase induction motor, the field winding consists of three separate sets of coils. Each of these is energized by one phase line, or *leg,* of a three-phase power system (Fig. 32-17A). When the motor is connected to a three-phase line, the currents in the coils produce what is called a *revolving,* or *rotating, magnetic field* (Fig. 32-17B). This magnetic field acts on the secondary magnetic field produced by the induced rotor current to keep the rotor moving.

A three-phase motor can be reversed by simply interchanging any two of the three power-line conductors. This is usually done with a magnetically operated switch called a *magnetic starter,* or a *motor controller.*

Because of their simple construction, high torque, and high efficiency, three-phase induction motors are found in all kinds of heavy-duty industrial equipment. Most three-phase motors operate at a voltage of 208 V or higher.

Fig. 32-17. The three-phase induction motor: (A) coil connections; (B) basic operation

Fig. 32-18. Making the connections to test a motor before certifying it as an energy-efficient motor (*Gould, Inc., Electric Motor Division*)

ENERGY-EFFICIENT MOTORS

Electric motors use about 64 percent of all the electricity produced in the United States. Three-fourths of this is used by motors that operate pumps, blowers, fans, and machine tools. These devices are used often in the chemical, metal, paper, food, and petroleum industries.

Because electric motors use such large amounts of electric energy, they also have great potential for energy conservation. The U.S. Department of Energy considers the development and use of energy-efficient motors by industry an important factor in the nation's energy-conservation effort.

Motors rated from 1 through 20 hp (0.746 to 14.92 kW) have the greatest conservation potential. Motor efficiency is a measure of mechanical work output compared to the electrical power input. A motor's *power factor* is a measure of how well the motor uses the current it draws (Fig. 32-18).

Energy-efficient motors have several important features. They operate at cooler temperatures. Thus, less electric energy is lost to heat energy. The motors are sized correctly to the load requirements. For example, if the equipment takes a 5-hp (3.7-kW) motor, the motor closest to that requirement should be used. Otherwise, the motor would be overloaded or underloaded. Having the right-size motor for the load is important in maintaining a good power factor.

The rotors of energy-efficient motors are made with more aluminum. This reduces losses resulting from current flowing in the rotor bars. More copper is used in the stators. This reduces losses in the motor. More steel and thinner laminations are used to reduce the stator and rotor losses. The air gap between the rotor and stator is less in an energy-efficient motor. A 1-hp (746-W) energy-efficient motor will use 70 W less under continuous operation than a standard motor of the same wattage.

MOTOR CARE AND MAINTENANCE

An electric motor is a very dependable machine. However, it will provide the safest and most efficient service only if it is used and maintained in the right way. The following suggestions will help:

1. Before installing a new or different motor, read the information on its nameplate. Make sure that the right voltage and system (ac or dc) are being used.
2. It is always safe practice to ground the frame of a motor. This is especially true if the motor is used in a damp location or near any grounded metal object.
3. If water enters the frame of a motor, the motor should be completely dried out and checked for shorts before being put back into operation.

4. Never try to stop a motor by grabbing its shaft.
5. Never overoil a motor. Apply a little oil to the bearings only. Too much oil may damage insulation and cause dirt and dust to collect. Some motors have sealed bearings that do not need oiling or greasing.
6. To prevent an ordinary motor from becoming overheated, keep the air openings in its frame clear.
7. Replace the brushes in a universal motor when they become shorter than ¼ in. (6.35 mm). Badly worn brushes will cause too much sparking at the commutator. Too much sparking is also caused by loose brush holders, by loose commutator segments, and by shorts in the rotor winding.
8. Unplug a motor if it seems to be working at a speed slower than normal. Otherwise, the motor could become overheated. The motor may be overloaded or it may have a shorted winding. Check motor speed with a tachometer.
9. Turn a split-phase motor off at once if it hums but fails to start after being turned on. This is very often due to a defective centrifugal-switch mechanism. If the motor is left on, the running winding may burn out quickly.
10. An induction motor draws much more than the normal working current as it comes up to full speed. For this reason, such a motor should be protected with a dual-element time-delay fuse. The correct sizes of the fuses to be used with several single-phase, 115-V induction motors are given in Table 32-1. Small portable motors are adequately protected by the fuse or circuit breaker in the panel supplying their power.

TABLE 32-1. SIZE OF FUSES USED WITH SINGLE-PHASE, 115-V INDUCTION MOTORS

Size of Motor (horsepower)	Equivalent (watts)	Fuse Size (amperes)
⅙	124	*
¼	187	*
⅓	249	*
½	373	*
¾	560	*
1	746	*
1½	1119	25
2	1492	30

*Motors rated at 1 hp (746 W) or less are considered protected by the branch-circuit fuse in the panel supplying their power. In most cases this will be a 15- or 20-A fuse.

LEARNING BY DOING

11. *A Simple Two-Pole Universal Motor.* As you have learned, electromagnetic energy is used to produce mechanical motion in an electric motor. By making this motor, you will learn more about the basic parts of motors and how they work.

MATERIALS NEEDED

1 piece of wood, ¾ × 4½ × 6 in.
(19 × 114 × 152 mm)
1 piece of band iron, ⅛ × ½ × 11⅝ in.
(3.18 × 13 × 295 mm)
1 piece of band iron, ⅛ × ½ × 6¾ in.
(3.18 × 13 × 170 mm)
2 pieces of sheet brass, ⅜ × 3⅛ in. (9.5 × 79 mm)
2 pieces of tin plate, ¼ × 1¼ in. (6 × 32 mm)

in.	mm
$1/8$	3
$3/16$	5
$1/4$	6.5
$5/16$	8
$3/8$	10
$1/2$	13
$5/8$	16
$3/4$	19
1	25
$1 1/4$	31
$1 9/16$	39.5
2	51
$2 3/4$	70
3	76
$3 1/8$	79
$3 1/2$	89
$4 1/2$	115
6	152
$11 5/8$	297

1 piece of tin plate, $1 1/2 \times 3$ in. (38×76 mm)

60 ft (18 m) PE magnet wire, no. 25 (0.45 mm); 40 ft (12 m) for the field winding and 20 ft (6 m) for the armature winding

Procedure

1. Assemble the materials and make the connections as shown in Fig. 32-19.
2. Connect the terminals of the motor to two D-size dry cells connected in series or to a battery-eliminator power supply adjusted to produce an output voltage of about 3 V.
3. Adjust the brushes so that maximum speed is obtained. The brushes should contact the commutator segments with the same amount of pressure. As brush pressure is increased, the motor speed will decrease.
4. Show how the motor can be reversed by using a dpdt switch wired as a reversing switch.

SELF-TEST

Test your knowledge by writing, on a separate sheet of paper, the word or words that most correctly complete the following statements:

1. An electric motor is a machine that changes _____ energy into _____ energy.
2. The size of an electric motor is given in terms of a _____ unit of power called the horsepower. One horsepower is equal to _____ watts of electric power.
3. In a series dc motor, the _____ and the _____ windings are connected in series.
4. The word *torque* means _____ force.
5. In a shunt motor, the field and the rotor windings are connected in _____.
6. The compound motor is a combination of the _____ and the _____ types.
7. Universal motors can be operated with either _____ or _____ current.
8. The direction of rotation in a universal motor can be reversed by interchanging the connections to the _____ windings or to the _____ windings.
9. A circuit using a silicon-controlled rectifier provides an efficient way of controlling the _____ of a universal motor.
10. Induction motors and synchronous motors can be operated with _____ current only.
11. The electromagnetic fields necessary for the operation of a split-phase motor are produced by current in the _____ and _____ windings.
12. The rotor of a split-phase motor does not have _____.
13. The starting torque of a capacitor-start motor is increased by connecting a nonpolarized electrolytic capacitor in series with the _____ winding.
14. In the shaded-pole motor, heavy copper _____ coils are wound around each pole piece or part of it.
15. The field winding of a three-phase motor consists of three separate sets of _____.

Fig. 32-19. Assembly and working drawings for Learning by Doing No. 11, "A Simple Two-Pole Universal Motor"

1. Explain how a simple motor works.
2. What does a commutator do in a dc motor?
3. How is the size of a motor given? Define this unit.
4. Describe the series, shunt, and compound motors.
5. Describe a universal motor.
6. Tell how the direction of rotation of a universal motor can be reversed.
7. How can the speed of a universal motor be controlled?
8. Name four kinds of single-phase induction motors.
9. Describe a typical split-phase motor. What is the purpose of its starting winding?
10. What is the centrifugal switch in a split-phase motor used for?
11. What is the main advantage of a capacitor-start motor?
12. For what purpose are shading coils used in a shaded-pole motor?
13. Describe a repulsion-start motor.
14. What is the main advantage of a synchronous motor?
15. Describe a three-phase induction motor.
16. Give six procedures that are helpful in using and maintaining electric motors.
17. Why are dual-element time-delay fuses used to protect motors?

INDIVIDUAL-STUDY ACTIVITIES

1. Obtain a commercial universal or split-phase motor. Disassemble the motor and describe its construction to the class. Also explain how the motor works.
2. Different kinds of motors can often be obtained from local appliance dealers, appliance-service technicians, and motor-service technicians. Show some of these motors to the class. Explain the major electrical and physical characteristics of each kind of motor. Discuss also the different kinds of equipment, tools, and appliances that use these motors.

UNIT 33   Producing Heat

Electric energy is converted into useful heat energy in a number of ways. In the home, electricity is used for space heating and to produce heat for a variety of uses. Electricity is also used to produce the heat needed for several industrial processes. These include welding, heat treatment, and steelmaking. Special electronic generators are used to produce the heat needed for certain medical treatments.

In the last few years, great strides have been made in manufacturing energy-efficient heat-producing equipment and appliances for industry and for the home. Many devices are more reliable, last longer, and are more easily controlled with the use of solid-state electronics. Sensing devices, for example, are being installed in modern clothes dryers to detect humidity levels. When the proper humidity levels are reached, the dryer automatically shuts off—thus saving time and energy.

RESISTANCE HEATING

Resistance heating uses the energy of moving electrons as they collide with particles within a conductor. If enough of these collisions occur, the friction that results will heat the conductor (Fig. 33-1).

The amount of heat produced in any conductor by resistance heating is related to the power formula $P = I^2R$. Thus, the heat produced is directly proportional to the resistance of the conductor and to the square of the current. This means, for example, that if the current is doubled, the amount of heat will be four times the original heat. However, if the current remains constant and the resistance is doubled, only twice as much heat will be produced.

Fig. 33-1. Resistance heating

Resistance Alloys. The conductors used for resistance-heating purposes are made of several materials. These materials have the amount of resistance needed to produce heat. The most common of these are alloys made of nickel and chromium; copper and nickel; and nickel, chromium, and iron.

Heating Elements. In many heat-producing appliances and products, the resistance alloy is in the form of a round or flat wire called *resistance wire*. This wire is wrapped around an insulator such as porcelain or mica to form a *heating element* (Fig. 33-2A). In other products, the resistance wire is in the shape of a coil or a rod enclosed in a protective metal tube (Fig. 33-2B). In this kind of heating element, the resistance

Fig. 33-2. Heating elements: (A) coiled resistance wire wrapped around insulators; (B) coiled resistance wire embedded in insulating material within a metal tube wire is usually embedded in a material such as magnesium oxide. This material is both a good electrical insulator and a good conductor of heat. Table 33-1 gives the wattage, resistance, and wire sizes for Nichrome-wire heating elements.

Table 33-1. RESISTANCE-WIRE HEATING ELEMENTS

Values for 115-V Operation			
Wattage Required (W)	Approximate Resistance at 75°F (24°C) (Ω)	Recommended Sizes of Nichrome Wire [AWG]	
		Minimum	Maximum
100	118.100	30	26
150	78.732	30	26
200	59.050	29	25
250	47.240	28	24
300	39.366	28	24
350	33.742	27	23
400	29.525	26	22
450	26.244	24	20
500	23.620	24	20
550	21.472	23	19
600	19.683	23	19
650	18.170	23	19
700	16.871	22	18
750	15.745	22	18
800	14.762	22	18
850	13.894	21	17
900	13.122	21	17
950	12.431	21	17
1,000	11.810	20	16

Fig. 33-3. Installing radiant heating cable (*L. N. Roberson Company*)

Radiant-heating Cable. Radiant-heating cable consists of resistance wire insulated with a heat-resistant rubber or thermoplastic compound. This cable is commonly used for space heating. The cable is placed in a concrete floor or in a plaster ceiling. In a ceiling installation, the cable is first stapled to plasterboard and then covered with plaster (Fig. 33-3).

Radiant-heating cable for space heating comes in several lengths. Each length is controlled by a thermostat. Each has a certain wattage rating, usually in the 400- to 5,000-W range. The individual lengths of heating elements are color-coded to indicate their wattage rating. The heating elements operate at either 115 or 230 V.

Radiant-heating panels are also available for space heating. Some panels are available in sizes of 2 × 4 ft (60.9 × 121.9 cm). They are designed to fit into a ceiling grid, replacing ceiling tiles. Two 220 Vac radiant-heating panels, each rated at 750 W, can provide sufficient heat to keep an average-size bedroom warm in winter.

Resistance Welding. Resistance heating is used for spot welding and for seam welding. In spot welding, the metals to be welded are placed between two welder electrodes. Current passes through the metals from one electrode to the other. The resistance of the metals to the current produces a very high temperature. This welds the metals together at the point of electrode contact (Fig. 33-4).

Seam welding is a special kind of spot welding. On a seam welder, the electrodes are wheels between which the metals to be welded are passed. As with spot welding, current passes through the metals, welding them together along a seam.

Fig. 33-4. Resistance welding in industry. Sparks from this process show as long white streaks in the photograph. (*Unimation, Inc.*)

ELECTRIC ARC

A simple way of producing an electric arc is shown in Fig. 33-5. To start the arc, the ends of the carbon rods are brought into contact with each other. The heat produced by the current through the point of contact causes a small amount of the carbon to vaporize, or turn to gas. If the contact between the rods is then broken and the ends are separated, current will *arc*, or pass, through the carbon vapor. This produces a very bright light and a very high temperature.

Electric-Arc Welding. In electric-arc welding, heat is produced by an arc formed between a welding rod and the metal object being welded. The rod is connected to one terminal of the welder. The metal object is connected to the other terminal (Fig. 33-6).

To strike the arc, the welding rod is touched to the metal. The heat produced as current passes through the point of contact vaporizes some of the rod, thus forming an arc. The heat of the arc is great enough to melt the welding rod and the workpiece. The extra metal needed for the weld is supplied by the rod.

The Electric-Arc Furnace. An electric-arc furnace is used to melt metals during the steelmaking process. In such a furnace, carbon electrodes are used to produce heat by means of electric arcs. The electrodes are lowered through the top of the furnace. The furnace contains a *charge,* or mixture, of scrap metals to be melted (Fig. 33-7). Arcs are then produced as current moves from the electrodes to the charge, melting the metal.

Fig. 33-5. Producing an electric arc

Fig. 33-6. Electric-arc welding

Fig. 33-7. The electric-arc furnace (*American Iron and Steel Institute*)

INFRARED HEATING

The prefix *infra* means below. *Infrared rays* are a form of electromagnetic radiation that people cannot see. They have a frequency just below that of the lowest-frequency visible light, which is red.

The infrared rays used for heating are usually produced by filament lamps (Fig. 33-8). The filaments of these lamps are operated at a much lower temperature than the filaments of ordinary incandescent lamps. Under this condition, the lamps produce little visible light but large quantities of infrared rays. When these rays strike a material that absorbs them, the energy of the rays is changed into heat with a high degree of efficiency.

Fig. 33-8. Infrared lamps: (A) tubular quartz; (B) reflector (*General Electric Company*)

Infrared lamps are used for drying ink, glue, varnish, and paint (Fig. 33-9). They are also commonly used for defrosting foods and for certain kinds of medical treatments.

Fig. 33-9. Automobile-body enamel-finish coat being baked in an infrared oven. Banks of infrared lamps provide the necessary amount of heat. (*The Fostoria Pressed Steel Corporation*)

INDUCTION HEATING

Induction heating takes place when a current is induced in a material by electromagnetic flux, just as in a transformer. In an induction heater, a high-frequency alternating current of from 5,000 to 500,000 Hz is passed through a heater, or work, coil. This coil can be compared to the primary winding of a transformer.

As the magnetic field around the heater coil cuts across a metallic object to be heated, voltages are induced in the object because of electromagnetic induction. These voltages, in turn, produce high-frequency alternating currents that move through the object. The resistance of the metal to these induced currents causes it to become heated very rapidly.

The amount of heat produced and the depth to which this heat will penetrate an object are easily controlled by induction heating. For these reasons, this type of heating is used in a variety of industrial processes. These include forging, heat treatment, and soldering (Fig. 33-10).

Fig. 33-10. An induction heater being used for soldering (*Induction Heating Corporation*)

DIELECTRIC HEATING

Dielectric heating is used to produce heat in nonmetallic materials. In their simplest form, the working elements of a dielectric heater consist of two metal plates.

The plates are connected to a high-frequency generator. The generator usually has an output with a range of 10 to 30 MHz. This produces a high-frequency electrostatic field between the plates and through the material to be heated. This field causes electrons within atoms of the material to be very rapidly drawn or distorted out of their normal paths. The electrons are forced to move first in one direction and then in the

Fig. 33-11. Principle of dielectric heating

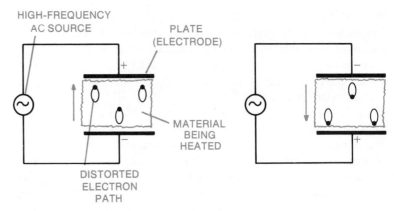

HIGH-FREQUENCY
AC SOURCE

PLATE
(ELECTRODE)

MATERIAL
BEING
HEATED

DISTORTED
ELECTRON
PATH

Fig. 33-12. Drying wood glue in a dielectric heater

Fig. 33-13. A modern microwave oven (*Admiral Home Appliances, Division of Magic Chef, Inc.*)

other (Fig. 33-11). The friction that results from this back-and-forth movement of the electrons causes the material to be heated very quickly.

Dielectric heaters produce heat that can be easily controlled. In addition, the heat is evenly distributed through all parts of a nonmetallic material. For these reasons, these heaters are widely used for drying glue and for heating wood, plastic, clay, and liquids (Fig. 33-12).

MICROWAVE OVEN

The microwave, or electronic, oven is able to cook foods in a fraction of the time needed for cooking with standard ranges (Fig. 33-13). The oven works similarly to dielectric heating units. Through the use of solid-state electronics, a modern microwave oven has, for example, a touch-control panel with memory programming, variable 10-level heat control, automatic defrost, digital clock, and a probe thermometer for cooking to an exact temperature.

Microwaves are electromagnetic radiations that, because of their ultrahigh frequency (UHF), have a very short wavelength. In the typical microwave oven, the frequency of the radiations is 915 or 2,450 MHz. These radiations are produced by an electron tube known as a *magnetron*.

In some ovens, microwave energy from the magnetron is beamed to a fanlike, motor-driven stirrer through a rectangular, metal, tubelike device called a *waveguide* (Fig. 33-14). The stirrer acts as a reflector, more evenly distributing the energy over the food being cooked.

The molecules in the food in a microwave oven try to keep in step with the ultra-high-frequency polarity reversals of the microwave electrostatic field. This produces heat evenly through all parts of the food by molecular friction.

Materials such as paper, plastics, and ceramics do not absorb microwave energy and so do not become heated. For this reason, food containers made of these materials are excellent for use in a microwave oven. Metal containers should not be used in a microwave oven because they reflect microwave energy and can damage the magnetron.

Fig. 33-14. Operation of a micro-wave oven (*Amana Refrigeration, Inc.*)

ELECTRIC RANGE

A typical electric-range heating element is shown in Fig. 33-15. The resistance wire of this unit is placed in a metal tube. It is insulated from the tube by an electrical insulation that is also an excellent conductor of heat.

Fig. 33-15. Construction of an electric-range heating element (*The Tappan Stove Company*)

Temperature Control. Current to each surface heating element is controlled by a heat-selector switch. This switch connects the sections of the heating element to the power line in different ways. For example, three-heat control of a simple two-ring heating element is shown in Fig. 33-16. Some ranges may have six or more heating-element rings that provide up to seven different levels of heat.

Fig. 33-16. Switching action for a two-ring, three-heat heating element for a range surface unit

The Oven Thermostat. A *thermostat* is a device used to automatically control the operation of heating appliances so that a desired temperature is maintained. It acts as a switch that can turn a circuit on or off. The temperature of the range oven is usually controlled by a bellows thermostat. The main parts of such a thermostat are the bulb, the capillary tube, the bellows, and the switch contacts (Fig. 33-17). The switch contacts are connected in series with the oven power-supply line. The bulb is filled with a liquid or a gas that expands when heated.

299

To set the oven temperature, the oven heat-selector dial is turned to the correct position. When the oven temperature increases above this setting, the pressure within the bulb forces the bellows to expand. The movement of the bellows is coupled to an arm that opens the circuit between the switch contacts (Fig. 33-17A). As the oven cools, the bellows contract and the switch is turned on (Fig. 33-17B). This action of the thermostat is repeated as often as needed to keep the oven at the temperature on the heat-selector dial.

Fig. 33-17. Basic operation of a bellows range-oven thermostat

Fig. 33-18. Operation of a bimetallic thermostat: (A) open; (B) closed

BIMETALLIC THERMOSTAT

The moving part of the common bimetallic thermostat used in many appliances is a strip of two different kinds of metal. These metals, which are rigidly joined together, expand at different rates when heated. As a result, the strip bends as it is heated. This bending is used to make or break a switching contact. The bimetallic strip may be straight or spiral.

Figure 33-18 shows how a simple bimetal thermostat works. In this thermostat, the bimetallic strip is placed near a fixed contact point (Fig. 33-18A). The thermostat is now in an open position.

When the thermostat is heated, the brass part of the bimetallic strip expands more than the iron. Because of this, the strip bends upward. It closes that part of the circuit connected to its terminals (Fig. 33-18B). When the strip cools, it bends back to its original position. This opens the circuit.

TOASTER

The heating elements of a toaster usually consist of flat, ribbon-shaped resistance wires. These wires are wound on sheets of *mica*. This is a mineral that is an excellent insulator. The elements are mounted in the toaster frame (Fig. 33-19A).

300

HEATING ELEMENTS

Fig. 33-19. The toaster: (A) heating elements in a typical automatic pop-up toaster; (B) circuit diagram

The main electric circuit of a typical toaster is shown in Fig. 33-19B. The four heating elements are connected in parallel. They have a total wattage rating of about 1,000 W. The main switch that controls current to the elements is turned on when the toaster bread carriage is pushed down.

The Timer. Automatic pop-up toasters have additional circuits and devices. They are used to time the toasting cycle and to control the carriage-raising mechanism when the cycle is completed. In many toasters, the timer mechanism is controlled by a bimetallic strip. It is heated by a resistance-wire heating element (Fig. 33-20A). This element is connected in parallel with a timer switch (Fig. 33-20B).

The Toasting Cycle. When a toaster is turned on, current passes through the bimetallic-strip heating element (Fig. 33-21A). This heats the strip, and it begins to bend. After the strip reaches a certain position, determined by the setting of the toaster light-dark control, it pushes against a trigger arm. This turns the timer switch on (Fig. 33-21B).

Fig. 33-20. Toaster-timer bimetallic strip connected to the toaster circuit

Fig. 33-21. Basic operation of a toasting-cycle control mechanism

Fig. 33-22. Construction of an electric water heater (*FauceHot Heater Company*)

Fig. 33-23. Sunbeam® Monitor™ Electronic Iron (*Sunbeam Appliance Company, a member company of Allegheny International, Inc.*)

Fig. 33-24. Inside view of the Sunbeam® Monitor™ Electronic Iron (*Sunbeam Appliance Company, a member company of Allegheny International, Inc.*)

The bimetallic-strip heating element is now shorted out of the circuit. This causes it to cool and bend in the opposite direction. It then pushes against a second trigger. This releases the spring-driven carriage, and the carriage moves upward (Fig. 33-21C). This action also turns off the main switch and the timer. The toasting cycle is then completed.

WATER HEATER

A typical electric water heater is shown in Fig. 33-22. The heating elements consist of resistance wire insulated from, and enclosed within, copper tubes. As the water in the tank heats, it circulates around the elements. It slowly rises to the top of the tank, where the hot-water outlet pipe is located. The water is automatically kept at the right temperature by bimetallic-strip thermostats. These control the current through the heating elements.

ELECTRONIC IRON

A modern electronic iron is shown in Fig. 33-23. Electronic circuitry has made this iron "smart." The electronic circuitry, including an integrated-circuit chip, senses the selected temperature setting and guards against the user's forgetting to turn it off.

Figure 33-24 illustrates the use of electronic circuits in the iron. One printed-circuit (PC) board is used for controlling and monitoring the various sensing units. Another PC board is used for the power supply.

This electronic iron is designed to shut itself down in 30 seconds or less if accidentally tipped or if left in the ironing or soleplate-down position and not moved. If left in the heel rest position, the iron will shut itself off in 10 minutes or less. The use of electronics makes the temperature control of the iron more accurate than that of a conventional iron.

Indicating LEDs provide information to the user. An amber light indicates that the electronic iron is plugged into an electric outlet. A red light indicates that it has been programmed to a heat setting and is heating or cooling to that temperature. A green light comes on to indicate that the iron has reached the desired setting and is ready for use. The electronic principles involved in this iron, which uses solid-state technology—integrated circuits and microprocessors—are discussed in detail in Unit 42, "Fundamentals of Computers."

SELF-TEST

Test your knowledge by writing, on a separate sheet of paper, the word or words that most correctly complete the following statements:

1. The amount of heat produced in a conductor by resistance heating is directly proportional to the _____ of the current and to the _____ of the conductor.

2. The most common materials used in making resistance-heating wires are alloys consisting of various combinations of _____, _____, _____, and _____.

3. The two most common kinds of resistance welding are _____ welding and _____ welding.

4. Infrared rays are _____ radiation having a frequency just below that of _____ light.

5. Induction heating is produced by high-frequency induced _____ moving through metallic objects.

6. Dielectric heating is used to produce heat within _____ materials.

7. A microwave oven uses _____ to cook food in a fraction of the normal cooking time.

8. The heat-sensing bulb of a bellows thermostat is filled with a liquid or a gas that _____ when heated.

9. A thermostat acts as a _____, which can be turned on or off by the application of _____.

10. The operation of a bimetallic thermostat depends on the fact that some metals _____ more than others when heated.

FOR REVIEW AND DISCUSSION

1. Define resistance heating.
2. What is resistance wire?
3. Describe the construction of two common kinds of resistance-heating elements.
4. Describe spot and seam welding.
5. Explain how an electric arc is produced between the ends of two carbon rods.
6. Describe arc welding.
7. Define infrared rays.
8. Give several examples of the use of infrared lamps for heating.
9. Explain induction heating. State the purposes for which it is commonly used.
10. Explain dielectric heating. For what purposes is such heating used?
11. What are microwaves?
12. Describe the basic construction of a microwave oven.
13. Describe the construction of a heating element of an electric range.
14. What is a thermostat?
15. Explain how a bellows thermostat works.
16. Describe the construction and operation of a bimetallic thermostat.

1. Prepare a written or an oral report telling about the industrial applications of resistance heating, infrared heating, induction heating, or dielectric heating.

2. Prepare a written or an oral report telling how the room thermostat in your home operates to control the heating and/or cooling system.

3. Obtain literature on heat-producing appliances from local appliance and home equipment dealers. Examine the literature in order to determine how manufacturers have improved the energy efficiency of their products through the use of solid-state electronics. Report your findings to the class.

UNIT 34   Refrigeration and Air Conditioning

The operation of refrigerators and air conditioners depends on the fact that liquids absorb heat when they *evaporate,* or turn into gas (Fig. 34-1). In cooling appliances, a liquid called the *refrigerant* is circulated through tubes made of thin metal. These tubes are formed into *evaporator coils.*

The refrigerant has a very low boiling point and evaporates in the evaporator coils. As a result, the coils are cooled. They absorb heat from the air around them. After each evaporation, or cooling, cycle, the refrigerant *vapor,* or gas, is compressed and cooled. This changes the vapor back into a liquid. The refrigerant is then ready to be used again.

REFRIGERATOR

Figure 34-2 shows the main parts of an electric refrigerator system. In this and in most other modern electric cooling appliances, the refrigerant used is a substance called *Freon.* Freon is basically a compound of fluorine, carbon, and hydrogen.

When the temperature in the refrigerator cabinet rises above a specific setting, the motor-driven compressor begins to operate. The compressor pumps Freon vapor from the evaporator coils. This reduces the pressure in these coils, allowing liquid Freon to move into them through the capillary tube. A bellows thermostat is used to control the temperature in the cabinet.

As the liquid Freon evaporates, it absorbs heat from the freezer compartment and from the refrigerator cabinet. The heated vapor is then drawn through the compressor and into the condenser. There it is cooled and changed into a liquid. The liquid Freon is then forced back into the evaporator coils. Here it evaporates once again to complete the cooling cycle. This action is continuous while the refrigerator is in operation.

As more and more heat is absorbed from the cabinet, the temperature within the cabinet drops. This causes the temperature-control-thermo-

Fig. 34-1. Liquids absorb heat when they evaporate.

stat contacts to open. This, in turn, turns the compressor motor off. The refrigerator remains idle until the cabinet temperature once again rises enough to cause the thermostat contacts to close and start the compressor motor.

The Motor-Starting Relay. The refrigerator compressor and the motor that drives it are contained in a sealed unit. The motor-starting winding is connected and disconnected from the motor circuit by means of a relay mounted on the compressor housing.

When the cooling cycle starts, the line voltage is applied to terminals L1 and L2 of the relay (Fig. 34-3). Current now passes through the running winding of the motor and the relay coil. The high starting current in the circuit causes the relay contacts to close. This completes the circuit through the starting winding of the motor.

The current through the running winding decreases in value after the motor has accelerated to its full speed. This causes the starting-relay electromagnet to lose strength. The starting contacts open. The motor then continues to operate with its starting winding disconnected from the circuit.

Overload Protection. The refrigerator motor-starting relay often has a protective device. This device opens the motor circuit when the motor becomes overloaded. An overloaded motor runs more slowly than usual. It may be seriously damaged by the increased amount of current passing through its running winding.

To prevent damage, a bimetallic thermostat is connected in series with the motor circuit. When an abnormally high current passes through the element, its temperature increases until the thermostat contacts open. The motor is thereby automatically turned off.

ROOM AIR CONDITIONER

A room air conditioner is a refrigeration unit that cools, dehumidifies, cleans, and circulates the air in an enclosed space. In general, the main parts of a typical room air-conditioning unit are similar to those of a refrigerator (Fig. 34-4).

Room air is drawn through the filter to remove dirt, dust, and other particles. The air then passes through an evaporator-coil assembly, where it is cooled. The cool air is then recirculated through the room by blowers.

As the air moves past the cold evaporator coils, some of the moisture in it *condenses,* or collects, on the coils. As a result, the air leaves the coils in a *dehumidified,* or drier, condition. This makes it more comfortable. The moisture that collects at the coils is discharged from the air conditioner as water or water vapor.

The cooling capacity of a room air conditioner is given in terms of the British thermal unit (Btu). The metric unit is the *joule.* One British

Fig. 34-2. Main parts of an electric refrigerator system

Fig. 34-3. Circuit of a refrigerator motor starting relay

Fig. 34-4. A typical room air conditioner (*Kelvinator, Inc.*)

CONDENSER FAN MOTOR   BLOWER   SOLENOID CONTROL   THERMOSTAT   FILTER

(COOLING) EVAPORATOR COIL

CONDENSER COIL

CONDENSER FAN   DRAIN TUBE (CONDENSATE)

AIR INLET GRILL

EXHAUST AIR OUTLET

thermal unit is the quantity of heat needed to raise the temperature of one pound of water one degree Fahrenheit. The Btu rating of an air conditioner is a measure of how much heat it will remove from a room during a certain period of time, usually 1 hour. The effectiveness of an air conditioner is also indicated by the amount of air it can move in a given period of time. The unit usually used is cubic feet per minute (cfm).

CENTRAL AIR CONDITIONING

A central air-conditioning system cools all areas of a house. In such a system, the condensing unit is located outside the house. When used in a house with a forced-air furnace, the evaporator-coil assembly is usually located above the furnace in the plenum, or main hot/cool output air duct (Fig. 34-5).

HEAT PUMP

The electrically driven heat pump is a combination heating-and-cooling unit. It transfers heat from one location to another in very much the same way as a refrigerator.

Winter Operation. When the heat pump is used as a heater, a liquid refrigerant is passed through an outdoor coil (Fig. 34-6A). As the refrigerant evaporates, it absorbs heat from the outside air. The heat-carrying refrigerant is then compressed. This raises its temperature to 100°F (37.8°C) or more. The refrigerant is then passed through the indoor coil. This acts as a heating unit. Cool air in the rooms is circulated over the warm coils. The warm air is then recirculated through the rooms.

During very cold weather, a heat pump may not be able to absorb

Fig. 34-5. Main parts of a central home-air-conditioning system installation (*Lennox Industries, Inc.*)

REFRIGERANT AND ELECTRICAL-SUPPLY CONNECTING LINES

FRESH AIR INTAKE

PLENUM OUTLET

EVAPORATOR COIL

FURNACE

CONDENSING (CONDENSER-COMPRESSOR) UNIT

enough heat from the outside air to provide proper space heating. In that case, auxiliary resistance-heating units are used. These units are automatically turned on by a thermostat when the temperature drops below a certain point. The units operate until the heat pump alone is once again able to provide enough heat.

Summer Operation. During the summer, the operation of the heat pump is automatically reversed by a temperature-control thermostat. Then warm air in the rooms is circulated over the indoor coil, which is cooled by the evaporation of the refrigerant (Fig. 34-6B). The refrigerant then carries the heat it has absorbed from the rooms to the outdoor coil. There the heat is released. The refrigerant condenses to begin another cooling cycle.

Fig. 34-6. Basic operation of a heat pump: (A) winter operation; (B) summer operation

ELECTRONIC AIR CLEANER

The residential electronic air cleaner removes very small particles that would normally pass through a filter (Fig. 34-7). It is usually installed in the cold-air return duct of a central forced-air heating or cooling system.

In a typical electronic air cleaner, air first passes through a prefilter unit. This traps the larger dust particles. From the prefilter, the air moves past a gridlike assembly of wires. These make up the ionizing section of the cleaner. The wires, suspended between grounded aluminum electrodes, are positively charged at about 6,000 V. This voltage is supplied by a high-voltage rectifier circuit. This causes particles still in the air to also become positively charged.

The air then passes through the collector section. This consists of aluminum plates negatively charged at about 6,000 V with respect to the grounded aluminum plates between them. There the positively charged particles are attracted to the negative collector plates, where they remain until they are removed by washing.

Fig. 34-7. Residential electronic air cleaner (*Whirlpool Corporation*)

SELF-TEST

Test your knowledge by writing, on a separate sheet of paper, the word or words that most correctly complete the following statements:

1. The operation of refrigerators depends on the fact that all liquids absorb _____ when they _____.
2. In cooling appliances, a liquid known as a _____ is circulated through thin metal tubes called _____ coils.
3. The most commonly used refrigerant is _____.
4. The purpose of the condenser in a refrigerator is to _____ the evaporated refrigerant and change it back into a _____.
5. A room air conditioner _____, or removes moisture from, the air. This occurs as moisture in the air _____ on cooled evaporator coils.
6. The cooling capacity of an air conditioner is given in terms of the _____ unit.
7. The electrically driven heat pump is a combination _____ and _____ unit.

FOR REVIEW AND DISCUSSION

1. What is the purpose of the refrigerant used in a refrigerator?
2. What is a common refrigerant material?
3. Explain how an electric refrigerator works.
4. Describe how a refrigerator motor-starting relay works.
5. How are refrigerator motors protected against overload?
6. Explain how a typical room air conditioner works.
7. Name and define the unit by which the cooling capacity of an air conditioner is given.
8. What is a heat pump? What is the purpose of the resistance-heating units used with this system?
9. Describe the basic construction and operation of a home electronic air cleaner.

Prepare a written or an oral report on the construction and operation of a refrigerator, room air conditioner, or heat pump.

UNIT 35   The Automobile Electrical System

The electrical system of an automobile has a number of electric circuits. These circuits distribute current to the devices and equipment in the automobile (Fig. 35-1). In addition, the modern automobile may contain several or all of the solid-state electronic products and circuit systems shown in Fig. 35-2. The sources of energy for these systems are a battery and an alternator, or ac generator. Fuses, circuit breakers, and relays protect the circuits.

HEATER

IGNITION
SWITCH

IGNITION
COIL

SPARK
PLUGS

DISTRIBUTOR

HORN RELAY   SOLENOID

GENERATOR
REGULATOR

STARTING
MOTOR

BATTERY

GENERATOR OR ALTERNATOR

Fig. 35-1. Basic automotive electrical system

BATTERY

The main purpose of the automobile battery is to furnish the electric energy needed to turn the cranking, or starting, motor. The battery is also used to operate other circuit loads when the engine is not running and when the alternator is producing less than a certain amount of voltage. One terminal of the battery, usually the negative terminal, is grounded. It is grounded by being connected to the frame of the auto-

Fig. 35-2. Example of the increasing number of solid-state electronic products and circuit systems found in the modern automobile (*Ford Motor Company*)

TABLE 35-1. CURRENT REQUIREMENTS OF COMMON ELECTRICAL AND ELECTRONIC ITEMS IN THE AUTOMOBILE

Device or Product	Current (amperes)
air conditioner	10–14
heater	5–7
ignition system	2–3
parking lights	4–8
low-beam headlights	8–14
high beam headlights	12–18
tail lights	1–2
radio	0.4–2
tape player	0.5–2
windshield wiper	2–3
summer starting*	100–225
winter starting*	225–500

*Starting current requirements vary with size of engine and viscosity of oil used.

Fig. 35-3. Starter-relay circuit

mobile with a heavy flexible cable. This reduces the number of circuit wires since the frame acts as a return circuit conductor for most of the circuits.

Most modern automobiles use a 12-V, 6-cell, lead-acid battery. This provides efficient starting and operates an ever-increasing number of electrical and electronic items (Table 35-1).

CRANKING CIRCUIT

When the ignition switch of an automobile is turned to the start position, a circuit is completed from the battery to a relay. The relay connects the battery to the cranking motor. In most automobiles, a series dc motor is used to crank the engine.

In some automobiles, the cranking relay is a separate unit mounted in the engine compartment. A diagram of this kind of cranking circuit is shown in Fig. 35-3.

In other automobiles, the cranking switch completes a circuit from the battery to a solenoid. This is mounted on the cranking motor frame (Fig. 35-4). The solenoid plunger acts as a relay to close the circuit between the battery and the cranking motor. It also operates a shift-lever. The shift-lever couples the motor shaft to the engine flywheel while the engine is being cranked.

RETURN SPRING
PLUNGER
SOLENOID
RUBBER GASKET
GROMMET
BRUSHING
SHIFT LEVER
PINION STOP
OVERRUNNING CLUTCH
FIELD COIL
ARMATURE
ASSIST SPRING

Fig. 35-4. The solenoid starting motor assembly

BREAKER-POINT IGNITION SYSTEM

As the crankshaft begins to turn, the cam-driven breaker points in the distributor start to open and close. This makes and breaks the primary circuit of the ignition coil. The ignition coil is actually a step-up transformer (Fig. 35-5). When the primary circuit is broken, by opening the breaker points, the magnetic field collapses quickly. This induces 20,000 V or more across the secondary. The high-voltage circuit is completed to the correct spark plug by the rotor under the distributor cap. As the rotor turns, the plugs fire in a desired order. This is called the *firing order*. It is usually found molded onto the intake manifold of the engine. This reference is handy in case the wires should ever become mixed up at the distributor cap.

When the breaker points open, the sudden collapse of the magnetic field also induces a high voltage in the primary circuit of the coil. This voltage would ordinarily cause extreme arcing at the breaker points. However, there is a capacitor across the points. This capacitor absorbs the induced surge and allows the ignition circuit to work properly. A faulty capacitor will cause poor ignition and point burning or no ignition at all.

Spark Plugs. The spark plugs provide the electrical gap in the high-voltage circuit of the ignition system. The gap at the tip of each plug is the site of the spark that ignites the fuel-air mixture in a cylinder of the engine. Spark plugs are exposed to extreme temperatures and pressures. Therefore, they are made of heat-resistant materials. Figure 35-6 shows the details of a typical spark plug.

Fig. 35-5. Conventional ignition system (A) circuit diagram; (B) ignition system and starting-motor connections (*Delco-Remy, Division of General Motors Corporation*)

Fig. 35-6. Construction of a spark plug (*Champion Spark Plug Company*)

Cylinders. When the spark plugs fire, the fuel-air mixture in the cylinders is ignited. The rapidly expanding gases produced by this burning push against the pistons. This causes them to move (Fig. 35-7). The movement of the pistons turns the crankshaft. Mechanical energy from the crankshaft is then passed onto the drive wheels through the transmission assembly.

ELECTRONIC IGNITION SYSTEM

In one common electronic ignition system, there are no breaker points in the distributor. A magnetic pickup assembly located over the distributor shaft contains a permanent magnet, a pole piece with internal teeth, and a pickup coil (Fig. 35-8).

As the distributor rotor turns, the teeth of its timer core move past the teeth of the pole piece. As a result, a moving magnetic field cuts across the pickup coil. This induces pulses of voltage across the coil.

The pulses are then applied to an amplifier in the electronic module. The output of the amplifier is connected to the primary winding of the ignition coil. A high voltage is induced across the secondary winding of the coil. This is then applied to the spark plugs through the distributor.

ALTERNATOR

After the engine has started and is running at a certain speed, an *alternator,* or ac generator, replaces the battery as the source of energy.

Construction. The typical alternator is a three-phase generator with a rotating field (Fig. 35-9). The rotor assembly consists primarily of a doughnut-shaped field coil. This assembly is mounted between two iron sections with interlacing fingerlike prongs called *poles.* Field current from the battery is passed to the field windings by two brushes that contact the rotor slip rings.

Most alternators are driven by the fan belt or by a separate belt that couples the rotor shaft to the engine flywheel. As the rotor assembly turns, the magnetic field produced by the field current cuts across the stationary windings of the stator assembly. This action induces an alternating voltage across the stator windings.

Rectification of Output. The voltage produced by the alternator is rectified by six silicon diodes. These are mounted inside the alternator end frame. Rectification is needed because the electrical system of the automobile operates with direct current.

Damage to Diodes. A reversal of the polarity of the automobile-battery voltage may seriously damage the diodes of the alternator or other parts of the electrical system. For this reason, it is important to use the correct polarity while connecting a new battery or a booster battery to the automobile.

ALTERNATOR REGULATOR

The voltage output of the alternator is automatically controlled so that it remains fairly constant at different engine speeds. This is done by the

Fig. 35-7. Effect of ignition in an automobile cylinder

Fig. 35-8. Exploded view showing the distributor assembly components of an electronic ignition system (*Delco-Remy, Division of General Motors Corporation*)

Fig. 35-9. The automobile alternator: (A) external view; (B) cutaway view showing main features (*Delco-Remy, Division of General Motors Corporation*)

alternator regulator. A typical regulator consists of two relay units, the voltage regulator and the field relay (Fig. 35-10).

The Voltage Regulator. The voltage output of the alternator increases as the engine speed increases. The voltage regulator limits the voltage so that it will not overcharge the battery or damage any part of the electrical system.

Fig. 35-10. Alternator regulator and regulator circuit

When the output of the alternator reaches about 14 V, the automatic switching action of the voltage regulator puts a resistor in series with the alternator field. This reduces the field current. The alternator output voltage is thereby also reduced.

The Field Relay. The field relay acts as a magnetic switch that closes when the relay is energized. This relay provides a low-resistance conductor path between the battery and the voltage-regulator coil. The relay also disconnects the battery from the field windings of the alternator. This system provides complete alternator regulation in a compact form.

LIGHTS

In the automobile, electricity is used to operate several kinds of lamps. Most are single- or double-contact lamps with a bayonet base. For safe driving, the headlights, the taillights, and the turn-signal lights are most important. Instrument, dome, parking, and backing lights are also common.

Headlamps. Modern automobiles use sealed-beam headlamps. In such a lamp, one or two filaments are sealed into a bulb that also serves as a lens and a reflector (Fig. 35-11). In a two-filament headlamp, the filaments are connected into the circuit so that either one of them can be turned on. This makes it possible to produce high and low beams of light.

After the lamps have been turned on by the main light switch, either the high or the low beam can be selected with the dimmer switch.

Many automobiles today are equipped with quartz headlamps. These are high-power output versions of the sealed-beam headlamps.

Stop Lights. In many automobiles, two-filament lamps serve as both stop lights and taillights. In other automobiles, separate lamps are used.

The stop-signal lamps are automatically turned on when the brake pedal is depressed. The pressure of the hydraulic fluid in the master brake cylinder forces a metal diaphragm over switch contacts. When the brake pedal is released, the diaphragm moves away from the contacts, and the lamps go off.

Fig. 35-11. Sealed-beam head-lamp (*General Electric Corporation*)

Turn-Signal Lights. The flashing of turn-signal lamps is generally controlled by a thermostatically operated flasher unit. This turns the lamps on and off about 90 times per minute.

HORNS

An automobile horn is a vibrating device that works very much like a door bell. In a horn, however, the vibrating arm is connected to a

HORN

RELAY
CONTACTS

RELAY
COIL

HORN

BATTERY

Fig. 35-12. The horn circuit

BIMETALLIC ARM
RESISTANCE WIRE
GAGE UNIT
HEATING
COIL

FLOAT

TANK FUEL

GROUNDED
SLIDING
CONTACT

TO
IGNITION
SWITCH

VOLTAGE REGULATOR
TO OTHER GAGES

Fig. 35-13. Fuel-gage circuit

diaphragm. The rapid back-and-forth movement of the diaphragm in an air column produces the sound.

Horns are usually controlled by a relay. When the pressure switch in the steering-wheel assembly is pushed, a circuit is completed from the battery or the alternator through the horn relay (Fig. 35-12). This causes the relay contacts to close. Current then passes through the horn circuit.

INSTRUMENTS

The fuel gage and the temperature gage are the most common electrical instruments in the automobile. In one kind of gage, a heating coil is wound around a bimetallic strip (or arm) connected to a pointer. As the coil becomes heated by current, the temperature of the strip also increases. This causes the strip to bend. The amount of bending determines the position of the pointer on the gage scale.

The amount of current in a fuel-gage circuit depends on the position of a float connected to a rheostat (Fig. 35-13). As the fuel supply in the tank decreases, the float causes the resistance of the circuit to increase. This, in turn, causes the pointer to move toward the E (empty) position on the gage scale. In a temperature gage, the current in the circuit is controlled by the temperature of the cylinder block.

ELECTRICAL ACCESSORIES

Common automobile electrical accessories include heaters, air conditioners, fans, windshield wipers, window operators, and seat adjusters. All of these are operated by small electric motors. The accessories are usually controlled by hand-operated switches located on or near the instrument panel.

FUSES AND CIRCUIT BREAKERS

Almost all the lighting and accessory circuits in an automobile are protected by either cartridge fuses or circuit breakers. In many automobiles, circuit breakers are used more widely than fuses.

Common automobile fuses include the 4-, 6-, 9-, 14-, 20-, and 30-A sizes. Each size has a different length. The larger the ampere size, the longer the fuse (Fig. 35-14). A wrong-size fuse cannot be inserted into the fuseholder or mounting clip. This is an important safety feature.

THE ELECTRIC CAR

The *electric car* is not new. It first appeared in this country about 1888. It was very popular at the turn of the century. But, by 1930, most electric cars had been replaced with the familiar automobile powered by a gasoline engine.

Many experiments are being conducted to test the usefulness of this type of vehicle. Commuting, short-distance deliveries, and demonstra-

Fig. 35-14. Automobile fuses

4 AMP   6 AMP   9 AMP   14 AMP   20 AMP   30 AMP

Fig. 35-15. An electric powered fleet car being used in a large metropolitan area (*Lead Magazine, Lead Industries Association, Inc.*)

tion vehicles are the main uses to which the electric cars are being put. At present, small to midsize production cars are being converted to electric propulsion for these experiments (Fig. 35-15).

The electric car as an alternative to the internal combustion engine has always been of interest to engineers and designers (Fig. 35-16). This car has many advantages. It is practically noiseless, producing only a hum or whine. The electric car does not pollute the air. It is very maneuverable on snow and ice, as the weight of the batteries gives good traction. It is small and lighter in weight than the internal combustion engine auto.

Fig. 35-16. Key features of an experimental electric car (*U.S. Department of Energy*)

The electric car does, however, have several disadvantages. It cannot match the gasoline car in range, versatility, performance, or speed. There is no nationwide system for maintenance or for battery recharging.

The electric car has four major systems. These are discussed below.

Power System. Because lead-acid batteries are presently available, some electric-car power systems are designed to operate with them.

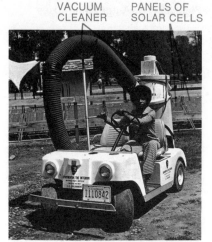

VACUUM CLEANER   PANELS OF SOLAR CELLS

Fig. 35-17. Solar (photovoltaic) cells are used to charge the batteries in an electric vehicle with a vacuum cleaner used for refuse pickup (*National Aeronautics and Space Administration*)

Eighteen 6-V, heavy-duty, lead-acid batteries are connected to produce 108 V. This system will allow a range of 25 to 40 miles (40 to 64 km), depending upon the weight of the vehicle and the speeds attained. The batteries are considered drained when they reach a 60 to 80 percent level of discharge, at which point they must be recharged.

Several new power systems are being considered for use in the electric car. Some of these use batteries made from nickel and zinc, nickel and iron, sodium and sulfur, zinc and chlorine, and lithium and a metal sulfide.

The objective is to develop a power system that can operate an electric car at a speed of 45 to 55 miles per hour (72 to 89 km/hr) with a range of about 150 miles (240 km) before recharging. A critical specification for batteries used in cars is the watts per pound of battery ratio. It is in this area that engineers are looking for great improvements.

There are two important reasons for using batteries. First, they are compatible with existing electric supply systems. Second, they involve a shift from a petroleum-consuming energy system to a system that uses an abundant or renewable source of energy (Fig. 35-17).

Control System. The control system has the instruments and switches needed to operate the electric car and support systems. Two important meters provide information about the condition of the power system. These are the *voltmeter* and the *ammeter*. The voltmeter reading indicates the charge in the batteries. The ammeter indicates the rate of energy consumption. Other controls include the switches for energizing various units, such as electric brakes, in the car. Because the electronic equipment used in the car is complicated, a central computer unit, called a *microprocessor,* is used to control it. For example, the accelerator uses solid-state devices to control the amount of energy that determines the speed of the car.

Electric Drive System. Some of the experimental electric cars use two dc drive motors, one for each drive wheel. Other electric cars use one motor with a transmission. These dc motors change the electric energy into mechanical energy to run the car.

Support System. The support system includes the accessory equipment, such as windshield wipers and washers, turn signals, heater, and air conditioner.

SELF-TEST

Test your knowledge by writing, on a separate sheet of paper, the word or words that most correctly complete the following statements:

1. Sources of energy for the automobile electrical system are the _____ and the _____ .
2. The _____ terminal of the battery is usually

grounded by being connected to the _____ of the automobile.

3. In some automobiles, the cranking switch completes a circuit from the battery to a _____ mounted on the _____ frame.

4. The breaker points in an ignition system operate as a _____ switch.

5. In a breaker-point ignition system, high voltage from the secondary winding of the _____ coil is applied to the _____ plugs by means of a _____ inside the distributor.

6. The desired order in which spark plugs fire is called _____ .

7. Excessive arcing across the breaker points is prevented by connecting a _____ across the points.

8. The ignition spark is produced in a _____ in the spark plug.

9. The typical alternator is a _____ -phase generator with a _____ .

10. The voltage output of the alternator is controlled by the _____ .

11. At present, electric-car power systems use _____ batteries.

12. The central computer unit in an electric car is called the _____ .

---

1. What is the main function of a car battery?

2. Why is one terminal of the automobile battery grounded to the frame?

3. What is the purpose of the solenoid in a cranking circuit?

4. State the purpose of the breaker points, the ignition coil, and the distributor rotor in a conventional ignition system.

5. Why is a capacitor connected across the breaker points?

6. What is the function of the spark plugs?

FOR REVIEW AND DISCUSSION

7. Briefly explain how one common kind of electronic ignition system works.

8. Why must the voltage output of an alternator be rectified? Explain how this is done.

9. How can alternator diodes be damaged?

10. What does an alternator regulator do?

11. State the purpose of the voltage regulator and the field-relay units of an alternator regulator.

12. Explain how the horn circuit works.

13. What are some major advantages of the electric car?

INDIVIDUAL-STUDY ACTIVITIES

1. Prepare a written or an oral report telling about the recent developments in the use of electronic devices in automobiles.

2. Prepare a demonstration for your class showing some automotive electrical units. Explain their operation.

ELECTRONICS IN AN INFORMATION AGE

UNIT 36 Basic Concepts in Communication

People communicate with each other by using one or more of the primary senses—hearing, vision, touch. The basic concepts in communication are shown in Fig. 36-1.

Note that communication is started by an *information initiator*. This is a person who has information to give to someone else, the *information user*. This information can consist of various kinds of messages, including music. The information user is the person who receives and makes use of the information. The information goes through several processes called *encode, transmit, carry, receive,* and *decode* in order

Fig. 36-1. Basic concepts in the communication process

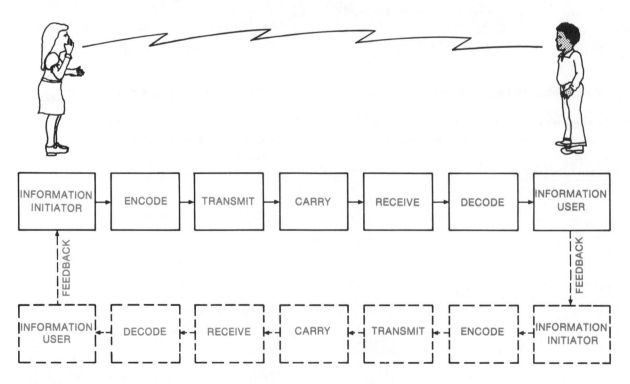

to be received by the user. *Feedback* enables the information user to let the initiator know whether the message has been received and understood. The initiator uses feedback to determine if the information needs further clarification. Feedback is essential to an effective communication system. The communication processes for several basic communication systems that use only hearing and vision are summarized in Fig. 36-2. Also shown are communication systems that use electricity and electronics. These systems allow people to communicate over long distances.

VOICE COMMUNICATION

Voice communication is the basic communications process. You engage in this activity daily—in school, at home, or at work. Actually, this process is very complicated. However, you have become so used to it that you do not think about it. You attach meanings to the sounds by the way you say vowels and consonants. This forming of the original language is the *encoding* process. The voice box produces the sound when air is expelled past the vocal cords. These vibrate rapidly and *transmit* an audible sound. The Earth's atmosphere is the medium that *carries* the sound vibrations to the ear—the *receiver*. If the language is heard but not understood by the information user, it must be translated into the language of the user. This process is known as *decoding*. Once the language is decoded, the brain interprets the message. If the language transmitted is the same as the language understood by the user, the brain automatically decodes the message. This makes it possible for the information user to understand the message. Feedback is provided by the reverse process (Fig. 36-1). However, voice communication can carry for only a limited distance.

VISUAL COMMUNICATION

The communication distance can be greatly increased by using visual means, such as flags, smoke signals, and flashing lights. Because of the curvature of the Earth, this distance is limited to a straight line of sight, about 20 miles (32.2 km). However, the distance can be increased to about 40 miles (64.4 km) by using a high building or a mountain.

As in voice communications, the information initiator starts the process. The nature of the flags (position, color, and so on), the variations in smoke puffs, or the duration of the flashing light are given meanings. This is the *encoding* process. For example, variations in the time a flashing light is on or off can have alphabetical meanings (A, B, C, and so on) and numerical meanings (1, 2, 3, and so on). These meanings are an *alphanumeric code*. Using this code, a flashing light can *transmit* a message. The *carrier* of this message is visible light. The *receiver* of this visual communication is the eye. The difference in time the light is on or off is easily detected by the eye. Therefore, the message can be decoded. Thus, the senses, especially hearing and vision, are essential to the communication process.

Fig. 36-2. Types of communication systems

Information initiator makes use of human senses	Processes and elements involved					Information user makes use of human senses
	Message encoding techniques	Transmitting elements	Carrying environment	Receiving elements	Message decoding techniques	
(A) Hearing *Voice communications*	Sounds spoken with vowels and consonants in the language are understood by person receiving message.	Human voice box (vocal cords, mouth, tongue, etc.) generates sound waves.	Earth's atmosphere (distance between communicators: about 275 meters or 300 yards)	Human ear	No need to translate if language is understood by communicator.	Hearing Ears receive sound waves. Brain interprets message.
(B) Vision *Visual communications*	Light flashes, flag positions, and smoke puffs have assigned alphanumeric meanings (code).	Light flashes, flags, smoke puffs	Visual light (distance between communicators: about 32 kilometers or 20 miles)	Human eye	Translate with same code.	Vision Eyes receive visual messages. Brain interprets message.
(C) Hearing and touch *Telegraph*	Hand-operated switch controls spurts of current which have assigned alphanumeric meanings.	Telegraph key	Wire (distance between communicators: worldwide)	Telegraph sounder	Translates electric pulses (current) into sound waves (clicks).	Hearing Ears receive sound waves. Brain interprets message.
(D) Hearing *Telephone*	Voice (sound waves) are translated or changed to electric (audio frequency) currents.	Telephone transmitter	Wire (distance between communicators: worldwide)	Telephone earphone	Reproducer (earphone) translates electric currents into sound waves (speech and music).	Hearing Ears receive sound waves. Brain interprets message.

	Encoding	Transmitter	Channel	Receiver	Decoding	Reception
(E) Hearing and touch *Wireless telegraph*	Encoding is the same as in a telegraph, but uses high-frequency (radio) currents.	Transmitter	Electromagnetic waves (distance between communicators: worldwide)	Receiver	Local oscillator signal mixes with high-frequency currents to produce audio frequencies; reproducer translates audio frequencies into sound waves.	**Hearing** Ears receive sound waves. Brain interprets message.
(F) Hearing *Radio*	Microphone changes voice (sound waves) into electric currents. These currents modulate radio-frequency currents.	Radio transmitter	Electromagnetic waves (distance between communicator: worldwide and interplanetary)	Radio receiver	Detector separates audio frequencies from radio-frequency currents; reproducer (speaker) translates audio-frequency currents into sound waves.	**Hearing** Ears receive sound waves. Brain interprets message.
(G) Vision and touch *Teletypewriter* *Computer* *Facsimile* *Real time writing*	Keyboard, tape, or microprocessor controlled. Alphanumeric meanings assigned to electric pulses.	Transmitter or sender	Wire (distance between communicators: worldwide)	Printer or monitor screen	Electric pulses translated into mechanical or electronic action to print alphanumeric characters or images on paper or monitor screen.	**Vision** Eyes receive visual image from printed paper or monitor screen. Brain interprets message.
(H) Hearing and vision *Television*	TV camera translates images (video) into electric currents. These currents modulate high-frequency currents. Microphone changes sound waves (audio) into electric currents, as in radio.	TV transmitter (video and audio)	Electromagnetic waves (distance between communicators: worldwide and interplanetary)	TV receiver (picture and sound)	Video detector separates video currents from radio currents; picture tube translates video currents into images; audio detector acts same as in radio above.	**Hearing and Vision** Ears receive sound waves from speaker. Eyes receive visual images from TV screen. Brain interprets messages.

ELECTRICAL AND ELECTRONIC COMMUNICATIONS

The use of electricity and electronics makes it possible to communicate over long distances. Figure 36-2 shows how the telegraph, telephone, wireless telegraph, radio, teletypewriter, computer, and other devices begin and end the process of communication through the primary senses. However, electric energy is used to encode, transmit, carry, receive, and decode the messages.

HOME TELEVISION, ENTERTAINMENT, AND COMPUTER CENTERS

The home electronic revolution has brought new electronic equipment to the attention of the homeowner. Home computers, portable television sets, compact disk players, car phones, video games, video cassette recorders, transceivers, video cameras, rear-projection large television screens, and others are all being produced for the mass market.

Figure 36-3 illustrates the variety of electronic equipment available for use in and about the home. The modern home may have a space designed as a television or entertainment center, another space for a home computer or telecommunication center, and the space outside the home for portable electronic equipment. The car phone, for example, under computer control using telephone line networks and satellites, makes it possible for you to communicate anywhere in the world while traveling in your automobile.

Modern electronic communication devices not only bring information to the individual but also allow the individual to interact with this information. We are, no doubt, living in an *information age*. The home or apartment dweller, for example, may stay at home and use the computer and telephone to send completed work to the office. This method of working is often called *telecommuting to work*.

Each unit in this section will expand your knowledge and understanding of the common information systems in use today. The units explain how the human voice, music, and data are amplified and changed so that intelligence can be transmitted and received at lightning speed all over the world.

SELF-TEST

Test your knowledge by writing, on a separate sheet of paper, the word or words that most correctly complete the following statements:

1. The three primary senses used in communication are _____, _____, and _____.
2. The person who starts the communication process is called the information _____.
3. The information _____ is the person who receives the messages.
4. The five basic steps in communication are _____, _____, _____, _____, and _____.
5. _____ is the process by which an information user lets an information _____ know whether the message has been received and understood.

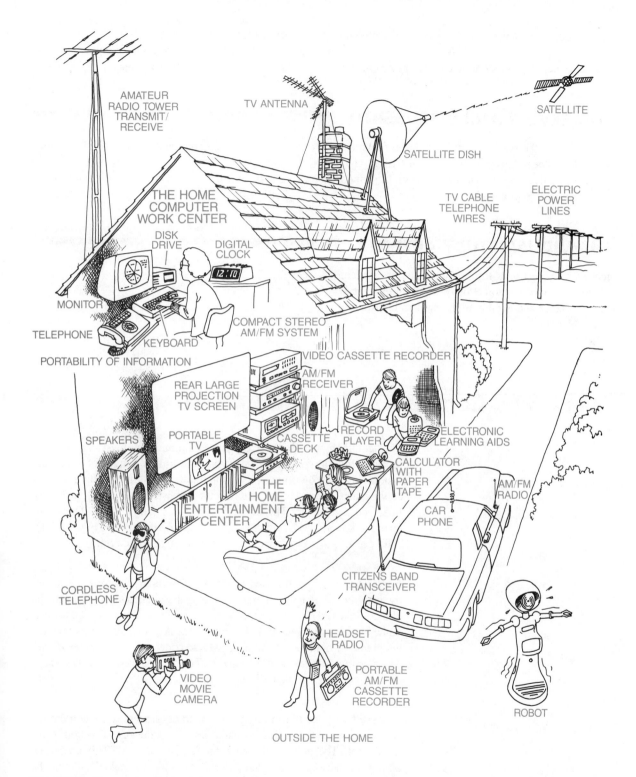

Fig. 36-3. Electronics in the information age

325

6. _____ communication is the basic communication process.
7. The meanings given to letters and numbers form

an _____ code.
8. In electrical and electronic communications, _____ transmits the messages.

FOR REVIEW AND DISCUSSION

1. Describe the basic concepts in the communication process between two people using voice communications. What are some of the limitations of this process?

2. Compare voice communication with visual communication.
3. List the electrical and electronic communications methods.

INDIVIDUAL-STUDY ACTIVITY

Identify 10 electronic information systems available for use in a modern home today. Rank them in order of importance and explain to the class the reasons for your selection.

UNIT 37   Common Information Systems

The telegraph was the first electrical communication system that allowed people to communicate beyond the limited ranges of voice and vision. Figure 37-1 shows basic telegraph circuits for sending and receiving messages. The electric circuit consists of a battery, a key, a line, and a receiver. The battery is the source of energy. The hand-operated key acts as a switch to open and close the circuit (Fig. 37-1A). This causes *pulses* of current to move through the circuit.

Encoding. The operator (the information initiator) controls the pulses by varying the lengths of time the key is switched on or off. In the United States, the code used in wire telegraphy is the Morse code. It is named in honor of Samuel F. B. Morse, the American who invented the telegraph. A modified form of the Morse code, called the *international Morse code,* is shown in Fig. 37-2. The international Morse code is often used for amateur radio communications.

Transmitting. The transmitting and encoding processes are done at the same time when the operator's hand first closes the key. This completes the circuit. The pulse ends when the key is released. This opens the circuit. A short pulse is called a *dot*. A long pulse is called a *dash*. The dot is about one-fourth of a second long. The dash is three times longer.

Fig. 37-1. Hand-operated telegraph systems: (A) telegraph key; (B) a sounder (receiver); (C) open-circuit telegraph system; (D) closed-circuit telegraph system

Transmission. The dots and dashes of the code are carried in the form of electric energy by wires. The signals are carried almost instantly through the wires from the transmitter to the receiver.

Receiving. The receiver, called a *sounder,* is a sounding device. It makes clicks loud enough to be heard (Fig. 37-1B). The sounder has an electromagnet and a movable arm. A pulse of current is sent through the electromagnet. The electromagnet then attracts the movable arm. The arm moves and makes a click. When the pulse stops, a spring returns the movable arm to its original position. This makes a second click. The time between the clicks represents a dot or a dash.

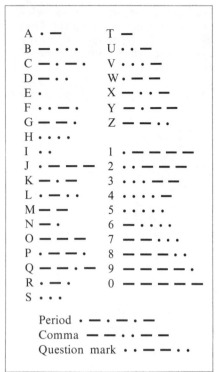

A · —	T —
B — · · ·	U · · —
C — · — ·	V · · · —
D — · ·	W · — —
E ·	X — · · —
F · · — ·	Y — · — —
G — — ·	Z — — · ·
H · · · ·	
I · ·	1 · — — — —
J · — — —	2 · · — — —
K — · —	3 · · · — —
L · — · ·	4 · · · · —
M — —	5 · · · · ·
N — ·	6 — · · · ·
O — — —	7 — — · · ·
P · — — ·	8 — — — · ·
Q — — · —	9 — — — — ·
R · — ·	0 — — — — —
S · · ·	

Period · — · — · —
Comma — — · · — —
Question mark · · — — · ·

Fig. 37-2. The international Morse code consists of combinations of pulses called dots and dashes.

Decoding. When the electric energy is translated into clicks by the sounder, the decoding process begins. The clicks, heard by ears, form the dots and dashes that represent the alphanumeric characters of the international Morse code. Thus, the message can be interpreted by the brain.

OPEN- AND CLOSED-CIRCUIT TELEGRAPH

Two basic hand-operated telegraph circuit systems are discussed below:

The Open-Circuit System. In this system, current or electrical pulses pass only while a message is being sent. When the telegraph is idle, no current flows (Fig. 37-1C).

The Closed-Circuit System. In this system, shown in Fig. 37-1D, the circuit remains closed until the operator wants to send a message. First the operator opens a switch connected across the key. This switch opens the circuit. The circuit can then be closed and opened rapidly by depressing and releasing the key. After the message has been transmitted, the key is closed. This completes the circuit so that other stations may use the circuit.

TELETYPEWRITERS

Modern telegraph systems use a variety of electrical and electronic equipment. The slow hand key and sounder cannot handle a large volume of messages. Instead, teletypewriters and automatic switching centers are used to send messages with great speed.

The early teletypewriter combined the basic elements of a telegraph and a typewriter so as to create coded electrical pulses (Fig. 37-3A). A transmitting unit, called a *sender,* can be operated like a typewriter keyboard or by a coded, punched tape. The receiver unit, called a *printer,* can produce regular printed messages on rolled paper or on paper tape. The printer can also produce messages punched as holes through paper tape. The punched tape is called *perforated tape.* Devices that can both send and receive messages are called *terminal units.* In addition to the keyboard, elements of the teletypewriter include a cabinet, electric power distribution panels, a transmitter distributor, and a page printer.

Messages are encoded into what is called the *teletypewriter* or *teleprinter code.*

The teletypewriter code works on a *binary system.* This is a system that has two different states—current *on* or current *off.* Using this code, each character—letter, number, or symbol—consists of seven electrical pulses within a time period, for example, 163 milliseconds (ms). When an electrical impulse is *on,* it is called a *mark.* When it is *off,* it is called a *space.* The standard five-unit, start-stop teletypewriter code is shown in Fig. 37-3B. Notice that each pulse is rectangular. A rapid rise and/or fall of current forms the marks and spaces. When a paper tape is punched with this code, the punched holes on the tape indicate current *on* (mark). The lack of holes indicates current *off* (space). Start and stop pulses do not appear on the tape. The five information pulses that are on the tape are called *bits*. One of the main advantages of perforated tape is that messages can be punched on the tapes and stored. They can later be sent at high speed.

Encoding Process. The mechanical linkage in the teletypewriter produces the right opening and closing of switches for each character. Figure 37-4A shows how the open or closed switches are sensed. When the key lever is pressed down by an operator, it acts on five crossbars. These, in turn, move locking levers to open or close five different switches. This is done according to the code for the key lever pressed down.

A

| CHARACTERS | | WEATHER SYMBOLS UPPER CASE | CODE SIGNAL | | | | | | |
LOWER CASE	UPPER CASE		START	1	2	3	4	5	STOP
A	−	↑		█	█				█
B	?	⊕		█			█	█	█
C	:	○			█	█	█		█
D	$	↗		█			█		█
E	3	3		█					█
F	!	→		█		█	█		█
G	&	↘			█		█	█	█
H	£	↓				█		█	█
I	8	8			█	█			█
J	'	↙		█	█		█		█
K	(	←		█	█	█	█		█
L	)	↖			█			█	█
M	.	.				█	█	█	█
N	,	φ				█	█		█
O	9	9					█	█	█
P	0	0			█	█		█	█
Q	1	1		█	█	█		█	█
R	4	4			█		█		█
S	BELL			█		█			█
T	5	5						█	█
U	7	7		█	█	█			█
V	;	∅			█	█	█	█	█
W	2	2		█	█			█	█
X	/	/		█		█	█	█	█
Y	6	6		█		█		█	█
Z	"	+		█				█	█
BLANK		−							█
SPACE						█			█
CARRIAGE RETURN							█		█
LINE FEED					█				█
FIGURES				█	█		█	█	█
LETTERS				█	█	█	█	█	█

Legend: □ SPACE ▓ MARK

B

Fig. 37-3. (A) An electromechanical automatic send-receive (ASR) Teletype (*Teletype Corporation*); (B) standard five-unit, start-stop teletypewriter code

Fig. 37-4. Electromechanical encoding process: (A) distributor for sensing the open or closed switches when the character R is depressed; (B) basic circuit of a teletypewriter; (a) ac synchronous motor; (b) key lever; (c) mechanical linkage; (d) switches; (e) distributor; (f) cam; (g) variable resistance; (h) selector magnet

WHEN A KEY IS DEPRESSED, MECHANICAL LINKAGE OPENS AND CLOSES FIVE SWITCHES ACCORDING TO THE 5-UNIT CODE. LETTER R SHOWN.

#5 OPEN
#4 CLOSED
#3 OPEN
#2 CLOSED
#1 OPEN

STOP CAM NOT SHOWN

DISTRIBUTOR

CAM SENSES SWITCH AS IT ROTATES PAST IT

START CAM NOT SHOWN

163 MILLISECONDS FOR EACH COMPLETE ROTATION

A

h

b

c

d

e

f

120 V DC

g

IN

OUT

DIRECT LINE (SERIES CONNECTED) TO ANOTHER TELETYPEWRITER

MOTOR

a

120 V AC

B

Each switch is matched with a rotating cam. The cams are placed around a distributor. This turns at a set speed. The no. 1 cam senses the no. 1 switch for a specified time, for example, 22 ms. If the switch is closed, current instantly flows through the cam. This indicates a mark. If the switch is open, no current flows. This indicates a space. Next the no. 2 cam senses the no. 2 switch for another 22 ms. This process is repeated for the other cams and switches until the rotation is complete. Thus, a character is encoded electrically by a mechanical motion. The pulses generated, including a 22-ms space for start and a 31-ms mark for stop, make up one character. These can be sent at a rate, for example, of 60 words per minute. Figure 37-4B illustrates the basic series circuit of a teletypewriter. The pulses generated by the transmitter, or sender, are carried over wires to the receiver, or printer. In radio telegraphy, the pulses are changed into high-frequency radio currents. These are carried by electromagnetic waves to receivers for decoding.

Decoding. Decoding is done by the *selector magnet* in the printer or receiver. The selector magnet is connected in series in the circuit. The pulses from the sending and/or receiving teletypewriter pass through it. The off-on pulses fed into the selector magnet are changed into mechanical action. The message is printed on paper in front of the operator. It can also be printed or punched on tape.

MODERN TELEPRINTERS

Modern teleprinters, called *keyboard printer terminals,* operate in a wide range of computer input-output applications (Fig. 37-5). Both keyboard printer terminals shown in Fig. 37-5 provide bidirectional printing at up to 200 characters per second on plain paper. They operate using the American National Standard Code for Information Interchange (ASCII). They also have special-purpose printing type and graphic capabilities.

ASCII

The American National Standard Code for Information Interchange is an important standard character set. It is used for the interchange of information among information processing systems, communications systems, and associated equipment. This standard, referred to as ASCII, is pronounced as-key.

Like the standard five-unit start-stop teleprinters code, this 7-bit coded character set works on a binary system (Fig. 37-6). With the use of 7 bits, 128 characters can be coded, each with a unique set of binary bits. Unit 41, "Digital Electronic Circuits," and Unit 42, "Fundamentals of Computers," provide further details on the binary system used in various electronic systems. The letter R is represented by the various bits shown in Fig. 37-6 (row 2, column 5) as follows:

$$b_7 \quad b_6 \quad b_5 \quad b_4 \quad b_3 \quad b_2 \quad b_1$$
$$1 \quad \ 0 \quad \ 1 \quad \ 0 \quad \ 0 \quad \ 1 \quad \ 0$$

Abbreviations such as NUL, SOH, STX, etc. are called "control" characters. They provide a method to modify, stop, or start an action. Table 37-1 provides the meaning associated with selected control characters.

Fig. 37-5. Modern Teletype, keyboard printer terminals: (A) desk top; (B) portable (*American Telephone and Telegraph Teletype Corporation. Teletype is a registered trademark and service mark of Teletype Corporation.*)

TABLE 37-1. SELECTED CONTROL CHARACTERS AND THEIR FUNCTION

Column/Row	Control Character	Function
0/0	NUL	Null (of no effect, none)
0/2	STX	Start of text
0/3	ETX	End of text
0/4	EOT	End of transmission
0/6	ACK	Acknowledge
0/7	BEL	Bell (bell sound)
0/8	BS	Backspace
0/12	FF	Form feed
7/15	DEL	Delete

Bits				Col.					$b_7 b_6 b_5$			
					000	001	010	011	100	101	110	111
b_4	b_3	b_2	b_1	Row→	0	1	2	3	4	5	6	7
0	0	0	0	0	NUL	DLE	SP	0	@	P	\	p
0	0	0	1	1	SOH	DC1	!	1	A	Q	a	q
0	0	1	0	2	STX	DC2	''	2	B	R	b	r
0	0	1	1	3	ETX	DC3	#	3	C	S	c	s
0	1	0	0	4	EOT	DC4	$	4	D	T	d	t
0	1	0	1	5	ENQ	NAK	%	5	E	U	e	u
0	1	1	0	6	ACK	SYN	&	6	F	V	f	v
0	1	1	1	7	BEL	ETB	/	7	G	W	g	w
1	0	0	0	8	BS	CAN	(	8	H	X	h	x
1	0	0	1	9	HT	EM	)	9	I	Y	i	y
1	0	1	0	10	LF	SUB	*	:	J	Z	j	z
1	0	1	1	11	VT	ESC	+	;	K	[	k	{
1	1	0	0	12	FF	FS	,	<	L	\	l		
1	1	0	1	13	CR	GS	−	=	M	]	m	}
1	1	1	0	14	SO	RS	.	>	N	⌃	n	~
1	1	1	1	15	SI	US	/	?	O	—	o	DEL

Fig. 37-6. Standard 7-bit coded character set for information interchange among information processing systems, communications systems, and associated equipment (ASCII)

When a stream of bits is transmitted by a keyboard printer terminal or similar device, there is a standard character structure and character parity sense for serial-by-bit data communications. This standard provides for *synchronous* and *asynchronous* data communications.

Synchronous Data Communications. The term *synchronous* means that something, such as signaling elements or bits, is happening at the same rate over a period of time. When synchronous transmission is used, the character structure consists of 8 signal elements or bits having equal time intervals—7 ASCII bits, plus 1 character parity bit (Fig. 37-7A). A parity bit is a binary digit 0 or 1 appended to the 7-bit ASCII code array to make the sum of all the 1 bits always *odd* or always *even* per character. The bit sense character parity for synchronous data communication is *odd* over the 8 bits (7 bits + 1 parity bit).

Asynchronous Data Communications. The term *asynchronous* means that something, such as signaling elements or bits, is not happening at the same rate over a period of time. When asynchronous transmission is used, the character structure consists of 10 signal elements or bits having equal time intervals (Fig. 37-7B). The 10 signal elements are as follows: one 0 (spacing) start element, seven ASCII bits, one character parity bit, and 1 (marking) stop element. The interval of time between the end of the stop element and the beginning of the next start element can be any length. The standard sense of character parity for asynchronous data transmission is *even*.

MODEM
The keyboard printer terminals are designed to function with computer time-sharing and terminal-to-terminal communication systems. They can be programmed just like a microcomputer. Programming is discussed in Unit 43, "Interacting With the Microcomputer." Included within the unit is a modem. The *modem* allows the operator to communicate online wherever there is a telephone available.

The term *modem* is a contraction of *modulator-demodulator.* The modem is the electronic device that connects data terminal equipment to a communications line. The modem at the sending end converts binary digital data (zeros and ones) from the terminal or computer into analog signals for use on telephone lines. A demodulator converts analog signals back to digital signals at the receiving end for use by the terminal. This device, therefore, provides an interface between digital and analog signals.

Communications lines that move data from one point to another in only one direction are called *simplex* lines. When two communications lines are used, one going in each direction, two-way communication is achieved. This is called a *full-duplex* communications system. The ordinary telephone is an example of a full-duplex system.

COMMUNICATIONS NETWORK
Figure 37-8 shows the interconnecting networks between the sender and receiver of information, and vice versa. In a complicated system, a teletypewriter send-receive (S/R) terminal can transmit a customer's

EQUAL TIME BETWEEN BITS

7 ASCII BITS

START BIT

ODD PARITY BIT

A

EQUAL TIME BETWEEN BITS

7 ASCII BITS

EVEN PARITY BIT

START ELEMENT (SPACE) BIT 0

STOP ELEMENT (MARKING) BIT 1

B

NOTE:
THE ORDER OF TRANSMISSION IN A AND B IS FROM LEFT TO RIGHT

Fig. 37-7. Character structure and character parity sense for serial-by-bit data communications (A) synchronous data transmission; (B) asynchronous data transmission

Fig. 37-8. Basic elements of an interconnected data communications system

order to the manufacturing plant, warehouse, and retail store all at once. In this way, identical information is received by all concerned with the business transaction. If there is a question, any S/R terminal can send a message to clear it up.

Note in Fig. 37-8 that the loop from the weather station teletypewriters goes by land line to a *relay center*. This is a switching center that can be a separate facility. It can also be located, as shown, in a *data control center* that also has equipment for transmitting and receiving information by radio.

A relay center can receive a message and redirect it to distant points by either radio or wires. This process can be repeated over and over until the message reaches its destination. An automatic switching system is shown in Fig. 37-9. The messages that come into this center have address codes that automatically direct them to certain places.

THE TELEPHONE SYSTEM

The telegraph and teleprinter used codes to transmit information. Let us now examine how the human voice is transmitted. A telephone system

Fig. 37-9. Installing an automatic (electronic) switching system (*AT&T*)

changes sound energy, usually speech, into electric energy at the transmitting, or sending, end. At the receiving end, the electric energy is used to reproduce the original sounds (Fig. 37-10A).

TELEPHONE TRANSMITTER

The part of the telephone system that changes sound energy into electric energy is the *telephone transmitter,* a microphone. Sound waves are actually a series of varying air pressures. These exert a force on the metal diaphragm of the transmitter. An increase of pressure pushes the diaphragm against a small container of carbon granules. The electrical resistance of the carbon is thereby decreased. This causes the current in the line to increase. When there is no pressure on the diaphragm, the electrical resistance of the carbon granules is high. This causes the current to decrease. The diaphragm vibrates against the carbon granules in step with the sound waves. This vibrating action changes the steady direct current in the telephone circuit into *pulsating,* or *varying, direct current.* The frequencies of the pulsating currents that result are, when changed to sound waves, within the hearing range of humans. Therefore, they are called *audio-frequency (AF) currents* or *analog signals* (Fig. 37-10C).

TELEPHONE RECEIVER

The AF currents produced in the transmitter are conducted through the circuit to a device called the *telephone receiver,* or *earphone.* In the receiver, the AF currents pass through an electromagnetic coil. The resulting electromagnetism causes a metal diaphragm in the receiver to move back and forth. It does this in step with the varying value and frequency of the pulsating current. The pushing of the diaphragm

335

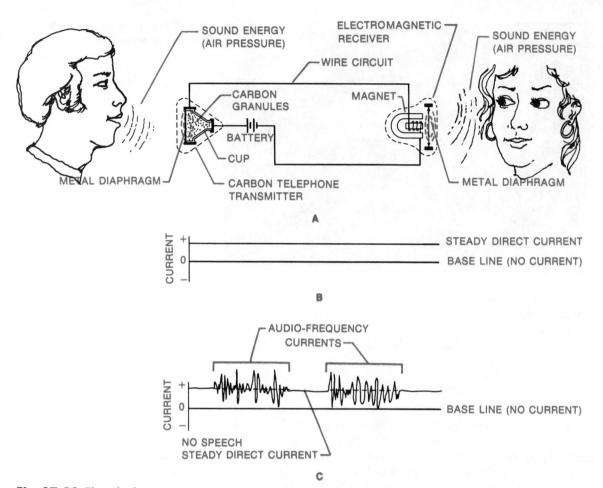

Fig. 37-10. The telephone transmitter changes sound energy into electric energy: (A) basic telephone electric circuit; (B) steady dc current flowing in wires; (C) comparison of steady direct current and audiofrequency currents

against the air produces sound waves. Thus, the message is first changed from sound energy to electric energy in the transmitter. It is then transmitted to a distant point. There the electric energy is changed back to sound energy by the receiver. A modern telephone has both the transmitter and receiver in one unit, called a *handset*. This is designed so that the transmitter will be near a person's mouth and the receiver near an ear (Fig. 37-11).

Volume and Frequency. You can hear better from the receiver if a person speaks louder or closer to the transmitter. This produces stronger pressures on the transmitter diaphragm. Greater changes in current are thereby created. As a result, the receiver's metal diaphragm vibrates more, and more air is set in motion. This produces a greater volume of sound. An increase or a decrease in the volume of a sound does not usually cause a change in the frequency of the sound.

Bandwidth. Humans can hear sounds that range from about 16 to 20,000 Hz. However, most of the significant content of speech falls in

Fig. 37-11. Cross-sectional view of a telephone handset

the frequency range below 3,000 Hz. For this reason, voice-communication receivers *attenuate,* or reduce, the high audio frequencies and boost, or increase, the lower frequencies. For example, the *bandwidth,* or frequency range, of a normal telephone channel is about 4,000 Hz.

The circuits that carry voice or analog signals, such as telephone lines, are designed to pass only certain frequencies. For example, the range of frequencies for the voice channel or *pass band* (bandwidth) is from 300 to 3,000 Hz. Any analog signal carried by the telephone lines beyond the pass band limit is an out-of-band signal. Because telephone lines are designed to carry analog signals within a specific pass band, digital signals from computers and other digital equipment must be converted to analog signals whenever telephone lines are used as the medium of transmission. As discussed previously, the device that makes the conversion is called a *modem.*

DIAL TELEPHONE

When you dial a telephone, you are actually encoding a message. For example, when you dial the number 555-1212, pulses of energy are produced by the dial mechanism according to a code. Each telephone number has its own code. After the dial is turned and released, spring tension returns it to its original position. The return speed of the dial is constant no matter what digit is dialed. But the length of time of the return is different for each digit. For example, it takes the dial longer to return after dialing the number 9 than after dialing the number 2. The dial mechanism acts as a switch to open and close the circuit 9 times during the return cycle when the number 9 is dialed. It does this only two times when the number 2 is dialed. These pulses have a meaning used by the switching equipment in the telephone company's central office.

HOW TWO TELEPHONES ARE CONNECTED

There are several ways to connect telephones. Early methods used switches operated by hand. Most systems now have automatic switching equipment.

Automatic switching is done by electromagnetic action or by solid-state devices. In electromagnetic equipment, relays open and close circuits. One such switching system uses a *step-by-step connector switch* (Fig. 37-12). The switch has a set of connecting arms with fingers

Fig. 37-12. A step-by-step connector switch (*Automatic Electric* Co.)

337

known as *wipers*. Each contact bank has 100 sets of metal contacts stacked in 10 curved rows. The upper bank is used to determine whether the called line is busy or idle. Each row has 10 sets of contacts. Each set of contacts represents the terminals of one telephone line. Electrical pulses from the dialing mechanism cause the connecting arm in the switch to step up or down to the proper level. Then a connector arm moves across terminals of the switch and stops on the proper contact point. This process is repeated until the entire dialing sequence is performed step by step.

Fig. 37-13. (A) A typical crossbar switch (*Bell Telephone Laboratories*); (B) the ferreed switch (*AT&T*)

A

B

Another kind of switching system uses the *crossbar switch* (Fig. 37-13A). It works in much the same way railroad cars are switched on tracks in a railroad yard. Only the track or tracks that are empty or not in use can be used. The *ferreed switch* is newer than the crossbar switch (Fig. 37-13B). It works faster and uses little power. It is used mostly to establish connections between electronic switching centers.

TOUCH-TONE TELEPHONE

In 1964, the Touch-Tone telephone was introduced. This kind of telephone has push buttons instead of a dial. When a button is pressed, two musical tones are generated at the same time. These tones are transmitted to the central switching office. They are then translated into a series of pulses similar to those made by the dial telephone. One of the main advantages of a Touch-Tone telephone is that a number can be punched more quickly than it can be dialed. The buttons marked * and # are for special services, such as routing calls to follow you when you are not at home. They can also be used to interconnect more than one phone at a time or to signal a busy phone.

The modern telephone, however, provides even more opportunities for personal communications. It is controlled with a microprocessor similar to a microcomputer. It has a touch-sensitive keypad and interchangeable cartridges and modules for additional functions not available on older telephones (Fig. 37-14). This personal communication

Fig. 37-14. A modern telephone—the Genesis™ telesystem. (*Genesis™ is a trademark of AT&T*)

system has many capabilities, such as putting calls on hold, group listening, redialing a previously dialed number with one touch, and memorizing and automatically alphabetizing 75 names and numbers for one-touch calling. If you own a microcomputer with a modem, the telephone is your link to a personal electronic mail service. The modem enables microcomputers to send printed messages over the telephone lines to other microcomputers.

LIGHTWAVE COMMUNICATIONS

Because the number of telephone calls and data communications is increasing, telephone wires are taking the form of hair-thin glass fibers (Fig. 37-15). Making telephone wires from glass fibers is a technology developed by the Bell Telephone Laboratories. This technology involves the use of a laser beam and glass fibers. For example, a small laser transmits pulses of electric energy at audio frequencies in the form of a light beam. The light beam is carried to its destination through glass fibers called a *lightguide* (Fig. 37-16). The popular term for this technology is *fiber optics*.

Fig. 37-15. Hair-thin glass fibers (lightguides)(*AT&T*)

There are several advantages in using glass fibers in place of copper wires and cables. Glass fibers are much lighter than copper wires. A single pair of hair-sized fibers can carry 672 conversations at the same time. Thus, much less space is used by glass fibers than by conventional wires and cables. The glass fibers are coated with a special organic compound that makes them stronger than steel. Laser beams are not affected by electromagnetic interference. Therefore, they can be used near electric power lines. The world's first lightwave communication system was operated in Chicago, Illinois, in 1977.

HANDWRITING BY WIRE

Figure 37-17 shows an electromechanical device that is capable of instantly transmitting or receiving handwritten messages, sketches, or other forms of graphic information over wires. It is called a *transceiver*. Information can be transmitted or received over any telephone line regardless of the distance. The use of this device is illustrated in Fig. 37-18. All departments, for example, in this hospital receive simultaneously on their receiver (or transceiver) the same handwritten message either on plain paper or on special printed forms. The various departments receive these messages without the problems of voice communications or messengers. Let us now examine the basic concepts involved in this transceiver.

Fig. 37-16. The telephone "wire" of the future—ultrapure glass fibers (*AT&T*)

TRANSMITTER

The main elements of the transmitter unit in a transceiver consist of the following: (1) transmitting pen or stylus, (2) writing table, (3) writing plate, (4) receiving pen, (5) pantograph, (6) vertical and horizontal

Fig. 37-17. Electrowriter® is a transceiver that combines both the transmitter and receiver functions in one unit. (*Infolink Corporation*)

ALERTING LAMP
AND BUZZER

RECEIVE
LAMP

SEND
LAMP

PAPER

PEN TIP

POWER
ON
LAMP

TRANSMITTING
PEN

Fig. 37-18. Various departments of a hospital are notified with one brief handwritten message on the Electrowriter® (*Infolink Corporation*)

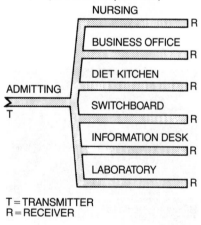

NURSING
R

BUSINESS OFFICE
R

DIET KITCHEN
R

ADMITTING
T

SWITCHBOARD
R

INFORMATION DESK
R

LABORATORY
R

T = TRANSMITTER
R = RECEIVER

Fig. 37-19. Transceiver functional block diagram (*Infolink Corporation*)

position transformers and servomotors, (7) vertical and horizontal coordinate oscillators, and (8) various electrical and/or electronic circuits (see Fig. 37-19).

Transmitting Pen or Stylus. This device has two switches located inside the handle of the pen. One switch, a mercury-operated switch, turns on the transmitting unit when the pen is raised (picked up) prior to writing a message. To begin writing, the transmitting pen or the stylus is pressed down on the pantograph's stylus ball and a pen-down switch is activated (Fig. 37-20).

Writing Table and Plate. Notice that the transmitting pen in Fig. 37-20 does not touch the paper but is located above the writing table on the clear plastic writing plate. When the pen is pressed downward, a pressure-activated, pen-down solenoid switch within the pen turns on a 120-Hz frequency-modulated oscillator. At the same time, a lamp lights up indicating that the transmitter is in the sending or transmitting mode.

Receiving Pen. The receiving pen of a transceiver is located below the transmitting pen. It has an inked pen point. During the transmitting mode, the receiving pen writes on the paper which is on the surface of the writing table. The receiving pen is located on the receiving arm and mechanically linked to the transmitting arm (Fig. 37-21). The receiving pen, therefore, follows the motions (up, down, sideways, etc.) of the transmitting pen as it moves across the clear plastic writing plate. The person writing the message, of course, can look through the clear plastic writing plate and observe the message as it is being written.

Pantograph. The arms of the transmitting pen and receiving pen are attached to a *pantograph*. This is actually a mechanical device that has

340

CONNECTING WIRE TO TRANSCEIVER

TRANSMITTING PEN OR STYLUS WITH TWO SWITCHES

PANTOGRAPH STYLUS BALL

TRANSMITTING PEN STYLUS ARM

UP-DOWN AND WRITING MOTIONS

CLEAR PLASTIC WRITING PLATE

RECEIVING PEN

MECHANICAL LINKAGE WITH PANTOGRAPH

WRITING SURFACE

TIP OF RECEIVING PEN

MOVEMENT OF PAPER

WRITING TABLE

RECEIVING PEN ARM

ROLLER

PAPER

ROLL OF PAPER

=== dotted lines indicate mechanical connection

Fig. 37-20. Transceiver: simplified cross-sectional view showing the relative positions of the main writing components

parallel hinged frames linked together. This linkage allows the transmitting pen to be moved easily in any direction. The frame of the pantograph is also attached to the shaft of the vertical and horizontal position servomotors (Fig. 37-22).

Position Transformers and Servomotors. The specially shaped vertical and horizontal position transformers with their servomotors cause audio-frequency signals to change in accordance with the position of the rotor of the servomotor. Thus, any writing motion causes the pantograph and the rotors to move. Figure 37-23 shows the close relationship of the position transformer windings and rotor windings of the servomotor.

Coordinate Oscillators. The transmitter has two basic oscillators—the vertical coordinate oscillator and the horizontal coordinate oscillator (refer to Fig. 37-19). These oscillators and related circuits generate specific audio-frequency signals that are used to define the position of a point on the writing surface. They are called *coordinate oscillators* because they function together. The vertical oscillator is tuned to 1,400 Hz. The horizontal oscillator is tuned to 2,200 Hz. These frequencies define the midpoint of the writing surface. The range of audio-frequency signals from the vertical coordinate oscillator is from 1,310 Hz to 1,490 Hz. For the horizontal coordinate oscillator, the range is from 2,060 Hz to 2,340 Hz. The frequencies of both the vertical and horizontal coordinate oscillators can be changed simultaneously by the movement of the transmitting pen.

It is helpful to visualize the vertical and horizontal audio signals as horizontal and vertical planes (Fig. 37-24). You can represent the horizontal frequency range of 2,060 to 2,340 Hz by equally dividing the distance on the x axis. Midpoint 0 would represent 2,200 Hz on the x axis. Likewise, the vertical frequency range of 1,310 to 1,490 Hz can be represented on the y axis. Midpoint 0 would represent 1,400 Hz on the y axis. If points A and B represent one-half the distance on their

PANTOGRAPH STYLUS BALL

TRANSMITTING PEN'S ARM

CLEAR PLASTIC WRITING PLATE

WRITING TABLE

RECEIVING PEN

RECEIVING PEN'S ARM

PANTOGRAPH MECHANICAL LINKAGE

TIP OF RECEIVING PEN

Fig. 37-21. Transceiver cover removed showing the relative positions of the transmitting and receiving arms, and the writing surfaces

WRITING PEN FROM ANOTHER NEARBY TRANSCEIVER

SHAFT OF HORIZONTAL SERVO MOTOR

SHAFT OF VERTICAL SERVO MOTOR

PANTOGRAPH LINKAGE

Fig. 37-22. View of the pantograph's linkage of two transceivers

341

RAISED COVER PLATE

HORIZONTAL POSITION TRANSFORMER COILS

PAPER FEED MOTOR

HORIZONTAL SERVO MOTOR

VERTICAL SERVO MOTOR

VERTICAL POSITION TRANSFORMER COILS

RELATED ELECTRONIC CIRCUITS

Fig. 37-23. View of position transformers and servomotors (*Infolink Corporation*)

Y-AXIS

WRITING SURFACE

1310 Hz

1355 Hz

HANDWRITTEN LETTER M

P

A

X   2130 Hz

X-AXIS

2060 Hz   B   0   2340 Hz

1490 Hz

Y

Fig. 37-24. Simplified concept of using two different frequencies to locate coordinate points on a graph

respective axes, then the frequency of the signals at these points would be 1,355 Hz at point A, and 2,130 Hz at point B. Point P, therefore, represents the coordinates of these two frequencies. Any other point on the writing surface can be represented in the same manner. The hand-written letter M illustrates the changes that occur in the horizontal and vertical frequency signals at several coordinates (points) represented by the large dots.

Basic Electronic Circuits. The block diagram Fig. 37-19 illustrates the various electronic circuits used in the electrical system of the transceiver. Notice that each vertical and horizontal system has its own oscillator for generating the audio signals. When the transmitting pen movement causes a mark on the paper, a 120-Hz frequency-modulated signal is added to the horizontal coordinate oscillator. Otherwise, the horizontal oscillator is the same as the vertical oscillator. This frequency-modulated signal causes the effective inductance to change in the same manner as if the receiver's position transformer servomotor's rotor were physically turned. [Note: Frequency modulation (FM) is discussed in Unit 39, "Radio and Satellite Communications."]

The transmitting output signals pass through a band-pass filter to the telephone wires and the receiving units. The output signal voltage is approximately 400 mV.

RECEIVER

When the transceiver is in the receiving mode, it uses the same type of equipment as the transmitter except that the receiver's equipment is *passive*. This means that the receiver responds to the audio signals received over the connecting wires, usually telephone wires. The block diagram, Fig. 37-19, illustrates the circuits that are connected when the transceiver is in the passive or receiving mode. At the left-hand side of the diagram, the input signals pass through a band-pass filter. This filter minimizes any unwanted signal frequencies entering the system. Next the signals enter the vertical and horizontal limiter amplifiers. These amplifiers increase the incoming audio signals to a precise level. The signals then enter the discriminator circuits and servoamplifiers. These circuits provide the varying frequencies at sufficient strength to operate the servomotors. A *servomotor* is a device in which a mechanical shaft is positioned in accordance with one or more input signals. In this case, the input signals generated by the transmitting unit can be compared to a loop feedback signal generated by a compatible or identical receiving unit. The feedback signals produce a loop error signal that, when reduced to zero by movement of the receiving unit, results in a shaft position identical with the position of the transmitting unit. A receiving pen, connected to the pantograph, follows the changing audio signals sent by the transmitter and records the message on paper located on top of the writing table. The receiving pen has an ink receptacle that holds sufficient ink for several days of constant writing by the receiving pen.

342

OTHER CONTROLLING CIRCUITS

After completing a message in the writing space provided, the transmitting pen is moved to the upper left-hand corner of the writing area. This action closes switches, and the paper-feed motor starts. The motor keeps operating until a new sheet is exposed on the writing surface. All receivers connected to the line will also advance their paper the specified amount. The paper that contains the message can be removed easily by pulling it across the tear-off blade. This leaves a blank sheet available for the next message. A 115-Vac rectifier provides the necessary power for the transceiver units. Indicating lamps show the status of the transceiver. The "send" lamp lights up when the transceiver is in the transmitting mode. A "busy" lamp lights up when the transceiver is receiving a message. The "on" lamp lights up when the power switch of the transceiver is turned on.

SELF-TEST

Test your knowledge by writing, on a separate sheet of paper, the word or words that most correctly complete the following statements:

1. A basic telegraph circuit consists of a _____ , a _____ , a _____ , and a _____ .
2. The telegraph key causes _____ of current to move through the circuit.
3. The telegraph code is carried as electric energy by _____ .
4. The _____ is the receiving element in a telegraph system.
5. In a _____ telegraph system, a switch is connected across the telegraph key.
6. The teletypewriter's transmitting unit is called a _____ .
7. The _____ is the receiving unit in a teletypewriter system.
8. A teletypewriter's message punched as holes on a strip of paper is called _____ .
9. The teletypewriter code works on a _____ .
10. A teletypewriter character consists of _____ pulses.
11. The term _____ indicates current on. The term _____ indicates current off.
12. The teletypewriter uses a _____ start-stop system.
13. The five information pulses in a teletypewriter system are called _____ .
14. Encoding messages in a teletypewriter is done by a distributor that has rotating _____ which

sense matching switches.

15. A central point in a communication network that is a switching center and can transmit and receive information by radio is called a _____ .
16. A telephone transmitter changes sound energy into _____ energy.
17. When the carbon granules in a telephone transmitter are compressed by the diaphragm, their resistance is _____ .
18. Pulsating electric currents generated in a telephone transmitter by the voice are called _____ -frequency currents.
19. Humans can hear sounds that have a range of about _____ to _____ Hz.
20. The telephone (voice) channel or pass band (bandwidth) is from 300 Hz to _____ Hz.
21. In a dial telephone, you actually _____ a message during the dialing process.
22. A _____ switch is a device that automatically makes the connections for the number dialed by step-by-step action.
23. A telephone switch that works like the switching system for railroad cars is called a _____ switch.
24. When a button is pressed on a Touch-Tone phone, two _____ are generated at the same time.
25. The abbreviation for the American National Standard Code for Information Interchange is _____ .

343

26. The bit sense character parity for synchronous data communications is _____.
27. The character structure used for asynchronous data communications consists of _____ signal

elements or bits that have equal time intervals.
28. The arms of a transmitting pen and receiving pen are attached to a _____ in a transceiver for handwriting by wire.

FOR REVIEW AND DISCUSSION

1. What are the basic parts of a telegraph circuit?
2. Describe the encoding process in a telegraph system.
3. Explain how a telegraph sounder works.
4. Describe the open- and closed-circuit telegraph systems.
5. What is the basic function of a teletypewriter?
6. Describe three kinds of teletypewriter terminal units.
7. Describe the pulses that make up the letter *R* on the teletypewriter.
8. Describe the functions of a data-control center in a communications network.
9. Describe the encoding process in a teletypewriter machine.
10. Describe the purpose of a modem.
11. Describe how sound waves are translated into electric currents.
12. Describe how a dialing mechanism works.
13. Explain how a connector switch uses the numbers dialed on a telephone.
14. Give two major advantages of the Touch-Tone telephone.
15. What are three advantages of using glass fibers in place of copper wires for telephone communications?
16. List the features available on some modern telephones that provide opportunities for personal communication.
17. Identify and describe the functions of the main elements on a transmitter unit used in the transceiver for handwriting by wire.

INDIVIDUAL-STUDY ACTIVITIES

1. Set up a hand telegraph system and demonstrate to the class how Morse code is transmitted and received.
2. Demonstrate how one phone is connected with another by dialing a number. Contact your local telephone company for illustrations and literature

on the subject.
3. Visit a business, hospital, hotel, motel, or factory that uses a handwriting electromechanical system. Ask the person in charge for a demonstration of their system. Report to your class on the system.

UNIT 38 Audio Systems

In the discussion of the telephone, you learned that a carbon microphone can change sound waves into *audio-frequency voltages* or *currents*. These voltages or currents are called analog, or audio-frequency (*AF*), signals. In this unit, we will discuss some devices that amplify or make use of these signals. Sometimes AF signals are amplified as a person speaks or as music is played, for example, in a school auditorium. Audio-frequency signals can be stored on a disk (record) or on *magnetic tape*. Audio-frequency signals can also be *digitized*. You will learn later in this unit how analog signals can be converted to digital signals (pulses) in a digital audio system.

The parts of a basic audio system are shown in Fig. 38-1. They include a microphone, connecting cables, audio amplifier, and loudspeaker.

Fig. 38-1. Basic elements in an audio-amplifier system: (A) monaural system; (B) common kinds of input devices; (C) block diagram

MONAURAL SYSTEM

The kind of audio-amplifier system shown in Fig. 38-1A is called a *monaural* system. This is because it uses only one *channel,* or path, for input, amplification, and output. Figure 38-1B shows several different input devices for use with a music system. Often a single amplifier is connected to two loudspeakers. If the amplifier has only one channel for amplification, it is a monaural system (Fig. 38-1C).

STEREO SYSTEM

Figure 38-2 shows a *stereo* sound system. This system has two amplifiers or two channels for the sound to be amplified. This makes it possible to amplify the sound from each microphone separately. The microphones can be put in different places. They can be used to pick up the sounds from the left side and the right side of the stage or the sounds from the stage and the echoes from the auditorium. Therefore, this system reproduces more lifelike sounds. Because two-channel sound makes the sound almost three-dimensional, it is called *stereophonic,* or *stereo* for short. The prefix *stereo* means three-dimensional.

Fig. 38-2. (A) Stereo sound system (two channels); (B) block diagram

LEFT-CHANNEL MICROPHONE

RIGHT-CHANNEL MICROPHONE

AF AMPL

HOUSED IN ONE UNIT

AF AMPL

B

LEFT-CHANNEL LOUD SPEAKER

2-CHANNEL AF AMPLIFIER

A

RIGHT-CHANNEL LOUD SPEAKER

FOUR-CHANNEL SYSTEM

Audio systems were further improved in an effort to obtain as natural a reproduction of sound as possible. A process involving four-channel stereo systems was developed. These were called quadraphonic, quadrasonic, multichannel, or surround-sound. All these systems may not produce true four-channel sound, but they were attempts to reproduce sound almost as your ears would hear it if it were played "live." This is called *high fidelity*. In a live concert or show, you hear not only what is in front of you but what is to the left, right, up, down, and behind you. A four-channel system tries to duplicate this condition. The basic arrangement for a four-channel sound system is shown in Fig. 38-3.

#1 FRONT #2 MICROPHONES

AUDIENCE SEATS

#3 #4

REAR MICROPHONES

3 4

1 2

AF AMPL

AF AMPL

AF AMPL

AF AMPL

B LOUDSPEAKER

#1 #2

LISTENER

#3 #4

1 2 3 4

4-CHANNEL AF AMPLIFIER

A

Fig. 38-3. (A) Four-channel sound system; (B) block diagram

346

COMMON ELEMENTS

Several elements are common to the monaural, stereo, and four-channel amplifier systems. These include microphones, phonograph cartridges, connecting cables, audio amplifiers, loudspeakers, and headphones. Microphones and phonograph cartridges are input devices. Other common inputs include the outputs of tape recorders and radios. Any of these can be monaural, stereo, or four-channel.

MICROPHONE

A microphone changes the energy of sound waves into electric energy. The mechanical energy of the moving air striking the microphone's diaphragm is changed into electric voltages and currents. These represent the audio frequencies and volumes of the original sound wave. There are several kinds of microphones. Two of the more common types are discussed in the following paragraphs.

Dynamic Microphone. The dynamic microphone has a diaphragm connected to a lightweight form with a small coil of wire wrapped around it. The form and, therefore, the coil are free to move over one pole of a permanent magnet (Fig. 38-4A). Sound waves striking the diaphragm cause the form and coil to move.

As the coil moves, it cuts across the magnetic field of the permanent magnet. A voltage is induced across it. The amount and frequency of this voltage vary according to the intensity and frequency of the sound wave. Therefore, the AF voltage developed across the coil is an electrical representation of the sound wave (Fig. 38-4B). Note that the AF voltage varies in value, first above the base line (+) and then below it (−).

High-fidelity dynamic microphones can respond to frequencies rang-

Fig. 38-4. Microphones: (A) dynamic; (B) af voltage from dynamic microphone; (C) crystal; (D) af voltage from crystal microphone

347

Fig. 38-5. (A) Record-player pickup arm with crystal cartridge; (B) record groove causes needle to vibrate (*Sonotone Corporation*)

Fig. 38-6. Basic construction features of a magnetic phono cartridge

ing from about 40 to 20,000 Hz. Since the moving coil of a dynamic microphone has only a few ohms of impedance, it generally has a built-in step-up transformer. This makes it possible to match the impedance of the microphone with that of the input circuit of the amplifier. The matching of the impedances is important. This makes it possible to transfer the maximum amount of energy from the microphone to an amplifier.

Crystal Microphone. The heart of the crystal microphone consists of Rochelle salt crystals or of a ceramic element. The crystals have properties similar to those of quartz. When the crystal is vibrated mechanically, an alternating voltage is developed between its two opposite faces (Fig. 38-4C). This is known as the *piezoelectric effect*. The AF voltages from dynamic and crystal microphones are similar. However, the output impedance of the crystal microphone is much higher.

CARTRIDGES

The two common kinds of cartridges used in pickup arms for audio systems are discussed below.

Crystal Cartridge. The crystal phonograph cartridge has a Rochelle salt crystal or a ceramic element, to which is fastened a needle, or stylus. The cartridge is mounted in a pickup arm (Fig. 38-5). As the needle moves in the grooves of a record, it swings from side to side. This mechanical motion is applied to the crystal, and a voltage is produced. This piezoelectric effect is the same as in the crystal microphone.

Magnetic Cartridge. The magnetic phonograph cartridge performs the same function as the crystal cartridge. There are several kinds of magnetic cartridges, but all work by electromagnetic induction.

In one common kind of magnetic cartridge, the needle is mechanically coupled to a soft-iron armature. The armature is located in the air gap of a permanent magnet (Fig. 38-6). As the needle moves in the grooves of a record, the armature is set in motion. This motion causes the air gap to vary. This, in turn, varies the flux density of the magnetic circuit. A moving magnetic field is produced. When the magnetic field cuts across a stationary coil, it induces a voltage across it. The strength of this voltage depends on how much the needle moves. Thus, the mechanical motion of the needle in the grooves of the record is changed to voltages and currents. These represent sound waves.

In the moving magnetic cartridge, the needle is fastened to a small permanent magnet. As the needle moves, the field of the magnet moves and cuts across stationary coils. This induces a voltage in the coils.

Two important characteristics are often used to compare magnetic phonograph cartridges: frequency response and compliance. *Frequency response* is the range of audio frequencies to which a magnetic cartridge will respond without distortion. In high-fidelity cartridges, this range may be from 20 Hz to 20 kHz. This means that the cartridge is made so its moving parts will vibrate at any frequency in this range without producing a voltage output representing a distorted signal.

Compliance is a measure of the ability of the needle to move easily within the cartridge assembly. The compliance of a cartridge is often indicated in centimeters-per-dyne (cm/dyn) units. An example would be 25×10^{-6} cm at an applied force of 1 dyn. A high cartridge compliance is desirable. It increases the frequency response of the cartridge and reduces needle and record wear.

AUDIO CABLES

For connecting the parts of an audio-amplifier system, coaxial shielded cable is best. Generally, no more than 20 ft (6.1 m) of cable can be used between a high-impedance microphone and an amplifier without distorting the sound. Connectors, such as cable plugs, phone plugs, and microphone connectors, should be fastened securely to the cable by soldering or by tightening all screws. Many problems in amplifier systems can be traced to loose connections or broken wires in the cables.

AMPLIFICATION

The main function of an audio amplifier is to increase the volume of the input signal. Figure 38-7 shows a block diagram indicating that 1 V of input signal is increased tenfold to 10 V at the output.

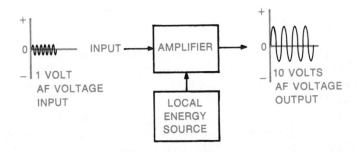

Fig. 38-7. Audio-frequency input voltages are increased by the amplifier.

THREE-STAGE AUDIO AMPLIFIER

Figures 38-8 and 38-9 show two kinds of three-stage audio amplifiers. One uses transistors and the other uses electron tubes. The following discussion relates mostly to amplifiers containing transistors since few are made with tubes today.

Input Signals. The audio-signal input for the amplifier in Fig. 38-8 could come from a high-impedance microphone or a phono cartridge in a record player. The jack J1 provides the cable connection to the ampli-

349

Fig. 38-8. Three-stage transistor audio amplifier

Fig. 38-9. Three-stage tube audio amplifier

fier. Capacitor C1 couples the input signals to the amplifier. C1 and resistor R1 working together form an impedance-matching network between the high-impedance transducer and the low-impedance input of transistor Q1.

The first audio-amplifier stage is made up of transistor Q1, resistors R1, R2, R3, and R4, and capacitors C1 and C2. The main current path is from the negative terminal of the battery (also connected to the chassis) through R4, into the collector of Q1, out the emitter, and through resistors R6 and R7 and switch S1 to the positive terminal of the battery. The circuit that establishes the bias for Q1 starts at the negative terminal of the battery and goes through R3, R2, R6, R7, and S1 back to the positive terminal of the battery. The bias for the base of Q1 is developed at the junction of R2 and R3.

Since the collector current of transistor Q1 differs according to the variations of the input signal, a varying voltage drop is produced across Q1. There is a voltage and current gain during this process. Thus, the input signal is amplified by the first stage of this amplifier.

Resistance-Capacitance Coupling. The signal output of the first-stage transistor Q1 is coupled to the second-stage transistor Q2 by capacitor C2. Resistor R4 acts as the collector load resistor for Q1. C2 is the dc-blocking capacitor that keeps the direct voltage at the collector of Q1 from appearing at the base of Q2. Resistor R5 is a current-limiting resistor through which the necessary base current is applied to Q2.

Transformer Coupling. Interstage coupling between transistor Q2 and transistors Q3 and Q4 (Fig. 38-8) is done by transformer T1. The primary winding of this transformer provides the needed load impedance for the collector (output) of Q2. The center-tapped secondary winding of T1 inductively couples the output signal of Q2 to Q3 and Q4. It acts as the circuit through which the base-emitter voltage is applied to these transistors. This amplifying stage is often called the *driver stage,* and T1, the *driver transformer.*

Transformer coupling is also used between the output stage (transistors Q3 and Q4) and the loudspeaker voice coil. Here, transformer T2 (the output transformer) acts to match the relatively high impedance of the transistor output circuit with the low impedance of the voice coil. Since this is a step-down transformer, its coupling action produces a low voltage across the secondary winding. As a result, the value of the current in the secondary-winding circuit is great enough to energize the voice coil to the level needed to operate the loudspeaker. Note that this transformer-coupling system is similar to the electron tube circuit (Fig. 38-9).

PUSH-PULL OPERATION

The final output, or power-amplification, stage of the three-stage, single-channel amplifier circuit (Fig. 38-8) is what is known as a *push-pull stage.* In push-pull operations, two transistors (or tubes) are used. When an amplifier circuit has only one transistor (or tube) in the final stage, the stage is called a *single-ended stage.*

The input signals to a push-pull stage are developed across the ends of the center-tapped secondary winding of interstage transformer T1. Therefore, the signal voltages applied to the input circuits of a push-pull stage from the secondary winding of T1 surge first in one direction and then in the other. When this happens, the signals are said to be 180 degrees *out of phase* with each other (Fig. 38-10). The output currents pass through transformer T2.

In this condition, the current from point 1 to the center tap of the primary winding of the output transformer T2 is increasing. The current from point 2 of the winding to the center tap is decreasing. Therefore, the magnetic field around one-half of the primary winding is expanding. The magnetic field around the other half of the winding is collapsing. This action is called a *push-pull effect.* The effects of these magnetic fields combine to induce the voltage across the secondary winding of the output transformer.

Fig. 38-10. The push-pull output signal from the transistors drives the output transformer T2.

One advantage of the push-pull amplifier stage is that it will deliver about twice as much power as a single-ended stage. Also, push-pull operation reduces the hum that power variations may produce in the output of an amplifier.

Power Output. The power output of an amplifier is rated in a number of ways. For example, music, peak, and RMS power output are common ratings. The abbreviation RMS means *root mean squared*. The RMS power rating is the most meaningful rating for comparing different amplifiers. This power value is obtained by applying a sine wave at different frequencies to the input. Next the power output is measured across a resistive load. The power values at the different frequencies are squared and totaled, and the mean, or average, is found. Then the square root is taken to give the RMS value.

LOUDSPEAKER

The loudspeaker changes electric energy into sound. Figure 38-11 shows a cross-section of a typical loudspeaker. In this loudspeaker, the voice coil moves freely over, but does not touch, the permanent-magnet pole piece. The voice coil is also connected to the secondary winding of the output transformer T2 (Fig. 38-10). The amplified audio signals are developed across the secondary winding of the output transformer. These signals are applied to the voice coil, thus energizing it. The electromagnetic field of the voice coil is then alternately attracted and repelled by the permanent magnetic field. This causes the voice coil to vibrate. The intensity of this movement varies with the audio signals

Fig. 38-11. The loudspeaker is one type of reproducer.

originally produced by the microphone. Since the voice coil is connected to the loudspeaker's cone, it causes large amounts of air to vibrate. These vibrations produce sound waves. If the microphone, amplifier, and loudspeaker are of high quality, the sounds amplified and reproduced will match the input signals almost exactly.

Kinds of Loudspeakers. A single loudspeaker can produce a good frequency response. However, high-fidelity systems often use three loudspeakers. These are called the *woofer,* the *midrange speaker,* and the *tweeter.* With three speakers, incoming frequencies are split. The low frequencies (20 Hz to 1,000 Hz) are handled by the woofer. The middle frequencies (800 Hz to 10 kHz) are handled by the midrange loudspeaker. The high frequencies (3.5 kHz to 20 kHz) are handled by the tweeter. High frequencies have little *dispersion,* or scatter. Thus, the tweeter is often fitted with a small horn (Fig. 38-12). A *crossover network* is used to split the input signals into frequency bands for the speakers. These networks, consisting of capacitors and inductors (coils), feed the correct range of frequencies to each of the loudspeakers.

Rating. A loudspeaker is rated by the size of its cone, the impedance and the power capacity of its voice coil, its frequency response, and the weight of its magnet (Fig. 38-13).

The cone diameter indicates whether the loudspeaker is small or large. For example, a 12-in. (304.8-mm) loudspeaker is generally a

Fig. 38-12. Tweeter fitted with horn (*Electro-Voice*)

Fig. 38-13. (A) A 15-in (381-mm) duplex monitor loudspeaker; (B) cross-sectional view (*Altec: Sound Products Division*)

A

B

PROTECTIVE CAP

DIAPHRAGM

HIGH FREQUENCY VOICE COIL

HIGH FREQUENCY EXPONENTIAL HORN THROAT

VOICE COIL

CAST ALUMINUM FRAME

CONE

CONE SURROUND

LOADING CAP

HIGH FREQUENCY PHASING PLUG/ POLE PIECE

HIGH FREQUENCY MAGNET

HIGH FREQUENCY POT STRUCTURE/ TOP PLATE

LOW FREQUENCY MAGNET

POLE PIECE

LOW FREQUENCY POT STRUCTURE/ TOP PLATE

FELT DUST PROTECTOR

MULTICELLULAR HORN

woofer. A 4-in. (101.6-mm) loudspeaker is a tweeter. Typical impedance ratings for loudspeakers are 4, 8, and 16 Ω. It is important that the impedance "seen" by the output of the amplifier matches that of the loudspeaker. Otherwise, the amplifier can be overloaded. This seriously distorts the signal. In addition, the power-handling capacity should be known for each loudspeaker. If the power amplifier can deliver 30 W, the loudspeaker should also be able to handle that.

The cabinet that houses the speaker is important for reproducing high-quality sound. For example, a properly designed cabinet keeps the sound waves in front and to the rear of the speaker's cone in phase with each other.

If similar loudspeakers have magnets of the same kind but of different weights, the loudspeaker with the heavier magnet will generally be more efficient. For example, the frequency-response range will be reproduced without significant distortion by a heavier magnet. The frequency-response range runs from about 50 Hz to 8 kHz in a low-cost loudspeaker. In more expensive loudspeakers designed for high-fidelity systems, the range is from about 20 Hz to 20 kHz.

COMPLEMENTARY SYMMETRY

Some audio amplifiers do not have an output transformer (Fig. 38-14). Instead, the circuit uses p-n-p and n-p-n transistors. Because of their polarity characteristics, these transistors provide the push-pull effect.

Fig. 38-14. Complementary-symmetry, audio-amplifier circuit. (*From Electronics Magazine, published by McGraw-Hill, Inc.*)

This kind of circuit is called a *complementary-symmetry, audio-amplifier circuit*. The amplifier has an input stage Q1, a driver Q3, and a power-output stage—transistors Q4, Q5, Q6, and Q7.

VOLUME CONTROL

The *volume* is the output sound level of a circuit. The volume control of an amplifier circuit is most often a potentiometer variable resistor. This is usually put into the input circuit of an amplifier stage (Fig. 38-15). The volume control acts as a voltage divider. As the shaft of the potentiometer is adjusted, the sliding arm moves toward either point 1 or point 2. When it moves toward point 1, a greater part of the voltage developed between points 1 and 2 of the control is applied to the input circuit of transistor Q3. As a result, the volume of the amplifier circuit is increased. Moving the sliding arm to point 2 decreases the volume.

Fig. 38-15. Volume-control circuit

TONE CONTROL

Tone refers to the balance of low frequencies, or bass, and high frequencies, or treble, in the sound output. A tone control lets you adjust the frequency response of an audio amplifier so as to affect this balance.

A basic tone-control circuit consists of a capacitor and a potentiometer variable resistor connected in series across the output of an amplifier stage. In Fig. 38-16, C2 has a capacitance value that causes it to present a low capacitive reactance to the higher-frequency signals in the output circuit of Q2. The capacitor then tends to bypass those high-frequency

Fig. 38-16. Tone-control circuit

signals to ground. This prevents them from reaching the loudspeaker. With the high frequencies weakened, the amplifier produces relatively more bass response. The degree to which this happens is determined by the setting of the potentiometer.

PREAMPLIFIER

A *preamplifier* increases the output voltage of the signal source so that the main audio amplifier can reach full power. A preamplifier can be either single-stage or multistage. It is connected between an input device with a low output level, such as a magnetic phono cartridge or a dynamic microphone, and the main amplifier. The preamplifier may be a separate unit, or it may be contained in the main amplifier.

STORING SOUND

There are two common devices for storing sounds—the record, or disk, and magnetic tape. The record player reproduces sound stored in the record, and the tape recorder does the same for tape.

RECORD (DISK)

A record is made, indirectly, by a recording machine. This machine changes the original sound into electrical vibrations. The machine's needle-sharp cutting head records these vibrations in a groove it cuts on a master record. During the cutting, the head moves slowly toward the center of the record. This forms an unbroken spiral groove. Inexpensive copies of the master are made from vinyl blanks.

The grooves on monaural records are irregularly wavy. The short waves are high tones. The longer ones are lower tones. The grooves on typical stereo records consist of "walls" cut at right angles (90°) to each other and at an angle of 45° to the record surface (Fig. 38-17). When the

Fig. 38-17. A stereo-record groove

stereo master is being cut, the vibrations from one channel are recorded on one wall of the groove. The vibrations from the other channel are recorded on the other wall. When a record is played with a stereo cartridge (Fig. 38-18), the vibrations from the two walls are picked up on the other wall separately. Thus, the sounds from the two channels are reproduced.

MOUNTING BRACKET

TERMINAL POSTS (4)

SILICON CHIP

COPPER-CLAD SUBSTRATE

NEEDLE

Fig. 38-18. A stereo cartridge (*Sonotone Corporation*)

MAGNETIC TAPE

Magnetic tape has a special coating of iron oxide. Sounds are induced on this coating electromagnetically. Two-track, four-track, and eight-track tapes are available today. On a two-track tape, one side is recorded or played on track 1. Then the tape is turned over, and the other track is used (Fig. 38-19). For stereo, four-track tapes are used. Two tracks are used at the same time, one for each channel. Then the tape is turned over, and the other two tracks are used.

TAPE HEADS

Tape heads record sounds on a tape, pick up sounds for playback, or erase the tape. The tape head is held closely against the tape during recording and playback. During recording, the head changes the audio signals into an electromagnetic field. This field magnetizes the oxide coating on the tape. During playback, the head detects the electromagnetic field on the tape. On some recorders, an erase head demagnetizes the tape by means of an ultrasonic-frequency electromagnetic field. An *ultrasonic frequency* is one that is above the audio range. Other ways of erasing the tape include passing the tape over a permanent magnet or

357

Fig. 38-19. Cassette tape cartridge

RECORD PLAYBACK

REWIND

REWIND

CASSETTE CARTRIDGE CASE

SPLINE FOR TAPE DRIVE

TAPE REELS

MAGNETIC TAPE IN RECORD OR PLAYBACK POSITION

RECORD PLAYBACK

GUIDE ROLLER

STATIONARY GUIDES

GUIDE ROLLER

MAGNETIC TAPE

PINCH ROLLER

FELT PAD

ERASE HEAD

RECORD AND PLAY HEAD

TAPE-TRANSPORT SYSTEM

TRACK 1

TRACK 2

ELECTROMAGNETIC IMPRINTS OF SPEECH OR MUSIC

DOUBLE-TRACK RECORDING TAPE

TRACK 1

TRACK 2

MAGNETIC TAPE

over an electromagnet energized by a direct current. The tape can be erased and reused many times before it is worn out. A motor and mechanisms pull the tape from a feed reel past one or more tape heads to a take-up reel called the *tape transport,* or *deck.* On some tape recorders, the tape can be set to run at any one of three standard speeds, 1⅞, 3¾, or 7½ inches per second (ips). In general, tapes operated at 7½ ips have superior sound reproduction.

COMPACT DISC PLAYER

The *compact disc (CD) player* is a digital audio system. Figure 38-20 illustrates a modern two-channel CD player. It uses an invisible laser beam to read the data on the disc. The diameter of the compact disc is 4¾ in. (120.65 mm). This disc rotates in an enclosed compartment. When the open-close button is pressed, the compartment comes forward

REMOTE CONTROL

COMPACT DISC PLAYER

Fig. 38-20. Compact disc player (CDP) with remote-control device (*Sony Corporation of America*)

358

automatically like a drawer to receive a disc. Once the disc is placed on the platter, the start button is pressed. The drawer closes automatically and the music sensor allows you to "leap" to the song you selected. The compact disc player has many features that allow you to enjoy the music without leaving your chair. It has, for example, a repeat capability and a front panel display that tells you which track is being played. The infrared remote control has 25 keys that allow you to perform all functions, such as play, pause, search, and access to a specific track number.

SOUND AND LIGHT

The technology that makes the compact disc player possible involves three new processes: (1) the creation of digital data that can represent the complex waveforms of music (sound); (2) the development of a laser beam with an optical (light) system that is tiny and sensitive enough to transmit and record digital data representing musical waveforms; and (3) the development of a mechanical system that can accurately control and play back the data approaching the original sound.

Analog-to-Digital Converter. Audio signals derived from a person's voice or from musical instruments are very complex audio waveforms. To convert audio signals into a digital form, a binary digital code is used. Since the binary system has only two states, on or off (1 or 0), a binary code can be used to indicate different levels of amplitude of an audio signal. The device that does this is called an *analog-to-digital converter* (ADC). An ADC is explained in more detail in Unit 43, "Interacting With the Microcomputer." Nevertheless, the fundamental principle of an ADC is illustrated by an artist's sketch in Fig. 38-21. A simplified analog waveform is shown in Fig. 38-21A. The voltage levels (-5 Vdc to $+5$ Vdc) of this waveform are coded into 16 different levels. The sketch illustrates selected binary codes and their associated binary digits (bits) representing the various voltage levels.

Each time a waveform is sampled (sensed), a binary code of the voltage level for that sample is established. Each sample is said to be *quantized*. That is, the magnitude of the voltage is measured and represented by a binary code 44,100 times a second. For every second, therefore, the musical (audio) signals are transformed into 1,411,200 individual 1 or 0 binary bits ($16 \times 2 \times 44,100 = 1,411,200$). The high rate of sampling and coding the sound waves makes it possible to reproduce the original music (sound waves) with very high fidelity.

Laser Recording. Because of the high rate of sampling, a laser beam is used to record the binary bits on the disc. One of the main advantages of the laser beam is that it consists of radiations that are nearly of the same frequency. This type of radiation is called *coherent light*. One of the important properties of the coherent light of the laser beam is that it does

Fig. 38-21. (A) One method of coding in binary form the amplitude change of an analog signal; (B) effect of sampling rates

not spread out very much even when it is far from its source. Because of this, the laser beam stays highly concentrated. Unit 29, "Lamps and Lighting," explains the laser in more detail.

The laser beam used in the CD player produces a beam that is 1.7 μm in diameter (one micrometer equals one millionth of a meter). The laser provides a constant light beam, and the spread, or diffusion, of the beam is negligible. In recording the music that has been converted into a binary digital code, the beam is directed at a blank plastic disc with a thin layer of *tellurium* or a similar substance. The thin layer is the active part of the disc. Tellurium is a rare silver-white element occurring in nature combined with gold and silver. During the recording process, the laser beam is focused on the disc and burns "pits" into the thin layer of active material. The pits change the reflectivity of a tiny area on the disc. Figure 38-22 shows an enlarged view of the pits. The pits and the absence of pits represent the music or sound recorded in digital form on a disc. A pit, for example, can represent a binary digit 1; and the absence of a pit, a binary digit 0. The length of the pit or the distance between pits varies according to the 16-level binary code derived from the analog-to-digital converter.

Laser Playback. The enlarged view of the pits created by the laser beam during the recording process does not indicate the magnitude of them on the disc. There are, for example, roughly *15 billion* pits passing the playback head every hour on the compact disc player. No traditional stylus could pick up that amount of information. Therefore, the playback process on the CD player uses a laser beam too.

A block diagram of the playback system is shown in Fig. 38-23. Notice that the optical pickup shows a laser beam aimed at the disc and reflected back to the optical pickup. The beam is sensitive enough to recognize each tiny pit with unerring accuracy. If the laser beam is reflected from its path unchanged, there is no pit. Therefore, a binary 0 is represented at the particular spot on the disc. If there is a perceptible change in the reflected beam, caused by a pit, a binary 1 is represented at that particular spot on the disc. The laser is so precise that nothing but a pit will cause a variation in the reflected beam.

Fig. 38-22. Greatly enlarged view of the pits formed by a laser beam on a disc (*Sony Corporation of America*)

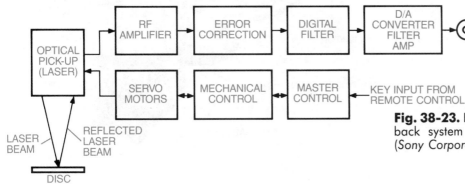

Fig. 38-23. Block diagram of playback system using a laser beam (*Sony Corporation of America*)

Figure 38-24 shows an enlarged view of the laser beam "reading the pit." The rectangular shapes on the outer edge of the disc provide electrical signals to the master control circuits. The master control serves as a center for all operations. For example, it controls the motion of three servomotors. One servomotor maintains the rotational speed of the disc for constant "linear velocity" as opposed to constant "angular velocity," which is found on traditional 33⅓ RPM record players. Another servomotor keeps the laser beam on track. A third servomotor adjusts the laser beam focus for discs that are not perfectly flat.

The block diagram, Fig. 38-23, shows that the detected binary-coded data bits are amplified and sent to an error correction circuit. The error correction circuitry can restore virtually any data lost during playback. The digital filter reduces unwanted frequencies and provides clear sharp digital signals. These signals become the input to the digital-to-analog converter (DAC). Its function is to change the digital signals that were

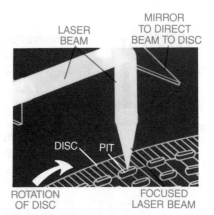

Fig. 38-24. Laser beam reading the "pit" (*Sony Corporation of America*)

processed by the digital circuits back into analog signals. The analog signals are filtered to reduce unwanted frequencies that could cause distortion, and then the signals are amplified for use by speakers. The sound reproduced by the speakers on a CDP has outstanding quality, depth, and range approaching the perfection of a live concert.

The entire CDP system assures that the music flows freely and without interruption. Figure 38-25 shows a cutaway view of the CD player laser-based playback system.

Fig. 38-25. Cutaway view of a laser-based compact disc player system (*Sony Corporation of America*)

SIGNAL PITS

OBJECTIVE LENS

COLLIMATOR (FIXED TELESCOPE) LENS

SEMI-TRANSPARENT MIRROR

GRATING PLATE

CYLINDRICAL LENS

LASER DIODE

PHOTO DETECTOR DIODE

FOCUS SERVO COIL

TRACKING SERVO COIL

TRACKING GUIDE RAILS

SELF-TEST

Test your knowledge by writing, on a separate sheet of paper, the word or words that most correctly complete the following statements:

1. The parts of a basic audio system are _____, _____, _____, and _____.
2. Four common input devices used with audio amplifiers are _____, _____, _____, and _____.
3. A _____ microphone has a diaphragm connected to a lightweight form with a small coil of wire wrapped around it.
4. High-fidelity dynamic microphones can respond to frequencies ranging from _____ to _____ Hz.
5. Two important characteristics often used to compare magnetic phonograph cartridges are _____ and _____.
6. _____ is best for connecting the parts of an audio-amplifier system.

7. Audio-amplifier stages are often coupled by _____ coupling and/or _____ coupling.
8. A _____ amplifier stage is used when the final amplifier circuit has only one transistor or tube.
9. The most meaningful rating for an amplifier is _____ power output.
10. Three kinds of loudspeakers found in a high-fidelity audio system are the _____, _____, and _____.
11. A _____ network is used to split the input signals into frequency bands for the speakers in a high-fidelity audio system.
12. One kind of transformerless audio amplifier is called the _____ amplifier.
13. A _____ and a _____ are two basic components used to form a tone control for an audio amplifier.
14. The two common means of storing sound are the _____ and magnetic _____.
15. The motor and mechanisms that pull the magnetic tape from a feed reel past one or more tape heads to a take-up reel are called the _____.
16. To convert audio signals into a digital form, a _____ digital code is used.
17. In a compact disc player, it is the high rate of _____ and coding the sound wave that makes it possible to reproduce original music (sound waves) with very high fidelity.

FOR REVIEW AND DISCUSSION

1. Distinguish between monaural and stereo sound systems.
2. What is the main function of a microphone?
3. Explain the difference between a dynamic microphone and a crystal microphone.
4. Explain the difference between the crystal and the magnetic phonograph cartridge.
5. What is compliance?
6. What is the main function of an output transformer?
7. Describe how an audio input signal is amplified.
8. Describe the advantages of a push-pull amplifier.
9. Identify three terms used to rate the power output of audio amplifiers. Which term is most meaningful?
10. Explain how a voice coil in a moving cone loudspeaker produces sounds.
11. What is the purpose of the horn attached to a tweeter loudspeaker?
12. Why is the weight of a magnet in a loudspeaker so important?
13. What is the basic function of a preamplifier in a stereo system?
14. Describe the grooves of a monaural record and of a stereo record. How does the cartridge pick up the sound from the record?
15. What is the function of an erase head on a magnetic-tape recorder?
16. Compare the differences between the compact disc player and the cassette tape player.

INDIVIDUAL-STUDY ACTIVITIES

1. Prepare a block diagram of a home audio system that would include such inputs as a microphone and phonograph and such reproducers as loudspeakers and headphones. The system might also include a tape recorder and a radio.
2. Visit a business that sells compact disc players. Request the owner to demonstrate the CD player for you. Report your experience to the class.

UNIT 39 Radio and Satellite Communications

Fig. 39-1. Two students operating a basic radio system using two transceivers (transmitter and receiver combined in one unit)

You have already learned how telephone wires are used to send messages from one place to another. Now you will see how speech and music can be transmitted *without wires*. This is done with a radio system. The radio system, like the telephone, has a transmitter and a receiver (Fig. 39-1). It does not, however, have connecting wires.

TRANSMITTER

The radio transmitter makes it possible to send music and speech by means of *radiated,* or emitted, energy. The radiated energy is transmitted through the air. Understanding how your voice works will help you understand how this is possible. Taking a deep breath is like opening an air bellows. You are forming the energy source for the air that will pass through your vocal cords, throat, and mouth when you talk. The *radio station,* where the equipment is located for transmitting speech and music, also has an energy source and a *high-frequency oscillator* in the transmitter. The energy source produces a high voltage. The oscillator causes a stream of electrons to vibrate back and forth at high frequencies (Fig. 39-2).

Fig. 39-2. Transmitting station: (A) power lines (energy source); (B) oscillator using coil and capacitor; (C) oscillator using a crystal; (D) carrier (electromagnetic wave)

RADIO WAVES

Sound waves are produced by your vocal cords. They are transmitted through the air as varying air pressures. In a radio transmitter, a circuit is used to create waves that, in some respects, are like sound waves. This circuit, the high-frequency oscillator, contains a coil and a capacitor. The oscillator causes a stream of electrons to vibrate, or *oscillate*. Similarly, vocal cords in a person's throat cause a stream of air to vibrate. This rapidly oscillating movement of electrons causes energy to be *radiated,* or sent through the air, in the form of electromagnetic waves.

Electromagnetic waves are a form of radiated energy that can do work. When a stone is thrown into the water, water waves radiate out from the point where the stone entered the water (Fig. 39-3). Electromagnetic waves can be compared to these water waves. Figure 39-4 shows this waveform. The higher the frequency, the shorter the wavelength. *Wavelength* is the distance between a point on one wave to a similar point on the next wave. Sound waves, water waves, and electromagnetic waves are similar. Radio waves, however, have a much higher frequency than sound waves do. A radio wave must have a frequency of at least about 10,000 Hz before it can be used for radio communication.

Ground and Sky Waves. Radio waves travel through space from the antenna of a transmitting station at the speed of light (186,000 miles per second or 300,000,000 meters per second). Some of these waves move along the surface of the Earth. These are called *ground waves*. Ground waves are soaked up rapidly by the Earth. They do not travel very far. Other radio waves move skyward. These are called *sky waves* (Fig. 39-5). Some sky waves are reflected back to Earth by a layer of ionized gas from 60 to 200 miles (97 to 322 km) above the Earth. This is known as the *Kennelly-Heaviside layer* (or *ionosphere*) in honor of the two men who discovered it. Some of the sky waves go through this Kennelly-Heaviside layer and never return to Earth. However, the sky waves reflected back to Earth make long-range radio communication around the Earth's surface possible. The following formulas can be used to calculate wavelengths:

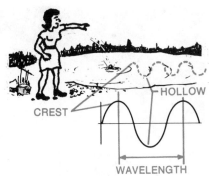

Fig. 39-3. Throwing a stone into water causes water to radiate out from the point where the stone entered.

$$\lambda = \frac{300,000,000}{f}$$

where λ = wavelength in meters
f = frequency in hertz

or

$$\lambda = \frac{300}{f}$$

where λ = wavelength in meters
f = frequency in megahertz

Fig. 39-4. Comparison of ac graph (sine wave) to a radio-wave form: (A) alternating current (low frequency); (B) radio wave (high frequency)

Carrier Waves. A radio wave of a certain frequency is assigned to a radio station. It is called a *carrier wave* because it "carries" speech and

Fig. 39-5. Transmitted radio waves: (a) sky waves; (b) ground waves; (c) Kennelly-Heaviside layer of gas

music from the radio-station transmitter to radio receivers. The frequencies of the carrier waves used for different kinds of radio broadcasting are assigned by the Federal Communications Commission (FCC).

Broadcast Bands. Commercial AM broadcast stations operate within a carrier frequency band that extends from 535 to 1,605 kHz. The carrier frequency of commercial FM broadcasting extends from 88 to 108 MHz.

MODULATION

When you speak, the vowels and the consonants of your speech are molded on the vibrating air stream. This is done by your tongue, lips, teeth, and the walls of your mouth and throat. This molding lets you send meaningful sound waves to another person.

In a radio transmitter, the process of molding the electron stream for speech or music is called *modulation*. A *modulator* is a circuit that combines speech or music information with the carrier wave.

A varying current is produced when sound waves strike a microphone. The microphone output is then fed into a modulation circuit. There the audio and carrier waves are combined. Modulation allows the carrier wave to carry information from one place to another by electromagnetic energy (Fig. 39-6). At the receiving end, this information is then taken from the carrier wave by special circuits in a radio receiver.

Amplitude and Frequency Modulation. The modulated radio wave is developed by combining the carrier wave and the alternating current from a microphone. Note that the frequency of the carrier wave does not

AMPLITUDE CONSTANT

A

CARRIER WAVE
(RADIO FREQUENCY)

Fig. 39-6. Amplitude of carrier wave modulated by an alternating voltage: (A) carrier wave; (B) alternating voltage; (C) modulated radio wave

AMPLITUDE OR STRENGTH VARIES

ALTERNATING VOLTAGE FROM MICROPHONE
(VOICE FREQUENCY)

B

AMPLITUDE VARIED

C

MODULATED RADIO WAVE

change after modulation (Fig. 39-6C). The alternating current from the microphone modulates the carrier wave by causing its *amplitude*, or strength, to rise and fall. This process is called *amplitude modulaion* (AM).

The carrier wave can also be modulated by changing its frequency. This process is called *frequency modulation* (FM) (Fig. 39-7). The changes in frequency are controlled by the signal from a microphone. Note that the amplitude does not change in frequency modulation.

LOW-POWER AM TRANSMITTER

A two-stage, amplitude-modulation (AM) transmitter is shown in Fig. 39-8. It is designed to transmit a frequency that can be received by an ordinary AM radio that you might find in your home. Despite its low power (400 μW), its energy can be picked up by a receiver 50 to 100 ft (15 to 30 m) away.

This transmitter contains five basic electronic circuits: power supply, oscillator, amplifier, modulator, and radiator. The input for the total system is a voice signal, for example, from a microphone. The output modulated amplitude is a radio frequency electromagnetic wave.

Power Supply. The power supply consists of a 6-V battery.

Oscillator Circuit. The oscillator circuit is composed of resistor R1, a crystal, Q1, capacitor C1, and coil L1. The movement of the electrons in the 300-pF capacitor C1 and the inductor L1 forms a parallel resonant

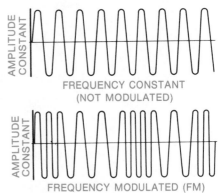

AMPLITUDE CONSTANT

FREQUENCY CONSTANT
(NOT MODULATED)

AMPLITUDE CONSTANT

FREQUENCY MODULATED (FM)

Fig. 39-7. The effect of frequency modulation

367

Fig. 39-8. Low-power, two-transistor, AM transmitter: (A) block diagram; (B) schematic wiring diagram

A

B

tank, or tuned, circuit. It is the action of this tank circuit that produces the continuous sine wave oscillations at a radio frequency rate, in this case, 670 kHz.

Amplifier Circuit. The radio frequency energy produced by the oscillator is coupled to the RF amplifier transistor Q2 through an eight-turn secondary-winding L2. The electron flow in the amplifier-circuit system is from the negative terminal of the battery to the chassis, then to L2, Q2, RFC, R2, and S1 before returning to the positive terminal of the battery. Practically all the battery power is dropped across the resistor R2.

Modulation Circuit. The modulation circuit allows intelligence (speech or music) to be superimposed on the radio frequency signal that can be radiated to distant receivers. Audio-frequency signals (voltages) are fed from the microphone in and out of C6, the coupling capacitor. These voltages are passed on to R2 and C2 at the base of Q2, the radio frequency amplifier. These voltages increase and decrease the base bias

368

voltage of Q2 at an audio rate. Thus, the audio input modulates the amplitude of the radio-frequency energy being radiated.

Radiating Circuit. The radiating circuit, as shown, consists of capacitor C3, and antenna matching network (L3, C4, C5), and a 3-ft antenna wire. Capacitor C3 acts as a coupling device for radio frequency energy into the *pi network* (so named because the schematic topology resembles the Greek letter π). The pi network is a tank circuit that acts like a transformer. This matching method (pi network) allows Q2 to work efficiently and "loads" up the antenna so that it radiates properly.

Although the radio transmitter shown in Fig. 39-8 uses only two transistors, the principles behind its operation are similar to those of larger and more powerful transmitters. The crystal provides stability. The tank circuits smooth out the energy pulse into a continuous-energy sine wave at a specified frequency. The tank circuit eliminates harmonics and thus reduces the chance of interference. The modulator circuit allows intelligence to be carried to distant receivers. And the matching pi network loads the antenna properly and increases its efficiency.

AMATEUR RADIO

A person interested in amateur radio can apply to the Federal Communications Commission (FCC) for a license to operate a station (Fig. 39-9). This activity can improve both your communication skills and your technical knowledge of radio.

The Federal Communications Commission provides the rules and regulations for the amateur radio service. At present, there are five classes of operator's licenses: novice, technician, general, advanced, and amateur extra. The novice class gives the beginner an opportunity to get on-the-air experience quickly. A novice must pass an international Morse code test of 5 words per minute. The examination also covers FCC rules and regulations and elementary radio theory. The amateur-extra class is the most advanced class. This class requires passing an examination on advanced radio theory and operation, including rules and regulations affecting amateur stations and operators and a code test of 20 words per minute. With each rise in class, certain privileges are gained. For example, specific frequencies, such as 3,500 to 3,525 kHz, are reserved for use only by amateur-extra-class operators. Common amateur frequency bands are 3,500 to 4,000 kHz (wavelength about 80 m), 7,000 to 7,300 kHz (wavelength about 40 m), and 14,000 to 14,350 kHz (wavelength about 20 m). Higher-frequency bands, such as 144 to 148 MHz (wavelength about 2 m) are also authorized.

Fig. 39-9. An amateur radio station (*American Radio Relay League*)

PERSONAL RADIO SERVICES

The Federal Communications Commission also publishes rules and regulations governing the operation of *Personal Radio Services*. These services include the stations discussed on the following page:

General Mobile Radio Service Station. This kind of station is intended to be operated between mobile and land stations or between mobile stations. These stations are licensed to be operated on an assigned frequency in the 460 to 470 MHz band with a transmitter power output of not more than 50 W.

Radio Control (R/C) Service Station. This kind of station is licensed to be operated on an authorized frequency in the 26.96 to 27.23 MHz band. For remote control of objects by radio, the frequency of 27.255 MHz is authorized. The 72 to 76 MHz band is authorized for the radio control of models used for hobby purposes.

Citizens Band (CB) Radio Service Station. This kind of station is licensed to be operated for radiotelephony only. *Radiotelephony* is the transmitting of voice messages. This station provides short-distance mobile radio communications for business or personal activities.

The CB authorized frequencies are in the 26.96 to 27.41 MHz band. Specific frequencies in this band are commonly called *channels*. There are 40 channels. For example, the frequency of 26.965 MHz is channel 1. The frequency of 27.065 MHz, channel 9, is used only for emergency communications. Channel 19, with an assigned frequency of 27.185 MHz, is very popular with truckers and other travelers. The CB equipment, called a *rig,* is authorized to operate with a maximum carrier power output of 4 W.

The latest rules and regulations of the FCC should be consulted for details as to who may operate CB equipment and the type of equipment authorized.

TRANSCEIVERS

A *transceiver* is a small unit that combines a transmitter and receiver. A small hand-held unit is popularly called a *walkie-talkie.* A modern transceiver often used in business for instant communication is shown in Fig. 39-10. Several small hand models are available. These are controlled by a crystal and operate at low power (100 mW) in the 49.82 to 49.90 MHz range. A pair of walkie-talkies is needed to carry on a two-way conversation (see Fig. 39-1). These units have 3 to 12 transistors each, depending on the quality and electronic circuitry. Since small transceivers are portable, a 9-V battery is often used as a power supply. The usual controls on these small units are (1) off-on switch with volume control, (2) push-to-talk button, (3) squelch control, and (4) jack for earphones. The *squelch control* eliminates background noises and unwanted noises between the transmissions.

SUPERHETERODYNE RADIO RECEIVER

In an attempt to improve radio reception, a special circuit called the *superheterodyne circuit* was invented in 1918. Edward H. Armstrong,

Fig. 39-10. A modern transceiver (ICOM America, Inc.)

an American, invented the circuit. This circuit helped make radio receivers more selective and more sensitive. A radio receiver is *selective* when it can pick out the modulated carrier wave from the desired broadcasting station and reject all the other carrier signals reaching its antenna. A radio receiver is *sensitive* when it can receive weak radio waves or signals. The superheterodyne circuit has made possible radio receivers that are both highly selective and sensitive.

BEAT FREQUENCY

The special circuits within the superheterodyne radio circuit are a *mixer*, or *converter*, stage and an oscillator stage called the *local oscillator*. The radio frequency signals generated by the local oscillator usually have a higher frequency than that of the carrier wave to which the receiver is tuned. The signals from the tuning circuit of the receiver and the signals from the local-oscillator circuit are combined in the mixer stage. The result is a signal with a frequency equal to the difference between the frequencies of the two signals being mixed. This is called the *beat frequency*. Producing a beat frequency is known as *heterodyning*.

Figure 39-11 shows how a beat frequency is produced in a superheterodyne radio receiver. The carrier signal to which the receiver is tuned has a frequency of 640 kHz. The signal generated by the local oscillator has a frequency of 1,095 kHz. These two signals are combined in the mixer stage. The output of that stage is the difference, or a beat-frequency signal of 455 kHz. This signal is called the *intermediate frequency* (IF). In the United States, most AM superheterodyne radio receivers operate at an intermediate frequency of 455 kHz.

In order to maintain a constant intermediate frequency of 455 kHz, the oscillator circuit must be adjusted whenever a different station is tuned in. This is usually done by means of a variable capacitor controlled by the main tuning knob. As a result, the oscillator output frequency is always 455 kHz higher than the frequency of the station selected.

Fig. 39-11. Producing a beat frequency (intermediate frequency)

STAGES IN AN AM SUPERHETERODYNE RECEIVER

The block diagram (Fig. 39-12) shows the electronic stages in a modern transistorized AM superheterodyne receiver. Electron tube receivers also have similar stages.

The Antenna. The antenna of a radio receiver may be compared to the secondary winding of a transformer. The electromagnetic fields of the radio waves radiated from the antenna of a transmitter cut across the receiving antenna. Thus, they induce voltages in the antenna circuit. These voltages represent the speech or music information with which the carrier wave has been modulated. The voltages are then applied to

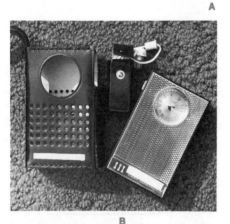

Fig. 39-12. (A) Block diagram of a superheterodyne radio receiver; (B) portable radio

the tuning circuit of the radio receiver. Since these voltages "carry" information, they are called radio frequency (RF) signals, or radio signals.

The Tuning Circuit. The tuning circuit for a superheterodyne radio receiver is shown in Fig. 39-13. The circuit consists of variable capacitor C1 and antenna coil L1. The variable capacitor is used to *tune,* or adjust, the circuit to different frequencies.

When the tuning circuit is adjusted to the frequency of a station, the circuit is said to be in *resonance* with the frequency of that station. In this condition, the inductive reactance of coil L1 is equal to the capacitive reactance of capacitor C1. The circuit now offers the least impedance to signals of the station carrier frequency. However, it offers a high impedance to carrier signals of other frequencies. Therefore, all the other carrier signals are rejected by the circuit.

Fig. 39-13. Tuner and converter (oscillator-mixer) circuits

You tune most home radio receivers by adjusting a variable capacitor. However, with other receivers, such as automobile receivers, you tune by varying the inductance of the tuning-circuit coil. This is done by moving a ferrite core into or out of a tube around which the tuning coil is wound. In tuning circuits of this kind, a fixed capacitor is used.

Converter (Oscillator-Mixer). In the converter circuit, incoming RF signals are heterodyned to the intermediate frequency of 455 kHz (Fig. 39-13). Transformer T1, capacitors C3 and C4, and transistor Q1 make up the local oscillator. C4 is *ganged,* or mechanically linked, to capacitor C1. C4 acts with the secondary winding of T1 to establish the frequency of oscillations for Q1. Note that the incoming radio frequencies are also coupled to Q1 through capacitor C2. Q1 heterodynes, or mixes, the two frequencies—a radio signal of 1,000 kHz and a local oscillator signal of 1,455 kHz—to produce the intermediate frequency of 455 kHz.

There are usually several stations broadcasting in an area. For example, three stations, each transmitting with its own frequency of 630 kHz, 980 kHz, and 1,500 kHz, could be tuned in on the receiver. However, no matter what the tuned radio frequency is, the intermediate frequency will always be 455 kHz.

Intermediate-Frequency (IF) Amplifier. The IF amplifier amplifies only one frequency, 455 kHz. Thus, its design can be made highly selective and efficient. The IF signals are coupled to their stages by tuned transformers like the first IF transformer T2 in Fig. 39-13. There are usually two IF amplifying stages before the audio signals are detected by a diode. *Detection* involves recovering the modulated audio-frequency signals from the carrier.

Audio Detector and AVC Circuit. The detector CR1, a semiconductor diode, removes the negative-going parts of the IF signals coming from the IF transformer T3 (Fig. 39-14). The audio output appears across the

Fig. 39-14. Detector, automatic volume control (AVC), and AF amplifier (driver)

373

volume-control resistor R13. It is coupled by capacitor C17 to the audio driver stage, Q4. The amplified audio signals are next fed into a push-pull amplifier and then to the loudspeaker.

The *automatic volume control* (AVC) provides high gain for weak signals at the incoming IF stages. It also reduces the strength of strong signals. For example, when a strong audio signal is detected, the voltage across C13 becomes more positive. The positive-going AVC signal is fed to the incoming IF stages and reduces their gain. The opposite happens when weak signals are received.

ALIGNMENT

Aligning is adjusting the variable trimmer capacitors and the variable cores of transformers and coils in the receiver circuit so that they will work efficiently. This is usually done with a *plastic alignment tool* (Fig. 39-15). Correct alignment of a radio receiver provides the best selectivity and sensitivity. The procedures for aligning different radio receivers are usually given in servicing manuals and handbooks.

Fig. 39-15. (A) Intermediate-frequency amplifier stage; (B) aligning the intermediate-frequency transformer by adjusting the movable iron cores in the coils

INTERMEDIATE FREQUENCY
TRANSFORMERS, T1—T2

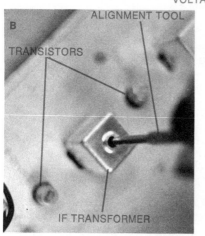

FM RECEIVER

The electronic-circuit stages of an FM superheterodyne receiver are shown in the block diagram of Fig. 39-16. These circuits include the antenna, RF amplifier, mixer, local oscillator, power supply, IF amplifier, FM detector, audio amplifiers, and loudspeaker. These electronic circuits have been discussed previously, except for the FM detector. The standard FM broadcasting band in the United States is from 88 to 108 MHz. The intermediate frequency used is 10.7 MHz.

FM Detector. Figure 39-17 is a schematic of an FM detector called a *ratio detector*. The input to this circuit is from the previous IF amplifier stages. The ratio detector recaptures the audio signals that are frequency

Fig. 39-16. Block diagram of FM receiver

FROM PREVIOUS IF AMPLIFIER

AUDIO-OUTPUT FOR FIRST AF AMPLIFIER

Fig. 39-17. FM ratio detector

modulated on the carrier signal. In frequency modulation, the audio signals cause the FM carrier signal to change frequency above and below the assigned center frequency.

In FM, the amplitude of the audio signal is porportional to the amount of frequency shift above and below the carrier frequency. Therefore, the ratio detector must be able to produce an output voltage that is proportional to the frequency of the carrier wave at any instant of time.

Advantage of FM over AM. Automobile ignition systems, lightning, and the making and breaking of circuit connections by switching actions create electromagnetic waves. These waves act on amplitude-modulated communications carrier waves and cause them to be disrupted or distorted. As a result, AM radio receivers often produce a noise commonly called *static*. Unwanted electromagnetic waves do not cause the frequency of a frequency-modulated carrier wave to change. Because of this, the FM radio receiver is able to reproduce information in the form of speech or music that is not distorted by static.

Fig. 39-18. Amplitude-modulated personal radio (*Radio Shack, a Division of Tandy Corporation*)

Fig. 39-19. A personal communication (paging) device (Metrocall Co.)

PORTABLE COMMUNICATIONS

Since the early 1980s, there has been a rapid growth in the use of personal portable radios, cordless telephones, personal message services, car phones, and radio control devices. These devices provide communications while you are "on the move."

Personal Portable Radio. The personal portable radio is very popular (Fig. 39-18). It provides a listening system that can go with you while walking, jogging, or traveling on a train. In fact, it can go just about anywhere. It can fit into your purse or shirt pocket. Headphones let you listen to your favorite station in private. It features a one-hand rotary volume control and requires a 9-Vdc battery for a power supply.

Personal Message Service. A *pager* provides a personal message service. It is a small radio receiver carried by a person (Fig. 39-19). Its basic purpose is to alert the person to an incoming message. This is done with a ringing tone, or tone and a message. The message is displayed digitally using alphanumeric characters. Some pagers can produce voice messages. Pagers can be operated automatically or manually. The radio frequencies used by these devices are in the very-high-frequency (VHF) range between 30 and 50 MHz and 138 and 174 MHz. Some operate in the ultra-high-frequency (UHF) range between 405 and 512 MHz.

Figure 39-20 illustrates an automatic paging system. To page a person (a subscriber using this system) several steps must be taken, as follows: (1) Pick up an ordinary telephone and dial the numbers (three digits) of the paging central office. Next dial the subscriber's paging code number (four digits). (2) The central paging office judges automatically if the number is correct. If correct, it automatically answers back with a tone sound or a recorded announcement. When you hear an answer-back sound, hang up the telephone and wait for the person paged to reach a public or private telephone. (3) The paging number called is converted by a transmitter into radio signals. (4) These signals are next emitted from the transmitter's antenna. (5) The emitted signals are detected only by the paging receiver that has the corresponding code number. (6) The person carrying the paging receiver responds to the alert by dialing a predetermined telephone number to receive the message.

Cordless Telephone. Many homes now have a cordless telephone (Fig. 39-21). The equipment necessary for this system consists of a base unit connected to the phone and power lines and a portable unit that can be carried about in the home or yard. The portable unit is basically a radio transmitter that can operate away from the base unit, the receiver.

The cordless telephone in Fig. 39-21 operates on frequencies between 46 and 49 MHz. It can be mounted on a desk or wall and have an

OFFICE NUMBER (3 DIGITS)

SUBSCRIBER NUMBER (4 DIGITS)

PUBLIC TELEPHONE

ORDINARY SUBSCRIBER'S TELEPHONE

SWITCHING OFFICE

CENTRAL PAGING OFFICE

(ANTENNA)

(PAGING TERMINAL)

(TRANSMITTER)

ALARM SOUND

(PAGING RECEIVER)

PAGING SUBSCRIBER

Fig. 39-20. Automatic paging system (*NEC Corporation*)

operating range of 1000 feet (304.8 m). Its features, for example, include two-way paging and intercom, last number re-dial, and billing security. This set is compatible with touchtone or dial pulse service.

Car Phone. Car phones enable individuals to make long-distance calls while in their cars (Fig. 39-22). Cellular technology has made this mobile system possible. *Cellular technology* is based on a grid system that covers a specific geographic area (Fig. 39-23). Each cell contains a low-powered radio transmitter and control equipment located in a building called a *cell site*.

The cell site is connected by wireline facilities to a *m*obile *t*elephone *s*witching *o*ffice (MTSO). This switching office is connected to a regular landline network through the telephone control office. With its electronic switching capability, the MTSO monitors the mobile units and automatically switches or "hands off" conversations in progress as the mobile unit moves from one cell to another.

Each cell has a set of radio frequencies, allowing reuse of every channel for many different simultaneous conversations in a given service area. As demands increase, dividing cells into smaller cells can meet customer needs even in the most densely populated areas. Because the service combines radio channels with landphone lines, customers can call any phone number in the world as long as the mobile unit is within the cellular service coverage area.

Fig. 39-21. A cordless telephone—the Nomad,® (*American Telephone and Telegraph Company*)

Fig. 39-22. A business executive using a car phone (*Bell Atlantic Mobile Systems*)

Fig. 39-23. Basic concept of cellular technology in a mobile car phone system (*Bell Atlantic Mobile Systems*)

LOCAL TELEPHONE OFFICE

CELL SITE

MOBILE TELEPHONE SWITCHING OFFICE

ANTENNA

HAND-HELD TRANSMITTER

ANTENNA

TOY AUTOMOBILE WITH RADIO RECEIVER MOUNTED INSIDE

Fig. 39-24. A simple radio control system

For the busy executive who spends an hour or more each day traveling to and from work, the mobile phone service cost can be offset by a saving of time. Dictation, for example, can be done while waiting in a traffic jam if the dictating machine has its own telephone number. Accidents can be reported as can other emergencies encountered while driving. Some automobile manufacturers are now offering cellular phones as options. On some airlines it is even possible to call your office or home.

Radio Control. A simple radio control device is shown in Fig. 39-24. This control system uses a hand-held portable transmitter and a receiver located in the toy automobile. The receiver is tuned to the frequency of the transmitter. The radio transmitter is powered by a 9-V battery as in the radio receiver. The automobile has an electric motor that turns the rear wheels of the car. Four AA batteries provide the power to operate the electric motor.

When the portable hand-held transmitter is turned on, it emits a radio signal. The receiver responds to the signal of the transmitter by causing the electric motor to reverse its direction—either backward or forward.

Through a mechanical linkage, the direction of the car is changed each time the car moves backward. Thus, the car can be directed in any direction simply by backing it up, then turning on the transmitter again, and the car moves forward in a straight line.

Radio control transmitting systems used for controlling toy automobiles and model airplanes generally have six basic electronic circuits: the RF oscillator (usually crystal controlled), the AF (tone signal) oscillator, the RF amplifier, the modulator, the antenna, and the power supply. The output of the transmitter is a radio wave modulated when the tone switch is closed. The radio control receiving circuits, located in the toy automobile or model airplane, detect the tone signals. The tone signals (AF currents), instead of operating a speaker, actuate a relay, solenoid, or some other device. The opening and closing of a relay, for example, causes an action to occur such as backing up in a toy automobile or moving the rudder in a model airplane.

Although these radio control systems are elementary, you will learn that satellites are radio controlled too. These control systems, however, are very complex and also provide a means to make and send measurements over long distances by using radio signals.

TELEMETRY AND SATELLITES

Telemetry is making measurements at one place and sending these measurements for recording and study to another place far away. The information obtained may be in a form suitable for display on a television tube, for recording on tape, or for use in analog or digital computers. In space explorations without astronauts, telemetry has helped scientists perfect the design of vehicles by monitoring their performance during flight. In flight with astronauts, telemetric signals add to the messages sent by the astronauts. Telemetry makes it possible to compute flight data with heavy equipment on the ground. Data include such information as facts and figures. These data are used for study or for making a decision.

POWER REQUIREMENTS

The power needed to send telemetric signals from satellites and space probes is much less than that needed for commercial radio and television stations. The space explorer, *Mariner IV*, sent data back to Earth from more than 191 million miles (307 million km) away with a 10-W transmitter. Radio contacts, but no telemetric data, were received from *Mariner IV* when it was 216 million miles (348 million km) away.

ANTENNA SYSTEMS

One of the reasons that so little power is needed on a spacecraft is that ground radio systems have very sensitive receiving equipment and high-gain antennas. For example, the antenna used with the Mariner spacecraft was 85 ft (26 m) in diameter. It was about 20,000 times more effective than the average rooftop television antenna. Ground stations with these antenna systems can use radio signals from satellites and spacecraft to track them with a high degree of accuracy. These systems also make it possible to communicate and receive data from spacecraft and satellites (Fig. 39-25).

Fig. 39-25. An 85-ft-diameter (26-m-diameter) parabolic antenna used for spacecraft and satellite communications (*General Telephone and Electronics Corporation*)

Fig. 39-26. (A) Block diagram of a programming and control subsystem of a weather satellite (*National Aeronautics and Space Administration*); (B) a weather satellite

PROGRAMMING AND CONTROL

One of the electronic subsystems used in a weather satellite is for programming and control (Fig. 39-26). This subsystem allows the satellite to be controlled either automatically or by command from ground stations in contact range. The satellite responds to a command-address unit. This unit allows one satellite out of a group to be contacted. For example, first an address tone of a specified frequency and duration is transmitted from the ground station. If the satellite is within range and the address tone is received, the programming and control subsystem is then activated.

Satellites have a number of auxiliary controls. The magnetic attitude control is an example. This control guides the spin axis of the satellite along a predetermined path. Other auxiliary controls are the despin control, spin-up rocket control, and telemetry and beacon controls. This last system has two continuous wave radio signals used to track the satellite. The beacon signals are also used as radio frequency carrier waves for telemetric signals.

One of the important elements in the satellite programming and control system is the satellite clock. A clock is like an oscillator. It generates periodic signals. The clock must be synchronized with the master clock at the ground station. The master clock at the ground station is calibrated with the standard time signals. These signals are transmitted by the U.S. National Bureau of Standards radio system, such as station

WWV. The satellite clock maintains proper synchronization and programming for the entire satellite system around the world. Different tone signals are used to set different clocks. Once set and working, the satellite clock helps control operating steps.

DATA ACQUISITION FACILITIES

Because of the large amount of data transmitted by communications satellites and other spacecraft, a system of ground stations has been built to receive and pass on this information. This system is called the Space Tracking and Data Acquisition Network (STADAN). *Acquisition* means "the act of obtaining or gaining." The network sends all its data to the Communications and Computing Center at the Goddard Space Flight Center of the National Aeronautics and Space Administration (NASA) in Greenbelt, Maryland. From there, the data are sent on to the users.

Figure 39-27 shows the basic parts of a weather-satellite system. The satellite provides television pictures of the Earth. The pictures show clouds, storms, and pollution. The pictures are relayed by radio to the ground station center. Other signals from the satellite are converted into usable drawings by facsimile recorders (Fig. 39-28A). These drawings

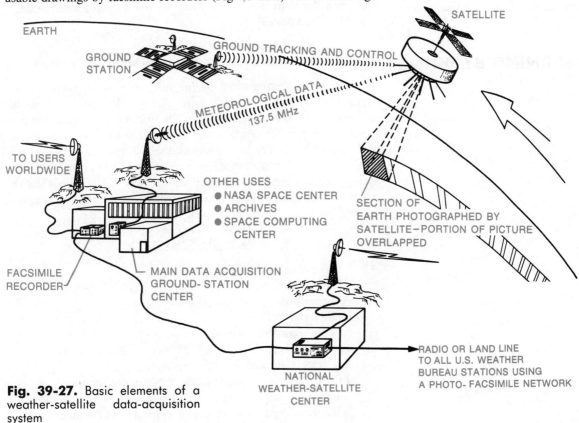

Fig. 39-27. Basic elements of a weather-satellite data-acquisition system

381

ANTENNA– POSITION INDICATOR

FM RECEIVER

ANTENNA– POSITION CONTROLLER

WRITING DESK

FACSIMILE TEST SET

POWER– DISTRIBUTION PANEL

FACSIMILE RECORDER

FACSIMILE PAPER– STORAGE DRAWER

STORAGE SPACE

A

B

Fig. 39-28. (A) Facsimile recorder control console (*National Aeronautics and Space Administration*); (B) photo of a tropical storm taken by a weather satellite (*National Aeronautics and Space Administration*)

or graphs are very helpful in locating hurricanes and other weather disturbances (Fig. 39-28B).

Other weather data, such as surface temperatures, are also received by the center at the same time. These are sent by radio-teletype or teletypewriter from about 1,500 local weather stations located throughout the United States.

LEARNING BY DOING

12. AM Radio Transmission. In this unit, we have discussed various types of radio communication. This activity will show you how this communication is accomplished (Fig. 39-29). You will send a tone over a very short distance. Radio communication of all types is controlled and licensed by the Federal Communications Commission (FCC); however, the transmitter described here is of such low power that no license is required to operate it. Standard connections and functions will be specified, but it may become necessary for you to refer to the operator's manual for your specific equipment.

MATERIALS NEEDED

Small portable AM radio
RF signal generator
AF generator
oscilloscope
cassette recorder/player with output jack
10 ft (304.8 mm) no. 18–no. 22 copper antenna wire
connector and cable for RF generator output
2 ft (60.9 mm), two-conductor cable with connectors to match the output jacks of the AF generator on one end and the audio-input jacks of the RF generator on the other end

2 ft (60.9 mm), two-conductor cable with connectors to match the auxiliary speaker output of the cassette recorder on one end and the RF generator audio-input connection on the other end

Procedure

1. Solder the antenna wire to the center connection of the connector compatible to the output of the RF generator. This will act as a transmitting antenna. Connect the antenna to the center terminal of the RF output of your RF generator.
2. Using the test leads for the oscilloscope, connect the antenna wire to the vertical input terminal of the oscilloscope. The common ground lead of the oscilloscope is connected to the common ground on the RF generator. The oscilloscope will allow you to observe the waveform being transmitted to the radio.
3. Connect the output of the AF generator to the audio input of the RF generator and set the selector switch of the RF generator to "external modulation."
4. Coil the antenna wire in a loose circle about 1 ft (30.48 mm) in diameter, and place it on the work surface with the AM radio near the coil.
5. Turn on the oscilloscope, RF generator, audio generator, and the AM radio.
6. Set the audio generator for 500 Hz and observe the waveform at point 1.
7. Set the tuning dial of the radio to a frequency that is not used in your area.
8. Set the frequency range selector of the RF generator to the AM band position (535 to 1605 kHz). Sweep through this band by adjusting the tuning control knob on the RF generator until a tone is heard in the radio.
9. Observe the oscilloscope and adjust the output level of the RF generator and the AF generator to get a pattern that closely approximates that shown at point 2 (Fig. 39-29).

Fig. 39-29. Equipment arrangement used for Learning by Doing No. 12, "AM Radio Transmission"

383

CAUTION

The equipment in this experiment may cause interference to radio and television reception in the area. If so, turn the equipment off. Set the power level of the RF generator to the minimum necessary to observe the signal on the oscilloscope. Try to eliminate interference by reorienting the antenna or relocating the test equipment.

10. Once you have an acceptable tone in the radio, sweep through the range of the AF generator, and observe the changes in the waveform on the oscilloscope and listen to the various tones in the radio.

11. Replace the AF generator with the cassette recorder/player. Do this with the cable compatible to the cassette player and the RF generator. Put in a previously recorded cassette tape and press the play button. Adjust the volume-level control until the pattern on the oscilloscope matches what you observed when there was an acceptable tone from the audio generator. Notice how the audio pattern on the carrier wave matches what you hear in the radio.

12. Draw on a separate sheet of paper the waveform observed when the cassette recorder is connected in step 11. Discuss the drawing with your instructor.

SELF-TEST

Test your knowledge by writing, on a separate sheet of paper, the word or words that most correctly complete the following statements:

1. A radio system consists basically of a _____ and _____ .

2. In a transmitter, the device that causes a stream of electrons to vibrate back and forth at high frequencies is called a high-frequency _____ .

3. The wavelength of a radio wave depends on its frequency. The higher the frequency, the _____ the wavelength.

4. A radio wave must have a frequency of at least about _____ Hz before it can be used for communication.

5. Radio waves travel at the speed of _____ .

6. _____ waves move along the surface of the Earth. _____ waves move skyward.

7. The radio wave of a certain frequency assigned to a radio station is called a _____ wave.

8. The process of molding the electron stream for speech or music is called _____ .

9. During modulation in an AM system, the _____ of the carrier wave rises and falls according to the audio input.

10. The pi network is a tank circuit that acts like a _____ .

11. In an FM system, the _____ is varied according to the audio input.

12. Commercial AM broadcast stations operate within a frequency band from _____ to _____ kHz.

13. When a radio receiver is able to select one radio signal and reject all others, it is said to be _____ .

14. A radio receiver is said to be _____ when it can receive especially weak radio signals.

15. The local oscillator of a superheterodyne radio circuit is tuned to a _____ frequency than the carrier frequency to which the receiver is tuned.

16. The standard intermediate frequency used in a superheterodyne radio circuit is _____ kHz.

17. The automatic volume control (AVC) provides _____ gain for weak signals.
18. Adjusting the variable trimmer capacitors and the variable cores of transformers in a radio receiver circuit is called _____ .
19. The intermediate frequency in FM superheterodyne receivers is _____ MHz.
20. The portable unit of a cordless telephone is basically a _____ .
21. A pager is basically a small _____ .
22. _____ technology has made the mobile car phone possible.

23. Little power is needed on a satellite because ground radio systems have very sensitive _____ and _____ .
24. The programming and control subsystem in a weather satellite responds to an address tone of a specified _____ and _____ .
25. The _____ signals provide the carrier waves for telemetric signals.
26. A satellite clock must be _____ with the master clock at the ground station.
27. Signals from satellites are converted into usable drawings by _____ .

FOR REVIEW AND DISCUSSION

1. What are the components of a high-frequency oscillator?
2. Compare the frequency of sound waves and radio waves.
3. What effect does the Kennelly-Heaviside layer have on radio waves?
4. Describe the difference between a sky wave and a ground wave.
5. Describe the processes of AM modulation and FM modulation.
6. Identify five basic electronic circuits in a transmitter.
7. Explain the purpose of a pi network as used in a transmitter.
8. Describe how a mixer, or converter, stage works in a superheterodyne radio-receiver circuit.
9. What are the main advantages of the IF amplifier stages?
10. Compare the assigned frequencies for the standard AM and FM broadcasting bands. List three AM and FM radio broadcasting frequencies in your local area.
11. List five common amateur radio bands. Identify their frequencies and wavelengths.
12. Describe the process of paging a subscriber using the automatic paging system.
13. Explain the term cellular technology as it pertains to the car phone.
14. Define the term telemetry.
15. Give two major advantages of telemetry in space exploration.
16. List four kinds of auxiliary controls in a weather satellite.
17. Explain the primary function of a satellite clock.
18. Describe the parts of a satellite data acquisition system.

INDIVIDUAL-STUDY ACTIVITIES

1. Obtain a schematic diagram of a complete AM radio. Identify the main components and circuits. Describe the function of each main section, such as the detector and the tuner.
2. Obtain a pair of walkie-talkie transceivers that do not require an FCC license to operate. Read and follow the operating instructions. Find the largest operating range that you and a friend can use to talk to each other. Discuss the effects that tall buildings, hills, vehicles, and trees have on the operating range?
3. Obtain and review descriptive literature on mo-

bile car phones. Give an oral report to your class on the basic concepts involved in cellular technology.

4. Prepare a report on the use of telemetry in the moon-landing, Voyager, Skylab, or Pioneer space programs.

UNIT 40 Television and Facsimile Systems

Of all the electronic devices available today, the television set is probably the one that has had more impact on the lives of individuals than any other single electronic device. And television images are improving steadily in quality.

The photos shown in Fig. 40-1 represent a new type of television picture. The photos are created using small to large picture elements called *pixels*. You can visualize a pixel as one square on an ordinary sheet of graph paper. The closer the vertical and horizontal lines are drawn on graph paper, the smaller the squares. In a digital television picture, each picture element has its own binary code. The device that creates the picture elements is called a video *digitizer*. The *intensity,* or brightness, of the picture element is also detected by the digitizer. Table 40-1 shows the number of horizontal and vertical divisions needed to establish the picture elements. As the number of picture elements increases, the *resolution,* that is, the ability of the individual parts (picture elements) to reproduce detail, is improved. This is shown dramatically by comparing the series of photos and the number of pixels shown in Table 40-1.

It is not possible in this text to discuss the details of digitizing a standard, or analog, television signal, but the basic concepts of developing, or digitizing, picture elements, as they pertain to a facsimile system, are discussed later in this unit. Although most current television systems use an analog video signal to reproduce images, future systems may be digitized. One of the advantages of a digitized television signal is that it can be interfaced with most computers and other digital processing equipment. Let us now examine the basic electrical and electronic concepts involved in the television system. These concepts will provide you with a foundation to understand the computer monitor, or screen, and other video devices.

TABLE 40-1. RELATIONSHIP OF PIXELS TO SCREEN RESOLUTION IN FIG. 40-1.

Photo No.	Resolution (Pixels)
1	512 × 480
2	256 × 240
3	128 × 120
4	64 × 60
5	32 × 30
6	16 × 15

FUNDAMENTALS OF TELEVISION

Two pieces of photographic equipment can be used to show how a television camera works. One is a camera with a ground glass in the back. The other is a light meter. The ground glass of the camera lets you

Fig. 40-1. Effect of picture elements (pixels) on a TV screen. (*Colorado Video, Inc.*)

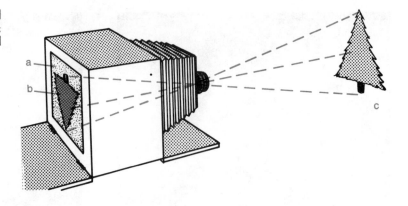

Fig. 40-2. An image on the ground glass of a camera: (a) ground glass; (b) image; (c) object photographed

see the image focused through the lens. This image is upside down (Fig. 40-2). Light rays travel in straight lines. If a straight line is drawn from the bottom of an object through a lens, it will meet the ground glass near the top. Thus, the bottom of an object is projected through a lens to the top of the viewing surface.

The light meter measures the *intensity,* or strength, of light striking it. The light meter helps you get the lens opening on the camera. On a dull day, the light meter reads low light intensity. On a bright day, the light meter reads high light intensity.

When light strikes certain substances, an electric current is produced. This *photoelectric effect* was discovered in 1873. This discovery led to other experiments and eventually to the first patent on a television system. This was taken out by V. K. Zworykin, an American physicist, in 1928. In the photoelectric effect, electrons are *emitted,* or thrown off, when light or other electromagnetic radiations strike a photosensitive surface. Two common photosensitive materials are cesium oxide and selenium. In a light meter, the emitted electrons from the photosensitive material are conducted by wires through a very sensitive meter. This measures the light intensity.

IMAGE ORTHICON TUBE

The heart of the television camera is the camera tube. The *image orthicon tube* and *vidicon tube* are two kinds in common use today. The basic parts of the image orthicon tube are shown in Fig. 40-3 and are discussed below.

Image Section. The image of an object to be televised is focused by lenses onto a light-sensitive material inside the tube. As in a camera, this image is upside down. The image causes electrons to be emitted from the light-sensitive material. The number of electrons emitted depends on the intensity of the light striking the material. A white dress on a performer, for example, would cause more electrons to be emitted than a dark dress.

A

B

FOCUSING COIL

HORIZONTAL AND VERTICAL
DEFLECTING COILS

DECELERATOR GRID #5

TARGET

ACCELERATOR GRID #6

PHOTOCATHODE

GRID #4

GRID #3

SCANNING
BEAM

ALIGNMENT COIL

GRID #2 AND DYNODE #1

ELECTRON GUN

FIVE-STAGE MULTIPLIER

RETURN BEAM

TELEVISED
SCENE

CAMERA
LENS

IMAGE
SECTION

SCANNING
SECTION

MULTIPLIER
SECTION

C

Fig. 40-3. (A) A television camera with three lenses; (B) an image orthicon tube (*RCA Corporation*); (C) schematic arrangement of an image orthicon tube (*RCA Corporation*)

The emitted electrons are attracted to the *target,* a thin glass plate. This plate is made so that the electron image is transferred to its opposite side, the side facing the scanning beam (Fig. 40-3C).

Scanning Beam. The scanning, or electron, beam transfers the picture information to the multiplier section of the tube. Just before the scanning beam strikes the target, it is *decelerated,* or slowed down. This makes the transfer of picture detail from the target possible. This scanning beam is focused like a light beam into a narrow stream.

The areas of the target where more of the electrons have been emitted are less negative. The scanning beam is repelled less in these areas. The areas where more of the electrons have been retained are more negative. The scanning beam is repelled more in these areas. The result is a return beam of electrons varying in density according to the details of the picture.

Return Beam. The variations in the return beam caused by the light and dark areas of the object being viewed make up the *video,* or *picture, signal.*

The return beam works like a photographic light meter moving across the sensitized image. A meter is more sensitive to light areas than to dark areas. The movement of the needle in the meter would register detail, as does the return beam (Fig. 40-4).

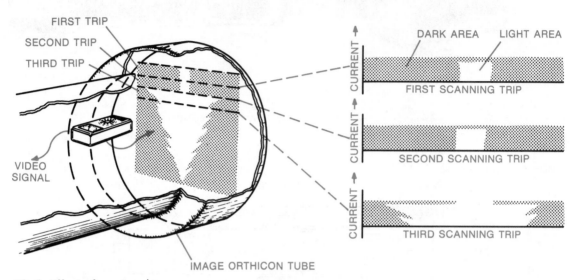

Fig. 40-4. Effect of a return beam using a photographic meter

Scanning Section. In order to reproduce an image, the scanning beam must *scan,* or view, the whole image. The scanning section causes the scanning beam to scan the image completely.

The scanning beam can be bent left or right by placing certain charges of electricity on horizontal plates like plates 1 and 2 of Fig. 40-5. The beam can be moved up or down by varying the charges on vertical plates 3 and 4. Figure 40-5 shows a greater positive charge on horizontal plate 2. This causes the scanning beam to swerve to the right, since it is attracted to the positively charged plate. The entire target can be scanned by placing various charges on the horizontal or vertical planes. A scanning beam can also be controlled by horizontal and vertical deflecting coils instead of plates (see Fig. 40-3).

Fig. 40-5. Charges on the plates cause the electron beam to scan in a specified area.

390

The scanning beam scans horizontally and vertically at the same time (Fig. 40-6). Therefore, each horizontal line of scanning slants downward a little. As each horizontal line is completed, the electron beam returns rapidly to the starting point of the next horizontal line. This point is always a little below the previous one.

Fig. 40-6. Scanning process

In television, a series of 30 frames is flashed on the screen every second. Each frame consists of 525 lines. Thus, the scanning rate is 30 × 525, or 15,750 lines, or hertz. A motion-picture film shows 24 frames per second to create the effect of continuous motion. The 30 frames per second of television has the same effect. Figure 40-7 shows the effect of a mechanical connection between scanning systems of the television camera and the television receiver. Actually, they have to be electronically *synchronized,* or locked in step.

Fig. 40-7. Television camera and receiver scanning systems must be synchronized, or locked in step.

VIDICON CAMERA TUBE

Figure 40-8 shows a simplified schematic diagram of a vidicon camera tube. One use of this kind of camera tube is in weather satellites, which

Fig. 40-8. Vidicon camera tube

take pictures of the Earth and its clouds. The vidicon camera tube does not have a return beam.

When the camera tube is taking a picture, the electrically sensitive material is exposed to the image. The image is converted into an electrical-charge pattern on the surface of this material by the emission of electrons. The electrical-charge pattern is transferred to the polystyrene layer. There it is *read out,* or scanned, by an electron beam moving across and down the surface. The pattern of the electrical charge causes the electron beam, or current, to vary. This variable current forms the video signal. The video-signal voltage appears across the load resistor.

COLOR CAMERA TUBES

To produce a *monochromatic,* or black-and-white, television signal, only one camera tube is needed. However, to transmit color, three or more camera tubes are used. One common kind of color camera has four tubes. One tube produces the *luminance* signal. This is just like a black-and-white signal. All the light reflected from the image is transmitted as the luminance signal. For color, an additional optical system is used. The light is filtered so that only red colors can be seen by the red camera tube, only green colors by the green camera tube, and only blue colors by the blue camera tube. Before transmission, the four video signals (luminance, red, green, and blue) are *matrixed,* or mixed together. Black-and-white television receivers accept the luminance signal. Color television receivers separate the red, green, and blue signals and reproduce them on their screens (Fig. 40-9).

TRANSMISSION OF TELEVISION SIGNALS

The video signal of television is transmitted somewhat like the audio signal of radio. Both video and audio signals are varying direct currents.

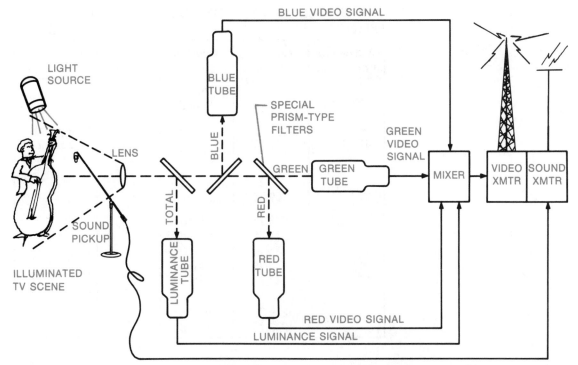

Fig. 40-9. Basic elements in television color transmission using a four-tube color camera

Each time the electron beam scans the image in the studio camera, this video signal is picked up and transmitted. Sound for a television program is transmitted at the same time as the picture, but on a separate frequency. In a television channel, therefore, there are two carrier frequencies, one for the picture and one for the sound.

Television and frequency-modulation broadcasting stations use high-frequency carrier waves. Television carrier waves are classified as very-high-frequency (vhf) waves (30 to 300 MHz) or as ultra-high-frequency (uhf) waves (300 to 3,000 MHz). Table 40-2 lists the bandwidths and video and sound frequencies for selected television channels. There are 12 vhf channels, numbers 2 to 13. Channel number 1 is not used now because that frequency band has been reassigned by the FCC to another kind of communication service. There are 70 uhf channels, numbers 14 to 83. These uhf channels provide for the expansion of television service, especially through the use of cable television. Cable television, as contrasted to over-the-air television, can provide a wide variety of television channels as well as two-way communication. This is done through a coaxial cable.

Because of the high frequencies used in television, the waves take on the characteristics of light waves. As a result, television broadcasting stations are limited to straight-line paths like light paths (Fig. 40-10). To get long-distance transmission, relay towers or satellites are used. Co-axial telephone cables are also used for long-distance transmission. At the local station, the programs are transmitted over the air to local viewers.

Maximum Bandwidth	Frequency (MHz)	Nature of Service	Channel Number	vhf or uhf
66–72	67.25 71.75	Video Sound	} 4	Very-high-frequency (vhf) range
180–186	181.25 185.75	Video Sound	} 8	
204–210	205.25 209.75	Video Sound	}12	
506–512	507.25 511.75	Video Sound	}20	Ultra-high-frequency (uhf) range
542–548	543.25 547.75	Video Sound	}26	
818–824	819.25 823.75	Video Sound	}72	

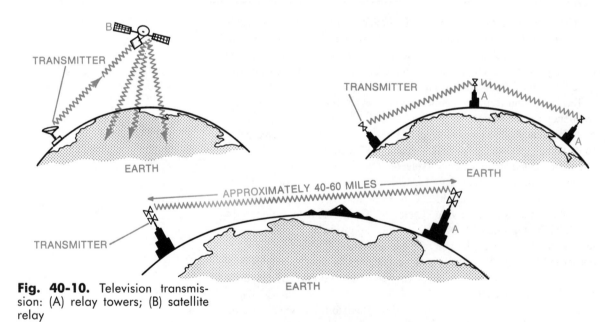

APPROXIMATELY 40-60 MILES

Fig. 40-10. Television transmission: (A) relay towers; (B) satellite relay

TELEVISION RECEIVER

The television receiver and the radio receiver are alike in many ways. The superheterodyne principle, intermediate frequencies, radio frequencies, amplification, and mixer and detector circuits are used in television as well as radio.

Modern television receivers also provide stereo capabilities (Fig. 40-11). Stereo sound on a television set adds a new dimension to home entertainment. Movies and other programming recorded in stereo can be played back in stereo too. Today the projection television receivers take about the same space as a console but offer "big-screen" enjoyment even in a moderate-sized room. The remote-control device allows you to scan 178 channels by using the channel-up and channel-down buttons. Channel selection can be made by the use of numbered buttons. Buttons are used to turn the television set on or off, to make the sound louder or softer, or to completely shut the sound off.

Fig. 40-11. Color television receivers: (A) 25-in. (63.5-mm) diagonal television set with built-in stereo speakers and stereo adapter for decoding new television broadcasts in stereo sound; (B) 45-in. (114.3-mm) diagonal projection television receiver with wireless infrared remote control (*Zenith Radio Corporation*)

REMOTE CONTROL

TELEVISION BLOCK DIAGRAM

Figure 40-12 is a block diagram of a color television receiver. A black-and-white television receiver would be similar. However, it would not have the circuits needed to process the color signals. Multiterminal modular packages used in a typical color television receiver are shown in Fig. 40-13.

Fig. 40-12. Block diagram of a color television receiver

Fig. 40-13. An example of an integrated-circuit (IC) color processing circuitry and associated components (*Zenith Radio Corporation*)

SUBCARRIER REGENERATOR IC

CHROMA-AMPLIFIER IC

221-42

COLOR DEMODULATOR IC

$\frac{1}{4}$ WAVELENGTH

32.6"

$\frac{1}{4}$ WAVELENGTH

32.6"

ANTENNA ELEMENT

(OVERALL LENGTH 65.2")

ALUMINUM TUBING

PARALLEL LEAD-IN WIRE

Fig. 40-14. Dipole antenna for channel 6

Fig. 40-15. Five-element television antenna

TELEVISION ANTENNA

Television antennas pick up both sound and picture signals. One of the simplest antennas for television reception is the *dipole,* or two-pole, antenna (Fig. 40-14). This is a half-wave antenna opened at the center. Each length of this antenna represents one-fourth of the wavelength of the incoming signal. For example, the length of one arm of a dipole for channel 6 is about 32 in. Connecting wires leading to the television receiver are fastened to the open ends in the middle of the dipole.

Figure 40-15 shows a five-element antenna. It is used in weak reception areas some distance from the television transmitter.

TUNER

The tuner of a television receiver lets you choose the channel you want. A rotary switching system is often used for this purpose. The rotary switch changes inductors and/or capacitors as needed for tuning in channels. The inductors and capacitors in the tuning circuit of a television receiver perform the same function as in a radio receiver.

Preprogrammed Tuner. A new computerized tuning system is now available on some television receivers. This system has the vhf and uhf channels plus all cable channels preprogrammed and stored in the memory of the *microprocessor*. This is a digital integrated circuit. It is considered the *central processing unit* (CPU) in a *microcomputer*. This microcomputer stores channel frequency information and recalls it on

396

demand (Fig. 40-16). The viewer just presses the channel number and then the "enter" button, and the station is tuned in instantly. A 10-digit keyboard is also available on the television set or in a remote location. This keyboard lets a person choose a channel by touching the proper digits.

AMPLIFIERS

As in a superheterodyne radio receiver, there are radio frequency amplifiers, IF amplifiers, and mixer stages in a television-receiver circuit. However, television IF amplifiers must be sensitive over a range of 6 MHz. This range includes both picture and sound carrier waves. The color television receiver in Fig. 40-12 has a video amplifier in addition to the audio amplifiers. The video amplifier increases the power of the video signals. A black-and-white television receiver would not have the circuits for the burst and chrominance amplifiers.

SOUND CIRCUITS

The FM sound circuit contains an intermediate-frequency amplifier, a ratio detector, and an audio amplifier. The efficient *intermediate-frequency amplifier* amplifies the sound signals and increases the sensitivity and selectivity of the receiver toward them. The *ratio detector* separates out the audio component in the frequency-modulation system. The *audio amplifier* increases the audio signal enough to operate a loudspeaker.

SYNCHRONIZING AND SWEEP CIRCUITS

The *synchronizing,* or *sync,* and *sweep,* or *deflection,* circuits receive the sync pulses from the televised picture signal and sweep the television picture-tube beam in synchronization with the camera-tube beam. Like the camera tube, the picture tube has vertical- and horizontal-sweep plates, or coils. These plates sweep the beam across and up and down the chemically coated screen to make the picture.

The horizontal-sweep circuit returns the television picture-tube beam to its starting point. This return sweep, called the *horizontal retrace signal,* is *blanked.* That is, the retrace signal cannot be seen by the viewer.

Several controls are used to adjust the operation of the sync and sweep circuits. The horizontal- and vertical-hold controls adjust oscillators within the range of the sync pulses. The height and width controls adjust the amplitude of the sweep. Other controls adjust the horizontal or vertical effect of the sweep to prevent distortion.

HIGH-VOLTAGE SYSTEM

A very high voltage is needed to light a television screen. A system commonly used in television receivers is the *flyback high-voltage* sys-

Fig. 40-16. Microprocessor has TV channel frequencies stored in its memory for instant recall. Ruler gives indication of size. (*Zenith Radio Corporation*)

tem. This system uses part of the horizontal-deflection circuit to develop a high voltage.

As the horizontal sweep flies back, or returns, to begin another pass across the television screen, its magnetic field induces a high voltage in the coil. This is similar to the way an automobile ignition coil works.

This flyback system does away with bulky transformers and large capacitors. This is because the frequency is high (15,750 Hz) and only a small current is needed to operate the television picture tube. Other electrical elements in the high-voltage system rectify the alternating sweep circuit and smooth any variations in the circuit. A typical color television receiver applies 27,500 V to the picture tube.

COLOR CIRCUITS

The major color circuits are shown in the lower right-hand section of Fig. 40-12. One interesting feature is the color automatic-frequency-control (AFC) section. This provides the precise signals needed to demodulate the complex color signal. Because of the interference that would result, the color carrier (about 3.58 MHz) cannot be transmitted with the other signals needed for television operation. However, the color carrier is required for color demodulation.

This problem is solved by transmitting short bursts of carrier during the horizontal retrace or flyback. During retrace, interference will not show on the screen. These *color bursts* are amplified and compared with an internally generated color-carrier signal. The comparison stage is called *color AFC*. It corrects the internal 3.58-MHz oscillator as needed. The color signals can then be properly demodulated. The original phase, or hue, relationships of the televised scene at the studio are preserved. The viewer can make small changes in these phase relationships by adjusting the hue, or tint, control.

After demodulation, the R-Y (red minus luminance) and B-Y (blue minus luminance) signals are matrixed, or mixed, to produce a G-Y (green minus luminance) signal. All three signals are then applied to the picture tube. There a positive Y signal from the video amplifier cancels all −Y components. Thus, a full-color picture is produced on the screen.

TELEVISION PICTURE TUBE

The television picture tube reproduces the image on the target of the camera tube in the television broadcasting station. Many of the elements in the television picture tube are similar to elements in the camera tube. The television picture tube produces an electron beam that scans the face of the tube. The scanning system uses either deflection plates or magnetic coils to deflect the beam. Figure 40-17 shows a simplified cross-sectional view of a black-and-white television picture tube.

RIM BAND
TENSION BAND
ELECTRON GUN ASSEMBLY
ELECTRON BEAM
SPLICE LINE
FACEPLATE

Fig. 40-17. Black-and-white television picture tube showing essential elements (*RCA Corporation*)

ELECTRON BEAM

The electron beam is actually a stream of electrons modulated according to the video signals placed on the control grid. The light intensity on the television screen depends on how many electrons strike it and with what velocity, or speed, they do so. The greater the number and the higher the velocity of the electrons, the greater the light intensity. Therefore, the clearness and contrast of the television picture depend on (1) the number of electrons, (2) their velocity, and (3) the kind of screen used.

TUBE SCREEN

On the inside of the face of the television picture tube is a coating of a *phosphor*. This is a material that glows whenever a beam of electrons or other radiated energy strikes it. This kind of illumination is sometimes called *cold light*.

Actually, this coating continues to glow after the electron beam has passed. A material that is able to do this is said to be *phosphorescent*. The glow remains for only a short time, but it keeps the picture from appearing to flicker.

In a black-and-white television receiver, the electron beam produces light, gray, and dark spots as it races across and down a screen. If the modulation allows a great many electrons to strike a screen, bright light appears. If only a moderate number are allowed to strike the screen, less light (gray) appears. If no electrons are allowed to strike the screen, no light (black) appears. These various shades make up the picture we see. A lighted television screen that is not receiving a picture is called a *raster*.

COLOR PICTURE TUBE

In one kind of color television picture tube (Fig. 40-18), the video signals (green, red, and blue) are beamed to excite 1,350,000 tiny phosphor dots. When the dots are struck by an electron beam, they glow red, green, or blue.

Fig. 40-18. Color television picture tube (*Zenith Radio Corporation*)

When this tube is made, 450,000 openings in an iris mask are used to apply the phosphors and a contrast area of jet black on the screen. The iris-mask openings are then enlarged. As a result, the electron beams are larger than the phosphor dots. Thus, the phosphor dots are illuminated completely. The black surround reduces light reflections and allows a clearer faceplate to be used to increase light transmission.

TUNING FOR COLOR

To receive color broadcasts properly, the television set should first be adjusted for black-and-white reception. Then the color controls, color gain and hue, should be adjusted as follows:

Color Gain. The color *gain,* or intensity, control should be turned clockwise to increase the color intensity. This control is moved to minimum for a black-and-white broadcast. If there is too little gain, the colors will appear pale and weak. If there is too much gain, the colors will appear flushed and poorly focused.

Color Hue. This control adjusts the *hue,* or tint, of the color. Adjust the control until the facial tones are natural. If the hue is turned too far counterclockwise, the facial tones will appear purple. If the control is turned too far clockwise, facial tones will appear green.

Once the color gain and hue are set properly, they usually do not have to be adjusted again. However, changing channels may require a slight readjustment. When all controls remain at their previous setting, the television receiver will automatically reproduce black and white or color, depending on the broadcast.

TELEVISION PICTURE INTERFERENCE

Many kinds of electrical apparatus can interfere with a television picture. Automobile ignition systems, flashing signs, electric motors, diathermy equipment, and other television and radio receivers and transmitters can all cause interference. Most television sets today reduce this interference to a minimum.

From Automobile Ignition Systems and So On. Interference from automobile ignitions, airplanes, electrical appliances, and so on cause speckled, streaked pictures. This condition is most noticeable in weak-signal areas.

From Diathermy Equipment. This kind of medical equipment produces a herringbone pattern and possibly one or two horizontal bands across the face of the picture. Weaker interference of this kind may cause a general fogging or blurring of the image.

From Radio Signals. Interference from radio signals may create moving ripples or diagonal streaks on a screen. These signals may be produced by nearby citizen, commercial, amateur, or police station radios. Other television or frequency-modulation receivers operating near the set may produce the same effect.

From Rebounding Signals. This interference accounts for a multiple image on the screen. It is caused by the rebounding of the television signal from a nearby building, hill, or mountain. Actually, this rebounding causes two or more signals to be received by the antenna. The rebounding signal is received a little later than the direct signal. The former appears as a "ghost" image on the screen.

From Fringe-Area Reception. At the fringes of the transmission area of a television station, the picture may appear as a snowy pattern on the screen. This condition can sometimes be partially corrected by moving the television receiver within a room. An outside antenna and rotator should be used for best reception in fringe areas.

CABLE TELEVISION

In the late 1940s, cable television became a reality. It is called the *c*ommunity *a*ntenna *t*ele*v*ision (CATV) system. This system brings television signals into communities located too far from the television station. It is also used in communities in which television signals are blocked by deep valleys or high mountains. The antennas of cable systems are located in areas with good reception. Then television signals are distributed by cable to subscribers for a fee. Cable fees vary from system to system but are usually charged on a monthly basis. Some cable services require an additional fee beyond that for the basic service. Installation fees are also charged new subscribers. Most cable companies distribute television signals through coaxial cables. These are strung over telephone poles or placed underground.

Since cable systems have more channels than are broadcast, they can provide additional services. Cable systems often have separate channels for weather reports, stock-market reports, wire-service news, FM radio, and movies. Cable operators also originate their own programs. They provide cable channels for use by the public, for education, for government use, and for lease.

New cable systems having more than 3,500 subscribers generally provide 25 or more television broadcast channels. Some systems have the capacity for two-way communication (Fig. 40-19). This allows subscribers to shop for merchandise, conduct banking business, reply to community surveys, and have utility meters read.

Pay cable service allows subscribers to view special programs, such as feature films and sports events. Since its beginning in late 1975, pay cable programming has become very popular and the number of systems has grown considerably.

Fig. 40-19. A cable television two-way communication system

Fig. 40-20. A modern high-fidelity stereo sound video cassette recorder (VCR) (*RCA Corporation*)

HOME VIDEO

Because video cassettes are playable on a home television set, the *video cassette recorder* (VCR) has moved the movies into the home. No longer do you have to wait in line at the movie theater. You can rent a prerecorded movie on a video cassette at one of many distribution outlets such as specialty video stores, supermarkets, bookstores and the like. A video cassette is a special cartridge having two reels that contain a magnetic tape designed for recording and playing back a television signal. Costs to rent a video cassette are quite low and many rental clubs give members access to thousands of tapes. Many public libraries have video cassettes too. A person with a library card can borrow a video cassette just as she or he would borrow a book. The VCR and video camera make it possible for individuals to create their own "instant replay" home video entertainment (Fig. 40-20).

Video Cassette Recorder. The electronic circuits in a VCR involve recording audio and video signals on magnetic tape, using digital circuits and microprocessors as well as adjusting servomotors. While a complete analysis of these circuits is beyond the scope of this text, the basic concepts will be presented.

Recording audio signals is much easier than recording video signals because the range of frequencies is much different. Audio frequencies range from about 20 Hz to 20,000 Hz. Video frequencies range from 30 Hz to 4 MHz. This difference presents several problems when video tape recording heads are used as contrasted to audio tape heads. As you may recall, an audio tape head picks up electromagnetic signals from the tape during playback. During recording, the audio tape head changes audio signals into electromagnetic fields. These fields magnetize the metallic oxide on a tape establishing an electromagnetic field. The same principle is used with video heads. The problem of recording high-frequency video signals is solved by moving both the head and the tape. This causes the relative speed between the head and tape to be fast enough to record and play back video signals.

Most home VCRs use the helical scan method of recording video tapes (Fig. 40-21A). The tape is wrapped around a rotating drum containing one or two heads. The heads travel at an angle to the direction of the tape travel. By selecting a cylinder head diameter, degree of tape wrap, tape speed, and cylinder head speed, it is possible to record a track long enough (across the tape at an angle—line AB in Fig. 40-21A) to hold a complete television field. Most VCRs use a half-wrap with two heads.

Figure 40-21B illustrates a simplified video track with sound and control signals. The control signals are needed to maintain proper timing so that the servomotor can adjust for any deviation from the desired performance.

Several methods are used to form the head-to-drum tape path. Some drums are vertical, others are at a slant (Fig. 40-22). The latter is very common because the video cassette can be loaded easily. The block

Fig. 40-21. Video cassette recorder principles: (A) helical scan recording track; (B) simplified track(s) on helical scan system (three tracks usually recorded) (*RCA Corporation*)

Fig. 40-22. Typical head arrangement in helical scan VCR (*Radio Corporation of America*)

diagram in Fig. 40-23 illustrates the typical play-record electronics for a VCR using two rotating heads. The block diagram of the electronic system indicates some of the complexities involved in a VCR. The heads serve a dual purpose: They record or play back the video and sound signals depending on the function selected.

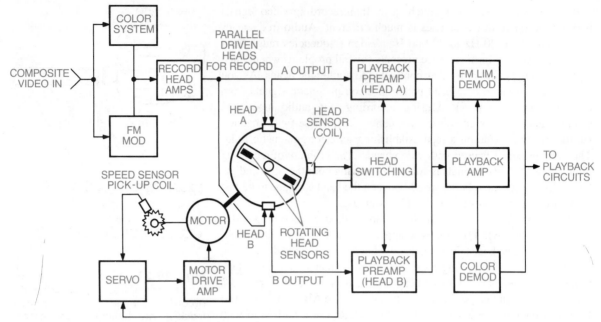

Fig. 40-23. Block diagram of a VCR using two rotating heads (*Radio Corporation of America*)

Fig. 40-24. Color video camera with zoom lens (*RCA Corporation*)

Portable Video Camera. The basic function of this video camera (color or black and white) is to convert light energy reflected from the subject scene into an electrical signal that can be recorded on video tape or displayed through a television set. The process is similar to that discussed earlier in this unit except that this camera is lightweight and portable (Fig. 40-24).

The block diagram (Fig. 40-25) illustrates the various electronic circuits in a portable video camera. The lens focuses the incoming light waves onto a pickup tube. The filters correct for the proper white light balance. Horizontal and vertical deflection circuits control the scanning process as the electron beam sweeps across and down the scene being televised.

The output video signal from the *preamplifier,* or prevideo signal, is applied to the signaling processing circuits. The red and blue video signals are first separated from the luminance signal. These signals are color corrected and encoded. The luminance signal passes through two low-pass filters and eventually is mixed with the color signals and the horizontal and vertical synchronizing pulses. The final video output signal must meet the standards established by the National Television System Committee (NTSC).

Indoor Antenna Connections. It is relatively simple to connect a VCR to a television antenna to record a television broadcast. Figure 40-26 illustrates the general principle. The VCR must be connected between the television set and the antenna. It is essential that matching transformers be used to match the type lead-in wires from the television

Fig. 40-25. Block diagram of a portable color video camera (*RCA Corporation*)

ELECTRONIC VIEW FINDER

VIDICON/CRT VOLTAGE SUPPLIES

EVF DEFLECTION

2.8 MHz LPF — Y_H — Y_H (LUM) PROCESS

3.58 MHz BPF

.5 MHz LPF — Y_L

Y/C MIX — NTSC VIDEO OUT

PREAMP

LENS/FILTERS

VIDICON

RED/BLUE SEPARATION — COLOR ENCODING

H/V SYNC BURST

SHADING TRACKING GENERATOR — VIDICON H/V DEFL — SYNC PULSE GENERATOR

ABBREVIATIONS USED IN DIAGRAM

PREAMP = PREAMPLIFIER
CRT = CATHODE RAY TUBE
H/V = HORIZONTAL/VERTICAL
BPF = BAND PASS FILTER (3.58 MHz)
EVF = ELECTRONIC VIEW FINDER
LPF = LOW PASS FILTERS (2.8 MHz AND 0.5 MHz)

Y_H (LUM) = LUMINANCE SIGNAL (Y_H = HIGH) (Y_L = LOW)
Y/C MIX = LUMINANCE/CHROMINANCE (SIGNALS) MIXED
SYNC/PULSE = SYNCHRONIZING PULSE
NTSC = NATIONAL TELEVISION SYSTEM COMMITTEE
(ESTABLISHES TV SIGNAL STANDARDS)

Fig. 40-26. Connecting a VCR to indoor antennas and television set: (A) vhf antenna; (B) uhf antenna

B
A
VHF   UHF

TV SET

300 Ω TWIN LEADS

VCR

UHF IN

VHF OUT   IN

300Ω

75Ω

UHF ANTENNA SPLITTER

300Ω TWIN LEAD

UHF   VHF

MATCHING TRANSFORMER (ADAPTER)

75Ω COAXIAL CABLE

75 TO 300Ω MATCHING TRANSFORMER

antenna to the VCR and television set. Most residential homes have a two-conductor (flat) 300-Ω lead-in wire. Most television sets have machine screws for connecting the terminals of these lead-in wires. These screws generally are located in the rear of the television set. Cable companies use the 75-Ω coaxial cable and VCRs are made to accept this type of cable. Figure 40-26 illustrates one method of connecting 300-Ω antenna lead-in wires to a VCR and television set.

The signal output of most VCRs generally is set for television channel 3 or 4. If channel 3 is an active channel in your area, then the VCR RF converter channel selector should be reset for channel 4. Because of the variety of VCRs and cameras available, you should review the manuals for your equipment. Detailed instructions are provided and should be followed carefully.

HOME EARTH STATIONS

Home earth stations use a *television receive only* (TVRO) electronic system to view broadcast transmissions from satellites. Figure 40-27 illustrates the basic concepts involved in receiving television broadcasts from satellites.

The TVRO systems make use of a satellite that is placed in a *geostationary orbit*. This means that the satellite is situated 22,300 miles (35,888.3 km) above the equator and revolves at the same speed as the earth. Therefore, to an observer on earth, the satellite appears to remain fixed in space, or stationary. Because the satellite is stationary with respect to a position on earth the dish-shaped antenna of the earth station can be aimed directly at it to receive its signals.

Essentially, satellites function as relay stations in the sky. Television programs that originate on Earth are converted into microwave signals at frequencies around 6 GHz. These signals are then transmitted in a narrow beam to the satellite. The transmitted beam from the Earth to the satellite is called an *up link*. The transmitted signals are received by the antenna of the satellite. After the up-link signals are received, they are passed to a *transponder*. The transponder changes the signal frequencies so that they have a broader beam. The signals are also amplified and retransmitted by the satellite back to Earth as a *down-link beam*. The down-link beam is transmitted at a different frequency, for example, 4 GHz.

Satellites are positioned so that the down-link signal is beamed to the Earth to provide the largest *footprint*. This is the area on Earth that can receive the signals without interference from other satellites (Fig. 40-27A).

The receiving antenna, like the transmitting antenna, is a parabolic-shaped dish. The shape of the TVRO antenna of the dish focuses the very weak signals from the satellite to a low-noise amplifier (LNA) (Fig. 40-27B). This LNA increases the strength of the weak signals to a usable level. Next the signals are down-converted from, for example, 4 GHz to a range of 2.2 GHz to 70 MHz. The television and sound

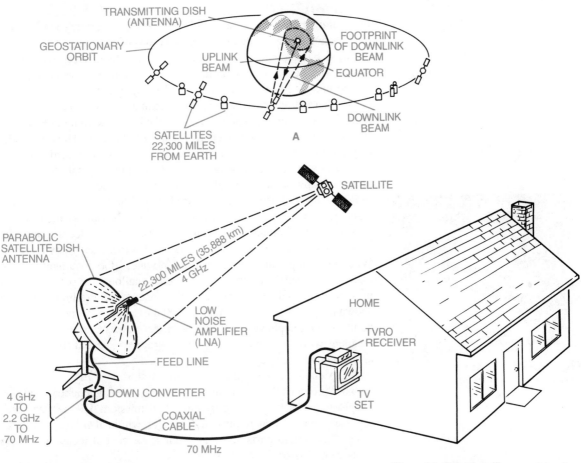

Fig. 40-27. Satellite communications: (A) satellites in geostationary orbit; (B) elements of a home earth station

signals are brought into the home via a coaxial cable. There they are demodulated to produce a television image and sound on a standard television receiver. Some satellite receiving dishes are motorized so they can be turned to aim at different satellites, thus increasing the number of channels available for viewing.

The satellite dish (antenna) used in this system is rather large, 6 to 10 ft (1.8 to 3 m) in diameter. However, the satellite-to-home television industry will use a *d*irect *b*roadcast *s*atellite (DBS). This DBS will emit television signals with sufficient strength to enable the use of a small 2-ft (0.6-m) rooftop dish antenna.

Beaming television programs from satellites directly to homes is envisioned as a means of providing television to areas not served by conventional over-the-air television channels or by cable television. In addition, the satellite relay station provides a clearer, sharper television picture and brighter color than was previously available from the continental ground-link television networks.

FACSIMILE TRANSMISSION

In facsimile transmission, a photocell is caused to perform a raster scan over a printed page or picture. The variations of print or picture density on the document cause the photocell to generate an electrical (video) signal. The raster scan is similar to a television scan, which was discussed previously in this unit. The video signal is used to modulate a carrier that is transmitted to a remote destination over telephone wires, radio, or cable communication links. At the remote terminal, demodulation reconstructs the video signal, which is used to modulate the density of print produced by a printing machine. The printing machine is synchronized with the raster scan at the transmitting terminal. As a result, an exact copy or facsimile of the document is produced.

Figure 40-28 illustrates an advanced "Fax Machine." This facsimile machine provides an electronic mail system that has an excellent degree of privacy and simplicity. You can send exact copies of letters, financial documents, contracts, and confidential reports to virtually any location. When incoming mail is identified as "private," the document is automatically placed in a "private electronic mailbox." To unlock it, a personal electronically encoded card is used. The facsimile machine shown in Fig. 40-28 can store up to 600 messages in its memory. After hours, when telephone rates are low, it can send messages to over 99 locations with push button ease. The messages are sent at speeds as fast as 14 seconds per page.

An example of a facsimile network is shown in Fig. 40-29. This network provides fast communications throughout the country either by telephone and cable lines or by radio transmission. The network uses regional "hubs" that retransmit messages within their respective region. This system costs less than having one central location sending messages all over the country.

Fig. 40-28. Advanced facsimile (machine) system (*Pitney Bowes*)

Fig. 40-29. A facsimile network can provide fast and reliable communications (*Pitney Bowes*)

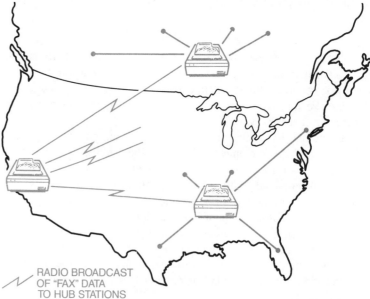

— TELEPHONE LINES FROM HUB STATION TO REMOTE FACSIMILE MACHINES

RADIO BROADCAST OF "FAX" DATA TO HUB STATIONS

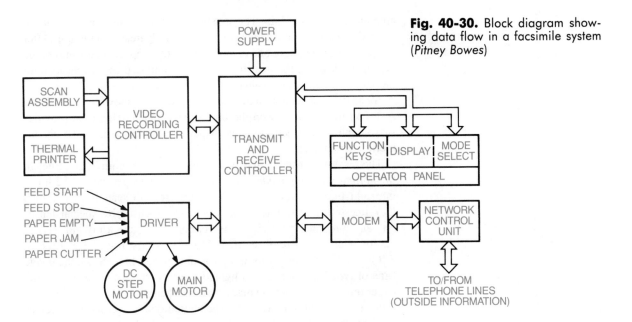

Fig. 40-30. Block diagram showing data flow in a facsimile system (*Pitney Bowes*)

The block diagram in Fig. 40-30 shows the data flow in a facsimile machine. The major elements of the facsimile machine are: (1) operator panel, (2) driver, (3) scan assembly, (4) video recording controller, (5) transmit and receive (transceiver) controller, (6) modem, (7) network control unit, (8) thermal printer, and (9) power supply. The telephone lines provide the connection between the machine and outside information. Notice particularly that the arrows indicate that the data flow is in both directions at the network control unit.

Operator Panel. This panel contains the SEND/RECEIVE control switches, mode select, and display indicators. Ten function keys also allow operators to control all modes of operation.

Driver. The drive system operates several electromechanical devices. A dc motor, for example, drives the document alignment mechanism. A stepper motor drives the paper-feed roller, eject roller, and the paper cutter. Electrical sensors automatically control the paper feed and stop the system if something goes wrong. Thirty documents can be loaded into the hopper. These documents are fed one at a time through the facsimile machine.

Scan Assembly. The scan assembly converts the image in the scan area to electrical signals suitable for processing by the transceiver controller. Each line on the document is focused on the light sensors by a lens. The electrical signals are next amplified and sent to a contrast control circuit. These circuits determine if the signal represents a white or black area on the scanning line. The signals, therefore, represent slices of the printed alphanumeric characters or light or dark areas of a picture. After the process of scanning one complete line, the stepper motor moves the document down to the next line and the scanning process repeats until the entire document is scanned.

An artist's conception of the scanning process is shown in Fig. 40-31. A strong light is shown on the line to be scanned. This light provides sharp contrast between the white paper and the black-printed alphanumeric characters.

The facsimile machine has two scanning modes: normal and fine. In the *normal scanning mode,* there are 97 scan lines per inch (3.82 lines/ mm). In the *fine scanning mode,* there are 196 scan lines per inch (7.7 lines/mm). The line to be scanned is focused by special lenses on an integrated circuit. The circuit has an array of 1,728 photodiodes. The size of the IC is $1\frac{1}{2} \times \frac{1}{2} \times \frac{5}{16}$ in. (38.1 × 12.7 × 7.9 mm). The frequency used for scanning is 500 kHz. Since the image (line of typed information) is lighted brightly, the white surface of the paper reflects light; but the black surface where the characters are typed reflects little light or none at all. The photodiode (detector) that receives the brightest reflected light will generate the highest voltage. And the photodiodes that receive the reflected light from the black characters will generate a low or no voltage at all. The scanning lines, therefore, will vary in voltage as they move across the surface of the page. The enlarged view of the artist's sketch illustrates the varying voltage generated by the scanning process for the letter T for each time period represented by t_0, t_1, t_2, etc. The picture elements, therefore, represent bits of information that can be processed by the video recording controller.

Video Recording Controller. This unit contains an automatic background control circuit. This circuit controls the shading correction function and converts picture information into binary data in relation to the amount of correction needed. The artist's sketch also illustrates the concept of how the picture elements are generated (Fig. 40-31).

Transmit and Receive Controller. This unit, also known as the *transceiver unit,* is the heart of the facsimile system. It is in reality a small computer. All information in the form of electrical signals is processed by this unit. The unit contains memory (RAM and ROM), a microprocessor, electronic drivers, input-output ports, and a clock. These components are described more completely in Unit 42.

Modem. The term *modem* stands for *modulator/demodulator.* It generates and detects tone signals necessary for signal interfacing between facsimile units and the telephone lines.

Fig. 40-31. Scanning process used to produce picture elements in a facsimile system

411

Network Control Unit. This unit provides the connection to the telephone network lines over which all signals are transmitted and received. It provides the connection to all outside information.

Power Supply. The power supply operates on 115 Vac, 50/60 Hz, single phase. The power needed varies depending on the function performed by the facsimile machine. The primary function and power requirements are: standby (15 W), transmission (80 W), reception (95 W), and copying (110 W). The power supply provides five output voltages to operate the system. In the standby mode, for example, 5 Vdc is supplied to the main circuit board.

Thermal Printer. The printer contains a thermal head. The head contains 1,728 tiny resistor heating elements arranged in a horizontal row of 27 segments, each containing 64 elements. The row is about 8½ in. long (215.9 mm). When an element heats, it causes the paper in contact with it to turn black. To print a solid line, for example, all heating elements would have to be heated. To prevent excessive heating, each of the 27 heating segments is energized serially (one at a time). After one row is printed, the paper advances and the cycle is repeated.

FACSIMILE TRANSMIT CYCLE

To transmit a document, first it is positioned properly in the facsimile machine. Then a telephone call is made to the person who is to receive the facsimile document. The telephone call establishes the electrical circuit between the sending facsimile machine (transmitter) and the remote receiving facsimile machine (receiver). When the "send" key is depressed, the circuitry in the network control unit switches the telephone circuit to the facsimile machine. Once the circuit between the transmitting unit and the remote receiving unit is complete, a process called *handshaking* takes place automatically. The handshaking process is controlled by a *protocol,* or specific procedures to establish compatibility with both the receiver and transmitter so that both units are in synchronization with each other. The protocol signals are generated by the transmit and receive control circuitry. These signals pass through the modem and network control unit to the telephone lines.

Picture information is generated by the scanner assembly, which converts the image on the document into electrical signals that are fed serially (one after the other) to the transmit-and-receive controller. The transmit circuitry first places the information in memory. Then the data are fed out of memory, controlled by a microprocessor in the transmit-and-receive control unit, to the network control unit. Each line of data on the document is scanned and transmitted in this manner.

FACSIMILE RECEIVING CYCLE

To initiate an automatic receive cycle, the standby power must be on. This puts the machine in the auto-receive mode. The network control unit contains a ring detection circuit that sends a called station identification signals. This is similar to a person calling your home telephone number. The transmit-and-receive controller responds by turning on full power and connecting the modem to the line. It also "answers" the ring by transmitting back to the "caller" signals at 1,850 Hz, 1,500 Hz, and/or 300 bits per second (bps) through the modem and network control unit. Again the handshaking process starts to establish compatibility between the transmitter and remote receiver. Once compatibility between the transmitter and receiver is established, the modulated picture signals will begin to be received at 9,600, 7,200, 4,800, or 2,400 bps. The data are sent to memory via the network control unit, modem, and transmit-and-receive controller. From memory, the data are sent to the video recording controller and thermal printer. The thermal printer prints one line at a time. The movement of the paper is controlled by the stepper motor until the document is completed. This process is repeated if more than one document is being transmitted.

COPYING CYCLE

In the copying cycle, the original document is fed and aligned automatically by the document-feed rollers. A photoelectric device senses when the paper is in the proper position, and it sends a signal to the stepper motor. The stepper motor causes a mechanism to position the document to the scan position in preparation for scanning. Once in position, the document is moved down into the facsimile machine by the stepper motor and related mechanism. This feeds the original document through this scanning area and records it on heat-sensitive paper. When the trailing edge of the document is sensed by a photoelectric device, the stepper motor causes a mechanism to activate a paper cutter and eject the original and printed copy. If no additional transmission occurs, a tone will be heard after the ejection process.

SELF-TEST

Test your knowledge by writing, on a separate sheet of paper, the word or words that most correctly complete the following statements:

1. Two common television camera tubes are the _____ and the _____ .
2. Variations in the return beam make up the _____ signal.
3. The scanning beam is bent left and right and up and down by charges on the _____ and _____ deflection plates.
4. Each frame on the television screen consists of _____ horizontal scanning lines.
5. When the television transmitter and receiver are locked in step, they are said to be _____ .
6. In the vidicon tube, the video-signal voltage appears across the _____ resistor.
7. All the light reflected from the image is transmitted as the _____ signal.
8. A television channel contains both _____ and _____ signals.

9. Television carrier-wave frequencies are classified in the _____ and _____ ranges.
10. There are _____ vhf and _____ uhf television channels.
11. A simple kind of television antenna with two arms is called a _____ .
12. A rotary switching system used in a television has _____ and _____ for tuning.
13. A tuner with a microcomputer is called a _____ tuner.
14. The _____ amplifier and the _____ amplifier are two amplifiers found only in color televi-

sion receivers.
15. The television picture tube, like the camera tube, has an _____ that scans the face of the tube.
16. The coating on the inside surface of a television picture tube is a _____ .
17. Video frequencies range from _____ Hz to _____ Hz.
18. A tape from a video cassette recorder (VCR) has three tracks: video, audio, and _____ .
19. A _____ is used to ensure a proper impedance match between the television antenna lead-in wire, the VCR, and the television set.

FOR REVIEW AND DISCUSSION

1. Discuss the common relationships of the principles of a television camera, a photographic camera, and a light meter.
2. Describe the image section, scanning beam, return beam, and scanning section of an image orthicon tube.
3. Describe the basic difference between the image orthicon tube and the vidicon tube.
4. How are the color signals developed in a color television camera?
5. Identify the electronic circuits found in a color television receiver that would not be found in a black-and-white television receiver.
6. List and explain the functions of the electronic circuits found in a typical television receiver.
7. Describe the function of the burst amplifier in a color television receiver.

8. Explain the purpose of the synchronizing sweep circuits in a television receiver.
9. Describe how the electron beam develops the picture in a black-and-white television receiver.
10. Describe the interference pattern most likely to be caused by automobile ignition systems, by diathermy equipment, and by rebounding television signals.
11. Explain why it is necessary to have the heads of a VCR travel at an angle to the direction of tape travel.
12. Satellites are often placed in a geostationary orbit. Explain what this means.
13. Identify the main electronic elements in a facsimile system.
14. Explain the electronic principles involved in the scanning process of a facsimile system.

INDIVIDUAL-STUDY ACTIVITIES

1. Find out if there is a cable television system available in your area. Describe the system, how a person may subscribe, and how the system is installed in the subscriber's home.
2. Investigate the local ordinances that must be met if a home owner wishes to install a home earth

station (TVRO) system. Report your findings to the class.
3. Investigate and write a report on the future applications of facsimile systems in business and in residential homes. Report your findings to the class.

UNIT 41 Digital Electronic Circuits

The operation of most digital circuit systems depends upon a series of switching actions performed in a sequence that produces the desired result. In this unit, you will learn about the basic switching actions that are related to the operation of logic circuits, adders, counters, and clocks. Other common applications of modern digital circuits include their use in computers and other data processing systems, in numerically controlled machine systems, and in test instruments. The term *digital* is also generally used to describe those circuit systems in which the output, or readout, is indicated by means of alphanumeric characters.

In many electronic circuit systems, the desired result, or output, is obtained by the use of signals that have many different levels and/or frequencies. *Signals* can be described as voltages or currents. For example, the loudspeaker in an amplifier system produces a wide range of sounds when currents of many different levels and frequencies are applied to it. The phrase *digital electronics* is used to describe those circuit systems which primarily operate with the use of only two different voltage levels or two other binary conditions. *Binary* means consisting of two parts.

BINARY CONDITIONS

The two different conditions, or states, by which digital circuits operate may be of several forms. They can, in the most simple form, consist of the opening and closing of a single-pole–single-throw switch (Fig. 41-1A). In this case, the closed-switch condition can be represented by 1 and the open-switch condition by 0. Likewise, the lighted lamp can be considered as being in the 1 condition when the switch is closed, while the unlighted lamp can be considered as being in the 0 condition when the switch is open.

A very common method of digital operation is achieved by using voltage pulses (Fig. 41-1B). Here the presence of a positive pulse can be represented by 1 and the absence of a pulse by 0. With a square-wave signal, the positive pulses can represent 1, and the negative pulses can represent 0 (Fig. 41-1C).

Another commonly used binary condition is obtained by the use of two different voltage levels, or values (Fig. 41-1D). In this case, a voltage that is positive with respect to a given point can be represented by 1 while a voltage that is less positive with respect to the point can be represented by 0.

LOGIC CIRCUITS

The term *logic* when used in connection with a digital circuit describes a circuit that provides a definite, predetermined output condition when

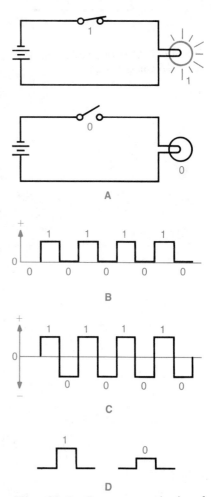

Fig. 41-1. Common methods of producing binary conditions

415

Fig. 41-2. Operation of a transistor as a switching device

one or more specific input conditions are satisfied. A circuit designed to operate in this manner is said to perform a logic function.

The input conditions of a logic circuit may be "set" by means of a combination of switches that are ideally suited for binary applications because of their ON (1) and OFF (0) actions.

In early logic gates, relays were very commonly used to perform switching functions. However, because of their slow operating speed and relatively large power requirements, relays have been replaced by switching devices such as transistors, diodes, silicon-controlled rectifiers, and other solid-state devices.

Integrated circuits containing many transistors are most commonly used as switching devices in digital electronics logic gates. The reasons for this are that they are capable of operating at extremely high speeds and are very compact.

A basic p-n-p transistor circuit that functions as an ON-OFF switch is shown in Fig. 41-2. In this circuit, the input signal (battery voltage) is controlled by switch S1.

With S1 open (position 2), the emitter-base junction of the transistor is reverse-biased to the cutoff point (Fig. 41-2A). In this condition, the current in the collector, or output, portion of the circuit is at a minimum. The transistor "switch" can now be considered as being turned OFF or in the 0 state.

When S1 is closed to position 1, a positive voltage is applied to the base of the transistor. Since this voltage does not affect the reverse-bias condition of the base-emitter junction, the transistor remains in the 0 state.

The transistor is turned on by closing S1 to position 3 (Fig. 41-2B). In this condition, a negative voltage is applied to the base of the transistor. The negative voltage overcomes the reverse-bias applied to the base-emitter junction by V_{BB}, and the transistor is "switched" to the conducting (ON or 1) state.

TYPES OF LOGIC GATES

The three basic types of digital logic gates are the AND gate, the OR gate, and the NOT gate. As with all logic gates, the output of each is binary, or in one of two states: ON (1) or OFF (0). Each of these output states is, in turn, produced by switching (on or off) actions or conditions that are applied to the inputs of the logic gate. The operation of the basic types of logic gates and a simplified example of the use of each are described in the following paragraphs.

The AND Gate. Let us suppose that in a manufacturing plant, two workers are stationed at an assembly line. Also suppose that in this system it is possible for the motor-driven assembly-line belt to move only when both workers are ready and that it is desirable for each worker to be able to stop the belt.

The problem of designing such a control-output system can be solved by using an AND gate (Fig. 41-3A). Since switches A and B are in series, both of them must be on (1) in order to apply a voltage to the motor so that it will operate. This voltage or output signal (C) can be represented by 1. If either switch A or switch B is off or in the 0 state, no voltage will be applied to the motor, and it will stop. This output condition can be represented by 0.

The operation of the circuit, in terms of its input-output relationships, can be described by what is called a *truth table* (Fig. 41-3B). From the truth table, it is seen that the output of an AND gate is 1 if and only if all inputs are 1. If any input or all inputs are 0, the output is 0.

Another very useful application of the AND gate is in digital circuits that compare quantities, conditions, or states to determine whether or not they are equal. Such a circuit is called a *comparator*. For example, a single, two-input AND gate can be designed so that its output is 1 only when two voltages reach a predetermined positive value. The output could then be used to activate an indicating device of some kind.

A basic AND gate using an n-p-n transistor is shown in Fig. 41-3C. Here switches A and B control the bias voltages by means of which the transistor is switched to provide a 1 or a 0 output across the emitter resistor. Notice that the truth table is also valid for this gate.

The operation of an AND gate is mathematically expressed by the equation $A \cdot B = C$. This can be read as "input A and input B equals output C."

Logic Mathematics. Note that the mathematics used to describe logic circuits is called *boolean algebra*. Although it looks like ordinary algebra, its symbols and operations are used in different ways.

The OR Gate. A very practical example of a simple OR gate is the combination of push-button switches used in a residential, two-door signal system (Fig. 41-4A). In this gate, switches A and B are connected in parallel. As a result, the buzzer will sound (output C is 1) when either switch A or switch B is closed (1) and when both switches are closed. The buzzer will not sound (output is 0) when both switches are open or in the 0 state. These relationships for the gate are shown by its truth table (Fig. 41-4B).

An example of a basic OR gate using an n-p-n transistor is shown in Fig. 41-4C. In this gate, switches A and B set the conditions by which the transistor switches to provide a 1 or a 0 output signal. The input-output relationships of this gate are also indicated by the truth table.

The operation of an OR gate is often expressed by the equation $A + B = C$. This can be read as "either input A or input B (or both) equals output C."

The NOT Gate. An important function of the NOT gate is to produce signal inversion or an output signal that is opposite in nature to the input

A

SYMBOL

Truth Table

Inputs		Output
A	B	C
0	0	0
1	0	0
0	1	0
1	1	1

B

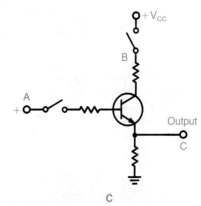

C

Fig. 41-3. AND logic gate

A

A—◁○— $\overline{A}$

SYMBOL

Truth Table

Inputs		Output
A	B	C
0	0	0
1	0	1
0	1	1
1	1	1

B

C

Fig. 41-4. OR logic gate

Fig. 41-5. NOT logic gate

A

418

signal. For this reason, a NOT gate is often referred to as an *inverter* or as a *complementary gate*. Such a gate has only one input.

A very common example of the operation of a basic NOT gate is given by the relationship between temperature and the operation of a gas furnace in a residential heating system. The control device in such a system is a thermostat that is affected by the binary conditions of a higher or a lower temperature. Let us assume that an input of a higher temperature to the thermostat is a 1 state and that an input of a lower temperature is a 0 state.

If the temperature in a room rises above the setting of the thermostat, the thermostat opens or "breaks" (Fig. 41-5A). This turns off the current to the relay that controls the gas valves, and the furnace goes off (or to the 0 state). If the temperature decreases below the setting of the thermostat (input 0), the thermostat closes, and the furnace begins to operate (a 1 state).

A basic NOT circuit using an n-p-n transistor is shown in Fig. 41-5B. When the input voltage to the base of the transistor is high enough in the positive direction (1), the transistor conducts heavily. At this time, the output voltage, or the voltage across the transistor, is low (0). When there is no input voltage or the input voltage is low (0), the transistor operates at cutoff, thus producing an output voltage which is high (or in the 1 state).

NAND AND NOR GATES

Any logic function or operation can be performed by the three basic gates that have been described. However, it is very often convenient to combine AND, OR, and NOT gates for the purpose of simplifying logic circuit structure. The two most commonly used combinations of these gates are the NAND gate and the NOR gate.

The NAND gate is a combination of an AND gate and a NOT gate (Fig. 41-6A). As indicated by its truth table, if the inputs to such a gate are in the same condition (both 1 or both 0), the output is in the opposite condition. If the inputs are not in the same condition, the output is 1.

The NOR gate is a combination of an OR gate and a NOT gate (Fig. 41-6B). The truth table for this gate shows that if both inputs are in the

SYMBOL

Truth Table

Input	Output
A	$\overline{A}$
1	0
0	1

B

1 condition, the output is 0 and if both inputs are in the 0 condition, the output is 1. When the inputs are not in the same condition, the output is 0.

SYMBOL

EXCLUSIVE-OR (XOR)

The XOR gate is a special gate. It is used when the logic desired is that only one of two states is true at any given time. As can be seen by the truth table in Fig. 41-7, when any one input is at a logic 1, the output will also be a logic 1. If the input logic has two logic 1s or two zeros, the output will be 0. An example of this is when you are playing a two-player video game. Only player 1 or player 2 can play the game at any given time. Both players cannot operate the game at the same time. Therefore, this is an exclusive-OR situation. If there are more than two inputs to an XOR gate, an odd number of input 1s will produce an output 1; an even number of input 1s will produce a zero output.

Truth Table

Inputs		Output
A	B	C
1	1	0
0	0	1
1	0	1
0	1	1

A

SYMBOL

LOGIC CIRCUIT DESIGN

Suppose a circuit with the following characteristics is needed: output C is 1 if inputs A and B are both 1; C is 1 if inputs A and B are both 0; C is 0 for all other inputs. Expressed mathematically, these statements are

(1) $C = 1$ if $A = B = 1$
(2) $C = 1$ if $A = B = 0$
(3) $C = 0$ if otherwise

Truth Table

Inputs		Output
A	B	C
1	1	0
0	0	1
1	0	0
0	1	0

B

Fig. 41-6. NAND and NOR logic gates: (A) NAND gate; (B) NOR gate

To design a logic circuit with these characteristics, each requirement is first fulfilled individually. They are then combined to give the output. Requirement 1 can be fulfilled with a simple AND, $C = A \cdot B$, as shown in Fig. 41-8. Requirement 2 takes a circuit that is 1 when both inputs are 0. This can be done with an AND circuit but with the inputs inverted. If both inputs are 0, then the inputs to the AND circuit are 1, and hence the output is 1.

These two circuits can be fed into the OR circuit so that either circuit gives an output when the right inputs are present. This circuit arrangement is called a *combinatorial circuit*.

A table for the first part of the problem can be made. First all the possible combinations of inputs are listed. With two inputs, there are four combinations. For each set of inputs, the output C is determined using the rules for the logic circuits used. With a specific set of inputs, intermediate logic values can be determined, and the output value is clear. This output value is listed in the truth table. A new set of inputs is then determined. This is done for all combinations. The final truth table is shown in Fig. 41-8. Note that the output C is 1 for the two input combinations 0-0 and 1-1 and 0 for all others. Also the third requirement in the problem is met automatically. This is often the case, but it should be checked.

SYMBOL

Truth Table

Input		Output
A	B	C
0	0	0
0	1	1
1	0	1
1	1	0

Fig. 41-7. Exclusive-OR (XOR) logic gate

419

C = A · B

AND CIRCUIT

A

C = Ā · B̄

AND CIRCUIT WITH INPUTS
INVERTED USING **NOT** CIRCUITS

B

C = (A · B) + (Ā · B̄)

COMBINATORIAL CIRCUITS

C

Truth Table

Inputs		Outputs
A	B	C
0	0	1
0	1	0
1	1	1
1	0	0

D

Fig. 41-8. Steps for designing a logic circuit: (A) the AND circuit; (B) the AND circuit, with inputs inverted using NOT circuits; (C) combinatorial circuit; (D) truth table for the conditions of the problem

The logic circuit design problem just described is a common circuit found in computers. It has a special name: *coincidence circuit.* Its output is 1 if its inputs are *coincident,* that is, both 1 or both 0.

THE BINARY NUMBER SYSTEM

To represent any number electronically using digits of the decimal system (0 through 9) would require 10 different circuit conditions or states. Each of these would represent a different digit. Although this could be done, it would necessitate the use of complicated circuit structures consisting of a tremendous number of components.

The logic circuits that have been discussed are binary in nature. This means their operation depends upon only two conditions, or states. These are very easily represented electronically by means of comparatively simple switching devices. In some digital circuits, however, there is a need for the expression of decimal numbers or groups of numbers. Examples of these are circuits found in counters, calculators, and data processing systems such as computers.

The binary number system can represent decimal numbers by a combination of the binary digits (usually called *bits*) 1 and 0. As a result, the mathematical operations of addition, subtraction, multiplication, and division can be performed with great speed by digital circuits.

The binary number system is based upon the fact that any decimal number can be represented by a number or by a combination of numbers using a base of 2. For example,

$$1 = 2^0$$
$$2 = 2^1$$
$$3 = 2^0 + 2^1$$
$$25 = 2^0 + 2^3 + 2^4$$

Several decimal numbers and their binary number equivalents are given in Table 41-1. A study of this table shows that, reading from right to left, the decimal number 7 is equal to

One (2^0) + One (2^1) or One (2^2)

or   1 + 2 + 4

or, expressed as a binary number,

$$7 = 000111 = 111$$

(Leading zeros may be omitted.)

The binary equivalents of decimal numbers are used in calculators and computers. People prefer decimal numbers. Therefore, the two sys-

TABLE 41-1. DECIMAL NUMBERS AND THEIR
EQUIVALENT BINARY NUMBERS

Decimal Numbers	2^5 (32)	2^4 (16)	2^3 (8)	2^2 (4)	2^1 (2)	2^0 (1)
			Binary Numbers			
0	0	0	0	0	0	0
1	0	0	0	0	0	1
2	0	0	0	0	1	0
3	0	0	0	0	1	1
4	0	0	0	1	0	0
5	0	0	0	1	0	1
6	0	0	0	1	1	0
7	0	0	0	1	1	1
8	0	0	1	0	0	0
9	0	0	1	0	0	1
10	0	0	1	0	1	0
20	0	1	0	1	0	0
30	0	1	1	1	1	0
40	1	0	1	0	0	0
50	1	1	0	0	1	0

tems have to be interchanged or converted back and forth as people work with the digital instruments.

As indicated by Table 41-1, each bit of a binary number represents some decimal number. This number is equal to 2 raised to a power. A binary number can be converted by summing equivalent decimal numbers. As the table shows, each of the decimal numbers equals 2 raised to the power indicated by the column in which the corresponding bit appears. This is true whether the binary number is read from right to left or from left to right. The important thing to remember when converting a binary number to a decimal number is that the powers of 2 begin with 2^0 in the right-hand column. The following example shows the conversion of 10110 to decimal:

$$\begin{array}{ccccc} 1 & 0 & 1 & 1 & 0 \\ 2^4 & 2^3 & 2^2 & 2^1 & 2^0 \end{array}$$
$$16 + 0 + 4 + 2 + 0 = 22$$

DIGITAL ARITHMETIC

The capability of performing mathematical operations is a vital part of the operation of many digital systems. As an example, the arithmetic unit of a computer system can add, subtract, multiply, divide, extract roots, and provide other means of processing information. Actually, all mathematical operations can be performed by adding circuits.

Addition of Binary Numbers. The rules for the addition of binary numbers are:

$$0 + 0 = 0$$
$$0 + 1 = 1$$
$$1 + 0 = 1$$
$$1 + 1 = 10$$

The 10 can be read as "one-zero," as 0 and carry 1, or as sum 0 and carry 1. Examples of the use of these rules are as follows, with decimal number equivalents written in parentheses:

011	(3)	1101	(13)	110	(6)
010	(2)	1111	(15)	011	(3)
101	(5)	11100	(28)	101	(5)
				1110	(14)

The Half-Adder. A *half-adder* is a digital circuit that is capable of adding two one-bit binary numbers (Fig. 41-9). This circuit provides an interesting example of the use of AND, OR, and NOT logic gates. The associated truth table gives the binary condition (0 or 1) at several points in the circuit when the various combinations of one-bit numbers are added.

The Full-Adder. The *full-adder* is a circuit that is capable of adding two bits plus a carry bit from a prior adding circuit. A basic full-adder circuit is a combination of two half-adders plus another logic gate. By using many full-adders, it is possible to add large binary numbers.

Subtraction, Multiplication, and Division. The processes of subtraction, multiplication, and division are all variations of addition. Subtraction is the inverse, or opposite, of addition; multiplication is a repetition of additions; and division is the inverse of multiplication. Because of these relationships, digital circuits that are variations of adders can also be used to perform other mathematical operations.

COUNTERS

Counters are one of the most common and useful digital electronics circuit systems. In addition to counting, they also provide a stable frequency division. For example, a 100-Hz signal can be divided to 10 Hz or to 1 Hz by digital counting circuitry.

The *bistable multivibrator* or *flip-flop* (FF), is the basic circuit used in most binary counters. This circuit has two stable output states and can be switched from one output state to the other. In the T type flip-flop, this is done by applying trigger voltage pulses to its input (Fig. 41-10). Here 1 represents an output voltage pulse and 0 represents no output voltage. In the symbol for the flip-flop, the bar Q ($\overline{Q}$) at one of the

Truth Table

Inputs		Points in Circuit						Answer	
A	B	1	2	3	4	5	6	C	S
0	0	1	0	0	0	1	0	0	0
0	1	1	1	1	1	0	0	0	1
1	0	0	0	0	0	1	1	0	1
1	1	0	1	0	1	0	0	1	0

Fig. 41-9. A half-adder circuit

Fig. 41-10. Basic switching action of a flip-flop

outputs indicates that this output is always the inverse of the other (Q) output.

The trigger voltage pulse applied to a flip-flop is often called a *clock*. When the pulse is a positive voltage, it is called an *up-clock*. Conversely, a negative trigger pulse is called a *down-clock*.

Each clock pulse causes a transition to occur in the output states of Q and $\overline{Q}$. When Q is at a high state 1, $\overline{Q}$ is at a low state 0. The outputs will remain at these states until another clock pulse causes a transition to occur.

A simplified counter circuit consisting of four T type flip-flops connected together in what is called a *cascade arrangement* is shown in Fig. 41-11. The $\overline{Q}$ outputs are connected to lamps that are the readout devices. The reset line allows a voltage pulse to be simultaneously applied to all the flip-flops. This pulse switches the flip-flops so that the Q outputs are in the 0 state. When reset, the readout of the counter is 0000. In this circuit, assume that a positive trigger pulse (a 1 state) applied to any flip-flop will cause it to switch or change states.

When the first positive pulse is applied to the trigger T of FF1, it switches this flip-flop, causing the $\overline{Q}$ output to become 1. Since, at this time, the Q output of FF1 is 0, the pulse does not affect FF2. Lamp 1 now lights, and the readout of the counter is 0001.

A second positive pulse applied to FF1 causes this flip-flop to switch back to its original state. Now the $\overline{Q}$ output of FF1 is 0, its Q output is 1, and lamp 1 goes out. As the 1 output of FF1 is applied to the trigger of FF2, this flip-flop switches, causing its $\overline{Q}$ output to become 1 and its Q output to become 0. As a result, lamp 2 lights and the readout of the counter is 0010.

A third positive pulse applied to FF1 causes it to switch, thus producing a $\overline{Q}$ of 1 and causing lamp 1 to light. The outputs of FF2 remain unchanged since its input, the Q output of FF1, is in the 0 state. Likewise, FF3 is not affected because the Q output of FF2 is also in the 0 state. In this condition of the circuit, lamps 1 and 2 are both lighted, and the readout of the counter is 0011.

By carefully "tracing" the operation of the counter beginning with the fourth pulse, it will be seen that the number 4 through number 15 pulses applied to the trigger of FF1 will result in the binary readouts indicated in Fig. 41-11. The maximum number of pulses that this

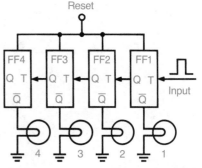

Binary Readout				Pulse Number
0	0	0	1	1
0	0	1	0	2
0	0	1	1	3
0	1	0	0	4
0	1	0	1	5
0	1	1	0	6
0	1	1	1	7
1	0	0	0	8
1	0	0	1	9
1	0	1	0	10
1	0	1	1	11
1	1	0	0	12
1	1	0	1	13
1	1	1	0	14
1	1	1	1	15
0	0	0	0	16

Fig. 41-11. A four flip-flop digital counter

counter can count is 15. The 16th input pulse automatically resets the counter back to 0000. A counter capable of counting additional pulses could be made by adding more flip-flops to the circuit.

A counter such as the one that has been described is called an *up-counter* since it counts events in an upward sequence (1, 2, 3, 4, 5, etc.). Conversely, a counter that counts in a downward sequence is called a *down-counter*.

FREQUENCY DIVIDER

Figure 41-12A shows the operation of a single flip-flop as a frequency divider. The first input pulse causes the Q output to go to 1 state and the $\overline{Q}$ output to 0 state. The second input pulse causes the Q output to go to 0 state and the $\overline{Q}$ output to 1 state. The third input pulse causes the Q output to go to 1 state and the $\overline{Q}$ output to 0 state. The fourth pulse causes the Q output to go to 0 state and the $\overline{Q}$ output to go to 1 state. Notice that it takes four clock input pulses to cause the output Q to go to a 1 state two times. The Q output, therefore, effectively divides the input pulses by 2. When the Q output is connected to the input of another flip-flop as shown in Fig. 41-12B, the input pulses at each flip-flop are divided by 2.

THE DIGITAL CLOCK

A simplified block diagram of a digital clock that operates from a 60-Hz power line is shown in Fig. 41-13. This diagram does not, of course, show the several different kinds of circuits involved in the operation of the clock. It does, however, provide an idea of how digital counters are used to "break down" a power-line frequency so that it can be used to accumulate seconds, minutes, and hours.

Fig. 41-12. Frequency divider: (A) basic operation; (B) flip-flops connected as a frequency divider

Fig. 41-13. Block diagram of a digital clock circuit system

60 Hz → Wave-Shaping Circuit → 60 Hz → By 60 Divider

1 Hz → Seconds Counter → 1 Cycle/Min → Minutes Counter

To Seconds Readout

To Minutes Readout

1 Cycle/Hour → Hours Counter → To Hours Readout

13. Making a Logic Probe. A very simple but useful digital instrument is the logic probe. It is used to test the logic level at important points in 5-Vdc digital circuits. The logic probe uses an AND gate and a pair of light-emitting diodes (LEDs). LED DS1 will light when the test logic is 0 and LED DS2 will light when the test logic is 1.

MATERIALS NEEDED

IC1 1-7408 Quad-two input AND gate
DS1 and DS2 two-light-emitting diodes, 1.5 Vdc, 5 mA or more
R1 and R2 2-1,000-Ω carbon-composition ¼-W resistors
1 piece of prototyping circuit board or breadboarding unit, 1 × 3 in (25 × 75 mm)
1 test probe
2 miniature alligator clips
2 pieces of red test lead wire, 20-24 gage, 14 in. (355.6 mm)
1 piece of black test lead wire, 20-24 gage, 14 in. (355.6 mm)
assorted lengths of solid-strand insulated hookup wire, gage to fit the selected circuit board
signal generator capable of producing a square wave at 5 Vdc

NOTE: The logic probe circuit obtains its power from the circuit being tested.

Procedure

1. Assemble the circuit, on a breadboard, as shown in Fig. 41-14.
2. Connect the alligator clip, pin 14, to a source of +5 Vdc.
3. Connect pin 7 to the common ground of the circuit being tested, the square-wave generator.

CONNECT TEST LEAD WIRE WITH ALLIGATOR CLIP TO +5 VOLT TERMINAL OF UNIT UNDER TEST

PROBE INPUT

LOW LOGIC LEVEL INDICATOR

HIGH LOGIC LEVEL INDICATOR

CONNECT TEST LEAD WIRE WITH ALLIGATOR CLIP TO COMMON GROUND OF UNIT UNDER TEST

Fig. 41-14. Logic probe circuit for Learning by Doing No. 13, "Making a Logic Probe"

4. Set the output of the generator to 5 V and the frequency from 1 to 5 Hz. The LEDs should blink.
5. Increase the generator frequency so that both LEDs appear to be on all the time. (Note the frequency at which this occurs.) Actually, the two LEDs are alternating on and off. This indicates a rapid train of logic pulses, a series of 1s and 0s. This can be verified by using an oscilloscope.

SELF-TEST

Test your knowledge by writing, on a separate sheet of paper, the word or words that most correctly complete the following statements:

1. Circuit systems that work primarily with two fixed levels of voltage conditions are called _____.
2. Another name for logic circuitry is _____.
3. Four logic gates are the _____, _____, _____, and _____.
4. The input to a logic gate can have one of two states _____ or _____.
5. A square wave with +5 Vdc high and 0 Vdc low is called _____ logic.
6. The mathematics used to describe logic circuits is called _____ _____.
7. The decimal number 9 can be expressed as _____ in the binary numbering system.
8. The addition of binary numbers (011 + 010) is equal to the binary number _____.
9. The basic circuit used in most binary counters is the bistable multivibrator called a _____ _____.
10. The logic circuit that converts a logic 1 to a logic 0 is called the _____ circuit.

FOR REVIEW AND DISCUSSION

1. Define digital electronics.
2. Name three methods by which binary conditions or states can be achieved.
3. What is a digital logic circuit?
4. Name, describe, and write the symbols for the three basic types of logic gates.
5. What is meant by signal inversion?
6. For what purpose is a truth table used in conjunction with a logic gate?
7. What is the function of a comparator?
8. Why is the binary number system used instead of the decimal number system in digital circuits?
9. What is a bit?
10. State the rules for the addition of binary numbers.
11. Describe a half-adder and a full-adder.
12. Briefly describe a flip-flop.
13. For what purpose is a symbol such as $\overline{Q}$ used with the symbol for a flip-flop?
14. What is meant by resetting a counter?
15. Briefly describe a digital circuit that can divide by 2.
16. Define the term *logic gate*.
17. Compare the truth tables for the following gates: AND, OR, NOT, and XOR.

INDIVIDUAL-STUDY ACTIVITIES

1. Prepare a written report or make an oral presentation to your class on the impact of digital electronics on American business and industry.
2. Using a catalog for integrated circuits, prepare a report on the types of digital devices available and how they are classified.

UNIT 42   Fundamentals of Computers

One basic need of business, industry, and government is to handle large amounts of information quickly with minimum error. Thus, systems are needed for gathering information, for making mathematical computations, and for storing information so that it can be easily obtained.

These and many other related functions are performed by computers and auxiliary units. A *computer* is a programmable electronic device that can store, retrieve, and process data. Computers and auxiliary units are known as *automatic data processing* (ADP) systems. There are two main kinds of computers. These are the *analog computer* and the *digital computer*.

COMPARISON OF THE BASIC ANALOG AND DIGITAL SYSTEMS

The automobile fuel-level circuit is an example of an analog measuring system. Its purpose is to first "sense" the quantity of fuel in the tank. This quantity is then indicated by a *readout*. This takes the form of the position of a pointer on a scale. Since the pointer can move to many positions on the scale, it continuously indicates fuel quantity. For this reason, an *analog measuring system* can be defined as one that is able to respond instantly to any condition of what may be a wide range of conditions.

An indicator light, such as the oil-pressure light in an automobile, is an example of a digital measuring system. In this system, the light is at any time either on or off. As you have learned, conditions of this kind are known as binary conditions. *Binary* means made up of two parts.

DIGITAL COMPUTERS

The circuits of a digital computer respond to one of only two conditions. These may be switches that are on or off, voltages that are either positive or negative, or two voltages that are different in value. Although the input and the output information to be processed by a digital computer may have different forms, the circuits that process this information are digital.

Most data processing is done by digital computers. There are many models and varieties of digital computers. They range from small portable computers to large, complicated systems. These systems are made up of many pieces of interconnected equipment. Figure 42-1 shows some of the kinds of equipment commonly found in a large computer center.

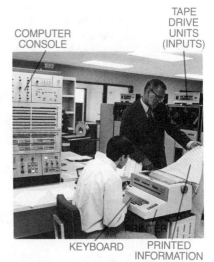

Fig. 42-1. Examining the printed output from an automatic data processing computer (*U.S. Department of Housing and Urban Development*)

BASIC ELEMENTS IN AN ADP SYSTEM

Generally all ADP systems have the following five basic elements: input, output, storage, arithmetic (logic), and control (Fig. 42-2).

Fig. 42-2. Basic elements in a computer-controlled ADP system

COMPUTER INPUT

The computer input device feeds data into the computer system. The main input devices used are paper tape, punched cards, magnetic tape, magnetic disk, and keyboard (Fig. 42-3). The holes punched in the paper tape and cards and the magnetic patterns imprinted on the magnetic tape and disks cause pulses of voltage to appear in the system. For example, a 5-V pulse many stand for the digit 1. The absence of a pulse may stand for the digit 0. These digits form what are known as *binary codes*. These are codes that are made up of only two parts. In this case, the two parts are the digits 1 and 0. These digits are called *bits*. A group of bits makes up one *alphanumeric character*. Such a character stands for a letter or number. This coding system is similar to that used for teletypewriter communications (see Unit 37).

Magnetic tapes are used to store large amounts of data. Large computer systems use equipment to handle magnetic tapes called *tape drive units* (Fig. 42-4). These units control the movement of the tape and can sense the bits that make up the characters on the tape.

COMPUTER OUTPUT

The output information obtained from a computer is often in the same form as the input: paper tape, punched cards, magnetic tape, or magnetic disks. Information printed directly on paper is also a very common form of computer output. In some computer systems, the output information is displayed on a cathode ray tube. This is similar to a television picture tube.

STORAGE

Data must be stored in the computer before it can be processed. One of the common ways of storing data is to magnetize tiny iron cores with

(PUNCHED HOLES)

PUNCHED TAPE

(PUNCHED HOLES)

PUNCHED CARD

(MAGNETIC-FIELD IMPRINT)

MAGNETIC TAPE

(MAGNETIC-FIELD IMPRINT)

MAGNETIC DISC
(RESEMBLES PHONOGRAPH RECORD)

KEYBOARD

Fig. 42-3. Computer inputs

428

each pulse of electricity. The magnetic fields that surround the cores represent stored data. These fields, and thus the data, can be sensed. Since the tiny iron core can retain its magnetic field, it has the property of *memory* (Fig. 42-5).

Other devices have "memory" too. For example, you have probably used a retractable ball-point pen. When you push down on the top of the pen and release, the point is in place for writing. When you push and release again, the point disappears. If you push up and down on the top of the pen in rapid succession, you will notice that the point appears *once* for every *two* pushes.

The ball-point pen action is similar to an electronic device called a *toggle flip-flop*. The toggle flip-flop is a kind of electronic switching circuit. The toggle flip-flop output is a digital 1 for every other 1 input. If the input signal is suddenly removed, the flip-flop output retains the same value it had after the last input signal. Because of this, you can say it has memory too.

A flip-flop can exist in many forms. The most common form uses transistors. Modern computers use tunnel diodes, metal oxide silicon (MOS) field-effect transistors, and integrated circuits as memory to store data. Each of these has some different advantage over the others, such as high speed, low cost, or small size. A more detailed discussion of the operation of a flip-flop is given in Unit 41, "Digital Electronic Circuits."

ARITHMETIC (LOGIC)

The arithmetic element of a digital computer has the ability to do comparisons, make decisions, add, and subtract. The computer does these things by rapidly counting and adding electrical pulses with specially designed logic circuits. Logic circuits are discussed in detail in Unit 41, "Digital Electronic Circuits."

CONTROL

In order to perform its operations automatically, a computer must be *programmed*. A *computer program* is a series of instructions for the computer to follow. The program is stored in the computer in the same way as the information it controls. The program can cause the computer to perform operations involving the stored information. These might include adding, dividing, reading a magnetic tape, or printing on paper.

MICROCOMPUTER

The *microcomputer* (sometimes called a *personal computer* or *PC*) is made up of many ICs that, when connected together, will perform one or more functions (Fig. 42-6). The main IC is the *microprocessor*. This is the center of all functions performed by the computer. As mentioned previously, the operation of the computer is controlled by a list of instructions called a *program*. The process of writing a set of step-by-step instructions for the computer is the job of the *programmer*. The pro-

Fig. 42-4. Installing a magnetic tape reel on a tape drive unit (*U.S. Department of Labor*)

Fig. 42-5. A typical core plane containing 1,024 sixteen-bit words. The inset shows an enlarged view of the cores with wires interleaved. Each circular core is 1 memory bit. (*Hewlett-Packard Co.*)

(A) MONITOR (VIDEO) SCREEN OR CRT DISPLAY

(B) DISK DRIVES

(C) KEYBOARD

Fig. 42-6. Typical microcomputer: the TRS-80® microcomputer (*Radio Shack, a Division of Tandy Corporation*)

gram is stored in computer memory. The *central processing unit* (*CPU*), located within the microprocessor, executes the steps one at a time. A simplified block diagram of a CPU is illustrated in Fig. 42-7. The arrows indicate the direction of data flow to and from the blocks in the diagram. The broad arrows indicate multiline data paths in parallel; however, 1 bit of binary data (0 to 1) is sent on each conductor at any given time. By grouping several of these conductors together, data can be sent in parallel: 4, 8, 16, or 32 bits (binary digits) at a time. This is an example of a *bus structure*. The single arrows are for single bits of information, generally for control purposes. The ALU is the *arithmetic logic unit*. It is within this unit that arithmetic functions (add, subtract, etc.) take place. The *accumulator* is a very special register within the CPU. Data contained in the accumulator can be used to perform mathematical functions with the ALU. *Flags* are used, for example, to indicate the results of the arithmetic and logic operations. Each flag is one bit of a special 8-bit group that can be individually set to a logic 1 or 0. A flag can indicate that the result of an arithmetic operation is equal or unequal to zero. A flag can also indicate a carry value that is generated

TRANSFER GATE t_a

S = SET
R = RESET
FF = FLIP FLOP

SYMBOL FOR B REGISTER

Fig. 42-8. A 3-bit register made up of three flip-flops

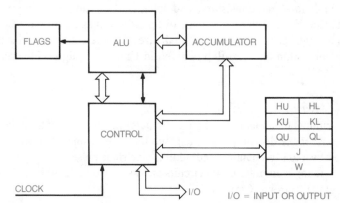

Fig. 42-7. Block diagram of a central processing unit (CPU).

by adding two numbers. Flags, therefore, can be used to control the operation of a program according to the condition of the flag. The *control* circuit gates, or transfers, information around the computer. As the name indicates, it is the function of this section to control the entire computer operation. All data leaving or entering the computer must pass through the control system. The block labeled with letters contains the *registers*. These are temporary storage spaces for data that are used later in the program.

REGISTER WORD

Flip-flops not connected to each other but considered together to form a "bank" of flip-flops utilize the memory feature to store data in the form of binary 1s and 0s. The bank is called a *register,* and the binary data in it are called *register words.* Figure 42-8 shows a register capable of holding (storing) a 3-bit word.

Input information A (A_1, A_2, A_3) is passed to the flip-flop inputs when the transfer gate signal t_a is 1. If an input is 1, a 1 appears at the set input and the flip-flop assumes a value of 1. If the input is a 0, a 1 appears at the reset input and the flip-flop assumes a value of 0.

The concept of *register transfer* is important to understand when considering data movement in a computer. Figure 42-9 illustrates the transfer of data in register A to register B. The large arrow indicates a data word of many bits. The t_1 indicates that the transfer takes place at a given time. In this case, t_1 could be set equal to 1 at some specific time known as t_1.

Register C in Figure 42-9 indicates a group of 12 binary bits contained in the register. The 12-bit configuration could represent the integer number 849, the letter S, the decimal number $+0.43 \times 10^{+1}$, or an instruction to ADD two variables. Register D in Figure 42-9 shows one possible interpretation of the register content that represents a decimal number. Figure 42-9 also shows that data can be transferred to and from several different units including memory, arithmetic unit, and input-output.

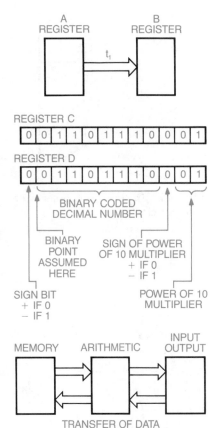

Fig. 42-9. Concept of register transfer and interpretation of binary bits in a register

PROGRAM

As previously noted, computer operation is directed by a set of instructions called a *program*. Each instruction requires a fixed number of steps to execute. Instructions are accessed from memory and worked on in sequential order. The time it takes to do a single step is called a *time state*. Early CPUs performed each function, one step at a time. Modern units contain multiple CPUs that handle several functions simultaneously. One of them might be for mathematical operations, another for graphic generation, another for input and output of data, and a fourth for the general operations that must be performed. By doing this, the speed of the computer can be increased by as much as four times. This is very important in office operations where computers are connected together to share information. This interconnection is called *networking*.

CLOCK

The *clock* is a square-wave generator that feeds a signal to the CPU. A crystal (XTAL) is used to control the frequency so that all signals within the computer are stable. In Fig. 42-10, the clock is outside the microprocessor IC. In other systems, it is a part of the microprocessor but performs the same function of timing. The desired clock frequency (for example, 1.023 MHz) designated Ø, is sent to the microprocessor. The CPU uses these clock pulses to control all other devices. In this way, all sections are made to work in time with each other. The period of each clock pulse is a time state t. A specific number of time states are used for each instruction. During execution, the CPU uses some parts of the computer for different purposes. It is, therefore, necessary that all sec-

Fig. 42-10. Microprocessor with external clock

tions be ready when the CPU sends it. The clock, therefore, is a very important part of a computer. One of the common functions that originates here is RESET. The reset function is usually initiated by the operator at the keyboard. The reset key is wired to the RESET connection on the clock. When this key is pressed the computer is forced to return to the *operating system* (OS), which is a program that is built into the computer.

Fig. 42-11. Parts of a square wave

LOGIC CIRCUIT PULSES

The pulses, or waves, of a logic circuit are rectangular in shape. Each pulse, however, has a distinct set of parts to describe the shape of the pulse or wave (Fig. 42-11). The time it takes for a change in state from 0 V to 5 V is called the *rise time* or the *leading edge*. Many circuits will trigger on the rise of the pulse. The 5-V level is called the *steady high*. The steady-high level is a constant 5 V for the duration of the pulse. The time it takes for the change from 5 V to 0 V is called the *fall time* or the *trailing edge*. The low level is called the *steady low*. It is near 0 V until the next rise is generated. Any one of these parts (leading edge, high, low, or trailing edge) can be used to trigger logic circuits.

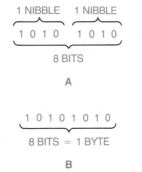

Fig. 42-12. Data word organization

DATA FORMATS

Information in the form of binary digits (1 and 0) is called *data*. Data can be a single 1 or 0 called a *bit*, which is short for *b*inary dig*it*. The bits can also be grouped into 4-bit units, which are called *nibbles* (Fig. 42-12A). Groups of 2 nibbles, or 8 bits, form a single *byte* (Fig. 42-12B). The 8-bit byte is a very common format for data. A byte is also called a *word* or *data word*. A computer that uses a single 8-bit byte for data transfer is said to be an "8-bit computer." When 2 bytes are used together as data, the computer is said to be a "16-bit computer." Some computers today can transfer data in 32-bit groups. These computers have the capabilities to rapidly perform a wide variety of tasks.

Data can be sent from point to point in a computer or from computer to computer. This is done by electrical impulses. Since digital informa-

432

tion is either a 1 (logical 1 or yes) or 0 (logical 0 or no), they can be represented by voltages. A very popular format is TTL (*transistor-to-transistor logic*). In this format, a 1 is represented by an energy level of 3 to 5 Vdc. Logic circuits receiving a voltage between these levels will read a logical 1. A logical 0 is received when 0 to 0.6 Vdc is sent to an input (Fig. 42-13). TTL is used primarily between the circuitry of a computer and the peripheral devices located generally close to the computer. If a distance of about 2 ft or less is needed, a *ribbon cable* can be used. This is a flat cable with all conductors running parallel. Over distances greater than 2 ft, the data will induce voltages between the conductors. This is called *cross talk*. If cross talk occurs, the data received at the end may not match the data that enter. To get greater distance (6 to 10 ft), a cable with twisted wire pairs can be used. In this type of cable, each data conductor is twisted with a signal return wire. This cuts cross talk to a minimum. Both cables can also have a conductive shield to minimize interference. The ribbon cable has a flat, woven wire mesh under the insulator, and the twisted-pair cable is wrapped with a metal foil.

Fig. 42-13. Allowable voltage variations for TTL levels

TIMING DIAGRAMS

When combinations of logic circuits are used, it is essential to know when the various input pulses will occur. Each time the signal enters a gate, it takes a period of time for the necessary switching to be done. This is called the *propagation delay*. If two signals are being presented to the inputs of an AND gate, they must be there at the same time. Figure 42-14A shows the pulses at input A and B arriving at the same time, t_0. The elapsed time between the rise and fall of the pulse is the same for both pulses. For this example, the time period between t_0 and t_1 is 0.5 microseconds (μs). If the pulse at A arrives late at the logic gate, there would be a time delay created by that circuit. The pulse, therefore, at input A would arrive later than the pulse at input B (Fig. 42-14B). If the AND gate is to function properly, pulse B must be of a duration long enough to accommodate pulse A. This can be shown by using a timing diagram as in Fig. 42-14C. As can be seen, if the delay of pulse A is 5 μs, then pulse B must be 5 μs longer than pulse A.

The timing diagram of a machine cycle for a microcomputer is shown in Fig. 42-15. After a delay, for example, from the falling edge of the WRITE signal, the address lines (A0 to A11) become stable. Data must be valid at the output lines of memory prior to the next failing edge of the WRITE pulse. The total access time is shown at *t*. This is the time when the address data are stable so that valid data can be placed on the data bus lines.

MEMORY

The computer has specific locations in which single bytes of data are stored. Data are stored as voltages, +5 V or 0 V (1 or 0, respectively),

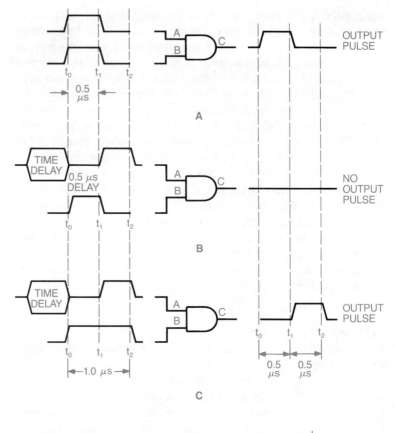

Fig. 42-14. Input timing for the correct operation of a logic gate

OUTPUT PULSE

t_0 t_1 t_2

0.5 μs

A

TIME DELAY 0.5 μs DELAY

NO OUTPUT PULSE

t_0 t_1 t_2

B

TIME DELAY

OUTPUT PULSE

t_0 t_1 t_2

t_0 t_1 t_2

←1.0 μs→

0.5 μs 0.5 μs

C

*Φ

* WRITE

*$A_{11} - A_0$ PREVIOUS ADDRESS   NEW ADDRESS

Fig. 42-15. Timing signals for an external main memory access (OP CODE FETCH) (*Mostek Corporation*)

*SIGNAL IS INTERNAL   ←———— t ————→   DATA VALID

which are held by special circuitry designed for that purpose. If the computer is an 8-bit machine, the memory locations will each contain one 8-bit data word. The total number of memory locations that a computer contains is one way of expressing how large that computer is. A *data word* is a small unit in memory. Many data words are needed to store usable amounts of information. Thousands of bytes, therefore, are combined together in groups of ICs to make up the total memory of the computer. For convenience, memory size is expressed in units of 1,024 bytes and written as 1 kilobyte or 1K. This is what is meant when a computer is said to have 64K or 128K of memory. Computers can have several groups of 64K bytes and are measured in terms of hundreds of thousands and millions of bytes (megabytes). The number of memory locations is based on the power of 2. One kilobyte is 2 to the 10th power (2^{10}), which is $2 \times 2 \times 2 \times 2 \times 2 \times 2 \times 2 \times 2 \times 2 \times 2 = 1,024$ bytes. Therefore, 64 kilobytes (2^{16} or $1,024 \times 64$) are really 65,536 usable bytes, expressed as 64K.

ROM/RAM. There are two general types of memory. ROM (*read only memory*) is permanent memory that contains the operating system programs that are needed to operate the computer when it is turned on. RAM (*random access memory*) is memory that can store a program entered by pressing keys on the keyboard or by loading the program from a peripheral device such as a diskette. When the computer is turned off, however, the information in the RAM is lost. When the computer is turned on, the RAM is loaded with combinations of ones and/or zeros. ROM, though, will still be the same when power is turned on again. This is why the operating system (OS) of a computer is contained on ROM. Programs in ROM are called firmware. Programs loaded into RAM are called software. Each time the computer is turned on, the OS must be running for the computer to decode the instructions the operator sends into the computer. A ROM integrated circuit has the program designed into the structure of the computer, and it cannot be changed. Because of the expense in design and manufacture of ROM, it is used when hundreds of thousands of units are needed. When a smaller number of units is needed, *programmable read only memory* (PROM) is programmed using special equipment.

PROM. The PROM integrated circuit allows manufacturers to have custom firmware in a less expensive format than ROM. Programming equipment electrically changes the condition of the memory cells, making them binary 1 or 0, as needed. Once a PROM has been programmed, it remains programmed and cannot be changed.

EPROM. A third type of ROM is user *erasable*. This is done by exposing the EPROM (*erasable programmable read only memory*) to ultraviolet light. The EPROM can be identified by a window on the top of the IC. This window allows *ultraviolet* (UV) light to cast onto the surface of the chip and change all locations to zero.

Electrical pulses are used to erase the EEPROM (*electrically erasable programmable read only memory*). The locations will be changed to logic 0 when voltages are applied to the connections that allow this to happen.

Each type of PROM is programmed through the use of special programmer circuitry called a *PROM programmer*. A computer is used to make checks as it goes through the process to make sure that the proper data are in the desired locations. Some computers have printed-circuit-

HIGH ADDRESS

0 0 0 1 0 0 0 1

LOW ADDRESS

0 0 0 0 0 0 0 0

Fig. 42-16. Low and high bytes of a memory address

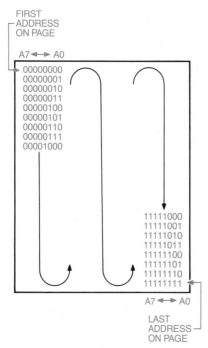

FIRST
ADDRESS
ON PAGE

A7 ◄─► A0

00000000
00000001
00000010
00000011
00000100
00000101
00000110
00000111
00001000

11111000
11111001
11111010
11111011
11111100
11111101
11111110
11111111

A7 ◄─► A0

LAST
ADDRESS
ON PAGE

Fig. 42-17. One page of memory

MSB 0 0 0 0 0 0 0 0 LSB
A7 ─────────── A0

Fig. 42-18. Lower 8 bits of the address bus

board slots where special boards can be placed to expand the function of the computer. Among these functions are printer drivers, speech synthesizers, or disk drive controllers. To operate these PC cards, a PROM is included within the controller circuitry to run the needed program.

ADDRESSING MEMORY

As discussed previously, the computer contains many individual bytes of memory. The operator must be able to access any one individual byte to obtain or alter the data contained at that point. It is for this purpose that a system of addresses has been created. It takes 2 bytes of data to address any one byte of memory. The bytes are called the *low* and *high* addresses. As illustrated in Fig. 42-16, each part of the address contains 8 bits. *Note:* During this discussion, you will be working with two numeration systems. A number with a base of 10 will stand alone, but a number with a base of 2 will be indicated by a subscript following the binary value, that is, 1101_2.

LOW ADDRESS

If a single binary bit is used to mark objects, two items can be identified, for example, item 0 or item 1. It can be easily seen that this would be insufficient, as a computer has many more than two memory locations. If the number of bits is doubled, the combinations increase to four: 00_2, 01_2, 10_2, 11_2. This is still not enough to be usable. If, however, the number of bits is increased to 8, or 1 byte, the combinations are increased to 256 identifiable locations. These 256 bytes (¼K) grouped together are said to be "one page of memory." As seen in Fig. 42-17, the 8-bit binary addresses on the page begin at 00000000_2 and continue with binary counting to 11111111_2. This system identifies memory locations that may contain stored data. The code for an address is sent to a memory chip on 16 conductors called the *address bus*. The low eight address bus lines are marked on drawings with the symbols A0, A1, A2, A3, A4, A5, A6, and A7. When several or all of the eight lines are considered, notations are written in simpler form, A0–A7. As noted in Fig. 42-18, A0 is called the *least significant bit* (LSB), as is the rightmost bit of any data configuration. A7 is called the *most significant bit* (MSB). The digit in the leftmost position of any binary data value is considered to be the MSB, no matter how many digits are in the value. With this system, many locations can be addressed by these combinations of digits. However, many more are needed to perform even the simplest tasks. To enlarge the addressable locations, the upper eight address lines are needed.

HIGH ADDRESS

As you have seen, the low address identifies the individual byte on a page. A system of individually identifiable pages is provided. Each page contains 256 low addresses. It is for this reason that the high address is employed. With a 1-byte high address beginning at page 00000000_2 and continuing in a binary count to 11111111_2, 256 pages can be addressed (Fig. 42-19). The lines of the high address bus are

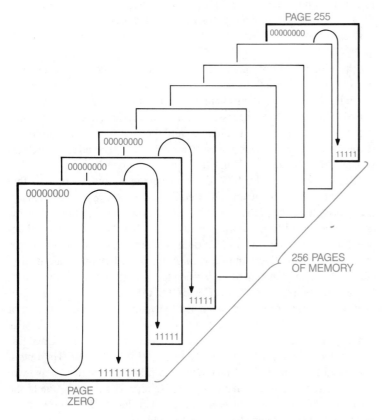

PAGE 255

00000000

11111

256 PAGES
OF MEMORY

00000000

00000000

00000000

11111

11111

11111111

PAGE
ZERO

Fig. 42-19. The high address defines the page number

marked A8, A9, A10, A11, A12, A13, A14, and A15. When the eight lines of the high address are considered as a group, they are marked A8–A15. Bit A8 is the LSB of the high address and bit A15 is the MSB (Fig. 42-20). By combining the high and low addresses (256 one-byte locations on each of 256 pages), a total of 65,535 locations can be addressed. This number is rounded off to 64K bytes for convenience. The first page number is zero, and on this page are locations 0 through 255. Zero is a valid number; therefore, there are 256 individual 8-bit memory locations. Next is page 1, and it has 256 locations, as do pages 2 through 255. By grouping blocks of 64K locations together and considering them one at a time, many blocks can be included in a computer and megabytes of memory can be used. Another way of increasing addressable memory is with a third set of address lines. This set is used to increase memory in 64K blocks. Two additional bits will identify four 64K blocks, 3 bits will identify eight blocks, and so forth. A full set of 8 bits will enable a computer to address more than 16 megabytes of memory.

MSB 1 0 0 1 0 0 1 1 LSB
A15 ◄——————— A8

Fig. 42-20. High 8 bits of the address bus

INPUT/OUTPUT (I/O)

The microcomputer alone is of little use to anyone if there is no way to get information in and out. Thus a microcomputer must be able to operate on data and perform some useful function. There are many forms of output devices available for a computer. A monitor (video) screen, a printer, a voice synthesizer, or machine-control circuitry are only some of these.

Latch. When a unit of data is sent to an output device, it remains there for only a short period of time. This time is typically only a few micro-seconds. There are few mechanical devices that can react in this time period. It is, therefore, necessary to have a device, called a *latch*, that will read the unit of data and hold it until the next unit of data arrives to replace it. You will see more clearly how this can be applied to circuitry in Unit 43, "Interacting With the Microcomputer."

A latch, such as a 74LS75 IC, is connected to four conductors that carry data. When conductors are used in groups of 4, 8, 16, or 32, each group is called a *data bus*. It is important that the data bus have only one device connected to it at any given time so that the data can be channeled to the right destination. To do this, the connections to all latches must have a very high impedance. A latch will draw little, if any, current from the bus when the impedance is high. Through the use of two enable pulses, a latch is selected for the receipt of data. Even if there is more than one latch connected to a data bus, the combination of two enable pulses can be gated to select only one device at a time. The enable pulses cause the impedance on the data line to go low. Once this occurs, the data are accepted by the device (Fig. 42-21A). The output lines send the data to the driven device and hold the logic at this level until changed. When the enable signals are removed from the latch, the input side of the latch returns to a high impedance. This sequence is illustrated in the timing diagram in Fig. 42-21B.

Tri-state Device. When it is necessary to bring data into a computer, another problem must be solved. The data must be presented to the bus only when the computer is ready to receive it. The tri-state IC is used for this purpose. It provides three states of impedance. When not enabled, it provides a very high impedance to the data bus. Thus, it does not load the data bus in this state. When the device is selected by the enabling signals, the input side accepts data and stores it. In the third state, the output side presents the data to the bus.

DEVICE SELECT BY BINARY CODES

When the program needs to send data to an output device, that device must be specified in some way. This can be done by using device-select (ds) codes generated by the computer. Binary codes between 0 and 255 individually define any one of 256 different possible output devices. The same codes are used to define a separate set of 256 input devices.

Fig. 42-21. A typical latch circuit with timing diagram

TIMING DIAGRAM FOR A LATCH CIRCUIT

The use of the same codes for different functions is possible because the computer also has a control bus. This bus is made up of a single conductor with a bit (0 or 1) that is set by the program instructions. The control bus is also connected to the enable pin of an IC. The enable connection allows a device to be active on the data bus when it is appropriate. This is important because only one device can be active on the bus during any single time state. Control lines are usually in an active state when at 0 V. This means that they are normally at a 5-V level and are changed to 0 V to activate a device. The word notation for this type of signal will have a line or bar across the top of the word (i.e., $\overline{\text{RESET}}$, $\overline{\text{ENABLE}}$). One example of several control lines is read as "$\overline{\text{IN}}$ not" or "$\overline{\text{IN}}$ bar"; both terms have the same meaning. If an input instruction is given, the $\overline{\text{IN}}$ control line will be changed to a logic zero. In the same way, if an output is to be executed, the $\overline{\text{OUT}}$ line goes low and an output device is enabled (Fig. 42-22). This system uses any or all lower 8 bits of the address bus (A0 through A7) to identify which device is to be selected, in this case A0. We are now using the address bus to supply a code for an individual device within a group of devices attached to the same bus. The use of a bus for several purposes during different time states is called *multiplexing*. A group of bits, input or output, is selected by the control bus. Two enabling pulses are gated through a NAND circuit and enable either the input or output port, allowing only one to function. Once a single device is identified, the data are carried to it on the data bus. These data are in groups of 8 or 16 bits in most microcomputers.

Fig. 42-22. Control signals generated to output data

ENABLE
(INPUT PORT
DISABLED BY LOGIC 1)

AO

IN

INPUT
PORT

DATA FROM
EXTERNAL
DEVICE

MICROPROCESSOR

8 BIT DATA BUS (D0-D7)

TO OTHER
FUNCTIONAL
ELEMENTS

OUT

OUTPUT
PORT

DATA SENT
TO EXTERNAL
DEVICE
SELECTED

ENABLE
(OUTPUT PORT
SELECTED BY LOGIC 0)

DEVICE SELECT BY MEMORY MAP

Another system used to select I/O devices is *memory mapping*. As illustrated before, there are 65,536 addressable memory locations when using 16 bits on the address bus. In micros that use memory mapping, some of these memory locations are set aside for I/O purposes. When the data from an input device is desired, the content of that particular location is read. This is done through the use of a memory READ instruction. To output data, a memory WRITE instruction is executed. The memory locations to which data are written are actually connected to an output device. An example of an input device is the keyboard that is connected to the computer. Each time a key is pressed, a code for that key is stored in a specific memory location. The CPU then reads that location and obtains the code. This information is decoded to determine which key was pressed. An output device is the monitor (video) screen, which is used to display the decoded information.

Video Monitor. Characters are ''printed'' in blocks on the TV-like screen of the video monitor. Each block is identified by a single memory address. A binary code has been assigned for each character that is to appear on the screen. One widely used system is called the *American National Standard Code for Information Interchange*, or ASCII. The ASCII code for an alphanumeric text character or graphic character is written in a desired location. When this location is selected, the character will appear on the screen. Typically, the screen format will be 40 characters to a row with 20 or 40 rows from top to bottom. This gives the ability to print 800 to 1,600 blocks on the screen which represent, for example, alphanumeric characters.

In addition to text printing, computers can display pictures or graphic shapes on the screen. Because of the size of each block, graphics come out very choppy in this format. Straight lines are fine, but angles and curves may not be acceptable. This method of graphics is called *low-resolution graphics* (LO RES mode).

High resolution (HI RES mode) can be used if more detail is needed. In this system, thousands of memory locations are used to identify individual dots on the video display. The dots are called *pixels,* short for *picture elements*. These are much smaller elements that make up the graphic display, giving a better resolution to the image (refer to Fig. 40-1).

TRANSMITTING DATA OVER LONG DISTANCES

When it is necessary to send data over great distances, TTL will not do the job. When data is to be sent between computers that are separated by hundreds of feet or even miles, fewer conductors are desirable. A very common standard data format is called RS-232. Details on this standard and updated versions are published by the Electronic Industries Association. Data from a microcomputer can be sent and received over a set of three wires labeled *send, receive,* and *ground*. Other wires can be used for control purposes. The data are sent 1 bit at a time in rapid succession, called *serial format*. The number of individual bits that is sent every second is called the *baud rate*. Common standard baud rates, or signaling rates, are 150, 300, 1,200, and 2,400 bits per second. Higher-speed signaling rates are 4,800, 7,200, and 9,600 bits per second. The baud rate for all communications equipment on the cable must be set at the same rate, either through the software or by hardware switches. When telephone networks are used, a modem is needed to properly interface the signals to the telephone lines.

The 1s and 0s of the data are sent in the form of $+12$ to $+15$ V for a 0 and a -12 to -15 V for a 1 (Fig. 42-23). Both the sending and the receiving devices will have at least three basic connections. A connector used for this format is the 25-pin D connector. A standard has been set for this connector so that data are sent on pin 2, received on pin 3. Pin 7 is the signal ground or common return (Fig. 42-24). For an example of a complete RS-232 format, refer to Fig. 25-17.

HEXADECIMAL AND OCTAL CODES

In order for humans to "communicate" easily with computers, high-level languages were developed. These languages use letter and number codes that have meaning to humans. The computer interprets these symbols into binary codes. Once we begin looking at data in memory locations, we must deal with the binary codes of the computer. The binary system is fine for the computer, but the human mind has a difficult time remembering hundreds of different combinations of 1s and 0s. For this reason, the binary code is changed for us into one of two easier codes. These codes are *hexadecimal* and *octal*.

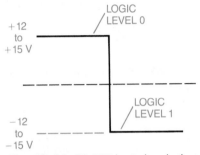

Fig. 42-23. RS-232 logic levels that represent the binary digits

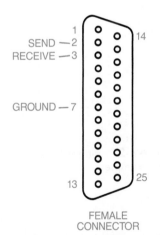

Fig. 42-24. RS-232 connection format to a DB-25 connector showing the connector side of a female connector

NIBBLE 2   NIBBLE 1

```
         8421 8421   HEX PLACE VALUE
MSB      1111 1111   LSB
                     ↓↓↓↓ HEX
         0000 0000 = 0
              0001 = 1
ETC       0010 = 2   ONE NIBBLE
          0011 = 3   PRODUCES
          0100 = 4   16 DIFFERENT
          0101 = 5   BINARY CODES
          0110 = 6   ($F)
          0111 = 7
          1000 = 8   TWO NIBBLES
          1001 = 9   PRODUCE 128
          1010 = A   DIFFERENT
          1011 = B   BINARY CODES
          1100 = C   ($FF)
          1101 = D
          1110 = E
    1111  1111 = F
     F     F
```

Fig. 42-25. Hexadecimal place value

```
8 4 2 1  8 4 2 1   HEX VALUE
1 0 0 1  0 0 1 1   BINARY NUMBER
8 + 1 = 9  2 + 1 = 3

            93₁₆
            or
            $93
```

Fig. 42-26. Binary-to-hex conversion

```
8 4 2 1  8 4 2 1         PLACE VALUE

0 0 0 1 0 0 1 1     1 0 0 0 1 0 1 0
    $13                 $8A

1 0 1 1 0 1 0 1     0 0 0 0 0 0 0 0
    $B5                 $00

1 1 0 0 1 1 1 0     1 1 1 1 1 1 1 1
    $CE                 $FF
```

Fig. 42-27. Binary-to-hex conversion examples

```
2 1 │ 4 2 1 │ 4 2 1   PLACE VALUE
1 1 │ 1 1 1 │ 1 1 1   BINARY NUMBER
 3  │   7   │   7     OCTAL
```

Fig. 42-28. Octal place value

442

Hexadecimal.

Many computers use the hexadecimal (hex) numbering system, which has a base of 16. In this system, the digits are 0, 1, 2, 3, 4, 5, 6, 7, 8, 9, A, B, C, D, E, F. With combinations of two of these digits, each of the 8-bit binary codes from all 0s to all 1s can be represented. It is much easier to remember two digits than it is to remember eight. A hex number is identified by the $ that leads the digits. For example, the binary number 00011010 is written $1A in hex. Many operating system programs in the computer ROM have firmware to display the hex value of any binary number contained in memory.

The conversion from binary to hex is a very simple matter that can be mastered with just a little practice. As seen in Fig. 42-25, the 8 bits of data are grouped into two groups of 4 bits or 2 nibbles. Starting at the rightmost bit (the least significant bit, or LSB), the bits are given a binary place value. The first bit on the right has the value of 1; the second bit, moving to the left, has the value of 2. The third bit is 4, and the fourth bit is 8. The values are repeated, right to left, for the next 4 bits receiving the values of 1, 2, 4, and 8 for the leftmost bit (most significant bit, or MSB). Each hex number will equal the sum of place values where a binary 1 appears in that group of 4 bits. Thus, it can be seen in Fig. 42-26 that 1001 0011 in binary equals $8 + 1 = \$9$ and $2 + 1 = \$3$, so the hex value is $93. If the sum of the place values is greater than 9, a single hex digit is provided by using the letters A through F. These are valid hex numbers for the base. Thus, 1010 is $8 + 2 = \$A$, or 1101 is $8 + 4 + 1 = \$D$. Figure 42-27 shows several more examples of this conversion.

Octal.

Another popular number system that is used is called *octal*. It has a *radix*, or base, of 8. The octal system uses three binary digits to represent an 8-bit binary number. Again, we assign place values to the digits. The digits are first divided into groups of three. Starting at the right, group the first 3 bits together. These have the decimal values of 1, 2, and 4, respectively, from right to left (Fig. 42-28). The next 3 bits are grouped and again have the value of 1, 2, and 4 from right to left. The 7th bit and the 8th bit, which is the most significant bit, have the values of 1 and 2. Any time a binary 1 appears in the data, the octal value for that place is added to the values in the group. The letter O is used to designate that a numeric value is an octal number. Thus, a binary value of 10 101 001 has an octal value of O251. With 8 binary bits, the octal numbers start at O000 and end at O377. More examples of octal conversions can be found in Fig. 42-29.

SINGLE-CHIP MICROCOMPUTER

Figure 42-30A illustrates a 40-pin, single-chip microcomputer. It has been designed to meet a wide range of applications that require some type of "intelligent" control. Because new devices are continually being added that use the same pin configuration and circuit design, referred to as the *architecture,* the Mostek MK 3870 "family" of microcomputers emerged. Figure 42-30B illustrates the part numbering used to indicate the generic part type and the ROM and RAM size (the memory space available on the chip). Figure 42-30C and D shows the names of the pins and the functions performed.

Figure 42-31 illustrates the variety of registers used on this single-chip microcomputer. Figure 42-32 shows, by arrows, the directions the data are transferred in and out of the registers. The *scratch pad* provides 64×8 bit registers that may be used as general-purpose RAM. The MK 3870/22 has extra RAM that is addressable. Software routines can be loaded into this RAM and executed. All MK 3870 family microcomputers execute a common set of more than 70 instructions. Designers can choose a device with the right combinations of ROM and RAM to suit the system requirements.

Information to and from the outside world is through the four parallel ports (I/O ports 0, 1, 4, and 5). These ports are shown on the block diagram (Fig. 42-33). Since information flows to and from the ports, they are called *bidirectional* or *I/O ports* (pronounced "eye-oh" ports). There are 8 bits available on each port. The ports can be used individually as either TTL-compatible inputs or as latch outputs.

```
2 1 4 2 1 4 2 1        PLACE VALUE

1 0 1 1 1 0 1 0      0 0 0 0 0 0 1 0
       272₈                002₈

1 1 0 0 0 1 0 1      0 0 0 0 0 0 0 0
       305₈                000₈

1 1 1 1 0 1 1 1      1 1 1 1 1 1 1 1
       267₈                377₈
```

Fig. 42-29. Binary-to-octal conversion examples

PIN NAME	DESCRIPTION	TYPE/FUNCTION
P0-0 – P0-7	I/O Port 0	Bidirectional
P1-0 – P1-7	I/O Port 1	Bidirectional
P4-0 – P4-7	I/O Port 4	Bidirectional
P5-0 – P5-7	I/O Port 5	Bidirectional
STROBE	Ready Strobe	Output
EXT INT	External Interrupt	Input
RESET	External Reset	Input
TEST	Test Line	Input
XTL1, XTL2	Time Base	Input
V_CC, GND	Power Supply Lines	Input

Fig. 42-30. A single-chip microcomputer: (A) the MK 3870, an 8-bit microcomputer integrated circuit; (B) part numbering example; (C) pin number and pin name; (D) summary of pin functions (*Mostek Corporation*)

Fig. 42-31. Block diagram of the MK 3870 single-chip microcomputer (*Mostek Corporation*)

WHAT THE FUTURE HOLDS

In the future, computers will control the production of more and more goods in the industries of the United States. Office work is changing rapidly because of *word processing* either by dedicated machines or through microcomputer software. This makes it possible to type rough drafts and view them instantaneously on TV monitors. The typist need not worry about typing errors, erasing, or starting the page over. Corrections can be easily made, stored in the device's memory and viewed on the screen. Once the draft is correct, a printer can produce the final copy at more than 600 lines per minute.

Electronic data processing by computer is even used in "fast-food" restaurants. No longer do the attendants write your food order on a piece of paper. As you state your order, they just press keys on a typewriter-like machine. When the transaction has been completed, you receive a printed paper tape. At the same time, the machine automatically stores the information electronically for future use. This information can be retrieved easily by managers for reordering or accounting purposes.

444

Fig. 42-32. The MK 3870 family programming model illustrating the I/O ports, CPU registers, scratch pad, and main memory (*Mostek Corporation*)

| SCRATCHPAD | SCRATCHPAD BYTE ADDRESS | |
	DECIMAL	OCTAL
	0	0
	1	1
	2	2
STATUS REGISTER W → J	9	11
DATA COUNTER DC → H { HU	10	12
HL	11	13
STACK REGISTER P → K { KU	12	14
PROGRAM COUNTER P0 → KL	13	15
DATA COUNTER DC → Q { QU	14	16
QL	15	17
PROGRAM COUNTER P0 →	16	20
	58	72
	59	73
	60	74
	61	75
	62	76
	63	77

Fig. 42-33. Scratch pad register map, illustrating data transfers between registers (*Mostek Corporation*)

SELF-TEST

Test your knowledge by writing, on a separate sheet of paper, the word or words that most correctly complete the following statements:

1. The letters ADP mean _____ .
2. The two basic kinds of computers are _____ and _____ .
3. A fuel-level circuit is a simple form of an _____ measuring system.
4. Stored data in a computer can be in the form of _____ .
5. Three basic logic circuits are the _____ , _____ , and _____ circuits.
6. A logic circuit can have one of two states, _____ or _____ .
7. The _____ logic circuit is similar in function to two parallel switches.
8. A circuit that produces an inverted form of the input signal is called a _____ circuit.
9. The part of the computer that is the center of all operations is the _____ _____ _____ .

10. The unit that sets up the timing for a computer is the _____ .
11. A word of data is made up of _____ bits.
12. The binary system of data uses _____ and _____ to represent single bits.
13. A two-digit system of numbers in base 16 is called _____ .
14. A group of 256 bytes of memory organized in sequence is called a _____ .
15. The value $3A in hex is _____ in binary.
16. The number value that represents a memory location is called the _____ of that location.
17. There are _____ bytes of memory in 64K computers.
18. One byte is formed with _____ binary digits.
19. Two bytes of data can address _____ memory locations.
20. Memory that can be programmed and will then hold that information until erased with UV light is called _____ .

21. The address of a byte of memory is made up of the _____ address and the _____ address.
22. A very common output device found with computers is the _____.
23. A very common input device for a computer is the _____.
24. The use of a bus structure for two or more purposes is called _____.
25. Using memory locations for I/O connections is called _____ _____ I/O.
26. Hexadecimal codes use _____ digits to represent an 8-bit value.
27. The octal number 275 equals _____ in binary.

FOR REVIEW AND DISCUSSION

1. Give some reasons for the increased use of computers by business, industry, and government.
2. List four operations performed by a computer from computer program instructions.
3. Define a logic circuit.
4. Describe the truth table for an AND logic circuit.
5. Draw a schematic diagram of an AND circuit.
6. Draw the symbols for the AND, OR, and NOT logic circuits.
7. Explain why binary numbers are used in computers.
8. Describe the courses available in your school that would help you prepare for a career in the computer field.
9. Discuss how you could get training in the computer field after high school.
10. Do research to determine how the following use computers in their occupations: programmer, operator, technician, engineer, data entry clerk, accountant, and researcher. Discuss how the use of a computer by each group is similar and how it is different.

INDIVIDUAL-STUDY ACTIVITIES

1. Visit a local company that makes use of automatic data processing. Tell your class what you have learned.
2. Prepare a written report or tell the class about how computers can be used to perform everyday tasks.
3. Go to a computer center where computers are used or sold, and find out how a person enters the various occupations.
4. Look in the advertisements section in your local newspaper for computer-related occupations. Prepare a report for your class on what you find.

UNIT 43 Interacting With the Microcomputer

Although the digital computer provides the mathematician with a rapid calculating device to solve complex problems, it is used increasingly, in one form or another, to control machines that perform simple or complex repetitive tasks. Microcomputers with a microprocessor, PROM, some RAM, and I/O ports can be programmed to run very complex machines that manufacture the goods we use every day. This application is called *dedicated control computing*. This type of computer has only one function to perform. Major program changes would have to be made to have it do other operations. However, the cost of dedicated control computing is so low that some toys now have this type of unit within them. In this unit, you will learn how the microcomputer can be used to control various devices.

INTERFACING

The microcomputer, or personal computer (PC), is much more costly and more versatile than the typical dedicated control computer. By constructing the needed circuitry, however, the PC can be made to control a device and perform a task. This task might be to control a light, a motor, or some other device of your choosing. Since these controlled devices are external to the computer, they are considered to be in the "real world." The process of connecting devices that are in the real world to the internal circuitry of a computer is called *interfacing*. The electronic circuitry needed to make the connection between a computer and the real world is a device called the *interface*.

Data. An important concept to remember from Unit 42 is that all the data in a computer are in the form of voltage pulses. Each bit of data is either a logical 1 or 0. Logic 1 is represented by a +5 V pulse that is gated by a TTL circuit. Logic circuits can supply base current to switch a transistor or the current needed to drive TTL-compatible devices. The logic 0, represented by a very low voltage or zero volts, is used to turn off a transistor or other device. These voltage pulses are controlled by a computer program. You will learn in this unit that the program provides specific step-by-step instructions that the computer follows in carrying out a task.

Fanout. The amount of current that can be sourced, or supplied, by a TTL logic circuit is not sufficient to operate many devices. The number of TTL devices that one TTL output will drive is called *fanout* (Fig. 43-1). Also the 5 V rectangular pulse wave, used inside the computer, is not compatible with most motors, relays, and other such useful devices. Therefore, some type of additional circuitry is needed.

Simple Interface. Figure 43-2 shows a simple interface circuit. A single data line is connected to a transistor in a common-emitter configuration. In this circuit, a transistor is used to control a relay. The base current is limited by the 1,000 Ω resistor (Rb). Resistor can be any convenient value between 500 and 5,000 Ω. The relay uses a 12 Vdc supply, and the relay coil provides the load for the collector circuit. A TTL voltage pulse at the emitter-base junction from the computer will produce a base current. This current will turn on the transistor, allowing collector current to energize the relay. As long as the base current con-

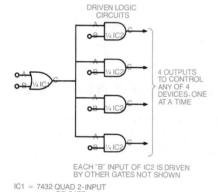

DRIVEN LOGIC CIRCUITS

4 OUTPUTS TO CONTROL ANY OF 4 DEVICES, ONE AT A TIME

EACH "B" INPUT OF IC2 IS DRIVEN BY OTHER GATES NOT SHOWN

IC1 = 7432 QUAD 2-INPUT OR GATE

IC2 = 7408 QUAD 2-INPUT AND GATE

Fig. 43-1. One TTL OR gate fanout to four TTL inputs

+12 V DC

N.C.

N.O. RELAY

D1

+5 V
0 V

Rb
1 KΩ

Q1
2N3055

TTL PULSE

Fig. 43-2. Transistor driver circuit

448

tinues, the relay will remain energized. If the base current is removed, the relay will return to the normal position. Diode D1 is connected across the relay coil to protect the circuit. The relay coil is an inductive load that can produce high transient voltages when turned on or off.

Latch. The instructions in a program take a very short period of time to execute. Data sent on a data line will last only until the microprocessor moves to the next time state. This is, at most, only a few microseconds. For this reason, the data must be sent repeatedly or it must be captured by a latch, as illustrated in Fig. 43-3. The 4-bit data bus is connected to the input side of the latch (pins 2, 3, 6, and 7). The controlled device is connected to the output side of the latch (pins 16, 15, 10, and 9). The action of the latch ciruit is controlled by the enable connections that are activated by signals from the computer. Since the byte of data is latched, the programmer must remember to send another signal that will turn off the motor, or other device, when the task is completed. If a logic 1 is used to turn the device on, a logic 0 is sent to turn it off.

ANALOG-TO-DIGITAL CONVERTER (ADC)

The internal circuitry of the digital computer is limited to logic levels of 1 and 0. The outside world, on the other hand, is not limited to two logic levels. Most devices use voltages in the form of continuous variable quantities. For example, there are unlimited values of color, temperature, light and dark levels, or resistance that exist in the real world. The audio amplifier and the operational amplifier are typical *analog devices* that operate on these variable quantities.

In order for a digital computer to determine one voltage or current level from another, an ADC circuit is used. Figure 43-4 shows a typical ADC used to convert analog signals into digital signals. As the ADC receives the analog signal at the input, it converts the analog signal to a digital code. The output of the ADC is digital in nature so the computer can use it. Most ADC devices can send data in either serial or parallel format, depending upon the format needed by the receiving device. The digital data is formed into a data table, which allows interpretation by the program. The data can then be used in equations, graphed, used to control the monitor screen, or put to some other meaningful purpose.

An inexpensive and simple ADC is shown in Fig. 43-5. This circuit uses a timer IC, the 555, and an *RC* network for control. Figure 43-5 illustrates a circuit that generates a free-running rectangular wave. The period of time for the rectangular wave at the low state is fixed. The period of time for the rectangular wave at the high state is determined by the value of the resistors R1 and R2 and the capacitor C1. The ratio of the duration of the high logic level to the duration of one full cycle, one high state plus one low state, is called the duty cycle. If the time of the high pulse is twice that of the low, the wave would have a 66 percent

Fig. 43-3. 4-bit data latch circuit

Fig. 43-4. Typical analog-to-digital converter (*BURR-BROWN Corporation*)

449

Fig. 43-5. ADC circuit using a 555 timer IC.

Fig. 43-6. Graph illustrating the 66 percent duty cycle of a 555 timer circuit

Fig. 43-7. Example of a digital-to-analog conversion (*BURR-BROWN Corporation*)

duty cycle, Fig. 43-6. As R1 is changed, the duty cycle of the wave is altered.

A computer program can be written so a determination of the level of the square wave can be made. For example, as long as the voltage pulse is low, no action occurs. When the logic level of the voltage pulse changes, an instruction in the computer program senses this change, and a "software" counter can begin increasing the count. The counter will continue the count until the logic level returns to zero, for example, at the end of the duty cycle. At this point, the computer has a digital value which represents the analog numeric value for the resistance.

DIGITAL TO ANALOG CONVERSION (DAC)

Sometimes it is necessary for the digital computer to generate an analog output in order to operate some device. The analog output is generally a varying voltage level. The voltage level is determined by a digital code sent by the computer to the DAC, which will vary between predetermined levels. Figure 43-7 is a typical DAC unit used to convert digital information into a continuous variable voltage output.

For both the ADC and the DAC accuracy of conversion from one format to another is called the resolution. Each digital value represents a point on an analog scale. For example, consider an analog scale from 0.0 V to 12 V. If 4 bits, or 1 nibble, are used for the data range, then the 12 V can be represented in 15 increments, as there are 16 combinations with 4 bits. In this case, each digital numeric value between 0000 and 1111 equals decimal 0.80 V (12 V/15). That is, 0000 = 0.0 V, 0001 = 0.80 V, 0010 = 1.6 V, and so forth, until 1111 = 12 V (Fig. 43-8). These increments of 0.80 V are quite large, but they are usable in some applications. Note that the change from 0.0 V to 12 V will not be a smooth transition but instead will be a staircase, stepped effect. However, by increasing to 8-bit resolution, the number of steps increases to 256, 00000000 to 11111111. This decreases the value of each step to 0.04706 V (12 V/255). If the computer is receiving data from a thermocouple that is measuring the temperature of a piece of experiment, this accuracy is necessary. When more accuracy is needed, 12- and 16-bit data can be utilized.

COMPUTER PROGRAMMING

A computer is operated through a set of instructions, or commands. The instructions, or commands, can be given in the *immediate mode* and in the *programmed mode*.

The immediate mode is often called the *calculator mode*. In this mode, the computer responds immediately, just like a hand-held electronic calculator, to instructions or commands. The following is an example of an instruction in the immediate mode:

PRINT "The cost of the transformer is 6 dollars."

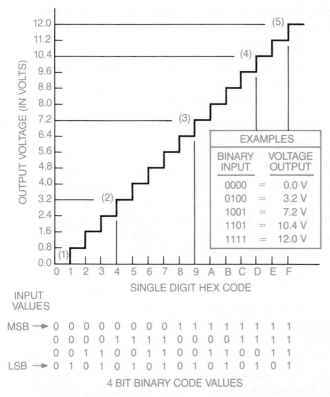

Fig. 43-8. An example of digital-to-analog converter voltage output (analog) for each possible input code (digital), using a 4-bit input

When the return key or enter key is pressed on the computer, it immediately responds by executing the instruction PRINT, and the following is printed on the CRT display screen:

The cost of the transformer is 6 dollars.

In the programmed mode, the execution of the computer program is deferred. The program that is written is stored in memory until it is executed with a command, for example, RUN. Line numbers make the programmed mode possible. A line number is a one-, two-, three-, four-, or five-digit number entered at the beginning of a program line. Some computer commands, however, do not use line numbers. The following is an example of instructions written in the programmed mode:

10 PRINT "The class designation letter for a capacitor is C."
20 PRINT "The class designation letter for an inductor is L."
30 PRINT "The class designation letter for a push button is S."
40 PRINT "The class designation for a transistor is Q."
50 END
RUN

After entering the command RUN (without a line number) and pressing

451

the return key, the computer will execute the program one line after the other and print it on the CRT display screen as follows:

The class designation letter for a capacitor is C.
The class designation letter for an inductor is L.
The class designation letter for a push button is S.
The class designation for a transistor is Q.

In order to get a computer to do a task, such as printing a statement, it must first be programmed. A *computer program* is a complete set of instructions arranged in logical order to do a task. Two types of programming languages are discussed in this text. The first type is called BASIC (*B*eginner's *a*ll-purpose *s*ymbolic *i*nstruction *c*ode). This is one of the most common languages used by programmers with microcomputers. The second language to be discussed is *assembly language*. This is the base language for the digital computer. Assembly language is used to do high-speed operations with the microcomputer.

BASIC

A computer language is actually a set of instruction codes or program statements in the form of words, abbreviations, and numeric characters. Figure 43-9 shows a program that will add two numbers. The numbers are entered from the keyboard by the input statements and then added together. The result is printed on the display screen, and the program is ended. Each instruction code causes the computer to perform a sequence of operations to complete the instruction. The number of operations a computer can perform is limited by the manufacturer's design. Some computers can execute 72 different operations (for example, PRINT, GOTO, +, and −). It is the programmer's job to determine which operation the computer is to perform and when to perform it. The set of instruction codes for each computer differs slightly, much as people of different parts of a country have different dialects of a common language. Figure 43-10 lists some BASIC instruction codes used to control devices external to the microcomputer. It will be helpful for you to have the programming manual for your computer.

INPUT and GET. Two BASIC instruction codes that will bring data into the computer are INPUT and GET. They are usually used to input data from the keyboard. However, by setting parameters with the instructions, other input ports can be accessed. These two instructions are fine if the ports are definable by number or a descriptive name. However, a more versatile instruction exists. If an instruction in the program states that $X = $ PEEK (16150), the variable X is assigned the data value that is contained at the indicated decimal address. Both the variable and the address can be changed to specify the desired locations.

PRINT. To output data, the PRINT statement can be used. The PRINT statement can include a designation for a particular output port, and the

```
10   INPUT"WHAT IS THE FIRST
     NUMBER TO BE ADDED?"; X
20   INPUT"WHAT IS THE SECOND
     NUMBER TO BE ADDED?"; Y
30   Z = X + Y: PRINT"THE SUM
     OF ";X;" + ";Y;" = ";Z
40   END
```

Fig. 43-9. A sample program in BASIC in which two numbers are added

452

INSTRUCTIONS	COMPUTER ACTION	INSTRUCTIONS	COMPUTER ACTION
HOME CLS CLEAR }*	Clears the monitor screen of all display and returns the cursor to the upper left corner of the screen.	POKE (address, variable)	Loads the indicated address with the data currently assigned to a variable or contained within the statement.
GOSUB (line number) GOTO (line number) CALL (variable) }*	The next instruction executed by the computer will be at the indicated line number or line number indicated by the variable value.	FOR NEXT	Used to repeat as routine within a program a specified number of times.
RETURN	Causes the computer to execute the instruction which follows the most recent CALL or GOSUB.	IF THEN	Conditionally causes action within a program; usually the condition will be the result of previous program action.
GET (variable) INPUT (variable) }*	Inputs data from the assigned device, usually a keyboard. The data value will be assigned to the indicated variable.	LET X = (value) X1 = (value) L$ = (value) }*	Assigns the value, numeric or string, to the indicated variable.
PR (designate drive) PRINT (variable) OUTPUT (variable) }*	Sends data to the device assigned by the variable in the statement.	REM	Allows the programmer to include information that will help describe what is going on in the program. The remarks, however, will not show up on the CRT display when the program is run. But, if a list is printed out of the program, the remarks will appear.
X = PEEK (address)	Assigns a copy of the data found at the indicated address, to a variable. Can be used to move data in memory or input data under memory mapped I/O.		

*Selected BASIC syntax examples from several popular microcomputers

Fig. 43-10. Some BASIC instruction codes used to control external devices

data will go to that port. Memory locations can be written to with the POKE (64325, 120) statement. The desired memory location is specified by the first number, called an *argument*. The value sent is set by the second number, called the *second argument*. The programming manual for your computer will specify the proper syntax needed for your computer. The term *syntax* refers to the arrangement of the words and abbreviations as well as the punctuation (that is, : and ;) in the instructional statements.

ASSEMBLY LANGUAGE

A second language exists that will allow the computer to speed up the sampling of data. BASIC is characteristically slow because each instruction must be decoded through interpretation by the computer before it can be executed. Assembly language, on the other hand, is very fast because it is in the form that is directly compatible to the microprocessor. Other terms that are applied to this language are machine language and assembler. Machine language is the system of binary codes that are sent to the microprocessor to execute a specific operation. These codes are very hard for humans to remember so, as you learned in Unit 42, the binary codes are changed to hex digits. Many computers have a program, usually called the *disassembler,* which will transform the binary codes into a more intelligible form of letters called *mnemonics* or *mne-*

monic codes. The word *mnemonic* means memory aid. Figure 43-11 shows a sample of a disassembled program from a common microcomputer. The mnemonic codes are abbreviations that tell what the hex operation codes mean.

ADDRESS HI LO	OPERATION CODE	MODIFIER	MNEMONIC	MODIFIER
$A000-	16	20	ASL	$20,X
$A002-	C9	FC	CMP	#$FC
$A004-	85	2E	STA	$2E
$A006-	20	FA FC	JSR	$FCFA
$A009-	A0	24	LDY	#$24
$A00B-	20	FD FC	JSR	$FCFD
$A00E-	B0	F9	BCS	$A009
$A010-	20	FD FC	JSR	$FCFD

Fig. 43-11. Disassembled assembly language program

STA. A good example of a mnemonic is STA, which is often used to take a data bit from one location called the accumulator to store it in another location, such as memory. The data can be set to operate a device connected to a latch. As you have learned, the latch can be identified by a memory location, and, therefore, the data in the accumulator will be stored in the latch. A device connected to the output side of the latch will be affected according to the data it receives.

JSR. Another typical instruction is JSR, which means to jump to a program subroutine, the address of which is defined by data in the next 2 bytes of memory. A *subroutine* is a programmed procedure that can be run by the computer but is not part of the main program. With the JSR, control of the microprocessor can be shifted around the program much as the GOSUB statement changes operation of a BASIC program.

Mathematical Operations. Data are changed by mathematical operations such as ADD and SUBtract and logic instructions such as AND, OR, exclusive-OR, and complement. These instructional codes can be used instead of hardware circuitry to perform logical operations. By combining several instructions, any logical operation can be performed. These operations are done 1 byte at a time (8-bit parallel operation), so a great deal of circuitry can be eliminated if these instructions can be used.

Time States. All instructions are executed in fixed numbers of time periods, called time states. Depending upon the instruction, this number will range from 2 to 15 time states. Each time state is a pulse from the clock, which typically lasts about 0.98 microseconds (μs). This is why assembly language is so fast. For example, a common personal computer can obtain data from a port, store it in a location, move to the next location, and return to get more data at the port in about 12 μs.

Using assembly language, many bytes of data can be gathered and stored for future use in a very short time. This is very helpful if the computer is collecting data from extremely fast equipment, such as charting the acceleration of a falling object as it passes sensors. Each type of microprocessor has a complete set of instructions that controls the operation of the computer. Each microprocessor is different, but there are many similarities between the various types. If you need to learn the assembly language for your computer, refer to the programming manual. It may look complicated at first, but once you experience using assembly language as a programming tool, you will be able to use your microcomputer in many innovative ways.

PULSE INPUT

Many computers have an input circuit that allows the use of a switch to input data. This input point is often called PB (push button) or fire button on game controllers. Figure 43-12 shows the pin location on some of these. This input pin can be used to read data from a variety of devices capable of generating a logical 1 or 0. This pin is assigned a memory location that will contain the current status of the switch, 1 or 0. All that is necessary is that the pulse generated by the input device be either +5 V or 0 Vdc when the program reads the memory location associated with that connection. By integrating software and hardware, useful tasks can be performed. A timer, for example, can be connected to allow external control of the program (Fig. 43-13). Sometimes it is necessary to stop or interrupt the sequence of the computer program. A pulse generated by this circuit will indicate to the program that an external device requires service of a predetermined nature. The pulse is read, and this makes the computer begin running a portion of the program that performs that service. For this circuit to work, the program must check the pulse indicator or memory address periodically.

Fig. 43-13. Timing pulse generator

Photo-operated devices that develop a 5 Vdc pulse can be used as a computer input. Figure 43-14 shows two typical circuits of this type. Photo transistors (Fig. 43-14A) or an infrared diode emitter-receiver pair (Fig. 43-14B), can be used to generate the required logic voltage pulse. Photo transistors are used to detect the presence or absence of

Fig. 43-12. Port pin assignments of some popular digital microcomputers

455

Fig. 43-14. Photo-operated devices: (A) photo transistor circuit (B) infrared diode-transmitter receiver circuit

light. The infrared diode pair circuit can be used to count the passage of items between the transmitter (emitter) and receiver.

Pull-up Resistor. As was previously discussed, the input to TTL devices must be within the proper voltage levels. To do this, a 1 kΩ resistor is connected as shown in Fig. 43-15. It is called a *pull-up resistor* because it makes sure that the voltage goes from 0 to +5 Vdc when needed. The value here is given at 1,000 Ω, but it can range from about 470 Ω to several thousand and still be effective. The resistor is connected to 5 Vdc on one end to provide the proper logic level. The other end is connected to the input of the IC and one side of the switch. The other side of the switch is connected to the common ground.

When the switch, SPST Push Button Normally Open (PBNO) Momentary contact, is in the normal "open" position, the input reads a logic 1. This is because the input has very high impedance, and very little current flows through the resistor. Therefore, there is almost no voltage drop across the resistor. For all practical purposes, the input appears to be connected directly to the +5 V and is held at logic 1.

An example of this is shown in Fig. 43-16A. Here we see a reset function on IC1, which requires a 0 logic to become active. In the normal position of S1, a logic 1 is applied to reset, and it will not cause the reset action to take place. When switch S1 is pressed and the contacts come together, Fig. 43-16B, current will flow through the resistor. Since it is the only resistive element in the circuit, all 5 V will be dropped across the 1 kΩ. The input is then brought to ground potential or a logic 0 (Fig. 43-16C). Without this circuit, the logic level cannot be predicted when the switch is open and therefore the data received would not be reliable.

The preceding discussion dealt with a normally open switch that changed the logic from 1 to 0 when it was closed. If the normally closed contacts of the PB switch are used in the circuit, the logic reverses from

Fig. 43-15. A pull-up resistor circuit to produce a logic 0 when pressed

0 to 1. For the circuit shown in Fig. 43-17, this is important. The SET connection on this IC requires a +5 Vdc pulse (logic 1) to function. When S1 is in the N.C. position, the SET pin is logic 0. Pressing S1 pulls the voltage to +5 Vdc (logic 1) and activates SET.

Debounce. In the previous discussion about a pull-up resistor and push button switch, the only pulse that was needed was the first one; therefore, no debounce circuitry was necessary. Since a switch is considered to be an input device for a computer, it can indicate if an event has taken place. Standard toggle, push button, snap action, or precision switches can be used for this purpose. The switch, however, must be connected between the PB terminal of an input port and ground. The computer program uses a read instruction at a memory location that is assigned to the switch. The data at this memory location will indicate the condition of the switch when it was read. A second method of determining the condition of a switch is through the use of 1-bit indicators called *flags*. Flags are either located in the CPU or in R/W memory. Each flag bit can be set, logic 1, or cleared, logic 0, by the action of a program or some external device such as a switch. Which method of switch reading is used is determined by the configuration of the computer.

When using a switch as a computer input device, you must give careful consideration to the action of the switch. If the switch is controlling a lamp, when the switch is closed, the lamp lights. However, when the switch closes, the contacts impact and bounce off each other for several tenths of a second. This bounce is no problem to a lamp, but a computer will have trouble. When that same switch is connected to a computer, the microprocessor can input data fast enough to read the bounce as a series of closures of the switch. Each closure of the switch, due to bounce, will be read as a voltage pulse. If a series of events are being counted, this would yield a false count.

Software Debounce. One way to get around this problem is to include a *software debounce routine* within the program. If the computer is only reading the input until data changes, then there will be no problem. Once it receives the first pulse, the program will go to another function after the switch closes the first time. It will not read the switch location again because it is performing another task. Therefore, it will not read the train of pulses produced by the switch while closing.

What happens, though, if the program is designed to count a number of quickly occurring events? To make the problem more difficult, assume that the events do not happen in any predictable pattern. That is, the span of time between pulses can be from a few milliseconds to several seconds in duration. The problem can be solved with the circuit found in Fig. 43-18. This is a hardware debounce solution. A single-pole–double-throw push button momentary contact switch is connected to the +5 Vdc source, through the pull-up resistors. The A input of each NAND gate is connected to one contact of S1. The B input of each

A

MOM = MOMENTARY

B

C

Fig. 43-16. Developing a logic 0 reset function with a pull-up resistor: (A) logic 1 at reset pin; (B) logic 0 at reset pin; (C) the closed push button switch effectively puts the reset pin to ground potential

457

NAND gate is cross-connected to the output of the opposite gate. The truth table in Fig. 43-19 shows that the output C will be logic 0 if logic 1 is on both inputs A and B. When the switch is in the normally open position (Fig. 43-18A), a logic 0 is applied to input A of NAND gate 1 and a 1 to input A of NAND gate 2. Referring again to the truth table (Fig. 43-19), a logic 0 on either input A or input B causes a 1 at the output. This logic 1 output is applied to input B of NAND gate 2. Since input A of NAND gate 2 has a 1 from the pull-up resistor, the output of NAND gate 2 is 0. This output is fed back to B of NAND 1. Even if the switch contacts bounce, the 0 on B of NAND 1 forces the output to stay as a 1.

When the switch is changed, as in Fig. 43-18B, the input logic changes. Input A of NAND gate 2 is changed to logic 0, which changes the output to logic 1. This logic 1 is applied to input B of NAND gate 1. Input A of NAND gate 1 has already been changed to logic 1 by the switch, and the output of NAND gate 1 becomes logic 0, which is applied to input B of NAND gate 2, thus forcing NAND gate 2 output to remain logic 1, without regard for the bounce of the switch.

IC1 = 7400 QUAD NAND GATE
S1 = SPDT TOGGLE SWITCH

Fig. 43-18. A debounce circuit for a manually operated switch

CONTROLLING PERIPHERALS

A common microcomputer has several ports available to the user. Each port requires edge connectors that match the number of pins and the particular spacing on the edge connector. Figure 43-20 illustrates a typical arrangement of these connections. Some microcomputers have a *general-purpose interface bus* (GPIB), also called the *expansion port*. There are other types of bus structures used in microcomputers. Some are very complicated. It is recommended that you refer to the user's manual to get specific information on the use of these busses.

User Port. The *user port* is a connector opening found in the rear of some popular computers. All active connections on this type of connector are on the top of the PC card and are numbered from left to right (looking at the back), 1 through 12 (Fig. 43-21). This access to the internal structure of the computer allows the use of the eight data lines (pins 3 through 10) for both input and output. This type of bus is called a *bidirectional data bus,* as the same lines are used in both input and output. There is one pin for signal ground (pin 1), which completes the circuit from the computer to the external device and back to the computer. As has been discussed previously, the computer must get a signal, or send a signal, to indicate when data are ready to be sent or when the computer is ready to receive data. The exchange of ready signals is called *handshaking.* The user port has two handshaking lines. Pin 2 on the connector is only an input handshake line to the computer that can receive a pulse from a device to acknowledge that data can be sent. Pin 11 is an input or output handshake line that can send or receive the needed control signals. Pin 12 is not used in this situation.

Data sent to an I/O port are in the form of TTL +5 Vdc and 0 Vdc signals. To get this data to the port, the necessary 1s and 0s are written to a memory location, memory mapped I/O. There are two locations with which you must be concerned. As previously mentioned, the port is bidirectional. This means that the input (I) or output (O) must be defined. This is done by a memory location called the *data direction register.* A decimal number, such as 59,459, is used to define this location. The individual bits of the 8-bit register are set to 1 or 0; 1 sets that line to output, and 0 sets a line to input. This allows individual lines of the port to be either input or output. Each line is independent of the others. As illustrated in Fig. 43-22, if the program instruction POKE 59459, $0F is executed, binary 00001111 will be stored there. This will set the lower nibble 1111 to output and the upper nibble 0000 to input. A POKE 59459, $FF configures an 8-bit output port 11111111, and $00 makes 59459 an 8-bit input port 00000000. On output, this location will expect a handshake signal. So handshaking must be provided. This can be accomplished by connecting pin 11 to ground, thus enabling it at all times, or by having the controlled device, the peripheral, send the logic 0. The same I/O port can receive data at a different location, for example 59471, without handshaking since it is not needed at this location. A set of relays being driven by data would not need handshaking. However, a printer that can accept only so much data before the printer *buffer memory* (memory built into the printer for the printer to store incoming data) is full and "overflows" needs handshaking to stop the data.

INPUT/OUTPUT PORTS

A common microcomputer has card slots on the main logic board. The PC card slots are used to plug in special-function circuits that enhance the operation of the computer. In addition, a single I/O port is provided, which is called the *game port.* The following discussion explains how data are moved from the internal circuitry to these I/O points.

Parallel PC Card. A parallel data I/O interface circuit card can be added to some expandable microcomputers. There are eight slots across

INPUTS		OUTPUTS
A	B	C
0	0	1
0	1	1
1	0	1
1	1	0

Fig. 43-19. NAND gate truth table

Fig. 43-20. Connector (port) locations on a single-board microcomputer

Fig. 43-21. A typical input/output pin assignment

459

Fig. 43-22. Half input, half output set of user port

REAR OF LOGIC BOARD

POWER SUPPLY

0 1 2 3 4 5 6 7

EXPANSION SLOTS

Fig. 43-23. Expansion slots location on several types of microcomputer

FEMALE CONNECTOR

PIN #   PIN #

1	IN 0		IN 4	14
2	GND		STROBE	15
3	IN 2		ACKN	16
4	GND		IN 1	17
5	OUT 0		IN 7	18
6	OUT 1		IN 5	19
7	NC		GND	20
8	OUT 2		IN 6	21
9	NC		OUT 3	22
10	NC		OUT 4	23
11	OUT 5		GND	24
12	OUT 6		IN 3	25
13	OUT 7			

IN = INPUT DATA PINS
OUT = OUTPUT DATA

Fig. 43-24. Pin location of a typical parallel interface connector

460

the back of the logic board on some common personal-use microcomputers. The slots are numbered 0 through 7, left to right, as in Fig. 43-23. Memory expansion is set for slot 0. The first two disk drives are connected to slot 6, and slot 1 is for a printer interface circuit card. These slots should be reserved for these purposes, as most software is written with this configuration. The parallel I/O card made for several compatible microcomputers can be placed in another available slot. On some models, the 0 slot is specifically assigned for an 80-column card and memory expansion. However, the other slots remain as in the earlier models.

A parallel I/O card is available from suppliers of computer hardware. The parallel card, when plugged into an available slot, provides an access to the bus structure of the computer. Eight data lines are provided for output, and eight more are provided for input. The selection and use of these data lines are controlled by the execution of instructions in the program to control the card circuitry. This circuitry is associated with specific memory locations into which the required data are stored. A pair of control lines are provided so that the computer and the peripheral device can communicate.

Strobe and ACK. The strobe-out signal (pin 15), a TTL voltage pulse, is provided so that the computer can indicate to the peripheral device that data are about to be sent. The peripheral device uses this pulse to get ready to receive data. ACKnowledge IN (pin 16) is used to indicate that the peripheral is ready to receive data and the computer may begin sending. The typical pin location of these and other connections is found in Fig. 43-24. The cable from this connector directly accesses the circuitry of the PC card in the slot.

Game Port. A *d*ual-*in*line *p*ackage (DIP), 16-pin socket is provided on the main board of some microcomputers. This allows connection to several 1-bit I/O ports, which will be described in detail. These ports are the strobe, *p*ush *b*utton (PB), *g*ame *c*ontroller (GC), and the *an*nunciator (AN). Figure 43-25A shows the location of this DIP socket on the logic board of one type of microcomputer. The assignment of each pin of the socket is illustrated in Fig. 43-25B. As one can see, +5 Vdc and ground are also provided here. These should be used to provide logic levels only. External circuitry should be powered by an appropriate power supply and not the computer supply. A 16-pin male connector pressed onto a 16-conductor ribbon cable, about 2 ft (60 mm) long is a good way to connect to this port.

Project 8 in Unit 50 shows a convenient way to terminate the ribbon cable and provide connections for experimentation. In addition to the 16-pin DIP socket, some models provide a 9-pin miniature D type female connector located in the rear cover panel. This device provides connections to the three push buttons, the four game controllers, +5 Vdc, and ground pins. Figure 43-26 shows the pin location of these connections. When soldering wires to the mating connector, the solder pins on the back of the connector must have the same configuration.

Strobe. Pin 5 on the DIP socket (Fig. 43-25) is assigned to a $\overline{\text{STROBE}}$ function. This is a TTL signal of short duration that can be used to enable circuits connected to the game port. Since the word *strobe* has a bar over it, the normal voltage to be expected is +5 Vdc, or logic 1. When data are sent from this pin, the logic changes to 0. This is accomplished by the X = PEEK (−16320) statement, which identifies a memory location −16320 or $C040. The negative sign in front of the decimal address means that the actual location relative to the highest possible address location is 65536 minus 16320, or 49216.

Since the duration of the strobe pulse is only 1 microsecond, this signal is used as an enable pulse. A problem exists when it is used as an enable pulse for an I/O device. The enable signal must be on the proper pin when the data arrive for input or output. Since the duration is only 1 microsecond by the time the program sequence moves, for example, from the peek $C040 to the next statement to POKE (annunciator), the $\overline{\text{STROBE}}$ signal will be gone and the external chip will not be enabled. Thus, it becomes necessary to stretch the enable pulse in some way. This can be done with the pulse stretcher circuit in Fig. 43-27.

Push Button (PB). Three 1-bit input ports, called PB0-PB2, are provided on the DIP socket (Fig. 43-25) to enable logical input for a program to sense some real-world event. As you have learned, a switch can change the logic level at a point in a circuit. Memory locations assigned to PB0-PB2 (pins 2, 3, and 4) are affected by this logic change, memory map I/O. The memory locations associated with these pins are $C061 PB0, $C062 PB1, and $C063 PB2. Each time a button is pressed, the memory location associated with it will change. If the program is written in such a way that it will read the data in the memory location, it can be directed to a section of the program through an IF THEN statement. The following program sample in BASIC reads a push button location and reacts to the logic level. The line numbers are used only as example, and this routine can be anywhere in the program.

```
450 X = PEEK $C062
460 IF X = 1 THEN 750
470 PRINT "BUTTON NOT PRESSED"
Program continues
```

The circuit shown in Fig. 43-28 need not be debounced externally because the hardware in the computer will do this. Bit 7 of the three locations associated with PB0-2 will be set to logic 1, when the appropriate push button input is closed. The instruction X = PEEK (−16287) will set the variable X to a value greater than 127 if the button is pressed. An IF THEN statement is used to test this value, and appropriate instructions are run if the condition is met.

Fig. 43-25. 16-pin DIP socket: (A) game port socket location; and (B) pin assignment

Fig. 43-26. Typical 9-pin D pin assignment

Fig. 43-27. Pulse stretcher circuit

+5 V DC

STROBE INPUT FROM GAME PORT SOCKET, PIN 5

2 8 4 3

STRETCHED STROBE OUTPUT

t_1 t_2

R1 1 MΩ   +5 V DC

IC1 555

7

6

TIME BETWEEN t_1 AND t_2 CAN BE CHANGED BY VARYING TIME CONSTANT BETWEEN R1 AND C1

C1 1.0 µF

C2 0.01 µF

1 5

GAME PORT CONNECTOR

NC	9	8	GND
GC1	10	7	GC2
GC3	11	6	GC0
AN3	12	5	STB
AN2	13	4	PB2
AN1	14	3	PB1
AN0	15	2	PB0
NC	16	1	+5 V DC

S1
PBN0

Fig. 43-28. Push button switch (S1) connected between PB0 and GND

Game Paddle. Four analog inputs are also provided on the game port. They are called *game paddles,* or *game controllers.* When a 100-KΩ potentiometer is connected between the +5 Vdc, pin 1, and game controller 1, pin 10, a number will be placed in memory location 49252. This number will be between 0 and 255 and will be proportional to the value of the resistance. The higher the resistance, the higher the count. The BASIC statements X = PDL (0) and PRINT X will return the value first to the variable X and second to the computer screen. The other locations associated with PDL are PDL 1 49253, PDL 2 49254, and PDL 3 49255. The instruction POKE 49264, 0 will reset all PDL values to 0. This will get the PDL memory locations ready for the next use. An example routine is as follows:

1010 X = PDL (0)
1020 PRINT X
1030 POKE 49264, 0

The paddle resistance is connected to one of the game controller (GC) pins (6, 7, 10, or 11) and the +5 Vdc pin (1). This places the resistance into an RC time constant circuit that generates a rectangular pulse wave. An internal counter is controlled by these pulses. The counter adds 1 to the then-current number until the duty cycle has ended and the rectangular pulse wave returns to 0 Vdc. The value of the count is then stored in memory by the circuitry for future reference.

Annunciator. Many personal computers have 1-bit output ports that can produce a 5 Vdc pulse. They are labeled AN0-AN3. Two memory locations are associated with each of the annunciators, one to set the output to +5 Vdc and one to set it to 0 Vdc. Figure 43-29 shows the locations of memory used for each of these functions.

Once an annunciator has been turned on, it will stay at this logic level until the program turns it off. This enables the computer to turn on a device and operate it for a period of time. The program can go on to

Annunciator	Memory Location	
	On	Off
AN0	−16295 $C059	−16296 $C058
AN1	−16293 $C05B	−16294 $C05A
AN2	−16291 $C05D	−16292 $C05C
AN3	−16289 $C05F	−16290 $C05E

NOTE: NEGATIVE NUMBERS INDICATE A LOCATION RELATIVE TO THE HIGHEST ADDRESS (65536)

Fig. 43-29. Typical microcomputer memory location assignments for controlling output with soft switches other tasks and return at a future time to end the operation. No external latch circuit is needed.

Using the digital computer to control devices can be very interesting and can open a new world of computing. Manufacturing processes, for many years, have been labor intensive and often very hazardous to humans. The computer is replacing human labor with sophisticated machines that free workers from repetitive and dangerous jobs. The worker of the future will need to know how to work with computers and how to use them effectively.

LEARNING BY DOING

14. Surface Roughness Gauge. Often data must be converted from an analog to a digital format in order for the digital computer to handle it. This activity illustrates one method of doing this data acquisition and the use of those data to rank a value on an appropriate linear scale (Fig. 43-30). The crystal phonograph stylus will produce a voltage when it is moved over a rough surface. The op-amp increases the signal strength and feeds it to the diode for rectification. This half-wave signal is fed to the always active AND gate. The AND gate will have an output pulse when the input level exceeds about 3 Vdc. Lesser voltages will be rejected. The output pulse will be sent to a PB connection of a computer. Each pulse will affect the memory location associated with the PB connection. This is done through the interaction of the hardware and the software, as was discussed in this unit.

MATERIALS NEEDED

Y1 crystal conical stylus, 1.5–2.5 g tracking or equivalent
R1 25 kΩ linear taper potentiometer, 5 W
IC1 741 operational amplifier
D1 germanium diode, 1N34A or equivalent
IC2 74LS08 quad 2 input AND gate

Fig. 43-30. Schematic diagram for constructing the surface roughness gauge in Learning by Doing No. 14, "Surface Roughness Gauge."

BT1 9-V battery
1 two-conductor 9-V battery clip connector
BT2 5-V power supply
1 prototype IC plug board for assembling the circuit hookup
wire as needed

Procedure

1. Construct the circuit as shown in Fig. 43-30 and connect the output
   of the two-input AND gate to a 1-bit PB input port of a computer.
2. Move the crystal stylus over a moderately rough surface (such as a
   piece of wood) and observe the output of the AND gate with an
   oscilloscope.
3. Adjust the potentiometer, R1, to obtain enough gain from the op
   amp so that a rectangular wave is present at the output of the AND
   gate.
4. Test some other surfaces to establish a comparison scale.
5. Experiment with a computer program in order to collect and tabu-
   late data on various types of surfaces.

15. Reaction Timer. This circuit is a simple electronic game (Fig. 43-
31). When the program is run and after a short delay, the computer will
turn the LED, D1, on. When the LED lights up, the push button S1
(PBNO) is pressed. A numerical value will appear on the CRT display
screen, which corresponds to the time it takes to press the button. The
object of the game is to get this number as low as possible.

In this activity, you will learn how to connect an interface circuit,
which has a flip-flop and a bilateral switch, to a microcomputer game
port. When this is done, you will experiment in writing a computer
program to operate the electronic game.

MATERIALS NEEDED

IC1 DUAL JK flip-flop, 74LS73
IC2 QUAD bilateral switch, 4066
2 14-pin DIP sockets
D1 light-emitting diode (LED), maximum forward current
   50 mA or higher
R1, R2 1,000 Ω resistors, ¼ watt, 5 percent
S1 PBNO momentary contact switch
prototyping IC plug board
No. 22 solid hookup wire, cut to length as needed
5 Vdc power supply, 150 mA minimum output (NOTE: Do
   not use the power supply from the microcomputer)
game port socket (16 pin) located on microcomputer, or
   equivalent input/output connector

464

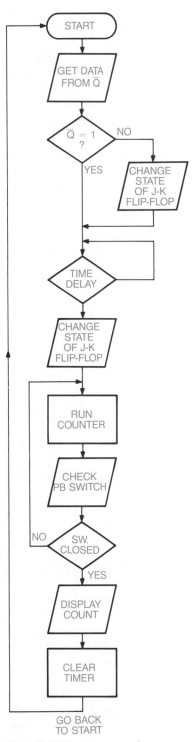

Fig. 43-31. Schematic diagram for constructing the reaction timer in Learning by Doing No. 15: (A) interface circuit; (B) timing switch; (C) game port pin connections used

Procedure

1. Construct the interface and timer circuit on the prototype board as shown on Fig. 43-31. NOTE: Be sure to provide a common ground.

2. Connect pin 5 of the flip-flop to a digital computer (Fig. 43-31A). NOTE: On some computers, pin 5 of the flip-flop can be connected to an annunciator (ANO), pin 15, of the game port socket (Fig. 43-31C).

3. Connect the push button PBNO (S1) timing switch to the bilateral switch control (pin 13) on IC2, 4066. The corresponding switch, pin 1, is connected to a push button (PBO), pin 2, of a game port socket (Fig. 43-31C).

4. Connect pin 8 of the JK flip-flop $\bar{Q}$ to a second bilateral switch control (pin 5) on IC2, 4066, and the corresponding switch on IC2, 4066, (pin 3) to PBI (pin 3) on the game port socket. This will enable the computer to determine the level of $\bar{Q}$ when the program starts.

5. Use the flowchart in Fig. 43-32 to guide you in writing, on a separate sheet of paper, the computer program to operate the Reaction Timer.

Fig. 43-32. Suggested program flowchart for reaction timer in Learning by Doing No. 15

Test your knowledge by writing, on a separate sheet of paper, the word or words that most correctly complete the following statements:

1. Two general types of computer memory are _____ and _____.
2. Connecting a computer to a device to be controlled is called _____.
3. The term used to describe the number of TTL devices that can be driven by a single TTL device is called _____.
4. A relay can be controlled by a computer by using a _____ driver circuit.
5. Measuring incremental values of 10 voltage settings of a potentiometer with an ADC yields _____ data.
6. If a computer is to control the speed of a motor by varying the voltage applied to that motor, the _____ data of the computer must be converted to _____ voltage values.
7. The set of instructions that operate a digital computer is called the _____.
8. The language called _____ is made up of a set of words, letters, and abbreviations.
9. The instruction _____ will send data to a designated location.
10. The input logic level of a switch can be ensured if a _____ resistor is used.
11. If a normally open push button switch is connected to a 1-bit input port and ground, the logic level when pressed will be _____.
12. The output of a NAND gate will be _____ when both inputs are 1.
13. A switch must be _____ because the contacts bounce when the switch is closed.
14. The connection called _____ _____ is used to complete the circuit for data lines that go to a peripheral device.
15. The computer and peripheral devices communicate through _____ lines to indicate when data are ready and can be received.
16. Some computers can use the same bus for both input and output because the _____ _____ register can be set to define the function of the lines.
17. When data are sent on multiple lines at the same time, it is said to be in _____ format.
18. When data are sent as a string of bits, it is in the _____ format.
19. A logic 1 is represented by a _____ TTL pulse.
20. A pulse train that is high for the same period of time that it is low has a 50 percent _____ _____.

FOR REVIEW AND DISCUSSION

1. What is dedicated control computing?
2. How does a computer use an interface circuit?
3. Why is an analog-to-digital circuit sometimes needed to enter data into a computer?
4. Why is it necessary to program a computer in order to use it?
5. Name three single component devices that can be used to input data into a computer.
6. Name three single-component devices that can take data from the computer and perform a function.
7. Why is a debounce circuit used with a switch?
8. What is meant by the term *bidirectional data bus*?
9. Define the term *parallel data*.
10. Define the term *serial data*.
11. Why is a pull-up resistor used with a switch to input data?
12. What is the difference between RAM and ROM?
13. What is meant by the term *resolution* when discussing digital-to-analog converters?
14. Describe what is needed to operate a 12-Vdc motor using a digital computer that sources 5-Vdc pulses at low current levels.

1. Explain the advantages of dedicated control computing for automation.
2. Prepare a written description of what would be needed to have a digital computer ring a three-chime door bell to play an eight-note sequence of tones used to indicate someone is at your door. Discuss this with your class.
3. Prepare a written or an oral report on how the digital computer has affected tools used in the home and workplace.

4. Compare the features of BASIC and ASSEMBLY LANGUAGE programming and what must be considered when deciding which language to use in an application. Present your findings to the class in an oral report.
5. Using the employment section of a major local newspaper, investigate the types of employment available that relate to computer use and operation.

ELECTRICITY AND INDUSTRY

UNIT 44   The Electric Power Industry

Fig. 44-1. Principle of a turbine. Air pressure forces the vanes (blades) of the pinwheel (rotor) to rotate.

The first electric power plant was built in New York City in 1882 under the direction of Thomas Alva Edison. Early electric power plants were small and generated direct current. One of the main reasons that small local plants were used then was that a direct-current output could not be transmitted economically over long distances. When direct current is so transmitted, much energy is lost in the conductors in the form of heat. The use of alternating current, which does not have such a large power loss, made large central power plants economical. Today huge electric power plants have almost completely replaced smaller plants.

Modern power plants are of three main kinds: (1) hydroelectric plants, (2) fossil fuel plants, and (3) nuclear plants. All power plants use large alternating-voltage generators, or alternators, to produce electric energy. This energy is delivered to users by transmission networks. The generators are usually driven by turbines, often called *prime movers*. These turbines are turned by the energy of moving water (in the case of hydroelectric plants) or by steam pressure (in the case of fossil fuel and nuclear plants). The basic principle of a simple turbine is shown in Fig. 44-1. Smaller generators are usually driven by gasoline or diesel engines.

Fig. 44-2. A vertical hydroelectric generator

HYDROELECTRIC POWER PLANTS

In a hydroelectric power plant, water from a river, a lake, or a reservoir created by a dam is directed against the blades of a turbine by gravity. The water pressure causes the shaft of the turbine to rotate. This shaft turns the rotor of a generator (Fig. 44-2).

A number of hydroelectric power plants in the United States are operated by the federal government. The dams built in connection with these plants are also important in flood control and navigation (Fig. 44-3).

Fig. 44-3. Aerial view of Shasta Dam and Shasta Lake—a large hydroelectric power plant near Redding, California (*U.S. Bureau of Reclamation*)

COAL PILE

Fig. 44-4. A large steam-electric plant

FOSSIL FUEL POWER PLANTS

Fossil fuel plants were the earliest kind of power plant and are still the most common. In these plants, water is heated in a boiler to create steam (Fig. 44-4). The fuel used to heat the water is coal, oil, or natural gas (called *fossil fuels*). In some electric plants, the steam is heated to 1,000°F (538°C) and is under a pressure of 3,600 pounds per square inch [24 800 kilopascals (kPa)]. This steam is directed at the turbine rotor (Fig. 44-5). The force of the steam jet is converted into rotary motion by a series of blades or buckets on the turbine rotor. After the energy of the steam is used up in the turbine, the steam is condensed into water and recycled to the boiler. This process is continuous. The

Fig. 44-5. A large steam turbine-generator unit. The turbine blades are mounted on the high-pressure (HP) rotor and the low-pressure (LP) rotor. (*General Electric* Co.)

TURBINE BLADES   STEAM TURBINE   GENERATOR UNIT

CONTROL MECHANISM
STEAM INLET (UPPER)
ADMISSION VALVES
STEAM INLET (LOWER)

L.P. DOUBLE-FLOW ROTOR
BEARING
NOZZLE DIAPHRAGM
H.P. ROTOR

EXCITER
HYDROGEN COOLER
WINDINGS
LAMINATED CORE
FIELD

generator turns at a constant speed even though the load requirements on the generator change. As more electric energy is needed, more fuel is burned. More steam is thus made available to be converted into mechanical energy and then into electric energy. This process is an *energy-conversion system*. Some high-efficiency steam-electric plants use as little as ¾ pound (0.34 kg) of coal to generate 1 kWh of electric energy. The efficiency of steam plants has been increased significantly by a system called *cogeneration*. In such a system the unused steam and hot water discharged by the turbine are used for air conditioning and heating, cooking, and other commercial and industrial applications before being recycled to the boiler.

NUCLEAR PLANTS

In a nuclear power plant, the fuel used is uranium. An atomic particle, the neutron, strikes the nucleus of a uranium atom and splits it about in half. This process is known as *atomic fission*. Fission causes the release of a large amount of energy and more neutrons. These neutrons split more uranium, and more energy and neutrons are released, and so on. The result is a *nuclear chain reaction*. In an atomic bomb, this chain reaction releases tremendous amounts of heat energy almost instantly. However, it can be controlled so as to release energy slowly.

In a nuclear power plant, a controlled amount of heat is produced by nuclear chain reactions in what is called a *reactor*. This heat boils water, and the steam produced is used to operate turbines. These turbines are similar to those in a steam-electric power plant.

The main elements of a modern nuclear power plant are shown in Fig. 44-6. Note that in this kind of atomic electric plant, the water is cycled directly from the main circulating pump to the reactor vessel. The reactor is inside the reactor vessel. The water surrounding the reactor is heated to about 600°F (316°C) and is changed into steam at a pressure of 1,000 pounds per square inch (6900 kP). The water used is

Fig. 44-6. The main elements of a nuclear electric plant. This is a direct-cycle, boiling-water plant.

demineralized. It thus helps slow down the neutrons, making them hit large numbers of atoms. A recirculating pump also helps regulate the fission. It does this by reducing the number of bubbles occurring in the water as the steam is produced. The fewer the bubbles, the greater the rate of the atomic reaction.

Reactor and Reactor Vessel. The reactor vessel in some plants is 65 ft (20 m) long and weighs nearly 700 tons (635 metric tons). It is supported in an upright position and is partly filled with water. The reactor contains the uranium fuel rods. The fuel rods throw off neutrons. During this process, some of the atoms split up, giving off heat energy.

Other rods of neutron-absorbing material are used to control the rate of the chain reaction in the reactor. The control rods are placed between the fuel rods. By moving the control rods in and out of the reactor, the amount of heat can be regulated. By controlling the heat from 115 tons (104 metric tons) of uranium in the core of the reactor, a plant can produce electric power equal to that obtained from 6 million tons (5.4 million metric tons) of coal.

Steam Generator. The steam generated at the top of the reactor vessel is directed through pipes at the turbine blades, making the blades spin. The turbine shaft turns the generator. In some modern plants, the generators convert over 800,000 hp (597,000 kW) into electricity. When the electricity is produced, it is transformed and distributed over regular transmission lines.

Steam Condenser. After the steam is used in the turbine, it is condensed to water in a *steam condenser*. There, large amounts of cold water are used to speed the condensation of the steam to water. The water is then recycled through the system by the main circulating pumps. Since this plant converts into steam the water that surrounds the reactor, it is called a *direct-cycle boiling-water plant*. Because of the large amounts of cold water needed by the condenser, plants that use steam turbines are usually found near large rivers or lakes. Some condensers use 250,000 gallons of water per minute (15.8 cubic meters per second) to condense the steam from the turbines.

Safety. Many safeguards are used in nuclear power plants. For example, in Fig. 44-6, a dry well surrounds the entire reactor vessel. Should a break occur in the reactor vessel, the steam and water would rush out into the dry well. The steam and water would then go through the vent pipes into the *torus,* the doughnut-shaped base of the reactor vessel, and the downcomer pipes. These pipes are placed around the torus with their openings under water. The water helps condense the steam, thus reducing the pressure. The large suppressor ring that surrounds the dry well has a chamber that acts as a cushion for any quick change in pressure. This protects the entire system from damage. If water is removed from the reactor vessel, the reactor will automatically shut down.

One of the major advantages of nuclear power plants is that they are operated with nuclear energy. This is available in practically unlimited quantities. The utilization of this energy, together with a wise use of coal, oil, and natural gas, can help meet energy needs in the future. However, safety factors are very important in the use of nuclear energy.

Nuclear power plants are massive and complex structures. They are designed to withstand earthquakes and tornados. They have many special safety devices and systems that help protect the plant, the plant personnel, and the public in the event of serious accident. However, in spite of these precautions, an accident did occur on March 28, 1979, at the Three Mile Island nuclear power plant. This plant is located near Middletown, Pennsylvania, on the Susquehanna River. The accident raised questions in the minds of many people about the use of nuclear energy to generate electricity.

It is important, therefore, that all citizens be fully informed about nuclear power plants. Learn about their safety devices. Discuss the methods used to treat and dispose of the wastes from nuclear plants. Find out what programs are used to train the people who operate the plants. Only when you know and understand the facts and risks involved can you help make intelligent decisions about the future of nuclear power. Nuclear power plants in the United States are operated under the general direction of the *Nuclear Regulatory Commission (NRC)*.

TRANSMISSION SYSTEM

To carry electric energy from power plants to the places where it will be used takes large transmission and distribution systems (Fig. 44-7). The main parts of these systems are discussed below.

Fig. 44-7. How electric energy is produced and delivered

Transmission Lines. Electric energy is transmitted from power plants by overhead wires supported by high towers. The center strands of these wires are made of steel to give them strength. The outer strands are made of aluminum because of its lightness and ability to carry current. The wires are insulated from the towers by porcelain insulators to prevent the loss of electric energy. Figure 44-8 shows line workers stringing wires for a high-voltage (250,000-V) transmission line. In some cases, especially in cities, wires run underground in ducts.

Through extensive laboratory and in-use testing, an underground transmission cable shown in Fig. 44-9 has proven successful. The double-tipped arrow in Fig. 44-9A shows a lead-foil–plastic-laminate insulating layer of the underground 35-kV cable against an actual cutaway. This type of design prevents water from leaking into the cable. This leakage problem is known as ''watertreeing,'' and such leakage can eventually render a power cable inoperative.

Transformers. In an alternating-current system, energy loss is reduced. This is so because the transformer makes it possible to raise the ac voltage to very high values. Some transmission systems are using 750,000 V. A higher voltage allows the same level of electric energy to be made available at a lower current. This results in lower energy loss, smaller transmission cables, and higher efficiency. Transformers make it possible to transmit electric energy economically over distances of 200 to 300 miles (322 to 483 km). In addition to stepping up, or raising, the voltage for long-distance transmission, transformers step down, or lower, the voltage to the requirements of the load.

Figure 44-10 shows two transformers connected in parallel being fed by isolated *buses,* or bars of copper, directly from a three-phase alternator. Each of the three phases of the alternator is isolated from the other. Each bus is separated by insulators in the center of a pipelike protector. The internal wiring connections are shown in Fig. 44-11. The high-voltage three-phase leads can be seen at the top of Fig. 44-10. These leads go directly to a substation.

Fig. 44-8. High-voltage transmission tower: (a) high-voltage insulators; (b) conductors

Fig. 44-9. Underground electric transmission cable: (A) cutaway view; (B) cross-sectional view of the core

A

INSULATION SHIELD
FILLED STRAND
INSULATION
COPPER NEUTRALS
CONDUCTOR

STRAND SHIELD
SEMICONDUCTING
FIBER TAPE
SEMICONDUCTING
POLY-LEAD
LAMINATED TAPE
JACKET
INSULATING OR
SEMICONDUCTING

B

Fig. 44-10. Two transformers connected in parallel (*Potomac Electric Power Co.*)

Fig. 44-11. Internal wiring connections from a three-phase generator to a three-phase transformer and transmission lines

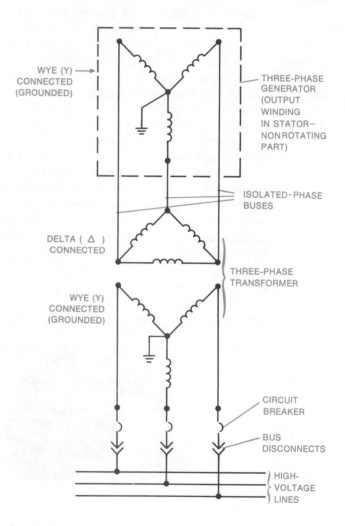

474

Substation and Distribution Networks. Figure 44-12 shows a *substation,* or distribution center. Substations step down the voltage for industrial and home use. They distribute electric energy conveniently to various loads. They make it easy to isolate any trouble in the distribution system.

Circuit Breakers. A *circuit breaker* is an automatic electric switch. It opens by itself whenever an overload causes excessive current. This protects the transmission lines and other parts of the circuit. Because of the high currents and voltages involved (as high as 34.5 kV and 1,200 A), the circuit breakers are placed in oil. Special devices are used to minimize the arc formed when the breakers open under load. Smaller circuit breakers operate in air. They are called *air circuit breakers.* Figure 44-13 shows two circuit breakers installed in a substation. Above the circuit breakers is a disconnect switch. Maintenance personnel can open this switch from the ground and thereby completely disconnect the load from the source. This allows work to be done on the system safely.

Fig. 44-12. Substation (*General Electric Co.*)

Fig. 44-13. Close-up view of substation switchgear

ORGANIZATION

An electric power company has many departments and working groups. These provide efficient service, maintain facilities, and plan the improvements and expansions needed to satisfy the demand for electric energy.

SELF-TEST

Test your knowledge by writing, on a separate sheet of paper, the word or words that most correctly complete the following statements:

1. The first electric power plant was built in the year _____.

2. The three main kinds of electric power plants are _____, _____, and _____.

3. The rods that regulate the chain reaction in a nuclear plant are called _____ rods.

4. Voltages as high as _____ V have been used in transmission systems.

5. At an electric power plant, the _____ from a three-phase alternator is connected directly to the three-phase step-up transformer.

6. _____ step-down the voltage for industrial and home use.

7. A _____ switch makes it possible for workers to safely perform their duties in a substation.

FOR REVIEW AND DISCUSSION

1. Explain why the dc power plants were generally small and provided only local electric service.

2. Explain why turbines are called prime movers.

3. What is an energy-conversion system?

4. Describe the main elements of a nuclear power plant.
5. List the main parts of a transmission and distribution system for electric energy.
6. What are three main functions of an electric substation?

INDIVIDUAL-STUDY ACTIVITIES

1. Visit a power plant in your geographic area and report to the class on your observations.
2. Investigate and report to your class on the power transmission system used to provide electric power to your home. Locate and describe, for example, the power plant and the various transformers, transmission lines, and substations that serve your home.

UNIT 45   Research and Development in Electronics

The term *research* means a thorough study or investigation of some topic or topics. In industry, one main purpose of research is the improvement of existing products and processes. The other is the *development* of new ones that are useful. New products and processes are most often made possible because of discoveries made by experimentation during research. Thus, research and development, or R&D, are closely related.

In the field of electronics, many areas are constantly being researched in an effort to improve and expand technology. These include studies of molecular electronics, solid-state physics, bio (life) functions, space exploration, data processing, and magnetics.

RESEARCH AND ENGINEERING

Research and engineering personnel work closely together. The engineers develop the ideas provided by research scientists into usable products and systems. An example of a product system that is the result of close cooperation among scientists, engineers, and technicians is shown in Fig. 45-1.

Research scientists and engineers are also responsible for tests and evaluations done on each piece of equipment or material developed. Environmental, electrical, mechanical, and physical-chemical tests are made. These provide data on the quality, performance, and dependability of a product.

Fig. 45-1. As a result of space suit research, the exoskeletal arm, as it is called, uses a complex system of electronic devices to duplicate the movement of a human operator's arm. (*National Aeronautics and Space Administration*)

DEVELOPING A NEW PRODUCT

The multilayer circuit board shows how the research and development process results in a specific product. This circuit board is made by compressing interconnected printed-circuit boards together so that they take up as little space as possible (Fig. 45-2).

Fig. 45-2. Lay-up of a multilayer, etched, printed-circuit board prior to bonding (*Melpar*)

There are several steps in producing a new and complex product of high quality. First, the materials and processes that will be involved must be determined. Second, their *parameters,* or ranges of limits and capabilities, and characteristics must be defined and measured. These steps provide information about the effects of the environment on the material. This information relates to temperature, shock, vibration, humidity, fastening methods, warp and twist, and so on. The third step is the setting up of effective and economical control procedures. The knowledge about the product gained through these steps is used to modify materials and processes as needed. The flow diagram in Fig. 45-3 shows the processes in the development of a new material or product and their interrelationships.

Fig. 45-3. Flow diagram of the various processes and their interrelationships in the development of a new material for the electronic industries (*Melpar*)

ENGINEERING SERVICES AND MANUFACTURING

The main function of a research and development company is to design and develop new products and/or materials. However, such a company needs a *manufacturing division* to support its other activities. The manufacturing division develops experimental models, prototype equipment, and fabrication and assembly procedures.

Engineering services are directed largely to marketing and sales. Engineering field services are provided in places where many of a company's products are being used. Engineering services include providing test equipment, determining spare parts availability, and training customer personnel.

DEVELOPING AN ELECTRONIC DEVICE

Figure 45-4 shows six main steps in developing an idea into a practical electronic device. An idea conceived in the mind of someone is the first step. Ideas for developing new products or materials come from two

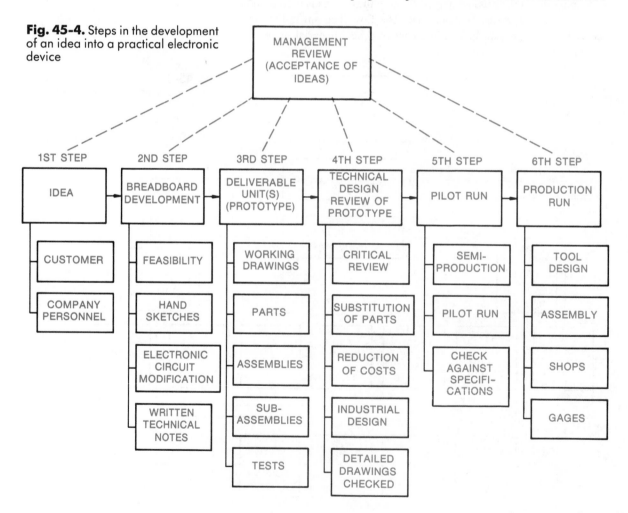

Fig. 45-4. Steps in the development of an idea into a practical electronic device

main sources: (1) from within the company, its scientists, engineers, management personnel, and others, and (2) from a customer who has a need. A customer may have a problem and ask for help to solve it. This idea or need is usually expressed in a written report or proposal. This gives specifications of the new product or material and an estimate of the time needed to produce it. The research and development company and the customer come to an agreement about the factors and costs involved. Then the work begins.

Exploring Ideas. Research and development generally involves solving new problems. Thus, much exploratory work is done first. This exploratory work is the second step in the research and development process. Its main purpose is to find out if an idea is practical. Computer-aided design (CAD) and computer-aided manufacturing (CAM) are very common today. Figure 45-5 shows an engineer exploring the practicality of ideas through the use of a computer. In industry, CAD/CAM reduce time and effort expended during the exploratory process of developing a new product. In the electronic industry, the exploratory process is called *breadboard development.* This is a design and development process in which scientists and engineers test theories. They want to find out whether their ideas work electronically. Rough pencil sketches are used to record ideas about new circuits. Technical notes are written down to record the results. It may take 6 to 8 months before a satisfactory circuit is found and accepted. At this point, a customer may want to order two or three deliverable *prototypes,* or units.

Fig. 45-5. Exploring the practicality of ideas using a computer (*Ball Corporation*)

Deliverable Prototypes. The engineering development process of making a deliverable prototype is the third step. The deliverable prototype is developed from the ideas found to be practical during the breadboard development. During this step, working drawings of the parts are made. These include the specifications and the designs for supporting parts, assemblies, and subassemblies. Tests are done during the development of a deliverable prototype to make sure that it continues to work and to improve the way it works.

Reviews. The fourth step in developing an electronic device from an idea is the *technical design review.* This involves taking a critical look at the whole process up to this point. Representatives from various divisions—such as manufacturing, engineering, purchasing, quality control and reliability, technical writing, and others—ask questions about the units already developed. This review is often called *value engineering.* This is a team approach to solving technological problems. Value engineering involves attempts to eliminate unneeded parts and to substitute new, lower-cost materials where possible. At this point, detailed drawings are reviewed. Any remaining mechanical and electrical design problems are solved.

479

Pilot Run. The fifth step is the *pilot run*. The pilot run is done to check a small number of the devices against the original specifications. The pilot run also provides a means of checking all tools and fixtures to be used in the manufacturing process. During the pilot run, the *process sheets* are brought up to date. These explain in detail the operations that must be performed to complete the work. They include details on the time of manufacture, number of parts, sequence of operations, and assembly operations. When all parts of this step have been completed, the device is released to production.

Production. Producing the device in the quantities needed is the sixth and last step in the development process. Manufacturing activities may include sheet-metal work, machining, welding, brazing, painting, and finishing. The model and tool shop has facilities for making models and building breadboards and experimental equipment. Wiring and assembly shops do wiring for all kinds of electronic equipment, including printed circuits and modular and chassis units. Some precise work is done in *clean rooms*. These have a controlled environment in which dust and other foreign particles are kept to a minimum and a constant temperature is maintained. The manufacturing division also controls the scheduling of all shop activities and shipping.

SELF-TEST

Test your knowledge by writing, on a separate sheet of paper, the word or words that most correctly complete the following statements:

1. Research is closely related to _____ .
2. A range of limits and capabilities is a _____ .
3. Development ideas come from company personnel and from _____ .
4. In the electronics industry, the exploratory process is called _____ .
5. The first deliverable units are called _____ .
6. Another term for technical design review is _____ .
7. A _____ explains in detail the operations in making a product.
8. A manufacturing site with a controlled environment is called a _____ .

FOR REVIEW AND DISCUSSION

1. Explain the relationship between research and development.
2. Name three steps in producing a new product.
3. List the steps in developing an electronic device.
4. What are the main sources of new ideas?

INDIVIDUAL-STUDY ACTIVITIES

1. Select a common household electronic device and try to trace its development to the present time.
2. Present an idea to your class for developing or modifying an electronic device to meet your needs. Your class or some interested student may want to follow the six steps suggested in the unit to develop your idea into a practical product.
3. Investigate three or more high-tech companies and report to the class how they use CAD and CAM in their work.

UNIT 46   Product Manufacturing

The manufacturing of electronic products is one of the major industries in the United States. In contrast to electronic research and development, electronic product manufacturing is done mostly by mass production (Fig. 46-1).

An electronic manufacturing company is often independently owned, with its own stockholders. It may also be an electronic division of a larger parent company. Electronic companies often have several divisions, such as chemical, laboratory, services, and engineering divisions. Each division has its own organization and functions. Cooperation between the divisions is directed by division managers and their assistants.

Fig. 46-1. Testing lamp motor blowers in a manufacturing plant (*Ametek, Inc.*)

DEVELOPING THE PRODUCT

The six basic steps in developing an idea into a practical electronic device are almost the same in product manufacturing as in research and development. However, in product manufacturing, the sales department is often the first to be aware of the need for manufacturing a particular product or device. This information is vital feedback data from which management makes decisions on a particular line of products to be manufactured.

Product manufacturing generally follows these seven basic steps: (1) developing finished drawings, (2) ordering raw materials and parts, (3) planning and controlling the manufacturing process, (4) fabricating the parts, (5) assembling the parts, (6) testing the parts (assemblies or sub-assemblies) against specifications, and (7) inspecting and shipping the final product.

Two important forms have been developed to control product manufacturing. These are the manufacturing process sheets and the manufacturing process specifications.

Manufacturing Process Sheets. Figure 46-2 shows a manufacturing process sheet. Note that the sheet has much information about the part, such as name, number, standard time of manufacture, and routing.

The *standard time* is the actual time it takes to do an operation. The times for operations are estimated before any parts are manufactured. Later these estimates are checked against the pilot run and corrected as necessary.

Manufacturing Process Specifications. These specifications describe briefly the steps to be followed during the manufacture of certain assem-

Fig. 46-2. A manufacturing process sheet

blies (Fig. 46-3). They tell the workers exactly what equipment is used, the specific operations in the process, and the maintenance needed to ensure quality. Manufacturing process specifications are kept up to date as changes and improvements are made.

QUALITY CONTROL

The purpose of *quality control* is to make sure that manufactured products meet specifications. Carrying out the sequence of operations listed on the manufacturing process and specifications sheet is a major factor in quality control. This ensures that each part will be treated in the same way. The inspection department is important in quality control. It is responsible for checking tolerances, specifications, and the like on parts as they move through the plant. The final inspection often includes touch-up and testing. Quality control is considered to be the responsibility of all persons in the company rather than of one person or department. Whatever the job, it should be done well. This is the foundation of any effective quality-control program.

COMPONENT MANUFACTURING

The component manufacturer plays a key role in the electronics industry. These companies employ anywhere from twenty to several thousand people. The range of components they make is as varied as the parts of electronic equipment. Some companies specialize in one item, such as a filter. Others make a variety of items, such as terminal boards, interlock receptacles, anode connections, test prods, and many others.

482

I.   Purpose

      To outline a process for dip soldering printed-circuit
      boards.

      NOTE: Dip solder is used primarily for boards over 3 1/2"
      in width and for boards with standoffs or terminal lugs on
      the circuit side. Boards with heavy land areas are better
      suited for wave soldering and, whenever possible, should be
      wave soldered.

II.   Equipment

      Dip-soldering machine

      Soldering flux formula no. 22

      Holding fixtures (4 available — 2 for boards of 1 3/4" to
        2 3/4" and 2 for boards 3" to 4 1/2"

      63-37 solder

      Flux remover type 6x

      Cleaner

      Thermometer

      Scraper (stainless steel with plastic
        handle for removing dross)

III. Preparation for dip soldering

      A. Turn thermostat knob on soldering pot to no. 5 (setting
         of 500°). This setting will heat the solder from 440
         to 470°F. Caution: This is the correct temperature for
         dip soldering and should be checked with a thermometer
         to verify prior to soldering.

      B. After checking the solder temperature, jog the sweep
         arm of the dip-soldering machine into a perpendicular
         position. Attach a holding fixture set to the correct
         width of the board to be soldered (or a dummy board of
         the exact width). Adjust the holding fixture to the
         correct height, without the board. The top of the
         solder should be even with the bottom of the notch in
         the holding fixture. With a dummy board, the board
         should rest on the top of the solder. Caution: Do not
         allow the board to submerge. Turn the machine on and
         return the board to its original position. The holding
         fixture should be to the right side of the machine.

IV.   Operation

      A. Adjust two fixtures to the correct width.

      B. Insert boards and dip in soldering flux no. 22.

      C. Clean dross from top of soldering pot with the scraper.

      D. Hang the fixture and press the start button. Allow to
         complete one cycle.

      E. Remove the board from the fixture and clean with
         cleaner. Reclean with flux remover type 6x.

V.   Touch-up and inspection

      A. Return the board to bench to be checked and touched up
         as required.

      B. After check and touch-up, return it to the ventilation
         booth to be spray-cleaned with cleaner.

      C. Submit boards to Quality Control.

         After acceptance, boards must be placed in plastic bags.

VI.   Maintenance of dip-solder machine

      When the solder on the boards assumes a dull, dingy, or
      stringy (solder skips on the land pattern) appearance,
      change the solder in the pot.

      Approvals:

      Originator   Manufacturing Engineering

      Production   Quality Control

Fig. 46-3. Manufacturing process specifications for printed-circuit boards: dip-soldering operation

Several elements are common to the organization of all companies, whatever their sizes. The product manufacturing process always includes five steps: (1) sales, (2) engineering, (3) prototype development, (4) production, and (5) shipping. These steps are quite similar in both small component manufacturers and large product manufacturers.

SELF-TEST

Test your knowledge by writing, on a separate sheet of paper, the word or words that most correctly complete the following statements:

1. In a product manufacturing company, the _____ department provides vital feedback information to management.
2. A document that contains information about a part's name, number, and routing is the _____ .

3. Specific manufacturing operations can be found in the _____ .
4. A system designed to make sure products meet specifications during the manufacturing process is called _____ .
5. Small electronic companies that manufacture selected electronic parts are called _____ manufacturers.

FOR REVIEW AND DISCUSSION

1. Describe the major organizational difference between a product manufacturer and a research and development company.

2. List the seven basic steps in product manufacturing.
3. What five elements are common to manufacturing companies, regardless of size?

INDIVIDUAL-STUDY ACTIVITIES

1. Obtain the organization chart of a medium-size electronics company. Discuss the functions involved in manufacturing an electronic product.

2. Develop an outline of a plan to mass-produce an inexpensive electronic device for each member of your class. Your class may wish to organize itself into an electronics "company."

TESTING AND TROUBLESHOOTING

UNIT 47   Electronic Test Instruments

In previous units of this book, you have learned about one basic test instrument, the multimeter. You have also learned about instruments used to test capacitors and transistors. Many testing and measuring instruments are used in the fields of electricity and electronics. Some of these are the oscilloscope (Fig. 47-1), the signal generator, the frequency counter, and the signal tracer. These instruments are used to test the performance of certain circuit systems. They are also used to adjust several kinds of circuits so that the circuits will work in the most efficient way. The operation of the signal generator involves two very important circuit functions, which are also briefly discussed in this unit. These are oscillation and modulation.

Fig. 47-1. Dual-trace oscilloscope (*Heath Company*)

OSCILLOSCOPE

The *oscilloscope,* or *scope* as it is often called, is one of the most important test instruments. It is used in all kinds of design, servicing, and maintenance activities (Fig. 47-2). The main purpose of the oscilloscope is to show a waveform, or picture of a voltage (Fig. 47-3). The amplitude of the wave represents various voltage values for the wave, and the horizontal axis of the screen is used to measure time between points on the wave. This makes it possible to test circuits by seeing if the waveforms of the circuit voltages at different points are correct and if the key points are in proper timing.

The Cathode Ray Tube. The waveforms shown by an oscilloscope are displayed on the screen of a cathode ray tube (CRT). This is in many ways similar to the picture tube of a black-and-white television set. An electron-gun assembly in the neck, or narrow end, of the tube produces

Fig. 47-2. Student using an oscilloscope to observe waveforms in a project

Fig. 47-3. Oscilloscope displays showing voltage waveforms present at different points of a television circuit

Fig. 47-4. The oscilloscope cathode ray electron tube: (A) tube construction; (B) tiny spot, or dot, of light appearing on the screen of a cathode ray tube (*Tektronix, Inc.*)

a beam of electrons, sometimes called a *cathode ray* (Fig. 47-4A). When the electron beam strikes the phosphor coating on the screen of the tube, the phosphor *fluoresces,* or glows. If the beam is not moving horizontally or vertically, a tiny spot of light appears on the screen (Fig. 47-4B). Some oscilloscopes can display two wave patterns at the same time. This type of oscilloscope is called a *dual-trace oscilloscope*. This system allows the technician to compare related patterns for amplitude and timing. Separate inputs and controls are provided for each beam and are referred to as channel 1 (Ch1) and channel 2 (Ch2), or A and B.

Electrostatic Deflection. The electron beam of the cathode ray tube in an oscilloscope is moved by a process known as *electrostatic deflection*. Since the beam is made up of electrons, or negative charges, it can be made to move by the electrostatic forces of attraction and repulsion. This is done by applying voltages to the horizontal and the vertical deflection plates in the tube (see Fig. 47-4A). Examples of horizontal and vertical deflection of the beam are shown in Fig. 47-5A and B. If one horizontal and one vertical deflection plate are made equally positive or negative at the same time, the beam will move across the screen diagonally (Fig. 47-5C).

Sweep Circuit. When the vertical gain control of an oscilloscope is turned down fully and the horizontal gain control is turned up, the electron beam *sweeps,* or moves, across the cathode ray tube in a horizontal direction. The beam spot moves so quickly that, because of a characteristic of our eyes known as *persistence of vision,* it appears as an unbroken line (Fig. 47-6).

The horizontal sweep of the beam is produced by an oscilloscope circuit commonly called a *sweep generator*. This circuit generates a sawtooth-shaped output voltage when a timed trigger pulse is applied to the generator circuit. In this way, the sweep will begin exactly at the same point on each wave displayed. The pattern will appear to be constant and stationary, and, therefore, it will be easy to observe. The main factor, however, is that the horizontal gradations on the screen will have

Fig. 47-5. Electrostatic deflection of the electron beam in a cathode ray tube: (A) horizontal; (B) vertical; (C) diagonal

HORIZONTAL DEFLECTION PLATES

ELECTRON BEAM

VERTICAL DEFLECTION PLATES

A　　　　B　　　　C

a time period assigned by the sweep rate. This time period will range from several seconds to fractions of microseconds for each gradation. When the sweep voltage is applied to the horizontal deflection plates, the beam is moved across the screen from left to right. It is then very quickly brought back to the starting position. The speed at which this action is repeated is determined by the frequency of the sweep generator. The frequency of the generator is varied by switching the time base control. This is usually a rotary switch with indicators of the time period at each position, for example, t/cm. There is often a variable sweep vernier control that adjusts the sweep rate to help the operator synchronize to a display. This control must be locked in the off position for the time base to be accurate.

Fig. 47-6. Horizontal line, or trace, appearing on the screen of an oscilloscope cathode ray tube (*Tektronix, Inc.*)

SIGNAL GENERATOR

A *signal generator* is a test instrument used to supply output voltages of different frequencies (Fig. 47-7). These voltages, or signals, are then applied to certain circuits such as those in a radio receiver. This is done to test and adjust the circuits so that the most efficient operation can be obtained.

Fig. 47-7. An RF signal generator (*Precision Apparatus Division of Dynascan Corporation*)

Oscillator Circuit. The heart of a typical signal generator is an oscillator circuit. Such a circuit produces an alternating current through the action of an inductance-capacitance circuit or a capacitance-resistance circuit.

A common inductance-capacitance oscillator circuit known as a *Hartley oscillator* is shown in Fig. 47-8. As direct current begins moving through the collector circuit of the transistor, it creates an expanding magnetic field around coil L1. This magnetic field induces a voltage across coil L2. The induced voltage excites the circuit consisting of L1, L2, and capacitor C1 into oscillation. This oscillation produces an alternating voltage across the output circuit. The combination of L1, L2, and C1 is commonly called a *tank circuit*.

While the tank circuit is oscillating, part of its energy in the form of a voltage is fed back through capacitor C2 to the input of the circuit. The input is at the base connection of the transistor. The feedback

Fig. 47-8. Hartley oscillator circuit

487

voltage is then amplified by the transistor. This resupplies the tank circuit with energy through the collector circuit. Because of this, the energy losses from resistance in the circuit are replaced. The circuit thus keeps oscillating. The frequency of oscillation is determined by the inductance of L1 and L2 and the capacitance of C1. Since C1 is a variable capacitor, the frequency of the output signal can be varied.

Audio-Frequency and Radio-Frequency Signal Generators. Audio-frequency (AF) signal generators produce output signals with a frequency range of from about 10 Hz to 100 kHz. Audio-frequency generators produce a sinusoidal, or sine-wave, output. Many also produce a square-wave output. Radio-frequency (RF) signal generators have a frequency range of from about 100 kHz to 100 MHz or more.

Modulation. In the typical radio-frequency signal generator, the signal from a 400-Hz oscillator circuit in the generator can be used to modulate the output signal. *Modulation* is varying the amplitude or the frequency of a carrier wave. In this case, the carrier wave is the sine-wave output voltage. When the amplitude is varied, it is called *amplitude modulation* (AM). When the frequency is varied, it is called *frequency modulation* (FM).

Because of its modulated outputs, the radio-frequency signal generator is very often used as a miniature radio transmitter for testing the circuits of radio receivers. In such testing, the signal generator is connected to certain parts of a radio circuit. If the circuit is operating properly, the 400-Hz signal, or tone, with which the carrier signal is modulated is reproduced by the loudspeaker. Special kinds of radio-frequency signal generators are also commonly used for testing and adjusting television receiver circuits.

Fig. 47-9. Wide-band frequency counter (*Sencore, Inc.*)

FREQUENCY COUNTER

The *frequency counter* is an instrument that can be used with the oscilloscope to study the frequencies of a circuit. This instrument counts the number of cycles present at the input leads for a very short period of time and then displays that count. This process is repeated periodically, and the display is updated.

The frequency counter, such as the one pictured in Fig. 47-9, has many uses. One application is to make sure that the output frequency of communications transmitting equipment is operating properly and within Federal Communications Commission (FCC) regulations. Another use is to aid in the setting of the local oscillator in a radio receiver.

SIGNAL TRACER

The *signal tracer* is an instrument used to trace, or follow, a signal voltage through circuits such as those found in amplifiers and radio receivers (Fig. 47-10). This is done by connecting different points of the circuit under test to the input of the instrument. If the circuit is operating properly, the signal tracer will indicate this by an audio output signal heard through a loudspeaker or headphone.

When a signal tracer is used with a modulated radio-frequency signal, it must have a detector circuit. This circuit separates the audio signals from the radio-frequency carrier. This is necessary since a signal-tracer loudspeaker will not respond to signals above the audio range of frequencies.

Fig. 47-10. Signal tracer (EICO Electronic Instrument Company, Inc.)

USING ELECTRONIC TEST INSTRUMENTS

The procedures given below are intended to provide basic information on operating the oscilloscope. The controls mentioned are those found on the typical, general-purpose instrument (Fig. 47-11). After learning to operate an oscilloscope in this way, you will be able to use the oscilloscope for various purposes. Many oscilloscopes have additional controls. Before operating an oscilloscope or other test equipment, you should carefully read its instruction manual. Basic information on the operation of a signal generator is also given in the following procedures. Notice that Fig. 47-11 is a drawing of a dual-trace oscilloscope. The following procedure applies to the operation of either of the channels.

Procedure

1. Turn the oscilloscope on. Adjust the following controls as stated:
   Volts/division   midrange
   Time base   midrange
   Intensity   approximate center of rotation
2. Adjust the vertical position control so that a horizontal trace, or line, appears through the center of the oscilloscope screen.
3. Adjust the intensity control so that the line can be clearly viewed without too much brightness. Then adjust the focus control so that the line is "clean," or well defined.
4. Connect an audio-frequency signal generator to the vertical input jacks of the oscilloscope. Set the output selector to square wave and adjust the frequency to 10 kHz. Set the output-level control to a midrange position.
5. Adjust the sweep selector to a range to 10 microseconds per millimeter. Adjust the volt per millimeter control to a position that yields a wave that is about ¾ of the full height of the screen.
6. Slowly adjust the output frequency of the signal generator and observe the display on the oscilloscope. The display should be stable and expand or contract as the frequency is decreased and increased, respectively.
7. Adjust the signal generator to produce a sign-wave output. Observe these waveforms at different frequencies.
8. Connect a crystal microphone to the oscilloscope. Observe the

Fig. 47-11. Typical dual-trace oscilloscope controls

voice waveforms generated by talking into the microphone.

9. Connect a 6-V battery in series with a door buzzer. Connect the vertical input leads of the oscilloscope to the terminals of the buzzer.

10. Adjust the necessary controls of the oscilloscope so that a clear pulsating-current waveform appears on its screen. This waveform is produced by the rapid action of the buzzer contacts in making and breaking the circuit.

SELF-TEST

Test your knowledge by writing, on a separate sheet of paper, the word or words that most correctly complete the following statements:

1. The main purpose of an oscilloscope is to show a _____, or picture, of a voltage.
2. Waveforms shown by an oscilloscope are displayed on the screen of a _____ tube.
3. The electron beam in the cathode ray tube is moved by a process known as _____ deflection. This is done by applying voltages to the _____ and the _____ deflection plates in the tube.
4. The horizontal direction on the oscilloscope represents the elapsed _____ of the waveform.
5. The instrument that displays the number of hertz for a waveform is a _____ _____.

6. An oscilloscope that displays the waveform of two signals at the same time is called a _____ _____ oscilloscope.
7. A signal generator is a test instrument used to supply output voltages of different _____.
8. The heart of a typical signal generator is an _____ circuit.
9. Two general kinds of signal generators are _____ signal generators and _____ signal generators.
10. When the amplitude of a carrier signal is varied by modulation, this is called _____ modulation. When the frequency of the carrier signal is varied by modulation, this is called _____ modulation.
11. An instrument used to trace a signal through circuits such as those in amplifiers and radio receivers is called a _____.

FOR REVIEW AND DISCUSSION

1. What is the main purpose of an oscilloscope?
2. How is a spot of light produced on the screen of a cathode ray tube?
3. Explain the process of electrostatic deflection in the cathode ray tube of an oscilloscope.
4. For what purpose is the sweep circuit used in an oscilloscope?
5. What is a signal generator? Why is it used?
6. Explain how a basic Hartley oscillator circuit works.

7. State the difference between audio- and radio-frequency signal generators.
8. Explain the difference between amplitude modulation and frequency modulation.
9. Why is a 400-Hz oscillator circuit used in a typical radio-frequency signal generator?
10. What is a signal tracer? For what purpose is it used?
11. Why must a signal tracer that is tracing a radio-frequency signal have a detector circuit?

1. Give a demonstration to your class on how an oscilloscope is used to show different kinds of waveforms. Describe the various controls on the front panel and show how they are used.

2. Give a demonstration showing your class how an audio-frequency signal generator is operated. An audio amplifier can be connected to the signal generator to provide audible tones of its output.

UNIT 48   Troubleshooting and Repair

Troubleshooting is the process of determining why a device or a circuit is not working as it should. To do this efficiently, you have to have a broad knowledge of how things work. Technicians who do troubleshooting, repair, or servicing must have a variety of skills and knowledge. They must know what test instruments and procedures are needed to find a defect. They must also know what tools and materials are needed to repair it. Finally, they must have the ability to *diagnose*. This means that they must be able to recognize the symptoms of a defective device or circuit and then form a plan of action to repair it.

When you build a project, very often it does not work the first time you power it up. If you have developed some of these same skills of the technician, you will be able to diagnose the trouble and get your project to operate properly (Fig. 48-1).

Fig. 48-1. Student diagnosing a problem in a project

TROUBLESHOOTING PROCEDURES

The troubleshooting process for a circuit often takes the form of a step-by-step procedure of specific instructions. For example, the following are the steps for troubleshooting a radio circuit.

1. Visually check all components, wiring, and printed-circuit boards for discoloring, burns, and breakage.
2. Check all batteries and replace any with low voltage.
3. Measure voltages at the leads of transistors for unusual voltage levels, high or low.
4. Test the voice coil of the loudspeaker with an ohmmeter.
5. Check potentiometers with an ohmmeter; clean or replace as necessary.
6. Clean contacts of headphone jack.
7. Check detector diode with an oscilloscope or ohmmeter; replace if necessary.
8. Test drive amplifier stages, especially the transistors and transformers.

In the general troubleshooting of devices and circuits, there are usually no definite rules to be followed. In the typical case, technicians must apply their knowledge of theory, test instruments, tools, and materials to solve a problem. This often involves mechanical skill. Many electrical and electronic devices and circuits depend to some extent on certain mechanical operations. Several suggestions for troubleshooting and repair are given in the rest of this unit.

VISUAL INSPECTION

Unless the probable source of difficulty is known, troubleshooting should usually begin with a thorough visual inspection. Loose connections, broken wires, poor solder joints, burned-out resistors, or even a burned-out fuse or a tripped circuit breaker can very often be found in this way.

For example, if you find that a floor lamp is not working, you might replace the bulb. If this does not correct the trouble, you might replace the lamp switch and then the lamp socket. If the lamp still does not work, you would have wasted your time.

Perhaps if you had inspected the plug before replacing anything, you would have discovered that a wire had become unfastened from a plug terminal screw. With this corrected, the lamp might have worked. Therefore, in this case, a thorough visual inspection would have saved some time and possibly some expense. In more complicated troubleshooting and repair jobs, more time and more money can be wasted in procedures that would have been unnecessary if a visual inspection had been made first.

Vision also plays an important part in troubleshooting television circuits since the picture tube can be used as a test instrument. Many technicians are able to quickly localize defects in a television circuit by observing the lack of a picture or the distortions that appear in a picture or in a test pattern.

SMELL, HEARING, AND TOUCH

In addition to sight, the senses of smell, hearing, and touch can be valuable aids in troubleshooting. Overheated resistors, transformers, choke coils, motor windings, and insulation materials can very often be detected by their odor. Each of these conditions produces a characteristic odor that the experienced technician can use to locate defective components. When the overheating of any component or part in a circuit is noticed, the circuit should be turned off at once.

Overheated transformers, choke coils, and motor windings will sometimes produce a cooking, or frying, noise that can easily be heard. In high-voltage circuits such as those in television receivers, the arcing of current between certain wires and the chassis or between two wires produces a chirping noise. By tracing this noise, it is often possible to quickly locate the source of the arcing.

The sense of hearing can also be used in troubleshooting a circuit that has a loudspeaker. By using the loudspeaker as a test instrument, the lack of sound or the distortions of sound heard through it can indicate specific circuit defects. An experienced technician can quickly locate defects using this procedure.

Overheated components can often be located by touch. This is especially true of transformers, choke coils, electrolytic capacitors, and transistors. If any of these components feels too warm, there may be a defect in the component or in the circuit wiring.

CONTINUITY TESTS

After the visual inspection and the smell, hearing, and touch tests have been done, the troubleshooting of many devices and circuits involves continuity tests made with an ohmmeter. Continuity tests should be made wherever an open-circuit condition is suspected (Fig. 48-2). The test can also be used to check for shorts. It is important to remember that an ohmmeter should never be used on a circuit to which a voltage is applied. Also a component should be isolated by disconnecting one of its leads before continuity tests are done.

CONTINUITY TEST POINTS

Fig. 48-2. Typical continuity test points used in checking the output transformer, headphone jack, and loudspeaker of a radio receiver

ELECTRON TUBES AND TRANSISTORS

Troubleshooting circuits with electron tubes usually begins with testing the tubes, unless a circuit defect is first noticed. The transistors in a circuit are generally not tested until there is definite reason to believe that at least one of them is defective.

VOLTAGE TESTS

After it has been determined that all power leads, fuses, switches, and electron tubes, if any, are in good condition, the next step in troubleshooting is to test the voltage at certain supply points. These include the secondary winding or windings of transformers, battery terminals, and rectifier outputs.

If the supply voltage is found to be normal, it is good practice to then measure the voltages at the electrodes of the transistors or the electron tubes. Unless these voltages are of the correct value, a circuit will fail to operate or will operate improperly.

Fig. 48-3. Portion of a radio-receiver schematic diagram showing the dc voltages that should be present between the electrodes of a transistor and the common (ground) point of the circuit

Fig. 48-4. Portion of a radio-receiver circuit showing the resistors that should be checked if correct voltages are not present at the electrodes of the transistor

Fig. 48-5. Troubleshooting a rectifier filter circuit

The voltages that should be present between the electrodes of transistors or electron tubes and the common point of their circuit are usually shown on the schematic diagram of the circuit (Fig. 48-3). If you do not have this diagram, it is often helpful to take a look at the schematic diagram of another circuit in which identical (or similar) transistors or electron tubes are used.

RESISTANCE TESTS

A lack of voltage or an incorrect voltage at a given point of a circuit is very often caused by a defective resistor or capacitor. In order to localize this defect, it is helpful to make resistance tests of that part of the circuit from which voltage is obtained for the electrode in question (Fig. 48-4). In this way, it is possible to locate defective components that may be preventing the correct distribution of voltage in a circuit.

WAVE PATTERN TESTS

Very often components will change characteristics enough to cause distortion in operation but not enough to fail completely. When this happens, the oscilloscope will show the deviations in wave patterns and aid in tracing the problem. By connecting a signal generator to the input of a circuit, such as Fig. 48-4, the technician can use the oscilloscope to observe the wave shape as it passes through the circuit. If the signal is present at the input to a component and not at the output, then the fault is usually isolated. Or (in Fig. 48-4) if a signal is seen on the oscilloscope at the base of the transistor and distorted at the collector, then the transistor is suspected.

DIAGNOSIS OF CIRCUIT TROUBLES

Defects in a circuit, such as a broken connection, a loose solder joint, or a worn-out component, can usually be taken care of by simple repair or replacement. However, a repair job often involves a further diagnosis of the reason or reasons for a defect. For example, a resistor, a diode, a transistor, or a solenoid coil will become overheated and burn out because of a second defective component in the circuit. If the first component is replaced without further diagnosis, it is probable that the replacement component will also be damaged.

Let us suppose that the carbon-composition resistor in the rectifier circuit of an amplifier is burned out (Fig. 48-5). Let us further suppose that an inexperienced person immediately replaces the resistor and finds that the replacement resistor also quickly burns out. Obviously, then, it is necessary to diagnose the situation more carefully.

First of all, fundamental theory tells us that the resistor burned out because it was forced to carry an excessive current. From experience, it is reasonable to assume that an excessive current is not caused by a defect in the resistor itself. The conclusion must be that the excessive current was caused by some other defect in the circuit.

In the circuit in Fig. 48-5, two electrolytic filter capacitors, C1 and C2, are connected across the rectifier output. We know that electrolytic capacitors can become shorted. If C1 were shorted, perhaps one or both of the diodes would be damaged. However, because of the circuit arrangement, this would not cause excessive current through the resistor. On the other hand, if C2 were shorted, excessive current would definitely pass through the resistor. Therefore, the solution to the problem is replacing both C2 and the resistor.

The situation just described is a very basic troubleshooting and repair job. It is, however, a good example of how knowledge of theory, practical experience, and the ability to diagnose trouble can be used in solving a circuit problem. The efficient technician must constantly do this in finding circuit defects and correcting them.

LOGIC PROBE

A *logic probe* is a test instrument used mostly to troubleshoot different families, or kinds, of integrated circuits (ICs) (Fig. 48-6). The logic probe detects pulses of voltage. In digital work, these pulses of voltage are called *logic levels,* or *threshold levels*. The logic probe also stores and displays the logic level. This logic level is displayed on a light-emitting diode (LED) readout.

By flipping a switch, the logic probe can be set to detect threshold levels of 2.25 V (logic 1) and 0.8 V (logic 0) for a family of ICs known as DTL or TTL. These abbreviations refer to *diode-transistor logic* (DTL) or *transistor-transistor logic* (TTL or T^2L). Switching to another position sets the probe to detect threshold levels for a family of ICs known as CMOS/HTL. These abbreviations refer to *complementary metallic oxide semiconductors* (CMOS) or *high-threshold logic* (HTL). In the CMOS/HTL ICs, the threshold levels for digital operation are determined by the *applied voltage* (Vcc). When a threshold level is greater than 70 percent of Vcc, it is logic 1. When the threshold level is less than 30 percent of Vcc, it is logic 0. Some logic probes detect pulse widths as narrow as 10 nanoseconds at a frequency of 50 MHz. These features make the logic probe an important troubleshooting instrument. The power supply of the circuit under test is also used to operate the logic probe. The following general procedures are suggested for using a logic probe:

1. Connect the clip leads to the power supply of the circuit.
2. Set the switch to the logic family to be tested (DTL/TTL or CMOS/ HTL).
3. Set the MEMORY/PULSE switch to the PULSE position.
4. Touch the probe tip to a node, or terminal, on the IC to be analyzed. The three LEDs (high, low, and pulse) on the logic probe will provide an instant reading of the signal activity at the node.

Fig. 48-6. Using a logic probe to check a digital-clock integrated circuit

If the logic probe is to store a pulse, touch the probe tip to the node under test. Then move the MEM/PULSE switch to the MEM position. The next pulse will activate the PULSE LED.

DIAGNOSTIC SOFTWARE TOOLS

The more complex a piece of equipment is, the more time-consuming the process of diagnosis becomes. If a technician were to test each circuit component in a computer until a fault were detected, much valuable time would be wasted. For this reason, software has been developed for most types of computers that will electronically test the circuitry in question to determine quality of operation. When a fault is found, the computer will report the results of the test on a video display terminal (VDT) or in printed form.

DATA COMMUNICATION TESTING

When computing equipment sends data from one location to another, many controlling signals are sent along with the data. The presence and timing of these signals is very important. Figure 48-7 shows a test set that can be connected in series with the data cable. Once in place, the technician can use a logic probe or oscilloscope to test for the key factors in data transmission.

Fig. 48-7. Data line test set (*Black Box Corporation*)

SELF-TEST

Test your knowledge by writing, on a separate sheet of paper, the word or words that most correctly complete the following statements:

1. The process of determining why a device or a circuit is not working as it should is called _____.

2. In addition to sight, the senses of _____, _____, and _____ can be valuable aids in troubleshooting.

3. Overheated components can often be located by _____.

4. The troubleshooting of many devices and circuits involves _____ tests.

5. The voltages that should be present between the electrodes of transistors and electron tubes are often shown on _____ diagrams.

6. Repair jobs often involve further diagnosis of the _____ for defects.

7. Integrated circuits can be analyzed with a test instrument called a _____.

8. CMOS refers to a family of integrated circuits called _____.

9. The oscilloscope is used to observe the _____ patterns in circuits under test.

10. A tool that saves time in determining the cause of trouble in complex computer circuitry is called _____.

1. What is meant by the troubleshooting of a circuit?
2. Name some of the things technicians should know and be able to do in order to be efficient at troubleshooting and repair.
3. Tell why a thorough visual inspection is so important in the troubleshooting of many circuits.
4. How can the senses of smell, hearing, and touch be put to use in troubleshooting?
5. What circuit defects can be located by means of continuity tests?
6. Explain how resistance tests can be used to locate defects in a circuit.
7. What can happen if you replace a part without making a full diagnosis of the trouble?
8. How can the oscilloscope and the volt-ohmmeter be used together to diagnose a circuit problem?
9. What safety procedures should be applied to a repair activity?
10. Make a list of the necessary personal characteristics required for a technician working in the repair field. It will be necessary for you to do some outside research for this.

INDIVIDUAL-STUDY ACTIVITIES

1. Give a demonstration showing your class the correct procedures to be followed in troubleshooting a device, an appliance, or an electronic circuit.
2. Demonstrate the safety procedures to be used when troubleshooting and repairing electronic equipment.

PROJECT PLANNING AND SUGGESTED PROJECTS

UNIT 49 Project Planning

Fig. 49-1. Constructing a project can be a valuable experience since it makes use of students' skills, initiative, and knowledge of correct work procedures.

Building a shop project that you choose can be one of the more interesting and useful activities in an electricity and electronics course (Fig. 49-1). Such a project will let you use some of the theoretical and practical ideas you have learned in this course. It will also give you an opportunity to do planning—the very important steps involved in "thinking through" a job. A project will allow you to work with devices and processes used in different kinds of electrical and electronics activities. Finally, successfully finishing a project can be very satisfying to you. It shows that you were both able and willing to do a job in the responsible way of an efficient worker.

One kind of project covered in this unit is what might be called a *construction project*. It often involves wiring from a schematic diagram and making certain components. You probably will build a chassis or some other form of base. On this chassis, you will assemble or mount a circuit. Other kinds of projects use materials from do-it-yourself kits. These often involve doing experiments. Still other project activities may center around repairing existing circuits. Each of these will give you valuable experiences.

CHOOSING THE PROJECT
The choice of a construction project should be based on several things: (1) the function of the finished project, (2) your interest and ability, (3) the availability of plans and materials, (4) the availability of tools and facilities, and (5) the cost.

Function. The project should be *functional*. That means that it should satisfy the need for a particular product. This will increase your desire to build the project and the satisfaction that you will get from it.

Interest and Ability. You should choose a project that you will find interesting. In addition, it should be something that you will be able to build. These two things are related. Being very interested in a job will often encourage you to gain a new skill. However, some projects may turn out to be too difficult. This can result in a waste of time and materials. It may discourage you from taking part in other shop activities. If you are not sure that you can make a certain project, choose a simpler one. You can then build on this experience and go on to do more challenging projects.

Plans and Materials. Unless a project is of your own design, its plans should include a schematic or pictorial diagram. It should also include a list of materials needed and any special hints for doing the job. Many project suggestions or plans do not include a chassis layout diagram. If the project is a printed circuit, a printed-circuit layout diagram should be prepared. Designing a chassis or a printed-circuit board can be an interesting and valuable experience.

Before making a final choice of a project, you should make sure that all the components and materials needed for it are available. Some of these can probably be found in your school shop. Others can be bought from local stores or ordered from catalogs.

Tools and Facilities. The choice of a project should depend on the availability of tools, equipment, space, and processes. Making the project should not require special tools, hazardous operations or processes, or any equipment not likely to be found in the school shop.

Cost. The total cost of a project should be included in any plan. This is important since, after starting a project, you may discover that it will cost more than you are either willing or able to pay.

PLANNING AND DESIGNING A PROJECT

Planning and designing an original project gives you a good opportunity to use theoretical information, knowledge of devices and materials, and skills related to problem solving. Even the simplest original project can test your ability to transform an idea into a practical product (Fig. 49-2). Engineers must have this ability. However, such ability is important for all who do technical work. Have a questioning attitude about the project.

What is it to be?
How can it be done?
How can it be done better?
Can it be done in a simpler way?

These are questions that challenge the mind. In design work, as in many other kinds of technical jobs, imagination is valuable.

The basic steps in planning and designing a small, low-cost radio are shown in a project-idea sketch (Fig. 49-3). Here you see the way in

Fig. 49-2. Planning a project means thinking through the problem to find a practical solution.

THE NEED — GOING TO CAMP THIS SUMMER — NEED A SMALL, LOW-COST RADIO

IDENTIFYING TECHNICAL PROBLEMS TO BE SOLVED —
WHAT SIZE SHOULD IT BE?
WHAT ELEMENTS MAKE UP A RADIO?
WHAT WILL IT COST? REAL CHEAP!
HOW LONG WILL IT TAKE TO BUILD?
WHAT COMPONENTS SHOULD BE USED?
WHAT TYPE CONSTRUCTION? CONTAINER?

POSSIBLE SOLUTIONS TO THE TECHNICAL PROBLEMS —
SIZE: SMALL, EASY TO CARRY
ELEMENTS: ANTENNA, TUNER DETECTOR, AMPLIFIER, REPRODUCER, POWER SUPPLY

1. ANTENNA:
   DIPOLE
   LONG WIRE ✓
   DIRECTIONAL

2. TUNER:
   BROADCAST BAND ✓
   POLICE BAND
   AMATURE BAND

3. DETECTOR:
   TUBE
   GALENA
   DIODE ✓

4. AMPLIFIER: NO

5. REPRODUCER:
   LOUDSPEAKER
   HEAD SET ✓

6. ENERGY SOURCE:
   BATTERY
   POWER SUPPLY
   RADIO WAVE ENERGY ✓

CIRCUIT SPECIFICATIONS

CR1
L1
C1 270pF
C2 0.001μF
HT

L1 = FERRITE ANTENNA COIL, BROADCAST BAND
CR1 = DIODE 1N34A
HT = HEAD SET, 2,000 Ω

CONSTRUCTION IDEAS
POINT TO POINT
PRINTED CIRCUIT (ETCHING SOLUTION) ✓
COIL SUPPORT —
ALUMINUM SHEET 1½ × ½ × 1/32 in.
(38 × 13 × 0.8 mm)
HOLE TO FIT COIL DIAMETER

TWO SMALL HOLES TO MOUNT COIL SUPPORT WITH MACHINE SCREWS
BEND

ASSEMBLY
TO — RED
PRINTED CIRCUIT (TOP VIEW)
L1
C1
CR1
C2
BLACK HOOK-UP WIRES
TO

SHORT LEAD, YELLOW HOOK-UP WIRES
TO

PRINTED CIRCUIT (BOTTOM VIEW) in/mm
C1
CR1
L1
C2
3.0 / 76
1.88 / 47

COMPLETE RADIO INSIDE JEWELRY BOX

NOTCHES CUT FOR LEAD-IN WIRES

DISCARDED JEWELRY BOX WITH HINGED COVER

COST: ABOUT $3.00 (NOT INCLUDING ANTENNA WIRE) IS PROJECT IN KEEPING WITH COURSE OBJECTIVES — YES
TIME: 8 CLASS PERIODS. ELECTRICAL CONCEPTS APPLIED: PRINCIPLES OF RADIO COMMUNICATIONS.

Fig. 49-3. An example of a project-idea sketch sheet

which an idea is expanded and refined until an overall final plan is developed. This process is really one of choosing. You test several different ideas on paper until you find what seems to be the most practical solution to the problem.

An example of a project plan sheet that can be used for making a project is shown in Fig. 49-4. When this plan sheet is filled out, it will have all the information needed for building the project according to the ideas developed on the project-idea sketch sheet (Fig. 49-3). These planning sheets can, in one form or another, be used with any project.

Name _____ Date _____	
Class _____ Project _____	Name of School City, State
	PROJECT PLAN SHEET

Quantity	Material Specifications	Unit Cost	Total Cost	
				Instructor's O.K. _____
				Approximate Number of Hours to Construct _____
	20% Cost of Finish			
	Total			Grade _____

Steps to follow in making this project (attach sketch or drawing to this sheet showing all dimensions and indicating special construction features):

Specification change: (Must be o.k.'d by instructor before change is made.)

1. _____
2. _____
3. _____

Electrical Theory Involved: (Clip other sheets to plan if needed.)

Fig. 49-4. A project plan sheet

PROJECT KITS

In recent years, many project materials have become available in kits. A kit usually has all the materials needed for a project. The kit generally has instructions that show and tell how the project is to be assembled and wired (Fig. 49-5). The instructions often include both pictorial and schematic diagrams of the circuit.

Fig. 49-5. Components of a volt-ohm-milliammeter kit and pages of the associated instruction manual (*Graymark Enterprises, Inc.*)

EXPERIMENTAL ACTIVITIES

The main purpose of an experimental activity is to show how a circuit or device works. This kind of activity can be very useful for demonstrating, in a practical way, how the theory and practice are related.

A number of ideas for experiments are given in the Learning by Doing activities included in many units of this textbook. You will find that building these projects and showing them to your class will be interesting and informative.

More experiments are given in the *Activities Manual for Understanding Electricity and Electronics Technology*. The manual first gives directions for making a circuit board, a power supply, and coils that may be used in doing many experiments. These experiments will give you valuable experiences that will increase your understanding of electricity and electronics. Working with circuits, devices, and common test instruments will help you see how they can be used in many ways. All these experiences will help make your electricity and electronics course both interesting and useful.

REPAIR PROJECTS

Repairing an existing circuit or device can give you much satisfaction and useful experience. The satisfaction comes from applying your knowledge to a problem and solving it. In doing repair jobs, you will learn about *troubleshooting,* or finding problems in components or circuits. This is similar to what professionals do. Thus, your experience can be put to use in a future career.

Most repair jobs require a knowledge of theory, components and materials, tools, test instruments, and testing methods. Procedures for using the basic test instrument, the volt-ohm-milliammeter, are given in various units. These procedures include the testing of devices and components such as resistors, capacitors, diodes, and transistors. Test instruments and troubleshooting methods are discussed throughout the book.

Repair projects should include a report (Fig. 49-6). In addition to being a record of your work, such a report gives you an opportunity to describe a job in writing. This can be a very useful experience. Written reports must be prepared as part of many technical jobs.

REPAIR-JOB REPORT

Name _____ Date _____

Product or Circuit Worked On _____

_____

For Whom This Job Was Done _____

_____

Description of Defect or Defects _____

_____

_____

_____

General Procedures Used in Doing the Job _____

_____

_____

_____

_____

_____

_____

_____

_____

Instruments Used _____   _____

_____   _____

Time Spent in Doing the Job _____

Approved   Yes _____ No _____

Fig. 49-6. Repair job report

SAFETY

Safety must be considered when designing and building any project. A project should always be made so that it is free of shock and fire hazards. If instructions are given, they should be clear, so that the project can be used easily.

While building a project, you must work safely by following established safety rules for the tools and equipment you are using. In addition, be sure to wear safety glasses when doing cutting operations of materials and component leads and when soldering.

SELF-TEST

Test your knowledge by writing, on a separate sheet of paper, the word or words that most correctly complete the following statements:

1. One of the main purposes of constructing projects is to use the _____ and practical ideas you have learned in the electricity and electronics courses.
2. The selection of a construction project is based upon several factors, such as the function it will perform; your interest and ability; the availability of materials, tools, facilities; and the _____.
3. The project-idea sketch is important because it is used to expand and refine an idea before an

_____ plan is developed.
4. Project kits usually include instructions for assembling the project, pictorial and _____ diagrams of the circuit.
5. _____ an existing circuit allows you to apply _____ to the solution of a problem.
6. A project should always be constructed so that it is free of _____ and fire hazards.
7. The process of finding and repairing a malfunction in an electronic unit is called _____.
8. Repair projects should include a _____ for future reference to provide information about the malfunction and the action taken to correct the problem.

FOR REVIEW AND DISCUSSION

1. Explain how construction of a project can provide a valuable learning experience.
2. Name five factors to be considered when choosing a project.
3. List and explain three factors involved in planning and designing a construction project.
4. Describe an experiment project.
5. What information is given on a repair job report?
6. List 10 general safety rules for safe operation of hand and power tools that drill, cut, shape, and connect the materials used in project construction.

INDIVIDUAL-STUDY ACTIVITIES

1. Prepare a written or an oral report describing the general procedures for planning, designing, and constructing a project.
2. Prepare a list of books, magazines, and other publications that include information about the construction of electrical and electronic projects. Report to your class about the project materials found in each.
3. Show your class a project you constructed. Demonstrate its operation. Describe any special construction features.
4. Ask your teacher about any project fairs or exhibits that are to be held in your area. If possible, plan to buld a project for the occasion.
5. Talk with a teacher in another class, such as math or science, and find out how electronics is applied to these areas. Plan and construct a project that demonstrates a concept studied in that subject. Either aid the teacher, or demonstrate your project to a class in the subject you selected.

UNIT 50   Suggested Projects and Technical Problem Solving

The following projects provide several practical and inexpensive circuits to build. Each project has a schematic diagram and a parts list. Hints that will help in the construction and the operation of a project are also given when appropriate.

Chassis construction and other mounting and enclosure information has been omitted purposely. This will provide an opportunity to exercise creative design skills in determining the appearance of the finished product.

The second part of this unit will give you some technical problems to solve. These selected problems are designed so that you will use what you have learned in electricity and electronics courses. You are to apply this knowledge in these specific situations to derive an appropriate solution. There is no one best solution to any of the problems, as the result is governed by several factors. Some of these factors are your experience, the materials available (commercial and scrap), and the tools available to you. Keep in mind that the basic purpose of these engineering and technical problems is to provide you with situations where you will apply your knowledge, skills, and creativity.

PROJECT 1 TRANSISTOR TESTER

Transistors, both n-p-n and p-n-p, can be tested using the circuit in Fig. 50-1. It will test the devices for short circuits, excessive leakage, and gain.

Fig. 50-1. Transistor tester

BT1, battery, 6 V or 4 size-C dry cells connected in series

M1, milliammeter, dc, 0 to 1 mA

R1 and R3, resistors, carbon-composition or film, 220 kΩ, ½ W

R2, potentiometer, 10 kΩ, ½ W

S1, switch, slide-type, TPDT (p-n-p or n-p-n selector control)

S2 and S3, switches, SPST, push button, normally open (N.O.) momentary contact type (p-n-p and n-p-n gain test controls)

Using the Tester

1. To calibrate the tester before testing any transistor, first adjust switch S1 to the p-n-p position. Then bring the alligator clips of test leads C and E into contact with each other. Next adjust R2 until the meter reads 1.

2. To test a p-n-p transistor, adjust S1 to the p-n-p position. Then connect the test leads to the proper leads of the transistor:

   a. If the meter shows a reading of 1, the transistor is short circuited.

   b. If the meter shows a reading of more than 0.2 but less than 1, the leakage current of the transistor is excessive.

   c. To test for gain, depress S2. If the meter reading is significantly higher than the reading before S2 was depressed, the transistor is good.

3. To test an n-p-n transistor, adjust S1 to the n-p-n position. Then follow the procedures given for testing a p-n-p transistor, using S3 to provide an indication of gain.

PROJECT 2 CONTINUITY TESTER

To determine broken or open connections as well as circuits shorted to ground, the continuity tester in Fig. 50-2 can be used. The presence of a completed circuit is indicated by either a buzzer signal or an indicator lamp.

*Lamp can be mounted in a miniature bayonet-base socket or an indicator-light assembly.

Fig. 50-2. Continuity tester

PARTS LIST

BT1, battery, 6 V or 4 size-C dry cells connected in series
DS1, pilot lamp, no. 47
LS1, buzzer, 6 V
S1, switch, toggle, SPDT with center off position

PROJECT 3 LAMP-DIMMER CONTROL

The circuit in Fig. 50-3 allows you to vary the light output of a 100-W incandescent lamp from zero to full brilliance. It is very convenient for controlling the operation of a study lamp or a lamp that is used as a night-light. This circuit can be used with any 60- to 200-W incandescent lamp. However, if you expect to use a lamp larger than 100 W, fuse F1 should be increased to 2 A.

Note 1: The center terminal (A) of the silicon controlled rectifier is internally connected to the mounting tab of the device. Therefore, as a safety precaution, the mounting tab must be completely insulated from any metallic enclosure within which the circuit is placed.

Note 2: For the safest operation, the shaft of the potentiometer, R2, should be equipped with a plastic control knob.

Fig. 50-3. Lamp-dimmer control

PARTS LIST

P1, 3-conductor polarized connector with male contacts, rated: 15 A, 125 Vac
C1, capacitor, 0.0022 μF, 200 WVDC
DS1, neon lamp, NE-2
DS2, incandescent lamp, medium-base, 100 W, with socket
F1, fuse, AGC, 1 A
R1, resistor, carbon-composition or film, 330 kΩ, ½ W, 5 or 10 percent tolerance
R2, potentiometer, 2 MΩ, ½ W
S1, switch, SPST (individual unit or mounted on R2)
SCR1, silicon-controlled rectifier, International Rectifier IR106B1 or equivalent

PROJECT 4 CODE-PRACTICE OSCILLATOR

The circuit in Fig. 50-4 shows an oscillator that provides adequate volume for either individual or group code practice. It is useful in preparing for the amateur radio operator's international Morse code examination. The most commonly used characters of the international Morse code and their dot-dash equivalents are given in Unit 37.

Fig. 50-4. Code-practice oscillator

PARTS LIST

BT1, battery, 9 V
C1, capacitor, 0.05 μF, 200 WVDC
C2, electrolytic capacitor, 100 μF, 25 WVDC
LS1, loudspeaker, 8 Ω miniature
Q1, transistor, n-p-n, SK3005 or equivalent
Q2, transistor, p-n-p, SK3444/123A or equivalent
R1, resistor, carbon-composition or film, 100 kΩ, 0.5 W
R2, resistor, carbon-composition or film, 100 Ω, 0.5 W
R3, resistor, carbon-composition or film, 10 Ω, 0.5 W
S1, telegraph key

PROJECT 5 MINI-ORGAN

This project (Fig. 50-5) is a multivibrator circuit similar to that used in several models of electronic organs. The fundamental output frequency is determined by the RC time constant established by C1 and R1. Changes in this frequency are produced when other capacitors (C2 through C8) are connected into the circuit by switches S2 through S8. A different tone is produced with each unique combination of resistance.

PARTS LIST

BT1, battery, 6 V or 4 size-C dry cells connected in series
C1, capacitor, 0.005 μF, 200 WVDC

Fig. 50-5. Mini-organ

* May or may not be required depending upon
the operational characteristics of Q2.

C2 to C8, capacitors, 0.02 μF, 200 WVDC
C9, capacitor, 0.001 μF, 200 WVDC
C10, capacitor, 0.2 μF, 200 WVDC
CR1, germanium diode, 1N54 or SK3087
LS1, loudspeaker, 2½ in. (63.5 mm), 8 Ω
Q1, transistor, n-p-n, 2N388 or SK3011
Q2, transistor, p-n-p, 2N408 or SK3003
R1, potentiometer, 1 MΩ, ½ W (tone control)
R2, resistor, carbon-composition or film, 1 MΩ, ½ W
S1 to S8, switches, SPST, push button, normally open (N.O.)
    momentary contact type
S9, switch, SPST (individual unit or part of R1)

PROJECT 6 LIGHT-CONTROLLED SWITCH

The relay-control circuit (Fig. 50-6) is operated by changes in the intensity of the light that strikes the active surface of a photoconductive cell. The relay contacts are used as a switch to control the operation of a load such as an incandescent lamp or a small motor.

Fig. 50-6. Light-controlled switch

509

BT1, battery, 9 V
K1, relay, miniature sensitive, SPDT, 500-Ω coil, with contact rating 600 mA at 50 Vac/dc or 2 A at 117 Vac
Q1 and Q2, transistors, p-n-p, GE-2 or SK3004
R1, potentiometer, 100 kΩ, ½ W (sensitivity control)
R2, photoconductive cell, Clairex no. CL704M or equivalent
R3, resistor, carbon-composition or film, 10 kΩ, ½ W
S1, switch, SPST (individual unit or part of R1)

PROJECT 7 ORNAMENTAL LAMP FLASHER

The lamp flasher circuit in Fig. 50-7 produces the attractive effect of neon lamps turning on and off in random patterns. This circuit is useful for lighting jack-o-lantern eyes, for holiday decorations, and for attracting attention to displays.

Dotted lines show circuit connections for additional lamp. More lamps can be connected into the circuit in a similar way.

All resistors are 10 MΩ and all lamps are type NE-2. Additional capacitors suggested are 0.15 µF, 0.18 µF, 0.22 µF, 0.27 µF, 0.33 µF, and so on.

Fig. 50-7. Ornamental lamp flasher

P1, three-conductor polarized connector with male contacts, rated: 15 A, 125 Vac
C1 and C2, capacitors, 0.1 µF, 200 WVDC
C3, capacitor, 0.12 µF, 200 WVDC
CR1, rectifier diode, 1 A, 200 PIV
DS1 and DS2, neon lamps, NE-2
F1, fuse, AGC, ½ A
R1 and R2, resistors, carbon-composition or film, 10 MΩ, ½ W
S1, switch, SPST

PROJECT 8 GAME PORT EXTENSION BOX

Some popular computers have a 16-pin DIP socket called the *game port*. This is located on the main logic board. The game port provides access to the I/O functions of the computer. The extension box project (Fig. 50-8) is designed to be a convenient method of interfacing cir-

Fig. 50-8. Game port extension box

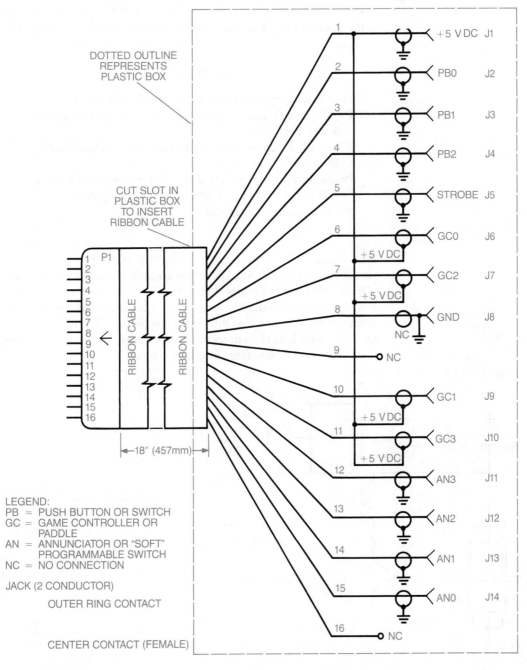

DOTTED OUTLINE
REPRESENTS
PLASTIC BOX

CUT SLOT IN
PLASTIC BOX
TO INSERT
RIBBON CABLE

P1

RIBBON CABLE

RIBBON CABLE

◄—18″ (457mm)—►

+5 V DC   J1

PB0   J2

PB1   J3

PB2   J4

STROBE   J5

GC0   J6
+5 V DC

GC2   J7
+5 V DC

GND   J8
NC

NC

GC1   J9
+5 V DC

GC3   J10
+5 V DC

AN3   J11

AN2   J12

AN1   J13

AN0   J14

NC

LEGEND:
PB = PUSH BUTTON OR SWITCH
GC = GAME CONTROLLER OR
     PADDLE
AN = ANNUNCIATOR OR "SOFT"
     PROGRAMMABLE SWITCH
NC = NO CONNECTION

JACK (2 CONDUCTOR)

     OUTER RING CONTACT

CENTER CONTACT (FEMALE)

511

cuitry to the computer. The testing of circuit design and operation is very important, and this project makes the testing process easier.

NOTE 1: The box must be made of plastic since the "ring" connections on some jacks are connected to ground and the ring connections of others are connected to +5 Vdc. It is helpful to arrange the jacks on the top of the box in groups according to function.

NOTE 2: The ribbon conductors at the free end of the cable are soldered to the jacks as indicated. Use a sharp knife and carefully separate the conductors.

PARTS LIST

J1-J14, RCA type chassis mount, female connectors
P1, 16-pin male DIP plug, compression type for ribbon cable header connection
Wire, 16 conductor parallel ribbon cable, approximately 18 in. (457 mm) length
Project box, approximately 2 × 3 × 1 in. deep (5.08 cm × 7.62 cm × 2.54 cm), Unibox No. 172 or equivalent
Assortment of hook-up wire

PROJECT 9 LIGHT-INTENSITY TRACKER

This circuit (Fig. 50-9) will allow your computer to detect the presence of light within the environment or to find the highest intensity of light. A computer program must be written to run the hardware, and this will determine the way in which this circuit can be used. The circuit can be applied to robotic devices or scientific experiments, or it can be used to experiment with rudimentary computer "vision."

Fig. 50-9. Light-intensity tracker circuit

NOTE: The cadmium disulfide (CdS) cell is mounted on the shaft of a slow-moving motor and is rotated to gather data to determine the relative light levels in the area. Although the motor turns slowly (2 RPM), the wires connecting the cell will wrap around the motor shaft; therefore, reverse motor after every revolution.

PARTS LIST

R1, resistor, carbon-composition or film, 1,000 Ω, ¼ W
R2, resistor, carbon-composition or film, 100 KΩ, ¼ W
R3, cadmium disulfide cell, resistance range 30–100 Ω
S1, switch, SPST
D1, D2, diodes, 1N34A or equivalent
Q1, transistor, n-p-n, 2N3055 or equivalent
K1, relay, 12 Vdc coil, DPDT, SIGMA R2-12DC-SCO or equivalent
Motor, 6 Vdc, 4 r/min, Hankscraft motors 184, 6 Vdc or equivalent
IC1, dual JK flip-flop, 4027 or equivalent. This IC should be mounted on a 16-pin DIP socket.
BT1, battery, 12 Vdc
BT2, battery, 6-Vdc or 4 1.5-Vdc dry cells connected in series

PROJECT 10 AUDIO AMPLIFIER

The audio amplifier, as in Fig. 50-10, takes a low-level audio-frequency signal as an input and boosts that signal so that a speaker can be driven to produce sound. The operational amplifier in integrated-circuit form is ideal for this function. It is small, requires few additional parts, can be operated on a simple power source, and the gain can be easily set and controlled. This circuit is useful since it can be used to amplify the signals from other projects you might make.

Fig. 50-10. Audio amplifier circuit

513

R1, resistor, carbon-composition or film 220 Ω, $\frac{1}{2}$ W
R2, resistor, carbon-composition or film, 3 Ω, 1 W
C1, electrolytic capacitor, 10 μF, 25 WVDC
C2, electrolytic capacitor, 500 μF, 25 WVDC
C3, C4, disk capacitor, 0.22 μF, 50 WVDC
C5, electrolytic capacitor, 1,500 μF, 25 WVDC
IC1, operational amplifier, LM 383 or equivalent
BT1, dry cell, 9 Vdc, with connector clip
LS1, speaker, 4 Ω, 10 W

PROBLEM SOLVING 1

Given This Situation: An amateur radio operator wishes to drill two holes, on the same horizontal axis, to accommodate two potentiometers that have ¾-in. diameter knobs. The potentiometer will be turned frequently by young adults. Each potentiometer operates independently of the other, and each adjustment is critical.

Solve This Problem: How close should the holes be located from each other on the horizontal axis to allow easy access to either potentiometer?

PROBLEM SOLVING 2

Given This Situation: A coil of No. 20 PE magnet wire is to be wound around a stove bolt core ¼ in. diameter by 2 in. long. The length of the coil is to be 1¼ in. The coil is to operate at 1.5 Vdc at 1.3 A.

Solve This Problem: Determine the number of turns of wire needed to lift 1 pound of soft iron. The range of accuracy for this problem is ±25 turns.

PROBLEM SOLVING 3

Given This Situation: An electronic device is inoperative because of the failure of a 1-W, 15-Ω resistor. You are in a location where there are no manufactured spare parts available. However, on your worktable there are a blotter, two pieces of writing paper, one ordinary wooden pencil, a jackknife, a small 3-in. piece of No. 25 bare copper wire and an ohmmeter.

Solve This Problem: Manufacture a temporary replacement part for the resistor from any of the materials mentioned that are on your worktable.

PROBLEM SOLVING 4

Given This Situation: An electronic technician wishes to test an A battery in a portable receiver while it is operating under normal conditions. However, the location of the A battery in the receiver makes it impossible to touch the poles of the battery with the regular voltmeter test prods.

Solve This Problem: Design a method to easily measure the voltage of the A battery when it is normally operating in a portable radio. Assume a standard flashlight battery is used and pressed into place against two metal terminals within a plastic cavity made especially for the battery.

PROBLEM SOLVING 5

Given This Situation: When performing the etching process in making a printed-circuit board, the board is placed in the etchant in a plastic container. The acid etchant must be agitated for the etching process to be efficient. Depending upon the temperature and strength of the solution, this process could take several hours. For this reason, some method of mechanical agitation is necessary. The speed of the action should be controllable so that the agitation does not become violent and spill the solution, thereby making a mess. Use materials that will not be affected by the corrosive nature of the solution and that can be found in the shops.

Solve This Problem: Design and construct a suitable agitator that will reliably perform this task with only occasional observation by the operator.

PROBLEM SOLVING 6

Given This Problem: An electronic instrument operates on a balanced circuit pair, which must have exactly the same amount of current in each of two fixed-value resistors. One resistor has been damaged and broken in two pieces and cannot be repaired. The only replacement parts available are several resistors of a value higher than the broken part. After attempting many of the possible combinations of series and parallel circuits, it is found that no combination will give the exact value.

Solve This Problem: Change the value of a fixed-value resistor so as to make a duplicate of the broken resistor.

PROBLEM SOLVING 7

Given This Problem: It is necessary to break a doorway in a masonry wall to make a passage between two rooms. It is known that the wall contains several large cast-iron pipes, and it is necessary to avoid the area of wall in which these pipes are located.

Solve This Problem: Design and build an electronic circuit that will detect and react to the presence of cast iron in the wall.

PROBLEM SOLVING 8

Given This Situation: In an industrial situation, it is desirable to monitor the condition of each leg of a high-voltage, three-phase electrical system. This is especially important in the delta configuration. Monitoring should be easily accomplished, and only normal operation or failure conditions need to be indicated.

Solve This Problem: Design a method of visually testing a 240-V, three-phase electrical system.

PROBLEM SOLVING 9

Given This Situation: Your science teacher wishes to use a microcomputer to collect data related to the swing of a pendulum. The available computer has a game port for a joystick controller and push button inputs.

Solve This Problem: Construct a circuit that will provide data to the computer through the game port.

GLOSSARY

A-D converter A circuit that changes analog (A) signals to digital (D) codes which are useable by a computer.

alphanumeric characters A system of standard alphabetic and numeric characters in combination to represent data.

ammeter An instrument used to measure the amount of current in a circuit. An ac ammeter measures alternating current. A dc ammeter measures direct current.

ampere The unit of measure for a specific quantity of electrons. A current of 1 ampere represents the movement of 6,280,000,000,000,000,000 electrons past a given point in a circuit in 1 second of time.

amplifier A device used to increase the amount of electric power output in a circuit by increasing either the input current or voltage, or both.

amplitude modulation A common method of radio broadcasting in which the amplitude, or strength, of a radio carrier wave is changed above and below a certain level. The changes in the strength of the carrier wave, when detected, represent the information that was transmitted.

anode The positive terminal of a cell or battery. In an electron tube, the anode, or plate, is that element within the tube to which a positive voltage is applied.

antenna The system of wires or other electrical conductors used to receive or to transmit radio waves.

armature The moving part or parts of a magnetically operated device such as a motor, generator, buzzer, bell, relay, or loudspeaker.

ASCII An acronym for American Standard Code for Information Interchange which is used to transfer data between computing equipment.

assembly language Programming language for a computer which is constructed of binary codes used directly by the computer.

atom The smallest part of a chemical element having the properties of the element.

automation The method of controlling the operation of machinery and equipment for the production of goods in such a way that the input and output of machines are controlled by the use of electron circuits and devices.

BASIC A programming language used extensively in personal computers. BASIC stands for Beginners All-purpose Symbolic Instruction Code.

baud A unit of signaling speed. Usually expressed in bits per second.

BCD An abbreviation for Binary Coded Decimal wherein each digit in a decimal number is represented by a 4 bit binary number.

binary The base 2 number system having 1 and 0 as the numeric characters.

binary code A system which uses binary notation to represent data.

binary digit One of the numbers in the binary system, either "1" or "0".

bit A shortened form of binary digit. The smallest unit of information represented by the binary digits 1 and 0. Computers store information in the form of bits.

breadboard A circuit arrangement in which electrical components are fastened together temporarily for testing or experimental work.

brush A carbon or metal object used to make contact with the commutator or slip rings of a motor or a generator.

bus A set of conductors over which data are transmitted from point to point.

byte A unit of data consisting of 8 bits, also referred to as a data word.

cable, coaxial A communication cable made up of one stranded or solid conductor insulated and placed in the center of a copper-braid shield. The outer jacket of the cable is generally vinyl-plastic insulation.

capacitance The property of a capacitor that enables it to store an electric charge. The unit of measurement for capacitance is the farad.

capacitive reactance The opposition that a capacitor presents to alternating current or to a direct current that is changing in value. Capacitive reactance is measured in ohms.

capacitor A device capable of storing electric en-

517

ergy. It is constructed of two conductor materials separated by an insulator.

cathode The negative terminal of a cell or battery. The part of an electronic device from which electrons are emitted.

cell, voltaic A device that produces voltage by means of chemical action. A voltaic cell is made of two different kinds of conductor materials placed within a paste or a fluid (electrolyte) that also conducts electricity.

charge, negative The electrical property of an object containing more electrons than protons.

charge, positive The electrical property of an object containing more protons than electrons.

charger, battery A device that supplies dc voltage to charge a cell or a battery.

chip A popular term for an integrated circuit.

circuit A system of conductors and devices through which electrons can move. A complete circuit contains conductors, a switch, a load, and an electrical source.

circuit, open An incomplete or broken circuit.

circuit, parallel A circuit in which the loads are connected across two wires or conductors of the power line.

circuit, printed A method of circuit wiring in which the conductors are copper strips on a sheet of insulator material.

circuit, series A circuit in which the loads are connected into one wire or conductor of the power line in a "one after the other" fashion.

circuit, short A circuit containing an extremely low resistance thus causing the electrons to bypass the circuit load.

circular mil The unit of measure for the cross-sectional area of a round wire. A round wire 1 mil or 0.001 of an inch in diameter has a cross-sectional area of 1 circular mil. The circular mil area of any round wire is found by squaring the diameter of the wire given in mils.

coil A device made up of turns of insulated wire wrapped around a hollow or a solid-core form.

commutator A device used to reverse the direction of current. A motor or a generator commutator is made of a ring of insulated copper bars, or segments, mounted on a shaft. The bars are connected to the coils of wire wound into the armature core slots.

conductor A solid, a liquid, or a gas through which electrons pass easily.

connector, D-type A common cable connector with 25 or more pins used with computers and associated peripherals. It generally has a hood or cover made from plastic or metal.

continuity test The test made to determine whether a circuit or a part of a circuit provides a complete electrical path.

CPU The Central Processing Unit of a computer, where the conditioning of data takes place.

crystal cartridge The device, mounted in a record player pick-up arm, used to change the physical variations of the record grooves into an electric current. The needle is fastened to the cartridge.

current The movement of charge through a conductor material.

current, alternating A periodic reversal in the movement of charge through a conductor, first in one direction and then in the opposite direction.

current, direct The movement of charge through a conductor in one direction only.

current, induced A current present in a circuit because of the voltage produced by means of electromagnetic induction.

cursor A highlighted mark placed on a computer display screen indicating where the next character will be placed when a key is pressed on the keyboard.

data Characters (alphanumeric or otherwise) which represent a value or condition used by the computer for the various functions performed.

data processing The conditioning of data to perform a function.

detector An electronic device or a circuit that changes the form of a current. In radio and television receivers, a detector is used to separate the audio or video portions of a carrier wave into currents that can be changed to sound or to a picture.

dielectric An insulation material.

digital Data configured in a binary format.

digital computer A computer that processes data in the binary format.

digitizer A device that converts information into digital values useable by the computer.

diode A two-terminal semiconductor device which offers greater resistance to the flow of current in one direction than in the opposite direction.

drive An electro/mechanical device that rotates or winds magnetic, memory medium, disk or tape.

electric car An automobile that gets its power from rechargeable batteries.

electricity, dynamic A form of energy present when electrons move through a circuit.

electricity, static A form of energy present within the space between two oppositely charged objects.

electrolysis The process of producing a chemical change by passing current through a conducting solution.

electrolyte A solution able to conduct current.

electromagnet A magnet produced by passing current through a coil wound around a core of iron.

electromagnetism The magnetism produced by an electric current.

electromotive force The electrical force that causes electrons to move through a conductor. Electromotive force is commonly known as *voltage*.

electron A negatively charged particle that revolves about the nucleus of an atom.

electron gun A device capable of producing a narrow beam of electrons.

electron tube A device consisting of two or more electrodes enclosed in a glass or metal envelope from which most of the air has been removed. Also commonly known as a *vacuum tube*.

electronics The study of electrons and how they move through space and through special conducting materials. The term *electronics* is usually applied to the study of how electrons flow in electron tubes and semiconductor materials.

electroplating An electrochemical process of plating with metal by passing current through a conducting solution.

EMI Electromagnetic interference.

energy The ability to do work.

facsimile process A method of transmitting documents from one place to another electrically. The variations of density of a document being scanned by a photocell cause the cell to generate a varying electrical (video) signal. These signals are transmitted to another point where they control the reproduction of an exact copy or facsimile of the original document.

farad The unit of measure for capacitance. A capacitor is said to have a capacitance of one farad when a voltage applied to it, changing at the rate of one volt per second, produces a current of one ampere in the capacitor circuit. Because the farad is such a very large unit, the term *microfarad, or one-millionth of a farad,* is most commonly used.

fiber optics A method of transmitting information using light and a conductor consisting of a glass or plastic filament.

filament A threadlike conductor found inside electron tubes and light bulbs. The filament glows to give off light and heat.

firmware Software that has been stored in read only memory.

flowchart A diagram that illustrates the operation of a program through the use of lines and symbols.

fluorescent lamp A lamp in which light is produced by the action of ultraviolet rays striking a phosphor-coated surface.

format The way in which data is arranged for processing or storage.

frequency The number of cycles of an alternating current completed in a certain period of time—usually 1 second.

frequency modulation A common method of radio broadcasting in which the frequency of the radio carrier wave is changed above and below a certain given frequency. The changes in the frequency of the carrier wave, when detected, represent the information transmitted.

friction A force that opposes motion.

fuse A protective device made up of a conducting material that melts and breaks the circuit when the current exceeds the ampere rating of the fuse.

fuse puller A tonglike device used to remove cartridge fuses from their mounting clips.

galvanometer An instrument used to measure very small amounts of current.

generator A machine used for changing mechanical energy into electric energy.

ground An electrical connection between a circuit and the earth, or between a circuit and some metal object that takes the place of the earth.

ground-fault circuit interrupter An electronic device that opens a circuit automatically when it detects excessive leakage current flowing to the electrical ground. This protects the user against serious shock.

ground wave A radio wave that travels on, through, or near the Earth.

hard copy Computer data or text printed on paper.

hardware computer The electronic components and units that make up the computing equipment.

headphones A device that changes audio-frequency current into sound. It is worn over the ears.

henry The unit of measure for self-inductance or mutual inductance. A coil is said to have an inductance of one henry when the current through it, changing at the rate of one ampere per second, produces a voltage of one volt across the terminals of the coil.

heterodyning The production of one frequency by combining two different frequencies. The frequency produced is equal to the difference between the two frequencies.

high-efficiency motors Electric motors designed to efficiently convert electric energy into mechanical energy by reducing mechanical and electrical losses.

high fidelity The faithful reproduction of sound by electronic devices such as loudspeakers and amplifiers.

hydrometer A device used to test the specific gravity of acid in a storage-battery cell.

impedance The total opposition of a circuit to alternating current.

incandescent lamp A lamp that produces light by the heating of a filament to a white-hot temperature.

induced magnetism The production of magnetism by placing magnetic material within a varying magnetic field.

inductance The property of a coil or of any part of a circuit that causes it to oppose any change in the value of the current flowing through it. The unit of measure for inductance is the henry.

induction The process of magnetizing an object or of inducing a voltage in an object by placing it within a varying magnetic field.

inductive reactance The opposition that a coil presents to alternating current or to a direct current that is changing in value. Inductive reactance is measured in ohms.

insulator A material that will not conduct current. An object made of an insulator material that supports or separates conductors in a circuit.

integrated circuit Complex circuitry formed on a single piece of base material such as silicon.

interface Electronic circuitry that links hardware to enable the passage of data.

I/O Input/Output, the transfer of data in and out of a computer.

ion A charged atom containing more or less than its normal number of electrons.

jack Any of several devices used to make a temporary and easily disconnected electrical contact in a circuit.

junction A point in a circuit to which two or more conductors are connected together.

key A hand-operated switch used for sending the international Morse code.

kilo A prefix meaning thousand.

kilohertz One thousand cycles per second.

lamp A device used to produce light.

laser An abbreviation for *l*ight *a*mplification by *s*timulated *e*mission of *r*adiation. A laser produces an intense directional beam of light.

lead Either the beginning or the ending wire of an electrical device or an external wire connected to a device such as a resistor, a coil, or a capacitor.

LED Light Emitting Diode.

Lenz's law A basic electrical law that states that the direction of a magnetic field generated by an induced current opposes any change in the field causing the induction.

load The device in a circuit operated by the current.

lodestone One of the common names for magnetite, a mineral that is a natural magnet.

logic gate A digital circuit with a number of inputs and one output.

logic probe A troubleshooting instrument for digital circuits.

loudspeaker A magnetically operated device that changes electric energy into sound.

lug An insulated strip of metal to which wires can be connected.

magnet An object with the property of magnetic polarity and that attracts magnetic materials.

magnetic field The space near a magnet in which magnetic forces are present.

meter A measuring instrument.

meter, analog A meter that operates with a continuous variable quantity.

meter, digital A meter that converts an analog quantity, for example, voltage, into a digital form.

meter, watthour An instrument used to measure the amount of electricity in kilowatthours.

mica A mineral that is a good insulator of electricity and heat.

micro A prefix meaning one-millionth.

microcomputer A small computer sometimes called a personal computer.

microphone A device used to change sound energy into electric energy.

microprocessor A complex integrated circuit containing hundreds of logic gates. It is the central control unit in a computer.

modem An electronic device that connects data terminal equipment to a communication line, such as a telephone line. The term modem is a contraction of modulator-demodulator.

modulation The process of changing the amplitude or the frequency of a carrier wave by means of an audio or a video signal.

MOS Abbreviation for Metal-Oxide Semiconductor.

motor A machine that changes electric energy into mechanical energy.

National Electrical Code® A set of guidelines for the safe installation of electric wiring and apparatus sponsored by the National Fire Protection Association under the auspices of the American National Standards Institute.

negative The electrical property of an object that contains more than the normal number of electrons.

neon lamp A device that produces light by passing current through neon gas.

nonmagnetic material A material that cannot be magnetized and is neither attracted nor repelled by a magnet.

numeric characters The digits 0 through 9.

ocean thermal energy conversion system An energy system under study that is expected to make use of ocean water to collect and store energy from the sun.

octal A number system in base 8 which uses the digits 0 through 7.

ohm The unit of electrical resistance. A circuit has a resistance of one ohm when one volt produces a current of one ampere.

ohmmeter An instrument used to measure resistance.

Ohm's law A basic electrical law that states the relationship between current, voltage, and resistance in a dc circuit.

operating system, computer The software program that allows the computer to perform the basic functions for which it was designed.

optical fiber A hair-thin ultratransparent filament of glass. Several fibers brought together form a fiberoptic communications transmission line.

oscillator An electronic device that generates an alternating current.

oscilloscope An instrument that produces the picture of a waveform upon the screen of a cathode-ray tube.

OSHA An abbreviation for the *O*ccupational *S*afety and *H*ealth Administration, an agency of the U.S. Department of Labor. This agency issues safety and health standards related to working conditions.

output device, computer A device that receives digital data from the computer and produces hard copy or a desired function.

output transformer A transformer placed between the output stage and the loudspeaker of a radio receiver, television receiver, audio amplifier, and so on.

PC Personal (micro) Computer.

peripheral computer A hardware device attached externally to a computer to enable the computer to perform various tasks.

phototube A two-element electron tube, the cathode of which emits electrons when light strikes it.

piezoelectricity The production of voltage by mechanically straining or pressing certain kinds of crystal substances.

pixels A contraction for picture elements. Individual dots or squares which make up a digitized scene on a television screen. As the number of picture elements increases, the resolution of the ability of the ''pixels'' to reproduce detail is improved.

plug A device inserted into a jack to make an electrical connection.

points, breaker A device that interrupts a continuous direct current. In an automobile, breaker points are part of the distributor unit.

points, contact A mechanism with special surfaces that make contact to complete, or separate to open, a certain part of a circuit. Contact points are found in switches, relays, circuit breakers, and so on.

polarity An electrical condition that determines the direction of current. In a circuit, electrons move from a point of negative polarity to a point of positive polarity.

polarization The process by which hydrogen gas is deposited on the positive electrode of a dry cell.

port, computer The part of a computer where data can be sent to or received from peripheral equipment via the appropriate connecting hardware.

potentiometer A variable resistor.

power The rate, or speed, at which work is done.

primary cell A cell that cannot be recharged.

program, computer A logical sequence of coded instructions which direct the computer to perform a function.

radio A general term used in connection with equipment that receives electromagnetic waves and changes them into sound energy. The process by which radio waves are sent through the air is called *radio transmission*.

RAM Random Access Memory. Computer memory that can be changed by writing to a specific location. Also known as Read/Write memory.

receptacle A socket or an outlet into which a plug is inserted to make an electrical connection.

rectifier A device that changes alternating current into direct current.

regulator, generator A device used to control the current and the voltage output of a generator.

relay (mechanical) A switch operated by electromagnetism.

resistance The property of a device or a circuit that opposes the movement of current through it. The unit of resistance is the ohm.

resistor A device used to insert electrical resistance into a circuit.

resonance The condition of a tuning circuit when the capacitive reactance of the circuit capacitor is equal to the inductive reactance of the coil in the circuit.

RFI Radio frequency interference.

rheostat A variable resistor usually used in circuits through which large amounts of current move.

ROM Read Only Memory. Computer memory which cannot be changed by a computer write function.

rotor The revolving part of a motor or generator.

scanning The process of moving an electron beam over the inner surface of the face of a cathode-ray tube.

selectivity The property of a tuning circuit that enables it to pass only one frequency at a time.

semiconductor A group of solid materials that are good conductors of current under one condition and poor conductors under another condition.

series-parallel circuit A circuit containing one or more combinations of series and parallel circuits.

signal generator An electronic device used to produce a variety of signals. It is often used to test and adjust an electronic circuit in radios and televisions.

signal tracer An electronic device used to trace the progress of a signal in a radio or television circuit.

software (computer) Another name for a program.

solar cell A cell, usually made of silicon, that produces current when light falls on it.

solenoid A coil of wire wrapped around a hollow form.

space-based power conversion system A solar energy system under study that can collect pollution-free energy from the sun and transmit it to Earth from a fixed orbit.

splice A form of permanent electrical connection—usually soldered.

switch A device used to open and close an electric circuit.

telegraph A system of communicating by means of coded signals.

telephone A system of communicating by means of audio signals.

teletypewriter An electrically operated typewriter that reproduces, in written form, the coded signals that it receives.

television Electronic apparatus that changes information transmitted by carrier waves into pictures and sound.

terminal A mechanical connecting point used to fasten wires to cells, batteries, switches, panels, and so on.

theory An idea that is thought to be true but has not yet been proved.

thermocouple A device consisting of two different kinds of metals joined at one end. When the junction is heated, a voltage is produced across the open ends of the metals.

thermostat A switch whose operation depends on changes in temperature.

tool, alignment A tool made up of insulating material used to adjust tuning circuits in communication equipment.

tower, transmission A tower on which a radio or television transmitting antenna is mounted.

transformer A device that can increase or decrease the voltage or current in an ac circuit.

transformer, toroidal A transformer whose magnetic core is shaped like a doughnut and, therefore, has no airgap. A *toroid* is the geometric term for a doughnut-shaped object.

transistor A semiconductor device used to amplify electrical signals.

transmitter The electronic apparatus that sends radio waves through the air.

tube, cathode-ray An electron tube containing an electron gun that can reproduce a signal in the form of a picture on its face.

tuner The circuit of a radio or television receiver that selects the carrier frequency desired.

TVRO A home-earth station which uses a Television Receive Only (TVRO) electronic system to view broadcast transmissions from satellites.

VCR A video cassette recorder. A device for recording and playing back video and audio signals on a special magnetic tape cartridge.

volt The unit of electromotive force, or voltage.

voltage The electromotive force that causes electrons to move through a circuit.

voltmeter An instrument used to measure voltage.

watt The unit of electric power.

waves, radio A form of electromagnetic energy that transmits information through the air.

wire, magnet Copper wire usually coated with insulating varnish. Magnet wire is used for winding many kinds of coils.

wire stripper A tool used to remove the insulation from wire.

wire table Table of sizes and properties of round copper wire.

wire wrapping A process of making an electrical connection by tightly coiling wire around a metal terminal.

write (computer) To record data in a computer memory location.

INDEX

ADC (analog-to-digital converter), 359, 449–450
Address bus, 436
AF (audio-frequency) signals, 344–345
Air cleaners, electronic, 308
Air conditioning
  central, 306, 307
  room, 305–306
Air-core transformers, 130
Air gap, magnetic, 128–129
Alkaline cells, 147
Alloys
  magnetic, 115
  resistance, 293
Alphanumeric characters, 428
Alternator regulators, 313–315
Alternators, 127, 158, 313, 314
Aluminum conductors, 271
Aluminum production, 264
AM (amplitude modulation), 367
Amateur radio, 369
American National Standard Code for Information Interchange (ASCII), 331–333
American National Standards Institute (ANSI), 13
American wire gage (AWG) number, 206–207
Ammeters, 95
  using, 97–98
Ampacity, 207
Ampere, 25, 43
Ampere-turns, 121–122
Amplifier circuits, practical, 180
Amplifiers, 252
  audio, 349–351
  operational, 191–193
Amplitude modulation (AM), 367
Analog computers, 427
Analog-to-digital converter (ADC), 359, 449–450
AND gate, 416–417
Angle of declination, 117
Annunciators, 462–463
Appliance service workers, 38
Architectural floor-plan diagrams, 16, 18
Armatures, 154, 279–280
ASCII (American National Standard Code for Information Interchange), 331–333
Assembly language, 453–455

Asynchronous data communications, 333
Atomic fission, 470
Atomic number, 2
Atomic weight, 2
Atoms, 2–4
Attraction, magnetic, 114
Audio amplifiers, 349–351
Audio cables, 349
Audio detection, 183–184
Audio-frequency (AF) signals, 344–345
Audio service technicians, 35–36
Audio systems, 344–362
  common elements of, 347–362
  four-channel, 346
  monaural, 345
  stereo, 345–346
Automobile, electric, 316–318
Automobile battery, 309–310
Automobile electrical system, 309–318
Automobile telephones, 377–378
Automotive service, 39–40
AWG (American wire gage) number, 206–207

BASIC instruction codes, 452–453
Basing diagrams, 253
Batteries, 144 (see also Cells)
  automobile, 309–310
Beat frequency, 371
Bells, 122
Bias voltages, 181
Binary codes, device select by, 438–439
Binary conditions, 415
Binary number system, 420–421
Binary system, 328–329
Bits, 329, 420, 428, 432
Block diagrams, 16, 17
Box connectors, 272–273
Branch-circuit wiring, 270–271
Branch circuits, 269–270
Breadboards, 225–226
  development on, 479
Breaker-point ignition system, 311–312
British thermal unit (Btu), 305–306
Broadcast technicians, 36
Burns, 20
Business-machine service workers, 38–39

Buzzers, 122
Bytes, 432

Cable fabrication techniques, 213–214
Cable television, 401–402
Cables, communication, 206, 211–213
CAD (computer-aided design), 479
Capacitance, 103–111
  unit of, 105
Capacitive reactance, 104
Capacitors, 103
  action of, 103–105
  charging rate of, 108–109
  color codes of, 109
  defects of, 109–110
  electrolytic, 106–107, 173–174
  kinds of, 105–106
  in parallel, 107
  safety of, 109
  testing, 110–111
  variable, 107
Car (see Automobile entries)
Carbon-zinc cells, 146–147
Carrier waves, 365–366
Cartridges, 348–349
Cathode ray tube (CRT), 485–486
Cathodes, 251
CD (compact disc) players, 358–362
Cells, 144–152
  alkaline, 147
  basic action of, 144–145
  carbon-zinc, 146–147
  current of, 145
  lead-acid, 149–152
  lithium, 149
  mercury, 147–148
  nickel-cadmium, 148–149
  in parallel, 84–85
  primary, 145
  secondary, 145
  in series, 75
  shelf life of, 146
  testing, 149
  voltage of, 145
Central air conditioning, 306, 307
Central processing unit (CPU), 430
Centrifugal switches, 284–285
Charging rate of capacitors, 108–109

Chassis, 13
  finishing, 245
  forming, 244–245
  layout diagrams for, 240
  location of components on, 240–241
  making, 240–245
Chassis blank
  cutting out, 241–242
  laying out, 242
Chassis punch, 243
Chemical cells (see Cells)
Chemical reactions, 260–264
Choke coils, 137
Circuit breakers, 27, 475
  magnetic, 124
Circuit-control devices, 8–9
Circuit diagrams, 10–18
Circuit packs, 199
Circuit trouble diagnosis, 494–495
Circular-mil area, 207
Clamp-on meters, 101
Clamping devices, 222, 223
Class designation letters, 12
Clips, 222
Clocks
  computer, 431–432
  digital, 424–425
Closed loop, 8, 69
CMOS (complementary-metal-oxide semiconductors), 187–188
Coaxial cable connectors and adapters, 224–225
Coincidence circuits, 420
Color camera tubes, 392
Color circuits, 398
Color picture tubes, 399–400
Color tuning, 400
Combinatorial circuits, 419
Common-emitter circuit, 178–179
Communication cables, 206, 211–213
Communications
  basic concepts in, 320–324
  electrical, 324
  lightwave, 339
  networks for, 333–334
  portable, 376–379
  radio, 364–379
  satellite, 379–382, 406–407
  types of, 322–323
  visual, 321
  voice, 321
Commutators, 156
  action of, 279–280
Compact disc (CD) players, 358–362

Complementary-metal-oxide semiconductors (CMOS), 187–188
Complementary symmetry, 354–355
Complex circuits, analyzing, 91–93
Compliance, 349
Component manufacturing, 482, 484
Compounds, 3
Computer-aided design (CAD), 479
Computer clocks, 431–432
Computer graphics, 441
Computer input, 428
Computer memory, 433–437
Computer output, 428
Computer peripherals, 458–459
Computer programming, 450–453
Computer programs, 429, 431
Computer storage, 428–429
Computers, 427–446
  analog, 427
  digital, 427
  future of, 446
  microcomputers (see Microcomputers)
Conductors, 8, 47–50
  aluminum, 271
  service-entrance, 267–269
Connection diagrams, 16, 17
Construction electricians, 39
Construction project, 498
Continuity tests, 100–101, 138, 493
Control grid, 252
Cords, electrical, 206, 210–211
Counter electromotive force (cemf), 108, 134
Counters, 422–424
CPU (central processing unit), 430
Cranking circuit, 310–311
CRT (cathode ray tube), 485–486
Current, 7, 42
  alternating, 44–46, 128
  of cells, 145
  direct, 43–44, 128
  excitation, 157
  induced, 126
  at junction points, 84
  in parallel circuit, 78–80
  in series circuit, 72–73
  in series-parallel circuit, 89–91
  in transformers, 132–133
Current-carrying capacity, safe, 207
Current loop, 69

DAC (digital-to-analog conversion), 450
Data, 432
  transmitting, 441
Data bus, 438

Data communication testing, 496
Data communications, 333
Data formats, 432–433
Debounce, 457
Decimal prefixes, 43, 44
Demagnetizers, 116
Demodulation, 183–184
Depletion region, 170
Depolarizing agent, 146
Desoldering tool, 204
Detector diodes, 183–184
Device select
  by binary codes, 438–439
  by memory map, 440–441
Diagnostic software tools, 496
Dial telephones, 337–338
Dielectric heating, 297–298
Dielectric strength, 51
Dielectrics, 103
Digital arithmetic, 421–422
Digital clocks, 424–425
Digital computers, 427
Digital electronic circuits, 415–425
Digital meters, 101
Digital multimeters, 101
Digital-to-analog conversion (DAC), 450
Diodes, 169–175, 251–252
  detector, 183–184
  light-emitting (LED), 189–190
  operation of, 172
  p-n-junction, 170–171
  photodiodes, 190, 191
  ratings of, 174
  testing, 174–175
Doping process, 169
Drilling holes, 242–243
Dry cells (see Cells)
Dynamic electricity, 42

Eddy currents, 131
Electric arcs, 295
Electric car, 316–318
Electric charges, 3–4
Electric circuits, 7–9
Electric energy, 46
  alternate sources of, 161–168
Electric generators (see Generators)
Electric motors (see Motors)
Electric power, 46
Electric power industry, 468–475
Electric ranges, 299–300
Electric shock, 19–20
Electrical Code, National, 266
Electrical communications, 324
Electrical cords, 206, 210–211
Electrical designers, 34–35

Electrical engineering, 34
Electrical impulse, 48
Electrical plugs, 219–221
Electrical system(s)
  automobile, 309–318
  home, 265–276
Electrical utility line workers, 40
Electrical wiring (*see* Wire *entries*)
Electricity, 1
  dynamic, 42
  measuring, 94–101
  occupations in, 32–40
  static, 4–6
Electrodes, 144
Electrolysis, 260–261
  of water, 261
Electrolytes, 144, 260
Electrolytic capacitors, 106–107,
  173–174
Electrolytic furnace, 264
Electromagnetic field, 120
Electromagnetic induction, 126–127
Electromagnetic interference (EMI),
  212
Electromagnetic spectrum of light,
  257
Electromagnetic waves, 364
Electromagnetism, 120–124
Electromagnets, iron-core, 121–122
Electromotive force (emf), 42
  counter (cemf), 108, 134
Electron tubes, 176–177, 250–251
  basic operation of, 251
  designation and substitution, 253
  testing, 253–254
Electronic air cleaners, 308
Electronic circuits, digital, 415–425
Electronic device development,
  478–480, 481–482
Electronic device manufacturing,
  481–484
Electronic ignition system, 313
Electronic irons, 302–303
Electronic revolution, home, 324,
  325
Electronic test instruments, 485–490
  using, 489–490
Electronics, research and develop-
  ment in, 476–480
Electrons, 2–4, 42
  free, 3–4
  valence, 3
Electroplating, 261–263
Electrostatic attraction, 251
Electrostatic deflection, 486, 487
Electrostatic field, 4, 104
Elements, 2–3

EMI (electromagnetic interference),
  212
Enclosures, ready-made, 245
Energy, 2–4
  electric (*see* Electric energy)
  heat (*see* Heat, producing)
Energy-efficient motors, 288
Energy levels, 3
Energy source, 7
Engineering services, 478
Engineering technicians, 35
Erasable programmable read only
  memory (EPROM), 435–436
Excitation current, 157
Exclusive-OR (XOR) gate, 419
Experimental activities, 502

Facsimile copying cycle, 413
Facsimile receiving cycle, 413
Facsimile transmission, 408–413
Facsimile transmit cycle, 412
Farad, 105
Federal Communications Commis-
  sion (FCC), 369
Feedback, 321
Ferrites, 115
Ferromagnetic elements, 114–115
Ferrous metal, 240
FET (field-effect transistors), 185
FF (flip-flops), 422–424
Fiber washers, 227, 228
Field-effect transistors (FET), 185
Files, 243
Flip-flops (FF), 422–424
Fluorescent lamps, 254–255
Flyback high-voltage system, 397–
  398
FM (frequency modulation), 367
Forward bias, 172
Fossil fuel power plants, 469–470
Four-channel audio systems, 346
Four-way switches, 274
Freon, 304
Frequency of current, 45
Frequency counters, 488
Frequency dividers, 424
Frequency modulation (FM), 367
Fuel cells, 165–166
Full-adders, 422
Full-wave-rectifier circuit, 174
Fuse panels, 268
Fuses, 24–27
  automobile, 316

Galvanometers, 95
Game paddles, 462
Game ports, 460–461

Gates, 172
Generators, 127, 154–160
  action of, 154–156
  alternating-current, 158–159
  basic, 154
  direct-current, 156–157
  three-phase, 159–160
Geothermal energy, 164
Glow lamps, 256–257
Graphic symbols, 11–16
Graphics, computer, 441
Green wire, 22–23
Grommets, 227
Ground connection symbols, 13
Ground-fault circuit interrupter, 28
Grounding for personal safety, 21–
  23

Half-adders, 422
Half-wave-rectifier circuit, 173–174
Hand wiring, 218
Hartley oscillators, 487
Heat, producing, 292–303
Heat pumps, 306–307
Heat sensors, 185
Heat sinks, 180–181
Heating
  dielectric, 297–298
  induction, 297
  infrared, 296
  resistance, 293–295
Heating elements, 293–295
Henry, 134
Hertz, 45
Hexadecimal codes, 441–442
High address, 436–437
High-altitude transmission of power,
  165
High-energy physics, 2
High-tech occupations, 37–38
Holes, drilling, 242–243
Home earth stations, 406–407
Home electrical systems, 265–276
Home electronic revolution, 324,
  325
Home television, 402–406
Horns, automobile, 315–316
Hydroelectric power plants, 468–
  469
Hydrogen, 152
Hydrometers, 150–151
Hysteresis loss, 131

IC (integrated circuits), 183, 186–
  188
IC test clip, 231

Ignition system
  breaker-point, 311–312
  electronic, 313
Image orthicon tube, 388–391
Impedance, 105, 135
Inadequate wiring symptoms, 275–276
Incandescent lamps, 249–250
Inductance, 133–134
  effect of, 135–136
  measuring, 138–139
Induction
  electromagnetic, 126–127
  magnetic, 115
  mutual, 129
Induction heating, 297
Inductive reactance, 134–135
Inductors, 136–137
  testing, 137–138
Information initiators, 320
Information systems, 326–343
Information users, 320
Infrared heating, 296
Input/output (I/O), 438
Input/output ports, 459–463
Instruments
  automobile, 316
  electronic test, 485–490
Insulating tapes, devices, and materials, 226–228
Insulation, 24
Insulators, 50–51
Integrated circuits (see IC entries)
Interfaces, 212
Interfacing, 448–449
International Morse code, 326, 328
I/O (see Input/output entries)
Ions, 4
Iron-core electromagnets, 121–122
Irons, electronic, 302–303
Isolators, 191, 192

Jacks, electrical, 219–221
Joule, 305
Jump starting, 85
Junction boxes, 272
Junctions, 71

Keyboard printer terminals, 331
Kilowatthour formula, 66–67
Kirchhoff's laws, 84

Lamps, 249
  fluorescent, 254–255
  glow, 256–257
  incandescent, 249–250
  mercury, 255–256

Lamps (Cont.)
  photoflash, 254
  three-lite, 250
Large-scale integration (LSI), 188
Laser playback, 361–362
Laser recording, 359–361
Lasers, 257–259
Latches, 438
Layout diagrams, 198
  for chassis, 240
Lead-acid cells, 149–152
LED (light-emitting diodes), 189–190
Lenz's law, 126–127
Light, 257
  coherent, 258
  incoherent, 257–258
  ultraviolet, 255
Light-emitting diodes (LED), 189–190
Lights, automobile, 315
Lightwave communications, 339
Lines of force, magnetic, 114
Lithium cells, 149
Load centers, 268
Loads, 8, 9
Logic circuit design, 419–420
Logic circuit pulses, 432
Logic circuits, 415–416
Logic gates, 416–418
Logic probes, 495–496
Loudspeakers, 352–354
Low address, 436
LSI (large-scale integration), 188
Lumen, 249

Machine screws, 245–246
Magnetic air gap, 128–129
Magnetic circuit breakers, 124
Magnetic compass, 117, 118
Magnetic fields, 114
  moving, 120, 128–129
Magnetic induction, 115
Magnetic materials, 114–115
Magnetic-particle inspection, 117
Magnetic poles, 113
Magnetic shielding, 116, 117
Magnetic starters, 287
Magnetic tape, 357–358, 428
Magnetism, 113–118
  eliminating, 116
  future uses of, 117
Magneto, 159
Magnetohydrodynamic (MHD) conversion, 166–167
Magnetrons, 298

Magnets, 113
  making, 115–116
Maintenance electricians, 39
Manufacturing, product, 481–484
Manufacturing process sheets, 481, 482
Manufacturing process specifications, 481–483
Matter, 2
Memory map, device select by, 440–441
Mercury cells, 147–148
Mercury lamps, 255–256
Message service, personal, 376
Metallic-oxide semiconductors (MOS), 187–188
Meter scales, reading, 98–100
MHD (magnetohydrodynamic) conversion, 166–167
Microcomputers, 429–430
  interaction with, 447–463
  single-chip, 442–445
Microminiaturization, 187
Microphone connectors, 221
Microphones, 347–348
Microprocessors, 188, 189
Microwave ovens, 298–299
Microwaves, 165, 298
Mil, 207
MK 3870 single-chip microcomputer, 442–445
Mnemonics, 453–454
Modems, 333
Modulation, 366–367
Modules, 199
Molecules, 3
Monaural audio systems, 345
Morse code, international, 326, 328
MOS (metallic-oxide semiconductors), 187–188
Motors, 278–289
  action of, 279
  alternating-current, 282–283
  capacitor-start, 285
  care and maintenance of, 288–289
  direct-current, 280–281
  energy-efficient, 288
  repulsion-start, 286–287
  reversing, 282
  shaded-pole, 285–286
  size of, 280
  speed control of, 282
  split-phase, 283–285
  synchronous, 287
  three-phase induction, 287
  universal, 281–282

Moving coil meters, 94–95
Multimeters, 95, 96
  digital, 101
Multi-outlet strips, 273
Multiplexing, 439
Mutual induction, 129

NAND gate, 418, 419
National Electrical Code, 266
Negative feedback voltage, 192–193
Neon lamp handitester, 23–24
Neon signs, 257
Networking, 431
Neutrons, 2–3
Nibbles, 432
Nickel-cadmium cells, 148–149
Nodes, 71
Nondestructive testing, 117
Nonmagnetic materials, 115
Nonsinusoidal waveforms, 46
NOR gate, 418–419
North magnetic pole, 113
NOT gate, 417–418
Nuclear chain reaction, 470
Nuclear power plants, 470–472
Nucleus, atomic, 2
Nutdrivers, 247

Occupational Outlook Handbook, 40
Occupational Safety and Health Act
  (OSHA), 29
Occupations in electricity, 32–40
Ocean heat, energy from, 164
Octal codes, 441–442
Ohm, 49
Ohmmeters, 95–96
  using, 98
Ohm's law, 60–63
  in parallel circuits, 79–80
Open circuits, 24
Open loop, 8, 69–70
Openings, making large, 243
Operating system (OS), 435
Operational amplifiers, 191–193
Optocouplers, 191, 192
Optoelectronics, 188–191
OR gate, 417
Organic materials as sources of en-
  ergy, 164
OS (operating system), 435
Oscilloscopes, 485–487
OSHA *(Occupational Safety and
  Health Act),* 29
Ovens, microwave, 298–299
Overloaded circuits, 79

p-n-junction diodes, 170–171
p-n junctions, 162–163
Parallel circuits, 9, 77–85
Parallel-resistance formulas, 81–84
Peak inverse voltage (PIV), 174
Peltier effect, 186
Pentodes, 253
Peripherals, computer, 458–459
Permeability, 115
Phones (*see* Telephones)
Photoconductive cells, 189, 190
Photodiodes, 190, 191
Photoelectric effect, 388
Photoflash lamps, 254
Phototransistors, 190, 191
Photovoltaic cells, 162
Pi network, 369
Pictorial diagrams, 10–11
Pilot runs, 480
Pin insertion method, 213–214
PIV (peak inverse voltage), 174
Pixels, 386, 387
Plates, 144
Pliers, 218, 219
Plugs, electrical, 219–221
Polarity, 71
  transistor, 181
Polarization, 146
Portable communications, 376–379
Potential barrier, 171
Power
  electric, 46
  high-altitude transmission of, 165
Power adapters, 101
Power factor, 288
Power formulas, 63–66
Power plants, 468
  fossil fuel, 469–470
  hydroelectric, 468–469
  nuclear, 470–472
Power rating, resistor, 54–55
Power strips, 28–29
Power supply block, 16
Power transformers, 132
Power transmission lines, 133, 473
Power transmission systems, 472–
  475
Preamplifiers, 356
Prefixes, unit, 43, 44
Primary winding, 29
Printed circuits, 197–204
  making, 200–203
  manufacture of, 198–199
  repairing, 203–204
Problem solving, 514–516
Programmable read only memory
  (PROM), 435

Programming, computer, 450–453
Project-idea sketch sheet, 500
Project kits, 501–502
Project plan sheet, 501
Project planning, 498–504
Project safety, 503–504
Projects
  choosing, 498–499
  planning and designing, 499–501
  repair, 502–503
  suggested, 505–514
PROM (programmable read only
  memory), 435
Protons, 2–3
Prototypes, 479
Pull-up resistors, 456–457
Pulse input, 455–458
Push-pull operation, 351–352
Pyrometers, 186, 187

Quality control, 482

Radio, amateur, 369
Radio communications, 364–379
Radio control devices, 378–379
Radio frequency interference (RFI),
  212
Radio receivers, superheterodyne,
  370–375
Radio services, personal, 369–370
Radio transmitters, 364
Radio waves, 364–366
Radiotelephony, 370
Random access memory (RAM),
  435
Reactance
  capacitive, 104
  inductive, 134–135
Reactors, nuclear, 470–472
Read only memory (ROM), 435
Reamers, 243
Records, 356–357
Rectifier circuits, 171, 252
Rectifiers, silicon controlled (SCR),
  184
Refrigerant, 304
Refrigerators, 304–305
Register words, 430–431
Relays, 123–124
Remote-control wiring, 274–275
Repair projects, 502–503
Repulsion, magnetic, 114
Research, defined, 476
Resistance, 48–50
  in parallel circuit, 80
  in series circuit, 71–72
  in series-parallel circuit, 87–89

Resistance heating, 293–295
Resistance tests, 494
Resistance welding, 295
Resistors, 52–57
    color codes for, 55–56
    defects in, 57
    fixed, 52–54
    fusible, 57
    variable, 56–57
Retentivity, 115, 121
Reverse bias, 172
RFI (radio frequency interference),
    212
RMS (root mean squared) value,
    352
ROM (read only memory), 435
Room air conditioning, 305–306
Root mean squared (RMS) value,
    352
Rotor assembly, 107
Rotors, 158, 279–280

Safety, project, 503–504
Safety glasses, 28
Safety rules, 19–29
Satellite communications, 379–382,
    406–407
Schematic diagrams, 11–16
SCR (silicon controlled rectifiers),
    184
Screen printing, 198
Screwdrivers, 246–247
Screws
    machine, 245–246
    self-tapping, 246
Secondary winding, 129
Segments, 156
Self-inductance, 133–134
Self-tapping screws, 246
Semiconductors, 169–175
    complementary-metal-oxide
        (CMOS), 187–188
    metallic-oxide (MOS), 187–188
    structure of, 169–170
Series circuits, 9, 69–75
Series-parallel circuits, 86–93
Service drop, 267
Service-entrance conductors, 267–
    269
Sheet-metal chassis (see Chassis en-
    tries)
Shield lead, 178
Short circuits, 24
Signal generators, 487–488
Signal tracers, 488–489
Signs, neon, 257

Silicon controlled rectifiers (SCR),
    184
Sine waves, 44–45
Single-chip microcomputers, 442–
    445
Slip rings, 154
Soft soldering, 232
Software debounce, 457–458
Solar cells, 162–163
Solder, 232–233
Solder flux, 232–233
Soldered connections, 226
Soldering, 232–238
Soldering guns, 235
Soldering irons, 233–235
Soldering method, 214
Soldering wires
    to hollow terminals, 237–238
    to lugs, 236–237
    preparing for, 235–236
    together, 238
Solderless connections, 225
Solenoids, 120–121
South magnetic pole, 113
Space Tracking and Data Acquisi-
    tion Network (STADAN), 381
Spark plugs, 311, 312
Specific gravity, 150
Speed control of motors, 282
Spray dust, 6
STADAN (Space Tracking and Data
    Acquisition Network), 381
Static electricity, 4–6
Stator assembly, 107
Stators, 158
Stereo audio systems, 345–346
Strapping devices, 222, 223
Substations, 475
Substrates, 186
Sulfuric acid, 150
Sunlight as source of energy, 162–
    163
Superconductivity, 50
Superheterodyne radio receivers,
    370–375
Surface-wiring devices, 273
Sweep generators, 486–487
Switch boxes, 272
Switches
    centrifugal, 284–285
    three-way and four-way, 274
Synchronous data communications,
    333

Tape heads, 357–358
Technical design review, 479
Telecommunication workers, 36–37

Telegraph systems, 326–328
Telemetry, 379
Telephone jacks, 220–221
Telephone receivers, 335–337
Telephone system, 334–339
Telephone transmitters, 335
Telephones
    automobile, 377–378
    cordless, 376–377
    dial, 337–338
    Touch-Tone, 338–339
Teleprinters, 331
Teletypewriter code, 329
Teletypewriters, 328–331
Television, 386–407
    cable, 401–402
    color (see Color entries)
    fundamentals of, 386, 388
    home, 402–406
Television antenna, 396
Television block diagram, 395
Television picture interference,
    400–401
Television picture tubes, 398–401
Television receivers, 394–395
Television signal transmission,
    392–394
Television technicians, 35–36
Terminal posts, 229
Terminal strips and lugs, 222, 223
Thermal energy of ocean, 164
Thermionic emission, 251
Thermionic energy conversion,
    167–168
Thermistors, 185
Thermocouples, 186, 187
Thermostats, 299–300
    bimetallic, 300
Three-lite lamps, 250
Three-way switches, 274
Thyristors, 184
Time-constant formula, capacitor,
    108
Timing diagrams, 433
Tinning, 234–235
Toasters, 300–302
Tolerance, resistor, 54
Tone control, 355–356
Toroidal transformers, 137
Torque, 280
Touch-Tone telephones, 338–339
Transceivers, 339–343, 370
Transformer coupling, 351
Transformers, 129–131, 473–474
    air-core, 130
    power, 132
    testing, 137–138

Transformers (Cont.)
  toroidal, 137
Transient response, 135
Transistors, 176–182
  field-effect (FET), 185
  kinds of, 177–178
  operation of, 178–179
  phototransistors, 190, 191
  testing, 181–182
  working with, 180–181
Transmission lines, power, 133, 473
Transmission systems, 472–475
Transmitters, low-power AM, 367–369
Triodes, 252
Troubleshooting procedures, 491–496
Tubing, insulating, 227
Turns ratio, 131
TVRO systems, 406–407
Two-to-three-wire adapters, 23

Ultraviolet light, 255
Underwriters' knot, 220
Unit prefixes, 43, 44
Unwrapping tool, 230
User ports, 458–459

Vibrating devices, 122
Video cassette recorder (VCR), 402–406

Vidicon camera tube, 391–392
Visual communication, 321
Visual inspection, 492
Voice communications, 321
Volt, 42–43
Voltage, 7, 42
  bias, 181
  of cells, 145
  counter, 134
  induced, 126, 130, 131
  negative feedback, 192–193
  in parallel circuit, 78–80
  peak inverse (PIV), 174
  in series circuit, 73–74
  in series-parallel circuit, 89–91
  in transformers, 132–133
  working, 106
Voltage dividers, 74–75
Voltage regulators, 314–315
Voltage tests, 38, 493–494
Voltaic chemical cells (see Cells)
Voltmeters, 95
  using, 97
Volume control, 355

Water, electrolysis of, 261
Water heaters, 302
Watt, 46, 249
Wave motion, energy from, 164
Wave pattern tests, 494

Wave soldering, 199
Welding, 295
Wind, energy from, 163
Wire gage number, American (AWG), 206–207
Wire markers, 228
Wire nuts, 221–222
Wire size, 206–207
Wire strippers, 218–219
Wire table, 207, 208
Wire wrapping and unwrapping, 229–231
Wired-to-chassis circuits, 23–24
Wires, 206–210
  common, 207, 209–210
  soldering (see Soldering wires)
  stranded, 206
Wiring
  inadequate, symptoms of, 275–276
  remote-control, 274–275
Wiring devices, 271–274
Wiring diagrams, 16, 17
Wiring tools and devices, 218–231
Word processing, 446

XOR (exclusive-OR) gate, 419

Z meter, 110, 111, 138–139